FOURTH EDITION

AT-RISK YOUTH: A COMPREHENSIVE RESPONSE

FOR COUNSELORS, TEACHERS, PSYCHOLOGISTS, AND HUMAN SERVICE PROFESSIONALS

J. Jeffries McWhirter
Arizona State University

Benedict T. McWhirter
University of Oregon

Ellen Hawley McWhirter
University of Oregon

Robert J. McWhirter
Federal Public Defenders Office, Phoenix, AZ

THOMSON
™
BROOKS/COLE

Australia • Brazil • Canada • Mexico • Singapore • Spain
United Kingdom • United States

THOMSON

BROOKS/COLE

*At-Risk Youth: A Comprehensive Response for Counselors, Teachers, Psychologists,
and Human Service Professionals,* **Fourth Edition**
J. Jeffries McWhirter, Benedict T. McWhirter, Ellen Hawley McWhirter, and Robert J. McWhirter

Senior Acquisitions Editor: Marquita Flemming
Assistant Editor: Jennifer Walsh
Editorial Assistant: Samantha Shook
Technology Project Manager: Inna Fedoseyeva
Marketing Manager: Meghan McCullough
Marketing Communications Manager: Tami Strang
Project Manager, Editorial Production: Rita Jaramillo
Creative Director: Rob Hugel
Art Director: Vernon Boes
Print Buyer: Judy Inouye

Permissions Editor: Bob Kauser
Production Service: International Typesetting
    and Composition
Copy Editor: Kay Mikal
Cover Designer: Irene Morris
Cover Images: Corbis, Gettyimages
Cover Printer: West Group
Compositor: International Typesetting
    and Composition
Printer: West Group

Printed in the United States of America
1 2 3 4 5 6 7 10 09 08 07 06

Library of Congress Control Number: 2006906114

ISBN 0-534-27236-3

Thomson Higher Education
10 Davis Drive
Belmont, CA 94002-3098
USA

For more information about our products, contact us at:
Thomson Learning Academic Resource Center
1-800-423-0563

For permission to use material from this text or product,
submit a request online at
http://www.thomsonrights.com.
Any additional questions about permissions can be
submitted by e-mail to **thomsonrights@thomson.com**.

CONTENTS

CHAPTER **3**

PART **2**

FAMILIES, SCHOOLS, AND SKILLS   63

CHAPTER **4**

PART **3**

AT-RISK CATEGORIES   123

CHAPTER **7**

CHAPTER 8

CHAPTER 9

CHAPTER 10

ANTISOCIAL BEHAVIOR, DELINQUENCY, AND YOUTH GANGS   179

CHAPTER **13**

CORE COMPONENTS OF PROGRAMS FOR PREVENTION AND EARLY INTERVENTION 256

CHAPTER **14**

CHAPTER **15**

PREFACE

Since 1983, when the National Commission on Excellence in Education issued its report *A Nation at Risk*, educators, counselors, and many other professionals within and outside of the human services began to use the term "at risk" to identify a wide range of social-psychological problems. The term "at risk" can be useful for describing many young people whose potential for becoming responsible and productive adults is limited by challenges within the ecology of their lives. These include problems at home, in schools, in communities; problems with some cultural norms and social messages that contribute to risk in children's lives; and problems within children and adolescents themselves.

Now in its fourth edition, our goals for this book continue to be to provide the reader with up-to-date information and research on the categories of problems experienced by at-risk youth and to provide the reader with effective interventions for these problems. More specifically, we have completely revised all chapters to reflect the most current information and statistics of each problem presented. We continue to present a unified and consistent conceptual framework for the categories. This framework includes discussions of all levels of the ecology of problem development and resolution related to youth at risk. Finally, we present a variety of practical educational, psychological, and counseling interventions for the prevention and treatment of the problems. For this edition, we have continued to describe empirically supported approaches and we have continued our focus on both teens and younger children along with their families and peers.

The information we present and the interventions we suggest can be used by a broad range of professionals, such as counselors, psychologists, social workers, human service professionals, and teachers. We direct our work primarily to graduate students in counseling, social work, education and special education, applied psychology, and other human service disciplines at both the pre- and in-service levels. However, we also write for teachers-in-training, as well as for undergraduate students in psychology, social work, justice studies, nursing, community psychology, and human services. We believe they may find this text useful. Many of the prevention and treatment methods we present here may also be used by school and community health, direct line human service, and mental health personnel—some directly and some with modification—in a wide range of settings, from birth-to-three enrichment programs to juvenile detention to family counseling.

As such, this book is intended as a textbook for courses in education, psychology, social work, special education, and human services. It is appropriate for developmental counseling courses as well, such as principles of counseling, school guidance, and agency counseling interventions. This book is also applicable to courses related to counseling students with special needs, maladjusted children, and, of course, at-risk children and adolescents. It may also be useful as a supplemental or primary text in courses in child and youth care, case management, child/adolescent behavioral and emotional problem management, educational administration, and community agency administration. Feedback we have received indicates that school and agency counselors as well as special education teachers find this book very useful.

In many ways this book reflects our belief about pedagogy, which is that three domains are important to learning: cognitive, affective, and behavioral. Whenever we plan a seminar, develop a workshop, or teach a class, we ask ourselves three questions: What is the most important information we want our students to know about the subject? How can we engage our students on an emotional/affective level? What new skills can we help our students learn to use? In this book we attend to the cognitive domain by providing up-to-date facts, research findings, and a theoretical and practical information base to stimulate thinking. We focus on the affective domain by presenting short readings at the beginning of each chapter and by presenting real-life case studies and sidebar stories to describe struggling young people and their families. We also include many specific behavioral strategies throughout the book to provide concrete and specific intervention skills to use with young clients and families. Although in Part 3 of the book we apply specific interventions to specific problems, nearly all of the interventions presented can be applied to a broad variety of problems and concerns experienced by children and adolescents.

This book may be used in a number of ways. We have used the entire text in the standard semester (or quarter) graduate counseling course at Arizona State and New York University and at the Universities of Oregon, Hawai'i, Texas-San Antonio, and Southern Maine. At the University of Oregon, we use this book as the principal text for a quarter-long undergraduate course in the human services. Educators can use parts of it as the basis for modular units elected by students in social sciences, human services, education, and psychology. For example, at Arizona State University we have offered several modules on a variety of topics within an upper-division educational psychology course taught by graduate assistants with various chapters providing the major content for the modules. This text has also been useful for training workshops and other forms of continuing professional education.

In this fourth edition, we have supplemented many of the chapters with additional prevention and treatment intervention suggestions. These include but are not limited to: refusal and resistance training; an Adlerian/Dreikurs intervention model; Glasser's Reality Therapy; Miller and Rollnick's Motivational Interviewing; crisis intervention strategies; parent training models; solution-focused interventions; and peer programs (such as cooperative learning, peer support networks, cross-age peer tutoring, conflict resolution, and peer mediation strategies). We have compressed the chapter on "school shooters" into the youth violence chapter. We have highlighted prevention strategies, especially anti-bullying programs and our own GOPEP (Group Oriented Psychological Education Program). On the inside of the front cover (and in Chapter 6), we provide a chart to help guide the reader in finding the strategies and in conceptualizing when to apply them in working with at-risk children and adolescents.

Based on feedback from instructors and students, we have added several other features to this edition that are available via the Brooks/Cole Web page. In reference to each chapter, we refer to further readings to supplement the information in the text. We also provide course instructors with an array of teaching materials—ideas, stimulas questions, exercises, test questions, and other aides. Concurrently, the student section of the Web contains useful handouts, worksheets, and video clips that help to make the book more vivid. Visit http://helpingprofs.com.

The book is divided into four major sections. In Part 1 we provide information on the background factors that contribute to risky behaviors. We focus on the ecology of children's lives, including the community and neighborhood environments that increase risk for children and adolescents. This ecological framework is augmented by legal and ethical concerns important to counselors and other human service professionals when working with at-risk youth. In Part 2 we turn to the family, school, and individual characteristics that provide a more prominent and direct influence on youth.

In Part 3 we present data about the five at-risk categories introduced earlier and we discuss major treatment and prevention approaches for each. In Part 4 we incorporate more prevention strategies that focus on the family, the school, the peer groups, and the individual. We suggest how and when prevention can be applied to meet the developmental needs of children, young teens, and families. Throughout the book we have used case studies to highlight, apply, and personalize the information in the text. Early in the book, we introduce the Andrews, Baker, Carter, and Diaz families. These families represent various ethnic/cultural groups from diverse socioeconomic and educational backgrounds and with different individual attitudes and behaviors. Each of the children in these families presents some risk of problem behavior. The background and circumstances of each family are described, and each family highlights and illustrates environmental, family, and school issues and concerns. The family members introduced in these case studies reappear throughout the book to illustrate specific issues. Readers will also find vignettes throughout the text that help to personalize and exemplify the issues being discussed.

It seems clear that if we do not confront the issues facing our young people and their families, our society will lose nearly a quarter of its youth to lifelong difficulty who might otherwise become productive, successful, and happy adults. We hope that this text increases awareness of the problems youth face and contributes to their solution.

Any book with four same-name authors seems bound to arouse curiosity, so perhaps we'd better explain who we are. Jeff is the father of Benedict and Robert, and Ellen and Benedict are married.

Jeff McWhirter holds a diplomate in counseling psychology from the American Board of Professional Psychology (ABPP) and is a fellow of the American Psychological Association (Divisions 17, 51, and 52), the American Psychological Society, the Association for Specialists in Group Work, and the Academy of Counseling Psychology. He is a professor emeritus in the Division of Psychology in Education and a founding member of the Emeritus College at Arizona State University. A former teacher and school counselor, Jeff received his Ph.D. in Counseling Psychology from the University of Oregon in 1969 and was awarded the College of Education Outstanding Alumnus Award in 2006. He has maintained a small private practice for 35 years and consults regularly with schools and agencies that work with at-risk individuals. He has published over 130 chapters, articles in refereed journals, training manuals, books, and monographs. He has been a Fulbright-Hays Senior Scholar to Turkey (1977–78), a Fulbright Senior Scholar to Australia (1984–85), and also participated in a Fulbright Intercountry Exchange to New Zealand. Most recently, he was awarded a Fulbright Senior Specialist grant to return to the same department and university in Turkey 29 years after his first Fulbright.

In 1989 he received the Arizona State University Distinguished Teacher Award. He has taught summer sessions or short courses at 22 other universities in the United States or internationally. He has been the principal investigator of several externally funded projects including a large Safe and Drug Free School and Community grant and a violence reduction grant for an alternative high school. His other areas of interest include group counseling, family counseling, learning disabilities, international aspects of counseling psychology, and grandchildren—not necessarily in the order listed.

Benedict McWhirter is an associate professor of counseling psychology at the University of Oregon and served for five years as Director of Doctoral Training. While he served as Director of Training, the Counseling Psychology Program received the American Psychological Association 2001 Suinn Minority Achievement Award for its efforts and success in contributing to the training of psychologists of color. Benedict received his Ph.D. in counseling psychology from Arizona State University in 1992. He was on the faculty in the Department of Educational Psychology at the University of Nebraska—Lincoln from 1993–1997, has taught at Arizona State University, and has been a teacher for seventh and eighth grades in Peru. He consults with schools on developing psychoeducational curriculum for high-risk youth. With Ellen, he also regularly conducts workshops with couples and provides counseling services to members of the community of Peñalolen in Santiago, Chile. He has extensively published and presented his scholarship at professional conferences in the areas of prevention for at-risk youth, training practices and multicultural training, college student development, loneliness, and counseling intervention approaches. Benedict received the 2001 University of Oregon Office of Multicultural Affairs Outstanding Faculty Award for his mentoring and support of students of color. He was a Fulbright Professor/Scholar conducting research and teaching in Chile during the year 2004.

Ellen Hawley McWhirter is an associate professor and Director of Training in the counseling psychology program at the University of Oregon. From 1993–1997 she was an assistant professor of counseling psychology at the University of Nebraska—Lincoln. Ellen received her Ph.D. in counseling psychology from Arizona State University in 1992. Her dissertation research was funded by a fellowship from the American Association of University Women. Her teaching experience also includes working with Head Start and teaching undergraduate students university academic survival skills. She has also taught and counseled Spanish-speaking children and parents. She has presented her research and scholarship at national conventions in the areas of career and vocational counseling, multicultural counseling and training, and empowerment. She is the author of *Counseling for Empowerment* (American Counseling Association Press). Ellen was awarded the 2001 Fritz and Linn Kuder Early Career Scientist Practitioner Award from the Division of Counseling Psychology of the American Psychological Association. She has been involved in evaluating school-based career exploration courses that include school-to-work transition components, and her empirical research includes a focus on the vocational development of adolescents of color. Ellen was named a Fulbright Professor/Scholar to teach and conduct research in Chile for 2004, and she continues to conduct workshops in Chile with Benedict.

Anna McWhirter was a co-author on the first two editions of this book and now focuses her attention and commitments on her family; she and her husband John have five children. We thank Anna for her past efforts and work on this book.

Our son and brother, Robert J. McWhirter, is the fourth co-author. Robert has been a practicing attorney with the Federal Public Defender's Office in Phoenix, Arizona, since 1989. He received his Juris Doctorate from Arizona State University in 1988 and clerked with Vice Chief Justice Stanley G. Feldman of the Supreme Court of Arizona until 1989. Robert has developed a specialty in criminal immigration law and teaches it to Criminal Justice Act Panel Attorneys, sponsored by the Administrative Office of the United States Courts. During a sabbatical from the Federal Public Defender's Office in 1998, Robert was a visiting professor of law at Catholic University of Chile and at the University of Chile teaching seminars in Spanish on free speech, privacy, and the Internet, and on American criminal procedure. More recently, Robert travels to Venezuela, Chile, Nicaragua, and Columbia where he teaches trial practice skills to public defenders and judges and consults with new public defender offices as part of judicial reform in those countries. Through support from the United States Department of State, Robert has also served as an advisor to the Venezuelan Constitutional Assembly drafting the new Venezuelan constitution. Related to his teaching and consulting, Robert has also published articles in the *Georgetown Immigration Law Review* and the *Criminal Practice Law Reports*. He is also the author of *The Criminal Lawyer's Guide to Immigration Law: Questions and Answers* (2nd edition, 2006; American Bar Association Press), *Criminal Law of Arizona* (2001; State Bar of Arizona Press), and *Strangers in an Even Stranger Land: Aliens and Immigration Law After September 11th* (2002; American Bar Association Press). He is currently working on another book: A "history behind the history" of the Bill of Rights to the U.S. Constitution.

Acknowledgments

Although we four are the most visible in this family project, other members (son and brother Mark J. McWhirter) of the clan contributed in many ways. We would particularly like to thank our daughter and sister, Dr. Paula McWhirter, an Assistant Professor in the counseling psychology program at the University of Oklahoma, who was a source of great ideas and resources. We especially thank Mary McWhirter (Jeff's wife and mother to Benedict and Robert) who has been a source of great support over the years and who cares for all the grandchildren so that her own children can write. We also thank Ben and Ellen's two daughters, Anna and Marielena, for their loving patience and humor.

About the Authors

This book is one of many McWhirter family projects that always seem to begin quite innocently around the breakfast bar but often take us far from home as they unfold. Such kitchen conversations led us to spend an intensive and exhilarating year in Turkey and another in Australia, both years as a Fulbright family. In Australia we developed a traveling road show with puppets and poems, music, and skits on learning disabilities, adult-child communication, and family enrichment. These discussions have also led us to pursue other international experiences along the way and most currently to help develop a center for family enrichment in Peñalolen, Santiago, Chile, one of the poorest communities of that great city, where we also annually conduct training workshops in Spanish on family communication, parent training, couples conflict resolution/mediation, and strategies for working with young people, families, and groups. This book has not taken us nearly so far geographically, but it has been a richly rewarding process.

AT-RISK CHILDREN AND YOUTH: THE ECOLOGY OF PROBLEMS

▲ Part 1 consists of three chapters. In Chapter 1 we discuss and define the term *at risk*, provide an overview of the book, and describe a metaphor and an ecological model for unifying various concerns for children and adolescents who are at risk. In Chapter 2 we provide an overview of environmental and societal issues that impact young people and families. In Chapter 3 we discuss legal and ethical issues that must be considered by helping professionals who work with children and adolescents. We also present two family case studies in Chapters 1 and 2 (and another two in Chapters 4 and 5 of Part 2) that are used throughout the book to illustrate specific problems and issues.

AN INTRODUCTION TO AT-RISK ISSUES

▲ *Rather than the hasty tinkering of the mechanic, the nurturing of life requires the patience of the gardener. The fast technological rush of society leads us to be mechanics. We must preserve the long patience of the gardener.*

CHAPTER OUTLINE

▲   The well-being of our society depends on our ability to prepare well-adjusted, responsible, well-educated young people to step forward as the older generation passes. Our and every nation's continuing stability and strength depend on our ability to ensure that youth are prepared to fill the courtrooms, boardrooms, classrooms, and industries of tomorrow. Young people will only be prepared to meet the demands of the future if schools, families, and communities are involved: Schools and school districts must provide optimal learning and social environments that are academically demanding, positive, and nurturing for all children; families must provide children and adolescents with security, affection, and discipline; and communities must support access to quality child care, education, health care, living wages, and opportunities for young people to work for the welfare of others.

In this chapter we highlight the problems that threaten children and youth and that put young people at risk. We present data to illustrate the severity of problems and personalize these data by describing one family. We then provide an overview of the entire at-risk arena, using the metaphor of a tree as an organizational device. The tree with all its parts—the soil (environment), the roots (family, peer, and school issues), the trunk (high-risk versus low-risk attitudes and behaviors), the branches (specific at-risk categories), and the foliage, fruit, and flowers (individual young people)—together with the gardener who provides pruning and nurturing (human service professionals who provide intervention) are a conceptual metaphor for understanding the complex interrelationships of risk and protective factors related to the problems that youth face. Finally, we review the ecological model as a conceptual framework for understanding environment and its effects on young people's development.

The Scope of the Problems: An Overview of the Ecology of At-Risk Youth

Although there were some sustained and rapid improvements in the lives of children in the United States in the late 1990s and very early 2000s, as a nation we have been unable to maintain most of these gains (Annie E. Casey Foundation, 2005; Federal Interagency Forum on Child and Family Statistics, 2005). The scope of the problem is enormous; so many children are at risk for psychosocial difficulties that it is reasonable to say that society itself is at risk. The data presented here are discussed in detail in later chapters, but for now they provide a reminder of the problems that confront young people in the United States and elsewhere. Professionals who work with young people already know the pervasiveness of these problems.

Facts of an At-Risk Society

- Thirteen million children live in poverty, an increase of half a million children since 2000, and 1 in 3 children will live in poverty at some point during their childhood.
- African American and Latino children are disproportionately poor. In 2000, 31% of African American youth and 28% of all Latino children were poor, with children of color under age 6 disproportionately poor.
- The majority of poor children live in families that work; 77% reside with a family member who worked in the last year.
- Four million children live with persistently unemployed parents. This is a 25% increase since the year 2000.
- In 2000 nearly 40% of children in single-parent households headed by women were poor.
- Violent youth crime occurs most often between 3 p.m. and 6 p.m. when almost 7 million U.S. children are at home alone. A child's chance of being a victim of crime triples after school.
- Even though juvenile crime is at its lowest level since 1980, more than 2.25 million juvenile arrests occur yearly, including more than 92,000 arrests for violent crimes such as murder, aggravated assault, forcible rape, and robbery.
- One in 1,000 children will be killed by guns before they reach age 20.
- In 1999, 14% of students reported being in a physical fight on school property, and 7–8% of 9th through 12th graders were threatened or injured with a weapon.
- Since 1996, there have been 39 instances of school shootings.
- The number of youth involved in gangs remains high, with female gangs a significant social problem. Gang involvement remains a powerful predictor of future violence.
- Teen pregnancy rates, although reaching a record low, are still much higher in the United States than in other developed countries—twice as high as in England, Wales, and Canada, and 9 times higher than in the Netherlands or Japan.
- About 30% of young adolescents report having had sexual intercourse by age 15. One fourth of all adolescents will be infected with a sexually transmitted disease before they graduate from high school.
- A sexually active teen who does not use contraception has a 90% chance of pregnancy; 78% of teenage pregnancies are unplanned.

- Males born to teen mothers are 13% more likely to end up in prison. Females born to teen mothers are 22% more likely to be teenage moms.
- Two thirds of all high school seniors have used illegal drugs; 90% of high school seniors have used alcohol.
- Seventy-seven percent of eighth graders report having used alcohol, with more than 13% of eighth graders and 27% of seniors using alcohol on a regular and heavy basis.
- School vandalism costs the United States more than $600 million each year.
- Seventeen percent of young people made plans to commit suicide in the last year, and 9% reported having attempted suicide at least once. Five children under the age of 20 commit suicide daily.
- Finally, in 2001 it was estimated that just 3.5% ($65.3 billion) of the federal budget was allocated for education, training, employment, and social services combined. In contrast, nearly 5 times as much ($299 billion, 16.1%) of the federal budget was spent on national defense. A recent federal tax cut, recovery efforts for major hurricanes and tornados in 2004 and 2005, and especially the U.S. war in Iraq have made this funding scenario appreciably more pronounced.

Even though there were hints of some improvement in the late 1990s, this gloomy catalog of the problems facing American children and adolescents shows a reversal of positive changes (Garbarino, 1998; Moore & Hagedorn, 2001). These numbers reflect millions of personal stories, some of which are reported under dramatic headlines about abandoned infants, battered and sexually abused children, suicides, and drug overdoses. The catalog also reflects millions of less "newsworthy" stories of troubled, depressed, and anxious young people: children who suffer at home and at school; young people afraid, bored, or angry; adolescents bewildered by family conflict, divorce, or absentee parents; and young people afraid of violence while at home and at school.

The Use of the Term *At Risk:* Definition Problems

During the past two decades the term *at risk* has appeared frequently in the literature on education, psychology, medicine, social work, and economics as well as in the legislation of various states and in federal government reports. Its origins are obscure, and its use in various contexts indicates a lack of consensus regarding its meaning. Psychologists, social workers, and counselors use the term to denote individuals who suffer emotional and adjustment problems. Educators use it sometimes to refer to young people who are at risk of dropping out of the educational system, sometimes to refer to youth who are not learning skills to succeed after graduation, and sometimes to refer to children whose current educational mastery makes their future school career uncertain. Medical workers use the term to refer to individuals with health problems. Economists and the business community label at risk those workers who do not have the requisite literacy and numeracy skills to obtain employment or to succeed at their jobs.

We use a definition of at risk in the context of working with children and adolescents that we believe attends to the most salient aspects of risk across these professional concerns:

> At risk denotes a set of presumed cause–effect dynamics that place an individual child or adolescent in danger of future negative outcomes. At risk designates a situation that is not necessarily current (although we sometimes use the term in that sense too) but that can be anticipated in the absence of intervention.

Minimal risk	Remote risk	High risk	Imminent risk	At-risk category activity

Favorable demographics | Negative demographics - - - - - - - - - - - - - - - ->

Positive family, school, and social interaction | Less positive family, school, and social interaction | Negative family, school, and social interaction - - - - - - - - - ->

Limited psychosocial and environmental stressors | Some stressors | Numerous stressors - - - - - - - - - -> | | At risk for more intense maladaptive behavior

Development of personal at-risk markers: Negative attitudes, emotions, and skill deficiencies - - - - - - - - - -> | | Young person's activity places him or her solidly in the at-risk category

Development of gateway behaviors and activities - - -> | At risk for other categories

Young person's children will be at risk

FIGURE 1.1   The at-risk continuum

For example, young people who use tobacco are at risk for alcohol use; young people who use alcohol are at risk for illicit drug use. Children and adolescents who use illicit drugs are at risk for drug abuse. Thus a specific behavior, attitude, or deficiency provides an initial marker of later problem behavior. Conduct disorders, aggression, and low achievement in elementary school become markers that predict later delinquent and antisocial behavior in adolescence. This is why the term *at risk* does not necessarily designate a situation that is current but that can be anticipated in the absence of intervention.

Perhaps even more important, being at risk must be viewed less as a discrete, unitary diagnostic category than as a series of steps along a continuum. Figure 1.1 illustrates this continuum from minimal and remote risk to personal behavior that anticipates imminent risk and finally precipitates the activities associated with being engaged in one or more types of risky behavior. The following definitions outline some of the descriptive characteristics that correspond to different levels of risk along this continuum. Although not all characteristics in each category are always predictive of outcomes, in general these clusters of risk and protective factors help determine each child's potential level of risk.

Minimal risk.   Young people who are subjected to few psychosocial stressors, who attend good and well-funded schools, who have loving, caring relationships, and whose families are of higher socioeconomic status are generally at minimal risk for future trouble. Because of the complex ecology of stressors that young people face, we do not use the term *no risk*. Young people in all circumstances may have to cope with a death, family discord, incapacity, or unpredictable family factors such as bankruptcy, divorce, or loss of home. Such stressors can appear at any time regardless of existing protective factors. Depending on the young person's age, developmental level, and personal characteristics, the environmental resources available, and a host of other factors, the consequences may or may not be negative in the long term. Further, neither favorable demographics nor "good" families and schools provide invulnerability (Mitchell, 1996). Affluent adolescents may reject positive adult values and norms. Neither money nor social status guarantees meaning and purpose in life. Finally, some "perfect" families harbor secrets—alcoholism, incest, depression— that stem from and perpetuate dysfunction.

Remote risk.   The point on the continuum at which risk, although still remote, seems increasingly possible is reached when markers of future problems appear. The demographic characteristics of low socioeconomic status, poor economic opportunity, poor access to good education, and membership in an ethnic minority group are associated with greater dropout rates, teen pregnancy, vulnerability, participation in violence, and/or other problems. Clearly risk factors do not emerge due to a person being a person of color, but membership in an ethnic minority group often suggests experiences of oppression, economic marginalization, and racism that negatively influence children and adolescents. That is, children of color who are poor are overrepresented in the at-risk behavioral categories. Of course, most poor African American, Latino, and Native American young people survive such difficulties and function well. Thus, even though these background factors are important, they are not predictive of risk for an individual child.

It is important to note that risk factors are also multiplicative. A young person who is from an impoverished, dysfunctional family and who attends a poor school in an economically marginalized neighborhood is potentially farther along the at-risk continuum than children who do not experience these conditions, especially if there are additional major psychosocial stressors. This is particularly the case when the individual child demonstrates personal characteristics that place him or her at even greater risk.

High risk.   Although dysfunctional families, poor schools, negative social interactions, and numerous psychosocial stressors nudge a young person toward higher levels of risk, the final push is supplied by the person's own negative attitudes, emotions, and behaviors. Characteristics that suggest a child is at "high risk" include aggression and conduct problems, impulsivity, anxiety, affective problems such as depression or bipolar disorder, and hopelessness, as well as deficits in social skills and coping behaviors. Of course, these characteristics both emerge from and enhance the negativity of the environment around the child; the causal pathway is dynamic. These personal markers signal the internalization of problems and set the stage for participation in gateway behaviors.

Imminent risk.   Individual high-risk characteristics often find expression in participation in gateway behaviors. Gateway behaviors are mildly or moderately distressing activities, frequently self-destructive, which often progress to increasingly deviant behaviors. A child's aggression toward other children and adults, for example, is a gateway to juvenile delinquency. Cigarette use is a gateway to alcohol and marijuana use, which can be a gateway to use of harder drugs. Although progression through each gate is neither certain nor predictable (for example, some evidence suggests that early use of marijuana among girls is actually a precursor or gateway to chronic cigarette smoking in adulthood and not the other way around), evidence linking gateway behaviors with more serious activities is so strong that such behaviors must be recognized as placing young people at imminent risk.

At-risk category activity.   The final step in the continuum is reached when the young person participates in those activities that define the at-risk categories. Here we confront the conceptual problem with the term *at risk*. Although the literature in this area continues to refer to young people at this level as "at risk," they have passed beyond risk because they are already engaged in the problems that define the category. Of course, activity in any at-risk category can both escalate as well as generalize to other categories. The young person who uses drugs can begin to abuse them and become addicted. The youthful delinquent can go on to commit violent crimes as a later teen and adult. Category activity by the adolescent can lead to lifelong involvement in self- and other-destructive behavior. Generalization means that individuals who participate in one category activity are at risk for engaging in others. The teen who drops out of school, for example, is at great risk for drug dependence, delinquency, and so forth. Consequently, we continue to apply the term *at risk* to behaviors and characteristics along the entire continuum, using the appropriate points along the way to anchor our discussion.

Assess the Context of Problems, Such as Poverty and Racism

The use of the term *at risk* has generated criticism and debate (Swadener & Lubeck, 1995; Tidwell & Corona Garrett, 1994). Viewing level of risk as a continuum that denotes future possibilities resolves some of the objections to the term (J. J. McWhirter, B. T. McWhirter, A. M. McWhirter, & E. H. McWhirter, 1995). But Swadener and Lubeck (1995) argue that an emerging ideology of risk emphasizes a deficit model that locates problems and pathology in the victim. The use of the term in the media, in casual conversations, and even by professionals suggests that risk is inherent in individual children and families. As will become abundantly clear (see especially Chapter 2), we place the blame for nearly 12 million children living in poverty firmly in the public domain. Adequate parental leaves, affordable child care, more accessible housing, increased employment opportunities and living wages, full funding of Women, Infants, and Children (WIC) and Head Start initiatives, and accessible health care will go a long way toward reducing risk. Equally problematic is the fact that children labeled "at risk" frequently are children of color from low socioeconomic environments. Rearing children and adolescents in the context of economic disparities, political marginalization, and a cultural and social milieu steeped in racism provide the soil that nurtures risk.

Chapters 1, 2, 4, and 5 each contain a case study describing a particular family to illustrate the social context and family dynamics related to the data presented here. We use these case descriptions to help clarify educational and counseling intervention strategies as well. The first family we present is the Andrews family.

CASE STUDY

The Andrews Family

The Andrews family consists of Jack, Alicia, and two children from Alicia's previous marriage. All are European American or "White." Mr. and Mrs. Andrews have been married for 8 years, and this marriage is the second for both. They live in a modest and rundown house in a working-class neighborhood of a major city.

Jack Andrews is a 46-year-old semiskilled laborer who was once employed as a technician in an electronics plant. About 5 years ago the plant was computerized, and the new technology reduced the labor force by 40%. Jack lost his job and has held a series of short-term, part-time jobs since that time. He currently has a part-time position pumping gas at a local service station. Thus the family income, which was never very high, fell drastically. Jack is an angry, hostile man with limited insight and a blustering, aggressive style in his interactions with his family.

Jack was an only child. He alludes to a stormy relationship with his own father, who apparently was quite strict and harsh. Jack is especially critical of his mother, with whom he had a very poor relationship. When he was 13, his mother had a "nervous breakdown," and he lived with his aunt for about a year because, as he said, "my mother didn't want me." He graduated from high school and served approximately 10 years in the army. He married during this time but divorced a few months later. He maintains no contact with his first wife. He met Alicia about 9 years ago, and after a brief courtship they married.

Alicia is the third of four children. She lived with her parents until they divorced when she was 6 . Her mother could not support the children, so Alicia spent the next 2 years with her grandparents. She then moved in with her father and his new wife. Alicia dropped out of school after the ninth grade and never finished high school.

Alicia went to work in a factory and married John Steiner at age 18. This marriage was difficult and stormy, beginning with Alicia's almost immediate pregnancy with Allie. John had dropped out of school, was a heavy drinker as a young man, and continued to indulge in periodic drinking binges. The drinking escalated after Paul was born. John physically abused the children and Alicia. When Alicia discovered that he was also sexually abusing Allie, the tensions in the family reached the breaking point, and she divorced him. Alicia retained the house as part of their divorce settlement. John was convicted of sexual abuse and served a prison sentence, and neither Alicia nor the children have had any contact with him since the trial. Alicia believes

The Andrews Family *(continued)*

or hopes that Allie has "gotten over" the sexual abuse and forgotten it. Neither one ever brings it up or acknowledges that it happened.

After divorcing John, Alicia worked as a waitress in a coffee shop until she married Jack. She is now 34 years old and works the lunch shift (11–2) at the same coffee shop. Alicia appears shy, unassertive, and somewhat depressed. She seems to be worried about the family interactions and often attempts to mediate family disputes and conflicts.

Mr. and Mrs. Andrews describe their marriage as an average one. They are somewhat hesitant to talk about their marital conflicts, but Jack has expressed his dissatisfaction with Alicia's complaints about his "laziness." Alicia says he is unwilling to do housework and neglects home maintenance, and she voices frustration about his limited income. They believe themselves to be fairly strict parents, and Alicia sometimes fears they are too strict.

Allie Andrews, 16, is in her second year of high school. She is an attractive girl of average ability. About 3 years ago Allie went through what her mother refers to as a "sudden transformation," changing from an awkward girl into a physically mature young woman. At the age of 14, she expressed a desire to date. Her interest in boys was reciprocated, and she seemed to be popular among the older boys in high school. Her parents reluctantly gave in but firmly stipulated the time she was to be home, the places she could go, the boys she could go out with, and so forth. During this time, her relationship with her parents became increasingly conflictual. Recently she has begun to violate her curfew and hang out with a "bad crowd." When she is grounded, she sometimes sneaks out to join her friends. Her school grades have been dropping although she continues to pass all her courses. She became a cheerleader this year. Allie is currently dating several different boys, including an African American classmate. She has been expressly forbidden to date African Americans, so she meets him away from home.

Allie is sullen around her stepfather. She believes that Jack blames her for most of the tension in the family, and she shows her hurt by constantly defying him. Days go by without a word between them. Their mutual dislike is a consistent part of their interactions. Jack uses the same harsh, authoritarian child-rearing style that he resented in his own father. He is the unquestioned decision maker and controls the children primarily through shouting, threatening to throw them out of the house, and grounding. Alicia is worried about Allie, blames herself for the sexual abuse that occurred, and wants Allie to be "happy" and have a

The Andrews Family *(continued)*

"normal family." Alicia absorbs conflict between the other family members, attempting to mediate and keep everyone calm. Over the past 2 years, Allie's parents, in particular her stepfather, have become increasingly suspicious and fearful. They suspect that Allie may be sexually active and fear she is not responsible enough to prevent pregnancy. They also suspect that her friends are drug users and fear that she will become addicted. Several times a week these issues erupt into loud arguments between Allie and Jack, or between Alicia and Jack. In the end, Allie, faced with her parents' lack of faith in her, feels hurt and misjudged. She responds with defiance, which invokes even more anger, and Jack tightens the restrictions. Lately she has threatened to run away if Jack doesn't let her choose her own friends, set her own timetable, and quit suspecting her of being a sexually promiscuous drug user.

The most recent confrontation occurred when Jack discovered Allie's dating relationship with her African American friend. This discovery has provoked a family crisis. Jack has threatened to "disown" Allie if she does not break off the relationship. Allie is sulking and threatening to run away. Alicia is frustrated and depressed about the antagonism between the two people to whom she feels most closely connected. Allie feels deeply hurt and sees running away as a means to hurt back. Her stepfather, in his own way, feels deeply hurt that his once compliant stepdaughter is now so unaccepting of his authority and protection. He expresses a strong dislike of his stepdaughter and is quite angry about her behavior.

Paul Andrews, 12, is a short, stocky eighth grader with an air of bravado. Underneath the bravado, however, he appears to be a very depressed and angry child. His parents' main concerns are Paul's dislike of school and his aggressive behavior, although Jack often tries to convince Alicia that Paul's behavior is "how boys are." Paul says he feels very sad at times for no reason. His aggressive behavior is a problem in the classroom, and he is suspected of stealing other children's lunch money. His behavior at home is no better. Two months ago he "accidentally" set fire to one of Alicia's dresses. He shows an intense interest in bloodshed, accidents, fires, and violent crimes. Between the incidents of aggression he seems overly controlled, and unless he gets help now, he may become increasingly violent or self-destructive as a teenager. He is also reaching the stage of development at which questions of personal and sexual identity are assuming some urgency for him. He seeks acceptance while at the same time rejecting pressures to conform. His relationship with both parents fluctuates from lukewarm to cold and back again several times a week.

AT-RISK PROBLEMS AND ISSUES

Cause or Effect?

One of the difficulties in trying to understand at-risk problems is fragmentation of knowledge. School dropout, drug and alcohol abuse, risky sexual activity, juvenile delinquency, youth suicide, and other problems are usually studied separately. In the real world, however, they interact, reinforce one another, and cluster together. Not only do problems cluster but so do the young people who have these problems; they tend to live in the same neighborhoods and to be exposed to many of the same influences. In addition, the problems reverberate within the community and frequently are intergenerational.

Much of the empirical research on at-risk youth has been correlational in nature. That two factors correlate does not mean that one is the cause of the other. Parent depression is correlated with child antisocial behavior, but the direction of causality is unclear. Perhaps the child's negative behavior contributes to the parent's depression; or perhaps the underlying depression of the parent results in inconsistent parenting that contributes to the child's predelinquent behavior; or likely both affect each other and are influenced by other factors as well. Circular or dynamic causality is operating—each problem and risk factor contributes to the other—so our knowledge of families like the Andrews illustrates that at-risk families and at-risk young people influence each other in many ways. In recent years, longitudinal research that tracks individual and contextual factors over time has assisted in answering some questions about "which came first," but overall it demonstrates the multi-directional influencing nature of community, school, family, and individual characteristics. In later chapters we identify the relationships between variables that contribute to risk and resilience and identify causality when it is possible to do so.

Vulnerable and Underserved

We know that the physical and mental health needs of many children and adolescents in the United States in general are underserved (e.g., Garbarino, 1998), but some children are treated even less equitably than others. Two groups of youth are particularly vulnerable and underserved. Children and adolescents of color usually do not receive culturally sensitive, relevant, and appropriate interventions and are more likely to be educationally and economically marginalized. Students of color also often must manage issues of acculturation, ethnic identity, and second language challenges along with all the other challenges of adolescence. The second group is gay, lesbian, bisexual, and transgender youth, who are particularly vulnerable to misunderstanding and bias and then subsequent marginalization and violence.

Children and adolescents of color.   Demographics in the United States are changing rapidly. By the year 2020 people of color will make up the majority in the United States. Asian Americans are the fastest growing ethnic group and are a very heterogeneous group. As many as 32 different Asian American ethnic groups are now identified in the United States. Soon, Filipino Americans will be the largest Asian group, followed by Chinese, Korean, Vietnamese, Indian, and Japanese. Nearly 60% of Asians in the United States are foreign-born, often recently immigrated, and represent a serious challenge to educational systems and to mental health professionals (Cheng, 1996). Our society is rich in cultural diversity, and this diversity is growing in virtually every region of the country.

The historical and contemporary marginalization of people of color continues an ethos of racism and inequitable opportunity in the United States. This has contributed to youth being "at risk." Many of the conditions that predict negative outcomes for youth, such as poor living conditions, poor quality and underfunded schools, and lack of economic opportunity, are correlated with being a child of color. To respond to this, existing prevention, early intervention, and treatment efforts need to be adapted to be valid for families and young people of color, and new intervention strategies need to be developed that take into consideration issues such as ethnicity, acculturation, religious norms, and the cultural and linguistic needs of specific communities in order to be effective.

Gay, lesbian, bisexual, and transgender youth. Although considerably fewer in number than children and adolescents of color, youth who are gay, lesbian, bisexual, or transgender (GLBT) are particularly vulnerable. Anderson (1994) and Savin-Williams (1995; Savin-Williams & Rodriguez, 1993) argue convincingly that gay and lesbian youth are ignored in most professional writing about children and adolescents. The increased social visibility of homosexuality has not been paralleled by greater attention to GLBT youth in the research or treatment literature. This lack of attention is particularly problematic because young people who are "sexual minorities" are disproportionately at risk for negative outcomes.

Most GLBT youth experience stress associated with their sexual orientation. They commonly experience disapproval, anger, and rejection from family and peers when they disclose same-sex attraction. Denial of same-sex attraction directly interferes with self-exploration and the ability to form healthy relationships critical to identity formation. That is, "living a lie" or "passing" can lead to incredible isolation and loneliness.

GLBT young people are particularly vulnerable to alcohol and drug abuse, depression, and a higher rate of suicide than heterosexual youth as they seek to cope with the isolation and rejection they experience (Sullivan & Wodarski, 2002). Homosexuals are frequent targets of hate crimes (Federal Bureau of Investigation [FBI], 2000). Educators do little to support them or are prohibited from doing so; GLBT youth often leave school before graduation. Although GLBT young people receive services from multiple systems, service providers frequently have not addressed their special needs (Lambda Legal, 2005; Mallon, 1998).

THE AT-RISK TREE: A METAPHOR

The cultural anthropologist Becker (1981) once observed that information accumulated in the last half of the 20th century has become "strewn all over the place, spoken in a thousand competitive voices. Its insignificant fragments are magnified out of all proportion while its major and world historical insights lie around begging for attention" (p. 14). Becker's statement is true today. Information about at-risk children and youth is indeed "strewn all over the place." What is cause, and what is effect? How does one situation relate to another? What is the relationship between various aspects of a child's problem? What are the underlying connections? In efforts to solve the problem, intertwined and complex issues are divided into manageable parts. Programs to reduce school failure, for instance, are isolated from efforts to prevent juvenile delinquency. Strategies to ameliorate teen pregnancy may ignore problems of substance abuse. Researchers and policy planners chip

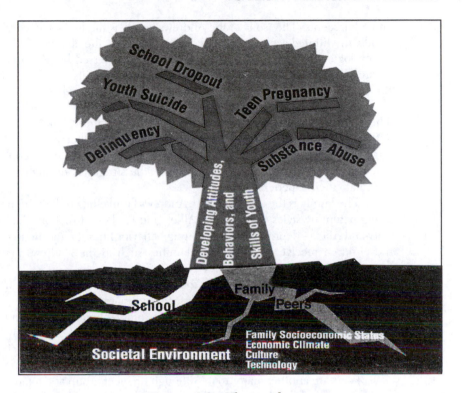

FIGURE 1.2   The at-risk tree

away at what remains unknown but often do not identify what is known. We attempt to determine the impact of narrowly defined interventions and strategies and ignore the powerful effects of a broad combination of strategies.

In this book we lay out a systematic framework to guide the reader toward an understanding of the scope and range of problems for which children and adolescents are at risk. The following metaphor is a conceptual and organizing framework. This metaphor integrates the various at-risk categories and intervention strategies and allows us to pull together information and knowledge that is "strewn all over" and focus on specific at-risk categories in a unifying framework.

We turn to horticulture for our metaphor. The analogy of a tree permits us to consider a range of issues that relate to at-risk children and youth. The soil of this tree is the individual's societal environment. The roots of family, school, and peer group connect the tree to the soil (that is, the environment) to provide support and nurturance. The trunk serves as the conduit of developing attitudes and behaviors of each individual child that lead to specific at-risk categories, which are the branches of the tree (see Figure 1.2).

The soil.   Various aspects of the environment, such as socioeconomic status, political realities, economic climate, and cultural factors, must be considered if we are to fully understand at-risk issues. The environment/soil also includes dramatic social changes. Urbanization, the feminization of poverty, the threat of violence and terrorism, and changes in technology are parts of the soil that nourish or fail to nourish at-risk children and adolescents. The "soil" of the Andrews family is the low socioeconomic status of the family, the limited access to mental health providers, the change of job status because of technological advances, and the racist attitudes expressed by Mr. Andrews; all indicate environmental pressures that mold this family and affect its members. This environment, this soil, potentially contributes to at-risk products—Allie and Paul.

The roots.   The at-risk tree has three primary roots: family, school, and peer groups. Just as the roots provide a network that anchors and nourishes life, so the family and the schools transmit culture and along with the peer group mediate young people's development. These primary social environments provide the structures through which the children assimilate their experiences.

The family is the taproot. In the Andrews family the conflict, friction, and vastly differing parenting styles contribute to Allie's and Paul's dysfunctions. Jack's anger and hostility and Alicia's depression and placating behavior limit the nurturance and support that the children receive. Multiproblem families such as the Andrews present a challenge because of the variety of issues they experience.

The school is another major root. Society looks to schools for help: to provide a secure environment for children, to foster appropriate learning experiences, and to attend to learning and emotional problems. Increasingly, schools teach essential life skills that families and churches taught in the past. The role of the school in the future of the Andrews children is critical. How the school handles Allie's and Paul's situations will have both short- and long-term effects on their attitudes toward school, learning, and life.

Peers are another major root. Although the peer group as a major influence usually starts later in a child's life—generally by preadolescence—it can be enormously powerful in transmitting culture, values, and norms that influence behavior. Failing to consider peers in understanding and intervening with young people has a high probability of leading to interventions that are ineffective.

The trunk.   The trunk is the support and brace for the tree's branches and the conduit from the soil and roots up to the leaves, blossoms, and fruit. The trunk of the at-risk tree consists of specific behaviors, attitudes, and skills of individual children and adolescents. It represents young people's strengths and weaknesses, talents and disabilities, and personal risk and protective factors. These behaviors, attitudes, and skills are also conduits to the branches, because specific characteristics such as inability to delay gratification, depression, anxiety, low self-esteem, and impulsivity lead directly to at-risk behaviors. In the Andrews family, Allie's oppositional and self-defeating behavior and Paul's anxiety, depression, and aggressiveness lead to specific at-risk behaviors.

The branches.   The branches of the tree represent children and youths' adaptation to society. Many young people are doing well. They are healthy and sound; they are integrated into society and preserve their cultural heritage; they will be productive as workers, as parents, as members of the community. Young people with this healthy adaptation contrast strikingly with those who isolate themselves from their cultural heritage, their families, and society through destructive attitudes and behaviors—those who are in specific at-risk categories.

The five branches that produce the most damaged fruit—that is, the five specific at-risk categories that seem most central to our concerns—are school dropout, substance abuse, risky sexual behaviors, delinquency and violence, and suicide. Both Allie and Paul are approaching school dropout. Further, Allie is at risk for teen pregnancy and drug abuse; Paul is at risk for delinquency and violence, and possibly for suicide.

Foliage, fruit, and flowers.   The fruits of the tree are individual and specific young people, such as Allie and Paul Andrews. Some young people are whole and healthy; others are bruised and damaged; still others drop from the tree. Although broken branches sometimes produce good fruit and healthy branches sometimes produce damaged fruit, the fact remains that certain branches—the maladaptive behaviors in the five major at-risk categories—increase the probability that at-risk behavior will escalate. Perhaps even more tragic is the probability that at-risk young people will themselves be the seeds of future generations of at-risk trees.

The gardener.   Like all growing trees, the at-risk tree needs pruning, staking and trimming, sun, water, and nurturing. Hence, this book is for the "gardeners"—the counselors and teachers, psychologists and social workers, youth recreation and juvenile justice personnel, and other human service workers—who nurture the Pauls and Allies of our society. Nurturing must be directed sometimes toward the soil, sometimes toward the roots, sometimes toward the trunk or branches; but always the intent is to improve the fruit of the tree. Throughout this text we recommend useful strategies for working with youth that will help you to be a better gardener.

The tree metaphor is a useful but informal framework for understanding and working with at-risk youth. A more extensive and elegant theory is the ecological model of human development.

THE ECOLOGICAL MODEL

The ecological model articulated by Bronfenbrenner (1979, 1989) posits that individual human development occurs within multiple embedded ecological systems. Bronfenbrenner identified these systems as the micro-, meso-, exo-, macro-, and chronosystems, with the individual at the center (see Figure 1.3).

The microsystem consists of the people with whom an individual comes into direct contact. For example, the family is the child's primary microsystem, and the child's school—including teachers, staff, and classmates—constitutes another. Each microsystem influences the child's development. The mesosystem refers to the interconnections between the different microsystems. Mesosystemic influences include the relationships between a child's parent and teacher and between the child's school and the surrounding neighborhood. The ecological model assumes that an individual's development is enhanced if the mesosystem—that is, the relationships among the microsystems—is consistent and positive (Bronfenbrenner, 1979, 1989). The exosystem consists of the interconnections between one or more settings that do not directly involve the individual. Public policy is an excellent example of an exosystemic factor. Public policy decisions regarding educational standards, teachers' wages, health care or school lunch programs have an impact on an individual and his or her microsystems (e.g., family, community, and school), but the individual may not be present in the environments in which public policy decisions are made (e.g., city council or state legislative sessions). The macrosystem

▲ Box 1.1

Carrie

Several years ago one of us was asked to work with a distressed, disturbed young girl named Carrie. At the personal level, 13-year-old Carrie was very self-defeating, angry, and fearful. She was obstinate and oppositional—a problem to her family, her school, and herself. Her behaviors and attitudes were more easily understood, however, when we analyzed the shifting ecology of her life.

Carrie had been raised in a rural community by a mother who worked part time as a waitress and received a modest monthly check for child support from her former husband. The mother was periodically anxious and depressed, and during these episodes Carrie assumed responsibility for herself, for her mother, and for their modest house. The living arrangements provided by both her mother and her other relatives (many of whom lived close by) could best be described as permissive and nonstructured, with a high tolerance for a wide range of behaviors.

Carrie attended the small local school and had known most of her classmates for years. Even though she gave evidence of a specific learning disability, Carrie's schoolwork was generally adequate, perhaps because the school's expectations were not high.

When her mother went through a particularly acute depressive episode, it was determined that Carrie should go to live with her father. Overnight she went from her small home in a peaceful, rural community to her father's huge house in a wealthy suburban neighborhood. Carrie's father, a self-made millionaire, had become successful as the owner and chief executive officer of a chain of drugstores. He worked long hours, drove himself very hard, and had high expectations of everyone with whom he had contact—suppliers, tradespeople, employees, school personnel, and family members.

Carrie suddenly found herself in a household that included her father, his woman friend (who was shortly to become Carrie's stepmother), a housekeeper, and a live-in nanny hired to support, tutor, discipline, and provide companionship for her.

Carrie enrolled in the local public school. Because of the high socioeconomic status of the neighborhood, the academic expectations and achievement norms were high. Her classmates were the sons and daughters of university professors, physicians, and business executives. Most students in this school went on to graduate from college, a large proportion of them from the most prestigious universities in the country.

Carrie might be considered a very "lucky" girl, rescued from a mother unable to care for her and provided with "every advantage" and a clear pathway to success. Her "ungrateful" behavior might be confusing from a perspective that narrowly focuses on socioeconomics. Considered from an ecological perspective, the deviant and pathological behaviors that brought Carrie to our attention are a logical and obvious reaction to her environmental change. Carrie was like a fern that is transplanted from a shaded corner of the garden into the hot, glaring sun. The fern cannot thrive; neither could Carrie.

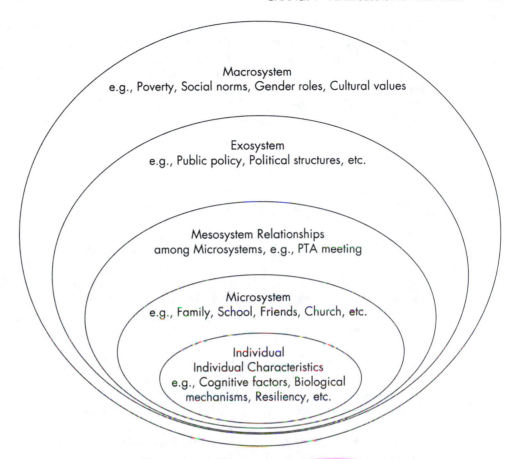

FIGURE 1.3   Bronfenbrenner's ecological model

represents a social blueprint: cultural values, belief systems, societal structure, gender-role socialization, race relations, and national and international resources (Bronfenbrenner, 1989). Research that examines the relationship between children's aggressive behavior and exposure to violent television is an example of studying macrosystemic influences on the individual. An additional concept is the chronosystem, which is the interconnection and interaction among individuals and the different levels of their environments over time.

The ecological model makes three explicit assumptions (Bronfenbrenner, 1979, 1989). First, the ecological model assumes that individuals and their environment are continually interacting and exerting mutual influence and, as a result, are constantly changing. The environment influences individual development and, in turn, the individual changes the environment. Second, the ecological model assumes that individuals are active participants in their development. That is, the individual is not merely acted upon by the environment but also exerts influence on the environment. Third, the ecological model assumes bi-directionality, or the idea that changes in one ecological system may influence changes in systems that are more proximal and distal to the individual.

For example, public policy decisions affect human development in more immediate or proximal ecological systems. In the same way, individuals, families, and communities in the micro- and mesosystems influence public policy decisions (exosystem) by writing government representatives, speaking at public forums, or protesting. This example illustrates bi-directionality and how factors in every system within the ecology can effect change in another system. Throughout this chapter, as in the entire book, many examples of risk and protective factors are located within these embedded and interacting systems.

HELPER INTERFACE

Counselors, psychologists, teachers, and human service professionals employed in both public and private settings can incorporate the intervention strategies we present in this text in their practice. The best interventions are ones that are fully integrated into other services provided by agencies and schools. To effectively implement strategies presented in this text on a day-to-day basis requires a high degree of professional collaboration with coworkers and administrators, as well as a sensible understanding of the specific agency culture and school climate (Massey, Armstrong, Burroughs, Hanson, & McCash, 2005).

Many of our suggestions can be used by a teacher with an individual child, a group of children, or an entire classroom. These interventions, with appropriate modifications, lend themselves to both individual and group work. They are most effective when concerned adults work together. When teachers, human service professionals, and parents collaborate in their efforts, putting the needs of an individual child or one classroom uppermost on their agenda, they increase the effectiveness of their work. Teachers, especially those in special education and in alternative schools, can incorporate in their classrooms aspects of the suggested programs that we present here. Human service workers in juvenile justice settings, in recreation centers, in day treatment programs, and elsewhere can utilize the strategies we present as well. There is an increasing need for adults to serve as mentors, to become positive role models for young people, and to provide practical information about communication and human relationships. Comprehensive life-skills training programs (discussed in Chapter 13) effectively meet this need. Teachers, perhaps in collaboration with counselors and trained parents, are in an excellent position to implement these programs. They need training, time, encouragement, and support in their efforts to do so.

The school or agency counselor or psychologist and other human service professionals are in a good position to consult with teachers about implementing life-skills programs. Counselors have the training to apply cognitive-behavioral approaches, small-group processes, and other developmental, cognitive-behavioral strategies to improve young people's social skills. The developmental and educational role of the counselor is crystallized in the concept of the counselor as a psychoeducator. Psychoeducational group interventions are applicable in a wide variety of problem areas and are especially useful for at-risk children and youth and their parents.

CONCLUSION

This chapter highlights the severity of the problems U.S. children and adolescents confront as they progress toward adulthood. The concept of an at-risk continuum is useful to teachers, counselors, psychologists, and human service professionals interested in identifying the nature and level of risk faced by the young people with whom they work. The ecological model provides a way of analyzing how varied dimensions of the environment support or decrease the likelihood of risk and risk category behaviors. The Andrews family, whom we will meet again in later chapters, demonstrates the complex interrelationships of family, school, and social problems that young people frequently experience. This book is intended to clarify the problems of youth at risk and to set the stage to help you provide multifaceted, comprehensive, practical, and ethical prevention and treatment.

Environmental/Societal Factors That Contribute to Risk

▲   *For the truly humanist educator (counselor, human service professional) and the authentic revolutionary, the object of action is the reality to be transformed by them together with other people.*

Paulo Freire
Pedagogy of the Oppressed

CHAPTER OUTLINE

▲ Heraclitus is credited with saying that "nothing is permanent except change." Perhaps at no time in history has this insight been clearer than it is today. Children and youth face the challenge of growing into mature, responsible, healthy adults amidst a maelstrom of economic, political, social, and technological change. Technological advances are occurring more rapidly than ever before in history. The resulting highly specialized systems of production and service, communication and transportation, add complexity to lives that are already complex. The World Wide Web, for example, is enormously promising in connecting our world and making it smaller, yet at the same time it provides children and adolescents with rapid exposure to information and social influences that are difficult to monitor and sometimes risky. The continuing mobility of the population, the declining influence of the extended family, the movement of industries from the North to the South, outsourcing of jobs to overseas locations, and extensive automation in the workplace make our society one in which very little seems certain. In addition, threats associated with terrorist attacks, international instability, and the nuclear capabilities of an increasing number of nations add to people's sense of change and insecurity, especially in this "post–September 11th" era. Our economy is globally interdependent, and the social and economic forces that affect other parts of the world also affect our young people.

In this chapter we review environmental influences that place young people at risk for poor outcomes. We discuss current economic policy trends, with particular attention to poverty, and describe the complex interactions between socioeconomic status, ethnicity, and public policy.

THE ECONOMY AND POVERTY

One major exosystemic influence in children's lives is the economy. Economic trends that greatly affect at-risk young people include (a) increasing poverty, (b) welfare reform, (c) the economic stagnation of the working poor, (d) single mothers, and (e) homeless families.

Poverty

Poverty is the risk factor most closely associated with family stress and highly correlated with school failure (Children's Defense Fund [CDF], 2001b), delinquency (Jarjoura, Triplett, & Brinker, 2002), and other problems, even though some children from poor economic backgrounds fare well. In the mid-2000s, nearly 17% of American children (13 million children) are being raised in poverty, and 1 in 3 children in the United States will live in poverty at some point during their childhood (Annie E. Casey Foundation, 2005; Federal Interagency Forum on Child and Family Statistics, 2005). Rural child poverty rates remain higher than those of urban children (21% versus 18%; U.S. Department of Agriculture, 2005) with the exception of geographically central cities, in which nearly a quarter of children live in poverty (Population Reference Bureau, 2004). Impoverished children also are far more likely to experience poor and inadequate education and health care.

Children of color are disproportionately poor: 28% of all Latino children and more than 31% of all African American children lived in poverty in 2000, compared with 13% of European American children (CDF, 2001b). Children of color under age 6 are even worse off: 33% of African American children and 29% of Latino children under 6, in contrast to 10% of European American children under 6, are poor (CDF, 2001a).

Among the detrimental effects Garbarino (1998) lists as ingredients for the "social toxicity" of poverty are increased risk of exposure to violence, racism, unstable care arrangements, economic deprivation, and community insecurity. Some of the by-products of these "toxins" are academic failure, learning disabilities, and child abuse (Garbarino, 1998). Children from poor families often begin school developmentally unprepared to succeed in the classroom.

Since the 2002 economic downturn, the United States has faced sharp rises in childhood poverty that resemble the increases in child poverty that accompanied recessions in the early 1980s and 1990s. Although the number of children living below the poverty line dropped to a 20-year low of 11.6 million in the year 2000, the number of poor children who live in families with a full-time, year-round worker rose to more than 4 million. Despite devoting more time to work, many low-income families remain poor. Promising news of fewer children living in poverty was an artifact of the late 1990s boom in employment (CDF, 2001b).

Welfare Reform

From 1995 to 2000 the number of children who lived in extreme poverty yet received no welfare rose 16%, coinciding with a 57% decline in the national welfare caseload. Previously, most extremely poor families received welfare. National welfare legislation passed in 1996 resulted in only 1 in 3 extremely poor families receiving such assistance in 2000

(CDF, 2001b). Such households rely increasingly on free school lunch and the Women, Infants, and Children (WIC) programs for subsistence (Winicki, 2003).

Meanwhile, research on the effects of the 1996 welfare reform has revealed poor outcomes (e.g., Wycoff, Bacod-Gebhardt, Cameron, Brandt, & Armes, 2002). In one study of 700 women moving off of welfare, Fuller and colleagues (2002) found that although mothers' incomes rose significantly, broader measures of the family's well-being deteriorated. For instance, one fifth of all mothers had cut the size of meals for their children because they didn't have enough cash to buy sufficient food. Even though a majority of women found jobs, few were able to climb above the poverty line (Fuller et al., 2002). Further, 2 in every 5 women (more than twice the national average) suffered from clinical depression, known to have significant detrimental effects on children's development (Fuller et al., 2002). The children displayed more developmental delays by age 3 or 4. Just 30% of the study children could write their first name correctly, compared to 66% in a sample of Head Start children and 70% in a national sample of 4-year-olds (Fuller et al., 2002). Moving off of welfare into low-wage jobs does not ensure that families or children are better off (Fuller et al., 2002).

Child care also is a major obstacle for mothers moving off of welfare. Two in 5 mothers reported that they had quit or passed up a job due to the lack of affordable child-care options (Fuller et al., 2002). Although children in day-care centers watched less television than children who were home (Fuller et al., 2002), many of the settings provided only limited, low-quality learning materials, lacked structured or positive interactions with caregivers, and lacked activities contributing to robust child development (Fuller et al., 2002).

Stagnation of the Working Poor

The majority of poor children live with a working parent. In fact, more than 77% of children living in poverty reside with a family member who worked in the last year and more than a third live with a full-time, year-round worker (CDF, 2001a, 2001b). In 2000 child poverty in families with a full-time worker hit its highest point in the 26 years on record. To some extent this is due to the federal minimum wage law, which in 2005 was $5.15 an hour. A single parent with two children working 40 hours a week at minimum wage earns $10,700 a year, $4,500 below the poverty line. But poor families must spend more income for child care than families who are not poor (Smith, 2002). What employment indices fail to reflect is that during a recession workers who lose their jobs and then are reemployed typically earn 20% less than they had earlier (CDF, 1995).

The economic problems faced by working poor families influence a child's development through parental attitude, disposition, and behavior. For example, parents with financial stress are more tense, irritable, and explosive and become increasingly arbitrary and punitive in child discipline (Schliebner & Peregoy, 1994). Further, adult mental health is affected by economic problems (McLloyd, 1989). Unemployed parents are more dissatisfied with themselves and with their lives, feel victimized, and are more anxious, depressed, and hostile than employed parents. The incidence of neurosis, psychosis, and suicide is higher among unemployed parents; they have more sleeping, eating, and somatic problems and consume more alcohol (Smith, 2002). These changes in attitude, disposition, and behaviors strain family relationships and harm children's development (Solantaus, Leinonen, & Punamaki, 2004). In Chapter 1 we introduced the Andrews family. Recall that technological changes resulted in the loss of Jack's electronic technician job, and that he now works part time in a service station. This change in his employment status and income level undoubtedly contributes to his feelings of anger, hostility, and powerlessness. These feelings in turn cause him to be less nurturing with his stepchildren and more punitive and arbitrary toward them. Allie Andrews's sullenness and defiance reflect her heightened stress and lowered self-esteem. Her sexual acting out (if indeed her parents' suspicions are correct) can be at least partially explained as a reaction to her stepfather's harsh and abrasive behavior. Similarly, Paul's depression, anger, and low self-esteem are exacerbated by his stepfather's situation. Paul's destructive behavior and poor school adjustment are among the consequences.

In short, the Andrews family illustrates several characteristics common to working poor families in the United States. Because of the parents' part-time work schedules, they do not require child-care services, which is an advantage many do not have. However, the low minimum wage and Alicia's and Jack's limited employment opportunities are important factors in the short- and long-term problems faced by this family.

Vulnerable and underserved families.   Families of color have experienced a disproportionate share of income and job loss, primarily because of structural changes in the economy. This has been exacerbated by the shift of manufacturing employment from the cities to outlying areas, including outsourcing to other countries. Because families of color reside in inner-city areas in disproportionate numbers and are overrepresented in the blue-collar jobs that have been disappearing, they are much more likely to be affected by displacement and unemployment. The problem is likely to be prolonged as the United States continues its transformation from a goods-producing economy to a service economy.

Workers of color continue to be overrepresented in less-skilled jobs. African Americans, for instance, are particularly concentrated in lower-ranking occupations in the United States. In 1995 African Americans made up 19.4% of all enlisted military personnel but only 11.4% of all officers. Similarly, African Americans made up only 4.2% of doctors and 3.7% of dentists; however, they made up 9.3% of registered nurses, 18.7% of licensed practical nurses, and almost 30% of nurses aides, orderlies, and attendants (Goldfield, 1997). This pattern is also seen in the federal workforce. African Americans make up almost 19% of the federal workforce but fewer than 7% of senior executive service positions (Zorn, 2001).

Poverty rates among African Americans are consistently 3 times higher than among European Americans; for Latino Americans they are 2.5 times higher. Female-headed households with children are particularly vulnerable to poverty; more than 39% of those living in such households were poor in 2000. This figure rises to about 50% for Latino American and African American children. Nearly 1 in 3 African American children and 16% of all children lived below the poverty line in 2000 (U.S. Census Bureau, 2001). More than 5 million of America's children live in extreme poverty, with family incomes less than 50% of the poverty threshold (National Center for Children in Poverty [NCCP], 2002). Native Americans are generally unaffected by national economic cycles because they consistently suffer high unemployment, especially on most reservations. Furthermore, the national poverty line or "threshold" is extremely low to begin with.

Young families.   If Allie Andrews continues her presumed sexual behavior, becomes pregnant (which is probable), and marries the father (which is less probable), and if she keeps her baby (also probable), she is setting herself up for a limited income and a heavy workload. She will assume most of the care for her baby and most of the household chores. She will probably also work outside the home.

Increasing numbers of young unmarried mothers are members of the workforce out of necessity, some because of the decline in real family income. In the United States today the minimum wage is $5.15 an hour. By contrast, in 1968 in current inflation-adjusted dollars, it was $7.67 an hour. Multiple attempts to raise the minimum wage closer to a "living wage" have been stalled in Congress. For workers to escape the federal definition of poverty, the minimum wage would have to be $8.20 an hour (Lind, 2001). In some families both parents must work simply to keep the family out of poverty, and young families are increasingly stressed to provide for their families.

In the Andrews family we see the effects of the first two trends we have discussed: job and income loss leading to economic stagnation, and young families. Two other areas of concern are now illustrated via the Baker family: single motherhood and homelessness.

Single Mothers

Young female-headed families are at the greatest risk of poverty and co-occurring problems. Children in families headed by a single parent are also more likely to be poor. In 2000, 40% of single-parent families headed by women with children under 18 were below the official poverty line. In contrast, 8.2% of dual-parent families with children were poor (CDF, 2001a). At least 20% of working single mothers need assistance such as food banks to make ends meet (Kim, Ohls, & Cohen, 2001). Indeed, the economic plight of most families headed by single mothers has steadily worsened in the last 25 years.

By the year 2000, births to unmarried females reached the highest level ever recorded (Center for Disease Control [CDC], 2001). One in 2 children will spend part of their childhood in a single-parent home (CDF, 2001d). The children and adolescents living in single-parent families are at greatest risk for poverty and all its co-occurring problems (Dickerson, 1995; Mulroy, 1995). On a more positive note, however, the national birthrate for U.S. teenagers declined steadily throughout the 1990s, with an overall drop of 22% (CDC, 2002).

When young teens become pregnant and carry their babies to term, many do not receive prenatal care, placing their child at risk for future problems. In 1996, 1 in 14 teenage mothers received no prenatal care or obtained it only in the last trimester. Only 2 in 3 received prenatal care during the first trimester (Ventura & Curtin, 1999). Lack of prenatal care influences the child's future health, well-being, and learning ability, and the consequences are borne by our schools and health care systems.

Homeless Families

At the end of 2001, the U.S. Conference of Mayors issued its status report on hunger and homelessness in 27 U.S. cities. In addition to the statistics listed here, all cities forecast increases for requests for emergency food assistance and for emergency shelter by homeless

CASE STUDY

The Baker Family

Sally Baker is a 28-year-old African American woman. She is legally married to George, the father of her 9-year-old son, Tyrone, and her 7-year-old daughter, Daniella, although she has not lived with George for 5 years. Her 3-year-old son, Jerome, was fathered by a boyfriend whom she has not seen for over a year. During most of her 9 years of motherhood, Sally's primary means of support has been Aid to Families with Dependent Children (AFDC). For several months she and her children have been residing at the Andre House, a shelter for homeless families.

Sally was born in rural Alabama. She never knew her father. When Sally was 8, she and her mother moved to Dallas with her brother and sisters. Sally remembers that her mother was not working and that "she couldn't afford to keep me and couldn't afford to send me back." As their situation became increasingly strained, her mother's frustration spilled over into abuse. After several years of intermittent abuse, at age 14 Sally refused to take any more of it and left home. She lived for several weeks in a local park but was then arrested for curfew violation and possession of alcohol and sent to a detention facility for status offenders. From there she went to the first of several foster homes. She indicated that after being sexually abused in this foster home, she went back to living on the streets. This became the pattern of her life over the next few years. She lived on the streets for several weeks or months until the police picked her up again and sent her to a detention facility, which placed her in another foster home. Her siblings were also eventually placed in foster care, and they maintained sporadic contact. When she was 18, she met and married George Tucker. For the first several months, Sally's marriage to George provided companionship and a home base. However, these elements were short lived. After 4 years of conflict and frequent separations, George availed himself of a "poor people's divorce": He walked out and never returned, leaving Sally to parent their two small children alone.

In the year before their arrival at Andre House, the Baker family's lifestyle mirrored Sally's earlier life—a chronic pattern of lurching from crisis to crisis. Sally had been living on AFDC in a Housing Authority complex in a small city. Because her unit was subsidized by the Housing Authority, she was paying hundreds of dollars less than she would have had to pay for a private unit, but she had to contend with drug dealers, gang activity, and considerable neighborhood violence. When Tyrone started to wear the "colors" of one of the local gangs, Sally decided to move in with her sister-in-law in a neighboring town. The safety of this new living arrangement was offset by the crowded

CASE STUDY

The Baker Family *(continued)*

conditions; there were now two adults and seven children in a two-bedroom apartment. Sally was able to stay for 3 months and saved some money, but not enough to get a place of her own.

Sally and her children moved back to Dallas to live with her sister, who also had a two-bedroom apartment. The sister and her boyfriend slept in one bedroom, the sister's three children slept in the other, and Sally and her three children slept on the living-room floor. Again there were problems. Her sister's boyfriend used and sold crack cocaine. Sally contributed a share of the monthly rent, but a few months later both families were evicted because the boyfriend was not paying the rent.

Sally and her children moved in with a friend, but once again drugs were a problem—this time because friends of the friend were using her apartment to make their deals. The police frequently came to the house because of the drug activity and finally threatened to take Sally's children away from her unless she got them out of the house.

Bit by bit Sally had been saving money from her AFDC checks, but the $100 she had managed to put aside was still too little to pay the first and last months' rent on a place of her own plus a security deposit. In any case, the fruit of her prudence and foresight disappeared when the apartment was robbed by the drug-dealing friends of the woman with whom she was staying. Sally was beaten, her life was threatened, and even her children were threatened. The elderly couple next door called the paramedics, who took her to a clinic. After all the threats to her life, she was too frightened to let anyone call the police. The counselor at the clinic found a shelter that had room for them and gave her money for the bus. And so the Baker family found themselves at Andre House.

Sally's children reflect the type of chaotic life she has led. Ty especially seems to have been negatively affected by his experiences. His behavior is highly impulsive. His attention shifts rapidly from one object or activity to the next. At school he is an "attention-starved" child. He must be first in line, the one to sit next to the teacher, the first to play with a new toy. At times he hurts other children and is destructive. Sometimes conflict with his mother erupts into aggressive outbursts and he lashes out at his 3-year-old brother.

Daniella, by contrast, has a good relationship with her family. She and Sally talk frequently, and Daniella is able to ask for what she wants and needs. Her calm, sweet disposition endears her to adults and apparently helps her with

---

CASE STUDY

The Baker Family (continued)

both of her brothers, even Tyrone. She is especially helpful in caring for Jerome. Even though this task is sometimes frustrating to her, she is quite responsible and affectionate with him.

Jerome is a shy, passive, sickly child who is fearful of strangers. He prefers to be left alone and makes few demands. He is apathetic and disinterested and when left alone mostly watches television. He seems indifferent to Tyrone's temper outbursts, even when they are directed at him. He tends to cling to Daniella, though, and follows her about closely.

---

families (U.S. Conference of Mayors, 2001). The problem of homelessness is widespread and getting worse. Here is a sample of what they reported:

- Requests for food assistance by families with children increased by an average of 19% from the previous year, and on average, emergency food assistance facilities had to turn away 14% of families in need due to lack of resources.
- Requests for shelter by homeless families increased by 22% between 2000 and 2001, and approximately 52% of requests by homeless families for emergency shelter went unmet due to a lack of resources.
- In 22% of the cities, families have to spend their daytime hours outside of the homeless shelter they use at night. In 52% of the cities, families must separate in order to be sheltered.
- Lack of affordable housing is the most commonly cited cause of homelessness identified by city officials. On average, families with children represent 40% of the homeless population.
- Families must wait an average of 16 months for public housing. The average wait for Section 8 certificates is 20 months, and for Section 8 vouchers, 22 months. Nineteen percent of the cities have stopped accepting applications for at least one assisted-housing program due to the excessive length of the waiting list.
- Barriers to homeless children enrolling and attending school include transportation, lack of official school records, immunization requirements, residency requirements, and providing birth certificates (Office of Elementary and Secondary Education, 2000).

Like poverty, homelessness is often explained at the individual, personal level. Sally Baker must be lazy or imprudent or unlucky. She didn't want to work. She should have put her savings in the bank. These simplistic arguments fail to account for the complex realities that have shaped her opportunities for decades. Homelessness, at the aggregate level, is caused by a lack of low-cost housing, which means many thousands of families will not have access to any housing. In these circumstances, poor people either pay more for housing, move in with friends or family members (Fuller et al., 2002; Office of Elementary and

Secondary Education, 2000), or become homeless. Basic arithmetic demonstrates that the Sally Bakers of this country have very limited choices.

Research on homeless families shows that they are disproportionately likely to be families of color, to be young, to be composed of parents who are more likely to have been abused as children and battered as adults, and to have limited social support networks (Styron, Hanoff-Bulman, & Davidson, 2000). Life in shelters or on the streets for homeless children and adolescents is linked to depression, anxiety, behavioral disturbances, and an assortment of educational problems (Anooshian, 2005). As might be expected, children of homeless families perform poorly in school and have more erratic attendance records (Office of Elementary and Secondary Education, 2000).

Here again the Baker family exemplifies the problems of homelessness. Sally's early physical and sexual abuse, chaotic and stressful living arrangements, and her lack of purpose and hope place Sally and her children at risk.

SOCIOECONOMIC STATUS

The social and economic environment in which children grow is a significant exosystemic predictor of their overall well-being. Almost all available data support the conclusion that children's education, later employment, future earnings, and health greatly depend on their families' socioeconomic status (SES). Membership in the lowest SES group—that is, families in extreme poverty—is clearly linked to a wide variety of problems among children and adolescents (Brooks-Gunn & Duncan, 1997; Garbarino, 1998).

Health Problems and SES

Children and adolescents from impoverished families have an increased risk of health problems (Bauman, Silver, & Stein, 2006). In contrast to middle SES children, they are more likely to have suffered neonatal damage, to have been underweight at birth and malnourished, to have had problems with vision and hearing that were unidentified and uncorrected, and to have experienced untreated childhood illnesses (Garbarino, 1998). Children who come from low SES families usually grow up with highly stressed immediate environments, or microsystems. They live in disorganized and impoverished neighborhoods, and their microsystems often involve socially isolated and very young mothers, no fathers, and minimal support from other family members (Garbarino, 1998). Further, low SES status is associated with problems of mental health, impaired parent–child relationships, and a high incidence of child abuse and neglect (CDF, 2001a).

At-Risk Categories and SES

Low SES status coupled with being a person of color is the strongest predictor of school dropout (Entwisle & Alexander, 1992). Low SES status is also related to juvenile delinquency (Jarjoura et al., 2002) and is the strongest predictor of teenage pregnancy (AGI, 1999). We will examine the relationship between SES and each at-risk category behavior more fully later in this book.

THE WIDENING GAP

For many reasons related to the changing economy, most U.S. workers are finding it more and more difficult to meet their financial needs. Meanwhile, they are also losing ground to the wealthy. For example, the income gap—that is, the disparity between the richest and the poorest—in Manhattan, New York, is worse than it is in Guatemala (Roberts, 1994). The combined wealth of the top 1% of American families is nearly the same as the combined wealth of the entire bottom 95% (Sklar, 1995).

The average family income in the middle and lower brackets has decreased while the income for the wealthiest families has increased. For instance, salaries for major executives jumped 571% between 1990 and 2000. Salaries for CEOs rose even in the year 2000, a year in which the S&P 500 suffered a 10% loss, and CEO salaries increased dramatically even in companies that experienced major layoffs. The explosion in CEO pay over the decade dwarfed the 37% growth in worker pay (Anderson, Cavanagh, Hartman, & Leonard-Wright, 2001). Stated another way, if the average annual pay for production workers had grown at the same rate since 1990 as it has for CEOs, the workers' 2000 annual earnings would have been $120,491 instead of $24,668. Likewise, if the minimum wage, which stood at $3.80 an hour in 1990, had grown at the same rate as CEO pay over the decade, it would now be $25.50 an hour rather than the current $5.15 an hour (Anderson et al., 2001). These income patterns have been accompanied by an increasingly lower standard of living among most workers and an increase in poverty in the United States overall. Because much of the shifting redistribution of wealth upward is based on income-producing assets—bonds, trusts, and business equity—this trend will likely continue.

ENNUI AND PURPOSE

The economic conditions of a major portion of our population contribute greatly to increasing risk factors for children and adolescents. It would be a mistake, however, to conclude that only poverty creates risk. Many young people from affluent backgrounds are also at risk. Affluent children typically spend a great deal of time on their own and often seek peer support and nurturance instead of parental and familial support (consider Carrie in Box 1.1). Among other problems, children and youth without family presence and adult support experience a great deal of "ennui."

Ennui refers to an emotional state of noninvolvement and boredom that comes from a lack of connectedness and a lack of life purpose. Many young people suffer from ennui, a lack of connectedness with others, themselves, and their own sense of future, which increases the possibility that they will be at risk (Karcher, Davis, & Powell, 2002; Townsend & McWhirter, 2005). Ennui can occur in children from all types of families; it both causes and is affected by aimlessness, alienation, and lack of direction.

POLICY PROPOSALS AND SUGGESTIONS

What can be done? In later chapters we try to provide some of the answers. Here we suggest several measures that may help to nurture the soil. These policy areas focus on child care, comprehensive preschool programs, 21st-century community learning centers, reading and work, and empowerment. Each of these suggestions requires the collaborative efforts of families, schools, and communities.

Child Care

Child care is a task that requires the joint efforts of families and communities to provide choices that are healthy and beneficial for children and their parents. The number of children who are cared for by people other than their parents during work hours continues to rise. Access to adequate child care enables parents to work without undue stress and concern for the welfare of their children. Adequate child care prevents parents from missing days of work because arrangements have fallen through, because quality care is not available, or because a child is ill. When both parents work, some of the socioeconomic limitations of their children's environment are likely to be overcome. The benefits of adequate child care are obvious—both by eliminating neglect, abuse, poor nutrition, and poor health that are likely in poorly run facilities and by providing the stable, consistent child care by providers who promote the healthy development of each child.

Fears and biases about child care have resulted in the failure to develop constructive social policies that ensure affordable, accessible, quality child care to people of all economic statuses. Studies that suggest negative effects of child care fail to account for variations in the type of care provided (from in-house caretakers to centers that care for more than 100 children), for the family/home environment (from abusive to highly supportive), and for the qualifications and training of care providers (from minimal attention by untrained caretakers to programmatic enrichment by highly trained child-care professionals). In sum, there is nearly complete consensus among developmental psychologists and early childhood experts that child care per se does not constitute a risk factor in children's lives; rather, poor quality care and poor family environments can together produce poor developmental outcomes (Scarr, Phillips, & McCartney, 1990).

The quality of child care is determined by the ratio of children to caregivers, the number of children cared for in the setting, the caring and responsiveness of caregivers, the stability of caregivers and settings, and the training and experience of caregivers (Gormley, 1995). The low pay and lack of benefits received by the majority of child-care workers result in a high turnover rate for this occupation. Many child-care workers cannot survive on the income that the position provides.

A national policy to shape and direct child-care services would help resolve this problem (Clarke-Stewart, Gruber, & Fitzgerald, 1994). A commitment from workplaces to reevaluate personnel policies that create difficulty for employees with families would also contribute to its solution. Currently, the social values that prevail in the United States generally require families to adjust to the demands of the workplace rather than expecting workplaces to modify policies to meet the realistic demands of families. In schools, teachers, counselors, and parent support volunteers can be effective advocates of parents by informing them of procedures for reaching their legislators. In addition, teachers and counselors might devise ways to facilitate exchanges of information on child care and to link parents interested in sharing child-care arrangements. Currently, many communities have nonprofit organizations that serve as clearinghouses for child-care service information, but even these services involve at least a nominal cost to families.

The lack of adequate day care is a persistent problem, particularly for the working poor. Parents are often prevented from securing employment because affordable day care is unavailable. Mishel and Bernstein (1994) suggested that mothers out of work due to child-care problems were disproportionately poorly educated, lowering their potential to earn a wage that might have allowed them to purchase the very child care they need. Thus they are stuck in a vicious cycle. Although the federal government subsidizes some day care through the dependent-care tax credit, Head Start, and Social Service Block Grant programs, the majority of poor people do not benefit from these services.

The dependent-care tax credit, for example, is the major federal support for child care. A family may deduct a portion of annual child-care expenses from their federal income tax, up to a maximum of $3,000 for one child—but the credit cannot be greater than the family's tax liability. The very poor rarely owe any income tax. Thus poor and single mothers whose children are at risk and who most need quality child care are least likely to receive any benefit from this policy (Burman, Rohaly, & Maag, 2002). The child-care tax credit primarily benefits middle- and upper-income families.

At the same time, poor families with an employed mother who paid for child care spent roughly 3 times as much of their budget on it as families who were not poor (20% versus 7%; Smith, 2002). The least well-off families, those with incomes under $15,000, spent an even greater percentage of their annual income on child care, nearly 25% (Smith, 2002). Securing safe and affordable child care remains a major obstacle for mothers moving off of welfare (Fuller et al., 2002).

Comprehensive Preschool Programs

Another effort that requires collaboration on the part of communities, schools, and families is the provision of comprehensive preschool programs for children who are identified as at risk. Evidence suggests that overcoming deficits in skills needs to begin early, so preschool is extremely important. The following results have been documented as a result of participation in early childhood interventions, including preschool programs: increased cognitive and emotional development, improved parent–child relationships, improved educational outcomes for children, increased economic self-sufficiency for parents and later for the child, decreased criminal activity, decreased child abuse and substance abuse, and increased maternal reproductive health (Greenwood, 1999; Karoly, Kilburn, & Cannon, 2005).

Head Start, a nationwide, federally funded program for economically disadvantaged prekindergarten children, is one comprehensive preschool program (Oden, Schweinhart, & Weikart, 2000). Head Start programs vary from locale to locale, but each provides a classroom-based, multicultural learning experience for 4-year-olds. Through Head Start, children with little structured home stimulation and lack of exposure to the resources of the middle class are given a "head start" on kindergarten. They learn school-related vocabulary and norms in a nonpressured, cognitively rich environment. Children are assessed for a variety of developmental problems and may be provided access to speech therapists, psychologists, and other professionals as the need arises. Head Start provides enrichment for the rest of the family as well (Oden et al., 2000). By actively participating in the daily events of the classroom and by receiving specific training in parenting, life skills, and health and employment issues, parents become engaged in an empowering process that extends beyond the 9 months of the school year (see Box 2.1). Although the success of Head Start varies with the quality of its implementation, Head Start programs have helped children from challenging economic backgrounds to persevere and eventually graduate from high school.

▲ Box 2.1

Mother Gets a Head Start

When her first child was 4, she shyly volunteered to help out in the classroom. Just for an hour. Over the weeks it became 2 and 3 hours and she even started looking children in the eyes. She was quiet, worked very hard, and seemed quite bright in a clandestine kind of way. When her next child turned 4 a year later, she was working on her GED. Her home, she told me, had been a smelly, dirty shack; her children were always barefoot and always hungry. When they weren't hungry, it was because she had given them change for candy bars and pop. "I weighed 250 pounds and I was still growing," she said, laughing. "I was disgusting even to me." And she had bruises, and permanent nerve damage in her left hand, and a husband who got mean when he drank.

She had bruises on her arm the first time I met her, and a welt under her eye, and she had been a Head Start teacher's assistant for 3 months. She was bringing her youngest to work and taking home a paycheck for the first time since she got married at age 18. Her husband didn't much like it but he had a little more beer money now. He really got mean when she insisted on cooking carrots one night. For the first time, she pressed charges. One incredible year, 82 pounds, and a divorce later, she was considering a community college course, "so I can be a teacher someday." And several years after she left Head Start, I heard she had done it.

Preschool programs generally have had a positive affect on children's cognitive and social development. In 1962, the High/Scope Perry Preschool Project began examining the lives of 123 low-income, African American children. Randomly divided into two groups as 3- and 4-year-olds, with one group receiving a high-quality preschool program and the other no program, the now 40-year-old participants demonstrate the value of preschool. On an initial investment of a little over $15,000 per student, preschool participants had committed fewer crimes, were more likely to have graduated from high school, earned higher salaries, and were more likely to hold onto jobs. In addition, both child-care assistance and comprehensive preschool programs have contributed to the effects of welfare-to-work programs (Oden et al., 2000). Stated in simple monetary terms, every dollar invested in early childhood interventions returns between 1.80 and 17.07 to society (Karoly, Kilburn, & Cannon, 2005), making failure to invest in early childhood interventions a strikingly foolish choice. The combination of inadequate child care and pervasive deficits in adult skills contributes to the stagnation of the poor and leaves our children at risk. If Sally Baker had adequate child care for her children, a reasonable wage, and support to enhance her work-related skills, she and her children might emerge from their cycle of instability. Unfortunately, the safety net our society provides for Sally and others like her is badly in need of repair.

TWENTY-FIRST CENTURY COMMUNITY LEARNING CENTERS

According to Zigler (cited in Dryfoos, 1994), a given community owns its public school buildings by virtue of having invested one to two trillion dollars in these properties. Based on this premise, Zigler advocates keeping schools open from 7 a.m. to 6 p.m. and establishing child-care centers for 3- to 5-year-olds as well as before- and after-school care for 6- to 12-year-olds. The centers would provide developmentally appropriate recreation and enrichment activities in a safe and well-staffed setting. These school-based centers would also offer home visits to all parents of newborns and organize and coordinate family day care for infants from birth to 3 years. Early childhood educators trained to bridge the gap between home and school would administer the center.

The 21st Century Community Learning Centers have implemented some of Zigler's ideas. Federal legislation pushed by then Vice President Gore, and initially supported by the Bush administration, resulted in federal grants that allowed schools to stay open before and after school hours, as well as on Saturdays and during summer. Most of the centers are organizational hybrids that include school-, city-, and community-based nonprofit organizations, each of which draws funding from a variety of sources. This decentralized arrangement leads each center to provide programs and services tailored to its unique combination of funders and constituencies (Moore, 2005).

Evaluations of the 21st Century centers find few gains in academic outcomes (Public Agenda, 2005). However, students enrolled in the programs were more likely to be supervised by adults after school and report feeling safer. Middle school participants missed one less day of school per year and were more likely to say they expected to graduate from college (James-Burdumy, Dynarski, Moore, Deke, Mansfield, & Pistorino, 2005). Policymakers tend to focus on the educational value of out-of-school programs. Interestingly, only 15% of parents and 12% of young people reported that academic achievement is the best reason to be involved in organized activities. Developing interests and hobbies and keeping young people engaged in positive activities and out of trouble were much more important outcomes according to parents and participants (Public Agenda, 2005). Unfortunately, limited academic achievement is often used as a basis for funding cuts or program elimination.

Reading and Work

Although the general level of education has risen in the United States over the decades (Berliner, 2001), a large number of Americans lack basic skills, and these deficits impede gainful employment. Reading is the single most important foundational skill for learning and an essential skill for all children. Slavin (1994) argues that virtually every child can become a successful reader in the early grades, and his Success for All program provides evidence that they can (Slavin, Karweit, & Wasik, 1994). He also presents evidence that the most effective approaches to preventing early reading failure are those that incorporate one-on-one tutoring of at-risk first-graders to help enhance their phonological awareness. Reading Recovery is one of the best documented approaches to preventing reading failure.

Reading Recovery is an early intervention program developed by New Zealand educator Marie Clay (1985). It is a one-on-one tutoring pullout program for first-grade students who are experiencing difficulty learning to read. It is based on the idea that high-quality, intensive intervention in the very early grades is an efficient and cost-effective strategy for preventing reading failure, a pattern of frustration leading to other long-term academic difficulties, and school dropout. This approach helps prevent children from developing ineffective reading habits. First, the Reading Recovery teacher assesses what the child knows as a means of tailoring the instructional approach. After this initial assessment period, each daily 30-minute session has a similar format. After identifying and working on problem words, the child re-reads two familiar books with an emphasis on fluency. When the child experiences difficulty, the teacher helps the child identify potential strategies for overcoming the problem. An unfamiliar third book is used to create a running record of the child's accuracy in reading. After the reading session, the teacher reviews the record with the student and asks questions: "How did you know that?" "What did you do here?" The teacher emphasizes the child's use of appropriate strategies in dealing with difficult sections. Next, the child dictates a one-sentence story to the teacher. This sentence is the basis for a writing activity and becomes part of the homework assignment. Finally, a fourth new book is introduced to the child, along with a packet to take home that includes another story and a copy of the student-generated writing. When children begin to perform at the average reading level of their classroom, they are released from the program.

Reading Recovery has had substantial success in New Zealand (Glynn, Crooks, Bethune, Ballard, & Smith, 1992), Australia (Center, Wheldall, Freeman, Outhred, & McNaught, 1995), and the United States (Pinnell, Lyons, DeFord, Bryk, & Seltzer, 1994; National Data Evaluation Center, 2005). Unfortunately, the size and mobility of the U.S. population, along with the intensive training and staff development required, make this tutoring program difficult for some schools to adopt. In Chapter 14 we discuss alternative one-on-one programs of peer and cross-age tutoring that can be implemented more easily.

About 1 in 4 Americans lacks a high school diploma, and 1 in 8 is illiterate. Basic competence in arithmetic, reading, and writing are essential in today's labor market, even in most entry-level jobs, and low proficiency in these skills is correlated with low educational attainment and low earnings. Basic skill needs have also intensified as our economy becomes increasingly "digital," and the problem is compounded by the fact that unskilled minimum-wage jobs provide less actual purchasing power than at any time in more than three decades. Contrary to popular notions, only 31% of minimum-wage workers are teenagers in their first jobs. Nearly half of minimum-wage earners are 25 years old or older, and 28% are heads of households (U.S. Census Bureau, 2001). More important for children and youth, the difficulties of the unskilled worker are often transferred to the next generation. The proportion of young people from households with low skills and low incomes who do not complete high school is twice that of youth from more affluent families (U.S. Census Bureau, 2001). Thus children of the unskilled and poor are more likely than children from affluent families to be poorly prepared when they enter the workforce, and their chances of escaping the cycle of poverty are very slim.

Finally, there is growing global competitive pressure for a highly skilled workforce. The United States is facing a tremendous mismatch between the jobs available and the ability of U.S. citizens to perform them. An undereducated and unskilled workforce that cannot keep pace with skill requirements will continue to lose jobs to international workers who meet the knowledge and skill-intensive work requirements and will carry out the work for significantly lower wages. Programs that enhance the basic and more advanced skills of our workforce are urgently needed within nearly all of our communities. Vocational education and programs that support the school-to-work transition are needed to assist in breaking the cycle of poverty and providing a skilled workforce for the nation.

EMPOWERMENT

Empowerment is another way in which adults can help at-risk children and adolescents address limiting environmental conditions. Empowerment helps people actively confront their environment rather than passively accept their conditions as unalterable (E. H. McWhirter, 1994, 1997).

The term *empowerment* is frequently used in education, social work, and counseling literature. We have elsewhere defined empowerment as "the process by which people, organizations, or groups who are powerless or marginalized (a) become aware of the power dynamics at work in their life context, (b) develop the skills and capacity for gaining some reasonable control over their lives, (c) which they exercise, (d) without infringing on the rights of others, and (e) which coincides with actively supporting the empowerment of others in their community" (E. H. McWhirter, 1994, p. 12). For young people this means learning how their lives are influenced by family, school, and the larger society; developing the skills to resist negative influences and make positive choices for their lives; and supporting the healthy choices of other young people in their families, schools, and communities. The benefits of contributing to the welfare of others is consistent with Adlerian principles and supported by findings such as those associated with service learning programs that reduce the likelihood of teen pregnancy (Kirby, 2001; see Chapter 9). Here we will discuss four aspects of empowerment in more detail: critical consciousness, skill development, exercising new choices and behaviors, and social activism.

Critical consciousness.   Part of facilitating empowerment means raising critical consciousness, which is awareness of the power dynamics that affect a person's life ecology, and critical self-reflection, or understanding the person's own contribution to that ecology (E. H. McWhirter, 1994). Critical consciousness leads to transformative action that increases a person's active direction of his or her life course (Martín-Baró, 1994). Analysis of power dynamics can focus on family systems, school and community factors, and local and national government policies; it can also be applied to racism, sexism, homophobia, ecology, nuclear weapons, pollution, and a multitude of other topics. The key is to help students understand how these issues affect them as individuals and as members of a community. The more immediate dynamics of popularity, peer pressure, and media influences such as advertising are especially salient to adolescents, and a basic knowledge of reality television shows and MTV can help facilitate discussions when discussing classroom social politics is not warranted. For example, "Who has ideas about why (character name) on *Survivor* got so angry in last week's episode? What kind of power do you think she has in her 'tribe'? How do others in the 'tribe' try to influence her behavior? What role do you think hunger plays in her decision making? What role does greed play? Has anything happened in the past 2 weeks at school that is similar to the way (the characters) are treating (the other character)?" Even young children can be taught in simple ways to examine how their behavior is influenced by context. For example, "I laughed at Sarah when all the other kids did, even though I didn't really think it was funny" is a statement of awareness many children could achieve. Adolescents are often quite willing to explore how their behavior is shaped by peers, the school, and the community, but they need assistance developing a norm and a language for doing so. Critical self-reflection, or understanding what they contribute to peer dynamics, social pressure, family tension, or class projects, requires a safe and nonjudgmental atmosphere that is free of blame. When they understand how they are influenced and can explore the choices they have made and are making without being criticized for those choices (that is, allowing natural and logical consequences to serve their powerful roles), adolescents have a basis for choosing different attitudes and behaviors. Power analysis and critical self-reflection, the two components of critical consciousness, can be integrated into a variety of standard subjects, including history, language arts, government, creative writing, and literature. Fostering critical consciousness helps young people identify social influences, identify what they are and are not able to change or control among those influences, and initiate desirable changes in their lives (Diemer & Blustein, in press). A young person critically conscious about pollution might be aware of the incentives and disincentives for local industries to control emissions and reduce waste and work with other young people to draw attention to the consequences of pollution in their community.

Skill development.   Empowerment also involves development of the concrete skills necessary for enacting responsible choices. Teaching children more effective social skills increases their power over their personal environment. Learning cognitive-behavioral skills helps them manage and cope better with their internal processes. Providing them with learning strategies facilitates their intellectual growth. Decision making and assertiveness training, imagery and relaxation techniques, and other psychological tools enhance people's ability to negotiate the barriers and take advantage of the opportunities in their environment. Training in other skills, such as conducting research, writing letters, organizing meetings, and public speaking, enable at-risk youth to take more active roles in negotiating various power structures influential in their lives.

Much of the discussion in the following chapters is designed to help teachers and counselors empower young people through the development of important skills. Kamps and Kay (2001) note that social skills programs that do not work are often characterized by poor teaching and modeling of the skill, inadequate reinforcement of skills over time, and negative modeling. Negative modeling could be group reinforcement of aggressive behavior in a group for boys with conduct disorder (e.g., Dishion, McCord, & Poulin, 1999) or could also refer to poor modeling on the part of the social skills trainer. A classroom teacher who instructs students on social skills and at the same time is disrespectful to them violates the basic principles of the skills that are being taught. Promoting skills development requires understanding components of the skill, the ability to model the skill, and providing consistent opportunities for students to practice the skill.

Exercising new choices and behaviors.   Through enhancing critical consciousness, the teacher or counselor helps at-risk youth realistically appraise the impact of socialization, economic stratification, and discrimination on their lives, as well as the more immediate influences of peers and family members. To ignore the political, economic, and social context within which the young person operates and survives is to risk identifying the source of the problems as the individual. It is the responsibility of the teacher or counselor to help individuals identify contributing factors, for many young people are all too willing to shoulder all the blame themselves. If young people are led to believe that "the system" caused all of their problems, however, their apathy and withdrawal may simply increase. Growing critical consciousness must be accompanied by the development of concrete skills and, equally important, the motivation and encouragement to utilize the skills, to identify new alternatives, and to change the individual's behavior. When the norms for behavior change within a classroom or a school, the child's environment is significantly affected. Empowerment suggests that although problems are often rooted in systems, individuals can and must share the responsibility for addressing and alleviating the problems. Identifying new choices and behaviors is essential, as is providing students with opportunities to practice those behaviors and actively pursue those choices. Otherwise, teachers and counselors will leave their students and clients feeling even less in control of their lives. Social activism is a natural outgrowth of the empowerment process.

Social activism.   One hindrance to the development of adequate services for youth is the fact that so many of the solutions require fundamental sociopolitical changes (Albee, 1995; E. H. McWhirter, 1998; Prilleltensky, 1997). Poverty, inadequate nutrition and housing, and discrimination cannot be prevented with crisis-oriented programs. Prevention requires changing the environment that fosters such problems. Thus some aspects of prevention must involve critical analysis of the structure of society and reflect the results of such analysis in planning, programming, and action. The issue of action is critically important. Empowerment, by its very nature, requires not just reflection and change on the part of those served by human service professionals but on the part of service providers themselves. We cannot facilitate critical consciousness in others without becoming aware of how we ourselves participate in maintaining systems that perpetuate inequity, injustice, and ongoing community and individual problems. We need to develop awareness of existing community organizations, support groups, neighborhood action committees, and other channels of collective effort. We need to inform our students, their families, our communities, and our colleagues of opportunities to participate in social and community affairs. We have suggested elsewhere (Chronister, McWhirter, & Kerewsky, 2004; E. H. McWhirter, 1994, 1997, 2001; J. J. McWhirter & E. H. McWhirter, 1989) that it is time to add a new dimension to the traditional roles of counselor and teacher. Traditionally, both teachers and counselors have been advocates of individual development and growth. With the growing acknowledgment of the role the environment plays in human development, however, social activism is the natural arena into which counselors and teachers must move if they are to remain faithful to that advocacy. Counselors especially can urge adoption of mental health programs that address specific environmental circumstances, limitations, and inadequacies. Teachers and counselors can make their views known to local and national leaders through votes and letters, publications, and seminars. All can work to be more aware of how local politics affect mental health policy in their communities. Teachers and counselors can enhance awareness of the influence of the environment, encourage recognition that change is possible, and facilitate development of resources and skills for creating change. The social and economic risk factors in the larger society can be directly modified only modestly at the grassroots level by mental health and school personnel. However, educational and mental health policy and practice at every level of government, preservice training, school district and building, and agency service can be modified to improve the health and learning of students at risk. Further, teachers and counselors need to be involved in the process of seeking change at the level of those who have the power to fund, to legislate, and to affect the structure of the environment. Teachers and counselors have both the resources and the knowledge to address the needs of the poor and to break the cycle of poverty. Counselors for Social Justice (www.counselorsforsocialjustice.org) is just one example of an organization designed to provide mutual support, information, and ideas for social action that promote community well-being. Although we refer to this as social activism, what we are referring to could also be described as citizenship: working conscientiously to make society better for all of its inhabitants, and especially for those who are most vulnerable.

Conclusion

Advocating for large and sweeping programs and strategies is an important way to enhance the potential of youth at risk. Ultimately, prevention of the conditions and systems that place youth at risk may require us all to be active in securing the type of public policy that benefits families who are economically struggling and socially marginalized. In this chapter we discussed the problems of poverty, the stagnation of the working poor, the struggles of young families, welfare reform, and how low SES is an important risk factor. We propose that improving social policy and funding around child care, comprehensive preschool programs, after-school programs, reading, worker skill enhancement, and empowerment of young people are some of the first steps to take to confront the environmental, exosystemic, and macrosystemic problems that place our children and adolescents at risk for future difficulty.

CHAPTER 3

LEGAL AND ETHICAL ISSUES

▲ *Federal law, state statues, court rulings, civil codes, administrative procedures, ethical codes . . . When two or more stretch out like railroad rails or telephone lines reaching perfectly parallel to an infinity point in the distance, the choice and the decision are easy. But sometimes two or more are like a pair of scissors—so joined they seem not to be separated, yet seemingly moving in opposite directions.*

Chapter Outline

▲ To work with at-risk youth is to be at the cutting edge of society's problems, which is also the cutting edge of the law. Psychologists, counselors, teachers, and other human service professionals (practitioners) and lawyers approach these problems differently. Rowley and MacDonald (2001) suggest that the different approaches are a "cross-cultural" phenomenon. In this chapter we provide insights about the legal "culture" and suggest important ethical considerations for practitioners working with youth.

In this chapter we treat ethical issues only within the context of their legal ramifications. Ethics codes of specific disciplines vary slightly, and all human service professionals should fully know and understand their profession's code of ethics and the specific state laws for the jurisdiction within which they practice. The American Psychological Association produces a series of state-specific books in its Law & Mental Health Professionals series. These books are a good place to start when seeking answers to specific legal and ethical questions and problems.

In this chapter we first generally explain the legal system and criminal, juvenile, and civil procedure. Next we focus on specific legal considerations related to the at-risk categories of substance use, sexuality, conduct problems/delinquency, and suicide. We also provide a guide to testifying in court. Finally, we list some "dos and don'ts" for working with at-risk youth to improve ethical decision making and avoid legal liability.

The Legal System

Although a complete discussion of the U.S. legal system is beyond the scope of this chapter, explaining the rudiments of how criminal, juvenile, and civil law works should clarify some issues.

Criminal Law

Criminal cases are the ones most often seen on television and in movies. Though the issues can be interesting, their relevance to most of us is often exaggerated. One can see a trend, however, toward holding practitioners and teachers criminally liable for failure to report suspected child abuse to authorities, which we discuss in detail at the end of this section.

General criminal law.   Criminal cases are tried by a prosecutor—a representative of the state or federal government who will often refer to him- or herself as representing "the people," "the commonwealth," or "the government." He or she has the burden of proving "beyond a reasonable doubt" that the defendant committed the crime for which he or she stands accused. The accused is usually defended by a lawyer, either retained private counsel or a public defender. Each side presents its case to a "trier of fact," usually a jury but sometimes a judge, who decides innocence or guilt on the evidence the prosecutor and defense attorney present at trial. Over several centuries our society has found this adversarial system to be the best way, despite its flaws, to find "truth."

The above description of criminal procedure, although accurate, is not commonplace. Instead, the defendant usually accepts a "plea" after the lawyer and the prosecutor "plea bargain." In a plea bargain, the defendant agrees to admit he or she has committed a crime in exchange for a lighter sentence or other consideration. Thus there is no trial but instead a "change of plea" hearing.

Human service practitioners are seldom concerned with criminal law because they do not confront criminal liability in their work. However, it is illegal to contribute to the delinquency of a minor, and it is possible for a practitioner with good intentions to run afoul of someone's idea of what constitutes a contribution to a minor's delinquency (Hopkins, 1989; Hopkins & Anderson, 1985). Obviously, providing drugs to a child or adolescent counts as contributing to delinquency. Suppose an adolescent such as Jason Carter (see Chapter 4) was using a drug as a form of self-medication and the practitioner, hoping to build a better relationship, facilitated his access to the drug. Pharmacists and osteopaths who prescribed dangerous drugs for minors have been convicted of contributing to their delinquency (*People v. Brac*, 1946; *State v. Tritt*, 1970). The best legal advice is obvious: do not provide illegal drugs to anyone.

Perhaps the most obvious situation in which a practitioner could be accused of contributing to the delinquency of a minor is sex. It is not earth-shattering advice that practitioners should never engage in sexual liaisons with underage persons. Moral and ethical considerations aside, states are increasing the legal penalties for such activity, and these penalties are increasingly applied equally to men and women practitioners.

The child-abuse quagmire.   Every state has mandatory child-abuse reporting laws (Walker, 1990), and the U.S. Congress has its version for practitioners working on federal land or in a federally operated or contracted facility (Crime Control Act of 1990). These laws require practitioners to report suspected child abuse, and the federal law even requires commercial film and photo processors to report evidence of child abuse. In addition, most states impose criminal liability for failure to report child abuse (Small, Lyons, & Guy, 2002). This section highlights the most important points, but see Kalichman (1999) for greater depth on the issue.

Practitioners are generally immune from criminal and civil liability for reporting suspected child abuse that turns out to be unfounded. States provide this immunity to obtain federal grant money (Small et al., 2002). The reporting, however, must still be "in good faith" with "reasonable cause" to believe the abuse happened. Small, Lyons, and Guy (2002) state that "to date, there are no reported cases in which psychologists have been denied immunity for failing to act in good faith" (p. 16). Generally, courts treat practitioners the same as psychologists. Conversely, there is no immunity for false reporting, and several states have laws that make this a crime as well (Small et al., 2002).

The extent of a practitioner's duty to report suspected child abuse varies, with some states requiring that practitioners report past abuse no matter how old. Others have time limitations. The Andrews family (see Chapter 1) conceivably might represent a reporting issue. If Allie Andrews confided that her birth father, John Steiner, had sexually abused her, in some states this admission would create a duty to report the abuse even though it occurred many years earlier. Practitioners must consult the laws of their own state to find their legal responsibilities. State and local professional associations may well have this information prepared, and Small, Lyons, and Guy (2002) provide a useful survey and helpful charts of state statutes.

Most state laws require reporting of child abuse when the practitioner has a "reasonable suspicion" of abuse. What constitutes reasonable suspicion is often left to the individual state court, legislature, or practitioner to decide (Walker, 1990). The best advice in an unclear legal situation is to trust one's own professional training and ethical standards. Talk with a supervisor or team of colleagues and document the conversation. Write it down or tape it so you can corroborate what you did and why (Renninger, Veach, & Bagdade, 2002).

Often even informed practitioners do not know the details of their state's reporting laws. Just knowing the definitions of "child abuse" and "reasonable suspicion" is not sufficient to assist practitioners in responding ethically. In a survey of psychologists, nearly one third of the respondents stated that they had seen children who they suspected were abused but did not report their suspicions to child protection agencies; only 15% believed that a subjective suspicion alone was sufficient to require reporting (Kalichmant & Brosig, 1993). Conversely, confusion exists among practitioners as to whether to report when someone tells them of abuse but they do not believe the abuse actually happened. After reviewing the literature, Foreman and Bernet (2000) concluded that the law generally does not require practitioners to report abuse allegations if they do not believe the allegation. They encourage practitioners to report abuse when the law requires it but not to make unnecessary reports out of confusion or misinformation.

Ambiguity in the statutes and lack of understanding of legal responsibility often lead practitioners to hesitate reporting suspicions that may, in the end, be unfounded. Perhaps the biggest factor in the failure to report, however, is the practitioner's concern regarding the negative consequences to the child and family.

To appreciate this problem, suppose a practitioner suspects a mother abused her child. Perhaps the practitioner knows the mother lost her job and that her own mother recently died, and that the abuse, if it occurred, was an isolated incident. The law views this matter in black-and-white terms, but to the practitioner this situation may be many shades of gray.

Another example might be when a practitioner suspects a child is abusing a younger sibling (see Box 3.1). Most child-abuse statutes mandate reporting. But if the practitioner believes the abusing child is very near a major breakthrough in therapy, reporting may be the more harmful alternative.

▲ Box 3.1

When the Abused Is the Abuser

Janey, age 8, was sexually abused by the son of her mother's best friend when she was 4 years old. Her mother, Tanya, at first attributed the change in Janey's behavior to the fact that she was absent for long hours. In addition to working full time, Tanya was taking care of her dying father and her newborn daughter, Kelsey. When Janey finally described the abuse to her mother, Tanya informed the authorities and sought counseling for herself and Janey. She responded quickly and appropriately and did everything she could to help Janey recover from her trauma. Two years later, however, she discovered that Janey was sexually abusing Kelsey. Janey was deeply ashamed and begged her mother not to tell anyone. Somehow Tanya found the courage to seek appropriate help once again and entered both girls in individual and group therapy for child survivors of sexual abuse. This is not an isolated case; the fact is that many child survivors of sexual abuse replay the abuse on other children. In this case, the mother's painful decision to report her older daughter's actions resulted in the provision of effective and appropriate support services for both children.

Practitioners should consider the study of Weinstein and colleagues (2000) when deciding how to handle these gray areas. The authors studied issues surrounding reporting and the client–practitioner relationship. They found that for the majority of practitioners, telling their clients before the therapy began that they had a duty to report child abuse did not deter clients from speaking. They also found that more than 35% of the clients were not informed of the practitioner's duty to report child abuse until after the practitioner suspected or knew of the abuse. Furthermore, the study reported that after the practitioner reported the abuse, about 20% of the therapy relationships ended, 7% deteriorated, 32% did not change, and 41% improved. The authors suggest that statewide consultation networks and training beyond "identification" of abuse be available to all practitioners because the nuances of this issue require it.

Fortunately, despite the universality of reporting laws, prosecution of practitioners under them is rare. In *Barber v. State* (1992), the counselor had not reported the alleged abuse because he found it unsubstantiated. But the alleged abuser later murdered the victim, and the counselor was subsequently convicted for failure to report the original child abuse (Small et al., 2002). Given the lack of other reported cases, the *Barber* case represents an extreme, and relatively rare, situation.

Juvenile Law

The juvenile justice system from the outside may look indistinguishable from the criminal system. The key difference is that juveniles who commit criminal acts are not guilty of a crime but rather of an "act of juvenile delinquency" (see, e.g., 18 USC § 5032). In this section we will use the Federal Juvenile Delinquency Act ("Federal Juvenile Act") as a model for explaining juvenile justice. Practitioners must be aware, however, that all states have statutes defining their own juvenile procedures to which the practitioner should refer.

Juvenile court.   A juvenile accused of an act of juvenile delinquency is charged with an "information" instead of the complaint or indictment used to charge an adult with a crime. Under the federal statute an act of juvenile delinquency is

> the violation of the law of the United States committed by a person prior to his eighteenth birthday which would have been a crime if it had been committed by an adult. (18 U.S.C. § 5031)

Thus the information charging the act of juvenile delinquency will include an allegation that the child is a "juvenile delinquent." If the judge finds that the juvenile committed the criminal act and that the child is a "juvenile delinquent," it is not a crime but rather a determination of the child's status. Thus it is neither a felony nor a misdemeanor.

To start the case, a prosecutor will file an affidavit alleging there is probable cause to believe that the juvenile committed an act of juvenile delinquency. (In federal court the prosecution must also file a "need certification" justifying why the case needs to be in federal court rather than the state court). Most states also require the prosecutor to file a "record certification," which requires delivery to the deciding judge of any prior juvenile record.

Under the Federal Juvenile Delinquency Act at 18 U.S.C. § 5033, whenever the police arrest a juvenile the officer must notify the child's parents. This is a "safeguard" for the rights of the juvenile. The statute thus involves parents in what is going on. Also, in rare cases, parents could have some liability for their children's criminal acts (Lockwood, 2000).

At this point the juvenile is "arraigned." This is a formal proceeding where a judge officially advises the juvenile of the charges. Unlike for an adult, this hearing is not public. At this hearing, if the juvenile's family cannot afford a private attorney, the court will appoint one. The court will also advise the juvenile of certain rights, including the right to remain silent. The juvenile also has a right to a preliminary hearing on whether there is probable cause to believe an act of juvenile delinquency occurred and whether the juvenile did it.

A juvenile has no right to a jury; rather, a judge will hear the case and decide. Juvenile statutes provide for an even speedier trial than for adults. A juvenile could choose, with the advice of counsel, to waive the juvenile proceedings and proceed as an adult, in which case the juvenile would have the right to a jury as well as other adult rights. The problem, of course, is that the juvenile faces an adult prosecution, and if the jury convicts him or her, an adult conviction. The facts of a given case, however, may warrant a jury.

Juveniles do not receive a sentence; rather, a judge enters a disposition. Most statutes require the judge in the disposition to focus mostly on "the needs of the child." Punishment and incarceration are not the goal; rather, the goal is the child's welfare and rehabilitation (see Box 3.2). A judge is limited in the incarceration that can be imposed on the juvenile: generally only until the juvenile is 18 years old. In certain circumstances, such as if the juvenile has his or her adjudication after age 18, the judge can impose incarceration until either age 21 or 23 (see 18 USC § 5037[c]). ("Spare the rod")

Transferring juveniles.   A "transfer" is when a juvenile's case, despite his or her age, is sent to adult court. If convicted in adult court, the juvenile will end up with an adult felony record (theoretically it could be a misdemeanor, but usually it is not). A transfer occurs under statutory procedures and can be one of two types.

▲ Box 3.2

Spare the rod, spoil the child!

One trend in society is to treat juveniles more punitively, which radically departs from the tradition of rehabilitation to salvage children into productive adults rather than making them a social burden with long prison terms. This dynamic played out in the author's case of Jonah R. V. Carmona, 446 F.3d 1000 (9th Cir. 2006). In 1999 the Federal Bureau of Prisons (BOP) change its policy and simply decided to not give juveniles credit against their sentence (disposition) for the time they spent incarcerated waiting the resolution of their case. The BOP did this despite the fact that adults receive this benefit.

One of the authors (R. J. McWhirter) successfully argued to the United States Court of Appeals for the Ninth Circuit that juveniles must receive this pre-sentence custody credit. In the first case of its kind, the Ninth Circuit ruled in favor of juveniles and the traditional rehabilitative approach. The BOP returned to its policy of granting juveniles the credit they deserve.

A "mandatory transfer" is when the statute requires that a juvenile of a certain age whom prosecutors charge with a given crime is automatically sent to adult court. No judge makes the decision, and if the juvenile fits under the statutory formula, the juvenile goes to adult court regardless of any mitigating factors.

A "discretionary transfer" occurs when the statutes provide that prosecutors can request that the judge decide whether to send the juvenile to adult court. The states still define the circumstances when this can happen, but they also recognize the judge's traditional role in deciding whether to transfer the child. The prosecutor must notify the defense of its intent to transfer the child within the time limits under the statute. Discretionary transfers usually involve an adversarial proceeding in which defense attorneys can present evidence and argue why the judge should not transfer the juvenile. Many times, the main issue is not whether the juvenile committed the act of delinquency but rather that the parties dispute transfer. Prosecutors often are influenced by strong political forces to transfer these children to adult court, with these forces overshadowing the underlying benefits to society of attempting to rehabilitate these children (see the case study of Johnny J.).

Congress periodically changes the federal transfer requirements; state legislatures do the same to the state statutes. Different states allow transfer at a much younger age under distinct criteria such as different predicate crimes. Under the federal transfer statute (18 USC § 5032), the court must consider the following when deciding whether to transfer a juvenile:

The alleged offence
The juvenile's prior record
The past treatment efforts
The juvenile's present intellectual development and psychological maturity
The juvenile's age and social background
The availability of rehabilitative and other programs

Johnny J.

Johnny J. first came to the attention of juvenile authorities when he was caught in possession of a firearm. The judge put him on juvenile probation and told him that if he possessed a firearm again he might be taken away from his family. Johnny did not want that to happen.

Johnny was the oldest of five kids. They all lived with their mother, Noreen, and each had a different biological father. Johnny always wanted to make sure that "we can all be together." He also said that his family life was "very happy." Child Protective Services (CPS), however, reported periodic abuse from both Johnny's father and other men in Noreen's life. CPS also reported that Noreen was a mother who alternated between being emotionally distant and overly sentimental. Whenever Johnny came to court, he looked to see if his mother was there and was often disappointed. When she did come, she was usually late. Johnny's public defender lawyers generally found her extremely passive and unhelpful. She did not provide much strength or guidance in the family, leading Johnny to feel more responsible for his younger siblings. He pressed the need to get out of detention so he could "take care of them."

While Johnny was on juvenile probation, he was in a car with older peers drinking beer. One of them threw a beer can out the window. A police officer saw it and pulled the car over. The other kids got out, but Johnny panicked. He had a loaded firearm and thought that if he got caught the judge would take him away from his family. In his panic he pulled the gun from his waistband and shot out the backside window.

The police officer, who was actually several feet away, opened fire, as did the backup unit that had arrived on the scene. Though Johnny did not know how to drive, he slid into the driver's seat and tried to drive away. He put the car in reverse and hit the front of the police cruiser. (The officers later alleged that he tried to assault them with the car by "ramming" the police cruiser after he "revved" his engine.) The police fired 47 rounds into the car, only two of which hit Johnny. The bullet that grazed his temple caused him to lose consciousness, and the car rolled into a ditch. Johnny was arrested.

Despite the fact that he did not have much of a juvenile record, the prosecutor immediately moved to transfer Johnny to adult court. Thus the attorneys were not dealing with the facts of whether Johnny committed an act of juvenile delinquency but rather with whether he should spend 10 to 12 years in an adult federal prison on an adult assault conviction.

CASE STUDY

Johnny J. *(continued)*

Johnny's public defender secured for him a very good placement pending trial. It was a juvenile detention facility geared to rehabilitation. Johnny was happy there. His mother and sisters were allowed to visit. One day, though, they violated the rules and snuck him cigarettes. When the staff found the cigarettes, they confronted Johnny, and he lied to protect his mother. Not wanting to lose her visits, he told the staff that he shoplifted the cigarettes at a recent outing. Because of this, the staff had to terminate him from the juvenile placement, and he went into a juvenile jail. He kept complaining to his public defenders that he could not understand why he could not go home to his "happy" family.

After considerable court battles, the judge decided to transfer Johnny J. to adult status. His defense attorneys appealed the transfer, and the court of appeals reversed his transfer.

After considerable work on Johnny's case and the passage of time, which watered down the political forces, the judge finally decided not to transfer Johnny. Instead the judge created a disposition where he would do the majority of time in juvenile custody. The hope is that Johnny will get rehabilitative services. Had the judge transferred Johnny, he would have gone into the adult prison system as a young man and come out, in all likelihood, more hardened and a greater threat to society.

During a transfer hearing, the prosecution and the defense present evidence on these factors. Evidence may include psychological testing information, counselor and social work reports, and testimony from police officers, family, or even from teachers or counselors. This gives the judge an idea of whether he or she should transfer the juvenile to adult status or whether the more rehabilitative system of juvenile justice best serves society's interests. Indeed, "the primary purpose of the FJDA [Federal Juvenile Delinquency Act] remains to rehabilitate children who have committed criminal acts, assisting them to become successful and productive members of their communities" (*United States v. Juvenile*, 347 F.3rd 778, 787 [9th Cir. 2003]).

Obviously, the issues in juvenile justice, especially on transfer questions, are complex, challenging, and politically charged. Often, however, politics loses sight of the "price our nation pays in filling our prisons with young people who have committed a crime that not only extracts an absorbent economic cost, but more importantly uses the full force of the law to create a human waste that cannot be measured" (Juvenile 347 F.3rd at 790 [Lay, J. concurring]).

Civil Law

Civil law is more likely than criminal law to affect practitioners as it includes the duty to warn and confidentiality.

General civil law. In civil law, unlike criminal law, nobody goes to jail. One exception to this is immigration law, which though civil in nature often leads to detention of the alien even if he or she is a juvenile (see R. J. McWhirter, 2006). In civil law, a person who believes he or she has been wronged (the plaintiff) sues another (the defendant). Both usually have lawyers. There can be several defendants and even several plaintiffs. The plaintiff has the burden of proving the case, but the standard of proof is lower than in a criminal case. "A preponderance of the evidence" is the required standard rather than "proof beyond a reasonable doubt." This means that to win, the plaintiffs have to convince the jury that their version of what happened is more likely than the other side's version. If the defendant loses a civil case, he or she must compensate the plaintiff. When the defendant is a practitioner, more often than not the defendant's insurance company has to pay.

One point to clarify here is that being sued is different from being liable. Anyone can sue for a moderate court fee, but winning the lawsuit is another matter. Without solid legal reasons and facts, a judge or jury will not hold a practitioner liable. Some people file lawsuits without much consideration for reason or even facts.

To establish the practitioner/defendant's civil liability, or malpractice, the client/plaintiff must prove four things:

1. The practitioner/defendant owed the client/plaintiff a duty of care. In this context this usually means that a professional relationship existed.
2. The practitioner/defendant was negligent in performing the duty. Again, the duty must be demonstrable, and the client/plaintiff must show the defendant practiced below the standard of care.
3. The client/plaintiff suffered a tangible harm or injury.
4. The practitioner/defendant's not meeting or "breaching" the standard of care was the "proximate cause" of the client/plaintiff's injury. In other words, the client/plaintiff's harm or injury was a reasonably foreseeable consequence of the practitioner/defendant's breach of care (Bennett, Bryant, VandenBos, & Greenwood, 1990).

Practitioners assume several duties when they accept a client. One of these duties is to conform to the ethical standards of the profession, including those of maintaining the client's confidentiality. If the practitioner violates this ethical standard, he or she also violates a legal duty by divulging a confidence and could be liable for damages. A plaintiff, however, must still show that the practitioner's conduct actually caused the plaintiff harm.

Suppose a psychiatrist fails to provide necessary medication to a young person, for example, to Jason Carter of Chapter 4. If Jason commits suicide, his parents, Doug and Lois, could certainly sue the practitioner for negligently failing to prevent Jason's death, and they might win a jury award of money. Again, this is because the practitioner assumed a duty, performed it negligently, and caused the harm to Jason's family.

This system of civil law, in which a jury decides that the defendant must pay if the plaintiff can prove duty, negligence, causation, and harm, helps to prevent or redress the more serious forms of negligence in society. This legal system encourages professional associations to establish a standard of ethical conduct to guide practitioners' behavior. Following these standards (or not following them) can make the difference in court. Because of this, practitioners who work with at-risk youth should always conform to the ethical standards of their particular human service profession.

Confidentiality and privilege in general.   The terms *confidentiality* and *privilege* are not synonymous, but they are related. Although both concepts exist for the benefit and protection of the client and not the practitioner (cf. McGuire, Parnell, Blau, & Abbott, 1994), important distinctions exist.

Confidentiality usually refers to the ethical obligation of the practitioner not to disclose confidential information obtained during the client relationship. Under rules of confidentiality, the practitioner must protect the confidence of the client. The rules of confidentiality are a professional standard of conduct. State statutes (laws passed by legislatures), case law (decisions of courts of appeals interpreting the statutes and other norms), or professional associations often define these standards. Confidential relationships are based on the idea that the practitioner and the patient have an understanding to protect the communication except in specific situations.

Privilege refers to the patient's legal right to prevent certain professionals (lawyers, doctors, psychologists, and possibly counselors) from providing information to a party in a lawsuit or from testifying regarding information the client gave them. Unless the law specifically mandates or allows the health care practitioner to reveal the information about the patient, the communication between patient and practitioner remains protected. Thus we often say that the client "holds" or "owns" the privilege.

The genesis of both concepts is that the law has long protected certain communications. This protection came from the relationship between priest and penitent, with all its sacramental overtones. A natural outgrowth of this relationship is the attorney–client privilege. Doctors and patients enjoy a similar privilege, and in most states so do psychologists, counselors, and other mental health practitioners. Of 45 states with a system of licensed professional counselors, 44 states have statutes or evidentiary rules granting privilege status to the counselor–client relationship (Glosoff, Herlihy, & Spence, 2000). However, the extent of the privilege varies from state to state.

In the federal context, the United States Supreme Court in *Jaffe v. Redmond* (1996) confirmed that a psychotherapist–patient privilege exists with such communications being "protected from compelled disclosure. . . ." The extent of this privilege is not absolute, however, nor is it with the "duty to warn" notion discussed in the following section.

Further complicating this problem is that in a given state the degree of privilege accorded a psychologist may differ from that accorded to another practitioner, such as a school counselor. Again, the best advice is to consult specific state law. This information is generally not too difficult to obtain; most states have an office that publishes a brochure or pamphlet on the issues, and state and local professional associations often compile this information.

Under the notion of privilege, practitioners can discuss clients' statements with colleagues, but those colleagues have the same duty to guard that communication as the practitioner. This is a critical point because practitioners must consult regularly with colleagues and discuss their client cases to effectively treat at-risk youth. Consultation is also important for avoiding civil liability, especially when dealing with ambiguous matters.

Confidentiality and privilege issues arise in schools. Some state courts hold that parents of public school children are entitled to inspect their children's records because they are public records. The reason is that because the youth is a minor the parents have the privilege and are therefore entitled to know their children's statements (Hopkins, 1989). Other states, however, hold that a young person's confidential communications should have the same protection as an adult's (Hopkins, 1989). One study found that among 354 licensed school psychologists in Minnesota there was great variability in the frequency with which practitioners told parents of communication with minors with whom they worked (Mannheim et al., 2002). There was also great variation in the professionals' willingness to share information with parents, even when in the child's best interests, in part due to the concern that divulging information would irreparably damage the client–psychologist relationship.

In certain situations, however, the law requires practitioners to reveal a confidence, such as in suspected child abuse (McGowan, 1991). Different states have carved out other exceptions for revealing confidential information, including the following (Glosoff et al., 2000):

- When the client's condition poses a danger to self
- When there is imminent threat of harm to a specific third person
- When the counselor knows the client will commit a crime
- When a dispute exists between the client and the practitioner
- When the client raises the issue of mental condition in court, including court-ordered psychological examinations
- For purposes of involuntary hospitalization
- When the practitioner knows a client is a crime victim, and in cases of harm to vulnerable adults

Again, practitioners should check the law in their states to see if these exceptions apply. Glosoff, Herlihy, and Spence (2000) provide a useful table outlining the exceptions to confidentiality in each state. In some situations, such as in group counseling, a client can waive confidentiality. Practitioners should discuss the limits of confidentiality in the relationship at the outset, especially when the therapy group includes the youth's family (Ford, Thomsen, & Compton, 2001).

Aside from these possible exceptions, a practitioner should not divulge any communication given in confidence, regardless of the client's age, unless a clear therapeutic benefit is possible or a court has ordered disclosure. Glosoff, Herlihy, and Spence (2000) recommend the following:

- Use disclosure/informed consent statements.
- Inform clients of the situation and involve them in the process.
- Take reasonable steps to protect client confidentiality.
- Provide minimal disclosure.
- With permission, contact the client's attorney.
- Document all actions and factors involved.
- Consult with colleagues regarding clinical judgments and with lawyers regarding legal obligations.

Even following these precautions, practitioners may still find themselves in court and ordered to reveal confidential information, despite being ethically and even morally bound not to do so. Refusal would truly put the practitioner at the cutting edge of the law and could lead to a jail sentence for contempt of court. One consolation is that given our current legal environment, a practitioner is not likely to suffer the fate of those priests who went to their deaths rather than break the seal of the confessional.

Duty to warn.   A practitioner may have a special duty to warn third persons of danger. In *Tarasoff v. Regents of the University of California* (1976), the California Supreme Court held that psychologists, and potentially all practitioners, have a duty to take reasonable steps to warn a specific third person or persons to whom the patient poses a danger. The important point is that in most states the patient or client must pose a serious risk to a specific third person before the practitioner has the duty to warn. A later California case holds that a psychologist may have a duty to warn even if he or she hears from a third person of the patient's threat to another (*Ewing v. Goldstein*, 2005).

The *Tarasoff* case concerned a patient at a university psychiatric center who stated during therapy that he intended to kill an unnamed but readily identifiable girl (Tatiana Tarasoff). The therapist did not warn the Tarasoff family of the threat, and when the patient killed Ms. Tarasoff, her family sued the university. The Supreme Court of California held that the family had the right to sue. Again though, what the Tarasoff family won was just the right to sue; the California Supreme Court's ruling did not mean that a jury found the therapist or university liable.

Not all states have a *Tarasoff* rule that includes a duty to warn, so practitioners must consult the laws of their own state. In states that do have a *Tarasoff* rule, practitioners who work with at-risk youth must consider whether any of their clients poses a possible danger to a specific third person. If the youth is dangerous, then the practitioner may have a duty to warn the third party or to take other measures to prevent imminent harm (Costa & Altekruse, 1994). Of course, as the American Psychological Association argued in *Tarasoff*, warning may well destroy the therapeutic relationship, leading to more harm in the long run.

This raises the question of how the privilege of confidentiality affects the legal duty to warn. As discussed with regard to the duty to report child abuse, a given state or federal court rule or statute may prevent divulging such information because it is privileged (*Jaffee v. Redmond*, 1996). Some states may provide the answer to this question via statutes, which the practitioner should check.

In a case following the United States Supreme Court's decision in *Jaffe*, the Ninth Circuit Court of Appeals ruled that a defendant could not have a case dismissed for making threats to FBI agents because his psychotherapist had betrayed his confidence (*United States v. Chase*, 2002). In *Chase*, the defendant, who had a history of bipolar disorder and was under the care of a psychologist, expressed anger at various officials and others, including FBI agents. The psychologist decided that the threats to "kill them" became concrete enough to warn the agents. The defendant was convicted at trial. On appeal, Chase argued that there was no "dangerousness" exception to the psychotherapist–patient privilege. The Ninth Circuit held otherwise and upheld his conviction. The court explained that though Chase never acted on his threats, they were tangible enough so that in the therapist's professional opinion there was an imminent danger that only disclosure of the communication could prevent.

Although *Chase* provides interesting guidance on the duty to warn in the context of a privileged or confidential relationship, the case does not end the question. The Ninth Circuit Court, in holding that an exception existed, sided with the prior Tenth Circuit case of *United States v. Glass* (1998) but against the Sixth Circuit case of *United States v. Hayes* (2000), which held that there is not a "duty to warn" exception to a privilege relationship.

Thus the best advice remains to consult with colleagues when one is in doubt as to the law or the gravity of the threat to the third person. Also, it is both a wise and expected practice to inform clients about the limits of confidentiality in the first session. Such a procedure clarifies the practitioner's responsibility and helps avoid the client feeling betrayed. We will return to the duty to warn when we address sexuality issues.

SPECIFIC LEGAL CONCERNS

The behaviors that put young people at serious risk—the use of illegal substances, irresponsible sexual activity, delinquency, and suicide—all present unique legal complications.

Legal Issues and Substance Use

In state-funded drug programs, state laws and regulations control the practitioner's activities. Programs that receive federal funds, however, follow guidelines found in the Code of Federal Regulations (CFR). Technical reports from the U.S. Department of Health and Human Services periodically explain these guidelines.

The general requirement for federally funded substance use programs is that a practitioner must maintain confidentiality in nearly all aspects of treatment (42 CFR 2.12[e]). This regulation applies to any program that provides treatment, counseling, assessment, or referral services for youths with alcohol and other drug problems. These regulations generally do not apply to teachers or practitioners in schools who may deal with substance problems of at-risk youth.

Practitioners can, of course, obtain a youth's consent to release information. Under this standard of confidentiality, it is hard to conceive of a situation in which a practitioner could be negligent for failing to disclose substance use. Indeed, federal regulations require the exact opposite. That is, in most cases, the practitioner must maintain confidentiality unless a young person has a specific self-destructive or suicidal intent (Brody & Waldron, 2000).

Legal Issues in Youth Sexuality

Although confidentiality is central to dealing with youth sexuality, a practitioner may have a duty to warn third persons of a youth's sexually transmitted disease (STD). As the number of sexually active teenagers in the country continues to be substantial (Brown & Eisenberg, 1995), sexuality issues are common topics in therapeutic settings.

Warning parents. The law is ambiguous as to whether a practitioner must tell parents of their child's sexual activity. Conversely, it would be very difficult for parents to prevail in a lawsuit against a practitioner who failed to report sexual activity among teenage clients because this communication ordinarily stays confidential to maintain the therapeutic relationship. Thus, when an irate parent calls a practitioner and demands to know if his or her child is sexually active, as Jack Andrews of Chapter 1 might do in his rage about Allie's behavior, the law is almost certain to support the practitioner's judgment not to reveal the information. However, this is the age of fatal and incurable sexually transmitted diseases. If Jack sought information from the practitioner as to whether Allie was sexually active and the practitioner refused to divulge the confidence, conceivably, Jack could sue the counselor if Allie later contracted AIDS. In this situation, Jack could come into court and say that if he had known that Allie was sexually active, he would have discussed "safe sex" with her. Because the practitioner refused him the information, he did not have the chance to protect her. Although the potential for this type of lawsuit exists, the practitioner certainly has defenses: Jack must have suspected that Allie was sexually active or he would not have asked, and nothing stopped him from discussing safe sex with her. A practitioner cannot be held liable for a parent's failure to communicate with his child. Consequently, though legal risks exist, practitioners cannot afford to let them get in the way of their work.

Contraception and abortion.   The laws relating to a practitioner's duties with regard to contraception and abortion are very inconsistent. If the counseling facility is not a family planning program, some state laws may require that practitioners notify parents of any contraception or abortion counseling they provide to minors. This presents special problems if the adolescent is homeless or orphaned (Blustein, Levine, & Dubler, 1999). However, because of the U.S. Supreme Court's decision on abortion in *Roe v. Wade* (1973) and the extension of that ruling recognizing that minors share in the constitutionally protected right of privacy regarding contraception and abortion (*Bellotti v. Baird*, 1979; *Carey v. Population Services International*, 1977), parental notification laws may not bind a practitioner.

As of now, parents have no right to know of communications between practitioners and minors despite state law to the contrary. The law here, however, is not fixed. Every new appointment to the U.S. Supreme Court as well as to the federal circuit court of appeals has a bearing on this question.

Thus the practitioner in a family planning program can provide access to contraceptives. In general the courts hold that the minor's right to privacy outweighs the parents' right to information. Consequently, even if Jack Andrews demands to know whether Allie is receiving contraceptives, the practitioner should not divulge the information to him if the practitioner works in a family planning program. If not, however, state law may require parental notification, although the age of the minor is an important factor that varies from state to state. Of course, any prescribing of contraceptives to a minor requires that the practitioner have the appropriate qualifications and medical training, without which the practitioner could be successfully sued.

The inconsistency of rulings on the confidentiality of contraception counseling extends to abortion counseling. The practitioner who does not work in a family planning situation may have a duty under state law to inform the parents of a minor's decision to abort. Conversely, these state laws will not cover a practitioner who works in a family planning clinic. In *H. L. v. Matheson* (1981), however, the U.S. Supreme Court held that a Utah law requiring a physician to notify a parent of an unemancipated minor's plans to abort was constitutional. If a given state law requires notification to parents but allows for a mature or emancipated minor to go independently to a judge for permission to abort, as of now the statute is constitutional. By extension, a practitioner can provide a minor abortion counseling and the opportunity to obtain judicial consent to abort without parental notification.

Most of the U.S. Supreme Court cases in this respect involve medical doctors. Mental health practitioners, however, need to stay abreast of the duties set forth for physicians and draw parallels with their own practice. In the right set of circumstances, the applications could as easily extend to teachers and practitioners.

STDs/AIDS.   The *Tarasoff* standard, imposing on a practitioner the duty to warn a third person of an explicit danger from the client, could apply to the threat of sexually transmitted diseases. A patient with AIDS can pose an "explicit threat" to a specific, fore-seeable victim. If Allie Andrews became infected with HIV, for example, and was sleeping with a specific noninfected person, the law might require the practitioner to warn that person of his or her risk. As of 1993, no courts had addressed a practitioner's duty to warn sexual partners in a case involving HIV (Harding, Gray, & Neal, 1993). Since then, however, Chenneville (2000) has summarized recent cases relating to a physician's duty to warn partners of HIV-positive adults. Some courts have held that hospitals and physicians are not responsible for disclosing HIV status to patient's spouses (e.g., *Diaz Reyes v. United States*, 1991/1992; *N. O. L. v. District of Columbia*, 1996; *Santa Rosa Health Care Corp. v. Garcia*, 1998), whereas others (*Chizmar v. Mackie*, 1995) found that physicians are free to inform a patient's spouse upon the diagnosis of a fatal sexually transmitted disease (Chenneville, 2000). How this relates specifically to adolescents is an open question.

Physicians have resolved this ethical problem by requiring all "reportable" or "communicable" diseases to be reported to the state or county department of health. These departments then take action to protect the public from the disease, which may include warning a third party at high risk. These departments protect confidentiality by not disclosing the source of the information.

Thus the practitioner has the option of notifying the state public health agency of possible communicable or reportable diseases, including AIDS and other STDs. Before reporting, the practitioner should find out how the agency will protect confidentiality. This protects both the third person and the client's confidence. Also, notifying a department of health of an at-risk youth's STD may protect the practitioner from civil liability. If a client transmits a disease to a third person, that person may sue the practitioner for being aware of the situation and taking no action. By confidentially reporting to a public health agency, the practitioner may be able to demonstrate that he or she took measures to prevent the harm. Although not perfect, this action provides at least a partial solution.

Legal Issues in Delinquency

In general, criminal law does not require practitioners to report criminal activity, with the exception of child abuse. Thus, even if you see a crime committed, the state will not likely prosecute you if you fail to report it. If you benefit from the crime or in any way facilitate it, however, you may be charged as an accessory (LaFave & Scott, 2002).

A practitioner who learns of a youth's crimes through confidential communications, then, is not likely to face criminal charges for failing to report them. Indeed, in federally funded programs for drug use treatment, a mental health practitioner cannot even request a court to permit the reporting of any crime less serious than a felony, such as homicide, rape, or kidnapping (42 C.F.R. 2.65[d][1]). Even in these circumstances, the practitioner must refer to a particular client by a fictitious name.

Under civil law, however, the practitioner may have a duty to warn in certain circumstances. Under *Tarasoff*, a mental health worker who knows of a danger to specific third persons may have a civil duty to warn them. For example, if a practitioner hears in a therapy session with a gang member that the gang is planning a drive-by shooting of a specific person at a specific time and place, the practitioner may have a duty to warn that person. If the person is killed, the surviving relatives could conceivably sue the practitioner and the institution for failure to warn the victim.

▲ Box 3.3

When Suicide Was a Crime

The legal system has never known what to do with suicide. Suicide was long a crime under English law. Punishments included refusal of burial in consecrated ground, mutilation of the body, burial at a crossroad, and a stake driven through the victim's heart. Although these sanctions were not transported to the United States, suicide was once a crime in most parts of this country (Marzen, O'Dowd, Crone, & Balch, 1985). This legal prohibition created obvious problems. How does one punish a suicide? The victim, of course, is immune to punishment, at least in this life. Sanctions, therefore, tended to be imposed on the surviving family. Partly in response to this inherent injustice and inconsistency, state legislatures abolished their suicide laws so that today it is no longer a crime to commit suicide (Marzen et al., 1985).

Legal Issues in Youth Suicide

Suicide.   Contrary to popular belief, suicide is no longer a crime in the United States, although aiding a suicide is still illegal in nearly all states despite the movement in support of assisted suicide for the terminally ill (see Box 3.3). Counselors, social workers, psychologists, and other human service professionals need not fear a criminal penalty if a client commits suicide unless the practitioner has aided the client in the act.

Traditionally, civil law has viewed suicide as an intentional, willful act by one individual, with no blame attaching to anyone else. This is not to say, however, that a practitioner may not be sued, and courts have allowed the victim's relatives and heirs compensation in exceptional circumstances (Jobes & Berman, 1993). After a youth's death, surviving family may seek an outlet for grief by casting blame elsewhere, and the practitioner may become the target. Numerous suits for malpractice reported by practitioners involve suicide or attempted suicide (Bongar, 1992). These lawsuits not only relieve guilt-ridden family members, they also protect the image of the victim. Given the psychological makeup of Doug Carter (see Chapter 4), no one would be surprised if he attempted to sue the practitioner if Jason commited suicide.

In the few suits filed against practitioners, families do not claim that the hospital, psychiatrist, or practitioner "caused" their loved one's death. Rather, they claim that the practitioner or institution had a duty to prevent the suicide and failed to meet that duty. Because it is difficult to prove that anyone has a duty to prevent suicide, practitioners are protected against most charges of malpractice in such instances.

The setting in which the practitioner works may also offer protection against lawsuits (J. J. McWhirter & R. J. McWhirter, 1988). The courts have reasoned that the primary responsibility of schools is to educate students, not to treat their emotional problems. Thus schools do not have a duty to care for the psychological health of students, so they do not have a duty to prevent suicide (*Bogust v. Iverson*, 1960). Although a school is not now liable for the suicide of a student, it is possible that under a particular set of circumstances a jury may find schools liable in the future (Anderegg & Vergason, 1992). It will depend on the circumstances.

A practitioner who works at a hospital has a greater chance of being sued if a patient commits suicide (J. J. McWhirter & R. J. McWhirter, 1988). Because the insurance industry recognizes that one need not be a psychiatrist to be a health care provider (*Blue Shield of Virginia v. McCready*, 1982), the courts may begin to hold nonmedical practitioners liable for the suicidal deaths of their clients. This acknowledgment, in combination with the fact that many practitioners now have malpractice insurance, increases the likelihood of lawsuits.

When the practitioner has acted with reasonable professional judgment, however, the chance of being successfully sued is minimal. The problem is that "reasonable professional judgment" is often not an objective standard (Berman & Cohen-Sandler, 1983). A practitioner may not believe, for example, that a patient's history of assaults and homicidal tendencies necessarily signifies suicidal tendencies. Another therapist may think otherwise. Courts usually hold a practitioner to the "generally accepted view of the profession" on a given point (*Fernandez v. Baruch*, 1968). Codes of professional ethics and discussions with colleagues are the best means to acquire information about the accepted professional standard of care (Jobes & Berman, 1993).

Attempted suicide.   Persons who have attempted suicide can conceivably sue their therapists for any injuries. Other legal considerations also enter the picture when a youth makes suicidal gestures. In certain circumstances, the courts may intervene after an adolescent attempts suicide. Although the courts generally do not punish people for attempting suicide, they may commit them to a psychiatric hospital (Wright, 1975). Most states have statutes that empower the courts to commit persons who pose a danger to themselves to the state psychiatric hospital. Courts are more likely to exercise this power when the person attempting suicide is an adolescent ward of the court.

When an adolescent's suicide attempt is serious enough to require hospitalization, an agency or hospital staff member should evaluate the patient. The evaluators may recommend a hearing to determine whether the court should commit the adolescent to the state hospital.

Underfunded state hospital systems often do not handle all mental health problems, especially those of children and adolescents. The Carter family, however, could probably afford a private mental health facility for Jason. When the family lacks the Carter's resources, the practitioner must diligently locate the resources available in the state mental health system through state agencies and mental hospitals. In some situations the only way to help a suicidal young person is for a court to order the client's commitment.

Practitioners should inject themselves into the state or county evaluation process. If no one contacts the practitioner after an adolescent's attempted suicide, the practitioner should contact the appropriate evaluating team or agency. The practitioner's recommendations may be invaluable, and the evaluation team may decide that it would be best for the practitioner to maintain the therapy.

Similarly, the practitioner should know the community's legal resources. If hospitalization is necessary, the therapist may have to find a suitable facility for a youth at risk of another suicide attempt. Contact with administrative agencies and the state court system often yields helpful information on how to make appropriate resources available to the client.

Testifying in Court

At some point in your career as a practitioner you might be called to testify. Under most rules of evidence, "every person is competent to be a witness except as otherwise provided in these rules" (Federal Rule of Evidence 601). Thus, unless an individual is determined to be "incompetent," due to a very young age or having a significant mental health problem, there is nothing to bar him or her from being a witness. The question, then, is whether to testify as a "lay" or "expert" witness.

Generally, lay witnesses only testify about something that they perceived at the time, such as something they saw. They could also testify as to what they touched or smelled. In short, they can testify to anything that they perceived with their five senses at the time as long as it is relevant. In fact, the only time a lay witness can give an opinion is when it is "rationally based on the perception of the witness, be helpful to a clear understanding of the witness's testimony or determination of a fact or issue, and not based on scientific, technical, or other specialized knowledge" (Federal Rules of Evidence 701).

Conversely, "expert" witnesses can offer opinions from their "specialized knowledge" (Federal Rule of Evidence 703). Their testimony is supposed to help the jury to better understand the evidence, not to testify as to "ultimate issues" (see Federal Rule of Evidence 702). For example, experts are not allowed to give an opinion as to whether the defendant is guilty. Thus an expert could testify as to cause of death but not who caused the death. The jury decides such "ultimate issues," not the expert.

Practitioners may testify as lay witnesses for what they actually perceived with their senses in a given situation. They may also testify from their specialized knowledge or skill as an expert witness. In some cases, a practitioner may end up testifying as both. The attorney who calls the practitioner as a witness should explain the type of testimony required at the time.

CONCLUSION

Practitioners can minimize the risk of lawsuits by understanding the legal system, ethical guidelines, and some of the legal quagmires entailed in working with at-risk youth (Jobes & Berman, 1993). Knowing the ethics code specific to a practitioner's field is paramount. The American Psychological Association, the American Counseling Association, the National Education Association, the National Organization for Human Services, and other professional organizations have written codes of ethics, which are available to their members. These codes define the standard practice on many points and are often produced to help professionals avoid legal as well as ethical problems. In addition, the following suggestions can both help the practitioner and benefit the young client:

Legal Dos and Don'ts in Work With At-Risk Youth

1. Avoid displays of anger or sarcasm toward the client, particularly in the tension of emergency situations. Paradoxical interventions are also highly risky. With a client who has recently attempted suicide, for example, a statement like "Next time cut vertically instead of horizontally and you'll get the main artery" would not impress a jury should the client later follow your advice.

2. Document actions fully and professionally. Documentation should include assessment of the risks involved in a particular treatment and the reasoning behind actions. The "reasonable professional judgment" standard will protect the practitioner against liability if the documentation indicates thoughtful professional decision making.
3. Consult frequently with colleagues on therapeutic, ethical, and legal questions. Common sense tells a juror that "two heads are better than one." If colleagues supported a decision at the time, a plaintiff will have a hard time proving negligence.
4. Maintain good staff communication. Bad communication between the "professionals" leaves practitioners more vulnerable to making poor decisions, and may also incline jurors to conclude that negligence is a factor.
5. Support and communicate with the family in the aftermath of a suicide or other traumatic event involving the young person, while maintaining the required level of confidentiality. This can help facilitate the family's resolution of grief. Such contact may also reduce the likelihood of a hasty, emotion-driven decision to file a malpractice suit.
6. Continuously update professional training, and keep a record of the seminars and classes attended. Ongoing training enhances the quality of practice, and may also convey to a jury or judge that you are a conscientious practitioner who works to provide the best for his or her clients.

These suggestions will help practitioners carry out their work with greater confidence, so that their energy can be focused on assisting at-risk youth rather than protecting themselves from lawsuits.

FAMILIES, SCHOOLS, AND SKILLS

▲ Part 2 contains three chapters. In Chapters 4 and 5 we deal with two primary microsystems that serve to reduce or enhance risky behavior: the family and the school. To extend our metaphor, they are two "roots" of the risk "tree." Peer influences are another root. Because the impact of peers occurs somewhat later, we only briefly touch on issues related to peers in this section. (Chapter 14 is devoted to peers and to peer-based interventions.)

Families and schools provide important resources to offset negative behavior. In families and schools, young people learn attitudes and skills that help them to survive and thrive. In Chapter 6 we describe resiliency and identify five important constructs that contribute to healthy, prosocial behavior. The case studies presented in Chapters 4 and 5 are used throughout the book to illustrate important issues and concerns.

CHAPTER 4

FAMILY PROBLEMS OF AT-RISK CHILDREN AND YOUTH

▲ *Why are some families bubbling fountains, filling goblets full of cold, clear water for thirsty people living there?*

While other fountains fill cups with dark, bitter liquid.

And yet other fountains are dead dry—nothing flows and mugs remain empty?

Too many children have either dusty-dry, empty vessels or bitter-brown, sewage-filled ones.

How do we turn on the fountains so that the cold, clear water flows?

CHAPTER OUTLINE

▲   As we saw in Chapter 2, shifting economic, political, and policy trends have created an often disturbing environment that directly affects the roots of the problems young people face. Nowhere is this more evident than in the family. The family microsystem is a major influence on individuals, and in this chapter we focus on family issues that affect at-risk children and adolescents.

SOCIETAL CHANGES AFFECTING THE FAMILY

The American family has undergone major changes in recent decades (Halpern, 2005). In fact, the American family has changed more during the last 50 years than at any other time in history. In Chapter 2 we considered the impact of SES and poverty and noted the increasing numbers of single parents and mothers in paid employment. Here we highlight two related trends that influence modern family life: divorce and the decline of extended-family networks.

Divorce and Single-Parent Families

The marked rise in the divorce rate that characterized the late 1960s and 1970s actually reversed direction (except for teens) during the 1980s and now remains stable. The divorce rate in the United States is very high and affects enormous numbers of people. Because divorce is more likely in younger marriages, two thirds of all divorces affect children living in the home (Arendell, 1995). Twenty-three percent of American children are now being raised in mother-only families (Riche, 2000) and 1 in 2 African American children live in mother-only households (Belsie, 2001). This statistic represents more than the divorce rate; in 2000 two fifths of single mothers had never been married (Bianchi & Caspar, 2000 change to Caspar & Bianchi, 2002). Divorce, out-of-wedlock births, and declining marriage rates have significantly altered the composition of the typical family.

Single-parent families are particularly stressed. Hilton, Desrochers, and Devall (2001) conducted a comparison study of child and parent functioning in single-mother, single-father, and intact families. They found that single fathers had better economic resources than did single mothers; single fathers had more positive parenting than married fathers, and they relied more on friends than did married parents. Single mothers, meanwhile, had less education, less prestigious jobs, lower incomes, and more economic strain. These mothers also had fewer social resources and more parenting difficulty than married parents. Children living with single mothers were found to have more internalized problems, and those living with either a single mother or father had more externalized behavior problems (Hilton et al., 2001). In addition, children living in single-mother homes were more at risk for school dropout (Pong & Ju, 2000).

The Erosion of Extended Family Networks

Not only is a mother or father more likely to be absent from the home now than at any time in history, but extended family members are also less likely to be involved in family life. In earlier generations the majority of children were raised through the collective efforts of a network of extended family relatives, in-laws, and friends who interacted with them throughout childhood and adolescence. Today children have fewer adults to help them develop responsibility, judgment, and self-discipline, even though the task requires more understanding, care, and awareness than ever before. Most young people do not have an extended family network of grandparents, in-laws, aunts, and uncles to support them and their parents. Today, when the extended family is involved in child rearing, it is typically not adjunctive—that is, supportive of the children's parents—but, in fact, replaces parental roles as primary or even sole caretakers. For example, among the nearly 20 million U.S. preschoolers, grandparents are leading child-care providers, taking care of 21% of preschool children (U.S. Department of Commerce, 1997).

Years ago the extended family provided a variety of role models, opportunities to anticipate and vicariously experience child-related problems, and individuals available to serve as resources. Today children and their parents have less access to the extended family as they face life crises. The family, once buffered with supports, is now stretched thin. Not infrequently, recreation, spiritual training, and education all take place outside the home. Among most U.S. families, children often become acquainted with the adult world through television, highlighted by programs that portray casual and unprotected sex (Kaiser Family Foundation, 2005), drinking, gratuitous acts of violence, and self-centered aggrandizement as routine behavior. Through commercials, television also sends negative messages about sacrifice, self-discipline, and patience. Many young people are unable to bond and connect with others; they lack a sense of being tied emotionally to other people, of sharing commitments to common values, and do not see themselves as part of society.

Divorce and the decline of the extended family do not necessarily result in a reduction of social networks for children and young people. Indeed, the increased complexity of family patterns may actually increase the availability of people who can serve as resources. Consider "Lisa." Her father had several children from a previous marriage with whom she interacted when they came for visits. When Lisa was 8 years old, her parents divorced. She lived with her mother but continued to see her father in the summer and on weekends. When Lisa was 13, her mother remarried. Lisa and her stepfather got along well and did many things together. Lisa continued to see her father, although less frequently, because he had moved to another state and married a woman with two children. Lisa graduated from high school and entered college. During two of her college years she lived with a man, and soon after graduation she married another man. She and her husband had a son. After several years, Lisa and her husband divorced and she was awarded custody of her son, who continues to see her ex-husband in the summer and on weekends. Three years later Lisa remarried. She and her second husband have two more children. During Lisa's life so far she has lived in nine families either part time or full time.

Lisa's situation is not typical, but neither is it unusual. Although the relationships in some of Lisa's families may not have been ideal, in each case there were people she enjoyed doing things with, wanted to continue seeing, and loved. This situation represents a substantial change from the experience of people who grew up several decades ago, when one might have been part of two or three families at the most. Some of these family experiences have the potential of enriching children's lives by providing more adults to serve as role models and by providing a greater variety of experiences. Unfortunately, for many youth these changing patterns and variable family experiences produce alienation, rootlessness, and disconnection.

Despite pervasive assumptions that poor children are at high risk and affluent children are at low risk, comparative studies of rich and poor children reveal more similarities than differences in socialization processes and adjustment patterns. Children of high socioeconomic status often manifest problems of depression, anxiety, and substance abuse. Such children often must deal with excessive pressures to achieve along with physical and emotional isolation from their parents. Family wealth does not automatically confer equanimity of spirit or wisdom in parenting. Children from wealthy families are privileged in many areas, but this does not remove potential threats to their psychological well-being (Luthar & Latendresse, 2005).

CHANGES WITHIN THE FAMILY

Even in the absence of structural changes arising from evolving societal conditions, the family normally changes over time. All changes necessitate shifts in the relationships of family members. At each stage the family has specific developmental tasks to accomplish, which lay the foundations for later stages.

The Family Life Cycle

The family life cycle is the name given to stages that a family goes through in its developmental history (Carter & McGoldrick, 2004). The family group begins with each newly married couple, even though the couple continues to be a part of their two original family groups. The fact that a new family cycle begins with each new marriage does not cut short the cycles of the families of origin of each partner. The couple continues the family life cycles of their earlier family groups at the same time that they begin their own family life cycle.

Duvall and Miller (1985) proposed an eight-stage model of the traditional family life cycle that remains useful today. This framework is appropriate for many families because most progress through certain predictable marker events or phases (such as marriage, the birth of the first child, the onset of adolescence, and so forth). Each stage is determined by the age of the oldest child, and each stage has its own set of tasks for the family to complete before it moves to the next stage. Carter and McGoldrick (2004) have outlined sets of developmental tasks for nontraditional blended families and single-parent families. They also add an initial stage—the unattached young adult—to the family life cycle. The inability of the family to negotiate developmental tasks at any of the stages contributes to the child's problems. Professionals need to be aware of the family developmental tasks and help the family to develop the necessary skills to negotiate them. The following stages are derived from the works of Duvall and Miller (1985), Carter and McGoldrick (2004), and Norton (1994). Movement between stages is sometimes difficult for traditional families; it is even more difficult for nontraditional families.

Unattached young adult stage.   The young adult must accomplish several developmental tasks at this stage. Young people must develop responsible habits that enable them to self-direct their behavior, manage their resources (e.g., maintain means of transportation, place of residence, secure food), and secure paid employment or some means of supporting themselves. These tasks are important even when single adults continue to live at home. In addition, it is important that young adults establish close peer relationships and begin to separate from the family of origin through an ongoing process of differentiation.

Establishment stage (married, no children).   This stage begins with marriage or a committed partnership. The young adult continues to break away from the family of origin. The major task for the couple at this stage is to establish their identity as a new unit. Making rules, defining roles within the marriage, and realigning relationships with friends and family are important components of this stage. For young adults who are gay, lesbian, or bisexual, this stage may include tasks associated with affirming their identity within their family of origin; interracial couples must often devote considerable time to negotiating the effects of racism on their relationship.

New parent stage (infant to 3 years).   These next stages apply to couples who have children. When the couple become parents, their duties and roles change. Their relationship as a couple must shift to accommodate the infant.

Preschool stage (oldest child 3 to 6 years).   Parents continue to develop their work and family roles. The major developmental task at this stage is learning and applying effective parenting skills to help the children learn how to interact positively with others.

School-age stage (oldest child 6 to 12 years).   The family becomes more involved with community and school activities as the children grow and develop. Members of the family must learn to renegotiate boundaries to include the children's peer group.

Teenage stage (oldest child 13 to 20 years).   The couple is required to deal with their individual, work, and marital issues along with the developmental tasks of their children and their own aging parents. The adolescent children, who are going through the individual developmental task of establishing their own identities and independence, challenge the boundaries and rules of the family system.

Launching stage (departure of children). Children and parents must separate emotionally and physically from one another. Of course, there is tremendous variation in the extent and nature of "healthy" separation. The primary task of the family at this point is to let go. Other tasks include reestablishment of the marital system as a dyad and negotiation of adult relationships between the parents and the children. Many families must cope with the death of a grandparent.

Two final stages. Two final stages, the postparental middle years and the aging family, are equally important in the family life cycle, but they do not bear directly on our subject so we will not describe them here.

Cultural variations. Cultural variations influence the nature of the tasks within each stage. In some cultural groups, for example, young people are expected to leave home at age 18 or soon thereafter, whereas other groups expect young adults to live with their parents until they marry, and in some cultures even after they marry. In any assessment of a family's passage through the stages and the completion of tasks, the cultural norms of the family must be explored.

Normal crises. Families undergo such profound changes as they move from one stage to another that the transitions present all families with normal family developmental crises. Most families negotiate these transitions adequately. Unfortunately, some families have such difficulty with the transitions between stages that they compromise the well-being of their children. Such families can become dysfunctional. If we are to understand dysfunctional families, we have to understand the family as a system. In addition, helping professionals need to view the cultural, ethnic, and unique aspects of families' backgrounds as resources and strengths that can be fostered and supported for their benefit. This appreciation of diversity is critical. Human service professionals need to develop and maintain an attitude that learning about culture and cross-cultural practice is an essential, ongoing, and ethical process synonymous with professionalism (Sue & Sue, 2003). This appreciation will also assist helping professionals in understanding similarities and differences in family systems across various cultural and ethnic groups.

The Family System

As discussed in Chapter 1, the family is a critical microsystem in the life of every child, and within which every child learns attitudes and behaviors that influence many long-term outcomes (Bronfenbrenner, 1989). The family is a system consisting of connected components (family members) organized around various functions that interact to maintain balance and a state of equilibrium. Each element is dependent on the functioning of other elements. Giving and receiving affection, child rearing, and the division of labor are some familiar family functions. Families are interdependent in that each member of the system influences and is influenced by each other member.

As they live together from day to day, families develop systematic patterns of behavior that serve to maintain the system in a state of equilibrium. Each family member contributes to this equilibrium or homeostatic balance. Homeostasis is represented by a particular family's ongoing behaviors, habits, expectations, and communication patterns.

To see the family as a homeostatic system, consider a family in which the husband/ father is an alcoholic. He serves as a scapegoat and maintains the system by receiving all the blame for the family's problems. Rather than accept the blame, he projects it onto his spouse. She internalizes the blame and enables him to continue his drinking by trying to improve her own behavior and the children's rather than confront his drinking. One child may try to keep the parents from fighting by diverting their attention to his or her own problems through drug use, pregnancy, or truancy. Another child may attempt to dissipate tension by being the family clown. These roles are not conscious attempts to keep the family in balance, however precarious this balance may be, but are patterns maintained at an unconscious level in a manner that is sometimes blatantly obvious and sometimes extremely subtle. When the patterns of behavior that maintain homeostasis are rigid and unyielding, the family system is considered "closed."

A closed system is dysfunctional because it is isolated from the environment, is less receptive to external stimuli, and is unresponsive to change. Because of its impermeable boundaries and nonreceptiveness to change, a closed system tends to move toward increasing disorder. Open systems, by contrast, interact with the environment and so may be capable of both adaptation and flexibility. Adaptation depends on maintaining enough stability to permit the family members to develop coherent, separate identities as they make the necessary accommodations to environmental changes.

Closed-system families contribute a disproportionate share of troubled children and youth to society because problem behaviors emerge more in closed family systems. Closed family systems typically demonstrate one of two major types of problems: detachment or enmeshment.

Detachment.   A detached family is one in which the individual members function separately and autonomously with little family interdependence. When one family member faces a time of stress, the family hardly seems to notice or respond at all. Detached families tend to be unresponsive because each member is isolated within the system. In such families, the boundaries are so rigid that only a high level of individual stress may activate support from other family members. The family members cannot get their social and emotional needs met within the family, nor do they learn appropriate ways to meet the needs of others. Although family members are not nourished or supported within their family, they often remain together because they seem to have no alternatives. Unfortunately, detached families produce young people who form inadequate or dysfunctional relationships outside the family because they have not learned how to have good relationships within the family. They do not know that other kinds of relationships are possible. Obviously, such youth are at risk for a variety of problem behaviors.

Enmeshment.   Enmeshed families demonstrate such intensity and closeness in family interactions that the members are overly involved and overly concerned with each other's lives. In enmeshed families, the children in particular experience a distorted sense of involvement, attachment, and belonging. They fail to develop a secure sense of individuality, separateness, and autonomy. When a member of an enmeshed family encounters a stressful situation, the family is likely to respond by rescuing rather than teaching constructive problem solving. Subsystem boundaries are weak, easily crossed, and poorly differentiated;

Mother keeping child in infantile state.

children may act like parents, and parental control may be ineffective. The young person's distorted sense of belonging and attachment interferes with his or her capacity to negotiate developmental tasks successfully. For example, a child may remain isolated from classmates and repeatedly feign illness so as not to "threaten" the mother–child relationship.

In the case study, the Carter family demonstrates the difficulties of negotiating the family life cycle and illustrates one kind of dysfunctional family. As you read this case study, take a few minutes to reflect on the family life cycle, the family as a social system, and issues of detachment and enmeshment.

The Carter family is at the transition point leading to the teenage stage of the family life cycle. Jason's underlying problems are intensifying precisely because adolescents begin to challenge rules and boundaries as they seek to establish their own identities. As the family is struggling to negotiate this transition, both Mr. and Mrs. Carter are attempting to cope with their own midlife transitional periods.

The Carters illustrate not only the family life cycle but also the family as a social system. The presenting problem—behavior difficulties at school—is an extension of Jason's role in his family. His "angelic" younger sister supports this role; his angry and depressed mother maintains it; and his isolated father covertly encourages it. Everyone in the family maintains homeostasis. Even though each of them is in some pain, the unknown (if Jason's position should change) is more anxiety provoking than the status quo. In other words, although Jason is the catalyst that prompts the Carters to seek an outside helper, the underlying causes of his behavior are embedded within the family's interaction. Each family member maintains equilibrium in the closed system of the family because each is vulnerable.

Christie is vulnerable because she builds her self-esteem on being the model child. If things shift, she may become the bad one—the "devil"—in the family. She does not know how to disagree or express negative emotions in a healthy way. She appears to be enmeshed in the family system. Mrs. Carter is vulnerable to a change in the homeostasis: if she loses the reasons for her depression (if Jason becomes cooperative and constructive), she might need to feel more guilt and be self-punitive to maintain her depression. Jason provides her with a scapegoat on which to vent her emotions. She would also have to develop a new relationship with Christie and begin to confront her husband, and such changes appear threatening. Mr. Carter might have to confront directly his anger and resentment toward his wife. He might also have to redefine Christie's role and change his behavior toward Jason. Jason is vulnerable because if his role changes, he might have to improve in school, risk failing when he is actually trying (instead of failing on purpose), and he will have fewer excuses for acting out. These shifts in perception, roles, and behavior are inevitably threatening. Thus each family member has a vested interest in maintaining his or her current functioning.

Families of Color

Family life cycle and family system theories are useful constructs in understanding family dynamics. Although useful in understanding and helping many families, the framework must be adapted to families of color and immigrant families. The professional helper's multicultural knowledge, awareness, and skills in working with people from diverse backgrounds are critical.

A specific example is the concept of enmeshment. What is enmeshment in the dominant culture may be collective sharing and interdependence in families of color. We must

CASE STUDY

The Carter Family

The Carter family came to our attention after Jason, a thin, pale, and intense 13-year-old, got into a particularly vicious fight. The other members of this middle-class family are Jason's parents, Doug and Lois Carter, and his 10-year-old sister, Christie. Jason was referred by his teacher because of fighting and other behavioral difficulties. He frequently disrupted his classes by harassing and fighting with other children and by talking back to teachers. His short attention span and apparent inability to sit still were the focus of a subsequent neurological examination, but no neurological impairment was indicated. Next Jason underwent an evaluation at school, consisting of a standard social history, psychological tests, and an intake interview.

The findings suggested that poor family communication and ineffective discipline might be the source of Jason's problem behavior. On the basis of this information, family therapy was strongly recommended. Referral to the neurological clinic, contact with school personnel, the social history, and the intake interview were all accomplished by a school social worker assigned to the case. She was also responsible for the family casework and referred Jason and his family to a mental health clinic that provided individual and family therapy.

Lois Carter, a chronically depressed European American woman, was torn by guilt over her perceived failure to rear a child who could function adequately at home and in school. She also seemed to have considerable unspoken anger, which was frequently directed at Jason. Mr. Carter, an engineer, was also a caldron of unexpressed anger. Emotionally locked out by his wife's depression, he seemed to resent Jason and to continually put the child in a double bind by subtly sending the message that his acting out was just a case of "boys will be boys" and at the same time reprimanding him for his behavior. He seemed unwilling or unable to follow through with punishment. In part, this behavior was an acting out of his own angry feelings toward his wife.

Mrs. Carter was the second daughter in her family of origin. She described her parents, who live only a mile from the Carters, in ambivalent terms. Her father was a chronic drinker, and he physically and emotionally abused his wife and children. He suffered brain damage as a result of drinking and had mellowed considerably in recent years. Mrs. Carter's mother was a passive-aggressive woman who turned to religion for comfort in her later years. Lois had an older sister who had twice married and divorced. After repeated attempts, the sister attained a college degree and now worked as an elementary school teacher. Mrs. Carter's two brothers expressed the family dysfunction more obviously. The

CASE STUDY

The Carter Family (continued)

youngest brother had committed suicide several years earlier. The other brother continued to live with his parents. At 30 he was unemployed and unmarried and existed on a small payment for service-connected emotional disability.

Doug Carter, of English and French descent, was the older of two brothers. His father, a bookkeeper for a small manufacturing firm, was a harsh, critical, and sarcastic parent. His mother was a pleasant though ineffectual woman who "adored" Mr. Carter's younger brother. A paternal grandmother, now deceased, lived in the home while Mr. Carter was growing up, and she tended to favor him. Mr. Carter and his brother had been very competitive as children and now have no contact. His parents reside in another state and contact with them is infrequent.

Christie was described by both parents as a "very good girl" who never caused any problems. She did well in school, was helpful at home when asked, and had a "nice little group" of girlfriends.

Both Jason and Christie Carter had been adopted as infants. Jason was considered the identified problem (patient), and Christie was regarded as a perfect little angel.

A counselor saw the family weekly for therapy that focused on their style of communication. During the first six sessions, the family discussed setting limits and the need for more direct communication. They reached an impasse, however, because the family members refused to listen to one another. Jason frequently pointed out, for instance, that his sister instigated many situations by teasing him. His parents refused to acknowledge that Christie could possibly do such a thing and reprimanded Jason for not listening to them and for trying to get his sister in trouble. Christie sat quietly and primly, in silent agreement with her parents. At the end of six sessions, the counselor felt that she was making little headway in helping the parents listen to Jason or to each other. Christie indicated little willingness to modify her secure position in the family structure. Jason continued to disrupt his classes and behave outrageously at school, in the neighborhood, and at home.

be cautious in relying on stereotypes to guide us; often families of color rely more on a larger social base and extended family support than do typical European American families. Among African American families, for example, extended family and friends are central. Arnold (1995) reports that most African American mothers in her study had a large and supportive social network of family and friends; the mean number of social contacts was

15.6 people for single women and 18.1 people for married women. The role of the church community also provides a rich network of support for many African American families. Among Native American families, the extended kinship system—including uncles, aunts, cousins, and grandparents—is central in children's lives, and multiple households that include non-blood-related individuals are often incorporated into the kinship circle. Many American Indian groups even have formal rituals to induct significant individuals into the family system. Asian American families often have close-knit and hierarchical family structures with particular authority being invested in the father and elders. Asian American relatives may participate in family life and in family decisions. And for traditional Latino families, the family structure is extended by formalized kinship relationships to the godparents. The term cousin may include many people—often same-age peers who are from non-blood-related families. With many families of color and immigrant families, loyalty to family and to their extended family takes priority over other social demands and dominant culture expectations. Clearly, there are cultural variations, group differences within ethnic groups, and individual differences within families of color as well as within European American families.

Families of Gay, Lesbian, Bisexual, and Transgender Youth

For many youth who are gay, lesbian, bisexual, or transgender (GLBT), family life is not a very safe life. Significant numbers of GLBT young people report that they have been verbally and physically assaulted at home (Sullivan & Wodarski, 2002). Many youth are rejected and become the focus of the family's dysfunction. In fact, the process of "coming out" is a major developmental task of homosexual youth, and GLBT youth often have a difficult time finding appropriate strategies for the coming-out process (Sullivan & Wodarski, 2002). Transgender youth are those whose "innate, deeply felt psychological identification as male or female, . . . may not correspond with the person's body or assigned sex at birth (meaning what sex was listed on a person's birth certificate)" (Human Rights Campaign Foundation, 2004). Society's lack of understanding of transgender individuals contributes to the enormous challenges faced by families of transgender youth, and these youth are at high risk for being rejected, shamed, and shunned.

Even more problematic is that lack of support and acceptance at home usually leads to other problems. Many GLBT youth run away; others are thrown out of the home when their sexual orientation or gender identity is revealed. Life on the street brings even more severe problems. Young people on the streets are not attending school; many are also using alcohol and drugs; many youth become prostitutes to support addictions, secure a place to stay, or ensure their "protection." Among runaways, GLBT youth have higher levels of early onset of sex and drug use and are at exceptionally high risk for HIV infection (Moon et al., 2000). Interventions within the family need to be sensitive to sexual orientation and gender identity.

FAMILY PROBLEMS AND PROBLEM FAMILIES

A focus on societal change, stages and transitions in the family life cycle, and the family as a system helps to identify stressors that may contribute to problems for young people. In addition, the possibility of young people developing problems increases rapidly as risk factors such as lack of parent–child bonding, family conflict and disorganization, ineffective parenting, and parental depression increase in comparison with resilience or protective factors (Kumpfer & Adler, 2003). Specific family problems contribute to the development of risky behaviors. Some family situations place all family members, and especially children, at risk.

Families Who Are Stressed

As we saw in Chapter 2, single-parent and poor families experience considerable stress. Two other kinds of families who are subject to stress are blended families and latchkey families.

Blended families.   Blended families (or reconstituted or stepparent families) are families in which the remarried partners bring children into the relationship. Because divorce and remarriage are increasingly common, blended families are becoming more and more numerous. Children in such families face an unfamiliar network of relationships, particularly with an adult with whom they have not fallen in love. They often suffer some degree of discomfort. These children may have few resources to draw upon in their attempts to cope with a new parent, new grandparents, possibly new stepsiblings, and a new family lifestyle. As the new couple shapes and ritualizes their lives, the young people face a whole new set of expectations, procedures, and interactions. Further, these children are struggling to adjust to their new conditions while the most significant people in their lives—their parents—are themselves adjusting and are consistently less available to them (Bray, 1999a; 1999b; 2001).

Viewed in the context of the family life cycle, the newlyweds must negotiate the establishment stage—a complex task in itself—at the same time that they must adopt a satisfactory and consistent system of child parenting and disciplining. The needs of the children are unlikely to coincide with those of the parents. Obviously, this situation causes problems and may be a major factor in the fragility of second marriages, which are more likely than first marriages to end in divorce.

Latchkey families.   Latchkey families are those in which one or more of the children are home alone before or after school and on school holidays. The increase in the number of mothers of young children in the workforce is one of the largest social changes in the last half of the 21st century (Halpern, 2005), and is an important factor in the latchkey phenomenon. In 2002, 66% of married women with a child under age 2 and 60% with a child under 1 year of age were employed (Trei, 2002). The traditional arrangement in which fathers are employed and mothers stay at home with the children is no longer the case for most families, for a complex variety of reasons including financial necessity, increasing equality in women's roles, and lifestyle goals. The combination of most mothers working and few fathers staying at home with the children means that more than 7 million children in the United States are latchkey children (U.S. Census Bureau, 2002).

Twenty-six percent of 11- to 13-year-olds and 5% of 5- to 10-year-olds take care of themselves either before or after school (National Center for Education Statistics, 2001). The average latchkey child is left alone for approximately 2.5 hours a day (Sadker & Sadker, 1987), and evidence suggests that a direct relationship exists between the number of hours spent in after-school self-care and problem behaviors (Ross, Saavedra, Shur, Winters, & Felner, 1992). Although physical well-being is of utmost concern to their parents, many latchkey children are unable to reach either parent by phone. Latchkey children are susceptible to accidents. They may also engage in acts of vandalism or delinquency (Dishion & Bullock, 2001). Not surprisingly, violent youth crime is most common between 3 and

6 o'clock in the afternoon, and a child's chance of being a victim of crime triples after school (CDF, 2001c). Unsupervised use of the Internet also occurs when children are home alone, which all too often can result in viewing pornography (even inadvertently), participating in chat rooms, and the formation of unhealthy and even dangerous relationships.

Carlos Diaz (see Chapter 5) spends his afternoons taking care of his sister. He is like countless other children who carry their keys in their backpacks and return to an empty house after school. Many latchkey children are bored, lonely, and frightened. These experiences can be even more intense when children do not have a structure to follow or responsibilities to carry out. As many as 1 in 4 latchkey children may be extremely fearful—fearful enough to arm themselves with a baseball bat as they watch television. For the latchkey child, television and the Internet become the babysitters, anesthetists, and constant companions. Given that parents must work and that the number of latchkey children will rise, widespread pre- and after-school programs that extend the number of hours children receive supervision are an important part of prevention efforts. Many after-school programs function as "afternoon schools." Such programs may seem too academic after a full day in the classroom, especially for young children. By the time students reach the age of 18, however, they will have watched 15,000 hours of television and attended school for only 11,000 hours (Sadker & Sadker, 1987). Indeed, the benefits of extra schooling and afternoon supervision may outweigh the possible excess of academia. This is particularly the case when after-school activities include games, sports, assistance with homework, counseling groups, tutoring, and opportunities to explore music and art.

If schools are unable to obtain the funds to offer pre- and after-school programs, they can still meet some of the needs of latchkey students. For example, the school counselor or psychologist can conduct workshops for parents or children to help children deal with the fears they encounter during their unsupervised hours. Children can be taught what to do in case of emergency or danger and how to maximize their safety. Latchkey children can be helped to devise productive ways to fill the time until a parent returns home, such as completing specific chores, doing homework, preparing nutritious snacks, and working on creative projects.

Families With Dysfunction

"Describe 4 types of family of Dysfunction"

All dysfunctional families subject children to stresses that may lead to risky behavior (Sander & McCarty, 2005). Substance abuse by the adult caretaker, interpersonal violence (Pettit, 2004), child abuse or neglect, and parental psychopathology are among those most likely to result in problems for young people. Most adults in such families experienced the same problems in their own families of origin and, as is common, perpetuate the same problems for their children.

Families experiencing substance abuse.   Children of alcoholic (or drug-using) parents are at risk for neglect and abuse. But even without overt neglect or abuse, parental alcoholism inflicts emotional damage on children. Such children may be predisposed to become alcoholic themselves or to enter into relationships with alcoholics (Wilens et al., 2002). Children are at high risk for emotional and social adjustment problems, including hyperactivity, relationship difficulties, aggression, depression, school absenteeism, and drug use (Watkins & Durant, 1996). The expanding literature on adult children of alcoholics documents the comprehensive and long-term impact that substance-abusing parents have on their children.

At best neglect - worst - abuse

Families experiencing violence.   Interpersonal violence is strongly correlated with children's problems. Of course, violence signals general marital discord, which is also associated with problematic behavior in children. Even when the child is not a direct target of family violence, exposure to adults who verbally abuse each other and who are not in control of their explosive anger can have long-lasting repercussions (Fincham, 1994; Fincham, Grych, & Osborne, 1994). The effect of family violence around the child is wholly negative, and violence exposure can destroy the child's self-esteem and confidence (Straus, 1994; Gelles, 1997). Such children are more vulnerable to stress disorders and other psychological disturbances. Violence also begets more violence. As violence in the family increases, it also increases the likelihood that the child will grow up to engage in violent and abusive behavior (American Psychological Association Presidential Task Force on Violence and the Family, 1996; Gelles, 1997).

Families with child abuse.   As another form of violence, child abuse occurs in many forms: physical violence, emotional abuse, psychological abuse, neglect, and sexual abuse. Physical violence is any physically harmful action against a child, from hair pulling and slapping to beating and burning. Emotional abuse occurs when children are subjected to harsh criticism, ridicule such as name-calling, irrational punishment, and inconsistent expectations. Psychological abuse occurs when parents manipulate children by withholding affection, giving inconsistent verbal and nonverbal messages, threatening suicide in front of children, and isolating children from peer contact, including making the home environment miserable so that peers never want to come over and play. Neglect occurs when a parent fails to safeguard the health, well-being, and safety of the child. Children who are not provided with healthy food and bathed regularly, who are left unattended, or who are consistently ignored are victims of neglect. Sexual abuse is any form of sexual behavior with a child, including molestation, incest, and rape, as well as systematic and consistent exposure to explicit sexual material. Children who grow up in such families find themselves at risk for future problems. The correlation of child abuse to teenage pregnancy and to later sexual victimization via unwanted sexual experiences is well documented (Kellogg, Hoffman, & Taylor, 1999; Smith, 1996). The age of first pregnancy is also linked with the presence of a family member with a drinking problem and with early physical or sexual abuse in the family (Kellogg et al., 1999).

Families with parental psychopathology.   Many young people are at risk because of parental psychopathology (Woolfenden, Williams, & Peat, 2002). Schizophrenia, bipolar disorders, and depression in adult caretakers seem to be particularly debilitating to young people. This can have long-term effects. For example, depressed teenagers growing up with depressed parents—especially depressed mothers—tend to have more frequent and severe depressive episodes as young adults than those with mentally healthy parents (Rohde, Lewinsohn, Klein, & Seeley, 2005). The family with depressed parents is usually characterized by poor marital adjustment and a low level of parent solidarity, warmth, and support. The parents' mental illness contributes to disturbed parent–child interactions, which leads to limited cognitive, emotional, and social development in the child. Teenagers in these families frequently have poor emotional and behavioral control and school adjustment problems. They may become easily upset, may disturb the class with unusual behavior, and have consistent discipline problems. These young people are at risk both for possible psychopathology themselves and for other risky behaviors.

In reality, the various types of dysfunctional families often overlap. Interpersonal violence, for example, is closely associated with alcohol use (60% of spouse batterers abuse alcohol), drug use (32% of spouse batterers use drugs), or both (22%; Walker, 1996). Violence between spouses is often accompanied by violence toward children; parent alcohol and drug use are associated with child neglect and physical abuse (Walker, 1996). Alcoholic fathers, for example, are 8 times more likely and alcoholic mothers 3 times more likely to abuse or neglect their children than parents who are not alcoholic (American Psychological Association Presidential Task Force on Violence and the Family, 1996).

When a child or adolescent exhibits at-risk behavior, it is important to consider the family in which the individual is being raised. The behavior of concern may be a reasonable—even if disturbing or dangerous—response to the stress of living in a dysfunctional family. The problems of the parents are sad and distressing; their effects on the children are tragic.

CHILD-REARING PRACTICES: THREE DIMENSIONS OF CHILD REARING

Over the years, researchers have reached a remarkable degree of agreement on the existence of three basic dimensions of child rearing despite the diversity of instruments, methodologies, and samples brought to bear on the subject. Researchers examining the basic factors involved in child rearing have consistently found three fundamental bipolar dimensions, although the names assigned to them vary (e.g., Arnold, O'Leary, Wolff, & Acker, 1993; Baumrind, 1995; Carlson, Grossbart, & Stuenkel, 1992; Vickers, 1994). These dimensions appear to provide an accurate description of parent–child interactions.

The permissiveness/restrictiveness dimension incorporates the constructs of control and power; permissiveness refers to low control and low power in parents' behaviors, whereas restrictiveness refers to high control and high power. The hostility/warmth dimension ranges from low to high levels of affection. The anxious, emotional involvement/calm detachment continuum ranges from high anxiety to low anxiety and reflects the emotional engagement or connectedness of the parent. These three dimensions appear to be relatively independent of one another and provide a key to understanding child rearing.

Figure 4.1 illustrates the three dimensions of child rearing in three-dimensional space. Note that the two end points of each dimension represent the extremes of parental behavior. The behavior of most parents tends to fall near the middle rather than the extremes on most dimensions. That is, a father is not likely to be either completely hostile or overwhelmingly warm; most mothers neither permit nor restrict everything their children want to do. It is typically parents with either extreme or inconsistent behaviors who place their children at greater risk.

Parental Inconsistency

The at-risk child's family life is often characterized by parental inconsistency as well as by the extreme behaviors. We know that consistent behavior by parents increases the child's ability to predict the environment and leads to more stable behavior patterns. Inconsistency has negative effects on children and may take various forms:

- Certain behaviors are permitted at one time but not at another, unpredictably: because of another child's behavior; because the parent's mood changes; because the parent is paying attention or not paying attention.
- What the child is told to do is inconsistent with what the child sees other family members doing, is rewarded for, or is punished for doing.

**Warmth
(high support)**

Understanding,
approval, much praise;
little punishment;
acceptance, affection;
child-centered home

**Anxious emotional
involvement
(high anxiety)**

Considerable emotion
related to child;
solicitous behavior/
attitude; protectiveness,
"babying"

**Permissive
(low control)**

Few rules or restraints,
little concern about
impulses, manners,
obedience, or noise

**Restrictive
(high control)**

Many rules and strict
enforcement in most
areas: emphasis on
obedience, manners,
boundaries; intolerance
of noise, aggression
toward peers/siblings/
parents

**Calm detachment
(low anxiety)**

Logical and controlled
behavior; never
punishes when angry;
lets child suffer
consequences of
his/her own mistakes

**Hostility
(low support)**

Considerable
disapproval and
punishment; little or
no understanding,
acceptance, affection,
or praise

FIGURE 4.1   Dimensions of child-rearing practices

- Patterns of rewards and punishments are inconsistent. The parent punishes a behavior at one time and does nothing the next time, rewards a behavior at one time and punishes it at another, threatens punishment and does not follow through, or promises a reward and does not give it.
- The degree of consistency the parent practices varies. One parent may be consistent in the overt goals set for the child but behaves in ways that subvert them; another may be so rigidly and literally consistent that the result is ludicrous.

Research findings on the effects of parental inconsistency have been limited because of variations in the way that inconsistency is defined and operationalized. Nevertheless, clear evidence of the deleterious effects of inconsistency emerges from the research literature on delinquency, which has repeatedly demonstrated a strong connection between inconsistent and erratic discipline (both between parents and within an individual parent) and a youth's antisocial behavior (Dishion & Bullock, 2002; Patterson, Reid, & Dishion, 1998). A related concern is the unstable home, or a home characterized by overstimulation and capricious discipline. Children may be teased, taunted, and encouraged to play roughly, for instance, and then punished for their boisterous behavior. Such unstable families produce children who lack social responsibility and display a low degree of conscientiousness. Capricious and coercive parental discipline contributes to conflict, aggression, and maladjustment (Bor & Sanders, 2004; Dishion & Bullock, 2002; Patterson et al., 1998).

Clusters of Child-Rearing Behaviors

To illustrate the interrelationships among the three dimensions of child rearing, we have transformed Figure 4.1 into a cubic model. Figure 4.2 depicts the resultant "parenting cube," which is made up of eight sections or clusters of parenting attitudes and behaviors. Sections 2, 4, 6, and 8, on the right, represent degrees of permissive parenting behavior, and sections 1, 3, 5, and 7, on the left, represent degrees of restrictive behavior. Sections 5 to 8, on the back half of the cube, represent anxious, emotional behavior, whereas the four in front, 1 to 4, represent calm detachment. The four cubes on the top, 1, 2, 5, and 6, reflect highly supportive, warm parental behavior; the four on the bottom, 3, 4, 7, and 8, reflect hostility or low support.

The parenting cube.   Each of the eight sections of the parenting cube represents a cluster of child-rearing practices that incorporate the three dimensions discussed earlier. The eight sections have been labeled with descriptive phrases that provide a rough generalization of the parenting behavior within sections. We consider each one in turn.

Section 1. Organized, effective behavior (restrictiveness, warmth, calm detachment). Parents who occupy this extreme position tend to control, shape, and evaluate the behavior of the child according to a high standard of conduct. The parents are positively involved with the child and use rewards, praise, and encouragement to engage the child. They discuss issues, values, and behavior without emotional turmoil.

Section 2. Democratic behavior (permissiveness, warmth, calm detachment). Parents who occupy this section usually encourage or permit discussion of family rules and regulations and tolerate a fairly wide range of behavior. The home environment is generally positive; the parents logically discuss the reasons a behavior is unacceptable.

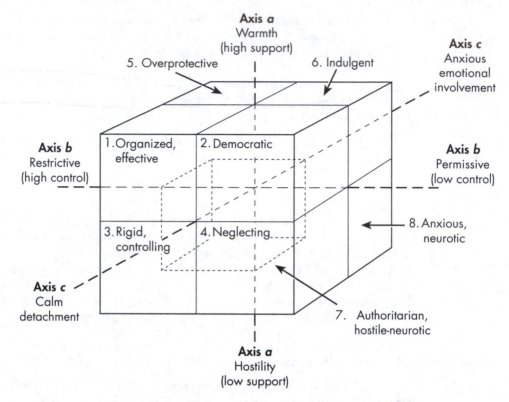

FIGURE 4.2 A cubic model of child-rearing practices

Section 3. Rigid, controlling behavior (restrictiveness, hostility, calm detachment). Parents in this category appear cruel in their interactions with their children. They generally have a large number of rules and regulations that they enforce in a cold, rigid, precise manner. The parents sometimes appear to relish punishing their children for misbehavior.

Section 4. Neglecting behavior (permissiveness, hostility, calm detachment). These parents allow their children to run free with few or no regulations. In extreme cases, the child's basic needs are not met because the parent is so uninvolved or hostile that the child is rejected and neglected.

Section 5. Overprotective behavior (restrictiveness, warmth, anxious emotional involvement). Parents in this cell offer consistent support along with many rules and regulations, but they do so with inappropriate emotional involvement and high levels of anxiety. They are often described as a mother bear (or father bear) protecting the young from a hostile environment.

Section 6. Indulgent behavior (permissiveness, warmth, anxious emotional involvement). The parents occupying this area can be said to spoil their children. The children have few rules, break those that they do have with few consequences, and tend to control the emotions and behavior of the parents.

Section 7. Authoritarian, hostile-neurotic behavior (restrictiveness, hostility, anxious emotional involvement). These parents establish many rules and regulations and rigidly enforce them, often with much anger, shouting, and physical punishment. Extreme behaviors in this cell may constitute child abuse.

Section 8. Anxious, neurotic behavior (permissiveness, hostility, anxious emotional involvement). The parents in this category are also potential child batterers, and in most cases they tend to exert little control over their children and exhibit little care for them. They tend to direct a lot of anger at their children (and others). These parents may do a great deal of ineffectual nagging and emotional battering with little expectation of modifying the child's behavior.

These eight categories of parenting styles affect child development. Some categories are likely to result in more at-risk behaviors than others. All have consequences for children's and adolescents' behavior.

Consequences of parenting styles.   These eight clusters of child-rearing styles provide a reasonable model of the complex relationships between parents and their children. But the efficiency of the model is offset by a lack of comprehensiveness: Some parental behaviors are not reflected in these clusters. Many factors influence the consequences of these parenting styles in the behavior of children and adolescents. The age of the child, the personality and constitution of the child, and the degree and duration of the unhealthy (or healthy) relationship with the parents all are of influence. Other factors include the child's perception of the interaction, the family setting, and other ecological factors. Nevertheless, there are some consistent consequences of each of these parenting styles on children and youth.

Section 1. Organized, effective parents; high-achieving conformers. These youth tend to be highly socialized and conforming. Often model children and adolescents, they may experience some internal conflict and may be timid and withdrawn but are rarely a problem to society. Children in this category are high in compliance, dependency, responsibility, leadership, and conscience. They are rarely referred for counseling, although intrapersonal stress sometimes forces them to seek treatment.

Section 2. Democratic parents; friendly, achieving bohemians. These children and adolescents tend to be active, socially outgoing, and friendly. Often they take an aggressive stance on social issues and assume adult role-taking behavior quite early. They are often creative, independent individuals who achieve when and if they decide it is important to do so.

Section 3. Rigidly controlling parents; delinquent runaways. These children often exhibit considerable fear and rejection of authority figures. Outwardly conforming, they may develop a repertoire of manipulative behaviors that passively express their aggression. Ultimately the child may explode into highly delinquent behavior or escape by running away.

Section 4. Neglecting parents; neglected children. These children are poorly equipped to take on adult roles and may eventually reject society's standards. They may develop self-punitive and self-defeating behaviors, becoming isolated and socially withdrawn.

Section 5. Overprotective parents; conforming, dependent children. These children are likely to show high compliance. They follow rules closely and with some anxiety. They may also be submissive, dependent, withdrawn, and timid. They frequently have a difficult time becoming independent.

Section 6. Indulgent parents; spoiled children. Children whose parents occupy this section tend to be pampered and spoiled. Often independent and creative, they can be disobedient, impudent, demanding, and "bratty." As they get older, they may develop anti-social, aggressive, or narcissistic behavior and then expect to be protected from the consequences.

Section 7. Authoritarian, hostile-neurotic parents; abused/aggressive children. Children in this category are fearful and angry and may eventually vent their rage against society. Often their rebellion takes the form of highly aggressive, delinquent, acting-out behavior. Some of these children run away.

Section 8. Anxious-neurotic parents; emotionally disturbed children. Children in this cell tend to be neurotic and disturbed. Often socially withdrawn, they may have poor peer-group attachment characterized by shyness and quarreling. They are likely to be unable to assume adult roles and have poor self-esteem.

These profiles are based on professional observation, descriptive reports in the literature, and a review of research studies. Although much needs to be done to expand knowledge in this area, some common parenting patterns have been identified with enough certainty to enable us to characterize the parenting styles seen in families. These patterns are crucial to the family environment and to the overall personal development of children.

Parenting styles in the Andrews family.   Let us consider Allie Andrews, whom we met in Chapter 1. It would be helpful at this point to review Allie's case. Recall that she and her stepfather were in open conflict regarding family rules and regulations and that their relationship had deteriorated.

Although the Andrews case study does not provide a great deal of information about Jack and Alicia's parenting styles, it does tell us enough to permit us to offer some tentative hypotheses about the family interaction and make a preliminary evaluation of the Andrews's parenting styles. This situation is not atypical. Indeed, one of the major problems for teachers and counselors is the difficulty of gaining access to the total picture. One is called upon to teach and counsel, to make judgments and evaluations, to provide treatment plans, and to respond to conflict and pain in the young person without knowing the full background and thus without completely understanding the life situation of the individual. Effective and competent counselors, teachers, and others are always working with hunches and tentative hypotheses.

When we review Allie's situation, several issues stand out. First, we find descriptions of parental behavior that represent each one of the three dimensions of child-rearing practices. Jack appears to be highly controlling and restricting. He sets firm, perhaps harsh rules and upholds them with punishment. He also seems to provide little warmth and low support for Allie. His apparent dislike for Allie and his punishments reflect a hostile style of interaction. Finally, his emotional involvement is negative and extreme—he is hurt, fearful, and angry, as well as suspicious and mistrustful.

We find less information on the parenting behavior of Allie's mother. We do know that she has assumed the role of the family mediator, however, and that she occasionally has absorbed some of the conflict. Her parenting style appears to differ from her husband's in the area of emotional involvement. And so we come to the second issue: inconsistency. Even though the mother's emotional response may have a calming and placating effect, Allie may view it as encouragement to act out. This inconsistency may be a strong clue to the dysfunction within the family system.

The third issue that emerges from the case study is the intensity of the stepfather's engagement in his parenting of Allie. On each of the three continuums, his behavior is

Warmth
(high support)

Anxious
emotional
involvement
(high anxiety)

Stepfather suspicious
and fearful,
angry, hurt

Permissive
(low control)

Restrictive
(high control)

Firm rules—
punishment,
restriction;
upholds
rules

Calm detachment
(low anxiety)

Mother mediates
and absorbs
conflicts

Hostility
(low support)

Strong
dislike

Comments: Allie's stepfather, Jack, operates out of Section 7
of the parenting cube and has become more reactive
and violent as Allie has reached adolescence. Mother's
parenting style is different (calm detachment), but the
case study does not provide enough data to locate her
precisely in the cube.

Section 7:
Authoritarian,
hostile-neurotic
parenting

FIGURE 4.3 **Parenting behaviors (the case of Allie)**

extreme. That is, he is quite restrictive and provides Allie very low support. He is obviously
very emotionally involved with her. This behavior places him in Section 7: He is authoritarian and hostile-neurotic. Needless to say, Allie's stepfather is a major negative influence on
her at this point. Figure 4.3 summarizes the behaviors that are involved in Allie's parenting.

The parenting issues raised in Allie's case suggest possible intervention strategies. The family system is already under considerable stress at this time and might be amenable to intervention. It is obvious that Allie's stepfather is a major influence in her life. This observation leads to several questions that may eventually need to be addressed. Should Jack be included in any treatment plans that are developed? Should Jack or the family as a whole be considered for intervention? Should school programs be arranged to provide Allie with a more reasonable limit-setting model? Possible answers to these questions will be provided in later chapters.

CONCLUSION

In this chapter we considered social changes that affect today's families and the rapid changes that occur within families in response to them. Helping professionals need to understand and appreciate cultural differences in families rather than impose dominant culture assumptions. Many families are characterized by detachment, enmeshment, poor parenting practices, or are dysfunctional in other ways. The Carter family illustrates a fairly common family dysfunction. As families progress through developmental periods, or stages of the family life cycle, some of the interaction patterns that developed early, such as parenting styles, must adapt to the changing needs of the children. When they do not, young people are often at risk for engaging in maladaptive and self-defeating behaviors. The conceptual model of the three dimensions of child rearing is intended to clarify the continuums of parenting styles. The parenting cube can also help counselors, teachers, and human service professionals teach and encourage positive behaviors among children and, as much as possible, within the whole family. As the case studies suggest, ineffective and poor parenting and family interactions have to be identified before steps can be taken to promote effective and positive interactions.

CHAPTER 5

School Issues That Relate to At-Risk Children and Youth

▲ *I started out in the hole, in school, because of my impression that I was a miracle of stupidity, and because I was afraid of my teacher. Her name was Mrs. Ida Homer and she wore cushiony shoes like nurses', only hers were red, and you could smell stale cigarettes and coffee on her breath . . . she made me stand in the wastebasket because I wrote on my desk and poked my neighbor, and because I did not follow directions. Instead of drawing pictures, I put words all over the sheet of paper. I loved the shape of letters in a word like shampoo. I got in trouble for coloring outside of the lines when we were drawing turkeys for Thanksgiving. . . . Mrs. Ida Homer said I didn't do my coloring right. She said I had to stay in for recess to get the colors inside the lines of the turkey.*

JANE HAMILTON
THE BOOK OF RUTH

CHAPTER OUTLINE

▲   In education, the term *at risk* refers primarily to students who are at risk of school failure. As we discussed earlier, at risk actually means much more than flunking reading or math, or even dropping out of school. Yet from an educator's perspective, educational concerns define at-risk issues. School problems and dropout are linked to many other problems expressed by young people (Beauvais et al., 1996; Jessor, 1991, 1993; Mahoney, 1998). The strong relationships between school difficulties and other problems, as well as evidence that educational involvement is a protective factor influencing resilience (Miller & MacIntosh, 1999), highlight the pivotal position of schools. In schools, prevention efforts can reach the greatest number of young people; therefore, examining the educational environment is critical.

THE VALUE OF EDUCATION

There are a number of indicators of the value placed on education in the United States. News reports compare the scores of students in the United States and in other countries on tests in geography and spelling, math and science. These reports consistently favor students in other countries. They imply that learning in U.S. schools is somehow not quite up to par. Does a student's ability to spell reflect his or her ability to think? Does recall of dates, locations, or facts indicate a student's problem-solving skills? The answer to these questions is "No." Learning is the act of acquiring knowledge or a skill through instruction or study, yet these comparisons suggest a view of learning that reduces this cognitive act to an isolated and mechanical process (Comer, 1996). In addition, these comparisons often fail to note that in the United States *all* children are expected to attend school through high school graduation, not just wealthy or middle-class urban or college-bound students.

How learning is valued is also reflected in the following statistics. According to the U.S. Census Bureau (2001), the average household income was a bit over $55,000 in 2000, but average teachers' salaries have hovered around $40,000 from 1987–88 through 1998–99 (NCES, 2001). Schoolteachers and counselors, most with master's degrees, are actually paid less than the national average and are poorly remunerated relative to other professionals. Low teacher salaries reflect the value society places on education and is one contributor to the current teacher shortage.

In response to the current shortage of 2.2 million teachers, many states are lowering teacher standards, with one fourth of new teachers not meeting state licensing requirements (CDF, 2000). During 1999–2000, more than 70% of the students in ESL/bilingual education classes had teachers without certification. In addition, 17% of high school physics students, 36% of high school geology students, and 29 to 40% of biology/life science and physical science students were being taught by teachers without certification (Seastrom, Gruber, Henke, McGrath, & Cohen, 2002). Students learn more from better teachers. Interestingly, more affluent schools attract teachers with greater academic skills (Wayne, 2002); a much greater percentage of teachers at poorer schools have poor academic skills. And the disparity between rich and poor schools is increasing (Berliner, 2001; Kozol, 1992, 2005). The richest school districts in the United States spend 56% more per student than the poorest schools. Economists, sociologists, and educators have known for decades about the link between the social and economic disadvantage and the student-achievement gap. To see real school reform, it is critically important to address the underlying social and economic conditions (Rothstein, 2004). Those schools serving large numbers of poor children are likely to have fewer books and supplies and more teachers with less training and experience (CDF, 2000). If U.S. schools are expected to combat the societal problems of at-risk students, we must commit to the education of our children and youth as our highest priority, which includes attracting and training enough qualified teachers and counselors, encouraging them to work in poor districts, and providing them with adequate compensation.

Federal funding and policies provide further evidence regarding society's support of education. During Carter's presidency, Congress elevated the subcabinet agency of education to the Department of Education (DOE). In the 1980s, the Reagan and the first Bush administrations insisted that the DOE bring about educational reforms by "leadership and persuasion"—not by new programs or funds. In fact, during every year of Reagan's administration, educational funding was level or reduced for programs that provided aid for disadvantaged children, bilingual education, and work-incentive child-care initiatives; educational funding fell from 2.3% to 1.7% of the total federal budget (Carville, 1996; Shearer, 1990). The expenditure per pupil (dollar level adjusted) in public schools only rose from $6,343 in 1989–90 to $6,662 in 1997–98 (NCES, 2001). The 1990s saw a disturbing trend in prisons versus education. For the first time, in 1995 states spent more on prisons than on colleges: university construction funds decreased by almost a billion (to $2.5 billion), and corrections funding increased by almost a billion (to $2.6 billion; Ambrosio & Schiraldi, 1997). New York and California further illustrate this relationship. The New York State prison budget increased by $761 million, and the higher education budget dropped by $615 million in the 1990s (Gangi, Schiraldi, & Ziedenberg, 1998). Between 1984 and 1994, there was a 209% funding increase in California's prison system, but there was only a 15% increase in state university funding (Taqi-Eddin, Macallair, & Schiraldi, 1998). The capital expenditure for a prison cell is $180,000; it costs $35,000 per year to house an inmate (Hora, Schma, & Rosenthal, 1999), a huge drain on public funds.

A society loses by producing nonproductive citizens. If schools do not provide a safety net for children, health and well-being are reduced. Investing in prisons instead of education and prevention is an expensive, wasteful, and failing long-term strategy. America spends 50% more incarcerating 1.2 million nonviolent offenders than the federal government spends on welfare programs, and 6 times more than on child care (Camp & Camp, 1999). Although the United States has only 5% of the world's population, it has 25% of the world's prisoners (Ziedenberg & Schiraldi, 1999) and the highest rate of incarceration in the world (Walmsley, 2005). Yet 1 in 2 of America's children will never complete a single year of college; 1 in 8 will never graduate from high school; and 1 in 3 are behind a year or more in school (CDF, 2000; Walmsley, R., 2005; *World's Prison Population List* (6th ed.), King's College London: International Centre for Prison Studies, retrieved [5-31-2006] from http://www.prisonstudies.org/)

The publication of *A Nation at Risk* (National Commission on Excellence in Education, 1983) led to more than two decades of public school education bashing and launched the high-stakes testing phenomena, in which consequences for not passing standardized tests include grade retention for the individual and decreased funding for schools that fail to achieve required pass rates (Amrein & Berliner, 2002). In *The Manufactured Crisis*, Berliner and Biddle (1995) provide convincing evidence of a political agenda underlying *A Nation at Risk* and present thorough and sound data indicating that public schools in the United States have done a marvelous job of educating American children. In fact, they demonstrate that children actually know more than earlier generations, compare very favorably to students educated in other countries, and perform better than ever before (see Box 5.1).

The No Child Left Behind (NCLB) Act of 2001 was signed into law by President George W. Bush in January 2002. This act has been described as the most sweeping reform of the Elementary and Secondary Education Act since its inception in 1965. It redefines the federal role in K–12 education and promises to help close the achievement gap between disadvantaged and minority students and their peers. NCLB contains four basic principles: stronger accountability for results (e.g., decreased funding for schools that do not meet pass rates for standardized tests), increased flexibility and local control, expanded school choice options for parents (e.g., parents can remove their children from failing schools), and an emphasis on scientifically supported teaching methods. While infusing resources to schools, there are significant concerns about the effects of the NCLB Act. For example, even more funding is likely to flow away from those public schools in most desperate need (Pierce, 2002). Some argue that the NCLB act undermines support for public education (e.g., Meier, Wood, et al., 2004). Others raise serious concerns about accountability and the ways that the NCLB Act may diminish attention to both above and below average students (Goldhaber, 2002; Reville, 2002). Schools required to show improvement will do so most efficiently by focusing resources on those children who test just below the minimum pass rates. Those children who have very poor test scores are unlikely to raise scores high enough to increase the school's pass rate, and those students with good scores are already part of the pass rates. Both the highest and lowest achieving students are less likely to receive support or services.

Most teachers work hard, are concerned about children, and try to do a good job of teaching. Teachers know that all children need support, care, and nurturing. They

▲ Box 5.1

Separate and Unequal 15-Year-Olds

A new look at the literacy of teens living in the industrialized world shows that American students are about average. "Average is not good enough for American kids," warns (former) Education Secretary Rod Paige. True enough—but Paige and the Bush administration miss the point. Hidden in those results is yet one more piece of evidence that American youngsters attend schools that are separate and markedly unequal.

The Program on International Student Assessment (PISA) seeks to understand what 15-year-olds in 27 industrialized nations learned in reading, mathematics, and science from school and nonschool sources. PISA's goal is to assess how well we teach youth to think and solve common, everyday problems in those three disciplines. With 85% of a student's waking hours up to graduation from high school spent outside school, this is really a study of how well our society educates our young.

The answer depends on whether the teens are White, African American, or Hispanic. Overall, American 15-year-olds were close to the international averages in all three areas of literacy; about 10% scored in the top 10% worldwide on all three scales. The three tests correlated so highly that national scores on any one measure of literacy were almost a perfect proxy for scores on any other measure.

In reading, our strongest area, teens in only three nations—Finland, Canada, and New Zealand—scored significantly higher than ours; in fact, 81% of U.S. teens scored at levels two and above on a five-level reading literacy scale (with Level Five being the top).

This is noteworthy because of what PISA says a "Level Two" teen can do: make a comparison or several connections between the text and outside knowledge, draw on personal experience and attitudes to explain the text, recognize the main idea when the information is not prominent, understand relationships or construe meaning within a selected part of the text, and locate one or more pieces of information, which may require inferences to meet several conditions. Only 12% of our teens, those classified in Level One, cannot reach this remarkably high standard. Even among the least-literate teens classified at Level One, almost half were able to successfully respond to the more difficult items in Level Two.

On all three tests, our youth didn't do badly overall—but we didn't shine either. Why? The answer becomes clear when the scores of different 15-year-olds are viewed separately.

PISA clearly shows we have some ill-educated 15-year-olds, and most of those are poor and minority children. On the reading literacy scale White students in the United States are 2nd in the world, but African American and Hispanic students rank 25th; in mathematics

(continued)

Box 5.1 (continued)

White students are 7th, African American students are 26th; in science White students are 4th, African American and Hispanic students are 26th.

The unpleasant reality is that the United States runs separate and unequal schools and neighborhoods. The conditions of the schools and neighborhoods for our poor, African American, and Hispanic youth are not designed for high levels of literacy in reading, mathematics, and science. We accept poverty, violence, drugs, unequal school funding, uncertified teachers, and institutionalized racism in the schools that serve these children and in the neighborhoods in which they live. These unequal conditions appear to be the major reason we fall short in international comparisons. We combine the scores of these ill-educated children with those of children who enjoy better resources. As long as these differences are allowed to exist, we will rank about average in international comparisons.

As PISA makes clear, accepting deficient schools and troubled neighborhoods for our poor and minority students diminishes our international competitiveness. In ignoring these data about who does well and who does not, we diminish our moral authority in the world as well.

PISA exposes what we have known for too long: that we have social problems to which we pay scant attention. In every international comparison of industrialized nations the United States is the leader in rate of childhood poverty. African American and Hispanic students attend public schools as segregated as they have ever been. Our poor and minority children are not getting the opportunities they need for the nation to thrive.

Politicians who spend their energy condemning the public schools for their supposed failure to educate American youth are ignoring what PISA tells the world: that we fail selectively, having organized our society to provide poor and minority 15-year-olds less opportunity to achieve. Shame on us.

David Berliner, Regents' Professor,
Arizona State University,
Tempe, Arizona

also know that with the decline of economic stability, the pressures facing parents, and the fragmentation of neighborhoods and communities, the support and care children receive at school is even more critical. Teachers are expected to do more than ever before in classrooms that some find increasingly unsafe. During the mid-1990s, 12% of all teachers were threatened with injury and 4% were physically attacked by a student (NCES, 2001). Much gang activity occurs around schools (Esbenson, 2000). School shootings leave teachers questioning whether such shocking violence could happen "at my school." Amidst these concerns, teachers are constantly bombarded about how "teachers are not doing their jobs," how "schools are inadequate and failing," and how teachers must "do more with less."

For public education to succeed, increased financial support is needed for struggling schools. Such expenditures will not be forthcoming unless our society as a whole understands the value of learning (Comer, 1996). School reform is critical to the development of more effective schools. However, in "our rush to reform education, we have forgotten a simple truth: Reform will never be achieved by reviewing appropriations, restructuring schools, rewriting curricula, and revising tests if we continue to demean and dishearten the human resource called the teacher on whom so much depends. Teachers must be better compensated, freed from bureaucratic harassment, given a role in academic governance, and provided with the best possible methods and materials" (P. Palmer, cited in Obiakor, 2001, p. 4).

RESEARCH ON EFFECTIVE SCHOOLS

Variables in Research on School Effects

Researchers have identified a number of elements common to effective schools (Good & Brophy, 1994; Taylor, Pressley, & Pearson, 2000; Wohlstetter & Smyer, 1994). These can be classified into the general categories of leadership behaviors, academic emphasis, teacher and staff factors, student involvement, community support, and social capital.

Leadership behaviors.   Effective schools have autonomous staff management at the school site. Administrators, teachers, and counselors make many decisions about programs and program implementation without the need to seek approval of the school board or the district. Effective schools have a clear mission and place an emphasis on strong instructional leadership.

Academic emphasis.   Effective schools provide a rigorous curriculum. Students are expected to perform, and they are frequently monitored. Academic achievement is recognized on a schoolwide basis, instructional time is maximized, and the curriculum is consistently improved.

Teacher and staff factors.   Effective schools are characterized by collegial relationships among the staff, encouragement of collaborative planning, and low turnover among the faculty. Further, staff development is provided on a schoolwide basis.

Student involvement.   Students at effective schools tend to have a sense of community, a feeling of belongingness, and to feel safe at school. They also are likely to have clear goals. Teachers and counselors work to help students feel connected. Student discipline is fair, clear, and consistent but not oppressive or punitive.

Community support.   The communities in which effective schools are located have high expectations of the schools and their students. Further, district support and supportive parental involvement are evident, and relationships between home and school are strong and positive.

Social capital. Social capital, the network of relationships that surround an individual child, is important for development (Coleman & Hoffer, 1987; Maeroff, 1998). One of the major reasons some schools perform significantly better than others is that they are so rich in social capital (Coleman & Hoffer, 1987). The nuclear and extended family, the neighborhood and church community, the social service agencies, and community organizations form a supportive enclave of adults who are united with school personnel around a system of similar educational beliefs and values. This network of relationships is extremely important to the education of all children. Most school systems are severely constrained today because of the general reduction of social capital in society (Maeroff, 1998).

Definitional Issues in Research on School Effects

Most research on effective schools measures effectiveness as students' performance on standardized achievement tests, an extremely narrow view of learning. Other cognitive criteria, such as decision making and critical thinking, are largely ignored (Adams & Hamm, 1994; Good & Brophy, 1994). Glasser (1990) states that "nothing of high quality, including schoolwork, can be measured by standardized, machine-scored tests" (p. 428). To judge school effectiveness by the narrow criterion of scores on standardized tests pressures teachers and districts to carry out test-driven curriculum. In one study examining a decade of data from 18 states that implemented high-stakes testing, Amrein and Berliner (2002) found that scores on standardized tests such as the ACT and the SAT did not increase after high-stakes testing was implemented, even when the high-stakes test scores increased. Scores on the ACT, SAT, and content measures stayed the same or actually decreased.

Results of research on school effectiveness must be viewed with caution. For example, schools with higher dropout rates potentially have higher test score averages than do schools that retain their lower achieving students longer. If effectiveness is judged by performance on high-stakes tests alone, a school that fails miserably with at-risk students by pushing them out may be deemed highly effective! Alternative indices, such as students' involvement in the community, attendance rates, the incidence of school vandalism and violence, or dropout rates, are seldom measured in school effectiveness research but these indices may be more relevant to the community. Obiakor (2001) suggests that "good" schools be redefined as those that are "culturally, racially, linguistically, and socioeconomically heterogeneous" and in which students "will not be misidentified, misassessed, mislabeled, miscategorized, misplaced, and misinstructed" (p. 129). Another dimension of school effectiveness is school culture. School culture focuses on aspects of education more directly relevant to at-risk youth. Let us consider the Diaz family case study.

School culture. Every social organization has its unique culture, and schools are no exception. School culture is determined by student involvement, teacher factors, community support, curricular focus, and educational leadership—factors that also define effective schools. A culture provides its members with two things. First, it establishes a set of rules, expectations, and norms for members. Carlos's teachers encourage an English-only norm. In Lidia's school, retaining students who do poorly is the rule. Essentially, school culture provides an informal understanding of the way things are done. Second, culture can enhance self-esteem through shared values, beliefs, rituals, and ceremonies. Students, faculty, and staff who take pride in their school culture are likely to do better than those who do not. Many of Carlos's teachers share negative views of bilingual education;

CASE STUDY

The Diaz Family

Enrique Diaz came to the United States from El Salvador 16 years ago when he was 23 years old. He was forced to flee El Salvador when his membership in a small labor union was revealed to the government authorities, and he left behind his parents, brothers, sisters, and extended family. He brought his sister's 2-year-old daughter Ramona with him because the baby's father had been killed for his labor union activity and his sister feared for her own life. A church group participating in the Sanctuary movement of the 1980s provided Enrique and Ramona with shelter in a local safe house, as well as assisting Enrique in finding employment. Enrique works as a day laborer for growers and lawn maintenance companies. He met Alicia, a Mexican American woman volunteer at the safe house, during his first week in the United States. Alicia began spending a great deal of time caring for Ramona, and she and Enrique married 10 months after his arrival. One of the things that attracted Alicia to Enrique was the fact that he was a very hard worker and did not drink alcohol. Currently Enrique continues to work as hard as ever during the day, but he now consumes one or two six packs of beer most evenings. Alicia is the second child in a family of nine children. Her parents came to the United States from central Mexico as young adults. Alicia works as a motel maid and has a second part-time job doing custodial work at her church. Alicia and Enrique have raised Ramona, now 18, as their own daughter, and also have a son, Carlos, who is 13, and another daughter, Lidia, who is 5 years old. They live in a small rented home and maintain a very modest standard of living. Enrique became a naturalized citizen just before the birth of Lidia.

Enrique understands but does not speak English. Alicia was raised in a monolingual Spanish household but learned to speak English in school. Although her English skills are solid, she is very reluctant to use English unless she has to because she believes that she makes many mistakes and feels self-conscious about her accent. Both of the parents express concern about their children because family life is curtailed by the long hours the parents spend at work. They are especially concerned about their children's educational problems. Neither parent completed high school, and both desperately want their children to have a better life. They view education as a necessary step toward that goal. Their communication with the school system has been complicated by language barriers. In addition, Enrique and Alicia are convinced that the teachers think they are bad and uncaring parents because they have not learned enough English.

Upon entering kindergarten, Ramona Diaz was placed in an ESL (English as a second language) program. She was transitioned into an English-only classroom

CASE STUDY

The Diaz Family *(continued)*

when she entered middle school because that was district policy; however, she did not seem prepared to enter this environment. Ramona associated only with other girls who were Spanish-language dominant and fell behind in all of her content areas. She resisted going to school, even skipping classes on occasion. In parent–teacher conferences, her teachers would consistently say that she was not turning in her homework, or would turn in work that was incomplete and inaccurate. Ramona would insist that she was turning it in but that her teachers were misplacing it and grading her unfairly because they thought she was "stupid" and didn't like her. Enrique was enraged by Ramona's attitude toward school, and they had explosive arguments two or three times per week, which were most likely to occur in the evening after Enrique had been drinking for several hours. Finally, at age 16, Ramona dropped out of school and began working five nights per week at ABC Burgers. Although Enrique and Alicia did not approve, they had felt somewhat out of control of Ramona and were unsure of how to help her in school. With Ramona out of the house at night, and because homework was no longer a constant source of tension, the fighting between Enrique and Ramona decreased. Enrique's drinking did not decrease.

Ramona tells her parents that she will eventually earn her GED. Alicia is concerned that Ramona will become pregnant and be stuck in low-paying jobs for the rest of her life. She rarely sees Ramona. Ramona arrives home from work after her parents are in bed and is still sleeping when Enrique and Alicia leave for work in the morning. Alicia suspects that Ramona has a boyfriend at work, but Ramona denies this and is very closed about her social activities. She has been contributing to the family income and is affectionate with her brother and sister when she sees them. Just last week, however, Ramona told her parents that she had lost her paycheck and would not be able to help out the family until the next one arrived.

Carlos Diaz is in the seventh grade. He has had a solid relationship with his parents, particularly his mother. Carlos has been in a regular classroom for the past 2 years. He has generally done well in his schoolwork, but he is not a model student. He has often had trouble with his peers and at times gotten into fights on the playground. Since he has moved into junior high school, his social problems have decreased somewhat. He has several teachers now, and the classes are larger than those in the primary school. He has begun to make friends, although his lack of free time outside of school has made this difficult.

CASE STUDY

The Diaz Family *(continued)*

Because of Ramona's job at ABC Burgers, Carlos has the responsibility of watching his little sister after school, and he has had difficulty completing school assignments. His after-school activities now include cleaning the house and helping to prepare dinner in addition to babysitting, so he has only a limited amount of time to complete the homework assigned by his five teachers. When his assignments require use of a computer, Carlos has to stay in from recess to use one at school because his family does not own one. Some nights he works on every subject for at least a short time, but on other nights he is able to complete an assignment for only one of his classes. At the time they entered counseling, Carlos was behind in every class and was falling asleep in school. Some of his teachers seem to think he is lazy, contrary, and unresponsive. Many of them seem frustrated that Carlos is not completely fluent in English "by now."

Carlos's social studies teacher, Ms. Bassett, has taken a particular interest in him. At first, she found him inattentive in class and unresponsive to her questions, and she assumed this behavior was a combination of language and lack of ability. She noticed, however, that when he did complete his homework it was usually well done and accurate. After consulting with the school counselor, she gave Carlos a more active role in his own education. She found ways to give him more responsibility for learning, provided a means for him to monitor his own progress, and generally encouraged him to be more active in learning. The counselor also suggested that cooperative learning groups might be especially beneficial to Carlos, not only academically but as a means to help Carlos develop better peer relationships. Ms. Bassett is currently struggling with ways to modify her teaching style in a school that bases evaluations of her teaching on direct instruction, a method that typically works well for social studies recitation classes but fails to allow students to take an active role in learning. Enrique and Alicia view Carlos as a very responsible young man and hope that he will continue on in school. They are aware that he is under a lot of pressure at home and in school but do not seem to know what to do about it. In spite of their concerns, they have not responded to Ms. Bassett's invitation to meet with them or talk on the phone. They seem to fear that she will be upset about Carlos's caretaking role and that she will not understand their family situation.

Lidia Diaz is in kindergarten this year. Last year she participated in Head Start, which greatly aided her language skills and helped prepare her for kindergarten. In spite of this advantage, she is progressing quite slowly. She is one of 30 kindergartners in the classroom. Some of her classmates attended private preschools and can already read. To deal with the large number of students in

CASE STUDY

The Diaz Family *(continued)*

her class, Lidia's teacher groups the children according to their ability in reading and arithmetic. Lidia knows that she is in the lowest group in both subjects. Like her older sister, Lidia often feels stupid. Lidia's teacher believes that Lidia has the potential for school success and wishes she could spend more time with her. Lidia's elementary school has a retention policy for kindergarten students who do not make certain gains in achievement. In spite of her teacher's belief in her abilities, Lidia fits the criteria for the district retention policy, and if things do not improve, she will probably be kept back next year.

Lidia's feelings of stupidity are due in part to her exclusion from her school's culture. Participation and attendance in school activities can greatly enhance school connectedness and pride. These activities are generally hard hit when resources are scarce, and even when available students such as Carlos are not able to take advantage of them. The culture of a school can be described in terms of student and teacher climate.

Student climate. Several aspects of student climate relate directly to children and youth at risk. Children's experiences with their peers provide them with an opportunity to learn how to interact with others, develop age-relevant skills and interests, control their social behavior, and share their problems and feelings. As children get older, their peer group relationships increase in importance. The child's recognition of belonging to a group is an important step in development, and students with more friends at school feel more connected to their schools (Karcher, 2004; McNeely, Nonnemaker, & Blum, 2002). But belonging to a group has both benefits and costs in the child's subsequent social development and behavior. Many students who are at risk for school failure know early that somehow they are different from—less acceptable and less accepted than—other students. Lidia Diaz is one such student. Consistently grouping students by ability heightens such self-perceptions. Who of us did not know by the second grade which groups constituted the "good readers" and the "poor readers"? More important, the expectations of students depend on the group they are in. Students who succeed in school have both high expectations of themselves and a strong, positive sense of belonging to the school community. Students who are at risk for school failure are often placed in the lowest ability groups and excluded from the academic success community. Exclusion from the school community limits the potentially positive effects of school culture on students at risk for failure (Korinek, Walther-Thomas, McLaughlin, & Williams, 1999; Meggert, 2000; Sinclair, Hurley, Evelo, Christenson, & Thurlow, 2002).

In addition to academically based groupings, student climate is influenced by the peer groups that students form. Peers influence one another by offering support, advice, and opportunities to discuss conflicting points of view, but peers may also negatively influence others by coercion and manipulation. Peer group pressure can be either a very powerful ally or a formidable antagonist, dissuading or encouraging problem behaviors (Dishion, Andrews, & Crosby, 1995; Kupersmidt, Burchinaal, & Patterson, 1995; Moffit, Caspi, Dickson, Silva, &

Stanton, 1996). Behaviors such as misbehaving in class, fighting or arguing, and neglecting to turn in homework all interfere with learning and are related to school failure (Knitzer, Steinberg, & Fleisch, 1990; Walker, Colvin, & Ramsey, 1995). Carlos's earlier playground fights demonstrate how poor decision making among students can hinder positive student climate. Efforts to improve students' problem-solving and decision-making skills have a positive effect on the at-risk population (Beyth-Marom, Fischhoff, Jacobs, & Furby, 1989; Shure, 1999; and see Chapter 13). Some schools have reported a marked reduction in disruptive behaviors after students have been taught to mediate disputes on their own. Significant benefits accrue when students teach and model social skills (Blake, Wang, Cartledge, & Gardner, 2000). The ability of students to solve their own problems and peacefully settle disputes directly and positively affects student climate. School mediation programs (discussed in Chapter 14) have been especially helpful in this regard (T. S. Jones, 1998; Lane & McWhirter, 1992, 1996; Smith & Daunic, 2002).

Peer involvement.   Because peers play such an important role in adolescents' risky behavior, prevention and treatment efforts should focus not only on individuals' problems but also on the peer group itself. Peer programs that emphasize training in assertiveness and other social skills have a good success rate (Herrmann & McWhirter, 1997). If these skills are not taught to the whole peer cluster, or if adolescents return to the same peer cluster after receiving treatment away from their peers, they often regress to past patterns.

Evidence suggests that adolescent girls—especially those who are talented—experience decreases in self-confidence and more social anxiety than in earlier grades (Colangelo & Assouline, 1995; Neihart, Reis, Robinson & Moon, 2002). Some have argued that there is an abrupt psychological shift at age 14 from needs for achievement to needs related to love and belonging. Talented girls see more disadvantages to their abilities than do their male peers. Compared to boys, girls receive inequitable instruction in the classroom, less attention from teachers, less informative responses from teachers, less detailed instructions on the correct approach to tasks, and more reprimands for calling out answers to questions and other "assertive" responses. There is consistent evidence that girls' self-esteem plunges between ages 11 and 17 (Brown & Gilligan, 1992; Kling, Hyde, Showers, & Buswell, 1999) and that rates of eating disorders, sexually transmitted diseases, and substance abuse increase.

Student climate is affected by students' ability to monitor their own behavior and progress, take responsibility for their own learning, and contribute to the school community (Eccles & Midgley, 1989; Eccles, Midgley, & Adler, 1984; Eccles et al., 1993; Korinek et al., 1999; McNeely et al., 2002; Shapiro & Cole, 1994). Most learning research focuses on methods and procedures that increase desired student behaviors and center on strategies teachers and counselors can use. More research is needed, however, on the ways teachers and counselors can modify the classroom environment and expectations in a manner that helps young people help themselves. At-risk youth are capable, thinking people who are able to see and monitor their own progress. They need to be taught how to do so. They need to be encouraged to develop a shared responsibility for learning.

Teacher climate.   The working environment for teachers and other school employees is also part of school culture. Levels of collegiality and collaboration among staff members, community support, autonomy, adequacy of funding, and the effectiveness of leadership all contribute to teacher climate within the school.

▲ Box 5.2

Teacher Climate

One of the authors of this text had the experience of spending 15 minutes in two different middle school teachers lounges in the same week during a research project. The atmosphere within the two lounges could not have been more different and provided insight into the teacher climate at each school.

In the first lounge, five teachers were filling coffee cups, organizing papers, and chatting energetically about the events of the week. One teacher approached the author/researcher, asking her name and making introductions to the others. Entering teachers were greeted by name. There was some joking about the "mountains of grading" that faced several of them.

In the second lounge, two teachers were silently grading papers when a third entered and immediately began talking about a student using crude and insulting language. The other two teachers offered comparable stories about difficult students, also using language such as "asshole" and "bastard." Then the third teacher stated, "God I can't wait to retire" and left the room; the other two teachers returned to their grading. All three teachers completely ignored the author/researcher and did not make eye contact at any time.

Consistent and focused meetings with teachers and support staff (psychologists, counselors, social workers) encourage stability, development, collaboration, and collegiality. Unfortunately, school personnel usually meet for curative rather than preventive reasons—ultimately a costly and inefficient procedure (Comer, 1996)—largely because of heavy demands on their time combined with limited understanding of one another's efforts and strategies. Moreover, they generally have no training in a collaborative, collegial model of working together to prevent problems. If Carlos's teachers were able to work as a team, as middle school teachers often do, they might gain a better understanding of his previous bilingual problems and devise potential solutions. Models of shared decision making and leadership organized around shared values, commitments, and beliefs can make a dramatic difference in teacher climate (e.g., Sergiovanni, 1994, 2001). Box 5.2 illustrates one dimension of how teacher climates can vary.

When teachers are identified as professionals, the effect on teacher climate is positive. Unfortunately, it is frequently the case that teachers are not treated as experts on learning, pedagogy, and curriculum. Teachers have a base of professional knowledge, a professional language, and bring specific skills to their job. Yet teachers often are required to simply follow mandates regarding curriculum and pedagogy. Educational practices that stifle teachers from utilizing their knowledge produce a poor teacher climate and ultimately a poor student climate. This is true for school counselors as well.

Educational writers (Johnson & Boles, 1994; Smylie & Tuermer, 1992) describe the need for teacher empowerment in the workplace, particularly with regard to curriculum, and Shannon (1989) advocates that teachers' knowledge about lesson preparation should prevail over the prepared lesson plans found in teachers' manuals. Some educators view teachers as capable decision makers and encourage involvement in school-based management (Cambone, Weiss, & Wyeth, 1992; Johnson & Boles, 1994; Sergiovanni, 1994, 2001). Team-teaching is a way in which teachers contribute to high-performance schools (Wohlstetter & Smyer, 1994). Teachers in the teams receive immediate feedback from one another. The team provides teachers with a support group to help resolve judgment decisions. Consequently, teachers perform better in specific situations (Phillips, McCullough, Nelson, & Walker, 1992). Further, teachers want to teach in a nonsexist way and are eager to learn how. Brief training workshops are effective in improving equitable behavior. How do schools typically respond to increasing incidences of disruption? Often, schools respond with "zero tolerance" policies, the addition of security guards and video cameras, and the suspension or expulsion of disruptive students. Although removing disruptive students from the classroom or the school provides some immediate relief to the affected teachers and students, these short-term policies have a series of negative consequences. They shift responsibility away from the school, reinforce antisocial behavior and an environment of control, devalue the adult–child relationship, and weaken the ties between academic and social behavioral learning. Positive Behavioral Support (PBS) is an alternative that involves a significant investment of resources and time, but it provides significant long-term benefits (Horner & Sugai, 2000). PBS is a systemwide approach to school behavior management that combines a system that supports teacher behavior with data that support effective decisions and practices that support student behavior. The purpose of PBS is to increase the effectiveness, relevance, and efficiency of academic and social learning for all students, and especially for those with emotional and behavioral problems by (1) increasing time devoted to teaching (instead of managing behavior problems) and (2) increasing students' academic engagement time and achievement. That is, PBS changes individual behavior by changing the context in which behavior occurs. PBS establishes a schoolwide system for discipline with clear procedures and behaviors expected of students and teachers and provides a clear continuum of reinforcement for positive behaviors and a continuum of discouragement for negative behaviors. Requiring collaboration throughout the school, school staff are encouraged to work "smarter instead of harder and longer" (Horner & Sugai, 2000).

Initiating PBS requires a commitment of several years, with maintenance of the system a top priority. Other requirements include a team-based approach, active administrator support, proactive instructional approach, local behavioral expertise, and the use of data-based decision making. Implementation of PBS requires an enormous amount of time, resources, and energy. So why would a school select this intervention? Answer: Results. In one school, the average daily referrals in December dropped from 21 down to 6 per day the following December. Four years later the changes were maintained, with an average of 5 referrals per day in December with similar effects every month. The savings of time and energy that go into dealing with office referrals, as well as the increased satisfaction and security experienced by school personnel, are enough to convince many schools to adopt this program.

EDUCATIONAL STRUCTURE: SCHOOLS AND CLASSROOMS

The structure of education can be manipulated at two levels: the school structure itself (grade configuration, type of building) and the classroom (the teacher's philosophy and teaching style, the instructional method). Reform may be needed at both levels to optimize the academic success of students at risk.

School Structure

Grade configuration has been the primary organizing principle of our system. The rapid growth of high schools in the United States after the Civil War led some sections of the country to operate under an 8–5 schedule: eight years of elementary school, five years of high school. Other areas used a 6–6 plan: six years of elementary school, six years of high school. Toward the end of the century, the 8–4 pattern became popular. In 1909 the first junior high school was introduced. Since then, grades have been configured in a variety of patterns (6–3–3, 6–2–4, 7–2–3, 5–3–4, 4–4–4) in attempts to group students by developmental needs and to increase the cost-effectiveness of education. Bickel and colleagues (2001) present evidence that contradicts the widely held notion that large schools serving a small range of grades are uniformly more cost-effective than single-unit (K–12 or K–8) schools. With respect to human costs, a larger size school is more damaging to disadvantaged students' achievement scores. After an in-depth analysis of a variety of indicators, Bickel and colleagues conclude, "If we were also interested in balancing expenditure per pupil with achievement-based equity, the best configuration seems to be a small single-unit school. . . . This makes the achievement advantage of small schools (where they are most needed, that is, in impoverished communities) more affordable than previously expected" It is important to engage in deeper-level examination of issues such as cost-effectiveness, and to raise questions such as "beneficial to whom?" and "cost-effective with respect to what dimensions?" and "what dimensions have not been considered?"

The school-within-a-school concept is one way of structuring the school so that smaller groups of students are clustered together (Cuban, 1989; Seidman & French, 1997). For example, the school population of a specific secondary school is divided into four "houses." These houses become the major vehicles for social interaction, intramural athletics, school activities, discipline, and so forth (think of the organization of Hogwart's Academy of Witchcraft and Wizardry, featured in the popular Harry Potter books by J. K. Rowling). The main reference group can be reduced in this way from, for example, 2,000 students in the comprehensive school to 500 students in the house, increasing the sense of community.

Some schools build before- and after-school supervised programs into their structure (Dryfoos, 1994; see Chapter 2). There is ample documentation that youth without supervision after school and who are with peers are more likely to engage in risky behaviors and to have poorer school achievement than unsupervised youth who are home alone, or youth who are with caretakers after school (Flannery, Williams, & Vazsonyi, 1999; Goyette-Ewing, 2000; Mulhall, Stone, & Stone, 1996). In addition, there are significant benefits to participation in quality after-school programs. The demand for school-based after-school programs exceeds the supply, and even existing programs are constantly threatened by decreasing funds. After-school care programs could be of significant benefit to at-risk students like Carlos and Lidia Diaz.

School Choice

School choice has been offered as a solution to poor-quality schools. The proponents of school choice include political conservatives who view public education as overly controlled by the government, religious conservatives who view public schools as damaging to children because of exposure to immoral values and practices, private schools seeking increased enrollment, and activist, urban parents of color seeking a higher quality education for their children (Miller-Kahn & Smith, 2001). Based on the belief that choice inspires competition and therefore higher quality, the school choice movement was supported by a 2002 U.S. Supreme Court decision upholding the constitutionality of the Cleveland school voucher program, which enabled students to attend private religious schools. The National Education Association, the National Association of School Principals, and the American Federation of Teachers immediately indicated strong opposition to the voucher system, believing that the effects will damage public education. For example, Miller-Kahn and Smith (2001) demonstrate how school choice policies reinforce and replicate inequities for lower SES, ethnic minority, and poor achieving students.

Charter Schools

The charter school movement has emerged from school choice (Wohlstetter & Smyer, 1994). Although charter schools are public schools that offer a free education, they differ from district-controlled schools in that they have a separate board of directors. Charter schools embody many different visions of school improvement. Charter schools have the freedom to be innovative and to become a source of good ideas. Supporters view charter schools as a promising way to raise academic standards, empower educators, involve parents and communities, and expand choice and accountability. Despite these promising possibilities, the variation in characteristics has made it extremely difficult to evaluate and compare their effects with one another and with traditional schools (SRI International, 1997). Charter schools clearly have the potential to be an important educational innovation. However, the accessibility of charter schools must be addressed with respect to transportation, enrollment procedures and requirements, and a thorough understanding of who actually enrolls. This is particularly important given the No Child Left Behind Act.

Classroom Structure

Classroom structure affects the academic experience of at-risk students. The structure of the class can give at-risk students a feeling of control over their situation. An environment in which students are treated as unique individuals who have unique contributions to make to the group yields positive results (Elmore, Peterson, & McCarthy, 1996). Such an environment produces an acceptance and appreciation of differences, an increase in creativity, an enhancement of personal autonomy, an improvement in mental health, and the ultimate overall quality of learning (McNeely et al., 2002). A caring relationship between teacher and student helps meet the needs of at-risk students (Birch & Ladd, 1997; Obiakor, 2001).

Class size also affects at-risk students. Certainly Lidia Diaz's teacher would be able to meet Lidia's needs more effectively if she were responsible for fewer children. Indeed, academic achievement and connection to school have been found to be related to class size (Finn, Gerber, & Boyd-Zaharias, 2005; McNeely et al., 2002). In fact, 4 or more years in small classes (13 to 17 students) in early elementary school significantly increase the likelihood of students graduating from high school. This is especially true for students from low-income homes (Finn et al., 2005).

Because Lidia's class is large, students have been assigned to smaller groups based on ability levels. Although little advantage accrues to students assigned to the high groups, students assigned to the low groups suffer great disadvantage (Slavin, 1993). Educational researchers now advocate smaller heterogeneous groups that work cooperatively in lieu of homogeneous ability groups (Johnson & Johnson, 1988, 1989; Sharan, 1994; Slavin et al., 1994; Slavin & Madden, 1989). When teachers and students are encouraged to work collaboratively, there is a positive effect on the overall school environment (Reminger, Hidi, & Krapp, 1992). Students who are at risk for school failure are usually several grades behind their age mates; school structures that emphasize cooperation over competition meet the needs of these students better (see Chapter 14).

Curricular and instructional practices also affect students who are at risk for school failure. Students have little enthusiasm for a curriculum that focuses simply on learning facts and isolated skills and over time become passive players in the schooling process. Further, controversial and sometimes very interesting content areas are being omitted from the curriculum (Glasser, 1990). Educators agree that it is their responsibility, as well as the parents', to pass down the common values of society (Adams & Hamm, 1994; Wilson, 1993). Yet anything associated with "values clarification," "values education," or "morals" sets off alarm bells in some segments of the community. Many districts tightly regulate classroom discussion of topics such as sexual behavior and pregnancy prevention in an effort to avoid controversy.

Curriculum Issues

A curriculum that ignores moral education, development of social skills, student dialogue, and critical thinking does not help at-risk students. For example, making contraceptives available to teens and providing information about effectiveness has been criticized as contributing to sexual activity among teenagers. However, even though sexual activity among teenagers is approximately equal in the United States and Europe, the teen birth rate is much lower in Europe, where contraception is available. In the year 2000, a narrowly defeated bill in Oregon would have prohibited school discussion of safe sex activities that prevent AIDS because of the unsubstantiated accusation that such information "promotes homosexuality." (We return to this important issue in Chapter 9.) The argument that children and adolescents should get their information at home is a hollow one in light of the vast numbers of families that do not provide this information at all.

Measures to assess the curriculum need to be broadened as well. Assessment of student learning should go beyond scores on standardized achievement tests to include critical thinking, decision making, and other factors (Cohen, McLaughlin, & Talbert, 1993). As a result of reforms in several states, students are required to pass benchmarks throughout K–12 that include social skills, problem solving, and other important career and life skills. Passing benchmarks in mathematics requires, for example, not simply providing the correct answer but being able to describe the reasoning process used to arrive at the answer, and to identify alternative strategies for finding the answer.

Vocational education is a critical element of all school curricula (Blustein, Juntunen, & Worthington, 2000). Bizot (1999) described the seven elements of a strong vocational foundation: (1) provides a sense of competence based on genuine achievement via opportunities to attempt challenging tasks; (2) exposes students to many areas of potential interest with the opportunity to explore some areas in greater depth and develop greater mastery; (3) fosters an ability to set goals, generate alternatives, evaluate options and results, and cope with obstacles; (4) provides a framework for understanding and organizing occupational information; (5) conveys respect for individual differences and an understanding of how individual values, interests, and skills lead to different choices, opportunities, and barriers; (6) provides for participation and opportunities to collaborate and contribute; and (7) imparts an understanding that education and career are lifelong, ongoing processes. Bizot (1999) noted that these key elements should be integrated into curricula. Perhaps if Ramona had been exposed to ongoing career education, and had a curriculum that made consistent connections between learning and life skills, she might have seen more benefits to staying in school. At a minimum, she may have had better-developed work and life skills when she did drop out.

ESL and bilingual education programs are also an important part of school curricula for students at risk. School dropouts are frequently poor, members of minority groups, lack skills in English, and have less access to English instruction (Watt & Roessingh, 1994). This group includes a great many ESL/bilingual students. Given the shortage of ESL teachers with appropriate credentials, and the fact that they live in a district characterized by many poor families, it is likely that the Diaz children did not have qualified teachers when they were in ESL classes.

J. Crawford (2002) points out that under No Child Left Behind, federal funds will continue to support the education of English language learners (ELLs) with the rapid teaching of English taking precedence at every turn. Annual English assessments will be mandated, and failure to show academic progress in English will be punished. Even though the additional resources provided by NCLB are good news for schools with substantial numbers of language-minority students, the money will be spread more thinly than before—between more states, more programs, and more students. Although districts will automatically receive funding based on their enrollments of ELLs and immigrant students, the impact of federal dollars will be reduced. Last year, for example, about $360 was spent per student in bilingual instructional programs. This year, despite the overall increase in appropriations, funding will provide less than $135 per student.

A final curricular issue we consider in this section is access to the World Wide Web—the Internet. The information available to schools via the Internet is virtually limitless, and support services to assist teachers to incorporate this resource into their teaching are evolving rapidly. By the fall of 2000, 98% of public schools had Internet access (NCES, 2001) across poverty levels and locations (e.g., urban, rural). By comparison, only 35% of schools were connected in 1994. Similarly, the percentage of instructional classrooms (including libraries and computer labs) with Internet access increased from 3% to 77%. Classroom access to the Internet continues to vary according to poverty levels. In schools serving 75% or more students eligible for free or reduced price lunch, only 60% of the instructional rooms have Internet access, whereas in schools with less poverty 82% of classrooms have access. When teachers are provided with the time and technological support to capitalize on the Internet, students benefit. And it is clear that access to and ability to navigate the Internet are critical skills for today's young people. Given the rapidity of change in this arena, we also offer some cautions about Internet use.

One of the primary functions of the Internet is for communication, and many proponents have convincingly described how the Internet expands the number of people with whom someone can be in easy communication. The social benefits seem obvious. However, results of one longitudinal study of Internet use raise serious questions. Kraut and his colleagues (1998) followed people age 10 and older using the Internet for communication during their first 2 years of going online. Increased use of the Internet was associated with decreases in family communication and the size of their social circle, along with increases in loneliness and depression. The more time adults spend using the Internet, the less time they spend engaging in family social activities (Nie & Erbring, 2000). As children and youth experience increased access, it will be critically important to monitor the effects of Internet use on their social interaction with family and peers.

CONCLUSION

Educators have control over some educational practices and policies and elements of school climate that may improve the learning potential of at-risk students. They can promote curricular and teaching practices that emphasize the entirety of students' learning and development. Second, educators can increase collaborative efforts that encourage collegial support and collaborative decision making to improve school climate. Third, student empowerment can be promoted, and students can be helped to approach their work and their interactions with tolerance and democracy. Teachers and counselors can be excellent models of such practices. Finally, educators can assist in raising public awareness about the value of extended support for children and youth who are at risk. Collaboration with researchers to provide evidence of successful prevention and intervention programs (or evidence that programs are not working) is one way to help draw attention to what does and does not work. Researchers, in turn, must consult with teachers to draw educators' first-hand classroom experience and wisdom into the development and implementation of prevention and intervention programs. Teacher expertise is a critical component of school-based programs that provide at-risk students with the skills and resources they need to be successful in school and in life (Aksamit, 1990; Dryfoos, 1994).

INDIVIDUAL CHARACTERISTICS OF HIGH-RISK AND LOW-RISK CHILDREN AND YOUTH

▲ *What makes some young people resolute and sturdy enough to chip away at the ore, locate the diamond, and polish it . . . while others weakly and feebly patter in the soil, haphazardly searching for a gem, finding only dirt?*

CHAPTER OUTLINE

▲   Within their unique family and community ecology, young people develop individual characteristics—likes and dislikes, talents and limitations, strengths and weaknesses. These individual characteristics emerge from the societal environment and from the roots of family and school conditions. Most young people develop adequate knowledge, positive behaviors, prosocial attitudes, and other healthy characteristics with lower risk of future problems. Other children and adolescents do not acquire the knowledge, behaviors, attitudes, and skills they need to become successful adults. They frequently exhibit interrelated dysfunctional patterns of behaviors, cognitions, and emotions early in life and especially in their early school years (Bellanti & Bierman, 2000; Schultz, Izard, Ackerman, & Youngstrom, 2001). If negative patterns are not reversed, they may develop into self-fulfilling prophecies, a downward spiral of multiple problems that could include school failure, drug use, teen pregnancy, delinquency, and suicide (Jessor, 1991, 1993).

Individual characteristics exhibited by children and adolescents form the trunk of the at-risk tree, which links the soil of environment and the roots of family, school, and peers to the branches of behaviors. These characteristics can nourish positive and healthful development or risky behavior. When studies of at-risk youth are reviewed, a "multiple-problem syndrome" becomes apparent. School dropout, drug abuse, delinquency, teen pregnancy, and youth suicide are all associated with similar sets of psychosocial variables and skill deficits (Beauvais et al., 1996; Younge, Oetting, & Deffenbacher, 1996).

Teachers, counselors, and psychologists realize that many young people are lacking in fundamental skills. The term *skills* refers here not merely to mechanically performed actions but rather to proficiency in the behaviors, feelings, and thought patterns that are appropriately applied in specific situations and circumstances. All youth, including those defined as at risk, are capable of learning more adaptive strategies for addressing their life challenges, and the incorporation of skills acquisition into educational and counseling interventions is critical (Algozzine & Kaye, 2002; World Health Organization, 1999).

Some young people manage to survive extremely difficult life circumstances. Somehow they rise above poverty, chaotic families, peer pressure, and poor school conditions—in short, those environmental conditions described in earlier chapters. These young people are considered to be at risk because their circumstances clearly suggest future problems. The greater the number of these risk factors, the greater their level of risk (Capaldi & Patterson, 1991; Deater-Deckard, Dodge, Bates, & Pettit, 1998). But resilient youth avoid falling into drug use, delinquency, and other risky behaviors. By examining their lives and circumstances, we may learn something that will inform our efforts with young people who are not so fortunate.

RESILIENCY

Despite extremely debilitating environmental, familial, and personal experiences, many young people develop normally. They exhibit competence, autonomy, and effective strategies to cope with the world around them (Haggerty, Sherrod, Garmezy, & Rutter, 1994; Werner & Smith, 1992). These children and youth have been called invulnerable, stress-resistant, superkids, and invincible. These terms have been subject to criticism because they imply that the well-being of these young people is due to internal or constitutional factors only, that they are successful across all domains, and that they are consistently successful across time (McGloin & Widom, 2001). The term *resilience* refers to those who demonstrate "a good outcome in spite of high risk, sustained competence under stress, and recovery from trauma" (p. 1022). Essentially, resilience is the capacity to adapt and function successfully despite experiencing chronic stress and adversity. Resilience is not a static trait, but it is influenced by both internal and environmental factors.

Garbarino (1994) contends that every child has a "tipping point" between doing well (having hope, positive attitudes about self, functional behaviors) and doing poorly (feeling despair, having low self-esteem, dysfunctional behaviors). Thus no child is immune to excessive exposure to negative social, familial, and educational environments, and the idea of a tipping point may be even more useful than the concept of resilience. Another criticism of the term is that the justice system has used resilience to help punish offenders—contending that a violent and abrasive upbringing provides no explanation for violent behavior because some youth who grow up in the same environment do not engage in violence. We acknowledge the validity of these criticisms. However, we find the concept of resilience useful to distinguish between young people who do well and those who do not.

FACTORS THAT CONTRIBUTE TO RESILIENCE

The development of resiliency is a function of three related but distinct areas that provide protection to the child (McCreanor & Watson, 2004). First, the social environment can provide children with opportunities for development and support despite adverse conditions. External support systems can enhance the young person's competencies and provide a sense of meaning or a belief system by which to live. Second, the family milieu has both direct and indirect influences on a youth's resiliency. Ties within the family provide emotional support at times of stress. Third, individual characteristics and attributes (e.g., cognitive skills, styles of communication, interpersonal skills) have positive influences on at-risk children and are related to resiliency. Also important are dispositional attributes of an individual, such as activity level, sociability, and intelligence (Werner, 1995).

Social Environment

Resilient children derive support from the social environment—their school, their community, and their kinship network. The school environment is potentially a mediating milieu for children who experience numerous risk factors (Korinek et al., 1999). When social support is low in one setting or microsystem, such as the family, other microsystems, such as school or the neighborhood, can compensate by providing assistance in rebuilding the support in the weakened area (Coleman, 1991). Caring relationships increase resiliency (Laursen & Birmingham, 2003), and supportive and encouraging teachers are particularly important. Counselors and psychologists can make a crucial difference as well. Resilient children often succeed in academic areas and may also achieve in art, music, drama, or sports (Werner, 1995). Positive contact with peers and adults in these extracurricular areas provide support.

The social support networks of the larger community also help to ameliorate the effects of stress on children. Resilient youth frequently use community networks—ministers, older friends, youth recreation workers, and others. Resilient children often have at least one adult mentor outside the family throughout their development. These adults provide emotional support, encouragement, and advice. Resilient children also have one or more close friends and confidants among their peers. These networks provide at-risk children and adolescents with resources that enable them to develop the skills necessary for survival and success.

Many young people develop specific survival skills that work in their setting. These skills provide them with mechanisms for coping with an unsupportive, negative, or destructive environment. Unfortunately, some of these survival skills are functional and effective only within the subculture of the neighborhood; using the same skills in other contexts is often ineffective or self-defeating.

Children of color in particular are often subjected to the stress of overt and covert racism and marginalization within the majority culture. Even though minority status is correlated with high risk, the way children learn to survive that stress makes a difference in their ability to maintain self-esteem and a positive identity. Some authors have articulated how many adolescents of color learn to navigate the traumas and stressors that they experience as systemic racism and actually transform such events into life-affirming experiences (e.g., see Holleran & Jung, 2005).

Carlos Diaz, whom we met in Chapter 5, is a potentially resilient young adolescent. His relationship with his mother has given him a secure foundation. His family responsibilities, although they interfere with schoolwork, have allowed him to develop important life skills such as cooking and caring for a younger child that improve his self-concept and self-esteem. Even though these responsibilities are stressful, knowing that he is contributing to his family gives Carlos an important role in the family's well-being. His academic difficulties are associated with not having time and resources (e.g., a computer), but the work he completes reflects that he is learning and academically competent. Also important is the special interest his social studies teacher has shown in him. Ms. Bassett's interest and support, coupled with reasonable expectations, provides a solid relationship with a caring adult. Further, her willingness to modify her classroom and teaching style encourages responsibility for learning and contributes to his resiliency.

Family Milieu

As we have seen, family environment is one of the most important influences on the psychosocial development of young people. The characteristics of a positive family environment include a lack of physical crowding, consistently enforced rules with strict but fair supervision, and well-balanced discipline (Rak & Patterson, 1996). The child who has a good relationship with even one caregiver demonstrates greater resiliency (Bushweller, 1995; Contreras & Kerns, 2000; Werner, 1995). Parental support and involvement are useful for autonomy and self-direction that contribute to resiliency.

Healthy communication patterns often prevail in the homes of resilient youth (McCubbin & McCubbin, 1988). The parents model such skills as attending, focusing, and sustaining tasks. Focused, flexible, well-structured, and task-appropriate communication leads to academic and social competence (Wolin & Wolin, 1993). Parenting characterized by warmth, affective expression, anticipatory guidance, active teaching of social skills, and involvement reduces risk (Pettit, Bates, & Dodge, 1997) and increases children's social competence (Mize & Pettit, 1997). Children in families who engage in "enabling" interactions—those that encourage and support the expression of independent thought and allow for give-and-take communication—are more likely to exhibit psychosocial competence (Baumrind, 1995). Parental monitoring and control is associated with better childhood outcomes in urban neighborhoods characterized by violence and poverty (Luthar, 1999; Tolan & Gorman-Smith, 1997). Good-quality parenting, parent support, and the quality of the mother–child relationship fosters resilience (Dubow, Edwards, & Ippolito, 1997; Klein, Forehand, & the Family Health Project Research Group, 2000). There is some cultural variation in parenting behaviors and outcomes, but these findings hold consistently across most cultural and ethnic groups in the United States.

The family also contributes to resiliency indirectly, through its influence on the children's support networks. Some parents, for example, selectively expose their children to religious and church-related organizations or to such community organizations as the Girl Scouts and Boy Scouts or 4-H clubs. Adults in these organizations provide a useful support network that builds resiliency.

Christie Carter, whom we met in Chapter 4, may be resilient. She emerges in the family as a prim and slightly unpleasant little girl. Her role as the family's angel relegates Jason to the role of devil, but perhaps her adoption of this role is what will save her. She does receive a great deal of attention, support, and reinforcement from both her father and her mother. The security that this support provides may be enough to inoculate her against the family dysfunction and prevent her from engaging in risky behavior.

Individual Characteristics of Resilient Youth

Resilient children frequently possess a number of the following individual characteristics and skills: better verbal communication, good social skills, an ability to form positive relationships with others (Flores, Cicchetti, & Rogosch, 2005), an internal locus of control, impulse control, reflectiveness, and positive self-regard (Berry, Shillington, Peak, & Hohman, 2000). Resilient children also demonstrate a well-developed sense of humor, an ability to delay gratification, and a future orientation. These skills reinforce further resiliency by eliciting positive reactions from family members and strangers (Werner, 1995).

Daniella Baker, whom we met in Chapter 2, has a special relationship with her mother. She has developed good communication skills and has the ability to make her needs known. Her sweet, calm temperament elicits positive reactions from her mother and from others. This is especially valuable in light of her frequent changes in living situations. Daniella also has assumed the care of her younger brother. Although this responsibility sometimes frustrates her, it enhances her self-esteem. These personality factors contribute to her resiliency and may mitigate the effects of her environment.

Research (Haggerty et al., 1994; Rak & Patterson, 1996; Werner, 1995) points to several characteristics that resilient children exhibit:

- An active approach to life's problems, including a proactive problem-solving perspective that enables the child to negotiate emotionally hazardous experiences
- An optimistic tendency to perceive pain, frustration, and other distressing experiences constructively
- The ability to gain positive attention from others, both in the family and elsewhere
- A strong faith that maintains a vision of a positive and meaningful life
- An ability to be alert and autonomous with a tendency to seek novel experience
- Competence in social, school, and cognitive areas

These characteristics act as protective shields that allow the young person to avoid, regulate, or cope with aversive environmental or developmental conditions, modifying the impact of stressors and leading to less damaging results.

Resilient children and youth cope constructively with challenges by balancing short- and long-term needs of both themselves and others. This allows them to reap mostly favorable outcomes that bolster their self-image and increase their future propensity for positive coping. These attitudes endear them to untroubled peers while alienating them from deviant peers.

Carlos Diaz, Christie Carter, and Daniella Baker are potentially resilient young people. All of them have personal characteristics that reflect influences from their social environment and their family milieu that may inoculate them against the stress of their current situations and help them to avoid future difficulty. The characteristics of resiliency correspond to specific skills that distinguish low-risk from high-risk children.

Skills That Characterize High-Risk Versus Low-Risk Youth: The Five Cs of Competency

As a result of our work in teaching and counseling at-risk children and adolescents, our discussions with other professionals, and an extensive review of research on resilient and at-risk children and youth, we have identified five characteristics that capture the major differences between low-risk and high-risk youth (J. J. McWhirter, B. T. McWhirter, A. M. McWhirter, & E. H. McWhirter, 1994). We call these characteristics the "five Cs of competency":

- Critical school competencies
- Concept of self, self-esteem, and self-efficacy
- Connectedness
- Coping ability
- Control

These characteristics discriminate between young people who move through life with a high potential for success and those who do not do well. Low-risk individuals exhibit proficiency, strength, or potential in the five Cs; high-risk individuals are deficient in one or more of these skills. The lack of these skills is closely related to the chronic dependency, aggressive behavior, or inability to cope with life that propels young people into the at-risk categories: school dropout, substance abuse, teen pregnancy, youth delinquency and violence, and suicide.

Of course, these skills overlap. Critical school competencies, for example, may lead to connectedness and relate to skills in coping and control. Self-concept interacts in very important and powerful ways with the other characteristics. All the same, we can grasp their importance more firmly if we consider each in turn.

Critical School Competencies

Critical school competencies comprise those skills that are essential to success in school: basic academic skills, academic survival skills, and self-efficacy expectations (Arbona, 2000). Because self-efficacy expectations also relate to the second C, concept of self, we discuss here only basic academic skills and academic survival skills.

Basic academic skills.   In a high-tech industrial society, young people must learn the basic skills of reading, writing, and arithmetic to survive. If they are to thrive, they also need information about themselves and the world around them. The lack of such skills reduces the prospects for a useful, productive life.

One of the most obvious characteristics of at-risk students is academic underachievement (Daly, Duhon, & Witt, 2002). Underachievement often results from a lack of basic numeracy and literacy skills. These academic deficits are an overwhelming cause of early school leaving and are often a contributing factor in many other problems. Mastery of academic skills encourages persistence in school. A lack of basic reading, writing, and arithmetic skills is often attributable to developmental delays, specific learning disabilities, a limited grasp of English, or emotional disturbance. These problems are compounded by contextual factors such as an inadequate educational structure, an uncaring and unresponsive school culture, limited instructional programs, or poor teaching. Elementary and secondary school students at risk for academic underachievement may be withdrawn and apathetic or, conversely, disruptive and overly aggressive (Coie, et al., 1993; Freeman, 1995). Early detection and intervention is critical to the prevention of ongoing academic difficulty (Daly et al., 2002).

Academic survival skills.   In addition to numeracy and literacy skills, a core of social-behavioral skills is necessary for student success (Kamps & Kay, 2001). The lack of these essential competencies or "survival skills" predisposes students to failure because skills such as attending to tasks, following directions, and raising hands facilitate the acquisition of knowledge. Some research indicates that these skills are actually more important than academic achievement. Fad (1990), for example, provides evidence that some social-behavioral variables are more important for students' success than academic achievement and demographic characteristics. Work habits, coping skills, and peer relationships are three important areas. She identifies 10 behaviors in each area that are highly correlated with overall functioning. Strategies for mastering these behaviors may maximize students' chances for success.

Ramona Diaz is at risk. She has not learned the basic academic skills she needs to function in society. Her lack of proficiency in English and her unconnectedness with successful peers probably reduced her academic self-efficacy expectations, and her decision to drop out of high school limits her potential for acquiring academic skills and developing more positive academic self-efficacy.

Concept of Self, Self-Esteem, and Self-Efficacy

The second of the five Cs refers to the self-concept. Self-concept is the view or perception that one has about oneself. Three terms that are often confused and are sometimes used interchangeably are important: self-concept, self-esteem, and self-efficacy. Although the terms seem similar, their differences are more than just semantic.

Self-concept refers to our beliefs about who we are. That is, how we define ourselves on various dimensions—traits, skills, characteristics, relationships, and so forth. Most often, self-concept carries with it an evaluative adjective. For example, a young teenager might define himself as a popular friend with really "cool" hair, a bad athlete, and an indifferent student who does really poorly at math but is okay in reading.

Self-esteem, on the other hand, refers to how good we feel about ourselves or how much we value ourselves given our self-concept. Well over a century ago, William James (1890) indicated that self-esteem decreases following failures and increases following successes in domains that are important to the individual's self-concept. In general, self-esteem is vulnerable when people experience failure in domains upon which their self-concept is contingent.

Self-efficacy expectations refer to beliefs about how capable we believe we are in performing specific tasks. Self-efficacy is domain specific, such that an adolescent girl might have very high self-efficacy expectations for tasks associated with playing basketball (dribbling, passing, shooting, guarding) but low self-efficacy expectations for the tasks associated with playing baseball (catching, throwing, pitching, batting). Another youth might have low self-efficacy expectations for playing all sports. Self-efficacy expectations are not necessarily accurate; individuals sometimes have low self-efficacy for tasks they are quite capable of doing, or high self-efficacy for tasks they do not do well. Self-efficacy expectations influence decisions about whether to attempt particular behaviors and how long to persist in those behaviors (Bandura, 1986).

Consider a teenage girl who has poor ability for playing on an athletic team at school, based on her performance in gym class and earlier attempts to participate in school and neighborhood sports. Her self-concept may include the belief that she is not the "athletic type." If she and her family highly value sports participation and her closest friends are all varsity athletes, then her self-concept might be "lousy athlete" and her self-esteem may be lower. If her friends and family are not interested in sports and she herself does not enjoy them either, her self-esteem is unlikely to be negatively affected by her lack of confidence and success in athletics. Her earlier experiences lead her to conclude that she cannot learn athletic skills. Because her self-efficacy is low, she is reluctant to attempt to participate in sports and is likely to give up easily if she does so. Obviously, if she never tries to develop a skill, she will not. Her self-efficacy expectations become a self-fulfilling prophecy. A young man who is not succeeding in school, lacks a sense of belonging, and does not feel good about himself might begin to experiment with disruptive or deviant behaviors. If these result in attention and admiration from deviant peers, he may shift his self-concept from "failing student" to "daring student," develop increased "skills" and more self-efficacy for disrupting class, begin to devalue school performance even more, and may actually experience increased self-esteem. A strong relationship exists between young people's self-evaluations and their performance (Arbona, 2000; Harter, 1990; Kliewer & Sandler, 1992). Thus the environment around young people influences the value they place on something (academic success, popularity, deviant behavior, and so forth) and to whom they compare themselves. The academically average student from a family of scholars is likely to have lower self-esteem than the academically average student from a family in which no one has graduated from high school. Both self-concept and self-esteem are "global"; they are derived from numerous experiences across many domains. Self-efficacy expectations are specific to domains.

Academic self-efficacy expectations are an important influence on children's school performance (Arbona, 2000). When children believe they are capable of doing something, they are far more likely to successfully do it. Poor self-concept and low academic self-efficacy expectations are critical determinants of school dropout. For example, one study of African American high school students found that self-esteem, as well as perceptions of the benefits of staying in school and perceived ability to overcome barriers to school completion, were significant predictors of intentions to stay in school (Davis, Johnson, Miller-Cribbs, & Saunders, 2002).

Low self-esteem does not predict delinquency when other factors are considered. In fact, there is little evidence that kids who bully or engage in delinquent behavior suffer from low self-esteem (Baumeister, Bushman, & Campbell, 2000). As we have mentioned, some young people may shift their self-concept to incorporate their delinquent or bullying behavior and in that way increase their self-esteem. However, Herrmann, McWhirter, and Sipsas-Herrmann (1997) found that young adolescents with lower self-concepts were significantly more involved as "wannabes" in street gang activity than peers who possessed higher self-concepts. Beliefs about their ability to have any impact on their world were particularly important. Middle school students who were involved with gangs had significantly less confidence in their ability to solve problems, obtain their goals, bring about desired outcomes, and function effectively within the environment. Perhaps this explains some of the confusion about whether gang membership increases a person's self-esteem. "Wannabes" who then become gang members may shift their self-concept, and because of their gang involvement increase their confidence in having an impact on their world.

Seligman (1995) demonstrates that it is not low self-esteem that causes low achievement at school, but the opposite: Low achievement causes low self-esteem. Low self-esteem may reflect a realistic appraisal of negative life experiences. Baumeister et al. (2000) conclude that there is little evidence that self-esteem influences achievement in any meaningful way. There is, however, considerable evidence to suggest that positive self-esteem should be pursued as an important outcome in itself. Opportunities to experience academic success via skill development and other supports may serve to bolster a young person's self-esteem more so than praise or encouragement alone (Seligman, 1995).

Allie Andrews, whom we met in Chapter 1, feels badly about herself and her behavior in part because of her negative relationship with her stepfather. As she becomes more distant from her stepfather, she adjusts her self-concept to that of a person who does not need her stepfather's approval. She develops distorted attributions with regard to herself, to adults, and to nondeviant classmates. As she rejects her parents' (and other adults') beliefs and values, she becomes more closely aligned with and influenced by a negative peer cluster. As the value she places on parental approval decreases and the value of deviant peer approval increases, her self-esteem may actually increase. Her self-efficacy expectations for pleasing her stepfather decrease—making her less likely to attempt to gain his approval and more likely to give up quickly if her attempt to be friendly at some moment is met with suspicion. Her self-efficacy for winning her friends' admiration increases as she begins to smoke, drink, and date more frequently in spite of her father's restrictions. Unfortunately, her behavior leads her down a path to potential disaster.

Connectedness

In earlier editions of this book, we identified "communication with others" as one of the five Cs of competency. Subsequent research (Draper, & Lee, 2001; Lee & Robbins, 1995, 1998, 2000; see Townsend & B. T. McWhirter, 2005, for a review) has convinced us that communication is actually subsumed under the broader and more encompassing construct of connectedness. Communication with others, of course, continues to be a very important construct and is, in fact, one of the main conduits that children and adolescents use to foster connectedness.

Connectedness is a ubiquitous and enduring experience of the self in relation to the world that includes a sense of close belonging in relationships with others (Lee & Robbins, 2000). In addition to communication, connectedness includes the idea of "mattering" (i.e., one knows that one matters to others), family, school, and community belongingness, peer clusters, and youth–adult linkage. Children and adolescents who lack connectedness experience social isolation or rejection and tend to suffer psychological distress and greater mental health problems as adults (Kupersmidt, Coie, & Dodge, 1990; Resnick et al., 1998).

Communication with others. Connectedness requires adequate social and interpersonal skills, and they play an important role in psychological adjustment and psychosocial development (Kamps & Kay, 2001). Basic interpersonal skills are necessary for competent, responsive, and mutually beneficial relationships and are perhaps the most important skills an individual must learn. The level of a young person's interpersonal skills has been related to several areas of adjustment in later life. A high incidence of mental health problems, juvenile delinquency, dropping out of school, and other at-risk behaviors has been related to social deficiencies in children and adolescents. Good social functioning in childhood and adolescence, in contrast, has been related to superior academic achievement and adequate interpersonal adjustment later in life (Dodge & Price, 1994). Further, an individual's ability to achieve and maintain positive interpersonal relationships is a prerequisite to success in work and in love.

Positive social interaction enhances social integration. Friendship is important not only for social reasons but also because of the interactive process involved in acceptable classroom and peer relationships (Richardson, Hammock, Smith, Gardner, & Signo, 1994). Children and adolescents who have positive peer relationships engage in more social interaction, and they provide positive social rewards for one another. They also use their abilities to achieve academically and to behave appropriately in the classroom. Positive relationships with peers and teachers are associated with better adaptation to school (Birch & Ladd, 1997; Ladd & Burgess, 2001; Ladd, Kochenderfer, & Coleman, 1996).

Perspective taking.   Perspective taking has been broadly defined as the ability to understand the perceptions, thoughts, feelings, and actions of others. Individuals must be able to distinguish the perceptions and reasoning of other people from their own. A young person's perspective-taking ability is related to his or her cognitive development and has implications for moral reasoning and empathy as well (Eisenberg, Fabes, Nyman, Bernzweig, & Piñuelas, 1994). Children with greater emotional knowledge are more empathetic and popular with peers and less likely to withdraw and experience peer social problems (Schultz et al., 2001).

At-risk children not only have distorted perceptions but also lack the core abilities that make for satisfying social relationships. For example, Bellanti and Bierman (2000) found that kindergarten children with low cognitive ability and inattention had prosocial skills deficits, were aggressive, and were rejected by peers in first grade. These children were at higher risk for poor peer relationships in elementary school.

Solving relationship problems.   The ability to solve interpersonal problems is an important skill. Shure (1999) describes problem solving as the integration of two skills: thinking of alternative solutions and understanding the consequences of behavior. Interpersonal problem-solving ability is related to interpersonal functioning in adults, adolescents, middle childhood, and children as young as 4 years old. Children usually develop this skill in the early grades (Shure, 1992a, 1992b, 1992c, 1999; Youngstrom et al., 2000). Even though Shure (1992a, 1992b, 1992c) has emphasized that the number of alternative solutions generated is most important, the work of Youngstrom and colleagues (2000) demonstrated that the quality of children's interpersonal problem-solving solutions was at least as important as the quantity of solutions. That is, the ability to generate two prosocial solutions would be better than the ability to generate eight aggressive or withdrawing solutions.

Jason Carter, whom we introduced in Chapter 4, is not connected. He has not developed adequate communication skills. He is at risk precisely because he cannot communicate his wants and needs without resorting to explosive, impulsive, and ultimately self-defeating behavior. His poor peer relationships, his lack of respect for adults, and his aggressive outbursts suggest serious deficiencies in communication skills. He has not learned those fundamental social skills that might help him deal more effectively with his dysfunctional parents, his competitive sister, his rejecting classmates, and his upset teacher.

Kamps and Kay (2001) overview core skills areas for elementary students that encompass communication, perspective-taking, and problem-solving skills: (a) classroom survival skills (e.g., asking for help, ignoring distractions, bringing materials to class), (b) friendship-making skills (e.g., beginning a conversation, joining in, apologizing), (c) skills for dealing with feelings (e.g., knowing and expressing one's own feelings, showing understanding of another's feelings, dealing with anger), (d) skill alternatives to aggression (e.g., asking permission, responding to teasing, problem solving), and (e) skills for dealing with stress (e.g., deciding what caused a problem, being a good sport, reacting to failure, dealing with group pressure). All of these skills help to foster connectedness. In Chapters 13 and 14 we discuss Kamps and Kay's (2001) recommendations for teaching social skills in more detail.

Coping Ability

The ability to cope effectively with anxiety and stress is another skill that differentiates low-risk from high-risk young people. All individuals confront situations that cause conflict and stress. All young people sometimes feel disappointment, rejection, fear, and anger in their interactions with others. How they cope with these emotions determines their adjustment.

Coping skills influence an individual's response to stress, which in turn affects the way that person deals with conflict. Some young people cope with humor and altruism, others by focusing their attention elsewhere. These methods result in a more relaxed and positive view of the situation. When young people are in a positive, relaxed state of mind, they are able to process information more objectively, exercise better judgment, and use common sense. They also demonstrate more effectiveness and competence in solving personal problems.

Some young people, unfortunately, are exposed to more stress and have greater difficulty coping with it, placing them at greater risk. They use evasive strategies such as compulsive acting out, withdrawal, and denial. Or they succumb to one of the twins of mental health problems: anxiety or depression. Anxiety interferes with the learning process, social judgment, and interpersonal relationships and often leads to aggressive and destructive reactions. Depression can lead to suicide, suicide ideation, and other self-defeating behaviors (B. T. McWhirter & Burrow-Sanchez, 2004). Both anxiety and depression in children and adolescents are associated with cognitive distortions, negative self-talk, and anticipation of more negative future outcomes (Epkins, 2000; Lodge, Harte, & Tripp, 1998). Anxiety and depression in children place them at risk for learning problems, academic underachievement, conduct problems, and poor social problem solving (Kovacs & Devlin, 1998). Fortunately, a number of programs have demonstrated effectiveness in enhancing children's skills for coping with stress, anxiety, and depression. For example, the FRIENDS program trains clinically anxious children and their parents to manage stress and anxiety while simultaneously fostering increased peer social support for children (Shortt, Barrett, & Fox, 2001).

Paul Andrews, Allie's brother, exhibits problems coping with stress. His bravado, aggressiveness, and destructiveness appear to mask considerable anxiety. His inability to modify his aggressive outbursts and his destructive hostility are a problem to him both at home and at school. His lack of skills in coping with the stress he feels foreshadows serious problems as he moves into adolescence.

Control

Lack of control—over decisions, over the future, over life—is a common characteristic of high-risk young people. Their inability to generate and follow through with sound decisions relates to failure to consider consequences, unwillingness to delay gratification, and an external locus of control. These problems influence the setting and achievement of goals. Many young people have an even more fundamental problem: Their sense of a purpose in life is limited, distorted, or lacking. Low-risk young people, by contrast, exert control over their environment and their behavior in developmentally appropriate ways.

Decision-making skills.   Decision making is a goal-directed sequence of affective and cognitive operations that leads to behavioral responses. Deficits in decision-making skills are clearly linked to at-risk behavior.

Low-risk children and adolescents have access to relevant information on which to base decisions. They accurately perceive, comprehend, and store this information. They personalize the information by relating it to their own beliefs, values, and attitudes. They evaluate their solutions by considering the consequences. They demonstrate behavioral skills in their efforts to implement these decisions in social situations. They have feelings of mastery and a belief in their personal competency (Harris, 1995). Young people who have high-perceived control and view their goals as important exhibit more mastery-oriented behavior, and have higher levels of achievement and satisfaction (Bandura, Pastorelli, Barbaranelli, & Caprara, 1999).

High-risk youth are deficient in the ability to make competent decisions (Cicchetti, Rogosch, Lynch, & Holt, 1993). Information on or knowledge of viable solutions is only part of the problem. Another problem lies in the ability to set constructive and attainable goals. Difficulty in this respect is significantly related to alcohol and drug use, delinquency, and low academic achievement. Further, high-risk youth are less likely to consider consequences fully (Bell & Bell, 1993), and they manifest an external rather than an internal locus of control. That is, they feel that forces outside of themselves control the events in their lives and even their own behavior and that they have no power to shape their own lives. Adolescents transitioning to middle school who did not believe they had control over their success in school and were not invested in success experienced significantly more school stress and depression (Rudolph, Lambert, Clark, & Kurlakowsky, 2001). Finally, many problems with decision making are related to an inability or an unwillingness to delay gratification.

Delay of gratification.   Individuals vary in their capacity to delay gratification even as early as preschool. In later years, lack of self-control expresses itself in an inability to delay gratification. Low-risk individuals voluntarily postpone immediate gratification, maintain self-control, and persist in behavior directed toward a larger goal to be reached when the appropriate foundation has been laid. At-risk young people value immediate gratification and behave in ways calculated to attain it. This behavior often becomes self-defeating. Inability to delay gratification is related to depression, low social responsibility, conduct disorders, antisocial behavior, and a variety of addictive disorders (Weisz, Sweeney, Proffitt, & Carr, 1993).

Tyrone Baker, whom we introduced in Chapter 2, is a young man who is unable to delay gratification. He is impulsive and lacks self-control. Because of the chaos in his home life, the lack of connectedness with his mother and siblings, and the absence of an adequate male role model, he simply has not developed skill in delaying gratification for the sake of a more important and more distant goal. His insistence on immediate gratification influences his decision-making ability and contributes to his potential for highly risky behavior.

Purpose in life.   Purpose gives life meaning. It is the positive end of a continuum whose negative end is meaninglessness or loneliness (B. T. McWhirter, 1990). Levels of future optimism and self-acceptance can discriminate between nonsuicidal adolescents and those who have attempted suicide (Gutierrez, Osman, Kopper, & Barrios, 2000). Lack of a purpose in life, with its accompanying sense of boredom, futility, and pessimism, is an essential mediating factor in the relationship between self-derogation, depression, and thoughts of suicide (Harlow, Newcomb, & Bentler, 1986; Seligman, 1995). Further, lack of purpose in life is related to the subsequent use of alcohol and other drugs. When life has no purpose, why worry about school or friends or goals or even life itself?

Low-risk youth have a purpose in life that is potentially attainable and that propels them forward. Their purpose in life orients them toward the future and often suggests short-term, realistic goals. Researchers have consistently found that goals are important

▲ Box 6.1

One Week at a Time

Young men and women who have just left high school or are close to graduation frequently struggle with the reality of poverty. Manolo, who lives in Huascar, Peru, is one such young man. His face is alive with enthusiasm and excitement. His wide grin often gets him out of trouble, and it also covers up some of his problems.

When we spoke during his last year of high school, he said to me, "You know, Peru is a great country, but I don't think about the future too much; not more than a few days ahead, anyway."

"Why is that?"

"Because I have no idea what will happen to me after next week. There are no jobs, a university costs too much, and when I'm at home, dry bread is sometimes the only thing we have to eat."

Then I asked him, "Are your high school studies going to help you later?"

"No," he replied with resignation. "School is taking up my time now, but what's the use? I'll never study in a university. I'll probably work in a factory somewhere, if there's a job to be found."

Educational opportunities in the Peruvian barrios and in American inner cities are extremely limited. For many young people, a career is out of the question; even a job is unlikely. What happens then to purpose in life and their hopes for the future?

---

predictors of student achievement (Arbona, 2000; Drazen, 1994). Students who had realistic and hopeful visions for themselves as successful in the future achieved; those with weaker visions did not. This echoes the view of Clausen (1993) who identified "planful competence" as a strong influence on adjustment and overall success in adulthood.

Many high-risk youth lack a viable life purpose (see Box 6.1). If young people do not perceive themselves as having a viable future, "just say no" has no meaning. They need to discover what to say yes to. When young people feel that they have a limited future, they have little to lose by expecting little of themselves or by engaging in at-risk behaviors, including unsafe sexual behavior, delinquency, substance abuse, and suicide.

THINGS TO DO CHART: INCREASING THE FIVE CS

We have included specific empirically supported interventions throughout the book that describe concrete and specific intervention skills to use with children and adolescents. Although these skills and activities are embedded in specific chapters, they usually have broader application beyond the particular problem area discussed. Most increase resiliency

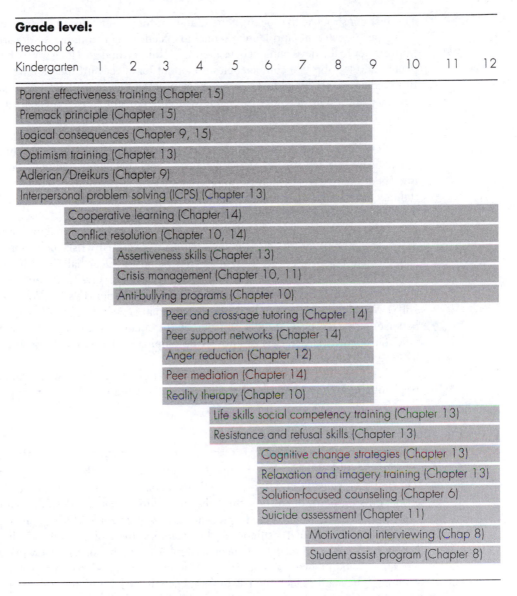

FIGURE 6.1   "Things to Do" Chart . . . and when to start doing them

and relate directly to one or more of the five Cs. On the inside of the front cover is a "Things to Do" chart that indicates the location of various activities and approaches that helpers can use with at-risk children, adolescents, and their families. On this chart we have suggested the most appropriate age groups and grade level for using each of the skills, strategies, and activities listed and presented throughout this book. We hope the "Things to Do" chart will help you locate intervention and prevention activities that work.

In addition to the interventions that are peppered throughout the following chapters, three very broad constructs are important in most of the interventions suggested in this text.

The first construct is that open, honest, and nurturing relationships between adults and young people who are at risk are essential to effective interventions. Adult caring relationships are key to the development of resilience in children and go a long way in helping young people develop the five competencies important for successful functioning. Laursen and Birmingham (2003) identified seven characteristics of these caring relationships that adults need to demonstrate: attention, availability, affirmation, empathy, respect, trust, and virtue.

The second construct is that faulty, negative, and self-defeating thought patterns that perpetuate risky behavior must be the focus of intervention when young people are mature enough to deal with their own insights (e.g., typically after fourth grade). While not totally universal, the negative spiral of faulty cognitions, poor expectations, reduced effort, and diminished performance is extremely common among many at-risk youth (see Figure 11.1). Understanding this negative spiral provides the helper with a variety of areas for focused intervention when working with youth.

The last construct is a "syndrome of negative affect." Emotional problems—anxiety, depression, and other mood problems—typically accompany risky behavior. Often, if we can alleviate negative affect, we reduce risky behavior. Over half of all lifetime cases of mental illness begin by age 14, but many people do not receive treatment until years after the first onset of symptoms of a mental or emotional disorder (Kessler, Wang, & Zaslavsky, 2005). We clearly want to help young people change self-defeating behavior and make better choices. To be optimally effective, it is critical to understand emotions and the potential "negative affect syndrome" in developing and implementing prevention and treatment strategies.

Each of these three core constructs needs to be considered when working with at-risk youth and when implementing the interventions presented in later chapters.

CONCLUSION

In this chapter we highlighted an important issue that we emphasize throughout this book: The problems faced by children and youth are mediated not only by their social, family, and school environments but also by the skills the children possess—skills they can develop to overcome their difficulties. One way we can assist young people is by recognizing how some of them have developed resiliency and by teaching these skills to those who are at risk. Professionals who can recognize the characteristics of high-risk versus low-risk youth are in a position to identify young people who are at greatest risk and to design well-focused interventions. They can reduce the risk to young people by helping them develop the competencies we have presented in this chapter. The five Cs of competency are attended to in greater detail in Part 3, in which we describe problems in the at-risk categories and treatments for them, and in Part 4, in which we suggest strategies for preventing them.

AT-RISK CATEGORIES

▲ In Part 3 we consider five specific categories that reflect some of the principal problem areas for at-risk youth: school dropout, substance use, risky sexual behavior, delinquency and youth violence, and youth suicide. Although these topics represent a substantial portion of child and adolescent problem areas, they do not reflect all areas of concern. Nevertheless, we believe these core topics are highly representative of other problems as well. In each chapter we provide (a) a conceptualization of the problem, (b) a discussion of the scope of the problem, (c) characteristics of the problem and strategies to identify and assess it, (d) consequences of the problem, and (e) specific intervention approaches that helpers need to know to reduce the problem. In addition, for each category we examine a major prevention and intervention strategy or two that address the specific areas described. Of course, the intervention ideas provided in each chapter can be applied to other areas as well.

CHAPTER 7

SCHOOL DROPOUT

▲ *Long day coming*
where any corner I turn
any door opening
any hallway minute
can end up with everyone watching
all those eyes seeing
and no one is there
Later you'll say 'just ignore them'
like it would be so easy,
like breathing
You'll tell me stories
listen to my plans
nod and then smile
and look at your watch
like I'm not even talking
like I'm not really there
We'll sit in your office
with posters of baby animals
on the endangered list
(they aren't the ones who belong on that list)
but you'll pretend, and then we'll both pretend
that our little talks make it better
that I will bravely endure
that this story has a nice quiet ending
and that I will be OK.

CHAPTER OUTLINE

▲   In this chapter we concentrate on young people who leave school before they graduate. In the following pages we (a) discuss changing literacy standards that define the term *dropout*, (b) discuss the scope of the dropout problem, (c) outline some of the roots of the problem, (d) highlight the economic and social consequences of dropping out, (e) present information to identify potential dropouts, and (f) describe pragmatic ideas and interventions designed to reduce dropouts.

DEFINITIONAL ISSUES OF THE DROPOUT PROBLEM

Literacy Standards

To understand the apparent decline in academic proficiency of students, we must note the changes that have taken place in educational standards. In 1890 only 6.7% of the nation's 14- to 17-year-olds attended high school. By the late 1990s, more than 95% attended high school. In 1890, 3.5% of America's 17-year-olds graduated from high school. By 1970, 75.6% did so, and by the late 1990s, 89% were graduated. In addition, the criterion for functional literacy has risen steadily from 3 years of schooling in the 1930s, to 6 years in the 1950s, to the completion of high school in the 1970s. These climbing standards have placed increasing demands on students (Berliner & Biddle, 1995).

Many more children with widely diverse backgrounds are being educated than ever before in our history. High schools of one hundred years ago were mainly open to the most privileged children, and only a handful of them were expected to graduate. Schools today are called upon to serve vastly larger numbers of children and to serve children from very different social, cultural, and language backgrounds. Schools also are expected to deliver many more services and to reach children with a much greater ability range. Today's high school dropouts are a major concern for educators and for society, and there are strenuous efforts to reduce the high school dropout rate to zero. Despite these challenges, the American educational system has been enormously successful (Berliner & Biddle, 1995).

Definition of a Dropout

A dropout is a pupil who leaves school before graduation and before completing a program of study. The U.S. Department of Education (DOE) has two classifications of dropout: event dropout and status dropout. *Event dropouts* are youth who withdraw from school within a specific time frame—during a given school year, for example. *Status dropouts* are nonenrolled youth ages 16 to 24 who are out of school without a high school diploma. The DOE uses school completion rates as well, both status completion rates (all completers, age 16 to 24) and the 4-year completion rate. These definitions provide consistent criteria for counting dropouts. However, educators, state governments, policymakers, and school district personnel sometimes use additional and inconsistent criteria, leaving us with statistics that are often imprecise and sometimes contradictory.

The quality of dropout data vary as a function of adequacy of school staffing, consistency of definitions of illnesses, leaves, and transfers, family transience, and specific state criteria for calculating dropout. For example, some states count students with equivalent high school degrees (GED) as graduates; others do not. Schools have a vested interest in keeping dropout rates low because their funds are often tied to student counts.

Even statistics based on common criteria rarely include students who dropped out before entering high school. For example, figures cited for Latino high school sophomores who drop out by their senior year may actually understate the dropout rate among Latinos. In one large secondary school district in Arizona, for example, eighth-grade students who do not register for high school are never counted in the high school census, and therefore they are not counted in the dropout rate. Latino students fit this profile in greater numbers than do African American or European American students (Kaufman, Alt, & Chapman, 2001).

SCOPE AND CHARACTERISTICS OF THE PROBLEM

Despite ongoing inconsistency in tallying dropouts, educators and researchers have made headway in their attempts to profile the student who drops out of school. Indeed, teachers know from their own experience that students who drop out are likely to be those who are unmotivated by their class work; who have had problems with either the school authorities, the police, or both; who skip classes or are often absent; who are pregnant or married; who are poor and must work; who have family problems; who have drug or alcohol problems; who are students of color; or who have fallen 2 or more years behind grade level (McMillen, Kaufman, & Whitener, 1995). The latter group includes many students who are learning English as a second language (ESL, also called second language learners, or SLL). In fact, students from non-English-speaking homes drop out in much higher numbers than do students from homes where English is the only language spoken (Fashola & Slavin, 1998). Recall that Ramona Diaz (Chapter 5) gets poor grades and dislikes school.

She does not think school is meeting her needs, and she feels as though she does not belong there. Her family's economic situation is difficult, and Ramona feels strongly that she should work to help support her family. She also feels bad about herself and does not believe she has the ability to compete at school. Ramona has little social involvement with the school, partly because of the family's economic situation and partly because of her struggle with the English language. These factors make Ramona a prime candidate for dropping out.

In 2000, 11% of 16- to 24-year-olds were out of school without a high school diploma. Although the status dropout rate remained fairly consistent from 1992 to 2000, it declined for young people as a group between the early 1970s and mid-2000. The rate of this decline, however, varied for European Americans, African Americans, Latino Americans, and American Indians (Kaufman et al., 2001). Considering graduation rates, American Indians/Alaska natives (51.1%) produce the lowest high school graduation rates from the ninth grade class of 2001. Latinos (53.2%) and Black, non-Latinos (52.2%) also had especially low graduation rates (Urban Institute, 2004). Between the early 1970s and 2000, the status dropout rate for European Americans was lower each year than the rate for African Americans or Latinos. During these years, the percentage of Latino young people who were out of school without a high school diploma was also higher than that of European Americans and African Americans in every year. In addition, status dropout rates for European Americans and African Americans declined by nearly 40%, whereas the rate for Latino young adults remained fairly constant.

Latino students are disproportionately represented among the status dropout rates in 2000 with a 27.8% dropout rate (Kaufman et al., 2001). This high dropout rate is partly attributable to the relatively greater dropout rate among Latino immigrants (44.2%) relative to first (21%) and second generation (15.9%) Latino youth.

Immigrant Students

Although all countries have experienced immigration, no country in the world has constantly experienced such a high immigration rate as the United States. More than 10% (or 28.4 million) of the U.S. population is foreign born (U.S. Census Bureau, 2001). Public school systems reflect these demographics, with children of immigrants accounting for nearly 1 in 5 of all U.S. schoolchildren. Most of the parents of these children arrived in the United States from Latin America and Asia. A major concern is the dramatically lower educational attainment of immigrant adolescents from Latin America with implications for their later employment, income, health, marriage, and housing (Fuligni & Hardway, 2004). This problem is likely to get worse as California, Arizona, and other states drop bilingual education programs in favor of state-mandated Structured English Immersion (SEI), putting a substantial proportion of immigrant children at even more risk. The SEI approach assumes that immigrant children, and others whose first language is other than English, learn English very quickly—generally within a year's time—under conditions of total immersion. Interestingly, studies have indicated that the development of oral English proficiency takes an average of 3.31 years ranging from 1 year to 6.5 years. Only 2.25% of students demonstrated English proficiency in a year's time; most achieved English proficiency in 2 to 5 years (MacSwan & Pray, 2005). In SEI programs, all subjects are taught in English regardless of whether the student understands. In effect, students lose a number of years of instruction.

Latino Students

The educational attainment gap between European American and African American youth narrowed in the 1970s and 1980s and has remained the same for the past 10 to 15 years. Unfortunately, the high school completion rate for Latinos is about as low today is it was in the 1970s (Fuligni & Hardway, 2004). The extensive literature on Latino dropouts indicates that there is not a single cause associated with the decision to leave school. For immigrants, the stress, confusion, and anxiety when first entering a U.S. school, combined with language problems, are issues. Other issues are poverty, pregnancy, poor academic achievement, parents' educational attainment, lack of motivation, low aspirations, disengagement from learning, and single-parent families (Velez & Saenz, 2001). A growing body of literature also points to school-related or institutional factors that play an important role in the dropout process. For example, Hess (2000) suggested that a self-fulfilling prophecy phenomenon might be occurring in schools, such that teachers hold and unknowingly convey lower expectations of Latino students. One case study by Conchas (2001) examined immigrant and U.S.-born Latino students' perspectives on how the school structure mediates academic success and school engagement. Latino students in this case study expressed how the stereotypes held by teachers and other students about Latinos in general (e.g., Latinos are lazy, don't try hard enough, and so on) affected their level of school engagement. For some students, such negative stereotypes foster pessimism about the usefulness of school.

Exceptional Students

In addition to students of color, immigrant, and English as second language students, dropout statistics include many students with disabilities. The dropout rate in special education is double that of general education despite the school's legal obligation to provide students with disabilities a free, appropriate education until they reach age 21 or receive a high school diploma, as mandated by the Individuals With Disabilities Education Act (IDEA) and the Americans With Disabilities Act (ADA). Students with specific learning disabilities who drop out of school are more socially alienated toward classmates and teachers than are students with learning disabilities who completed school. These young people also have far to go to reach the goals of adult adjustment. In one study, only 56% of learning disabled high school dropouts were employed full time, and most were working in service work or labor occupations (Sitlington & Frank, 1993). Results are similar for adolescents with attention deficit hyperactivity disorder (ADHD). Gifted students, who often demonstrate high ability and intelligence, high creativity, and a strong drive to initiate and complete a task, drop out of school more often than one would think. In fact, they drop out more often than their nongifted peers. All of these exceptional students must be kept in mind when we discuss the scope of the dropout problem.

Gay, Lesbian, Bisexual, and Transgender Students

Another group of students who are particularly at risk of dropping out of school are gay, lesbian, bisexual, and transgender (GLBT) students. Many of the school problems of these adolescents are related to the physical and verbal abuse they receive from peers. Peer harassment contributes to poor school performance, truancy, and withdrawal from school.

School is a dangerous and punishing place for many GLBT students who often experience threats, physical and psychological abuse from peers, and bias from teachers and other school personnel (Glimps, 2005; Rivers & D'Augelli, 2001).

Unfortunately, too many educators do little to support GLBT teenagers in a world that reviles them and in a school environment that permits them to be called "dykes," "faggots," and an assortment of other names (Glimps, 2005). Ironically, although educators will challenge and correct other derogatory terms, the words *dyke* and *faggot* often go unnoticed or at least unchallenged. Making school safe for GLBT youth is the responsibility of all educators. GLBT youth are susceptible to depression and are at high risk for suicide because of internal turmoil and environmental harassment (see Chapter 11). They also consistently report significant stress associated with school and related activities, no doubt contributing to their high dropout rate (Ryan, 2001).

Adjudicated Youth

Adjudicated young people are less likely to graduate from high school. More than two thirds of juvenile offenders of high school age fail to return to school following their release from custody. These adolescents are often alienated from school by below grade level academic performance, a lack of necessary high school credits, school reenrollment procedures, chronic truancy, and a need for special education services (U.S. Office of Juvenile Justice and Delinquency Prevention, 2005). These young people present a particularly thorny problem because in addition to their potential for dropping out of school they present multiple problems. Eight in 10 incarcerated juveniles suffer from learning disabilities. Nearly 4 out of 5 youth arrested for juvenile crimes in 2000 were involved with drugs or alcohol, and 92% tested positive for marijuana. Unfortunately, only a very low number of these youth receive substance abuse treatment once they enter the juvenile justice system. Up to three quarters of all incarcerated juveniles had a diagnosable mental health disorder. Most often educational programs fail to meet state standards, and mental health services are scarce (National Center on Addiction and Substance Abuse, 2005).

THE CONSEQUENCES OF DROPPING OUT

Dropping out of school has a significant impact on the life of the individual, but the costs go far beyond individual consequences. School dropout has serious economic and social repercussions for society as well.

Economic Consequences

Students who drop out of school are at an economic disadvantage and will be throughout their lives: Unemployment and underemployment rates are high among high school dropouts; they earn significantly less over their lifetimes than high school graduates and less still than those graduates who attend some college (Grubb, 1999), and their unemployment rate is considerably higher.

Another aspect of the relationship between school, society, and dropping out is important. A high school diploma no longer ensures gainful employment as it did in the past; our economy needs large numbers of people to work at jobs that are not intellectually challenging. Unfortunately, most of these jobs do not pay well (Berliner & Biddle, 1995). Many adolescents do not see employment opportunities as contingent upon a high school diploma, so many working high school students see no need to finish their education. The perception of a lack of employment opportunities—sometimes a realistic perception—accounts for the widespread belief among adolescents that school is irrelevant.

The economic consequences of the dropout problem include loss of earnings and taxes, loss of Social Security, and lack of qualified workers. A high school diploma is the minimum qualification for participation in the U.S. economy. A worker without one can find work in only the most menial occupations. The factory jobs that once allowed workers to make a good income without a high school diploma are diminishing or are being transferred out of the country; the educational requirements for jobs in general are increasing. The high school dropout is not easily absorbed into the workforce due to this ever-increasing demand for highly trained workers. Students who drop out of high school will lack the necessary skills to participate in the high-tech job market and are likely to be destined for marginal employment or outright dependence on society. A male dropout working full time in 2002 earned nearly $24,000; a male dropout working full time in 1971 earned more than $35,000 in 2002 dollars (Educational Testing Service, 2005). This is a 35% decline. Furthermore, the cost to society of one youth dropping out of high school followed by a life of drug abuse and crime is $1.7 million to $2.3 million (Cohen, 1998).

Not long ago, the Social Security checks of retirees were paid for by as many as 17 employed workers; people who retire in the next 20 years, however, will draw their Social Security from the wages of only 3 workers (Sklar, 1995), one of whom will be a person of color. As discussed in Chapter 2, projections indicate that the percentage of people of color entering the labor force will continue to increase over the next 15 years. Schools, communities, and legislators must ensure that adolescents of color graduate in increasing numbers both to meet the needs of the national labor market and to provide equal representation of people of color in society's labor force.

Social Consequences

Students who leave school before completing their program of study are at a disadvantage in other ways as well. Dropping out of school often has an impact on an individual's psychological well-being. Most dropouts later regret their decision to leave school (Kortering & Braziel, 1999). Dissatisfaction with self, with the environment, and with lack of opportunity is also associated with lower occupational aspirations among young people. When high school dropouts are unemployed or earn less money than their graduated peers, their children also experience negative consequences because they live in lower socioeconomic conditions. Proportionately few of these homes provide the study aids that children of graduates can expect to have. Parents who are poor are less likely to provide non-school-related activities for their children than parents of higher socioeconomic status. Further, low wages require parents who are dropouts to work such long hours that it is difficult for them to monitor their children's activities. Because high school dropouts have lower occupational aspirations than their graduated peers, they also have lower educational expectations for their own children. The Andrews, Baker, and Diaz families (of Chapters 1, 2, and 5) are prime examples of this situation. In each of these families, at least one of the parents did not complete high school, and the children must face the consequences.

Dropping out of school truncates educational and vocational development in a manner that dramatically increases the probability of a downward spiral into greater physical, emotional, and economic problems. Less-educated adolescents are more likely to become pregnant outside of marriage and to rely on public assistance. Dropping out of school is also highly correlated with such conditions as alcohol and drug abuse, delinquent and criminal activity, and other social problems to which communities of color are sometimes even more vulnerable (Cohen, 1998; Orthner & Randolph, 1999).

The idea that dropouts beget dropouts conveys an unnecessary hopelessness. Not all dropouts have children who want to drop out, and not all students at risk for school failure today are children of dropouts. Nevertheless, a continuing cycle of leaving school early seems likely if schools do not take action. Schools can break the cycle in a variety of ways.

PREDICTIVE INDICATORS AND TYPE OF DROPOUTS

Effective implementation of dropout prevention programs requires identification of students at risk. To facilitate this, we turn to research that teachers, counselors and psychologists, and other human service professionals may find useful in their daily work with students.

Differences Between Stayers and Leavers

More than 20 years ago, Ekstrom and her colleagues (1986) focused on a sample of high school sophomores over a 2-year period. They found that those who stayed in school (stayers) differed significantly from those who left (dropouts) across a variety of dimensions: socioeconomic status, race/ethnicity, parent support for education, family structure, school behaviors, and attitudes/abilities toward schoolwork. Students who left school were more likely to be poorer, older, male, and ethnic minorities. They tended to come from homes with fewer study aids and fewer opportunities for non-school-related learning than students who stayed in school. Dropouts were less likely to have both birth parents living in the home, more likely to have employed mothers (who had less education and lower educational expectations for their children), and had less parental monitoring of their activities.

The students who dropped out of school also differed from the stayers in a variety of behaviors. The dropouts were less likely to be involved in extracurricular activities and had lower grades and lower test scores than the stayers. Interestingly, the gap between stayers' and dropouts' grades was greater than the gap between their scores on achievement tests. Dropouts did less homework: an average of 2.2 hours a week as opposed to the 3.4 hours reported by the stayers. The dropouts also had more discipline problems in school, were absent and late more often, cut more classes, got suspended from school more often, and had more trouble with the police.

Differences between dropouts and stayers also emerged in the affective domain. Many of the dropouts reported feelings of alienation from school. Most were not involved in clubs, sports, or student government. Not surprisingly, few dropouts reported feelings of satisfaction with their academic work. Dropouts did not feel popular with other students, and their friends were also alienated from school and had low educational expectations. Finally, the dropouts worked more hours than the stayers, and their jobs were more enjoyable and more important to them than school.

Ekstrom and her colleagues (1986) also investigated what had happened to the students who had dropped out of school between their sophomore and senior years. They found that 47% of them were working either full or part time (more Whites and males reported working for pay than did minorities and females), 29% were looking for work, 16% were homemakers, 10% were enrolled in job-training programs, and 3% were in military service. Of these dropouts, 58% hoped to finish high school eventually, and 17% reported that they had already enrolled in an educational institution. Fourteen percent had already obtained a General Educational Development (GED) high school equivalency certificate. Very little has changed since Ekstrom's original report.

Predictive Variables and Dropout Types

Although the profile developed by Ekstrom and her colleagues (1986) tells us some of the characteristics of young people who drop out of school before graduation, it does not tell us enough about the complex interaction of variables or about why younger students leave. Indeed, dropping out of school is a culmination of a developmental process that involves a complex ecology. Dropping out is a process that begins early in development, typically before a child even enters school, and continues through the time a student formally withdraws. In one study, the quality of early care giving, the early home environment, peer competence, and problem behaviors predicted high school status 15 years later (Jimerson, Egeland, Sroufe, & Carlson, 2000). Early experiences may affect a student's sense of agency and self-concept. These may directly influence school performance and later decisions to stay in school. Early experiences also lay foundations for relationships with teachers and differential interactions with peers that further propel the individual along the pathway toward dropping out. Success in school requires numerous capacities for behavioral control and self-regulation that are formed in earlier years.

In a study designed to test five theories of early dropout behavior, Battin-Pearson and her colleagues (2000) identified poor academic achievement as assessed by standardized achievement tests and grade point averages as consistently one of the strongest predictors of dropping out of high school early. Engaging in deviant behavior such as substance abuse or delinquency, having close connections to antisocial peers, and coming from a poor family increased risks for leaving school by age 14, even when the student had not experienced academic failure or difficulty. Clearly, dropout prevention efforts should be focused directly on improving academic achievement at early ages, but prevention programs should also focus on poor families, youth who associate with deviant peers, and those who participate in aggressive behavior and drug use.

Good dropout prevention programs have the ability to closely match their methods and content to the specific strengths, vulnerabilities, and needs of the participants. One helpful typology of dropouts comes from the work of Janosz and his colleagues (2000). Combining three axes of school-related behavior—academic achievement, school commitment, and behavioral maladjustment—Janosz and colleagues identified four basic, reliable, and valid dropout types: disengaged dropouts, low-achiever dropouts, quiet dropouts, and maladjusted dropouts. Each type has unique characteristics to consider in designing interventions.

Disengaged dropouts.   Although they believe that they are less competent than other students, disengaged dropouts obtain surprisingly high achievement scores considering their lack of school involvement. These young people care little about school grades and have few educational aspirations, generally do not like school, do not recognize the importance of education, and accord little value to both school and education in their lives.

Low-achiever dropouts.   Although they have relatively few behavior problems, low-achiever dropouts have a very weak commitment to education, experience poor grades, and learn little. Of all the dropout types, low achievers are distinct in their lack of ability to fulfill minimal course requirements.

Quiet dropouts.   Young people who fit this dropout category have few external problems although they exhibit poor school performance. They hold positive views about school attendance, appear to be involved in school activities, and do not create disciplinary trouble. They do not get very good grades but also do not misbehave much and do not react openly to school difficulties. They generally go unnoticed until they drop out.

Maladjusted dropouts.   Dropouts in this category have high levels of misbehavior. They demonstrate a weak commitment to education, have poor school performance, invest little in school life, and frequently are in disciplinary trouble. Due to the variety and severity of difficulties, these dropouts have the most negative school profile of the four types.

Knowing these dropout types will assist counselors and educators to identify potential dropouts. Clustering variables that predict dropout types will improve interventions to reduce dropouts because prevention efforts can target specific behaviors and attitudes.

We must also consider another contributing factor: the student's instructional environment. Lunenburg (2000) argues that the instructional environment can seriously magnify a student's dislike for school, lack of motivation, and low self-concept. For example, at-risk, low-achieving students are treated differently from high-achieving students, and this kind of differential treatment can literally "push" them out of school. Differential treatment of at-risk students includes that they are called on less, given less wait time to answer questions, given less praise, and given less eye contact and other nonverbal communication of responsiveness (Janosz, LeBlanc, Boulerice, & Tremblay, 2000). At-risk students sense the teacher's lower regard for their personal worth as learners, come to believe it, and live up to those expectations.

SPECIFIC INTERVENTION STRATEGIES FOCUSED ON SCHOOL DROPOUTS

Students at greatest risk for dropping out of school are identifiable, although many disengage from school and drop out for a variety of reasons for which there is no one common solution. School districts and specific schools can improve their retention rates by organizing programs that directly address the personal and idiosyncratic issues of individual dropouts in their region. At a minimum, though, efforts to prevent pupils from leaving school should include methods to reduce antisocial behaviors, increase academic achievement, improve connection with other students and adults, and in other ways encourage positive school commitment. Insufficient attention is paid to alienated, lonely, and disliked students (Thomas & Smith, 2004). The teenager who speaks to us in Box 7.1 (a possible quiet or disengaged dropout) expresses concerns that are common to many high school dropouts:

▲ Box 7.1

Reflections of a Future Dropout

I wish I could leave school. It's so boring that I just daydream all day anyway. Why can't they just let me leave now, instead of waitin' till I'm 16?

When I leave, I'm gonna help Mama in her restaurant. It's her own business and she runs it, but she also has to take care of my little sisters. We have it all worked out. I already help her every night when I get home from school. This week she let me work in the kitchen. I figured out a new way to make salad dressing, and it's really good. Mama says it's gonna be a house specialty. The first time we served it, I had to figure out how to make a batch for 100 people without messing it up.

Mama also lets me do the books. She don't have time for everything. If I didn't have to go to school, I could help her a lot more. Three weeks ago, we had a taxman in here checking through the books. He said he was impressed with the figures. We couldn't let him know I did them cuz I'm too young to work. Mama brings 'em home for me, and I do 'em at night. I'm usually right. I wish I could be like that in school. But man, those questions in my homework just get me all confused. I mean, once I was s'pose to figure out when two trains would meet if they was goin' toward each other and leavin' at different times and stuff like that. I mean, who cares? Someone's already got the train schedule all figured out so they don't run into each other, and I ain't never gonna be a train engineer, so why ask me? Usually, though, it don't make much difference cuz I'm so busy addin' up customers' bills that I don't have time to set down and figure out what some smart guy has already done. Mr. Larson is sorta gettin' used to me not turning in my homework. So is Mr. Poland. He says I better start thinkin' about what I'm gonna do for the science fair or I'm gonna flunk his class. Well, excuse me, but I just don't have time to figure out how to make an atom bomb. I wish he'd just get off my case and stick to buggin' the smart kids.

If I didn't have to go to school, I could help Mama by takin' the kids to the library. They have story time, and my little sisters like to hear it sometimes. I just set and read the encyclopedias. The other day I was readin' that a kangaroo can have as many as three babies suckin' on her tits at once. There can be an embryo that attaches itself to the nipple, a newborn inside the pouch, and an older baby (they're called "joeys," in case you weren't aware) that hops in for some chow. I really enjoy the library. Especially in summer cuz the air conditioner works real good. Some of those librarians are real nice to me. Mrs. Bishop is my favorite. She always asks me about the books I check out, if I liked 'em, and then she says what's another

(continued)

BOX 7.1 *(continued)*

good one to read. One librarian there is kinda mean, but she's nothing like the one at the school library. Man, that lady won't even let you read the inside cover flaps cuz it'll mess up her nice clean shelf. She looks at me like I'm lookin' to take something all the time. Mama says she must have a board up her butt. I just hate goin' in there. Anyway, it doesn't matter much cuz we're only allowed to go to the library with our English class, and I never finish my work in that class. I just can't get into prepositions and garbage like that. I mean, who cares anyway? In Mama's restaurant, nobody says I'm not talkin' right, and I know I never heard anybody discussin' conjugatin' verbs while they was eatin' a French dip roast beef sandwich. I sure wish I could leave school so I could start learnin' something.

a lack of relevance between the school's curriculum and the circumstances of students' lives and a lack of belongingness. This teen, however, at least has a goal: She is going to help her mother manage a restaurant. Clearly she is interested in learning, but the school she attends is not where most of her learning takes place. Because she seems to be so eager to learn science, to read, and to use math skills, it is indeed a shame that she does not see the school curriculum in these areas as relevant to her life. Curricula that highlight the connection between learning and the "real world" should be selected whenever possible, with support for teachers to promote those connections. She would also benefit from a curriculum that encompasses goal-setting techniques. Identifying and writing down long-term goals, developing a plan to implement those goals, and periodically reviewing the actions taken to achieve the goals are useful skills. Tyrone Baker, for example, would benefit from such a curriculum. (We discuss goal-setting techniques in Chapter 13.)

Schools can also organize programs to bring truant students—disengaged, quiet, or maladjusted potential dropouts—back to the classroom. For example, requiring a daily after-school study group might enable truant students to catch up, work at their own pace, and receive credit. These last-resort study sessions could be a key element in a dropout prevention program.

Social interaction, especially with antisocial peers, influences the decision to leave school. An opportunity to get involved with a social group and to work with the other members in a positive manner might be beneficial to the quiet potential dropout (Davalos, Chavez, & Guardiola, 1999). Perhaps if 9-year-old Tyrone Baker could get involved in healthy social activities run by the school, he would not be so susceptible to gang activities. School arts, music, and athletic programs provide support and opportunities for disadvantaged students to participate in sports, clubs, and activities. Most school arts programs provide valuable outlets for young people and give them a sense of accomplishment, as does participation in the school band or choir. Too often, when funding is tight, the prevention value (in human and economic terms) of school arts programs is ignored.

Peer and cross-age tutoring, mediation, leadership, and facilitation (counseling) programs can also help young people at risk for dropping out of school. Such programs have great potential because they blend learning and responsibility with the development of social skills and a positive self-image. In Chapter 14 we provide an extensive discussion of the use of peer and cross-age programs. In addition, classroom techniques that provide students with the opportunity to communicate with each other in a positive manner help to improve their social relationships and connectedness. Jason Carter and Ramona Diaz would benefit greatly from working with other students in supportive groups. Some specific classroom practices are discussed in Chapter 14, including peer support networks and cooperative learning groups.

The more effective dropout intervention programs identify and track young people at risk for school failure and maintain a focus on students' progress toward educational achievement. They are designed to influence enrollment status and to address various indicators of student engagement. They address issues related to student mobility, alternate time lines, and routes for school completion that often include alternative education programs (Christenson & Thurlow, 2004).

Alternative Education

Besides prevention and early intervention, accommodations must be made for students who are at imminent risk of early school withdrawal or who have already dropped out. Alternative education programs provide ways for these young people to experience academic and personal success in technical vocational schools, alternative middle or secondary schools that may include schools for pregnant teens, homebound programs, career academies, and evening high schools. Such interventions need adequate staffing by effective teachers and professional counselors. The Educational Testing Service (2005) provides information related to consistent school dropout rates. School counselors are scarce, with only one certified counselor available for every 285 high school students, leaving counselors with very little time to work with students at risk of dropping out. In addition, there has been a decline in federal investment for second-chance educational opportunities (from about $15 billion in the late 1970s to about $3 billion currently). In earlier years, students who left school before graduation had a wider range of opportunities.

Dynarski and Gleason (2002) summarizes findings from a comprehensive evaluation of federally funded dropout prevention programs. Alternative middle schools with an intensive intervention approach were more effective at preventing early dropout than schools that only provided supplemental services. An intensive intervention approach involved teaching students in smaller classes; implementing competency-based curricula that allowed students to work independently and progress at their own rate; developing challenging curricula that required students to use knowledge from several subject areas to address real-world issues; and pushing students to learn more and faster, so that those who were behind grade level could accelerate their progress.

In contrast, the supplemental program provided only tutoring or occasional classes to promote self-esteem or leadership and had almost no impact on student outcomes (Dynarski & Gleason, 2002). An evaluation of alternative programs suggests that although supplemental services were relatively straightforward to implement, they did not appear to keep students in school or improve their attendance or academic performance. Alternative programs that provide more attention to students, that create an environment geared to their specific needs, and that provide a more personal atmosphere with smaller classes seem to work best for students at risk for dropping out.

Most important, the choice of teachers was a more influential factor than the choice of curriculum. The evaluators observed inspired and creative teachers engaging students intellectually with traditional material. More often, however, they observed classes with interesting subject material but with traditional teaching formats. Students were not engaged (Dynarski & Gleason, 2002).

Specific Intervention: Comprehensive, Competency-based Guidance

Placements in alternative school settings are less critical when schools are systematically organized to intervene consistently. Research shows that most students who leave school before graduation did not receive school interventions to help them stay in school (Coley, 1995; Mattison, 2000). More than 60% indicated that no one on the school staff had tried to talk them into staying. Less than one fourth saw a counselor or social worker to discuss their troubles or dropout plans. For many of these students, it was clear that they were struggling with academic and other problems in their final 2 years, and no one caught the problem early enough to prevent dropout.

The 1990s have seen a major push by the American School Counseling Association and other concerned groups to encourage schools to adhere to the national standards for school counseling programs (Campbell & Dahir, 1997). The national standards are closely aligned to the Comprehensive, Competency-Based Guidance (CCBG) model. Comprehensive, competency-based guidance and counseling programs are rapidly becoming the program of choice for managing guidance and counseling in schools (Gysbers & Henderson, 2006). It is currently estimated that more than half of the states promote the use of CCBG programs.

Comprehensive, competency-based guidance programs are developmentally focused and are designed to provide all students with experiences to help them grow and develop. These programs change the traditional responsibilities, roles, and contributions of school counselors. Although counselors continue to meet the immediate counseling and crisis management needs of students, their major task is to identify competencies among all students and to provide planned activities on a regular basis to assist students to achieve competencies and to learn new skills. Within the CCBG model, counselors provide a full range of services and activities—assessment, information sharing with teachers and parents, consultation, prevention, counseling, referral, placement, and follow-up work with children and youth and their families. CCBG programs typically incorporate the following unique components:

- A guidance curriculum that infuses career exploration in the academic curricula.
- Individual planning that consists of advising, assessing, and supporting students individually with their academic and career goals.
- Responsive services that include individual counseling, small-group counseling, large-group or classroom-level interventions, prevention work (also often through classroom delivery), consultation, and referral.

The student development aspect of CCBG encompasses a variety of desired student learning competencies. These competencies are comprised of specific knowledge, attitudes, and skills. They form the foundation of the developmental school counseling program. All students gain the specific competencies they need to be successful students and successful adults. The three areas or domains of student development in the CCBG model are as follows:

- Academic development—that is, young people acquire the knowledge and skills that contribute to effective learning in school and across the life span.
- Career development—specifically, students employ strategies to achieve future career success and satisfaction.
- Personal/social development—students acquire the attitudes, knowledge, and interpersonal skills to help them understand and respect themselves and others.

Developmentally appropriate competencies in each of the three domains are identified at all levels, pre-K through 12. Typically, counselors are assigned to and become an expert in a particular domain. All students are systematically provided with opportunities to develop competencies through classroom and small-group presentations according to the master calendar developed by the counseling staff.

In the CCBG model, school counselors are more fully engaged in implementing prevention and intervention activities for all students. They move out of marginalized positions and into roles that more effectively promote essential education and career objectives for students. Substantial research (e.g., see Gysbers & Henderson, 2006; Lapan, Gysbers, & Petroski, 2001) indicates that implementation of CCBG programs is associated with improving student success and safety.

In later chapters we provide a wide range of programs, strategies, and interventions that fit extremely well with the CCBG model. For example, in Chapter 12 we present two universal prevention strategies—the Group-Oriented Psychological Education Prevention (GOPEP) program and a bullying prevention model—both of which can be used in a CCBG counseling program. Our colleagues, Barbara Kerr and Sharon Robinson Kurpius at Arizona State University, developed an interesting and unique service-learning-research program for a group of girls who had never previously been studied: at-risk talented girls who had a capacity for extraordinary intellectual achievement especially in math and science. Using a series of grants from the National Science Foundation (NSF), they created the Talented at Risk Girls: Encouragement and Training for Sophomores program, which was followed by a program called Guiding Girls into Math and Science (Robinson Kurpius, 2005; Kerr & Harkins, 2004).

The two programs provide a day-long intervention followed by a booster session several months later. Identified girls spend a day on the university campus participating in individual and small-group activities and receiving feedback and support about their career interests and personality characteristics, risky behaviors, and strength and resilience assets. Participation in the "A Future Day Fantasy" activity and in a small-group counseling session on career aspirations and barriers seem to be particularly meaningful (Foley-Nicpon & Kerr, 2005). A modified program has been used with adolescent boys, and the program components are probably applicable and effective with other at-risk populations.

In the traditional school counseling model, not every student receives the same quality or quantity of information from the counseling staff regarding postsecondary educational opportunities, career opportunities, or life-coping skills. Students with the most obvious personal difficulties and students with top academic skills receive the most attention from counselors. In this traditional counseling model, counselors are passive and wait for students to contact them, which is particularly disadvantageous to the potential school dropout. In the CCBG model, the potential dropout at least knows that somebody is attending to multiple dimensions of his or her development. Of course, because of the increase in the school counselor's job responsibilities, opportunities for long-term counseling of individual children are few, and outside referrals to appropriate counselors, social workers, or psychologists in the community may increase. The CCBG model provides more support and guidance to more students, and adoption of such a model can be a significant step toward dropout prevention.

Specific Intervention: Solution-Focused Counseling

How can a school be transformed from a problem-focused environment into a solution-focused environment that fosters and highlights positive change? Solution-focused counseling is a positive and competency-based response to the problems experienced by children, adolescents, adults, and even organizational systems (Gingerich & Wabeke, 2001). Rather than focusing on what is wrong and how to fix it, this approach looks for what is already working and how to use and augment it. Its usefulness within the school system and its effectiveness with school problems have been well reported (Bruce, 1995; Durrant, 1995; Metcalf, 1995; Murphy, 1997; Murphy & Duncan, 1997; Sklare, 1997). The limited time frame of the solution-focused approach and its positive, competency-based, goal-oriented emphasis make it very well suited for counselors operating in a comprehensive, competency-based guidance model.

Our focus here is on the use of a solution-focused approach within the context of counseling. However, the techniques are also useful to administrators working with teachers, parents, and students; in administrative meetings; and in case conferences. Teachers have found many of the strategies, skills, and concepts to be helpful in working with parents and students.

There are several key assumptions of solution-focused counseling:

- Change can occur rapidly, and often a small change is all that is needed to prompt other changes.
- Problems are usually not pervasive; there will be times when the problem is less intense or not present at all.
- Students are more likely to change when they have a clearly defined goal and are able to generate solutions that fit.
- People have strengths and resources and are already doing some things to solve their problem.
- The problem is the problem, not the student, teachers, or parents.

Consistent with these assumptions, encouraging a student to make small changes in behavior has the potential to lead to bigger changes in behavior. Encouraging a student to complete a small portion of her English paper rather than complete the entire assignment is based on the idea that she needs success and encouragement to get some momentum started in her life. In addition, small shifts in role by one person in a relationship have the potential to cause the role shift of others in that relationship. Initially, the counselor's job is to push for small changes.

Using solution-focused questions helps the client identify exceptions and potential solutions to the problem. The counselor helps the client identify those times when the problem is not present or is less intense ("Can you describe a time in the past week when your teacher was not angry with you? What were you doing?"), and these exceptions can be transformed into solutions. Next, the counselor builds on asking the client how the exception happened and how the client could make it happen more often.

The following pragmatic points appeal to clients' common sense:

1. If it works a little, try to do more of what is working.
2. Build on and add behaviors to what works.
3. If it is broke, stop what's not working and do something different to fix it.
4. "If it ain't broke, don't fix it."

In solution-focused counseling, goals are stated in positive and observable terms. Clients do better in obtaining goals that are specific and quantifiable. For example, the goal of "study harder" is inferior to the goal of "complete one homework assignment per day in study hall." Time in the counseling session is devoted entirely to increasing exceptions (doing more of what works) and identifying and pursuing specific goals. No time is spent trying to determine the cause of a problem, describing the history of a problem, or rehashing old, past experiences.

One simple strategy that counselors can use to implement solution-focused counseling is the "miracle question" (de Shazer, 1990). The miracle question is a future-oriented question that is very useful in goal setting and in shifting from focusing on the problem to focusing on the solution. In essence, the client is asked to visualize what his or her life would be like if the problem was suddenly solved. For example, "Suppose a miracle occurs tonight while you are sleeping. When you wake up, you realize that your problems are solved. What would things be like? What would you be doing that would tell you that the miracle had actually taken place?" A form of the miracle question useful for children is, "If I were to wave a magic wand and all of your problems went away, what would you do? If we could videotape you for one day, what would we see?" Older children and adolescents might respond better to a visualization of what their life would look like 6 months or a year from now if the problem were solved. "If we were to meet in a year and the problem we are talking about didn't exist anymore, what would you be doing differently and how would you know that things were okay?"

The miracle picture is elaborated through the use of solution-focused questions, such as "What else?" "What will others see?" "How would that make you feel?" and "How would that happen?" By engaging in this process, students are essentially able to explore the positive change they would like to see occur and come up with possible solutions that they would like to implement.

Solution-focused counseling is nonblaming and emphasizes normalizing young people's experiences and problems. Solution-focused counseling may be especially effective with youth at risk for early school dropout for the following reasons:

- Students are less likely to feel that the counselor is attacking or blaming them for the problems they are experiencing.
- Students feel empowered knowing that the counselor believes they are capable of becoming their own agents of change.
- Students are able to recognize that they have many options besides dropping out of school.
- Counselors hone in on realistic solutions that can be readily implemented, thereby maximizing the effects of their brief encounters with each at-risk student.

Counselors should keep in mind the following five principles when working with at-risk youth from a solution-focused perspective (Davis & Osborn, 2000):

- Make the most of each brief encounter with a student, as it may be the only one that you have.
- Honor and respect students, especially the resources and strengths they already have, because these are the ingredients for positive change.
- Help students to transfer what they've heard and learned in their counseling interactions with you to the hallway, lunch room, gym, the bus or subway, and so on.
- As much as possible, engage in a collaborative, nonconfrontive exchange with students and their families.
- Instill in students a reason to be hopeful because hope fuels change, and change is always possible.

Solution-focused brief counseling is uniquely suited to the school setting. It emphasizes resources and strengths and natural forces within the environment, and it uses effective, simple, and positive strategies to help students change behavior.

Research on the efficacy of solution-focused brief counseling is limited; much of what is known is from anecdotal reports of solution-focused brief counseling. However, the research that is available demonstrates that brief counseling has been effective when applied to students with behavioral disorders, anxiety, depression, and suicide risk (Dielman & Franklin, 1998; Durrant, 1995; Randell, Eggert, & Pike, 2001; Triantafillou, 1997). This approach allows a busy school counselor to have an impact on a larger number of students and is of great potential value in limiting risky behavior.

CONCLUSION

As literacy standards rise along with the demands of our increasingly technological society, we expect more from our young people than ever before. Unfortunately, these demands come at a time when economic resources are unequally distributed, and many communities and families are unable to meet young people's educational and motivational needs. When we recognize the family, school, social, and personality issues involved, as well as the effects of the experience of failure, we are in a better position to understand why young people drop out of school. We must attempt to effect changes in all of these areas if we are to make any headway against the dropout problem and its wide-ranging consequences.

If at-risk children and adolescents do not stay in school, they move beyond the reach of effective prevention and intervention strategies that can be administered by and through the schools. And if young people do not develop the fundamental skills that schools can provide, they will continue to be dependent, unproductive, and discouraged members of society.

CHAPTER 8

SUBSTANCE USE AND ADDICTION

▲ *There is an assumption here that perhaps should be argued out rather than taken for granted. It is that the self is worth being.*

There is a philosophical dialogue that turns on the question of whether people are born good and become corrupted or are born evil and become civilized.

My own opinion is that each is equally true.

Thus, I cannot claim that if you strip yourself of the encrustation of attitudes and defenses, you are going to expose an angelic, euphoric, and expansive person.

But, certainly, neither are you going to find the cretinous and willful monster that most of us fear is lurking underneath.

There will be a human being, with the assets and limitations inherent in the definition of human being but, for the first time and most importantly, with the choice not to be ugly and cruel and stunted. . . .

To give the self permission to be the self, a leap must be taken across the chasm of dread that the self may be little and mean and nasty toward a certain faith that the self is a good thing to be and that spontaneous behavior can be trusted.

J. J. MCWHIRTER
SEEK WISDOM

CHAPTER OUTLINE

▲   In this chapter we describe the severity of substance use by children and adolescents, the problems associated with it, and potential solutions to this widespread problem. This discussion is especially pertinent to the United States, which has the highest rate of alcohol and drug use by adolescents among industrialized nations (Johnston, O'Malley, & Bachman, 2003). Throughout this chapter, we use the terms substances and drugs interchangeably, and include tobacco and alcohol as examples of drugs. In the following sections, we (a) describe some of the definitional and assessment problems associated with substance use, (b) illustrate the scope of substance use among adolescents, (c) outline personal and social determinants leading to drug use and addiction, (d) discuss some of the consequences of alcohol and drug consumption, and (e) highlight child and adolescent substance use treatment and prevention approaches found to be effective.

DEFINITIONAL DIFFICULTIES AND ASSESSMENT

To determine the abusive nature of drug use, one must consider the context, frequency, and purpose for which a drug is used. There is often a fine line between drug use and drug abuse. The causes of substance use are often linked to social influences (e.g., peer drug use), whereas substance abuse may be more tied to internal processes, for example, using drugs as self-medication against persistent emotional distress. Yet for adolescents and preadolescents, most of the correlates of substance use are identical to those of abuse. The term *substance abuse* is also an ideological term, suggesting that the results of drug use are always negative or harmful, which can be misleading. We use the term *substance use* throughout this text because it does not negate the harmful consequences of drug use nor does it exaggerate them.

Although tobacco products and alcohol are accepted and legal for adults, they can have severe negative consequences even when they are used in relative moderation. Alcohol and tobacco use are responsible for significant physical and personal problems and have greater social costs than all other drugs combined. Miller and Blincoe (1994) estimated the total dollars spent or lost for alcohol misuse in one year in the United States was $116.5 billion. Cigarette smoking is estimated to account for more than 430,000 premature deaths each year (National Center for Chronic Disease Prevention and Health Promotion [NCCDPHP], 2000). Nevertheless, we do not define the occasional smoker or drinker as an abuser of substances.

Criteria have been established for identifying substance abuse and substance-induced disorders, including substance intoxication, in adult populations. The *Diagnostic and Statistical Manual of Mental Disorders* (DSM-IV-TR; American Psychiatric Association, 2000) distinguishes between substance dependence and substance abuse without making separate provisions for children and adolescents. Substance dependence is addiction. It involves the physiological responses of tolerance (increasingly larger doses of a particular drug are needed to maintain its physiological effects) and withdrawal (painful physical and psychological consequences result when the drug is withheld from the body). Substance use is maladaptive in DSM terminology if use of a particular substance causes impaired social, school, or occupational functioning. Drug use is identified as being "with or without physiological dependence," and the specific courses of drug use are identified as "early full remission," "early partial remission," "sustained full remission," or "sustained partial remission." Although not specifically listed as DSM criteria, substance abuse can be determined by examining (a) the frequency of use, (b) the quantity typically used, (c) the variety of substances used at the same time (polydrug use), (d) the social context in which drugs are used (Is the user being dared to try drugs? Does the user usually use drugs with friends, alone, or with strangers?), and (e) the emotional state of the abuser (Is the user typically depressed or feeling positive before engaging in drug use?). Examining these criteria help to clarify the nature and extent of substance use and abuse among children and teenagers.

THE SCOPE OF THE PROBLEM

Although the overall use of drugs in the United States has fallen by 50% in the past 20 years, the past 10 years have shown some increase in drug use by adolescents (Johnston et al., 2003). The National Institute on Drug Abuse (NIDA), through its Monitoring the Future Study (MFS), for example, found that 50% of high school seniors regularly use alcohol, with 26% having engaged in binge drinking. More than 20% of 10th-graders had engaged in binge drinking within 2 weeks of the survey (Johnston et al., 2003). Also, experimentation with tobacco during adolescence is quite prevalent, and many children experiment with tobacco as early as age 9. Though daily use rates are declining, 10th- and 12th-graders still have substantial use rates of 10% and 17%, respectively. In addition, about 5% of 8th grade boys and 12% of 12th grade boys had used smokeless tobacco (chewing tobacco, snuff, or dip) in the past 30 days (Johnston et al., 2003). The use of tobacco and alcohol are critical because both are considered "threshold" or "gateway" substances, which often precede use of illicit drugs such as marijuana, methamphetamine, inhalants, and coca-based substances.

Close to 30% of high school students had been offered, sold, or given an illegal drug, often marijuana, on school property at some point during the 12 months preceding one survey (Grunbaum et al., 2004). These data are serious, especially because marijuana smoking may actually precede heavy tobacco smoking or alcohol abuse among girls (which suggests it is a gateway drug for girls). Furthermore, marijuana use is often a forerunner to smoking heroin and using cocaine or methamphetamine (Golub & Johnson, 2001). More than 10% of students nationwide had tried marijuana before age 13, with male students more likely to use than female students across all ethnic groups (Grunbaum et al., 2002). Additionally, nearly 10% of adolescents have at least once used a form of cocaine (e.g., powder, "crack," or "freebase"), with Latino (15%) and European American students (10%) significantly more likely to do so than African American students (2%). It is also estimated that nearly 15% of adolescents have used inhalants (sniffed glue, aerosol spray, or paint) to get high. Among 12th-graders, use of tranquilizers and barbiturates has been steadily rising since the 1990s (Johnston et al., 2003). An increasing problem among youth is methamphetamine use; nationwide, nearly 10% of adolescents have used methamphetamines with European American (11.4%) and Latino (9%) young people using significantly more than African Americans (2%). However, recent informal information from health and human service workers on the street suggests methamphetamine abuse is an extremely serious problem.

Within these data there are points of hope. There is no evidence of increase in early onset of drug use. Use of most illicit drugs decreased or was stable in the early 2000s, and perceptions of risks associated with smoking and using most illicit substances increased (Johnston et al., 2003). Although these data are positive, drug and alcohol use among U.S. children and adolescents continues to be a serious behavioral, social, and health problem. The continuous introduction of new drugs, as well as the tendency for youth to "forget" the dangers associated with older drugs such as heroin, requires ongoing effort to educate the public (Johnston et al., 2003).

The often-held stereotype that adolescents of color abuse substances more than European American youth is not supported by research. African American youth are significantly less likely to use cigarettes, alcohol, and illicit drugs than European American youth (Johnston et al., 2003). In 8th grade, Latino youth have the highest use rates for all substances except amphetamines. It is European American youth who tend to have the highest use rates for all substances in 10th and 12th grade (Johnston et al., 2003). Native American Indian adolescents use alcohol, tobacco, and other drugs significantly more than other groups, resulting in problems that include a high incidence of fetal alcohol syndrome (Plunkett & Mitchell, 2000).

Adolescents who are gay, lesbian, bisexual, or transgender (GLBT) are at highest risk of substance abuse (Jordan, 2000). These young people are at risk because of an increase in suicidal ideation, levels of depression and hopelessness, and experiences of victimization (Russell & Joyner, 2001). Estimates suggest that more than a third of GLBT youth are frequent and problematic users and are more likely to engage in polysubstance use, with marijuana and alcohol used most (Radkowsky & Siegel, 1997). Of course, gay and lesbian teenagers abuse drugs for the same reasons as straight youth, but the additional challenges and oppression they experience as members of a sexual minority group may drive many GLBT youth to use drugs as a way of buffering the social exclusion, ridicule, and torment that they experience (Radkowsky & Siegel, 1997). Clearly, a better understanding of substance abuse among GLBT young people can help the development of targeted prevention and treatment programs, and a greater awareness and sensitivity to this underserved community can improve our prevention and intervention efforts right now.

SOME DETERMINANTS OF SUBSTANCE USE AND COMMON CHARACTERISTICS OF USERS

Family and peer influences, individual behavior, and personality characteristics consistently relate to child and adolescent substance use (Johnston, O'Malley, & Bachman, 2000; Scheier, 2001). Counselors and human service professionals can use knowledge of these factors to assess the likelihood of drug use and to provide appropriate interventions. Correlates and predictors of child and adolescent drug use influence one another in a variety of ways (e.g., Dishion, Kavanagh, Schneiger, Nelson, & Kaufman, 2002). Understanding the complex ecology of children's lives and how each aspect of their environment—social policy, media advertising, parenting practices, family and peer drug use, and individual characteristics—interrelates in predicting substance use and its outcomes is important. Although correlates to adolescent drug use are presented here in discrete categories, these variables are highly interrelated and mutually influential.

Environmental and Social Correlates of Substance Use

A variety of environmental factors contribute to drug use. The soil that nurtures drug use (see Chapter 2) includes poverty, racism, community and interpersonal violence, lack of educational and job opportunities, the dissolution of communities, and interpersonal and family problems. In economically depressed communities, young people often use drugs in response to the bleakness of economic and social conditions, as we see in the Andrews and Baker children (Chapters 1 and 2). Traumatic events, poor neighborhoods, adverse school conditions, and negative peer influences also contribute to increased use of substances (Johnston et al., 2000) and to aggression. Consistent with this, drug use is typically heavier among lower socioeconomic groups.

The U.S. "war on drugs" has been unsuccessful in large part because it has been a military/geopolitical response to what is fundamentally a social and public health issue. The "war" also underscores that the United States focuses much effort on dealing with drugs and their related problems through the criminal justice system, contributing to the U.S. status as the most incarceration-oriented country in history. But this response does not address the reasons adolescents turn to drugs in the first place. This is a war that we cannot win.

Drug use is also reinforced through the media, which inundate the market with images of drug use as a helpful solution to all physical complaints and psychological problems. Alcohol is portrayed as necessary to lead the "good life." Movies depict marijuana use either in a positive way (52%) or as neutral (48%) (Gunasekera, Chapman, & Campbell, 2005). These messages of drug acceptability further communicate to young people the usefulness of drugs as part of mainstream U.S. culture (Stern, 2005). The profit motive also leads advertising to glamorize products to appeal to and entice young people, such as using cartoon characters to advertise cigarettes. Finally, modeling by older siblings, parents, and peers is highly correlated with drug use among children and adolescents (Kosterman et al., 2000). Two of the most important and direct predictors of adolescent drug use are peer drug use and low parental monitoring, or parents who are detached and disconnected from the everyday activities of their child's life (Dishion et al., 2002).

Peer Influence on Substance Use

Peer groups strongly influence a young person's decision to use drugs, and they predict the age of initial drug use, especially alcohol, marijuana, and tobacco (Dishion et al., 2002; Kosterman et al., 2000). Thus interventions that focus on the peer group may be the most effective for preventing and treating substance use and associated problems. Unfortunately, peer group and peer pressure have been used so loosely that their meanings are ambiguous. Peer cluster theory (Beauvais et al., 1996; Oetting & Beauvais, 1986), which we discuss in greater detail in Chapter 14, provides a specific framework for understanding and explaining the influence of peers on a young person's decisions and decision making. Peer cluster theory emphasizes that drug use is linked to peer relationships. Peers provide information about drugs, shape attitudes toward them, create a social context for their use, give rationales for using them, and make them available.

This theory has been tested and supported by a series of research studies that highlight the importance of attending to peer clusters in both prevention and treatment (Beauvais et al., 1996; Oetting & Beauvais, 1987; Swaim, Oetting, Edwards, & Beauvais, 1989). This theory has also enjoyed some support in describing problem behavior among adolescents in other cultures (P. T. McWhirter, 1998), suggesting that the theory may be culturally sensitive and broadly applicable.

Adolescent drug use is also a function of positive reinforcement. When children and adolescents use certain substances, they frequently experience not only physiological reinforcement (e.g., euphoria, stimulation) but also social reinforcement by peers who bestow attention and status on the using adolescent. Such reinforcement is a powerful force for maintaining substance use and for experimenting with more potent drugs.

Family Correlates of Substance Use

Research consistently identifies family factors, such as parenting style, as central to the etiology of multiple problem behavior outcomes, including early-onset substance use (Webster-Stratton, 1997). Lower socioeconomic status and parental substance use are predictors of onset of alcohol and tobacco use (Dishion et al., 2002; Kirisci, Vanyukov, & Tarter, 2005). Low parent monitoring, in particular, predicts early alcohol, tobacco, and marijuana use. Therefore, increasing parental monitoring serves as a key protective factor for reducing substance use among children exposed to it by their siblings or peers (DiClemente et al., 2001). Poor parent–child relationships, deficient parental limit setting, and weak problem-solving and communication skills within families all predict higher use as well (Dishion & McMahon, 1998; Kosterman et al., 2000). At the same time, authoritarian and punitive approaches in schools and in families also tend to contribute to higher drug use among children and adolescents. And teens are more likely to use drugs if their family environments are disruptive or disorganized, include an adult who uses drugs, or have no family religious affiliation (Webster-Stratton, Reid, & Hammond, 2001). Thus the children in the Andrews, Baker, and Carter families are at serious risk. Jason Carter's dysfunctional family, his poor school adjustment, and his underlying emotional distress provide particularly fertile ground for the development of drug-use problems. Because family factors are central to the risk of adolescent drug use, it is not surprising that family-based approaches are quite promising for reducing early-onset substance use and would be quite helpful to each of our described families (Dishion et al., 2002; Hawkins, Catalano, Kosterman, Abbott, & Hill, 1999; Kumpfer, Molgaard, & Spoth, 1996).

Personal Correlates of Substance Use

Although some adolescents never experiment with drugs, others experiment briefly and never use them again, and others develop long-term patterns of use. Drug dependence may be associated with two additional critical factors: psychic pain and inability to cope (Clark & Sayette, 1993; Simons, Whitbeck, Conger, & Melby, 1991). Psychic pain can emerge from pervasive self-criticism and a chronic sense of failure that often leads to lower self-esteem and to young people believing that they are primarily responsible for the problems they experience. Many adolescents internalize these attributions for problems and experience subsequent depression and anxiety (B. T. McWhirter & Burrow-Sanchez, 2004; B. T. McWhirter, J. J. McWhirter, Hart, & Gat, 2000). Adolescents with poor coping skills are vulnerable to intense emotional pain, and drug use can become a relief-seeking behavior aimed at alleviating both internal problems (frustration, stress, depression, feelings of low self-worth) and external problems (poor school performance, family discord, violence). These kinds of pain can be overwhelming and draw many young people into substance use as a form of self-medication (see Box 8.1). But because relief through drugs is only temporary, drug use itself becomes part of a downward spiral and is ultimately self-defeating. Jason Carter of Chapter 4, for example, is experiencing considerable psychological pain, and his coping methods are ineffective and exacerbate his distress. He is a prime candidate for potential chronic drug abuse and dependency.

Pervasive substance use, rather than experimentation, is associated with a variety of other personality characteristics. Among these are pleasure- and sensation-seeking behaviors (Comeau, Stewart, & Loba, 2001) such as rebelliousness; nontraditionalism, tolerance for deviance, adventuresomeness, and need for excitement (Kirisci et al., 2005; P. T. McWhirter, 1998); and an acute desire for independence and autonomy, along with low interpersonal trust and low impulse control with poor ability to delay gratification (Comeau et al., 2001). Indeed, increasing evidence suggests that adolescents' brains are less developed than previously believed, and impulsive and risky behavior may result (Rosser, Stevens, & Ruiz, 2005). Drug interventions should focus on the problematic aspects of these personal risk factors. Some of these characteristics (e.g., high risk-taking behavior and adventuresomeness) are not necessarily a problem and, in fact, can be used in treatment. Some prevention and treatment programs use adventurous activities to help adolescents channel their energies in a positive direction along with building self-efficacy and appropriate trust in self and in peers.

Finally, cognitive dissonance and personal attribution make abstention from drugs difficult for adolescents. Cognitive dissonance is a result of conflicting internal messages. For example, the statements "I don't smoke anymore" and "After 3 months without a cigarette, I just smoked most of a pack" are inconsistent. They create dissonance, which brings on feelings of guilt, depression, and failure. These feelings are relieved when the internal messages are made harmonious: "I just smoked most of a pack" and "I'm a smoker."

▲ Box 8.1

Joe

One of us worked with a 13-year-old boy named Joe for 2 months after Joe's mother requested that he receive counseling. She and her husband, Joe's stepfather, were concerned about Joe's poor school performance, his acting out, his group of "delinquent" friends, and his alternately hostile and completely withdrawn behavior at home.

Joe's stepfather was a machine operator who provided severe yet inconsistent discipline. Joe disliked his stepfather, and he reported that the dislike was mutual. He described his mother as "nicer" but complained that she did not permit him to do what he wanted. His mother was primarily a homemaker, but occasionally she did temporary office work. She frequently placated her husband so that he would not get angry with Joe. She felt Joe needed to change, however, and believed that counseling might "fix" him. Joe's parents refused to come in for counseling as a family because Joe was the problem.

Joe spent a great deal of time with his friends both during and after school. He reported smoking marijuana and cigarettes fairly regularly. Shortly after our first counseling session, he was arrested for possession of drug paraphernalia. His parents refused to let him see any of his friends after the arrest.

Joe's school performance and effort were poor. Joe probably had a mild learning disability, but a recent psychoeducational evaluation had been inconclusive. Joe's primary problem at school was his acting out. Unfortunately, when Joe got into trouble with a teacher, he was inadvertently rewarded for his disruption. He could effectively avoid the schoolwork that he found so difficult and distasteful by sitting in the assistant principal's office

Personal attribution is the act of placing responsibility for a break from abstention on personal weaknesses and inadequacies. Despite situational factors that may greatly influence their behavior, such as unusually strong peer pressure or the actual addictive properties of the drug, people blame themselves for using substances again after they have decided to quit. The feelings of loss of control, failure, and guilt that result from both of these cognitive processes can lead abstainers to turn again to substances in an effort to cope, to alleviate their negative feelings, and to engage in behaviors consistent and congruent with their self-concept.

Effective child and adolescent drug prevention and intervention must address many of these fundamental contributing factors to be successful (August, Realmuto, Winters, & Hektner, 2001; Kosterman et al., 2000). The most effective interventions do attend to underlying problems, skills deficiencies, and systemic problem deficiencies (such as poor family life, lack of school programs) that are core to successful intervention and prevention programs.

"listening to stupid stories." Joe was doing so poorly at school and misbehaving w...
frequency that his stepfather threatened to send him to a strict boarding school un...
behavior improved. Joe said that would be fine with him because he had heard that the
work was easier there. His stepfather's threat to cut his hair short was the only consequence
he seemed concerned about.

Joe primarily used marijuana, which did not change during the 2 months he was in
counseling. We don't know whether Joe experimented with more powerful substances
because he showed a great deal of resistance to coming to counseling and seemed very disinterested in changing himself, although he did want his stepfather to move out. Joe was a
frustrated and angry adolescent who resented his parents and received little direction or consistent structure from them. He was unsure of their expectations, hated school, felt isolated from
his friends, and could see no solution to his problems. He directed his anxiety and poor self-
esteem inward and acted out by skipping school, talking back to his teachers, or roaming the
streets with his friends.

Like many other young people, Joe faced difficult challenges in life and had few
resources for coping with them. He had never learned to delay gratification, he did not know
how to relate to others in a healthy and positive way, he received no consistent discipline and
failed to develop a sense of responsibility for his actions, and he felt mistreated and betrayed
by the school and by his parents. Drug use was simply a means for Joe to escape from the
problems that troubled him so much.

Joe's parents did not accept that his difficulties might be symptomatic of larger family
problems. They refused to enter family therapy and eventually withdrew Joe from counseling.

SOME CONSEQUENCES OF SUBSTANCE USE

The long-term consequences of substance use require additional research, but some of the
physiological and psychosocial consequences are clear. Examples of each are briefly presented here.

Physiological Consequences

The physiological consequences of drug use vary with the drug. Most substances (alcohol, nicotine, marijuana, narcotics, hallucinogens) have relatively immediate physical
effects with alterations in one's sense of reality, judgment, and sensory perceptions.
These effects are caused by interference with the normal functioning of the central

nervous system. The effects may be felt for hours (as with alcohol) or for days (as with marijuana). Part of the difficulty with communicating the physiological risks of substance use to young people is that not all substances have severe or immediate consequences. Although marijuana impairs perception and judgment, for example, it is not physiologically addictive when it is used in moderation (although its ability to become psychosocially addictive is quite high). Focusing exclusively on the short-term negative effects of marijuana actually reduces the perceived truthfulness and therefore the effectiveness of the helper.

Although short-term feelings associated with use of a substance are obvious, the long-term consequences of drugs are more severe. In the United States, alcohol is a factor in approximately half of all adolescent deaths from motor vehicle crashes, and long-term alcohol misuse is associated with liver disease, cancer, cardiovascular disease, and neurological damage (NCCDPHP, 2000). One of the most troublesome effects of marijuana smoking is impairment in processing newly learned material and storing it for future use (Ameri, 1999). Like tobacco, marijuana use also has adverse respiratory effects: chronic cough, recurrent bronchitis, and irritation of the respiratory tract (Lynskey & Hall, 2000).

Physiologically addictive substances (cocaine, crack, heroin, other narcotics) used over a long time can cause severe impairment of the nervous system and internal organs. Addiction is typically defined as a physiological state in which the body needs increased amounts of a substance to maintain homeostasis (physiological balance). Users become tolerant of a drug and need increasing amounts of it to achieve the desired effect. Withdrawal is a painful physical experience that occurs when the drug is withheld from the system and the body reacts. When the use of substances results in tolerance and withdrawal processes, treatment often includes inpatient detoxification because physical dependence on the drug needs to be eliminated for behavioral and psychological interventions to be effective.

Psychosocial Consequences

Typically, drug use during childhood and adolescence leads to more serious problems in early adulthood. Early and risky sexual involvement, failure to pursue educational opportunities, early entrance into the workforce, and unemployment or underemployment are associated with high levels of drug use (Dishion, Kavanagh, Schneiger, Nelson, & Kaufman, 2002).). Essentially, adolescents enter into adult roles before they are ready, without critical life skills, leading to even poorer outcomes for themselves and their offspring (Gragg & McWhirter, 2003). Young people who are "stoned" also miss out on important developmental learning necessary to thrive in society. Alcohol use has been linked to physical fights, academic failure, occupational problems, and juvenile criminal behavior (NCCDPHP, 2000). Drug use contributes to HIV/AIDS and to infant morbidity and mortality (NCCDPHP, 2000). Adolescent cigarette smoking is associated with poorer achievement on standardized tests (Jeynes, 2002). Interestingly, moderate use of alcohol in the later teen years tends to increase a young person's sense of being integrated with others, positive self-feelings, and positive affect, while reducing loneliness and self-derogation (Shedler & Block, 1990). But heavy use of more serious drugs (e.g., intravenous drugs, cocaine-based derivatives such as crack, methamphetamines) during adolescence increases loneliness, depression, and suicide ideation and decreases social support (Newcomb & Bentler, 1989).

SPECIFIC INTERVENTION STRATEGIES FOCUSED ON DRUG USE

School Intervention Programs

Prevention programs are a common form of drug use intervention because many young people have not yet experimented with drugs or alcohol. In addition, treatment to deal with the use of tobacco and alcohol as gateway drugs is also considered prevention for use of other drugs. Because some children experiment with drugs early, universal and indicated prevention programs should begin in the early school grades, commensurate with the prevention–intervention framework we present in Chapter 12. The goals of drug use prevention programs generally have two goals: to delay age of first use and to reduce the use of gateway substances. Delaying the age of initial drug use is associated with better outcomes in nearly all indices: social, academic, and economical (Kosterman et al., 2000). Exposure to prevention programs is significantly related to reduced susceptibility of gateway substances such as tobacco (Huang et al., 2000) although some research (Wiehe, Garrison, Christakis, Ebel, & Rivera, 2005) suggests that there is little evidence to support that prevention programs reduce smoking among youth. Nevertheless, the role of schools in prevention programs is extensive and varied (August et al., 2001; Botvin, Schinke, & Orlandi, 1995; Dishion et al., 2002; Durlak, 1995; Huang et al., 2000).

Some school intervention programs provide alternative activities, such as adventurous recreational activities and service-related community projects. Others provide better opportunities for drug education, increase teachers' awareness of drug use, provide more drug counseling, and support law enforcement efforts to limit drugs on the school campus. Some schools enlist family and community organizations. Indeed, the most successful programs are ecological in nature; they include work to strengthen the relationships between families, schools, and communities (e.g., August et al., 2001; Dishion et al., 2002).

Family Interventions

Inconsistent parents who do not monitor their children's activities contribute to high risk for drug use (Dishion et al., 2002). Thus efforts targeting parents' management practices and family norms regarding adolescent substance use are promising for preventing early initiation of substance use (Kosterman et al., 2000). Parent training in improving monitoring of their children is particularly important. In Chapter 15 we review a variety of examples of family interventions.

Community Intervention Programs

Most juvenile programs are patterned on the traditional drug-free treatment models developed for adults in the 1960s, but programs in the later part of the 1990s began to respond more to the developmental needs of youth. Although more research is needed to demonstrate the efficacy of such interventions, programs tailored to youth have demonstrated promise in reducing adolescent drug use (Hser et al., 2001). A serious shortage of programs for adolescents is a major problem in most communities. Examples of community intervention programs for youth include the following:

- Drug-free programs offer outpatient counseling and use no medication. Some offer drop-in services; others are organized around activities, such as camping trips or challenge experiences.

- Therapeutic communities are residential programs that utilize a structured environment relying on peer influence and confrontation to change self-destructive values and behavior.
- Psychiatric residential programs are operated by profit-making corporations that operate on a mental health residential rehabilitation model.
- Day-care programs provide alternative schooling, counseling, recreational, and social activities for several hours daily and include greater attention to ecology.
- Aftercare programs incorporate therapeutic elements such as professional contact and participation in self-help groups like Alcoholics Anonymous or Narcotics Anonymous after the young person has been discharged.

Student Assistance Programs

Because of the limited programs for young people, school-based Student Assistance Programs (SAPs) have great advantages. Student assistance programs deal directly with two major problems. First, students involved with alcohol and other substances are hesitant to seek counseling services. Second, the illegal nature of substance use contributes to the reluctance of adolescents to seek assistance and accentuates the denial of problems associated with abuse. The typical SAP has a team that includes representatives from key units in the school and a substance abuse specialist (Moore & Forster, 1993). The composition of this team includes administrators involved in student discipline, school counselors, and faculty representatives. SAPs have a structure and process for identifying substance-abusing students, a network to community resources that provide treatment and recovery interventions, and a reentry program that includes case management and follow-up for students returning to school after treatment.

One particularly important component of follow-up is the school recovery support group. The type of support received when a young person leaves a treatment center and reenters the "real world" is extremely important in preventing relapse. On average, teens who take a leave of absence from school for drug treatment are faced with pressure to use drugs again within the first 20 minutes of returning to school (Hanson & Peterson, 1993). The recovery support group provides an opportunity for students to discuss emotional difficulties of being clean and sober. Because they include students who are "working a program," they accentuate a prosocial peer cluster. In fact, it is detrimental to a school recovery support group to include students who are not actively engaged in their own recovery. Other types of group counseling should be available to drug-using adolescents who choose not to be committed to a drug-free lifestyle.

SPECIFIC INTERVENTION: MOTIVATIONAL INTERVIEWING

Motivational interviewing (MI) is a counseling approach that has been applied to drug and alcohol use problems, is well supported by research, and includes the core components of best practices (Millers & Rollnick, 2002). Using the "Stages of Change" metatheory proposed by Prochaska and DiClemente (1983, 1986), MI is based on the idea that people proceed through a process of preparing to make a change before actually doing so. Motivational interviewing helps to "motivate" people to both desire and prepare for making a life change. The assumptions of MI are that people who are abusing alcohol or drugs will not change their behavior (that is, quit) unless they are ready. Thus intervention focuses on helping the individual realize that the negative consequences outweigh the positive effects of drug use and understand how the costs are greater than the benefits. Thus, instead of the confrontational approach traditional in drug and alcohol intervention, MI provides people with personalized feedback and focuses on pointing out discrepancies and inconsistencies in people's self-view with their actual behavior. The counselor is always supportive throughout the process. Studies (e.g., Stephens, 2001) indicate that MI is effective in reducing adolescent smoking by increasing adolescents' motivation to change and by increasing their interest in participating in smoking cessation programs compared to students who received a school-based tobacco education group intervention (Stephens, 2001). In one randomized study, MI reduced young people's use of cigarettes, alcohol, and marijuana, with greater reductions among heavier users of these substances. Reduction in marijuana use was also greater among teenagers considered high risk according to other criteria (McCambridge & Strang, 2004).

Relying on the Prochaska and DiClemente (1983) stages of change model, MI is designed to motivate people to progress along the change process, regardless of where they are in the process. The stages of change suggests that people change when they are ready and that the change process is dynamic: People move through established stages from one to the other, but they also can move in and out of stages depending on a variety of circumstances and the specific nature of the problem. Therefore, intervention helps people progress through the stages and develop their readiness to change, and it provides the skills needed to effect and maintain change.

Prochaska and DiClemente (1983) describe the stages as follows:

- *Precontemplation.* Example: Not considering quitting drug or alcohol use.
- *Contemplation.* Example: Considering quitting within a specific time frame, such as within the next month.
- *Preparation.* Example: Characterized by making active plans and attempts to quit drug or alcohol use, sometimes characterized by following through with at least one quit attempt.
- *Action.* Example: Being engaged in and actively involved in treatment.
- *Maintenance.* Example: Typically defined as maintaining abstinence for a specific time period after treatment.

These stages of change describe the discrete steps in the process of an individual's intentional behavior change during treatment. Assessment of where people are along this sequence may also help to monitor and guide substance use treatment and prevention planning in adults and in adolescents (Annis, Schober, & Kelly, 1996; Prochaska & DiClemente, 1983, 1986, 1992; Prochaska, Velicer, DiClemente, & Fava, 1988; Werch & DiClemente, 1994). The appropriateness and potential impact of any given intervention is contingent upon the young person's readiness to change. For example, the clinically appropriate response to a relapse is qualitatively different when an adolescent is in an initial stage of the change process (that is, internally more at the preparation stage) than at the final stage (maintenance). Fundamentally, interventions designed to enhance readiness to change may be necessary before people engage in and benefit from other active treatment strategies (Freeman & Dolan, 2001). For example, young people in the preparation stage were 25 times more likely to quit smoking than those in the precontemplation or contemplation stages (Dino, Kamal, Horn, Kalsekar, & Fernandes, 2004).

Motivational interviewing includes core intervention components, and one MI-like system referred to as FRAMES provides a good model. Each letter stands for one of the following important, but not sequential, aspects of counseling:

- Feedback of personal status allows the counselor to simply reflect back behavior to an individual without judgment or pressure to change. Sometimes showing a mirror to a client can be very powerful.
- Responsibility for change is an emphasis that keeps counseling focused on the choices, consequences, and personal responsibility of the adolescent for changing and reduces focus on external excuses that adolescents may make for engaging in behaviors that they have chosen.
- Advice to change allows the counselor to simply suggest that the adolescent may be much better off if he or she considers and follows through with a behavior change. Advice always comes after developing a trusting relationship with the client.
- Menu of change options allows counselors to suggest treatment alternatives to teens and to parents. As opposed to narrowing options, this method lets adolescents and families choose what they believe will work for them at any given time. Providing a menu of treatment options is central to the idea of allowing adolescents and families to make choices about the treatment they receive.
- Empathetic counselor style is something that occurs from the very outset of counseling and highlights the importance of accepting people where they are, being nonjudgmental about their behavior, and accepting them as people who are struggling. Acceptance facilitates change, and skillful reflective listening is a powerful intervention for understanding clients and for helping them to feel heard.
- Self-efficacy for change means that adolescents develop the skills needed to quit or reduce use, find and enter into more positive social and support environments, and develop confidence that they can quit.

Some of the fundamental principles of MI are well integrated into the FRAMES list. Expressing empathy is paramount. Helping clients develop discrepancies is also critical. This involves helping clients see for themselves the consequences of their actions, and that the consequences of their actions are often in conflict with stated goals. By pointing out discrepancies, clients present their own arguments for change rather than the counselor doing it for them as is more common in traditional interventions. Avoiding argumentation is important because arguments are counterproductive. Defending a position (e.g., "Abstinence is the only way to improve your life!") nearly always breeds defensiveness in clients and enhances their resistance to change. Rolling with resistance means that instead of "boxing with" clients (that is, trying to get clients to see the counselor's point of view and entering into a power struggle with clients) it is best to "dance with" clients (that is, see their resistance as a coping strategy, which suggests that clients have some important strengths that you can build on; Miller & Rollnick, 2002). Finally, supporting self-efficacy means communicating belief in clients' ability to change. Providing clients with hope and with a range of available behavioral alternatives that they might use to act differently is a powerful motivator. Supporting self-efficacy means to communicate clearly to clients that responsibility for personal change rests solely within them and that they have the capacity to make the change.

Motivational interviewing meets the core components of best intervention practices. It is multimodal. It is well adapted to include individual counseling, can be applied to family counseling (e.g., Stormshak & Dishion, 2002), can involve peers in the treatment process, and is sensitive to cultural and individual differences. Motivational interviewing also highlights the notion of perceived choice. Adolescents make their own decisions about change, and interventions are based on where an adolescent is along the change path. Using the stage model framework, therapeutic interventions at each stage incorporate stage-appropriate strategies to motivate and prepare the adolescent for the next stage. These interventions increase the adolescent's intrinsic sense of choice throughout treatment. Motivational interviewing is also sensitive to individual, cultural, and ethnic group differences. This is essential because studies show that the reasons adolescents use drugs vary according to their ethnicity. Youth of color may have a higher risk of posttreatment relapse due to the greater number of environmental and contextual risk factors they face (e.g., possibly greater overall presence and availability of drugs within some communities). Motivational interviewing accounts for potential cultural and environmental differences and is flexible enough to integrate specific risk and protective factors. Fundamentally, MI is very respectful of clients' worldview, helps clients to identify their own strengths, and supports their own decisions of what changes to make and when. Similar to the solution-focused brief therapy model we presented in Chapter 7, we encourage you to read more about MI as an effective approach to working with adolescents who have a drug or alcohol problem.

CONCLUSION

Drugs and alcohol are widely used, and their abuse imposes great social, economic, and personal costs on individuals, communities, and society as a whole. The most effective prevention strategies involve schools and families, and treatment is most effective when families, schools, and the community collaborate. Understanding and attending to the influence and attitudes of the peer cluster are critical for both deterring and treating the problems caused by drug use. Only by helping young people to understand themselves, their motives and coping strategies, and their responsibility for their actions and for creating change in their own lives will the negative influences of alcohol and drug use among adolescents be diminished.

CHAPTER 9

Teenage Pregnancy and Risky Sexual Behavior

▲ *A young girl-woman, without education,*
without resources, stressed and depressed,
rears her baby alone and
bends like the poplar.

Gentle summer rains nourish the soil . . . but
where do the poplars and the waters meet?

CHAPTER OUTLINE

Problems related to adolescent sexual activity are broad-ranging and complex, including pregnancy, abortion, sexual identity difficulties, human immunodeficiency virus (HIV), acquired immunodeficiency syndrome (AIDS), other sexually transmitted diseases (STDs), childhood molestation and incest, and sex-related violence. No one chapter can fully attend to the interpersonal, psychological, and social implications of these issues. We focus on two critical problems related to a young person's sexuality, sexual development, and sexual activity: the problem of "babies having babies" and HIV/AIDS and other STDs.

More specifically, in this chapter we discuss (a) the incidence and frequency of teenage sexual behavior and teenage pregnancy, (b) factors associated with teen pregnancy, (c) the consequences of teen pregnancy, (d) incidence of AIDS and HIV among teens, and (e) prevention and treatment strategies.

THE SCOPE OF THE PROBLEM

After steady increases in the 1980s, teen pregnancy and birthrates have declined in the United States since the mid-1990s (National Campaign to Prevent Teen Pregnancy, 2001). This decline is attributed to decreased sexual activity and increased use of contraceptives (Ventura, Martin, Curtin, Mathews, & Park, 2000). Teen birthrates are now at their lowest recorded level ever (National Campaign to Prevent Teen Pregnancy, 2001). Overall sexual experience decreased 11% among high school students between 1991 and 1997, except among female and Latino students (Centers for Disease Control and Prevention [CDCP], 1998b). Even with the reported decreases, 6 out of 10 teens have sex by the time they graduate from high school, 1 in 5 report having sexual intercourse before age 15 (National Campaign to Prevent Teen Pregnancy/Child Trends, 2005), and more than 1 in 3 teenage girls get pregnant before age 20 (National Campaign to Prevent Teen Pregnancy, 2005).

Even with recent declines, the United States still has the highest teen pregnancy and birthrates among comparable industrialized nations: twice as high as Great Britain and 10 times higher than the Netherlands (National Campaign to Prevent Teen Pregnancy, 2001). The United States has higher teen pregnancy rates than at least 50 developing nations (McDevitt, 1996). In countries with lower teen pregnancy rates, contraceptive services are confidential, widely available, and very inexpensive or free (Brown & Eisenberg, 1995). Approximately 78% of teen pregnancies are unplanned (Alan Guttmacher Institute [AGI], 1999), with childbirths among unmarried girls higher among African Americans than European Americans (Dixon, Schoonmaker, & Philliber, 2000).

Eight in 10 girls and 7 in 10 boys are sexually inexperienced at age 15—so most very young teens have not had intercourse (AGI, 1999). By the time they graduate from high school, however, about two thirds of all students have had intercourse. The younger women are when they first have intercourse, the more likely they are to have had involuntary or unwanted first sex (National Campaign to Prevent Teen Pregnancy, 2001). Regular use of alcohol, cigarettes, and marijuana by 14- and 15-year-olds is also related to their engagement in sexual intercourse (AGI, 1994). According to the Youth Surveillance Survey by the CDCP (2002), among the 33.4% of currently sexually active students nationwide, 25.6% had used alcohol or drugs at their last sexual intercourse. Male students (31%) were significantly more likely than female students (21%) to have used alcohol or drugs at their last sexual intercourse. Overall, European American and Latino students (28% and 24%, respectively) were significantly more likely than African American students (18%) to have used alcohol or drugs at their last sexual intercourse (CDCP, 2002).

Although contraceptives can prevent pregnancy, they can be complicated to use and difficult and expensive to obtain. They may also seem unnecessary to teenagers, even though a sexually active teenage girl who does not use contraceptives has a 90% chance of becoming pregnant within one year (AGI, 1999). Teen girls use contraceptives much more sporadically than older women (AGI, 1999). Teenage contraceptive use at first intercourse rose from 48% to 65% during the 1980s, mostly due to the doubling in condom use. By 1995 contraceptive use at first intercourse reached 78% (AGI, 1999). However, more than 1 in 5 students failed to use condoms at last sexual intercourse, leaving them at risk for pregnancy and sexually transmitted diseases (Kann et al., 1998). Meanwhile, consistent contraceptive use has been significantly related to factors such as high academic expectations, good relationships with both parents, lower rates of involvement in delinquency and substance use, lower association with deviant peers, and for males, more frequent attendance of religious services (Costa, Jessor, Fortenberry, & Donovan, 1996).

About 33% of students in grades 9 through 12 nationwide reported that they were currently sexually active (CDCP, 2002), and more than 40% reported that they had not used a condom during last sexual intercourse. Male African American students were more likely to report condom use than European American or Latino students. Female and European American students reported birth control pill use more than male, Latino, and African American students. Teenage women would experience an estimated 385,800 additional unintended pregnancies annually if publicly subsidized contraceptive services were not available; therefore, publicly funded contraceptive services annually avert about 154,700 teen births, 183,300 abortions, and 47,800 miscarriages or spontaneous abortions every year (Forrest & Samara, 1996).

The response of adolescents to pregnancy is changing as well. The teen abortion rate in the United States declined by 21% between 1991 and 1995, and more teens chose to give birth rather than to terminate their pregnancies (Henshaw, 1998). Nonetheless, teenagers receive more than 25% of all the abortions performed in the United States, giving the United States the highest rate of teen abortion among developed, industrialized countries (Brown & Eisenberg, 1995). In addition, formal adoption among teens has declined sharply in recent decades, with less than 1% placing their children for adoption (Child Trends, Inc., 1996). Children of teens in Latino, African American, and Native American families are often parented or informally adopted by a member of the extended family. Current trends also suggest that adolescent girls would rather have an abortion than carry an unwanted pregnancy to term and relinquish the baby for adoption.

The rise in adolescent sexual activity and subsequent pregnancies, abortions, and births that occurred up until the mid-1990s has been attributed to a variety of factors. We review these next.

PRECURSORS OF TEEN PREGNANCY: COMMON BACKGROUND CHARACTERISTICS

Family and social issues as well as psychological and interpersonal characteristics contribute to teen pregnancy. In this section we discuss (a) issues related to adolescent development; (b) antecedent characteristics that set the stage for teen pregnancy; (c) interpersonal influences, such as peer relationships and family dynamics; and (d) the media.

Adolescent Development

In view of the normal challenges of adolescence, it is not surprising that many teens are involved in sexual activity or that pregnancy so frequently results. One of the primary ways in which adolescents attempt to negotiate the transition from childhood to adulthood is through sexual activity. Even though more than 80% of teenage parents never expected or wanted to conceive a child, many teens see sexual activity as a way to develop adult identity (Melchert & Burnett, 1990; Musick, 1993). Teens look to the opposite sex for validation and approval. Sexual behavior also provides a means of challenging parents on the way toward independence (Musick, 1993).

Adolescence is an important time in the formation of sexual identity. Experimentation with sex is often a part of the learning experience. Interestingly, young people engaging in same-sex activity often do not identify as gay or lesbian. One study of male adolescents who reported same-sex intercourse found that only 54% identified themselves as gay (Ryan & Futterman, 1998). Models of gay or lesbian identity development characterize the process of developing a positive gay, lesbian, or bisexual (GLB) identity as a series of nonlinear and potentially reoccurring stages (Fassinger, 2000; E. H. McWhirter, 1994; O'Connor, 1992). For GLB teens of color, the process of developing a positive ethnic identity may conflict with the development of a positive sexual identity. GLB adolescents confront the task of forming a stigmatized identity just at a time when sameness and affiliation with peers are very important, and they may withdraw from their peers, stifle expression of their feelings and experiences, or develop a false identity. All of these strategies create anxiety. Not surprisingly, drug use, running away, family rejection, and risky sex are significant problems among GLB adolescents.

Preparation for career, marriage or partnership, and family life is part of this developmental period for all adolescents, and sexual activity serves as a way for young people to test these future roles. When an unwanted pregnancy occurs, the developmental process is accelerated. Adolescents must cope immediately with adult roles: parenthood, finding a job, and dealing with social isolation and loneliness. In many cases they become dependent on public aid for survival. For many girls, pregnancy limits life options. However, if already restricted in opportunities, having a child may not alter their beliefs about options.

Antecedent Characteristics

Personal and demographic characteristics place teens at risk for premature pregnancy. Higher self-esteem decreases the risk of pregnancy for Latino and African American teens (Berry et al., 2000), but delinquent activity and alcohol use often precede teen pregnancy (Hockaday, Crase, Shelley, & Stockdale, 2000). Among urban African American girls, living in a more disorganized neighborhood, having low school expectations, holding deviant values, being a gang member, and engaging in early status offenses are the greatest risk factors for sexual activity. For these girls pregnancy may represent a source of gratification and independence (Lanctot & Smith, 2001). Pregnant African American girls are proportionally more likely to participate in status offenses than their sexually active but nonpregnant peers (Berry et al., 2000). Teens at risk for pregnancy are also likely to reject social norms, to have limited knowledge of their own physiology, to have difficulty using information about birth control, to be biologically mature, and to be less religious (Brown & Eisenberg, 1995; Haveman & Wolfe, 1994). Finally, a young woman's socioeconomic status (Berry et al., 2000), perception of opportunity, and educational expectations are crucial determinants of pregnancy (Hockaday et al., 2000; National Campaign to Prevent Teen Pregnancy, 2001).

Teens born to poor and less-educated teenage parents are more likely to bear children during adolescence (Berry et al., 2000; Haveman & Wolfe, 1994; National Campaign to Prevent Pregnancy, 2001). Lower educational and career opportunities and coming from a single-parent family or from a family with marital strife and instability also increase risk. School dropouts are more likely to start sexual activity earlier, fail to use contraception, become pregnant, and give birth (Brewster, Cooksey, Guilkey, & Rindfuss, 1998; Darroch, Landry, & Oslak, 1999; Manlove, 1998). Teens who give birth are much more likely to come from poor or low-income families (83%) than teenagers who have abortions (61%) or teenagers in general (38%; AGI, 1999). Finally, early childbearing is associated with conduct disorder as well as with lower IQ, lower educational attainment, and lower SES (Jaffee, 2002).

Interpersonal Influences

A teen's relationship with his or her parents is associated with adolescent pregnancy. Perceptions of high levels of warmth, love, caring, and connection with parents, as well as parental disapproval of teen sex, have been associated with delay of sexual activity among teenagers (Resnick et al., 1998). A close mother–daughter relationship, in particular,

> ▲ Box 9.1
> ### Daddy's Girl
> When 16-year-old Susan and her father came for counseling to work on their relationship, she appeared sullen, depressed, and angry. When I met with her alone, she explained that her father had tricked her into coming by telling her he was taking her shopping. She confided that she was pregnant, that her father did not know, and that she hadn't been able to hold down food for three straight days. Susan's mother had "run off years ago." Susan reported that she had had one abortion already and was very reluctant to have another one. When I saw her father alone, he told me that he knew she was pregnant—"Well, that's why I brought her to you." He emphasized several times, "I'm a hundred percent behind her. I support Susan all the way." He told her the same thing when the two were brought together and she acknowledged her pregnancy. In the same breath he told her, "The decision is totally up to you. But, of course, if you decide not to get an abortion, you'll have to live somewhere else."
>
> Susan did not show up for her next appointment. She sounded tearful when she answered the phone.
>
> "Couldn't you make it in today?" I asked.
>
> "No, I'm sick. Well . . . I had an abortion this morning."
>
> Despite repeated calls and letters to her father, he would not bring her in for additional counseling. So far as her "supportive" father was concerned, Susan no longer had a problem.

encourages girls to turn to their mothers for nurturance. Communication between mother and daughter about sexual issues, feelings, and behaviors can significantly help daughters learn and practice responsible sexual behavior. Girls who are close to their mothers are more likely to abstain from sex or to practice birth control (Dittus & Jaccard, 2000; Levin, Whitaker, Miller, & May, 1999). A good mother–daughter relationship provides a girl with a model for responsible sexual behavior and for maintaining a good relationship with a future partner (Apter, 1990).

Families characterized by poor interpersonal relationships, ineffective communication, and limited problem-solving skills typically encourage teens to turn to peers, which often leads to risky behavior and irresponsibility. In one study, Cowley and Tillman (2001) found that boyfriends' attitudes toward having children was the only significant predictor of teenage girls' attitudes about pregnancy. Peers can provide support, fairly clear norms, and the structure that most adolescents want and, along with the media, are a primary source of information about sex. Unfortunately, adolescents who confidently share information may lack knowledge and may encourage premature and irresponsible sexual decisions.

Finally, once a girl becomes pregnant, her mother usually has the most influence on the outcome, but not always (see Box 9.1). Often the mother pressures her pregnant daughter to keep the child. In this case, the relationships between mother, daughter, and baby tend to become confused, with the new grandmother taking on primary responsibility for the infant. Although these teen mothers may indeed have family support, the decision to keep the baby in the family usually restricts their educational and occupational attainment (Haveman & Wolfe, 1994). Often this choice places the babies in a similar situation of restricted future options, and the cycle of "babies having babies" is perpetuated.

Media Influences

Young people are bombarded with sexual messages and images in the media that reflect premature, risky, and irresponsible sexual behavior. More than two thirds of the programming on television has some form of sexual content (Brown, Halpern, & L'Engle, 2005). The effect of television on teenagers' sexual behavior increases as a teenager watches more sexual content. The impact on those teens in the 90th percentile of viewing sex on TV was twice as high as on those teens in the 10th percentile (RAND Corporation, 2004). In addition, the CDCP (2001) found that nearly 40% of students watch television for more than 3 hours per day during an average school day, with male, African American, and Latino students having the highest rates of television viewing. Rock music videos, rap music, cable channels, and movies are even more sexually explicit than television. Virtually every R-rated movie contains at least one nude scene with some containing as many as 15 instances of sexual intercourse in less than 2 hours (DuRant et al., 1997). Finally, children have easy access to pornography on the Internet. Children's chat rooms have linked sexual perpetrators to their victims. Among young people 10 to 17 years of age who regularly use the Internet, one fourth had encountered unwanted pornography and one fifth had been exposed to unwanted sexual solicitations or approaches (Finkelhor, Mitchell, & Wolak, 2000). Parental monitoring of children's Internet use is critical; however, sexually explicit websites may be entered even when there are no indicators of sexual content at that link.

Running parallel to media inundated with sexual content is a reluctance to depict contraception use. For instance, in 2001 only Fox, CBS, and NBC permitted condom advertising, which was largely restricted to late night television (Wilke, 2001). These policies are far more conservative than the average American. In a national random survey of adults, 60% believed that cigarettes and 47% believed that hard liquor should not be advertised on television, whereas only 25% believed that condoms should not be advertised (Princeton Survey Research Associates, 2001). Nearly 40% of the sample believed that condom advertising should be permitted throughout daytime and nighttime television.

Interestingly, 95% of U.S. adults and 85% of U.S. teenagers think children and teenagers should receive a strong societal message that they should abstain from sex until after high school, and nearly 60% of U.S. adults think sexually active teenagers should have access to contraception (Princeton Survey Research Associates, 1997). Just as the mass media can encourage risky sexual behavior, it has an undeniable potential for presenting helpful and healthy information. For example, more than half of the high school students in a national survey reported that they had learned about birth control, contraception, or preventing pregnancy from television; almost 66% of the girls and 40% of the boys said they had learned about these topics from magazines (Sutton, Brown, Wilson, & Klein, 2002).

CONSEQUENCES OF EARLY CHILDBEARING

When a teenage girl becomes pregnant, her physical, social, educational, and career development is significantly altered. An unwanted child has consequences for the mother's socioeconomic status, educational attainment, health, and family development.

Socioeconomic Consequences

A teenage girl who decides to keep her baby is likely to suffer consequences in the form of substandard housing, poor nutrition and health, unemployment or underemployment, an end to her schooling, inadequate career training, and financial dependency (Robinson, Watkins-Ferrell, Davis-Scott, & Ruch-Ross, 1993; Way & Leadbeater, 1999). She is 3 times more likely to live in poverty than women who delay childbirth until age 20 or older, earns half the lifetime income of her counterparts who mother after age 20, and is far more likely to require public assistance (National Organization on Adolescent Pregnancy, Parenting, and Prevention, 1995; Robin Hood Foundation, 1996). Had the teen birthrate not declined during the 1990s, an additional 428,000 children would be living with single mothers and another 400,000 children would be living in poverty than actually did so by 2002 (National Campaign to Prevent Teen Pregnancy, 2005).

Educational Consequences

Teen pregnancy is associated with low achievement scores and limited vocational and educational expectations. Clearly, youth at risk for becoming parents are also at risk for dropping out of school and are more likely to be unemployed or underemployed throughout much of their lives. In recent years, the proportion of teenage mothers with high school diplomas has increased, in large part because many school districts now provide alternative high schools or school programs for student mothers. Although 70% of teenage mothers eventually complete high school, they are much less likely to go on to college (AGI, 1999).

The educational problems faced by adolescent parents are frequently carried over into the next generation. A disproportionate number of the children born to teenagers show more emotional and behavioral problems while growing up (Thomson, Hanson, & McLanahan, 1994; Zill, Morrison, & Coiro, 1993). These children also have more erratic attendance records, poorer school performance, and lower college expectations (Astone & McLanahan, 1991; Moore, Morrison, & Greene, 1997). As might be expected, teen parents' children have been found to have less supportive and stimulating home environments, poorer health, and lower cognitive development (National Campaign to Prevent Teen Pregnancy, 2001).

Health-Related Consequences

Pregnant adolescents commonly experience poor nutrition, poor health, and limited access to and use of health services. One third of pregnant teens receive inadequate prenatal care. Prenatal, perinatal, and postnatal problems are more common among younger than among older mothers, and more of their babies die, likely because younger mothers rarely seek prenatal care in their first trimester. The younger the mother, the higher the incidence of pregnancy-related problems such as anemia, toxemia, infections of the urinary tract, cervical trauma, and premature birth (Advocates for Youth, 1994). Of course, these problems are compounded for teenagers who live in poor socioeconomic conditions. In comparison with older women, younger girls also have problems with premature delivery and are at greater risk of very long labor (American College of Obstetricians and Gynecologists, 1993). The maternal mortality rate for mothers under age 15 is 60% greater than for mothers in their 20s (Advocates for Youth, 1994).

Children of teenage mothers also have serious health problems. Babies born to teen mothers are more likely to have childhood health problems and to be hospitalized than those who are born to mothers in their 20s or older (National Campaign to Prevent Teen Pregnancy, 2001). They are also more likely to be low-birth-weight babies; low-birth-weight babies are more likely to have several developmental problems during adolescence and to have lower IQs at age 20 than comparison children. Girls are more withdrawn, anxious, and depressed, and have more attention problems. Boys grow up to have thought problems (Hack, Youngstrom, Cartar, & colleagues, 2004).

Infant mortality is highest among younger teen mothers, especially African American teen mothers (Ventura, Matthews, & Hamilton, 2002). Low birth weight, congenital problems, and sudden infant death syndrome account for nearly half of infant deaths in the United States (Ventura et al., 2002).

Family Development

Few teen pregnancies actually involve marriage. Of the girls who do marry, nearly a third are divorced within 5 years, compared to 15% among couples who marry later. Most children born to teen mothers will spend at least part of their lives in single-parent homes (AGI, 1994). Indeed, many teenage fathers never acknowledge parenthood. Some of these boys never know that they are fathers, but many do know and are simply unwilling to deal with the responsibilities of parenthood (Arendell, 1995; Kiselica, 1995).

Teenage mothers are at a great disadvantage when they attempt to create a healthy and stimulating environment for their children. They are often forced to work long hours and may have little time to spend with their babies. These problems may be compounded by neglect because teen mothers often know little about what babies need to thrive. Teen mothers experience a great deal of stress, and the potential for child abuse is significant (Becker-Lansen & Rickel, 1995). Boyer and Fine (1992) and Walker (1996) suggest that the high rate of maltreatment inflicted by adolescent mothers on their children is more likely due to their histories as abuse victims rather than their immaturity. In one study, 65% of pregnant and parenting teen mothers reported nonvoluntary sexual activity, and 44% reported having been raped. The average age of first rape was 13.3 years (U.S. Department of Health and Human Services, 1998). Children of adolescent mothers are 83% more likely to become mothers before age 18, 2 to 3 times more likely to run away from home, and more than twice as likely to become victims of abuse and neglect as children of mothers in their 20s or older; and sons of teen mothers are 2.7 times more likely to end up in prison (Robin Hood Foundation, 1996). The challenges that adolescent mothers deal with often result in a lack of optimal development of the baby, which lays a foundation for a continued cycle of teen pregnancy.

Psychosocial adjustment is an important predictor of a variety of outcomes for teen mothers. For example, one longitudinal study found that prenatal socioemotional adjustment (as measured by social competence, self-esteem, depression, anxiety, and attachment to mother) predicted later parenting stress, child abuse potential, and maternal socioemotional functioning, and was also the best predictor of their children's later socioemotional adjustment (Whiteman, Borkowski, Keogh, & Weed, 2001). Finally, Hunt-Morse (2002) found that teenage mothers with higher levels of psychosocial development experienced less parenting stress, reported using fewer dysfunctional parenting practices, and were more confident in their maternal role and in their ability to overcome parenting barriers.

AIDS AND OTHER SEXUALLY TRANSMITTED DISEASES

Sexually transmitted diseases (STDs) have extremely serious health consequences that may be irreversible and, in the case of herpes and AIDS, are incurable. Chlamydia, an infection of the vagina or urinary tract, is the most frequently diagnosed STD among adolescents. Gonorrhea, genital warts, herpes, and syphilis are also common. Approximately 1 in 4 teens contract STDs every year (Kirby, 2001). In a single act of unprotected sex with an infected partner, a teen girl has a 1% risk of acquiring HIV, a 30% risk of getting genital herpes, and a 50% chance of contracting gonorrhea (AGI, 1999). African American teenage girls are 24 times more likely to contract gonorrhea than their European American counterparts (CDCP, 1997).

Each day 54 young people under the age of 20 are infected with HIV. The total number of reported AIDS cases among 13- to 24-year-olds in the United States exceeded 31,000 in the year 2000, and most of those in the 20- to 24-year-old age group were infected during their teens. African American and Latino youth are vastly overrepresented in AIDS cases in the 13- to 19-year-old age group, representing 61% and 21% of new AIDS cases, respectively (Devieux et al., 2005). Young people are most likely to have contracted AIDS via sexual contact with men, with only about 10% of reported cases resulting from intravenous drug injection (CDCP, 2000). Finally, although rates of contracting AIDS are declining overall, there has not been a comparable decline in HIV cases among youth (CDCP, 2002). Forty-six percent of a nationally representative sample of high school students had experienced sexual intercourse, and only 19% reported condom use. One in 6 teenagers have had a sexually transmitted infection (SDI), and half of all new HIV infections in 2001 occurred in those under age 25 (CDCP, National Center for Health Statistics, 2003).

Knowledge regarding STDs is low among teenagers. For example, one survey found that only 12% of teens were aware that STDs infect as many as one fifth of people in the United States, and 42% of teens could not name a single STD other than HIV/AIDS (American Social Health Association, 1995). Even more alarming, in a study of sexually active female adolescents, 81% indicated that they had "never done anything that could give them a chance of getting AIDS," and most believed that their chance of contracting HIV was "very low" (36%) or "nonexistent" (37%). Their reasons for feeling safe included that they were currently monogamous, they believed their partner was safe and faithful, they believed that they were good at choosing partners carefully, they used condoms, and they did not use injection drugs (Overby & Kegeles, 1994). Note that only one of these reasons, using condoms, is a reliable (though not guaranteed) means of reducing risk of HIV transmission.

Teens tend to feel invulnerable to something as catastrophic as AIDS—"It can't happen to me!" or else "Even if I get it, there will be a cure before it affects me." That attitude, coupled with sexual activity, multiple sex partners, and ineffective, sporadic, or no condom use, makes teenagers very vulnerable for contracting HIV/AIDS. Sexually active adolescent gay males are particularly vulnerable to HIV infection (Besner & Spungin, 1995; Cranston, 1991). When adolescents experiment sexually with both male and female partners, teenage boys who experiment with unprotected sex with other males may not see themselves at risk if they do not self-identify as gay, which many do not (Ryan & Futterman, 1998). Research on young men who have sex with men indicates high rates of risky activity. Two studies indicated that 38% to 55% or more of respondents reported unprotected anal intercourse (HIV Epidemiology Program, 1996; Valleroy, MacKellar, & Jacobs, 1996).

INTERVENTION STRATEGIES FOCUSED ON RISKY SEX

For every dollar spent on adolescent pregnancy programs, one cent is spent on primary prevention (Feijoo, 1999). Given the consequences of risky sexual activity among teens, primary prevention requires far greater resources. The U.S. Surgeon General issued a Call to Action in 2001 in which he described the deplorable state of sexual health in the United States and requested nationwide collaboration in providing, among other things, high-quality sex education in schools and communities (Office of the Surgeon General, 2001). In his review of the empirical literature on pregnancy prevention, Kirby (2001) divided prevention programs into three categories: those that focus on the "sexual antecedents" of pregnancy (i.e., sexual attitudes, beliefs, and skills), those that focus on "other antecedents" (i.e., poverty, parental relationships, school failure, depression), and those that address a combination of the two. Programs focused on sexual antecedents are typically referred to as sex education or HIV prevention programs.

Programs focusing on the nonsexual antecedents of teen pregnancy addressed such issues as poverty, school detachment, lack of parental connections, and lack of vocational aspirations. Kirby (2001) categorized these programs into several subgroups: early childhood programs, service learning programs, vocational education programs, and other youth development programs. Although more research is needed, interesting findings are that vocational education programs alone were *not* effective in decreasing sexual activity, pregnancy, or contraceptive use. The most effective nonsexual antecedent programs were service learning programs. That is, engaging young girls and teens in service programs reduced their rate of teen pregnancy. School-based interventions for pregnant and parenting adolescents also significantly decreased the occurrence of repeat births (Key, Barbosa, & Owens, 2001).

Of course, nonsexual antecedent programs contain common elements that address a variety of risky behaviors above and beyond those of a sexual nature. Many of the recommendations for program development that we make throughout this book involve content, attitudes, skills, and processes that are broadly helpful for many at-risk children and adolescents. To avoid redundancy, we leave the discussion of these programs to future chapters (e.g., see Chapter 13).

Children and adolescents from the early school years through high school have been found to benefit enormously from family life education programs that address health, development, information about sexuality, family life stages, family transitions, and so on. Yet many young people receive little systematic information about sexuality from their parents. Many parents are intimidated about the subject, and some possess limited or inadequate information themselves. Many parents appear to be excessively skeptical about birth control methods. For example, only 47% of parents believe that condoms are "very effective" in preventing sexually transmitted diseases. Only 52% believe that the pill prevents pregnancy "almost all the time." When used consistently, the pill has been shown to be 99.9% effective, and condoms are successful 97% of the time (AGI, 2004).

Although sex education is still controversial in some communities, less than 5% of parents excuse their children from sex education classes (Haffner, 1994). Despite sentiments to the contrary, HIV and sex education programs do not increase the frequency of sexual activity or hasten the onset of intercourse (Kirby, 2000, 2001; Kirby et al., 1994). The National Campaign to Prevent Teen Pregnancy (2001) reports that many sex and HIV education programs have actually been found to delay the onset of sex, reduce its frequency and number of partners, and increase contraceptive use. An overwhelming majority of Americans support providing sex education in junior and senior high schools. Most parents want students to have information to protect themselves against unplanned pregnancy and STDs and oppose the portion of the federal law that funds abstinence-only-until-marriage education (Advocates for Youth, 1999; Smith, 2000). Of course, teaching young people about contraception while denying them access to it is unlikely to be effective when young people begin to have sex.

Abstinence, although a critical element in prevention programs, cannot be counted on as the major means to reduce unintended pregnancy or HIV/AIDS among teenagers. In fact, programs promoting both abstinence and consistent contraceptive use have demonstrated delay of sexual activity if the information is provided in a culturally specific fashion. Longer-term intervention programs also show more lasting positive affects (National Campaign to Prevent Teen Pregnancy/Child Trends, 2005), especially if they include booster sessions (Pedlow & Carey, 2004). Access to information about human sexuality, reproduction, and birth control is a prerequisite for responsible sexual behavior, and adolescent well-being is optimized when sexual intercourse occurs in the context of a personal commitment based on caring, mutual consent, the exercise of personal responsibility, and includes steps to avoid both STDs and unintended pregnancy.

Sexual antecedent programs have common characteristics (Kirby, 2001). They deliver and consistently reinforce a clear message about abstaining from sexual activity, and if sexually active that condoms and other contraception methods are essential. They focus on reducing risky sexual behavior. They provide basic and accurate information about the risks of teen sexual activity and ways to avoid intercourse or use protection and include activities that address social pressures that influence sexual behavior. Successful programs provide examples of and practice with communication, negotiation, and refusal skills, and they tailor program goals, methods, and materials to the age, sexual experience, and culture of the students. Such programs are based on theoretical approaches that have been demonstrated to influence other health-related behavior as well. They identify specific important sexual antecedents to be targeted, employ teaching methods that involve the participants and personalize the information, last a sufficient length of time, and select teachers or peer leaders who believe in the program and provide them with adequate training (Kirby, 2001). By and large, to avoid negative outcomes people need a variety of skills, such as skills in decision-making, assertiveness, and learning how to regulate intimacy and how to behave in accordance with their personal values and boundaries (Kirby, 2001).

Any skill-building program designed to alter sexual behavior needs to personalize the information so that young people apply it directly and concretely to themselves. Self-understanding aids in personalizing information and increasing motivation. Awareness of the purpose and goals of one's behavior is an extremely important component of self-understanding. Young people at risk for pregnancy need to be encouraged to explore and understand why they are engaging in sexual activity, and especially why they are unwilling to use methods that prevent pregnancy and disease. Such understanding helps the young person make better decisions. Adults who work with young people at risk for pregnancy need to understand these underlying goals and purposes as well because they are in a position to help young people make better decisions. A method to expose these goals and purposes is described in the following section.

SPECIFIC INTERVENTION: AN ADLERIAN MODEL

One of the best models for understanding child and adolescent behavior is found in Alfred Adler's (1930, 1964; Ferguson, 2001; Hoffman, 1994) concepts of social interest, mistaken goals, and purposive behavior. Rudolf Dreikurs (1964, 1967), the foremost interpreter of Adler's ideas as they apply to the American scene, added another concept: the goals of misbehavior. These concepts are useful for understanding and dealing with a wide range of adolescent problems and issues, and we apply them here specifically as a tool for responding to teenagers in the sexual realm (Clark, 1994; Pryor & Tollerud, 1999; Sweeney, 1998). The concepts are also helpful for younger children. Indeed, Adler, and later Dreikurs, developed child guidance clinics that provided education and counseling to families and parents, not infrequently with very young children. Many school counselors use these ideas to assist young children as well.

In the following paragraphs, we first present the general framework of the model, and then we detail its specific application to issues of sexuality. These recommendations are not a substitute for sexual health education but are adjunctive to it.

According to Adler, much individual behavior is directed toward finding a place or position in the group. All young people need a sense of belonging and an arena in which to contribute. Low-risk children find belonging first in their families and later in the school environment with peers and adults. In their interaction with their social environment, they find ways to contribute to the common welfare. These contributions increase their social interest, build their feelings of self-worth, and solidify their sense of belonging. Unfortunately, other young people struggle to belong and are frustrated in their attempts to contribute to the social group. But the need to belong continues, and these youth often behave in ways that are less acceptable in the mistaken belief that a particular action will fulfill a certain social need. These mistaken beliefs contribute to what Dreikurs calls the goals of misbehavior. Negative, antisocial, and self-defeating behavior has an underlying purpose — to allow the individual to fit into the group. One way to help at-risk children is to attend to the underlying purposiveness of their behavior: first, to understand their mistaken goals and to respond more appropriately to them, and second, to reveal to the young people their own underlying goals and the purposiveness of their actions.

Purposiveness of Behavior

Purpose is not the same as cause. Cause is past-oriented; purpose is future-oriented. Cause implies a need to search through past history to identify what event, person, or situation brought about the child's present behavior. It also implies that the individual has no agency or influence over his or her own behavior. Purposiveness reflects the goals the youth wants to achieve and the consequences he or she anticipates. In this sense, the young person's behavior is a means to an end and is based on his or her perceptions of reality. Young people behave in ways that they believe will lead to desirable consequences and help them avoid unpleasant ones. Purpose operates in the present and looks toward the future, toward the outcome of behavior, and therefore is more directly open to intervention. The purpose of adolescent sexual activity has been associated with an underlying tendency to nonconformity; Lanctot and Smith (2001) suggest that girls are more likely to respond to this tendency by being self-destructive rather than destructive to others. Adolescent pregnancy may be considered self-destructive behavior, especially when prenatal care is neglected (Lanctot & Smith, 2001).

Goals of Misbehavior

In the Adler/Dreikurs model, a young person's misbehavior may be designed to achieve one or more of four goals: (a) attention (the child wants service and attention), (b) power (the child wants to be boss), (c) revenge (the child desires to hurt others), and (d) inadequacy or assumed disability (the child wants to be left alone). Although young people usually do not think about their behavior in these terms, they do see their actions as logical. Whether they seek attention, attempt to assert power, take revenge, or capitalize on their inadequacy, the corresponding misbehavior is designed to get special recognition. Their behavior, regardless of their goal, results from the belief that this is the most effective way to function in the group, which includes the family and the peer cluster.

Attention.   When children do not achieve acceptance and belonging through useful contributions to the family, they may seek inclusion through attention. At first they may seek attention through socially acceptable means. If these efforts are unsuccessful, they may try any of a vast array of negative behaviors calculated to get attention. The purpose of such attention-getting mechanisms (AGMs) is to engage the adult. The young person's underlying goal is to get adults to pay attention. The adult's intervention reinforces the young person's desire for attention, because it's better to be punished than to be ignored.

Attention-getting behaviors are usually negative, but overly cooperative behavior may also be a bid for special attention. It is sometimes difficult to distinguish between behavior that stems from a genuine willingness to be helpful and behavior that is aimed primarily at getting attention. If the youth's behavior seems directed to becoming the best or better than the other children (the teacher's pet), he or she is probably motivated by a desire for attention. Children and adolescents need to be able to derive satisfaction from performing positive, cooperative behaviors rather than simply from the reinforcement that follows. Consider an adolescent girl who gains satisfaction from her prosocial acts only when adults notice them. If her siblings (at home) and classmates (at school) are more successful at gaining adults' attention, she may try to gain attention by being the worst among her peers. Many youth behave negatively because the positive roles they really want are already "taken."

Recognizing when attention is the goal of misbehavior is not simple, but it may be inferred when the adult's initial reaction to the behavior is annoyance, irritation, or surface anger, and the child responds to correction by temporarily stopping the disturbing action. Essentially, the scolding, coaxing, helping, reminding, and so forth provide the desired attention, so the behavior stops—temporarily. Understanding the purpose of irresponsible sexual behavior is a more complex task because the behavior may be aimed not only at adults but at peers as well. In some cases, AGMs evoke attention and concern from permissive or indifferent parents. In other cases, AGMs derive from a desire for attention and affection from peers or a specific peer. Sometimes the AGM is directed toward the idealized infant in the hope that the baby may fill an emotional gap left by rejecting parents or the romantic partner. In each instance, the need to belong, to feel needed, to be loved, or to feel increased self-esteem underlies the AGMs.

As part of a research project, one of the authors was debriefing eighth-grade students after they filled out questionnaires about stress. One student, a 12-year-old eighth-grader, offered shyly, "Well, I don't have a boyfriend, but I met a boy at the mall and I let him put it in me. I know that's how you get a baby, but he said he took it out in time. I hope he's gonna meet me there again." In the course of a subsequent conversation, it was quickly apparent that she was not interested in physical pleasure, nor did she seem to have romantic notions about babies; she simply wanted to feel special.

Boys exhibit purposiveness and mistaken goals in their sexual behavior in experiencing sexual interaction as a means of gaining affection and attention from girls. Sometimes boys establish desired reputations as their sexual exploits gain the attention of their male peers. In some subgroups, fathering a child increases the boy's status and brings him into what he perceives to be a more mature and powerful stage of development.

Power.   When the goal of misbehavior is power, young people attempt to establish their position in the group by dominating, controlling, and manipulating adults and peers. They demonstrate their control and power by refusing to be commanded and by breaking rules. Many use manipulation to demonstrate to themselves and to the world that they do have power over others. If the adult responds to the power struggle by exerting more control or power to force compliance, the young person becomes even more convinced of the value of power. The goal is less to win the struggle than to get the adult involved in it. Once the adult engages in the battle, the teenager has won, regardless of the outcome.

If the adult's anger goes beyond mere annoyance and if the anger is coupled with feelings of being challenged and provoked, then the young person's goal is probably to gain power. The sentences that run through the adult's mind at this point also provide clues to the nature of this power struggle ("I'll show you who's boss around here." "I'll make you do it." "You can't get away with that."). When the adult behaves in accordance with these thoughts, the adolescent may escalate his or her actions or comply outwardly while subtly sabotaging the adult's efforts. Either way, the teenager wins the power struggle.

The underlying goal of power in sexual acting out may be directed against parents who are inconsistent, too permissive, or too strict. On the surface the young person appears to be expressing independence, but in reality the behavior is designed to establish a position vis-à-vis the parents. Willingness or unwillingness to engage in sex may provide girls and boys with perceived power over others or over a specific partner. Willingness to coerce a girl into unprotected intercourse may be based on the mistaken belief that a subsequent pregnancy would secure the relationship. Boys may use sexual activity to demonstrate independence and power over their parents. With their partner or even someone unknown to them, boys may use sex as a physical expression of domination or control through rape and other forms of sexual assault. Sometimes the boy's domineering attitude and his unwillingness to use a condom are attempts to demonstrate power. Assuming that girls are responsible for contraception and denying fatherhood when pregnancy occurs are other ways in which the young male may express domination and power over others through sexual behavior.

Revenge.   The child who seeks revenge is extremely discouraged and poses the greatest problem. If children have not been able to attain and maintain a desired position by gaining attention or power, they may consider that the only other way to gain attention is to hurt someone. It is as if they conclude, "I can't be liked and I don't have power—but I can be hated." This often violent antagonism provides them with a specific role to play in the group.

Revenge is sought only after a long series of failures has convinced the young person of his or her utter lack of belonging. Revenge is frequently the result of an unrecognized

▲ Box 9.2

Lying for Revenge

Some years ago I was co-conducting a consultation with several teenagers and their families. The model we were using called for a large-group meeting that included both parents and teenagers, in which participants discussed family and school concerns. We then broke into smaller groups, the adults in one group and the young people in another.

After several weekly sessions, a girl who had a particularly stormy relationship with her mother used the large-group session as an opportunity to tell her parents that she thought she was pregnant. Her mother's horror and embarrassment were vividly evident. Later, during the session with peers and siblings, the girl reported that she was not pregnant and currently wasn't even sexually active. Her earlier false self-disclosure, she concluded, was intended to hurt her mother: a clear instance of revenge. In a later family session, this incident became a springboard that enabled us to help her look at the self-defeating aspects of her behavior and to help her family confront their own dysfunction.

problem (depression, severe learning difficulties, conduct disorder) and of unrealistic expectations and pressures by significant adults. The unrecognized problem may prevent the young person from accomplishing a particular task. Assuming negative motives, adults punish the youth for "not trying." Young people are hurt by such encounters and want to hurt back. In taking this position, they are likely to evoke responses that justify the continuation of revenge, and the cycle escalates.

Feelings of intense anger with underlying hurt and shock in response to a young person's behavior indicate to the adult that the goal of misbehavior is probably revenge. The adult may think: "How could he possibly do that to me?" "This kid is just nasty and unlovable." "How could she be so vicious and cruel?" If the adult's response is full of anger, the adolescent will continue trying to get even. If the adult responds with hurt, sadness, and tears, the youth may actually smile (see Box 9.2).

Premature and irresponsible sexual activity is sometimes a way to get back at parents. One of the authors of this book worked with an angry father whose son had dressed in women's makeup and clothing and had sexually explicit pictures taken of himself on the family's front porch in daylight. The son left these photos for his father to find, which achieved the desired effect. Sexual behavior can also be used to obtain revenge on the partner if one feels rejected. The person who acts out sexually may intend to get back at the former partner. So, ultimately, the dynamics of revenge are played out not only within the family but also between partners.

Assumed inadequacy.   Children and teenagers who expect failure rely on their assumed inadequacy to escape participation in the group and family system. They want to be left alone. As long as nothing is expected of them, they can still appear to be members of the group. Some children and adolescents believe that by hiding behind a display of real or imagined inferiority they can avoid even more embarrassing and humiliating experiences. Those who feel inadequate and incapable of functioning will not try, whether their deficiency is real or merely assumed.

This goal poses serious problems for parents, teachers, and counselors because these young people realize that underachievement and lack of effort are the most effective ways to keep adults involved with them. Thus it is convenient for them to continue their lack of effort even when it is no longer necessary. Adults often fail to distinguish between a real lack of ability and a lack of ability that the child or adolescent merely assumes.

Feelings of despair, frustration, and hopelessness in the adult are good signs that the young person is operating on the assumption of inadequacy. Adults should reflect carefully upon the feelings aroused by a young person's misbehavior because whatever they feel is often exactly what the young person intends them to feel. Despair and hopelessness may be what the child wants, but when the adult responds with despair, inadequacy is reinforced. Such responses encourage continued inadequacy.

Assumed inadequacy in the sexual realm may be expressed by lack of assertiveness regarding sexual activity. The term *assumed* suggests that these adolescents have the skills to resist sexual pressure—from a partner or from peers—or to insist on protection if they do engage in sex, but that they do not use these skills. Of course, we know that some young people's inadequacy is not assumed; the lack of skill is real. In such situations the concerned adult can use specific cognitive and behavioral strategies to provide success experiences and reduce the young person's sense of inadequacy. In Chapter 12 we provide a model for building skills, and in Chapter 13 we discuss specific cognitive and behavioral strategies from which young people may benefit.

Summary.   Having reviewed the four goals, we must emphasize that young people are often in pursuit of more than one goal at the same time and that their goals can shift depending on the people with whom they interact. Some young people actually pursue all four goals at one time, a situation that causes parents, counselors, teachers, and other adults a great deal of distress. Some children or teenagers may have one goal at school, another goal with their peers, and still another at home. If the misbehavior is to be understood, the child's actions have to be seen as a whole, as part of the total social environment, not as emanating solely from one situation.

Sexual behavior does not have an underlying negative purpose for all teens. Needs gratification, reinforcement, pleasure, and desire for warmth, closeness, and validation are all components of sexuality. When teens become pregnant, mixed goals are probably the rule rather than the exception. Allie Andrews, for example, appears to use sex to gain attention from boys. Further, lacking a positive position at home, she has progressed from sex-as-attention to sex-as-power to show her stepfather that she counts. Unfortunately, his criticisms and accusations have led her now to use sex to shock and hurt him. She has adopted the goal of revenge (on her stepfather) and uses her sexual behavior, at least partly, as a way of getting back at him.

Among the methods that have proved helpful in efforts to intervene with young people who are struggling with these four mistaken goals are corrective procedures, logical and natural consequences, and encouragement. We describe these techniques in the context of risky sexual behavior; however, they can be used with any kind of misbehavior.

Corrective Procedures

Corrective procedures involve (a) altering adults' responses to adolescents' risky sexual behavior and (b) helping young people to interpret the goals of their sexual activities. Altering the adult's responses (e.g., the parent, teacher, or counselor) begins with identifying the feelings aroused by the youth's behavior (anger, disgust, resentment, despair, and so forth) and then not acting on those feelings. Helping young people interpret their goals is a bit more complex. If you ask them why they didn't use a condom, the response may be an honest "I don't know" or a hindsight rationalization rather than a factual account of motives: "I just finished a period and didn't think I would get pregnant" rather than "At that moment, I didn't care what happened to me, even if I got some disease, I was so lonely." The sensitive counselor or teacher can help young people by proposing some possible goals of their behavior. Such a confrontation can be the first step toward change. To confront the behavior, however, is not to label it ("You're being stupid"). Labeling has no meaning for the young person, does not explain the behavior, and does nothing to change it. Confrontation helps adolescents understand their own motivation and gives them the option of continuing or discontinuing their behavior. Sometimes the behavior loses its appeal once the underlying intention has been brought into the open; other times the young person is able to identify more effective and less harmful ways of getting his or her needs met.

The most useful approaches are tentative, beginning with "Could it be that . . ." or "I was thinking that maybe . . ." All questions must be asked in a nonjudgmental way, and not during an argument. It is not enough to help young people identify their goals; it is important to provide them with alternative and less self-defeating goals. All corrective procedures should be geared toward helping young people choose more constructive goals and behaviors.

Corrective procedures for AGMs.   When the goal of risky sexual behavior is attention, the following questions may be helpful: "Could it be that you want him to see you as more special than other girls, by sleeping with him?" "Do other guys respond differently, say, with more respect or admiration, when they know you've had sex?" Recognize that punishing, giving service, coaxing, and scolding are forms of attention and may only serve to reinforce the negative behavior. Although ignoring the behavior while it occurs is normally a corrective procedure for AGMs, this strategy isn't useful in the case of risky sexual behavior because adults are not typically present. However, if the young person is bragging about his or her sexual escapades, ignoring the behavior in the moment may be the most appropriate response.

Corrective procedures for power.   Interpretive questions for power-seekers might include, "Could it be that you want to show your mother that she isn't in control of you?" or "It seems to me as though you want her to see you as stronger and in charge, as if that will make her think you are more masculine." It is important to recognize and acknowledge that the young person does indeed have power and choices regarding sexual behavior, even though that behavior has consequences. Refrain from engaging in arguments over sexual behavior, and rather than insisting that rules be followed, put energy into being consistent about imposing consequences when rules are broken. Be willing to negotiate on issues where it is possible for you to do so. And, outside of the context of arguments, help the young person identify other means to establish a sense of power in ways that do not pose health risks to him- or herself or to others. This may include broadening the youth's circle of activities and engaging his or her leadership and responsibility skills.

In addition to interpreting goals, provide alternative goals that are less self-defeating. One of the authors worked with an adolescent male client who had been having unprotected sex with an older young woman in his father's garage. He quite readily admitted that part of him wanted to be caught, to show his father he was "practically a man" now. After several counseling sessions he decided to, at least temporarily, abandon this tactic and get his ear pierced instead. This action provoked a confrontation with his father that allowed him to express some of his resentment quite directly. When last seen, he and his father had begun a tense but hopeful process of negotiating a new set of freedoms and responsibilities.

Corrective procedures for revenge. It is of critical importance that the adult refrains from punishment and retaliation and does not take the young person's revenge behavior personally or show feelings of hurt. When the adult is also the parent, this can be especially difficult, and the parent will need support and time to learn better responses. Questions to help the young person identify his or her goals might include, "Could it be that you want to punish your mother for her boyfriend's behavior?" or "I'm wondering if you are consciously trying to hurt me, and if you are, I want to understand that."

Corrective procedures for assumed inadequacy. When the child sees him- or herself as a failure, it may be helpful to ask, "Do you think you're going to flunk out, so you might as well have a child to take care of ?" or "I wonder if you think you don't deserve to be protected against diseases." It is important that the adult helper shows encouragement and optimism in the face of the young person's despair. Arranging situations in which he or she can experience success may be critical, and this may require engaging the assistance of teachers, tutors, parents, and siblings.

Some general suggestions for corrective procedures in response to risky sexual activity also include participation in skill-building groups and activities to increase self-esteem, assertiveness, and self-efficacy (see Chapter 13); individual, group, or family counseling; social competency skills building; and sex education for the young person and parents. It is important that all interventions and corrections be geared toward empowering adolescents to identify healthier ways to meet their goals of belonging, inclusion, and recognition.

Natural and Logical Consequences

Natural and logical consequences are also effective ways of dealing with misbehavior. Traditional discipline involves reward and punishment: Adults punish kids for unacceptable behavior and reward them for complying with their wishes and commands. Natural and logical consequences differ from reward and punishment in a number of ways and have certain advantages. The goal of consequences is to teach young people responsibility, cooperation, respect for order and the rights of others, good judgment, and careful decision making, and to give them a sense of control and choice. The goal is not to force submission and compliance, nor is it to obtain retribution and revenge (often the real goal of punishment). To some degree, reliance on consequences removes from the adult the function of meting out rewards and punishment, which de-emphasizes the traditional authority position of the adult. When authority is de-emphasized, young people feel more independent, and that feeling itself decreases undesirable behavior.

Natural consequences result directly from the behavior. Examples are getting an STD or becoming pregnant. Because natural consequences in this case threaten health and safety, logical consequences should be used in the hope that the natural consequences will never be experienced. Clear and unequivocal communication about the natural consequences of risky sexual behavior should be accompanied by encouragement to engage in healthier behavior. Logical consequences are determined in advance, are logically connected to the behavior, and are applied when the misbehavior occurs: for example, "If you have your boyfriend over while I'm at work one more time, you will not be permitted to have any friends over for one month." It is important that logical consequences are not arbitrary or invoked during the heat of an argument. Consequences are administered and experienced in an impersonal, matter-of-fact fashion, without moralizing, judgment, or excessive emotional involvement.

Sometimes another young person can share natural consequences in a way that communicates more effectively than adults can do so. A student of one of the authors gave a speech on how becoming pregnant earlier in high school had drastically changed her life. She did not "preach" to her classmates, nor was she dramatic in her descriptions. She simply told her story. Her straightforward, unromantic portrayal of daily life had a profound effect on her classmates and generated a lively discussion on the belief that "it could never happen to me." Although the actual effects of her speech cannot be measured, her matter-of-fact and nonjudgmental approach certainly provoked a good deal of nondefensive discussion. Exposing students to the natural and logical consequences of risky sexual behavior through other people's lives may promote some behavior change so they do not have to experience the consequences themselves.

Reliance on consequences is intended to help children develop responsibility for their own behavior. It is not meant to be a vehicle to express the adult's displeasure or anger. Care should be taken that the nonverbal aspects of the interaction do not turn it into covert punishment and thereby defeat the purpose of the entire procedure.

Encouragement

Encouragement greatly enhances the relationship between child and adult and reduces the child's need to resort to undesirable behavior to feel significant. Encouragement is the process of increasing young people's sense of worth and self-esteem by focusing on their actual strengths and assets, not on expected or potential strengths. Encouragement conveys to young people that the adult has faith in them, trusts and respects them, and values them as people despite any mistakes or flaws.

All too often children and teens are exposed to ongoing discouraging experiences. Some adults focus only on the mistakes children make, attributing them to basic defects of character or ability (e.g., "He's just lazy," or "She's always been clumsy."). Some adults set standards that are difficult or impossible to reach; they compare young people to each other in such a way that there is always a loser. The discouragement and self-doubt that arise from these practices may be manifested in misbehavior and in useless, inappropriate attempts to gain recognition.

Encouragement should be a regular aspect of interactions with all adolescents and children. When a young person is deeply discouraged, the teacher or counselor has the difficult task of counteracting a host of negative experiences. Adults can offer encouragement by recognizing effort and improvement as well as accomplishment, expressing appreciation, separating the deed from the doer when the deed is unacceptable, focusing on the child's or teenager's unique talents and contributions, and treating youth with respect and courtesy. Nonverbal messages are also important. Listening without interruption, using a friendly, nonjudgmental tone of voice, treating mistakes as opportunities for learning rather than as failures, and choosing the right moment for a remark are as important as the choice of words.

Keep in mind that some words that purport to be encouraging have the opposite effect. Some ill-advised attempts at encouragement include competitive encouragement ("See what you can do when you try?"), coupling encouragement with expectations ("You got an A; that's great. Now let's keep up that average."), expressing surprise at success ("You did? I never thought you could do it!"), using someone else as an example ("If Kristin can do it, you can too, I'm sure."), and blaming someone else for a young person's failure ("If it hadn't been for that referee, I'm sure you'd have won.").

In general, anything that perpetuates low self-esteem, that lowers confidence in a child's ability to master problem situations, or that fosters feelings of inadequacy and insignificance is discouraging. Anything that gives a sense of being an important member of the group and a feeling that the child's participation, contribution, and cooperation are valued is encouraging. Above all, it is important for young people to learn that they are good enough as they are.

CONCLUSION

Premature and irresponsible sexual activity, teen pregnancy, and HIV/AIDS are significant social problems. Understanding some of the environmental, family, and peer dynamics that young people encounter and helping adolescents change the goals of their misbehavior may help prevent some of these problems. Because of the long-term consequences of teenage sexual activity, it is critical to provide young people with accurate, comprehensive sex education, including the skills they need to carry out their own informed decisions about sexuality. The growing literature on successful prevention programs indicates that there are specific characteristics associated with reducing pregnancy and unprotected sex, increasing abstinence, and delaying first intercourse.

Young people's optimistic and positive beliefs about themselves and their capacity to set the direction of their future are an important part of a comprehensive effort to prevent pregnancy and risky sexual behavior. According to Edelman (1987), "The best contraceptive is a real future" (p. 58), and a future requires opportunities to build academic and work-related skills, job opportunities, and life-planning skills. As such, we believe that greater funding to support prevention is an important method to reduce problems related to teen sexual activity.

CHAPTER 10

ANTISOCIAL BEHAVIOR, DELINQUENCY, AND YOUTH GANGS

▲ *In my side of the 'hood late at night,*
the cluck walks around in spandex too tight
looking high and low for a rock,
hoping the dealer's still on the corner of the block.

In my side of the 'hood people do see
how the dealers make crack money.

Little kids play in the streets,
watching the deals and listening to gangsta beats.

Then one day those kids that play,
think that dealing will make cash someday.

Then the game goes from hide and seek,
to slang the crack and dodge the heat.

In my side of the 'hood guns go bang,
and everybody thinks the only way is a gang.

Broken bottles, razor blades, crack deals, and hand grenades,
Little kids that lose the dream, these are the things, I have seen—
In my side of the 'hood.

JEREMY STEEN
RITES OF PASSAGE, 1995-96
JEFFERSON HIGH SCHOOL, LITERARY MAGAZINE, PORTLAND, OR

CHAPTER OUTLINE

THE SCOPE AND NATURE OF ANTISOCIAL
BEHAVIOR, DELINQUENCY, AND GANGS
Family Aggression and Violence
School Problems
Vandalism
Juvenile Delinquency
Gang Membership

ORIGINS OF THE PROBLEM
Society
Guns
Media
Television
Videogames
Rap and acid rock
Communities and Neighborhoods
Risk Factors in Society, Communities,
    and Neighborhoods
Family and Home Environment
    Risk Factors
School Environment and Risk Factors
BOX 10.1 TRAINING FOR VIOLENCE
Peer Group Environment
    Rejection by low-risk peers
    Membership in a deviant peer group
Onset of Delinquent Behavior
Gang Involvement
Gang Risk Factors

SCHOOL SHOOTERS
Identifying Potential Shooters
Profiling and Checklists

Predicting Versus Preventing
Targets of Intervention
BOX 10.2 THE WORDS OF A SHOOTER:
    KIP'S JOURNAL
BOX 10.3 THE WORDS OF A SHOOTER:
    KIP'S LETTER
    Emotional pain and confusion
    Aggressive hatred toward self and others
    Planning and leakage
    Vigilante motivation
Intervention Strategies Focused on Youth
    Violence

SPECIFIC INTERVENTION: REALITY
THERAPY
Assumptions of Reality Therapy
BOX 10.4 MIKEY THE MENACE
Theoretical Components of Reality Therapy
    Involvement
    Rejection of irresponsible behavior
    Relearning
The Seven Principles of Reality Therapy
    Involvement
    Current behavior
    Evaluating behavior
    Planning responsible behavior
    Commitment
    Accept no excuses
    No punishment

CONCLUSION

▲ In this chapter we discuss (a) the nature and scope of antisocial behavior, delinquency, and
    gang activity; (b) the roots of conduct disorder; and (c) the development and consequences
    of delinquency and youth gangs. The developmental and ecological model of antisocial
    behavior (see Figure 10.1) has relevance here. Because society repeatedly has witnessed an
    increasingly lethal dimension of youth violence, we include a section specifically on the
    school shooter and highlight differing experiences and ecological pressures that contribute
    to school shootings. We also present several interventions that focus on youth violence,
    including Glasser's choice theory and reality therapy.

THE SCOPE AND NATURE OF ANTISOCIAL BEHAVIOR, DELINQUENCY, AND GANGS

Antisocial behavior refers to any activity that conflicts with social norms. Sometimes it includes criminal activity, but not always. Delinquency implies breaking the law. Not infrequently, antisocial behavior and delinquency include violence. Violence takes many forms, among them organized gang violence, school and community shootings, and self-inflicted violence. Antisocial behavior, delinquency, and violence have common roots and similar consequences. Some of the most frequently encountered antisocial behaviors are (a) expressions of aggression within the family and school, often becoming conduct disorder; (b) problems such as fighting and vandalism; (c) non-index crimes such as substance use and running away; (d) index crimes such as theft, robbery, and larceny; (e) gang membership; and (g) school shootings. Although these areas are related, we discuss them separately to make clear their unique characteristics.

Family Aggression and Violence

Family aggression and violence occur with alarming frequency and can lead to the development of severe antisocial behavior with children witnessing 10 to 20% of the nation's homicides (Pynoos & Eth, as cited in van Dalen & Glasserman, 1997). Violence is the leading cause of injury to women in the home. Between 2 million and 4 million women are battered by their partners each year (Hughes & Hasbrouck, 1996). An estimated 3.3 million children witness violence in their homes (Krajewski, Rybarik, Dosch, & Gilmore, 1996).

Chronic exposure to violence can have a detrimental developmental effect on children, including identification with the aggressor, truncated moral development, and pathological adaptation to violence. Children who observe parents using violence observe not only the violent behavior but also the circumstances, the emotional triggers, and the consequences of violence (Fehon, Grilo, & Lipschitz, 2005). These observations significantly influence behaviors.

A related problem in families is poor parental response to challenging children who are irritable, inattentive, and impulsive. These difficult children are often responded to with anger and hostility, followed by attempts to appease the child, leading to inconsistent discipline. Children who view the world as hostile and inconsistent attempt to get their way regardless of social rules. These children tend to be violent later in life (Osofsky, 1997).

School Problems

Problem behavior at school is often a precursor to more severe antisocial behavior. In fact, well-developed antisocial patterns coupled with high levels of aggression early in a child's life are among the best predictors of delinquency in later years. The general principle is that less serious problem behaviors precede more serious delinquency. Thus disruptive and delinquent behavior generally progresses in an orderly, sequential fashion from authority conflict (e.g., defiance and disobedience), to covert actions (e.g., lying and stealing), to overt actions (e.g., fighting, delinquency, and violent behavior).

Overall aggression in the classroom increases individual aggression (Aber, Jones, Brown, Chandry, & Samples, 1998). Children in classrooms with higher overall levels of aggression are at increased risk of higher levels of aggressive strategies, aggressive fantasies, and hostile attributional perceptions. This higher level of classroom aggression even affects future behavior. Overall classroom level of aggression in the first grade increased boys' risk of being aggressive in middle school. Further, the more aggressive first-grade boys who were in more highly aggressive first-grade classrooms were at a markedly increased risk for aggressive behavior 6 or 7 years later (Kellam, Ling, Merisca, Brown, & Ialongo, 1998). Early aggression patterns characterized by high frequency, intense severity, and occurrence across multiple settings predict a number of ominous outcomes later on, including victimization of others, delinquency, and violence (Loeber & Farrington, 1998).

Conduct disorder (CD) and its less severe diagnostic cousin, oppositional defiant disorder (ODD), encompass most of the antecedent, precursor behaviors that relate to delinquent and violent behavior. CD refers to clinically severe antisocial behavior including physical aggression, stealing, fire setting, truancy, and running away. The effects of CD and associated delinquent behavior patterns constitute a major social problem; evidence suggests, for example, that disruptions in the classroom interfere with teaching (U.S. Department of Education, 1998). Even more important, boys who carried a concealed gun were 4 times as likely to be diagnosed with conduct disorder, and those who carried concealed guns as adolescents were more likely to commit crimes as adults (Loeber, Burke, Mutchka, & Lahey, 2004). Some researchers (Delligatti, Akin-Little, & Little, 2003) argue that girls are underrepresented in CD research because of the focus on externalizing behaviors rather than covert relational aggression, which is often exhibited by girls. Even so, this disorder is of serious magnitude with a prevalence rate of up to 16% (Sommers-Flanagan & Sommers-Flanagan, 1998).

Vandalism

Vandalism accounts for millions of dollars in damage to school property (Goldstein, 1996) and millions more in damage to parks and playgrounds, street signs and billboards, museums and libraries, buses and trains, and numerous other venues.

As "high-level" aggression—student fights, assaults of teachers, weapon violations, youth gangs—became an increasing issue, vandalism diminished as a concern. This indifference comes at a substantial cost. Aggression toward both property and people is learned behavior. Just as the oppositional child may develop into the conduct-disordered preadolescent and ultimately into the delinquent adolescent, so too may young vandals evolve into assaultive youth. Indeed, the motivations for vandalism suggest underlying feelings and attitudes such as disconnection from school and peers, vindication for perceived wrongs, anger, rage, and frustration and indicate more serious future problems (Office of Community Oriented Policing Services, U.S. Department of Justice, 2005).

Juvenile Delinquency

In 2002 the juvenile arrest rate for offenses in the Violent Crime Index (robbery, aggravated assault, forcible rape, and murder) reached its lowest level since 1980, less than half its 1994 peak level. Even though this decline is encouraging, more than 2.25 billion juvenile arrests occurred in 2002, and more than 92,000 of them were Violent Crime Index offenses (Office of Juvenile Justice Delinquency Prevention [OJJDP], 2005.) Ironically, most people continue to believe that juvenile crime is increasing, perhaps because the media sensationalize crime, particularly when it is violent and involves young victims or perpetrators. Following the national trend of "get tough on youth crime," a number of states enacted laws to prosecute young juvenile offenders as adults. A 14-year-old alleged murderer being tried as an adult makes headline news, continuing reports of the trial often go on for weeks and months, and subsequent legal and sentencing ramifications—especially possible execution—go on for months and years. In addition, the public may believe that youth crime is increasing because the average age of first offense has become increasingly younger, making the problem seem worse (Snyder, 2000). Finally, child and adolescent use of certain drugs, particularly methamphetamines, has risen since 1995, and substance use is highly correlated with other law violations by young people. The use or possession of alcohol and other substances has also led to the arrest of many boys and girls. Thus crime and drug use are related, and their relationship influences social perceptions.

The decrease in youth crime is encouraging, but this is no time for complacency. The Surgeon General still reports that between 30% and 40% of boys and between 15% and 30% of girls have committed a serious violent offense by age 17 (Office of the Surgeon General, 2001). About 2.5 million children 10 to 17 years of age—10% of our youth—were arrested in 1999 (Snyder, 2000) and about the same in 2000 (Lykken, 2001). In addition, the number of girls in the juvenile justice system has increased both in percentage and numbers (OJJDP, 2005). For example, in the last decade loitering and curfew violations for girls have increased 150%, and drug violations have increased almost 200%.

Gang Membership

A youth gang is a group consisting primarily of adolescents and young adults who interact frequently with one another, share a common identity expressed through a gang name and common symbols, claim control over a certain geographical area, and are deliberately involved in illegal activities. Although down somewhat from 1998, there were still 21,500 gangs active in the United States in 2002, with nearly 732,000 total members (Kelly, 2005). Youth in these gangs were responsible for a wide variety of offenses, including street crime, drug trafficking, and witness intimidation, and they are highly likely to use firearms in an assault crime (Esbensen, 2000). A high percentage of gang activity occurs in high schools (95%) or intermediate schools (91%), and involvement with gangs remains one of the most powerful predictors of violence (Office of the Surgeon General, 2001).

When one gang gains power and control in an area, rival gangs sometimes relocate to other areas, even to other cities. Divisions of power and region are frequently related to ethnicity, although a new type of hybrid gang is emerging. Hybrid gangs are characterized by mixed racial and ethnic participation within a single gang and are driven by drug sale profits (Starbuck, Howell, & Lindquist, 2001). Economic opportunities (e.g., new markets for drug profits) also play a part in a gang's decision to relocate or expand. Many neighborhoods untouched by organized violence now find themselves threatened by gang activity. The proliferation of youth gangs in recent decades is of concern, and of particular concern is the spread of homegrown youth gangs to rural communities (Esbensen, 2000). These findings highlight the importance of continuing a systematic response in combating youth gang problems.

ORIGINS OF THE PROBLEM

The origins of conduct disorder, delinquent activity, and gang involvement are developmental and ecological. The model of antisocial behavior we present here provides one way to conceptualize this multifaceted and complex problem. In this model, society, community, and neighborhood are viewed as remote predictors of antisocial and delinquent behavior (see Chapter 2). As depicted in Figure 10.1, family, school, and peer influences as well as individual characteristics of youth all contribute to the ecology of the problem.

Society

The ecological model (Bronfenbrenner, 1989) highlights the importance of the microsystems of community and neighborhood as well as other environmental influences in predicting and understanding antisocial behavior. Economic conditions—prosperity, employment rates, family income—are important and help to predict the degree and severity of antisocial behavior and delinquency. In fact, significant correlations between rates of unemployment and juvenile delinquency have been found in more than 100 American cities, and youth crime is most common in urban areas that are economically depressed (Esbenson, 2000). The impact of media and the access to guns are important societal components as well.

Guns

The ownership of firearms in the United States has persisted throughout American history and is unique among Western industrialized nations. In fact, the United States has more firearms than any other industrialized nation in the world. A police officer is killed by a gun every 5 days, and a child dies of a gunshot wound every 2 hours in the United States. Over a 10-year period, 2 times as many children under the age of 10 died as a result of firearms as U.S. soldiers killed in Somalia and the first Persian Gulf War combined.

Firearm-related death rates for both boys and girls reveal that the most vulnerable group are youth 15 to 19 years of age, a group in which the death rate from guns jump precipitously from younger teens and children. However, a child under the age of 15 in the United States is 15 times more likely to be killed by gunfire than a child growing up in Northern Ireland. Finally, the overall firearm-related death rate among U.S. children under 15 years of age is nearly 12 times higher than that of children in 25 industrialized countries (Prothrow-Stith, 2001).

The easy and excessive availability of firearms is a major contributor to the problem. The availability of guns makes youth violence more lethal and provides school shooters with access to the means to create their mayhem. A recent report suggests that a disproportionately high number of children fall victim to homicide (and suicide and accidental shooting as well) in those areas where purchase and possession of guns is especially prevalent (Miller, Azrael, & Hemenway, 2002). A comparison of five states with the lowest gun availability compared to the five states with the highest gun availability shows the number of non-gun murders is similar. Those states with high gun availability, however, have 250% more shooting murders of children. When compared to other upper-income nations, the homicide rate for U.S. children is 17 times higher (Miller et al., 2002). Among

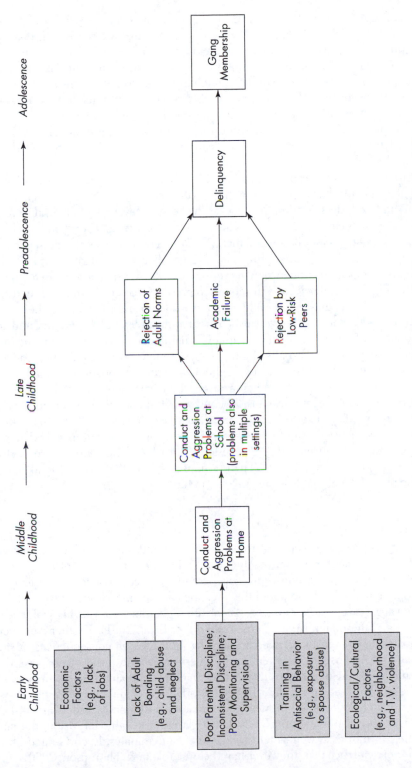

FIGURE 10.1 A developmental and ecological model of antisocial, delinquent, and gang behavior

Source: Adapted from Patterson, DeBaryshe, & Ramsey, 1989.

urban youth, 40% report that a gun is available in their homes. Eighty-eight percent thought it acceptable for children and teens to have guns, yet nearly half (47%) stated that a gun had injured either a relative or themselves (Kahn, Kazimi, & Mulvihill, 2001). Adults have increased gun accessibility to young people during the last two decades. Canada (1995) points out that young people have come to believe they need handguns for their own protection. Handgun manufacturers have been quick to take advantage of this situation, making their guns more attractive to teens and marketing their product to them. In spite of efforts to raise awareness of the problem of gun accessibility, stricter gun legislation has not been passed, typically in the name of misinterpreted Second Amendment rights.

Student access to weapons is common and is especially critical for school shooters. Most of the shooters had a history of gun use with some demonstrating a fascination with weapons and explosives. Most of the attackers had easy access to weapons and were able to take guns from their own home or from a relative or friend. Harris and Klebold, the Columbine shooters, easily purchased them. Some received them as gifts from parents. The Glock used by Kip Kinkel, the Springfield, Oregon, shooter, was a gift from his father, an attempt to demonstrate confidence in the young man who was such a concern to his parents.

Relying on metal detectors in schools to prevent weapons from entering the building provides false security. Most of the shooters made no effort to conceal their weapons. In addition, metal detectors are very expensive, require at least two operators, and are subject to relatively frequent breakdowns with high maintenance costs. In discussing this issue with young people in an alternative high school, the adolescents we talked to scoffed at the idea of metal detectors. They told us, "School starts at 8:15. Security people get here at 7:30; so we just get here at 7:15." When we asked them what happened if the school locked the doors until 7:30, the response was, "We just give it (the weapon) to the girls. They (the security officers) don't like to check purses." We asked further, "Well, what if they did check the girls' purses?" "All of us get there at 8:10, they don't want us to be late to class, so we all rush by the machine." We persisted, "But what if they don't let you get by the machine and just mark you tardy?" Their response, "Oh, in that case, a friend goes in, we go to the outside fence and toss the gun over to him."

Media

Television.   Over five decades of research on film and television viewing have documented the consistent exposure of American children to high levels of media violence. The relationship between television viewing and violence has been empirically established: There is absolutely no doubt that increased acceptance of aggressive attitudes and increased aggressive behavior are correlated with higher levels of viewing violence on television (e.g., Huesmann, Moise-Titus, Podolski, & Eron, 2001). Further, younger children's exposure to media violence can have harmful lifelong consequences. A study by Bushman and Anderson (2001) reaffirms modern society's exposure to massive doses of violent media. By the time the average American child graduates from elementary school, he or she will have seen more than 100,000 assorted acts of violence (e.g., rapes, assaults) and more than 8,000 murders on network television (Bushman & Anderson, 2001). If the child has access, as most do, to a VCR, DVD player, or to cable television, the numbers are higher. In movies as well as television, violence dominates. Even G-rated films now contain more violence than they ever have before (Yokota & Thompson, 2000).

Videogames.   Media games also contain violence, with 62 to 85% of the most popular videogames containing violence. Even young children play violent videogames. Fourth-grade boys and girls reported that the majority of their favorite games were violent (Buchman & Funk, 1996). Playing violent videogames—on average from 7 to 9 hours per week—can increase aggressive thoughts, feelings, and behavior in real life (Anderson & Dill, 2000). Violent videogames teach children aggressive solutions to conflict, and prac-ticing aggressive strategies during the game makes it more likely that children will use those strategies when real-life conflicts arise. Repeated exposure to videogames with vio-lent content is associated with academic difficulties, aggression, trait hostility, and lowered empathy (Funk, Baldacci, Pasold, & Baumgardner, 2004; Gentile, Lynch, Linder, & Walsh, 2004; Uhlmann & Swanson, 2004). Some of the most worrisome games are: Doom, Doom2, Duke Nukem (videogames played extensively by Harrison and Klebold, the Columbine shooters), Destrega, and Carmageddon. The latter two are advertised by "Let the slaughter begin!" and "More fun than shooting your neighbor's cat."

Rap and acid rock.   Music is another media influence that is often imbued with violence. The FBI surmised in its study that all the school shooters had listened to music lyrics that promoted violence (Band & Harpold, 1999). Youth today have access to gangsta rap and acid rock with lyrics of murder, violence, and aggression—raps about slitting parents' throats and sticking needles through eyelids—and other viciously disturbing images. Most school shooters listened to acid rock and rap more than 40 hours per week (Buchman & Funk, 1996). This overwhelming saturation by the combined media highlights aggressive and antisocial behavior and promotes an appetite for more violence. In addition, teenagers fear becoming victims, which sets the stage for "justified" violent behavior. At the same time, media violence has led to increased desensitization to violence and depersonalization toward the victims of violence.

Other social influences such as racism continue to be a major factor. Racisms' effects continue to be insidious and far reaching, with large portions of our ethnically diverse com-munities experiencing serious violence, crime, and continued economic, social, and educa-tional marginalization. Such marginalization is associated with poorer parenting, lower levels of parental monitoring, and less-integrated family structures all of which have been associated with criminal behavior (Dishion & Kavanagh, 2002; Patterson, Reid, & Dishion, 1992).

Communities and Neighborhoods

Because parents who are struggling with social, economic, and community problems are often less able to provide the structure young teenagers need, many young people are drawn to gangs, which provide structure (such as rules and norms) and a sense of belonging and group and individual identity. Adolescents of color living in inner cities have much higher levels of personal victimization than national norms (Sheley, McGee, & Wright, 1992); for these youth, gangs also provide a sense of safety.

Most studies suggest that gay, lesbian, bisexual, and transgender (GLBT) youth have a higher incidence of negative encounters with police, including jail, than do het-erosexual youth (Rotheram-Borus & Langabeer, 2001). But more important than crime done by GLBT adolescents is the violence done to them. GLBT youth are uniquely sub-ject to violence resulting from societal homophobia. Forms of violence in school and in the community range from name-calling to "gay bashing" to physical attacks, and there is a high and increasing number of hate crimes directed toward GLBT persons in the United States (Herek, Gillis, Cogan, & Glunt, 1997). This amplified vulnerability to victimization of GLBT youth is especially problematic because of the distinctive developmental struggles reported by GLBT youth during their adolescent years (Savin-Williams, 1995).

Antisocial behavior is a developmental process that begins early in life and continues throughout childhood and adolescence and into adulthood (Patterson, 1993). Chronic delinquency emerges in a series of predictable steps that place young people at increasingly greater risk for long-term criminal behavior. Unfortunately, by the time offenders come to the attention of the juvenile justice system, they may have spent several years committing minor offenses and developing serious behavior problems that eventually led to crime. Next, we review risk factors that contribute to this developmental process.

Risk Factors in Society, Communities, and Neighborhoods

Although the primary social environments for most children are family and school, children also interact with others in their neighborhood, with peers who attend other schools, and with other adults. Children develop a set of expectations about themselves and others in these social contexts and are faced with many challenges. Among other things, the following risk factors provide an environment that makes antisocial behavior, delinquency, and gang activity more likely.

- Poor economic prosperity of the nation as a whole and unequal distribution of wealth
- Limited transportation, health, and social services
- Ready access to guns and drugs
- High rates of unemployment, underemployment, and limited work opportunities
- Failure of communities to meet their economic and educational expectations, and poor community response to economic marginalization
- High frequency of social marginalization and racism in the community, including the presence of hate groups and hate crimes
- Public policy that fails to meet community, economic, family (e.g., accessible quality day care), and educational needs
- High frequency of neighborhood vandalism, crime, gang activity, and violence
- Low family income and high likelihood of economic hopelessness

Family and Home Environment Risk Factors

The family can mitigate against delinquency or encourage it. Parents whose discipline is harsh and inconsistent, for example, who have little positive involvement with their children, and who do not monitor their children's activities foster early aggressive behavior, which is strongly related to later delinquency (Baumrind, 1993; DeBaryshe, Patterson, & Capaldi, 1993). When parents and grandparents are negative and inconsistent in their parenting styles, are explosive, and when parents are antisocial themselves, aversive and aggressive behavior is reinforced (Fry, 1993). Family stressors, such as family violence, marital discord, divorce, or stresses related to acculturation or bicultural adjustment all contribute to the development of a youth's antisocial behavior.

Certain family demographic features are also highly correlated with delinquency. SES is not directly related to the incidence of delinquency, but ethnicity, the type of neighborhood, and parents' education, occupation, and income can influence the type of delinquency children exhibit (Tolan & Guerra, 1994). Children who live in poor communities, whose parents have unskilled jobs or are unemployed, and whose schools and community economic opportunities are poor are at greatest risk for violent forms of delinquent behavior (Knoester & Haynie, 2005). This risk is partly attributable to the difficulty of raising children in a poor environment and to parents' lack of education, resources, and problem-solving skills. Parents with this profile often monitor their children less, show little involvement with them, and provide less educational stimulation and positive reinforcement for prosocial behaviors (Dishion & Kavanagh, 2002; Dishion et al., 2002).

Early parenting patterns can lead to antisocial behavior in two ways. First, a negative and hostile interaction style and inconsistent discipline lead to poor bonding between parent and child. This lack of bonding contributes to the child's failure to accept society's values and to develop internal control mechanisms. This problem is exacerbated when the family is isolated. Second, coercive and violent behaviors may be modeled and reinforced by grandparents, parents, and siblings. Children learn to use aversive and aggressive behaviors to counteract the hostile and negative behaviors of other family members, and aggressiveness is rewarded. Learned aggressiveness in such an environment is functional for survival, and hitting, screaming, and other aggressive behaviors are sometimes accepted as normal early in life (Bor & Sanders, 2004).

Families that reinforce aggressive and antisocial behavior fail to provide the appropriate skills that children need for survival in the school and social environment. The significance of positive parental involvement, healthy parent–child interaction, and consistent discipline is supported by the fact that when parents change their discipline and monitoring styles to become more consistent, more positive, less physical, and more aware and observant, their children's antisocial behavior almost invariably declines significantly (Cunningham, Bremner, & Boyle, 1995; Kumpfer & Tait, 2000). Conversely, if children receive training in antisocial behavior in the home, they will likely experience significant difficulties in and out of school (see Box 10.1).

School Environment and Risk Factors

Coercive behavior learned at home usually leads to aggression at school and often an assessment of ODD or CD. School aggression also leads to academic failure. Uncontrolled behavior adversely affects a child's ability to concentrate, to stick to a task, and to complete homework. The correlation between antisocial behavior and poor academic performance is strong (Catalano & Hawkins, 1996; Stormshak, Bierman, & the Conduct Problems Prevention Research Group, 1998).

The link between aggression and poor academic performance is due to several factors, most of which have developmental roots. Children who are aggressive are disruptive, and disruption itself means less on-task behavior, leading to less concentration and study. Disruptive young people are more often placed in time-out, are sent to the principal's office, spend more time in a responsibility room, and are suspended more often. All of these consequences contribute to less learning time, leading to poor performance. Limited academic achievement contributes to the student's negative self-perception, which encourages more negative behavior that in turn leads to even more limited academic achievement.

▲ Box 10.1

Training for Violence

At one time I was a school counselor for two brothers, Tom, a freshman, and John, a sopho-more. Almost every week one or the other or both got into a fistfight at school—sometimes with each other, more often with another student. The vice principal provided appropriate dis-cipline, which progressed from talking to detention to more detention to in-school suspension to suspension. Because the parents refused to attend parent–teacher or parent–administrator conferences, and because I worked with the boys in a counseling relationship, the vice prin-cipal asked me to make a home visit to discuss the problem with the parents.

The boys' father was home when I arrived. It quickly became clear that the boys' prob-lem was their dad. The overriding family value he expressed went something like this: "Don't take nothing off of nobody. If someone bothers you, hit him." In this family, aggression and violence were not only being modeled and reinforced, they were being actively encouraged through verbal instruction.

Once I understood the situation, I was able to work with the boys to help them under-stand their aggression, to develop different standards of behavior at school, and to learn more appropriate problem-solving skills.

Many of the risk factors that emerge in the school environment are symptomatic of other problems, such as learning disabilities, emotional problems, or a temporary difficulty in the family. Nevertheless, some of the following risk factors in the school environment lead to or are symptomatic of more severe antisocial or delinquent behavior expressed out-side of school:

- Behaving aggressively or violently toward other students and toward teachers in the classroom or on the playground
- Using money as a means of winning other students' approval and acceptance
- Disrupting the classroom by failing to attend to the tasks of the class, staying in their seats, responding appropriately to the teacher, or participating in appropriate classroom behavior (such as raising a hand before speaking)
- Vandalizing school property and classroom materials
- Making sexual gestures toward other students and teachers
- Performing poorly in academic work, regularly scoring low on tests, and consistently failing to complete classroom and homework assignments
- Spending free time with older students who behave aggressively in and out of the classroom
- Describing themselves as "bad" or "dumb," or in other ways deriding their ability to do the required schoolwork and behave appropriately around other students and teachers

Peer Group Environment

Rejection by low-risk peers.   As young children become socialized to the behavioral standards and norms of society, they gradually reduce their level of aggressive and acting-out behavior. However, older children with antisocial behavioral patterns display rates of aggression that are more typical of younger children. They are usually not cooperative or helpful in their social interactions. Indeed, antisocial students seem to have a particular disinclination to cooperate with others in peer-related activities. Their aggression leads to eventual rejection by low-risk peers (Fraser, 1996). They have difficulty entering positive peer groups: they misperceive peer group norms and inappropriately interpret peer reactions. Considerable evidence suggests that even benign actions by other students—an innocent, accidental bump in a crowded hallway, for instance—are interpreted as hostile, deliberate, aggressive attacks (Dodge & Price, 1994).

Membership in a deviant peer group.   Antisocial behavior ultimately leads young people to join deviant peer groups for support and acceptance. Aggressiveness and antisocial behavior learned at home is exacerbated by academic failure and rejection by normal peers and becomes a precursor to membership in a deviant peer group. But the relationship between inappropriate and aggressive behavior and academic failure and peer rejection may be circular. That is, school failure and social rejection may in fact stimulate behavior problems, enhance aggressiveness, and contribute to delinquent and hostile reactions by the struggling student. This relationship needs to be assessed more carefully, however. Some studies suggest that training in academic and social skills can be effective but must be introduced early in the child's life to prevent or reduce antisocial behavior (Goldstein, Harootunian, & Conoley, 1994; Kazdin, 1994; Lipsey, Wilson, & Cothern, 2000).

As we mention in Chapters 5 and 14, the peer cluster is a major training ground for the development of a young adolescent's attitudes, beliefs, and behaviors. Peers supply the attitudes, motivations, rationalizations, and opportunities for engaging in antisocial and delinquent behaviors. Furthermore, delinquent peers reinforce deviant behavior and punish behavior that is socially conforming (Cho, Hallfors, & Sanchez 2005; Dishion et al., 1999; Kaminer, 2005). Pressure from the peer cluster makes it difficult for children and adolescents to modify antisocial behavior once they have started to engage in it. Many delinquent youth actively resist efforts to change their behavior. If they adopt more positive social behavior, they may alienate themselves from their major source of companionship and acceptance.

Onset of Delinquent Behavior

The age of onset of aggressive and delinquent behavior is an important factor in determining severity. Youth who begin delinquent activities early are at greatest risk for becoming chronic offenders (Patterson, Reid, & Dishion 1992; Walker et al., 1995). Boys who are first arrested between the ages of 6 and 10, for example, have more criminal charges and convictions than "late starters," or those who commit their first offense in middle adolescence. About one half of conduct-disordered children become adolescent delinquents, and one half to three fourths of adolescent delinquents become chronic adult offenders (Blumstein, Cohen, & Farrington, 1988). These data argue for the importance of early assessment and intervention.

The developmental perspective (Patterson, Crosby, & Vuchinich 1992; Patterson, DeBaryshe, & Ramsey, 1989) and the ecological model (Bronfenbrenner, 1979) show how ecological, cultural, and economic factors place external pressure on families, schools, and children. As young people develop, their interactions with families, schools, and peer groups change. Identification with a deviant peer cluster encourages delinquent behavior and, for some, eventual membership in a gang.

Gang Involvement

Gangs have significant negative consequences not only for society but also for their young members. However, a gang may be the only means many young people have to satisfy their need for affiliation and affirmation (Jackson, Bass, & Sharpe, 2005). Gangs also provide an opportunity for economic gain and an image of success for young people who have no other means to establish it. Gangs provide security, protection, companionship, and opportunities for excitement. Thus gang membership gives young people ways to enhance their perception of their worth and acceptance (Howell, 1998).

In one of our studies (Herrmann et al., 1997), we found that high gang involvement was associated with low competence and low self-concept. That is, those middle-school-aged students who were most involved (members) or wanted to be involved (wannabes) in gangs believed they had very little impact or influence on their environment, with adults, or with their peers. Apparently, if young people believe themselves impotent, gang membership is viewed as a way to increase their competency and power. These consequences of gang involvement make intervention a complicated and challenging task and further highlight the importance of early prevention.

Gang Risk Factors

Researchers have identified risk factors for juvenile gang membership at a variety of levels: individual, peer group, school, family, and community (Dishion, Nelson, & Yasui, 2005; Howell, 1998). These risk factors range from lack of parental role models to academic failure to neighborhood drug availability. Many duplicate the risk factors in community, families, and schools noted earlier. Some of the most important risk factors that lead to gang membership are as follows:

- A community characterized by poverty, residential mobility, and other examples of social disorganization often avowing cultural norms that support gang behavior.
- Families experiencing extreme economic deprivation.
- Parents with management problems and violent attitudes, and households with siblings with antisocial behavior.
- Low commitment to school with low achievement test scores and low school attachment; high levels of antisocial behavior in school; and identification as being learning disabled or conduct disordered.
- Interaction with and high commitment to delinquent peers coupled with a low commitment to positive peers; friends who use drugs or are drug distributors or who are gang members.
- Problem attitudes and behaviors including hyperactivity, drinking, lack of refusal skills, externalizing behaviors, and early sexual activity.

All of these risk factors and the contexts in which we find the roots of the problem of youth violence and delinquency need to be considered in prevention and intervention.

Youth gangs represent a particularly acute concern because gang members account for a disproportionate number of delinquent acts and for a greater number of more serious crimes. In addition, substance use and abuse, drug trafficking, and gang membership are related (Bilchik, 1999).

SCHOOL SHOOTERS

An unprecedented number of school shootings—39 instances since 1996 (Department of Justice, 2005)—that resulted in the deaths of students and teachers in Arkansas, Mississippi, Kentucky, California, Oregon, Colorado, and Minnesota have created widespread concern about school safety. These seemingly random and irrational acts have demonstrated that school violence extends far beyond poor, inner-city schools.

Tragic events like the shooting at Columbine High School in Colorado captured public attention, but most adolescent homicides are committed in inner cities and outside of school. They most frequently involve a single victim and an interpersonal dispute with a clear territorial, retaliation, or economic motive. Most of the perpetrators of school shootings have been from affluent and middle-class communities, and many are from intact families. The majority of the shooters are academically able students, and most are European American.

Even though teenage violence has decreased, young people do not feel safe at school. One in 5 Latino and African American teens indicate that the threat of crime and violence have kept them from attending school (Butts, 2002). In one large national survey of 6th through 12th grade students, children and youth reported that they had considerable distress because of school violence. Fifty percent of the students knew someone who moved to another school to feel safer; 37% did not feel safe in their school; 45% avoided school grounds; 43% avoided school restrooms; and 20% avoided school hallways (Ansley, 1997, p. 5). The ripple effect of concern and fear is manifested in settings far from those in which the shootings took place. It is really not very surprising that so many members of the American public, including young people, think that school is not safe: We are all exposed to repeated televised pictures of students who have used handguns to kill their fellow students; media broadcasts and newspaper stories describing a teacher disarming a student in the classroom; telephoned weapon threats that necessitate closing down schools for a thorough search, while students stand and shiver in parking lots and on sidewalks, watching. These are powerful images that encourage the belief that schools are no longer safe regardless of the facts.

Even though school shooters share some of the characteristics described for antisocial youth, they represent a distinct subcategory of antisocial behavior. Identifying the potential shooter before tragedy occurs continues to be a major concern.

Identifying Potential Shooters

In the aftermath of violence by school shooters, professionals have taken increased steps to prevent violence. Often, their efforts have focused on providing resources, funding, and hiring of school security officers. They have increased physical security with metal detectors and cameras. They have developed tactical plans for responding when a shooting occurs. Although some of these approaches might be moderately helpful, they do not get to the root of the problem (Hyman & Perone, 1998). Two other approaches consist of profiling and problem checklists. These approaches have been recommended to identify future shooters.

Profiling and Checklists

Historically, profiling has consisted of carefully studying a crime scene and, based on the physical evidence, generating a set of hypotheses about the demographic, physical, personality, and other characteristics of the person most likely to have committed the crime. Profiling has been very helpful in identifying suspects and solving crimes. More recently, profiling has been used in an attempt to identify perpetrators of violence before an incident occurs; it is based on studying the characteristics of past school shooters. Prospective profiles of school shooters include the "classroom avenger" profile (McGee & DeBernardo, 1999) and the FBI profile (Band & Harpold, 1999) to predict an individual student's potential for violence. Unfortunately, profiling potential shooters is not an exact science. Accurate prediction requires a very high degree of concordance, and many students who fit shooter profiles do not become shooters. For example, shooters are described as moody, confrontational, angry, and have low self-esteem. This description fits almost any young person at some point in adolescence. Undoubtedly, the use of profiles will fail to identify some dangerous students who share only a few characteristics with prior attackers and will identify as dangerous many students who do not actually pose a risk to others.

Checklists of warning signs are a less scientific alternative to profiles that are designed to help identify potentially violent youth without assuming that all young people fitting the description are potential shooters. Several agencies and groups, including the Department of Education, the FBI (Band & Harpold, 1999), and the National School Safety Center, have provided checklists of warning signs and risk factors. The best use of these checklists is usually to motivate schools to develop prevention and early intervention procedures, as well as safe school plans, because warning list items are so commonly found among adolescents at a given school. Most developers of checklists emphasize that the list is not intended to predict future violent behavior by otherwise nonviolent students. The Department of Education warning sign checklist explicitly cautions that their list does not constitute a profile and was never intended to serve as a predictor of violent behavior. Yet even explicit cautions are disregarded (Sewell & Mendelsohn, 2000), and many checklists are applied as profiles. This can result in the unfair labeling of students who do not pose a threat to the school, particularly students who differ from the majority with respect to sexual orientation, race, and appearance. Lonely, isolated, "weird," young people who dress "funny," have quirky personality characteristics, and otherwise don't fit the norms of their peer group are likely to receive even more harassment, rejection, and ostracism than they already do. Warning lists may actually promote the profiling concept, creating an environment of both suspicion and false security (Bender, Shubert, & McLaughlin, 2001; Lord, 1999).

Predicting Versus Preventing

Predicting future incidences of school violence is fraught with methodological and practical problems. Predicting any low base rate or infrequent behavior, even if reasonably accurate, results in many false positives for every true positive (Mulvey & Cauffman, 2001). Although social scientists are able to predict with some accuracy the approximate number of individuals in a given cohort group who are likely to behave in a certain way, their ability to predict which and when a specific individual is likely to engage in the behavior is poor (Borum, 1996, 2000; Mossman, 1994; Otto, 1992).

There is an important distinction between predicting violence and preventing it (Reddy et al., 2001). Violence prediction involves maximizing the accuracy of predicting who will be violent and under what circumstances the probability of violence is greatest (Sewell & Mendelsohn, 2000). Violence prevention emphasizes not who and when but identifying common underpinnings of violence and intervening to maximize protective factors and minimize risk factors.

A recent collaboration between the U.S. Secret Service and the U.S. Department of Education (Reddy et al., 2001) focused on 37 school shootings from 1974 to 2000, involving 41 attackers. Shootings that were drug related, gang related, or stemming from disputes that just happened to occur on school property were not analyzed. Rather than building a profile of attackers from a set of personality traits and demographic characteristics, the Secret Service focused on behavior and motives, tracing the shooters' thoughts and actions from the day of the attack back to when the perpetrator first developed a notion to make the attack. Based on a systematic analysis of investigative, educational, judicial, mental health, and other files, along with interviews of some of the shooters, the report provides useful information about the patterns of relationships, emotions, and attitudes of others in the shooter's environment.

Bender, Shubert, and their colleagues (Bender et al., 2001; Shubert, Bressette, Deeken, & Bender, 1999) came to remarkably similar conclusions as those of the Secret Service, even though they proceeded with different data sources. Using national press reports, the researchers constructed a list of factors consistently associated with the shooter's psychological and social environment. They used the term *invisible kids* to describe the school shooters, underscoring the finding that these students were not known for overt behavior problems or aggression; indeed, they were simply unknown.

Targets of Intervention

Drawing together the results of the reports by Reddy et al. (2001) and Shubert et al. (1999), four clusters of emotions and behaviors emerge as critical indicators of potential violence: emotional pain and confusion, aggressive hatred toward self and others, planning and leakage, and vigilante motivation. Each of these is an important target of intervention, and the four areas are the basis for intervention with antisocial young people.

Boxes 10.2 and 10.3 provide a glimpse inside the mind of a school shooter in his own words. These excerpts from Kip Kinkel's (the Oregon shooter) journal and letters were included with the documents presented at his hearing. They graphically illustrate the four target areas we now describe. Notice that these target areas do not refer to personality traits, family background, or demographic characteristics per se. Rather, they address specific thoughts, behaviors, and plans that represent the ecology common to school shooters.

Emotional pain and confusion. Very few of the shooters had been diagnosed with any mental illness. Relatively few of them had histories of alcohol or drug abuse, but most demonstrated an incredible range of conflicting emotions. Each of the students responsible for school shootings demonstrated some type of emotional trouble. More than half had a history of feeling extremely depressed, almost desperate. Most threatened to kill themselves, made suicidal gestures, or tried to kill themselves before the attack. A number did kill themselves during the attack.

▲ Box 10.2

The Words of a Shooter: Kip's Journal

These excerpts are from a journal hidden in the loft of Kip Kinkel's home. Investigators discovered the black, hard-cover book tucked away in a chest. Passages read in court are filled with violent images: with Kinkel's wishing for his own death, with visions of his classmates' deaths. The journal offers a window into Kinkel's state of mind leading up to the tragic shooting at Thurston High School in Springfield, Oregon. It also illustrates the concepts discussed in this chapter.

Aggressive Hate

I sit here all alone. I am always alone. I don't know who I am. I want to be something I can never be. I try so hard every day. But in the end, I hate myself for what I've become.

Every single person I know means nothing to me. I hate every person on this earth. I wish they could all go away. You all make me sick. I wish I was dead.

The only reason I stay alive is because of hope. Even though I am repulsive and few people know who I am, I still feel that things might, maybe, just a little bit, get better.

I don't understand any (expletive) person on this earth. Some of you are so weak, mainly, that a 4-year-old could push you down. I am strong, but my head just doesn't work right. I know I should be happy with what I have, but I hate living.

Motivational Vigilantism

Every time I talk to her, I have a small amount of hope. But then she will tear it right down. It feels like my heart is breaking. But is that possible? I am so consumed with hate all of the time. Could I ever love anyone? I have feelings, but do I have a heart that's not black and full of animosity?

Plan and Leakage

I know everyone thinks this way sometimes, but I am so full of rage that I feel I could snap at any moment. I think about it every day. Blowing the school up or just taking the easy way out, and walk into a pep assembly with guns. In either case, people that are breathing will stop breathing. That is how I will repay all you (expletive) for all you put me through.

Motivational Vigilantism

I need help. There is one person that could help, but she won't. I need to find someone else. I think I love her, but she could never love me. I don't know why I try.

End. New day. Today of all days, I ask her to help me. I was shot down. I feel like my heart has been ripped open and ripped apart. Right now, I'm drunk, and I don't know what the hell is happening to me.

I gave her all I have, and she just threw it away. Why? Why did God just want me to be in complete misery?

Aggressive Hate

Oh, (expletive). I sound so pitiful. People would laugh at this if they read it. I hate being laughed at. But they won't laugh after they're scraping parts of their parents, sisters, brothers, and friends from the wall of my hate.

Please, someone, help me. All I want is something small. Nothing big. I just want to be happy.

It is clear that no one will help me. Oh, God, I'm so close to killing people. So close.

Every time I see your face, my heart is shot with an arrow. I think that she will say yes, but she doesn't, does she? She says "I don't know." The three most (expletive) words in the English language.

I need to find more weapons. My parents are trying to take away my guns. My guns are the only things that haven't stopped me—that haven't stabbed me in the back.

Emotional Pain/Confusion

I want you to feel this, be this, taste this, kill this. Kill me. Oh God, I don't want to live. Will I see it to the end? What kind of dad would I make? All humans are evil. I just want to end the world of evil.

I don't want to see, hear, speak or feel evil, but I can't help it. I am evil. I want to kill and give pain without a cost. And there is no such thing. We kill him—we killed him a long time ago.

Anyone that believes in God is a (expletive) sheep.

If there was a God, he wouldn't let me feel the way I do. Love isn't real, only hate remains. Only hate.

▲ Box 10.3

The Words of a Shooter: Kip's Letter

This second document is the text of a letter written after Kip Kinkel killed his parents. He left it on the living room coffee table. We have divided it into segments to provide examples of key points in the text.

Emotional Pain/Confusion

I have just killed my parents. I don't know what is happening. I love my mom and dad so much. I just got two felonies on my record. My parents can't take that. It would destroy them. The embarrassment would be too much for them. They couldn't live with themselves. I am so sorry.

Aggressive Hatred

I am a horrible son. I wish I had been aborted. I destroy anything I touch. I can't eat. I can't sleep. I didn't deserve them. They were wonderful people. It's not their fault or the fault of any person or organization or television show. My head just doesn't work right. God damn these voices inside my head!

Emotional Pain/Confusion

I want to die. I want to be gone. But I have to kill people. I don't know why. I am so sorry.

Why did God do this to me? I have never been happy. I wish I was happy. I wish I made my mother proud, but I am nothing. I try so hard to find happiness, but you know me: I hate everything. I have no other choice. What have I become? I am so sorry.

The shooters were young people bursting with anger and rage. But under the anger and rage was an enormous range of feelings including pain, fear, shame, and sadness. These conflicting emotions interfered with reasonable problem solving. Many of the shooters saw the attack as the way to solve a personal problem: a parent planning to move the family, a lost or unreturned love, or a school suspension. For these emotionally confused shooters, their problems appeared to be devastating and without solution. For those who did not commit suicide, most experienced intense regret, remorse, and guilt afterward. Developmentally appropriate life-skills training would have assisted them in dealing with negative feelings, disappointment, and loss, as well as learning skills in developing and maintaining intimate friendships.

Aggressive hatred toward self and others.   The shooters had very favorable and narcissistic views about themselves, concurrent with very poor self-esteem. They believed that they were different from other people, and at the same time, they disliked those who were different. Along with narcissism, they were filled with self-loathing. Apparently these narcissistic young people with fragile, unstable self-esteem erupted into violence when their egos were threatened (Baumeister, Bushman, & Campbell, 2000).

Almost all of the attackers had come to the attention of someone, often fellow students, for their disturbing behavior. Behind this disturbing behavior were feelings that exemplified a callous disregard for the lives of others and for their own lives. Some wrote poems about homicide and suicide. One student talked often of putting rat poison in the cheese shakers at a local pizza restaurant. One shooter claimed that he did not dislike his English teacher, whom he killed. His goal was to kill two people because killing any two people made him eligible for the death penalty. She happened to be an opportune target. Because other teens may have knowledge of potential problems, peer assistance programs and supportive, compassionate adults are important components of an environment that increases protective factors of support and belonging.

Planning and leakage.   In almost all of the incidences of school shootings, the attacker developed the idea to harm the target well before the attack, most at least 2 weeks earlier. The attacks were neither spontaneous nor impulsive. The attackers developed the idea, acquired weapons, and most developed a plan at least 2 days prior to the attack. These young people took a long, planned, public path toward violence.

Prior to most incidences, the shooter told someone about his plan. The FBI describes this communication as "leakage." In more than half of the incidents, the shooter told more than one person about his plans. In virtually all of the cases, the person told was a peer—a sibling, a schoolmate, or a friend. Sometimes the attackers told their friends directly, providing detailed information about the plan and the target. In other cases the information was oblique with the peers knowing that something spectacular was going to happen at school on a particular date. In almost half the cases, the shooters were encouraged or influenced by other students.

Even though the shooter told a sibling, schoolmate, or friend about his ideas about a possible attack before it occurred, in almost no case was that information relayed to adults. Thus a few young people at school usually knew what would happen because the shooters had told them, but these bystanders didn't warn anyone. Ironically, this disturbing pattern gives hope: If shooters plan, there is time to intervene; if shooters tell peers, adults might be able to learn what is planned.

Vigilante motivation.   School shooters had more than one motive, with the most frequent motive being revenge. Most of the shooters were known to hold a real or imagined grievance against the targets. Coupled with the grievance was the shooter's difficulty in coping with a major change of a significant relationship or with a personal failure prior to the school attack. These young people had built up such a huge reservoir of pain, resentment, hostility, anger, and rage that, in the end, it took relatively little to tip the scale.

A precipitating event alone did not cause the shooters to act. Rather, most had been persecuted, threatened, attacked, injured, or bullied by others prior to the incident. Shooters described experiences of being bullied in terms that approached torment. They described behaviors that, if they occurred in the workplace, would meet the legal definitions of harassment.

The experience of bullying appeared to play a major role in motivating school attacks. More important, perhaps, was the common belief held by most of the shooters that they had not been safe at school. They had come to believe that adults would not or could not protect them, and they concluded that adults did not care.

We followed the sentencing hearing in Lane County Circuit Court for Kip Kinkel, a 15-year-old high school student from Springfield, Oregon. On May 20, 1998, Kinkel was suspended from school for stashing a stolen pistol in his school locker. That evening he killed his mother and father at home, and the next morning he took several guns and hundreds of rounds of ammunition to school and proceeded to shoot 26 of his high school classmates. Two were killed. At the time of his hearing, Kinkel had accepted a 25-year prison term after pleading guilty to killing his parents and two classmates. The hearing was held to help the court decide whether to add more prison time for the 26 counts of attempted murder and for trying to stab a police detective after his arrest. His final sentence was for 112 years without possibility of parole.

Intervention Strategies Focused on Youth Violence

An effective plan for prevention of school shootings, as well as other types of youth violence, should target the four areas just discussed. Quiet, withdrawn, or "strange" youth who are frequently rejected, disrespected, teased, and bullied by classmates and who have a tenuous relationship with parents need appropriate attention and listening from compassionate adults. The presence of a caring and involved adult may be the single most effective school safety measure available. Teachers, para-educators, as well as administrative, cafeteria, and maintenance staff can all be taught improved skills for listening and identifying troubled students.

In almost every school shooter case, adults were not especially concerned or even knowledgeable about the behavior and feelings of the perpetrators prior to the shootings, but other students knew something was wrong. Schools can creatively use peer groups as a vehicle to identify and assist young people at risk for violence. Peer support networks, cross-age and peer tutoring, mediation, and leadership programs provide links to connect understanding adults to the youth peer culture. Through connecting the troubled teen with positive peers—in itself a great help—the responsible adult has access to adolescents who may be on the fringe in a meaningful way. What also seems clear is that students must believe that telling an adult is an appropriate and positive behavior and that telling an adult will lead to positive outcomes. If they do not believe both of these, students are unlikely to confide in adults.

Uncontrolled feelings of anger, hostility, and rage are a major factor in shootings. The anger was often connected to experiences of rejection, isolation, and persecution, and hurt and fear was underlying the anger. Although expressed in different ways, these feelings are often a component of other antisocial behaviors.

In addition to learning to deal with feelings, young people can learn to behave more responsibly if they are taught to do so. Schools in which rules and expectations for behavior are clear to children are very effective in managing school discipline. For instance, programs such as unified discipline—a proactive, schoolwide approach for managing problem behavior—are very important in maintaining discipline (White, Algozzine, Audette, Marr, & Ellis, 2001). Schools that have a consistent, clear, and graduated consequence for misbehavior and that provide recognition for positive behavior reduce antisocial behavior and conduct disorders (Sugai & Horner, 1999, 2001).

The school can also play an effective role in mitigating the influence of gangs. Effectiveness depends on the level of communication among school personnel and the speed of their response to a potential crisis or violent acts. School personnel need to be in close communication with one another, with each employee having a clearly designated response role when the threat of gang activity is present. However, because delinquency generally precedes gang membership, efforts should not be limited to gang intervention or suppression within the school (Esbenson, 2000).

Schools can also play a crucial role in developing communication with the community and in building coalitions with community organizations and law enforcement. Community groups that are recruited and educated by schools can help to minimize violence and gang activity. Youth service centers, recreational centers, and religious organizations can meet an adolescent's need for inclusion, affirmation, and acceptance and can serve to discourage gang involvement by providing a healthy alternative. Developing and nurturing school, community, and family relationships (the mesosystemic level) is very important for preventing youth violence. Proactive citizen groups have been developed in some communities to deal with youth gangs (Esbensen, 2000). Such community groups can make a positive difference, especially when closely coordinated with schools, churches, youth agencies, and police to provide a better general environment for managing youth violence in the community (Spergel et al., 1996). At the same time, to deal with a specific troubled youth, a specific intervention, such as reality therapy, is called for.

SPECIFIC INTERVENTION: REALITY THERAPY

William Glasser and G. L. Harrington developed reality therapy, one of the more promising approaches to the deterrence of delinquency. When Glasser was a resident in psychiatry at the Veterans Administration Neuropsychiatric Hospital in West Los Angeles, California, in the 1950s, both he and his supervisor, Harrington, were frustrated by the inability of traditional psychotherapy to solve the problems of many of their patients. Harrington was in charge of a "back" ward that had a very low success rate. The 210 patients averaged 17 years of confinement; the last discharge had occurred 2 years earlier, and the patient had returned within a short time. Although the staff was compassionate and well intentioned, the patients were not getting better. Harrington began to confront the patients, chiding them for their unacceptable behavior and supporting them when their behavior improved. Nurses and aides began to follow suit; they became more involved with the patients and less tolerant of their "crazy" symptoms.

At this time Glasser was taking a similar approach to delinquent girls at the Ventura School for Girls, an institutional facility of the California Youth Authority. In view of the populations they were serving, both men were achieving a remarkable degree of success. Forty-five patients on Harrington's ward went home the first year. They were followed by 85 the second year, and 90 the third year. Many returned, of course, as they were encouraged to do, but only a very few remained more than a month after their return. The others reentered mainstream society immediately. Glasser obtained similar results at the Ventura School for Girls. Roughly 400 girls, with offenses ranging from "incorrigibility" to murder, were confined there for 6 to 8 months for rehabilitation. After applying the new therapy, Glasser reported that 80% of the girls were released and did not return.

Reality therapy grew out of the experiences and discussions of Glasser and Harrington. Glasser first described this treatment in *Reality Therapy* (1965), and he has continued to elaborate and expand his approach through numerous publications (Glasser, 1972, 1976, 1984). In his most recent work (Glasser, 1998, 2001, 2002), Glasser has developed the concept of choice theory, in which reality therapy is embedded.

Assumptions of Reality Therapy

Reality therapy and choice theory are based on the assumption that human beings must have human communication and contact to thrive, much like the notion of connectedness that we present as one of the five Cs of competency in Chapter 6. Within the context of this communication and contact, people must balance their five basic drives: (1) belonging, (2) power, (3) fun or enjoyment, (4) freedom, and (5) survival (Wubbolding, 2000). Humans have a basic desire to be with other people, to care for others, and to be cared for in return. Individuals who seek help or who are sent for help suffer from one basic inadequacy—they are unable to achieve such contact successfully.

Striving for human contact reflects two fundamental needs: to love and be loved and to be worthwhile as a person. Low-risk young people are able to satisfy these needs in an appropriate way. They develop a success identity that enables them to be involved with respected people who care for them and for whom they care. They have the capacity to give and receive love. They have at least one other person who cares about them and one person whom they care about. They also develop a feeling of personal self-worth. They believe they have a right to be in the world, and they behave in socially responsible ways.

High-risk young people are unable to satisfy these two basic needs. Instead, they either ignore or deny reality. In the process, they develop a failure identity. Young people who ignore reality cope with life by acting as if the rules do not include them (see Box 10.4). They are described as antisocial, sociopathic, delinquent, or criminal. Those who deny reality cope in one of two ways, through substance abuse or mental illness. The young person who says "The world is no good, so I must change it" and proceeds to change the world by getting "high" or "wasted" is essentially denying reality and escaping it. Withdrawing from the world through delusions and other symptoms of mental illness is another way of denying reality.

The reality therapist assumes that all problems result from an inability to fulfill essential needs (Brown & Swenson, 2005). Psychological problems are caused by lack of responsibility, the choice of behaviors, and toxic relationships (Glasser, 2001). Individuals must fulfill their needs without preventing others from fulfilling theirs. The person who cannot do so is irresponsible, not mentally ill or bad. Perhaps more than any other approach, reality therapy holds that it is impossible to maintain self-regard while living irresponsibly. The practice of reality therapy is based on teaching at-risk individuals satisfactory standards of behavior, praising them when they act appropriately, and correcting them when they are wrong. Self-respect comes through self-discipline and closeness to others. In learning to face reality, young people fulfill their needs. In doing so, they become socially responsible people who can achieve honest human relationships.

Theoretical Components of Reality Therapy

Reality therapy has three basic components: involvement, rejection of irresponsible behavior, and relearning. We consider each of these components in detail as they might apply to Tyrone Baker of Chapter 2.

▲ Box 10.4

Mikey the Menace

When Mikey arrived at the classroom door each morning, the atmosphere changed. A subtle wave of tension would pass among the children as he entered the room shouting, "Hi every-body!" Within minutes, someone would be crying, complaining, or retreating from his awk-ward overtures and fast-moving fists, and he would be temporarily relocated to the time-out chair. He would beam at me from the chair. "Teacher, I'll be good." And he tried.

Mikey is the youngest of seven children. His father was in prison for selling drugs, and his mother had described her current boyfriend as a "damn scary alcoholic." Child Protective Services closely monitored the family and was close to taking the younger children away from the mother. During one home visit, I observed the mother grab Mikey roughly, pull his hair, and hit him on the head, all in response to appropriate attention-seeking behavior. Each time he was punished, Mikey scowled and then quickly turned his sunniest smile back on; each time, his mother failed to notice.

One evening I was still working in my classroom as darkness fell, and I was suddenly startled to hear him shout, "Hi, every . . . Where's the kids?" There was Mikey in the door-way, cheerful as ever, having just walked seven long blocks through projects so crime-ridden that the classroom mothers had warned me to "never go in there." Mikey was very disap-pointed to learn that "the kids" had gone home. His desperate efforts to gain affection and attention were all that a 4-year-old could do. Mikey should be 19 years old now. What new methods has he learned?

Involvement.   Involvement is the initial and most difficult phase of counseling and requires the most therapeutic skill. Involvement, and the process of developing it, is a pre-requisite to the other steps and forms a consistent theme running through the entire helping relationship. In creating involvement with young people, it is important not to give up or push too hard. In the language of choice theory (Glasser, 2001), if Tyrone is internally controlled, the adults cannot work "on" him (external control); they can only be effective by working "with" him, and to do that a good relationship is necessary.

In Tyrone's case, the helper must be able to become emotionally involved with him and must be able to accept him uncritically at first. The adult cannot be frightened by or angry about Ty's behavior, thoughts, or attitudes. By demonstrating interest, warmth, and sensitivity while discussing Ty's values, interests, hopes, and fears, the adult helps Tyrone grow beyond his problems. The counselor must know and understand Tyrone and express interest in him as an individual with great potential.

Further, the helper must be open and present him- or herself as a model of trans-parency and integrity. Glasser says that helpers must be willing to have their own values tested. The helper must be tough and able to withstand Tyrone's intense criticism and anger. In addition, the helper must be willing to admit imperfection and yet demonstrate to Tyrone that he has the ability to act responsibly. The helper, in effect, supports and strengthens Ty's conscience by demonstrating honesty, concern, and personal authenticity.

The counselor develops an "I/you" pattern of interaction. The personal "I," Glasser says, must be used instead of the more impersonal "we," "the school," and "they." The adult says, "I'd like you to do your homework for me." "It's important to me that you're here every day." "I'm concerned about you and interested in you." "I want to explain how your life can go better." Such statements emphasize the personal; they lead the adult to involvement not only as helper to client but as person to person. They communicate that the adult cares enough to risk an emotional, personal involvement. This allows Tyrone to look at his unacceptable behavior and to learn better ways to lead his life. By being responsible, tough, and sensitive, the helper shows confidence that Tyrone can change his irresponsible behavior. The counselor thus creates a sense of belong for Ty (Wubbolding, 2000).

Rejection of irresponsible behavior.   In the second phase of treatment, the client's irresponsible behaviors are rejected first by the counselor and later by the client. The counselor ignores the past and works in the here and now with a view to the future. The focus is on Ty's behavior rather than on his feelings and attitudes. In fact, the feelings and emotions that accompany deviant behavior are de-emphasized.

The counselor working with Tyrone insists that he recognize and assume responsibility for his own behavior. Tyrone is helped to evaluate and to judge his behavior against an established standard of social responsibility. The counselor does not accept excuses or help him justify irresponsibility. Ty is helped to "own" his behavior and to view that behavior in light of his values and needs and of society's system of values and needs (Glasser, 2001). "The skill of therapy is to put the responsibility upon the client and, after involvement is established, to ask him why he remains in therapy—if he is not dissatisfied with his behavior" (Glasser, 1965, p. 29).

Of course, emphasizing responsibility is fruitless if the client is not ready. Irresponsibility is discussed with stubborn clients only when they are ready to change. Even then, the counselor should discuss only the fact that the client's behavior is irresponsible and that only the client can do something about it. Tyrone's recognition that his current behavior is irresponsible or wrong and therefore not effective in getting his needs met provides powerful motivation for positive change. Consequently, the counselor is free to pose questions such as, "Are you taking the responsible course of action?" or "Are you doing right or wrong?" Questions of this sort underline the unrealistic aspects of negative behavior and set the stage for the next level of interaction.

Relearning.   The third procedure employed by the reality therapist is to help clients learn more realistic ways to fulfill their needs. By modeling consistently responsible behavior, the counselor can guide Tyrone toward an understanding that happiness results from responsibility.

Counselors instruct clients to examine their "constructive" thinking about the present and future, in other words, to evaluate their plan for getting what they want out of their current situation so that they can be where they would rather be (Glasser, 1965). By working out this plan of action with Tyrone, the counselor helps identify alternatives to his negative, self-defeating behavior. Developing a realistic plan of action that accords with Tyrone's previously articulated values serves as a means for the counselor to teach responsibility.

After the counselor and the client jointly agree on a plan, they make a mutual commitment to resolve the problem. Tyrone's plan, for instance, must lead to behaviors that will enable him to satisfy his needs for acceptance and connection with others. The mutual planning and mutual commitment demonstrate that the counselor does not accept Tyrone's negative behavior but cares about him and is willing to help him do something definite that will lead to the fulfillment of his needs. The plan and the commitment always involve much positive reinforcement for Tyrone's responsible behavior and the rejection of excuses for irresponsible, self-defeating behavior.

When Tyrone behaves irresponsibly, the counselor refrains from punishing him. The helper does, however, freely express praise when Tyrone behaves responsibly and shows disapproval when he does not. In varying degrees, then, the counselor teaches Tyrone more realistic ways to meet his needs.

The Seven Principles of Reality Therapy

Glasser has elaborated his three-stage framework by providing seven principles of reality therapy. These principles constitute the essential mechanics of reality therapy. We briefly describe each principle here with sample statements that reflect the interactions of client and counselor.

It should not be assumed that every session will incorporate all seven principles. Involvement is essential in every session, but the other principles emphasized will depend on the particular client, the circumstances, and the progress of counseling. Early sessions tend to focus on identification and evaluation of current behavior. Later sessions tend to deal with planning and commitment issues.

Involvement. Involvement means development and maintenance of a close, emotional relationship between client and helper. It implies a positive, caring attitude and gives the relationship a warm, personal quality. The thread of involvement is woven throughout the therapeutic process and intertwines with all other principles. (Client: "I'm going out of my head. I've got to get some help quick." Helper: "I'd really like to help you.")

Dozens of studies have provided evidence of the importance of an empathetic therapeutic relationship in achieving positive outcomes (Garfield, 1994; Orlinsky, Grawe, & Parks, 1994; Sexton & Whiston, 1994). It is critically important for difficult and defiant adolescents as well (Bernstein, 1996; Hanna, Hanna, & Keys, 1999). Furthermore, a strong relationship based on mutual respect and trust is one of the seven attributes of effective prevention programs (Schorr, 1997).

Current behavior. The focus is on behavior here and now. The counselor helps the client become aware of his or her current behavior and its ramifications. The client is also helped to see that this behavior is self-selected and therefore the consequences of the behavior are self-inflicted. (Client: "My mother is always angry at me. She's always been angry at me. I never do anything right." Helper: "What are you doing now about that situation?")

Evaluating behavior. The client is made to look critically at his or her behavior and judge whether the behavior is in his or her best interest. The counselor helps the client make value judgments about what is contributing to a lack of success. At this stage, the client realistically determines what is good for him- or herself and what is good for people the client cares about or would like to care about. (Client: "To keep her off my back, I don't stay home much." Helper: "Is that productive for you?")

Planning responsible behavior. The counselor helps the client develop a realistic plan to implement the identified value judgment. At this stage the counselor is strongly involved in teaching responsibility to the client. Working with the client to develop a realistic plan for changing behavior is an important step in teaching responsibility. (Client: "It's not productive because when I do come home she complains even more." Helper: "Is there a plan that we could make together that would keep your mother from complaining so much?")

Commitment. When the plan of action has been agreed upon, the client and counselor make a commitment to follow it. The commitment may be a written agreement, but usually it consists of an oral exchange. Equivocations—"I'll try," "Maybe," "I think I can do it"—are not acceptable. (Client: "Yes, I guess I could stay home a couple of nights a week." Helper: "Are you willing to make a commitment to stay home two nights next week?")

The principles of reality therapy are designed to help clients learn to become involved with others in a responsible way and to learn to say yes and no at appropriate times. Clients are also encouraged to try new patterns of behavior to fulfill their needs, regardless of fears that these behaviors may not work. Essentially, clients learn not only to face reality but also to fulfill their needs. They commit themselves to a plan that has no loopholes. In the process they evaluate their current behavior and develop a plan for the future.

Reality may be painful, but when at-risk young people can admit to the irresponsibility of their actions, the last phase of counseling—the relearning process—can begin. Then there is potential for growth, fulfillment, and self-worth. When at-risk young people take responsibility for their actions, they gradually find better ways to meet their needs and change inappropriate patterns of behavior. At-risk young people can learn to control themselves (Glasser, 2001).

Accept no excuses. The helper must help the client gain the experience that will enable the client to keep the commitment he or she has made. In addition, the new behavior needs time to become satisfying and thus self-reinforcing. Consequently, the helper cannot accept excuses for failure to keep a commitment. Glasser makes it clear that counselors, teachers, parents, and other adults who care about young people must not make excuses for them. Nor should adults tolerate the excuses that young people offer. (Client: "Yes, I'll stay home unless something more important comes up." Helper: "If you make the commitment, no excuses are acceptable. You have to decide now whether to commit yourself or not.")

No punishment. A counselor will not implement sanctions that have not been agreed upon in the commitment. Punishment changes the relationship that is necessary for success and reinforces the client's loneliness and isolation. (Client: "What will happen if I don't stay home two nights?" Helper: "Well, then we'd have to restudy the plan and the commitment. I would be disappointed; you wouldn't have helped your situation. It would be better to come up with a plan you can live with than not to follow through on your commitment.")

Engaging adolescents in a process that reflects the assumptions and principles of reality therapy can be very helpful to counselors, teachers, and parents. Adults who use this approach can effectively confront a potential or current delinquency problem. Although the principles of reality therapy were developed in a structured, controlled setting, they can be applied successfully in many less-controlled environments.

CONCLUSION

Unfortunately, many young people with interpersonal, personal, and environmental pressures react to these pressures through aggressive acting out. Unless we help young people identify and manage their own behavior, and unless our interventions help modify and change school and family environments to support more positive and prosocial responses, children with conduct problems may develop antisocial behavior, engage in more severe crime, or become involved in gangs as teens. Moreover, even though there has been a decrease in youth crime and school violence in the last decade, sensational incidences of school shootings have created concern and fear for all communities. The characteristics of shooters are different from the characteristics of other perpetrators of youth violence, but their access to guns, emotional pain and confusion, aggressive hatred, and vigilante motives mark them distinctly as at risk.

The problems of delinquency are multifaceted, so understanding the problem as well as prevention and intervention strategies must focus not only on the individual youth but on family, school, peer group, and the community as a whole. Professionals and parents alike should develop ways to systematically listen more to young people regarding their experiences within their environments, engage peer groups in prosocial ways, reduce the incidence of bullying within schools, and provide improved training in anger management and other social skills. We have also identified more specifically how the principles of reality therapy can be usefully applied to help adolescents understand the consequences of their actions and form a plan for changing self-defeating and destructive behaviors.

YOUTH SUICIDE

▲ *Wet the top of the glass*
and run your finger around the rim.
That's me in the shimmering squeal; the sound of glass.
Drop the vase to the floor
and listen to it shatter.
That's me in the piercing shatter; the sound of glass
Crush the mirror and watch the image
crack and splinter.
That's me in the crack, the splinter, the sound of
glass.
There is not much left of me.
Why not just silence the sound of glass, too?
If only I could find
some meaning for myself that
death won't take away.

CHAPTER OUTLINE

▲   To prevent suicide we must understand the influences that contribute to suicidal behavior. They may range from a child's chaotic family life to not knowing how to manage relationships, from a child's perception that the future is doomed to a teenager's feeling that the present is hopeless. To prevent suicide, we also should know the warning signs and available intervention strategies.

Among the aspects of suicide discussed in this chapter are (a) the incidence of childhood and adolescent suicide, (b) precursors to suicide and the characteristics of suicidal children and teens, (c) warning signs and behaviors, (d) common misconceptions of suicide, (e) identification and assessment of suicide ideation, and (f) prevention and intervention strategies, including early intervention, crisis management, and follow-up treatment. Particular attention is given to childhood and adolescent depression and early onset of bipolar disorder. Finally, for each intervention, we focus on the potential role of the teacher, counselor, psychologist, and other human service professionals and the role of the school, family, and inpatient settings in effecting change.

▲ Box 11.1

Accidental Death

Jarrod was a senior in high school who loved to play the guitar and compose songs. He had dreamed of being a musician for as long as he could remember. It was a dream his parents did not share. Jarrod was the oldest child in the family and had hoped to study music in college, but his parents insisted that he attend a business school because they didn't want to "send good money after bad." Jarrod expected a lot of himself, and he knew that his parents also expected a great deal of him. He had few friends, but the friendships he had were quite intense. His friends looked up to him and had high expectations for his career in music. They were disappointed about his parents' plan to send him to business school and told him to "fight for his rights." Feeling unable to live up to his friends' expectations, he retreated from them. That spring Jarrod was sleeping only 3 to 4 hours a night. He alienated himself from his friends and his parents and grew increasingly distraught over his seeming inability to please the people he loved. Four days after his high school graduation, local newspapers reported that Jarrod, aged 18, had died in a car accident. Investigators could not explain why, in the absence of traffic or bad weather, he had suddenly veered off the road and crashed at high speed into a very prominent cement wall.

THE SCOPE OF THE PROBLEM

Suicide is the third leading cause of death among adolescents in the United States after unintentional injury and homicide (CDCP, 2001; McIntosh, 2000; National Center for Health Statistics, 2000). In the United States teen suicide rates tripled over several decades in the 20th century but have declined slightly since the mid-1990s (Moskos, Achilles, & Gray, 2004). In recent years, approximately 5,000 individuals whose death certificate indicated suicide were between the ages of 15 and 24; five children under the age of 20 committed suicide every day (CDF, 2002). Research suggests that 9% of young people attempt suicide each year, 15 to 17% develop a plan to do so, and 19% seriously consider it. This rate climbs to about 33% among troubled adolescents (Tomlinson-Keasey & Keasey, 1988) and to 61% in some groups of juvenile offenders (Alessi, McManus, Brickman, & Grapentine, 1984). The suicide rate among adolescents is predicted to increase (McIntosh, 2000; Robertson & Mathews, 1989). Suicide rates among children and adolescents are highest in the western regions of the United States and lowest in the Northeast (National Center for Health Statistics, 2000).

These estimates are probably low. Many suicides are not reported as such because of the family's embarrassment or religious beliefs or the discomfort of the school and community in acknowledging that a suicide has occurred (see Box 11.1). Consider also that accidents, the leading cause of death among adolescents, are often associated with recklessness and use of alcohol, both of which are related to suicide ideation. Many accidental deaths may result from a wish to be dead. Similarly, drug overdoses, recorded as accidental deaths, may be unrecognized or unreported suicides. These deaths are considered passive suicides. Of course, researchers are unable to determine the number of passive suicides that occur each year.

Sex differences have been found in the rates and the lethality of suicide attempts. Three times as many females as males attempt suicide, but about 3 times as many males as females are successful (Canetto & Lester, 1995; McIntosh, 2000).

Differences can be partially attributed to the lethality of the method. Males tend to choose more violent means to kill themselves, such as firearms, whereas females more often use pills and poisons. Six out of 10 suicides among all adolescents are through the use of firearms (McIntosh, 2000). For boys, having access to a gun in the house is the single most important factor that distinguishes between adolescent males who just think about suicide and those who attempt it (Bearman & Moody, 2004). Indeed, some modest declines (8.3%) in the rate of suicide among 14- to 17-year-olds is attributed to child access prevention laws in some states. Those states with laws that require gun owners to lock away firearms to prevent access by young people had reductions in suicide. Minimum possession age and minimum purchase age for firearms produced no effects (Grossman et al., 2005).

Latino children and adolescents have a higher rate of suicide than European American youth (Queralt, 1993; Smith, Mercer, & Rosenberg, 1989). The suicide rate of African American teens has increased, and although the rate is still lower than for European Americans, the gap is closing. African American females have a low rate of suicide compared to other ethnic groups (Range et al., 1999); however, increases in suicide attempts by male and female African Americans are quite dramatic (CDCP, 1998a).

Although there is considerable variability from tribe to tribe, Native Americans have the highest adolescent suicide rate of any ethnic group in the United States (Gould & Kramer, 2001). The high suicide rate has been associated with factors such as substance abuse and alcoholism, child abuse and neglect, unemployment, the availability of firearms, and lack of economic options leading to hopelessness (Grossman et al., 2005; Middlebrook, Lemaster, Beals, Novins, & Manson, 2001). Although few data exist for Asian American adolescents, some researchers hypothesize that cultural values may contribute to lower rates of suicide among this group (Range et al., 1999).

Suicide among gay, lesbian, bisexual, and transgender (GLBT) youth has received considerable attention during the last several years. Rates of attempted suicide range from 20% to 42%, with suicide the leading cause of death among gay, lesbian, and bisexual youth primarily because of the debilitating effects of growing up in a homophobic society (Gould, Greenberg, Velting, & Shaffer, 2003; The rate of suicide among gay and lesbian youth is considerably higher than that for heterosexual youth: They are 2 to 3 times more likely to commit suicide and constitute 30% of all adolescent suicides. Several researchers (Noell & Ochs, 2001; Remafedi, French, Story, Resnick, & Blum, 1998) suggest that suicide attempts by this population are frequently linked with sexual milestones such as self-identification as homosexual, coming out to others, or resulting loss of friendship. GLBT youth often report higher rates of intravenous drug use, a lifetime history of suicide attempts, and recent depression and suicidal ideation (Noell & Ochs, 2001). Such risk factors increase when homosexual youth are faced with additional difficulties, such as homelessness. According to French, Story, Remafedi, Resnick, and Blum (1996), homosexual males are also more likely to report poor body image, binge eating, or purging behaviors. Gay male suicide attempters tend to adopt a homosexual identity at a younger age, express more feminine gender roles, and often come from dysfunctional families (Savin-Williams, 1994).

Attempts are most likely to occur after same-sex sexual activity or when individuals question their heterosexual identity. During this period, they are faced with additional stressors and experience feelings of social isolation, self-revulsion, disenfranchisement, and rejection from family and peers (Remafedi et al., 1998; Savin-Williams, 1994). In this particularly high-risk group special attention is required to reduce suicide attempts.

Disability status may also be a factor in youth suicide. Children and adolescents with disabilities often feel isolated (Bauer, 2001) and are frequently the only member of their family with a disability. Although the presence of disabilities can affect both male and female children, some researchers have noted the multiple minority status for females with disabilities (Bauer, 2001). Feelings of isolation and "differentness" can cause additional stress leading to loneliness, depression, and thoughts of suicide.

RISK FACTORS AND CHARACTERISTICS OF YOUTH SUICIDE

To understand the causes of suicide among children and adolescents, it is helpful to recognize behaviors that are considered "normal" during development. Many adolescents of all cultures enjoy life, are happy most of the time, and are able to develop nurturing friendships (Diener & Diener, 1996). They feel positive about their development and their future. They experience physical changes and new social roles without undue trauma, even though they may regularly experience situation-specific anxiety. For the most part, they are able to cope with the changes that are taking place in their lives.

For other adolescents, however, this period of change and growth is filled with stressful events and adjustments. Depression, aggression, and divergent thinking are common during this transitional period. These characteristics can be exacerbated by low socioeconomic status, absence of parental support, and lack of educational and economic opportunity. Girls tend to express more negative feelings toward themselves than boys, and report more loneliness, sadness, and vulnerability (Tang & Cook, 2001). These experiences may provide fertile ground for suicide ideation and attempts.

It is often difficult for parents, teachers, and mental health professionals to differentiate between the normal turmoil that occurs during childhood and adolescence from turmoil that is life-threatening (King, Price, Telljohann, & Wahl, 2000). Many children and adolescents at risk for suicide have been mistakenly viewed as simply "going through a stage." Certain psychological and relationship characteristics help to identify those who are at risk for self-destructive behavior.

Interpersonal, Family, and Psychosocial Characteristics

A variety of interpersonal, family, and psychosocial characteristics are associated with suicidal ideation and suicide attempts. We describe several here, but this is not an exhaustive list.

Substance abuse. Alcohol and drug abuse are often related to adolescent risk for suicide (Gould & Kramer, 2001; Hull-Blanks et al., 2004). Although adolescents who are chemically dependent are generally at higher risk for suicide, interrelated factors, such as homelessness or social isolation, can add to the likelihood of a suicide attempt (Noell &

Ochs, 2001). Substance abuse can exacerbate suicide risk in myriad ways. For example, alcoholics or drug users are often inaccessible for suicide prevention and may not seek the support they need (Roy, 2001). Chapter 8 provides detailed information about the risks associated with substance use.

Under- and overachievement.   Academic underachievement has been linked to suicide although impaired academic functioning may follow and be a consequence of suicide attempts (Lewinsohn, Rohde, & Seeley, 1993; Mazza & Eggert, 2001). Perfectionism, overachievement, and living up to high expectations are characteristic of many academically talented suicidal children and adolescents. Talented girls with high levels of impulsivity and aggressiveness and low levels of harm avoidance may be particularly at risk for suicide (Robinson Kurpius, S. E., Kerr, B., & Harkins, A. (Eds). (2005). Deterioration in the academic performance of young people, whether they are high or low achieving, can be a warning sign of suicidal potential.

Catastrophic worldview.   In addition to negative thoughts and feelings about the self, a negative or catastrophic view of the world and the future is associated with suicide risk. Some children and adolescents view the world as an unpredictable, dangerous, and hostile place. These intimations of catastrophe are exacerbated by threats of nuclear weapons, the AIDS crisis, racism, poverty, regional wars, and civil violence. Consequently, some young people feel desperate and helpless and are potential victims of a suicide crisis. Unfortunately, music, video games, films, and television influence catastrophic feelings by modeling and glorifying violence and death (Gould & Kramer, 2001).

Cluster suicides.   Cluster suicides are suicides that follow or imitate another suicide. They may also follow a television program or movie that depicts teenage suicide (Capuzzi & Golden, 1988; Gould & Kramer, 2001; Gould & Shaffer, 1986). When one child or adolescent commits suicide, the act somehow becomes normalized for others. After one suicide, those who have already been experiencing despair may begin to see suicide as a viable response to their stress and feelings of hopelessness. Adolescents who are at risk for self-destructive behavior are even more vulnerable after someone they know or know of commits suicide (Cerel, Roberts, & Nilsen, 2005). Suicide reports in the media primarily affect teenagers and young adults as opposed to young children (Gould & Kramer, 2001). Suicide clusters, often trivialized as "copycat" suicides, are a particular problem on American Indian reservations (Tomlinson-Keasey & Keasey, 1988). For this reason, appropriate postvention or follow-up treatment after a suicide crisis is essential.

Disruptive family experiences.   Suicidal youth often come from dysfunctional or disintegrated families (Fergusson & Lynskey, 1995). The rise in single-parent households as well as lack of skill and experience in parenting, communication, and discipline (see Chapter 4) exacerbate the risk of suicide. Depressed parents, especially depressed fathers, are particularly problematic for their sons. Depressed male teenagers with depressed fathers are 7 times more likely to attempt suicide as young adults than depressed male teenagers with unaffected fathers (Rohde et al., 2005).

Family interactions that are characterized by anger, emotional ambivalence, and rejection are also associated with self-destructive behavior in youth. Adolescents are more likely to have serious suicidal thoughts if they engage in fewer activities with parents

(Bearman & Moody, 2004). When single parents are overloaded with work and financial obligations and have limited support from others, they have less energy to devote to the parent–child relationship. "Blended" families or stepfamilies may also be at high risk for suffering from uncertain, inconsistent, and confusing family interactions. Parental support and consistency are important protective factors against children at risk for suicide, and youth who lack family stability are at increasingly higher risk for suicide (Mazza & Eggert, 2001; Randell et al., 2001).

Violent families.   Violence is common in the families of many suicidal children as is a history of sexual abuse (Gould et al., 2003). In one study, attempters were 3 to 6 times more likely to have experienced sexual or physical abuse at home (Blumenthal, 1990). Suicide is also more prevalent among young people whose families have a history of suicide (Gould & Kramer, 2001; Gould et al., 2003; Pfeffer, Normandin, & Kakuma, 1994). One study found that relatives who attempted suicide in the previous year greatly increased adolescents' suicide thoughts (Bearman & Moody, 2004). The age of a child is also significant: As many as 75% of children who were under 11 years of age when a family member committed suicide attempted suicide themselves when they became adolescents (Roy, 1983), a greater percentage than older children who experience this tragic event.

Poor communication.   Children who grow up in a dysfunctional family system frequently develop inadequate communication skills. Young people who grow up in an environment where communication of their thoughts and feelings is unsafe do not learn to express their distress to others. As feelings and thoughts fester and become increasingly negative, these children may withdraw into themselves, making it difficult for others to recognize and respond to their increasing pain, depression, and possible suicidal feelings. The progressive isolation that results from poor communication skills can be a warning sign of self-destructive behavior (Marttunen, Aro, & Lonnquist, 1993). Other children may begin acting out, which is also associated with higher levels of suicide risk (Evans, Marte, Betts, & Silliman, 2001).

Loss and separation.   Suicidal youth are more likely than other youth to have experienced the loss of a parent through separation, divorce, or death (Marttunen et al., 1993). Even when one has not lost a parent or other close relative, suicidal thoughts may arise in response to the loss of a friendship or dating partner (Tang & Cook, 2001). Separation and differentiation from parents is an important developmental task of adolescence, but death and divorce are life-changing events over which a child has no control. The natural feelings of grief, abandonment, and anger call for coping skills that not all children have developed. The surviving parent may be experiencing tremendous emotional adjustment as well and may be unable to provide the direction and support the child needs. In contrast with steadily nurturing autonomy, the loss of a parent may push children rapidly into adult roles before they are ready.

Intrapersonal and Psychological Characteristics

Certain intrapersonal and psychological characteristics are associated with suicide ideation, attempts, and completions. These deserve specific attention.

▲ Box 11.2

She Didn't Want to Die

Jennifer was a 12-year-old girl, just finishing her sixth-grade year in elementary school. Unlike other girls her age, she began developing physically and emotionally into a young adult during the school year. Although Jennifer had a close circle of friends, she often worried about other girls teasing her and gossiping about her behind her back. She felt different than everyone else. She was ashamed to shower after gym class and uncomfortable about her rapid physical development. Jennifer often found herself hanging around boys several years older than herself and enjoying their company. She no longer felt comfortable giggling and gossiping with her friends. She was too ashamed to tell her parents how she felt and believed her friends would not understand. Slowly Jennifer started speaking with her friends less and spending more time with her older male buddies.

One day after school, Jennifer headed home and flipped on the television as she normally did. There on the news she saw a young girl in high school who had committed suicide the previous week. The news coverage was quite extensive, showing her memorial service, her saddened classmates, and all of the flowers around the school laid out for her. It was at that moment that Jennifer grabbed a bottle of pills and swallowed over 30 of them in hopes of recovering some sense of importance and belonging. Later, in the emergency room, she told her mother that she really didn't want to die; all she wanted was to stop feeling so unbearably alone.

Self-image.   Low self-esteem, poor self-concept, and feelings of worthlessness are typical of suicidal children and may predispose a child or adolescent to suicide ideation. Poor self-esteem and self-concept often lead to feelings of hopelessness and depression. A distorted view of the self can also lead to irrational and unrealistic expectations of others, the world, and the future. For example, adolescents who are underweight or overweight are only slightly more likely to report suicidal tendencies. However, teens who perceived themselves to be very or slightly underweight and slightly or very overweight were more likely to report thoughts and attempts of suicide compared to those who said they were "about the right weight" (CDCP, 2005). Children and adolescents who dislike themselves and who are unable to see themselves in positive ways require special attention from counselors, teachers, and parents. Girls are at an increased risk of problems with self-esteem, especially during middle school (Tang & Cook, 2001). Female adolescents who physically mature earlier than others and date at an early age may have particularly negative outlooks on their body and appearance (see Box 11.2).

Anger.   Anger, aggression, and anger control difficulties are also predictors of risky suicidal behavior (Randell et al., 2001). As discussed in Chapter 10, inappropriately expressed anger is a major problem, and suicidal adolescents often display increased levels of hostility.

In a recent study conducted in the Rocky Mountain region, the area with the highest rate of adolescent suicide, researchers found a relationship between reported suicide risk and initiation of fights, threatening of other children, and use of weapons to assault (Evans et al., 2001). Those who act aggressively toward their peers, are victims of violence, or witness such hostility are at increased risk for suicidal behavior.

Loneliness. Loneliness, isolation, and lack of connectedness are clearly implicated in suicide (Mazza & Eggert, 2001; B. T. McWhirter, 1990). Most suicidal children and adolescents have problems with their peers and are sensitive to rejection. Loneliness usually begins in childhood and continues into adolescence. Teenagers who feel lonely and isolated in a period marked by developing social relationships do not experience the support of friends. Without these nurturing and bonding relationships, children feel expendable and unnoticed—feelings that often lead to suicide ideation. For girls especially, being socially isolated and having conflicts with peers means it is more likely that they will consider suicide (Bearman & Moody, 2004).

Impulsivity. Impulsivity is often related to a suicidal response in young people. Teenagers and preteens who are part of a peer cluster, for example, may attempt suicide out of an impulsive reaction to someone else's self-destructive actions. Impulsive children are also influenced by others' responses to suicide and by the impact that a suicide has on others (Gould & Kramer, 2001; Lipschitz, 1995). The restriction of firearms (Gould & Kramer, 2001) is very important here. In the United States the most common method for attempting suicide is through the use of firearms. Having a gun in the home is a significant suicidal risk factor, especially for boys. Girls who attempt suicide often choose a medication overdose.

Impulsivity is also related to a risk-taking style. Although young people may be ambivalent about ending their lives, an impulsive or daredevil reaction to stressors often leads to suicide. In other words, adolescents may not be intent on killing themselves, but they may attempt to gain attention or approval from others through risky behavior. High-risk behaviors and impulsivity, fairly common during adolescence, allow young people to test their fears of death against their feelings of immortality (Bell & Bell, 1993). Impulse control may be a key predictor of the outcome of a suicidal crisis: Impulsive children who contemplate suicide may attempt it before they have time to think of an alternative.

Depression and hopelessness. Depression and related psychiatric disorders are clearly a strong contributing factor to youth suicide (Gould et al., 2003). Recent studies have suggested that 14% of young people ages 12 to 17 have experienced at least one major depressed episode in their lifetimes, and about half of them thought about killing themselves (Bridge, Goldstein, & Bren, (2006)). Depression is linked to suicidal thoughts and behaviors among children and adolescents in both clinical and nonclinical settings (Gould & Kramer, 2001; Mazza & Eggert, 2001). Interestingly, antidepressant medication apparently has significantly lowered the suicide rate of older adolescent boys (ages 15–19) from lower socioeconomic circumstances (Olfson, Shaffer, Marcus, & Greenberg, 2003), suggesting that depression is a component of some adolescent suicides. As we have argued elsewhere (B. T. McWhirter & Burrow-Sanchez, 2004), depression may not be present in all cases of youth suicide but remains an important dimension among most.

Hopelessness, one component of depression, is a solid predictor of the feeling or state that leads some young people to self-destructive behavior (Gould & Kramer, 2001; Levy, Jurkovic, & Spirito, 1995; Metalsky & Joiner, 1992; Whisman & Kwon, 1993). Other psychological disorders, such as anxiety disorders, obsessive-compulsive behavior, hostility, and psychosis, also play important roles in some teenage and child suicides. Recognition of the signs of depression and other psychopathology in children may help to avert a suicidal crisis.

Adolescents who develop depression are at increased risk for a variety of adverse outcomes later in life (Fergusson & Woodward, 2002), including subsequent depression, anxiety, suicidal behavior, nicotine dependence, difficulties in academia and employment, and unplanned pregnancy. As many as two thirds of those between the ages of 14 and 16 showing depression will experience another episode before the age of 21 (Fergusson & Woodward, 2002).

Thinking patterns.   Faulty thinking and irrational beliefs such as cognitive rigidity and cognitive distortion are consistently found in conjunction with depression and low self-esteem and are prevalent among suicidal youth (Metalsky, Joiner, Hardin, & Abramson, 1993). Children at risk for suicide possess fewer positive coping strategies and often do not seek assistance for their problems (Randell et al., 2001). If faulty thinking can be modified earlier, many suicide crises may be avoided. Here are some thinking patterns common to suicidal children and adolescents.

- *Cognitive constriction:* the inability to see options for solving problems and the conviction that the current bad feelings will never end. This leads to dichotomous thinking.
- *Dichotomous thinking:* the individual is able to see only two solutions to the problem: (a) continue to exist in a living hell or (b) find relief through death. (For example, "I will feel this way forever unless I kill myself.") A number of negative thinking patterns are common to suicidal children and adolescents, but the most important one is dichotomous thinking, which is common in the critical stages of suicide ideation.
- *Cognitive rigidity:* a rigid style of perceiving and reacting to the environment, which restricts a person's ability to cope with stress and to formulate realistic alternative approaches to problems. Cognitively rigid individuals see the problem, their inability to solve it, and the future as catastrophic. (For example, "I have no place to live and no one to help me; there's absolutely nothing I can ever do about it.")
- *Cognitive distortion:* overestimation of the magnitude and insolubility of problems. The difficulty of a problem is also generalized to all situations. Distorters assume that they are the cause of the problems they have. (For example, "I didn't get an A on that test, so I must be stupid and everything in my life is a complete mess.")

These consuming negative beliefs about the self, the insolubility of problems, and the future are pervasive. They can lead to withdrawal, to an inability to create change, and ultimately to suicide. Faulty thinking patterns are self-defeating, and tend to spiral: once young people begin to see their problems as insolvable, the problems themselves grow increasingly worse, and their ability to conceive of solutions becomes increasingly limited (see Figure 11.1).

FIGURE 11.1   Spiral of self-defeating cognitions

WARNING SIGNS OF SUICIDE

Suicide Motivations

The reasons that young people attempt suicide are, themselves, initial warning signs, if they can be detected. Suicide can be a method of self-punishment to deal with guilt or shame. Self-punishment is not uncommon for a young girl who discovers she is pregnant, for a teenager who begins to have memories of sexual molestation, or for an adolescent in conflict about sexual orientation. Suicide may also seem to provide absolution for past behaviors; this motivation is not uncommon among alcoholics who end their lives to absolve themselves of past behaviors. Suicide may be motivated by perverted revenge, a perceived means to get back at those who caused the individual pain, such as parents who got divorced. Retaliatory abandonment is another motivation for suicide. A boy who has been dumped by his girlfriend can "retaliate" by showing her how awful she was to cause him to end it all. He would rather leave than to be left by someone. Both perverted revenge and retaliatory abandonment may have been operating in the case of the girl described in Box 11.3. Fantasy of omnipotent mastery is a desire to have absolute control over the self and others, to control life and death itself, and to be completely autonomous. Finally, children or adolescents may attempt suicide not intending to end their lives but rather as a cry for help; of course, these attempts can be just as lethal. Decreasing suicidal ideation is essential in reducing actual attempts, and being aware of suicide motivations can assist in detection and prevention.

▲ Box 11.3
The Girl Who Had Everything

Shelley was an intelligent, beautiful, and popular high school senior. She was dating the homecoming king, was earning straight A's, was the star of the girls' softball team, and was liked by everybody. She seemed to have everything her girlfriends wanted without even trying. When her parents went through a sudden and angry divorce, Shelley continued to be the same smiling, fun-loving friend; her girlfriends believed that this "courage" was just another strength that their talented friend possessed.

One weekend she got into a fight with her mother just before her mother and brothers were to leave for an overnight visit with friends. In what was probably an attempt at revenge, Shelley called a large number of her friends and had a party at her mother's house. After several hours of drinking, Shelley got into another argument, this time with her boyfriend, and he broke off the relationship. Her girlfriends reported that Shelley seemed to be her "normal, laughing self" for the rest of the evening; at the time, they assumed she thought the breakup was only temporary. But when her family arrived home the next morning, the car was running in a closed garage, and Shelley had been dead for hours.

She left no note. Shelley had not done or said anything to her friends to suggest that she wouldn't be around the next day. It appeared to be an impulsive decision, carried out in haste. Clearly her outgoing high spirits and bravado were masking despair and anger. Perhaps they also masked the fact that this girl who "had everything" had never really learned how to cope with disappointment and pain.

Verbal Messages

Most children who feel self-destructive give verbal hints that life is too difficult to handle and not worth living. Children and adolescents may say any of the following or similar statements:

- "I don't see how I can go on."
- "I wish I were dead."
- "There's only one way out of my problems."
- "I won't be around much longer."
- "I'm tired of living."
- "You'll be sorry you treated me this way."
- "Pretty soon my troubles will be over."

These young people are hinting or saying directly that they are considering suicide.

Suicidal children also talk about death, wonder aloud what it will be like to be dead, and may be preoccupied by thoughts of others who have died. They may also joke about killing themselves. Many messages that are communicated as jokes are actually indications that a suicidal crisis is imminent; these jokes should not be taken lightly. In an effort to get help or to find out how others will respond, some children make direct threats of suicide. Verbal warnings should be taken seriously and not seen as just a "stage" that children go through. Failure to respond to a verbal warning or to a direct threat of suicide may be interpreted as confirmation that the child is worthless, expendable, and unloved. These feelings only increase the risk of a suicide attempt.

Behavioral Changes

Parents, teachers, and counselors can help prevent suicide attempts in children and adolescents by familiarizing themselves with behavioral changes that may suggest the risk of a suicide attempt (Mazza & Eggert, 2001). These include the following:

- Mood swings or fluctuations
- A change from happy and positive interactions with others to withdrawal and negativity
- Apathy or a lack of activity, such as neglect of hobbies that once were important to the person
- Changes in sleeping or eating patterns—insomnia or lethargy, lack of appetite or ravenous hunger
- Giving away prized possessions

School personnel in particular may recognize the following behavioral changes (Mazza & Eggert, 2001):

- A decline in the child's productivity and performance
- An increase in truancy
- More acting out in class
- Possible drug or alcohol use and hanging out with the "wrong crowd" at school and after school hours
- Higher levels of social activity than the average student if the youth is at risk for school dropout as well

General Risk Factors

As we observed earlier, suicidal children typically have a rigid and unrealistic style of thinking (Randell et al., 2001). The content of their preoccupations may also be a warning sign. When children seek to escape from a situation, to join a dead friend or family member, to be punished for their actions, to get revenge or to hurt someone else, to control their death, or to solve a problem that they see as intolerable or unresolvable, they are at risk for self-destructive behavior (Capuzzi, 1994; Capuzzi & Gross, 1996). A negative outlook and poor self-image are also warning signs. Most children will express their thoughts in some way. Knowing the state of mind and the style with which a child resolves or fails to resolve problems is the first step in preventing suicide. Strategies for cognitive change are discussed in Chapters 12 and 13.

As we saw in Chapter 1, Paul Andrews exhibits many of the warning signs of suicide. The conflict with his parents, although less focused than that of his sister, Allie, may be a precursor to a suicide attempt because parent–child conflict is a common prelude

(Randell et al., 2001). Paul's stepfather, Jack, either is overtly aggressive toward him or ignores him completely. His mother passively encourages Paul not to upset Jack. Paul acts out in school, is aggressive with other children, and yet at times is very withdrawn. He also receives attention (and subsequent rejection) from other children by repeating gory news stories related to death and human pain. Paul's interactions with his peers reinforce both his aggressiveness and his feelings of guilt, worthlessness, and anger at himself and at the world. Paul demonstrates warning signs in those areas that serve as red flags—verbal messages, behavioral changes, and cognitive preoccupations. Unfortunately, his strategies for getting attention and support are not effective.

COMMON MISCONCEPTIONS OF SUICIDE

There are a number of common misconceptions or myths about suicide (King et al., 2000; Moskos, Achilles, & Gray, 2004).Here are some of the most common ones:

- A person who has considered or attempted suicide will always be suicidal. In fact, most children and adolescents think about suicide at some point. Most suicide attempts are a desperate means of crying out for help. If the crisis is resolved effectively, many will not become suicidal again, with those who did not actually attempt suicide at lower risk of future attempts.
- After a suicide crisis has passed, the child is no longer at risk for suicide. Although children may not continue to feel suicidal after an attempt, they are not out of danger. Because suicide attempters have already overcome a social taboo by trying to kill themselves once, subsequent attempts are easier for them. If parents, counselors, psychologists, and school personnel do not attend to the child and the reasons for the attempt, a subsequent attempt is possible. Suicide takes a great deal of emotional energy. A child or adolescent who displays a calm reaction after an initial suicide attempt may be gaining strength for another. Later suicide attempts frequently involve more lethal methods. In one study, adolescents with a history of suicide attempts were almost 18 times more likely than those with no attempt history to try to commit suicide during a 1-year time period (Lewinsohn, Rohde, & Seeley, 1993).
- Talking about suicide can make people more inclined to make an attempt. Talking to children and adolescents about suicide can allow them to express their feelings and concerns and can lead to increased supports and coping skills. Adults should not avoid the topic of suicide; there is no evidence that this increases risk.
- People who commit suicide always leave a note. Actually, only a small proportion of children and teenagers who commit suicide leave a note, even though they may leave numerous clues or hints. This misconception can perpetuate a family's bewilderment after a suicide. Not only are they helpless to change what happened, but they are also uncertain about the reason for the suicide. Many suicides are classified as accidents because no note has been found and the deaths are not recognized as suicides.
- Suicide happens without warning. Though few people who are thinking about committing suicide actually spell out their intention directly, most do give numerous clues and hints of despair and suicidal ideation. After a young person has committed suicide, it is not uncommon for friends and family members to retrospectively identify many of the warning signs that we have reviewed.

- The person who talks about committing suicide never actually does it. Nearly every suicide has been preceded by some kind of warning. Even if such threats seem to be bids for attention, it is better to respond to a child's potential risk than to regret a completed suicide. Always take threats seriously.
- Suicide occurs more frequently among the lower socioeconomic groups than among the more affluent. Although age and gender differences persist (suicide is on the rise among children and adolescents) and some ethnic differences persist (Native Americans have the highest suicide rate), suicide is a problem in all socioeconomic and ethnic groups.
- Suicidal people are mentally ill or severely depressed. Suicide is an ineffective, maladaptive solution to a problem that appears unsolvable. Suicidal youth usually are not mentally ill, nor can any genetic markers for the incidence of suicide be distinguished from ineffective coping mechanisms learned from others in the environment. And even though many suicidal children and adolescents are depressed, not all are. Some children and adolescents who are not depressed consider suicide in the absence of adequate problem-solving skills.

Awareness of these misconceptions about suicide helps parents, teachers, and counselors to identify suicidal behaviors and risk among children and adolescents. Next, we consider specific identification and risk assessment strategies.

IDENTIFICATION AND ASSESSMENT STRATEGIES

Several useful strategies have been devised to determine whether children will act on suicidal thoughts. Recognizing signs of depression and familiarity with its various forms and manifestations can be very helpful. Two other methods are clinical interviews, which can disclose the severity and lethality of suicide ideation, and self-report measures.

Forms of Depression

Building on earlier works on adult suicide, two studies (Garrison, Addy, Jackson, et al., 1992; Lewinsohn, Rohde, Seeley, & Fischer, 1993) focused on increase of depression among children and adolescents. Depression affects approximately 30% of the adolescent population with similar trends present in young children. The assumption is that the precursors of depression begin quite early in a child's life. Referring to "epidemic proportions" of depression, Seligman (1995) suggested that we are in an "Age of Melancholy." Early onset bipolar disorder is also being more effectively identified and is more pervasive than previously thought (Papolos & Papolos, 1999). One tool for more clearly understanding depression and bipolar disorder in young people is the *Diagnostic and Statistical Manual of Mental Disorders* (DSM-IV), which has been published with a revised text (TR), or DSM-IV-TR (American Psychiatric Association, 2000).

The DSM-IV-TR clarifies differences in the expression of depression in childhood, adolescence, and adulthood. For example, children commonly display irritable moods rather than depressed moods, somatic complaints, and social withdrawal. Depressed adolescents typically display psychomotor retardation and hypersomnia. Also, children typically display major depressive episodes along with disruptive behavioral disorders, anxiety disorders, and ADHD. Adolescent depression is more commonly associated with ADHD, disruptive behavior disorders, anxiety disorders, substance-related disorders, and eating disorders.

Mood disorders in the DSM-IV-TR are divided into three major categories: depressive disorders, bipolar disorders, and mood disorders due to a general medical condition. The depressive disorders include major depressive disorder, characterized by one or more depressive episodes without a history of mania, and dysthymic disorder, characterized by conditions indicating mood disturbance that has been chronic or intermittent for at least 2 years but without the degree of severity to warrant the diagnosis of major depressive disorder.

Bipolar disorders include bipolar I disorder, bipolar II disorder, and cyclothymic disorder. Bipolar disorders are distinguished by the presence of a manic episode. Cyclothymia, a milder form of bipolar disorder, is indicated by the presence of numerous episodes with hypomanic symptoms and numerous periods with depressive symptoms that do not meet the criteria for a major depressive episode. The final category includes mood disturbances judged to be of medical origin. This condition is found with increasing frequency among younger populations. The DSM-IV-TR also describes conditions such as seasonal affective disorder, in which people become more depressed during certain times of the year, and adjustment disorders, in which the adjustment to a major external stressor is accompanied by depressed mood. In sum, the DSM-IV-TR is a useful tool for clarifying certain types of depression in childhood and adolescence.

In view of the relationship between depression and suicide, the use of depression inventories is warranted in efforts to determine the risk of suicide. Two that are useful for children and adolescents are the Beck Depression Inventory (BDI), which has an adolescent version (Beck, Ward, Mendelson, Mock, & Erbaugh, 1961), the Child Depression Inventory (CDI; Kovacs, 1981; Kovacs & Beck, 1977). The BDI contains 21 items that yield a single score reflecting a client's symptomatology for depression. It indicates whether an adolescent may be severely depressed and at risk for suicide. The CDI was modified from the BDI for use with children between the ages of 8 and 17.

Later in the chapter we present strategies for early intervention, crisis intervention, and postvention for child and adolescent suicide. Interventions to prevent depression itself are extremely important in preventing suicide. Two such programs, optimism training (Seligman, 1995) and the SOAR program (Gilboy, McWhirter, & Wallace, 2002), are described in Chapters 12 and 13.

Interviews for Suicide Lethality

Interviews are probably the most effective and informative way to assess suicide risk (J. J. McWhirter, 2002). Interviews are conducted with parents, teachers, and the child or adolescent who appears to be at risk of suicide. Because suicidal children are typically angry at themselves, upset at the world, and caught up in emotional turmoil, it is critical to establish a professional relationship that expresses confidence, helpfulness, and trust.

The interviewer should attempt to assess (a) the history of the presenting problem (e.g., depression, anxiety, loneliness), (b) the family constellation and family relationships, (c) a developmental, medical, and academic history, (d) the status of interpersonal relationships, (e) verbal and behavioral warning cues, and (f) any current stressors that may trigger a suicide attempt. Changes in behavior, in sleep and eating patterns, and in emotional status as well as any previous suicide attempts should be noted. Discrepancies between the parents' and the child's reports may indicate a problem. The following high-risk factors should receive particular attention:

- Symptoms of clinical depression and hopelessness
- Recent loss of an important relationship or life goal
- Serious family problems, such as divorce, alcoholism, physical abuse, or incest
- Personal history of physical disability, alcohol or drug abuse, or psychiatric treatment
- Interpersonal impoverishment, or the absence of friends, family, church members, or others who can provide direct emotional support in a crisis

When suicide ideation is present, the lethality of the risk must be assessed. The severity of the threat depends on the specificity and the lethality of the method of choice. Ideation alone is not a great risk. Progressively worse are (a) ideation with a plan, including a time, place, and method; (b) a lethal method (such as a gun or a leap from a tall building); (c) accessibility of a means to commit suicide (such as a loaded gun in the house); and (d) a history of previous suicide attempts (Pfeffer et al., 1994).

Holinger, Offer, Barter, and Bell (1994) have devised useful guides for determining many of these risk factors. Consult their work and other sources, such as J. J. McWhirter (2002), for sample interview procedures.

Self-Report Inventories

Researchers have developed a variety of inventories to identify suicidal children and adolescents (see Thompson & Eggert, 1999, for a review of these). In particular, the Suicide Risk Screen is a pragmatic and effective method for identifying suicide-risk students among potential dropouts in school settings (Thompson & Eggert, 1999). In addition to his depression measures, other scales by Beck and his associates are the Beck Hopelessness Scale (BHS; Beck, Weissman, Lester, & Trexler, 1974) and the Scale of Suicide Ideation (Beck, Kovacs, & Weissman, 1979). The Scale of Suicide Ideation includes questions related to attitudes about living or dying, the characteristics and specificity of suicidal ideation, and background factors such as previous suicide attempts. These measures can help identify the risk of suicide among children and adolescents.

Schoolwide screening strategies have demonstrated encouraging results in preventing suicidal behavior (Gould & Kramer, 2001). Through the use of interviews and self-report inventories such as those described here, preventive screening methods in schools can generate information about suicidal ideation, substance abuse, depression, and previous suicide attempts. This is critical for identifying those who are at risk.

Specific Intervention Strategies Focused on Suicide Crisis

When involved with a young person who is seriously contemplating suicide, it is very important for the helper to assume a different stance than that which is ordinarily assumed by counselors. After all, suicide is the one mistake that young people can make that is not correctable. Thus the counselor or other helper becomes active, authoritarian, and engages other significant people. Suicide treatment is a response to a threat of suicide, and the following six steps must be taken to defuse a suicide crisis:

1. Listen and show respect for the feelings a suicidal youth expresses. Suicidal children feel that their problems are severe, and their feelings should not be brushed aside. Schools should incorporate peer assistance programs to aid in crisis intervention and decreasing suicidal behavior (King et al., 2000).
2. Reinforce the child for seeking help. Admitting suicide ideation or attempting suicide brings shame and embarrassment. These feelings should be acknowledged. The counselor can also help the child recognize and voice the part of him or her that wants to survive. This can help deter a later attempt.
3. Be specific about assessing lethality. Ask direct questions: "Are you thinking about killing yourself?" Be particularly specific about assessing the concreteness of the plan. Ask: "How do you plan to kill yourself?" "Do you already have the pills?" "Have you attempted suicide before?" Don't be afraid that asking such questions will increase the risk for a suicide attempt.
4. Make decisions. Children or adolescents who give indications that they will attempt suicide within the next few hours should be hospitalized for consistent care and monitoring.
5. Have the youth sign a written contract. An oral contract may be adequate, but a written contract is more powerful. Sometimes the suggestion of hospitalization is enough to persuade a child to sign a written contract. Be very careful about this tactic though. The child who feels coerced into signing a contract may feel under no obligation to abide by its terms.
6. Use the resources that are available. Community mental health agencies and private therapists are often the primary resources for helping children and their families after a suicide attempt or acute suicidal ideation.

We elaborate on these points in more detail shortly.

Prevention, Early Intervention, and Postvention

Primary prevention involves the removal or modification of environmental and interpersonal characteristics that are commonly associated with suicide. Early intervention programs target early detection and treatment of depressive disorders, anxiety, loneliness, stress, and family problems. Parents and teachers, the adults most accessible to the child and adolescent, play crucial roles in early intervention, but other school personnel and community professionals are also important (King et al., 2000). Early intervention programs in the school minimize the frequency and severity of the suicide ideation experienced by high-risk youth. Early detection can be managed conveniently and inexpensively through group screening devices. Suicide threat can also be detected through gatekeeper training programs (Gould & Kramer, 2001; Grossman & Kruesi, 2000). In these programs, adults who come into contact with youth in school on a daily basis are trained to identify suicidal youth. The principle behind these programs is that suicidal children and adolescents are often underidentified. Had such an early intervention program been in place in Paul's school, he might have been identified earlier and appropriate interventions could have been implemented before the suicide crisis emerged.

School crisis response teams are an important part of deterring suicide and providing support when a suicide or other tragedy occurs (Allen, Burt, et al., 2002; Allen, Jerome, et al., 2002). Of course, a crisis response team also deals with other tragedies, such as school shootings or localized terrorist attacks. Response teams are made up of trained teachers and administrators, school counselors, school nurses, social workers, and educational paraprofessionals (Allen & Ashbaker, 2004), as well as parents and community members (Maples et al., 2005). Although response teams are designed for crisis intervention, part of their purpose is to provide education and intervention before an actual crisis emerges.

Several early intervention activities are central to the response-ready crisis team (Brock, Sandoval, & Lewis, 2001; Johnson, 2000). The school must develop a prevention and early intervention plan. Referral resources should be prepared and procedures established so that team members can take direct, immediate action when it is needed. Schools should involve families and parents in this program. In addition, schools must incorporate the unique experiences of diverse populations into their early intervention plan.

- Teams coordinate their activities with those of mental health agencies and other organizations that serve families and children in the community. They may also engage law enforcement agencies, private therapists, medical professionals, and church and hospital personnel. Developing a network is critical for preventing suicide and for dealing with attempts.
- Response teams can participate in education and training. Continuing education on suicide risk and response should be provided to teachers, other school personnel, and parents (King et al., 2000). Response teams can also maintain appropriate audiovisual materials and a library of information on suicide and intervention resources. In one study, researchers found that after viewing videos on suicide, parents' knowledge increased regarding suicidal signs, responses toward suicidal youth, and appropriate help-seeking and prevention strategies (Maine, Shute, & Martin, 2001).
- Response teams should review and maintain the program to ensure that referral resources are updated, procedures are efficient, and the prevention and early intervention activities are appropriate for the students.

Finally, response teams should consider the following recommendations when instituting suicide prevention and early intervention procedures:

1. Plan your response before a crisis.
2. Deal with suicide issues openly and honestly. Don't avoid talk about suicide.
3. Prepare significant adults first, especially teachers and other school personnel, to deal with a suicide crisis. This will help to prepare students to deal with suicide.
4. Always prepare adults about suicide issues and discuss the content of educational films about suicide before showing them to students. Be sure to reserve time after showing an educational film on suicide to discuss the content and to allow students to share their thoughts and feelings about it. The same is true for parents.

Crisis Management and Response

A suicide crisis is managed with the same concern and immediacy as any other emergency. Counselors, teachers, and administrators who are members of the response-ready crisis team should free themselves from normal duties to respond to such an emergency.

Mental health professionals, such as school counselors, play primary roles in a crisis response.

First, counselors need to assess the lethality of the suicide threat (Holinger et al., 1994; J. J. McWhirter, 2002). If a suicide plan is specific and lethal or if an attempt has been made, counselors must assess whether the child or adolescent is stable, using referral procedures as needed. Hospitalization may be called for.

Second, a written contract is developed between the student and the counselor. This contract establishes an agreement that the student will not attempt suicide before talking to or seeing a counselor again. Most children who sign a contract comply with it. Providing the child with an emergency crisis number is also important. Crisis hotlines have been used for decades to prevent suicidal behavior (Gould & Kramer, 2001). Suicidal behavior is often related to a crisis, and "cries for help" can be handled by trained workers at crisis centers. Although hotline resources may be especially important for at-risk teens, few studies have examined their efficacy.

Third, observation is critical. The child or adolescent must be monitored during the crisis for a period of at least 24 to 72 hours. This may involve arranging for hospitalization or a "suicide watch," during which family members and friends keep constant track of the youth's affect and behavior (Capuzzi, 1994; Capuzzi & Gross, 1996). Counseling should be action oriented, directive, and aimed at dealing first with the danger of suicide. Once a child is stabilized, the underlying causes of the suicide crisis can become the focus of intervention.

Finally, counselors must notify parents of the danger of suicide when they are aware of suicide ideation. Parent–counselor contact is often the first step of a crisis response. Although this contact may break confidentiality, it is an ethically and legally appropriate response to a child's suicide threat. The counselor must make clear to all minor clients and to relevant adults the limits of confidentiality at the onset of the relationship. The counselor who informs others of the danger of suicide shows concern for the youth's welfare.

Immediately after a crisis.   After a nonfatal attempt, school personnel or the crisis team should attend to a number of other issues. Because most suicide attempts are not made at school, a member of the crisis team should call the parents to verify the suicide attempt. The call also provides an opportunity to offer assistance to family members. After this call, a team member should notify teachers and administrators, emphasizing confidentiality. It is also important to monitor the attempter's friends, to follow up on others who are perceived to be at risk for suicide, and to respond to friends who may be traumatized by the attempt. While the student is recovering, a team member should keep the student informed about what is going on at the school and encourage the parents to report on the child's progress.

This collaborative relationship is continued when the student returns to school. Members of the crisis team should help to make the student's return to school as comfortable as possible. Teachers should also remain aware of the appropriate steps necessary when a student returns to school after a suicide attempt (King et al., 2000). Both individual and group counseling have been effective in helping a child deal with the aftermath of a suicide attempt, although group counseling should be postponed a few months so that the attempter is not the primary focus of the group (Robertson & Mathews, 1989). Medications for depression and anxiety may also be effective after a suicide attempt and may be used in conjunction with therapy. It is important that the prescribing physician is aware of the young person's suicide attempt (Grossman & Kruesi, 2000).

Family interventions.   After a suicide attempt, family treatment is often recommended in place of or in addition to individual interventions. An attempt at suicide by any member of the family is very stressful for all the other members, particularly when the family is already struggling. Even when the family is relatively healthy and functioning well, normal nurturance and family care may not be adequate to deal with a child's stress, anxiety, depression, and suicide ideation.

When working with families, counselors must emphasize certain key issues (McLean & Taylor, 1994). First, counselors must establish the significance of the problem. Although parents may see their child's concerns as minimal, they may be overwhelming to the child. Parents must understand that a suicidal child's problem is a family problem. The involvement of Paul's parents, for example, is critical because much of his despair is rooted in family problems.

Second, counselors must deal with the shame, guilt, and anger that parents often experience when their child is suicidal—and with the denial that may be operating within the family. Oftentimes, individual meetings are helpful after a suicide attempt in a family (Grossman & Kruesi, 2000).

Third, the family must begin to recognize that the problems that led up to the suicide crisis have developed over a long time and recognize the extent to which they reflect family dynamics. Families should be encouraged to recognize, understand, and modify these dynamics as a means of managing a suicide crisis and of effecting long-term change. Finally, counselors should assess for suicide ideation among each member of the family.

Family counseling is probably the most effective method for dealing with the primary causes of self-destructive behavior. For example, modifying the communication styles and helping each family member to clarify and modify his or her role in keeping the dysfunctional family in balance would be useful for Paul and his family. Unfortunately, many suicidal children and adolescents do not have a family and are in the child protection system. In these situations, interventions should involve alternative caretakers (Grossman & Kruesi, 2000). Family counseling interventions are discussed in Chapter 15.

Postvention and Follow-Up Treatment

If a young person completes suicide, the focus shifts to damage control. A great deal of suffering is felt in the aftermath of a teen's or child's suicide. Surviving family members, friends, and schoolmates of the suicide victim often need follow-up treatment, or postvention. Individual, group, or family counseling may be needed to help them deal with the event. Sharing information about the suicide and discussing it with community members and with fellow students helps to prevent cluster suicides. Indeed, mental health professionals and school personnel have important responsibilities after a successful suicide (King et al., 2000). Most postvention efforts involve the school and the family.

Schools.   The school is the major setting not only for prevention and early intervention but also for attention to the aftermath of a student's suicide. School personnel can provide information about suicide, help survivors cope with their loss, and offer counseling to students who may need special attention. Suicide should be discussed because a fear of discussing self-destructive behavior actually increases the risk to other students. In discussions of the suicide, the deceased child should not be glorified or romanticized, but students should be allowed to grieve. For example, the school should not hold a memorial for the student or plant a tree in honor of the student. However, students should be allowed to miss school if necessary to attend the funeral service of the deceased student. Neglect of these factors may increase the possibility of cluster suicides and complicate the grieving process for students.

Postvention, like crisis intervention, is the responsibility of the crisis team. The response team should take the following steps after a student has committed suicide (Grossman, Hirsch, Goldenberg, & Libby, 1995; King et al., 2000):

- Administrators should call an emergency faculty meeting to relay the facts and to give teachers "talking points" for class discussions.
- Designated team members call parents and offer assistance, contact the district counseling department, and prepare written information for parents about the event, the school response, and how to support their children and secure outside support as needed.
- The school should not hold an assembly to announce the suicide or issue a public statement about it. Some students may perceive these actions as positive consequences of suicide. In addition, the school must prepare for possible media coverage of the suicide.
- The school should not hold a memorial service, nor should it prepare a memorial statement for publication in the student newspaper. These activities can increase the perception that suicide is an acceptable form of death.
- Opportunities should be provided for friends and schoolmates to meet to share their grief, and emergency or crisis hotline numbers should be made available to students. The school may need to enlist community resources to manage these groups and to provide emergency and information services.
- Depending on the nature of the event, the school should hold a critical incident stress debriefing (CISD) of staff members (Juhnke, 1997; E. H. McWhirter, 1994). This process includes a structured review of the event and allows personnel to ventilate their feelings, fears, and frustrations. Although the usefulness of CISD has been questioned (Mayou, Ehlers, & Hobbs, 2000; Rose, Bisson, & Wessely, 2001), its use very soon after the incident and its continuing use (Campfield & Hills, 2001) suggest it has value in preventing future problems.
- The school should identify and monitor the well-being of close friends of the student who committed suicide.

Families. Some of the strategies used in working with families after a suicide attempt are also useful for postvention. Families may experience feelings of guilt, shame, and embarrassment, but family members also feel grief, loss, and helplessness after a suicide. Those who must deal with a youth suicide must pay particularly close attention to the needs of the surviving family after the death.

CONCLUSION

Suicide attempts and completions can have a catastrophic effect on children and adolescents and on those around them. The prevention of suicide and the provision of early intervention in the presence of suicide ideation are essential. Because teachers, school counselors, and other school personnel play primary roles in the lives of children and adolescents, their knowledge of the symptoms, causes, misconceptions, warning signs, and related problems of adolescent and child suicide is of particular importance. Understanding child and adolescent risk factors can help to prevent suicidal behavior, and prevention and early intervention strategies will help minimize the likelihood and long-lasting effects of self-destructive behavior.

PREVENTION, INTERVENTION, AND TREATMENT APPROACHES

▲ In Part 4 we provide a wide range of empirically supported prevention and intervention strategies to help young people. In Chapter 12 we describe a systematic conceptual framework and model of prevention, early intervention, and treatment of children and teenagers at risk. We conclude the chapter by describing two universal prevention programs. In Chapter 13 we return to resiliency and the five Cs of competency discussed in Chapter 6 and provide a variety of interventions demonstrated to be helpful: social skills, cognitive-behavioral strategies, and other approaches aimed at decreasing negative behaviors and attitudes and increasing positive ones. In Chapter 14 we describe several intervention programs that can be used to help young people by harnessing prosocial peer group influences. Chapter 15 focuses on family-based interventions. Thus we conclude the book with a presentation of interventions that have been found very helpful for working effectively with children, youth, and families in need.

CHAPTER 12

A Prevention, Early Intervention, Treatment Framework and Other Environmental Considerations

▲ *Ten old men gather for an evening of conversation and drink. They each bring their own bottle of Chinese wine, to be mixed together, warmed up, and shared.*

One of them thinks: "Why should I bring wine? The other nine will. I shall fill my bottle with water instead," which he did.

Unfortunately, so did the other nine. And the old gentlemen suffered the evening, silently and ruefully, drinking warm water.

This vignette comes from an old Cantonese story. A family, school, or community is greater than the sum of its members. How often do we, as parents, educators, counselors, human service professionals, and as a society bear only "water" instead of bearing "wine"?

FROM SEEK WISDOM BY J.J. McWHIRTER

Chapter Outline

▲   In this chapter we introduce a multifaceted prevention and treatment framework that integrates the concepts addressed throughout the book and provides an overall context for the interventions described. We precede our description of the framework with clarification of the relationship of prevention, treatment, and risk and with a brief history of prevention strategies. We define prevention. After a thorough description of the framework, we address two universal programs that can reduce child and adolescent risk.

A Comprehensive Prevention, Early Intervention, Treatment Framework

What serves as a treatment intervention for one problem frequently serves as a preventive strategy for a more advanced problem. Problem behaviors exist along a continuum. If we involve Tyrone Baker (of Chapter 2) in a smoking-reduction group, for example, we are providing a treatment for his cigarette smoking; but because cigarette smoking puts Ty at risk for the use and possible abuse of alcohol, marijuana, and other drugs, our treatment also serves as a prevention strategy. If we engage the Carter family (of Chapter 4) in treatment for their troubled family system, we are providing treatment for their ongoing negative interactions. We are helping Jason Carter deal more effectively with both his maladaptive and self-defeating behaviors, and we are also potentially preventing Jason's further progression toward one or more of the at-risk categories.

Risk also forms a continuum, from remote risk to imminent risk. Factors that contribute to risk include demographic characteristics such as social class and economic conditions; family, community, and school stressors; and personal characteristics, attitudes, and behaviors. As discussed in Chapter 6, some young people are resilient enough to flourish even though their environment and context place them at risk. Other youth are fortunate in having enough protective factors to counterbalance the risks. Unfortunately, some young people develop specific personal behaviors that interact with poor family and social contexts to increase their potential for problems and place them at further risk for even more severe problems. As risk factors increase without a concurrent increase in protective factors, children and adolescents become increasingly likely to be at imminent risk. Our continuum framework incorporates the relationship between prevention and treatment as well as the continuum from remote to imminent risk.

In understanding risk, it is especially important to consider protective factors. Clearly, protective factors serve to buffer or protect young people who might otherwise be at greater risk. Just as risk factors can be thought of with respect to individual characteristics, family, community, and other contextual characteristics, so too are protective factors potentially present at each level. Individual protective factors include but are not limited to social skills and intelligence; familial factors include authoritative parenting and strong attachments between parents and children; community factors include accessible resources such as social and medical services and parks, as well as strong linkages between family and community. Prevention efforts that support and maximize protective factors while reducing risk factors are more likely to be successful.

Any model that incorporates prevention, early intervention, and treatment raises complex issues. The role of the school, the linkage between the problems of young people and prevention, and the interplay between treatment and prevention are all important considerations in formulating such a model (Conyne, 2004; Conyne & Cook, 2004; O'Shaughnessy, Lane, Gresham, & Beebe-Frankenberger, 2002). It is also important to understand previously successful and unsuccessful efforts at prevention to improve interventions now.

HISTORY OF PREVENTION PROGRAMS

During the 1960s, drug prevention programs emerged with a focus on providing information. Early efforts were based on scare tactics, moralizing, and often inaccurate information; many programs contained fear-arousal messages regarding the social and health consequences of drug use. The emphasis was on the drugs themselves rather than on the reasons people used them. Perhaps even more significant, youth reported that the information lacked credibility, and drug use actually increased among adolescents during this time. A consensus emerged that relying on knowledge alone to change problem behavior is misguided (Dielman, 1994; Montagne & Scott, 1993).

By the 1970s, drug prevention programs began to address personal and social factors that correlated with drug abuse and to provide more accurate information. Affective education became the major preventive approach. Rather than focusing on drug abuse, educational efforts focused on apparent factors associated with the use of drugs and attempted to eliminate the presumed reasons for using drugs. Affective education programs targeted self-esteem on the assumption that if young people understood their motivations for drug use and had greater self-esteem, they would not want to use drugs. This approach also failed to lower substance-abuse rates. Indeed, trying to eliminate most problem behaviors by focusing on self-esteem alone is not effective. During the 1980s, prevention efforts began to emphasize behavioral strategies. These programs focused on developing social competency and prosocial coping, often subsumed under the rubric of "life skills." Following the behavioral tradition that includes a strong empirical foundation, research was conducted across some at-risk areas to test the efficacy of prevention and early intervention programs. The results of this research are promising, and life skills education has been adopted around the world as an important prevention tool (World Health Organization, 1999).

The 1990s built on these previous efforts. Models developed in the 1990s began to systematically incorporate affective, cognitive, and behavioral areas and emphasized development of both skills and prosocial attitudes. Programs became more comprehensive and broad-based. Some efforts were made to develop programs to increase protective factors, but the main focus continued to be on eliminating risk.

Concern with program effectiveness also emerged in the 1990s and continues in the 2000s. Unfortunately, relatively little is known about the effectiveness of the hundreds of commercially marketed youth prevention and intervention programs currently used in communities and schools throughout the United States. It has become evident, as serious attempts have been mounted to evaluate program impact, that many well-intentioned prevention programs are ineffective and may even have negative effects on their young participants.

To deal with this concern, some university institutes (e.g., Blueprints Program at the University of Colorado) and a number of federal agencies (e.g., National Institute of Mental Health, Substance Abuse and Mental Health Services Administration, Safe and Drug Free Schools and Communities, and the Office of Juvenile Justice and Delinquency Prevention) have utilized expert panels to consider the level of evidence for classifying empirically supported programs. This has come about because state and federal agencies are mandating that practitioners spend public funds only on effective programs. Lists of acceptable scientific programs help facilitate this. The highest level of evidence is usually based on the Chambless and Hollon (1998) criteria, which in turn are based on the American Psychological Association Task Force on Psychological Intervention Guidelines (1995). It is the gold standard for defining empirically supported therapies and includes at least two randomized control trials by two independent teams of investigators. Unfortunately, practitioners are not implementing these evidence-based interventions routinely, compared with practitioner-developed or commercially marketed programs, which often have no tested outcome results. There are probably very good reasons for this, not the least of which is the gulf that exists between university researchers and school and community practitioners. Some programs are very expensive because in addition to materials, workbooks, and audio- and videotapes they require considerable training to implement. In restricted school and community budgets, the practitioner looks elsewhere. Some programs are not particularly user-friendly, and most have to be adapted anyway to accommodate local community and school norms and circumstances.

To confuse the issue further, the federal agencies use somewhat different criteria to produce incompatible lists and different qualifying terms—exemplary, model, promising, best practices, evidence-based, and so forth—and in somewhat different ways to define the level of evidence of effectiveness.

Nevertheless, proven programs are likely to be more helpful to children and adolescents. Understanding how programs are identified as effective should be helpful. Almost always, the procedures include establishing a set of evaluation standards for selection. This most often includes an experimental design, evidence of a statistically significant effect, replication of the original study with an experimental design that demonstrates effects, and—sometimes—evidence that the effect was sustained for at least 1 year posttreatment. Based on adherence to criteria, programs are designated by evaluative category. For example, the Safe and Drug Free Schools and Communities (SDFSC) Program of the U.S. Department of Education (2000) has a rigorous process for identifying prevention and intervention programs that have evidence of being successful. Using expert field reviewers, programs are submitted, reviewed, and evaluated according to the criteria. Evidence of program efficacy is a critical dimension of their evaluation; other criteria include program quality, educational significance, and usefulness to others. After a series of field reviews, the full expert panel then meets to consider all of the reviews and to make recommendations to the Secretary of Education of those programs successfully meeting the criteria. Programs are designated as Best Practices or Promising Programs. In this text, we offer descriptions of many of the programs that have been deemed valid and effective through this process or a very similar one.

PREVENTION DEFINED

Commensurate with this brief history of prevention programs, definitions of prevention have varied over time and across disciplines (e.g., Caplan, 1964; Conyne, 2004; Gordon, 1987; Mrazek & Haggerty, 1994; Romano & Hage, 2000). Literally, prevention means to stop something before it happens (Romano & Hage, 2000). In 1964 Caplan added the categories of primary, secondary, and tertiary prevention. These terms refer to the reduction of new incidence rates of a disorder (primary), prevalence rates for those at risk of developing a disorder (secondary), or the harmful effects of an existing disorder (tertiary). In 1987 Gordon created a different classification system, making distinctions among universal, selected, and indicated prevention. This classification system identified targeted populations, including everyone in a population (universal), an individual or subgroup of a population (selected), or only individuals and groups at high risk (indicated). More recently, the Institute of Mental Health defined prevention efforts in a very limited way as only those that occur before the onset of a disorder (Mrazek & Haggerty, 1994).

There are several criticisms regarding the applicability of these more recognized definitions and classification systems to the prevention of mental disorders (Lorion, Price, & Eaton, 1989; Romano & Hage, 2000). Caplan's (1964) and Gordon's (1987) prevention definitions, for example, were originally created to classify prevention efforts for physical disorders. Unlike most physical disorders, however, it is more difficult to identify the cause or origin of a psychological disorder and to classify complex mental disorder prevention efforts into a single category such as primary or universal prevention. Similarly, the Institute of Health's prevention definition (Mrazek & Haggerty, 1994) has been criticized for using a disease-based prevention model, excluding social and political change and health-promoting interventions as part of prevention. Romano and Hage (2000) addressed these criticisms and created a new definition for the prevention of mental disorders.

Romano and Hage define prevention efforts as those having one or more of the following five dimensions: (1) stops (prevents) a problem behavior from ever occurring; (2) delays the onset of a problem behavior; (3) reduces the impact of an existing problem behavior; (4) strengthens knowledge, attitudes, and behaviors that promote emotional and physical well-being; and (5) supports institutional, community, and government policies that promote physical and emotional well-being. This definition of prevention encompasses the goals of primary, secondary, and tertiary prevention practices and also includes strategies for risk reduction and promotion of protective factors. Moreover, this definition includes prevention efforts within larger social systems and acknowledges counselors' and other human service professionals' role as agents of social change. To engage in prevention efforts along any of these dimensions, however, counselors are challenged to determine which prevention practices and implementation strategies will be most effective with what individuals and communities at what time. This requires consideration of individual and context-specific factors as well as the interaction among these factors in the creation and implementation of interventions (Bronfenbrenner, 1979, 1989; Conyne & Cook, 2004). The framework we describe next is designed to assist toward this end.

DESCRIPTION OF THE FRAMEWORK

This comprehensive framework is conceptualized as operating along several continuums and provides intervention components that encompass society and community, family, and schools. Universal primary prevention, secondary prevention and treatment programs (that is, early intervention and selected programs), and second-chance treatment intervention strategies are included. Figure 12.1 shows the several continuums that comprise the framework.

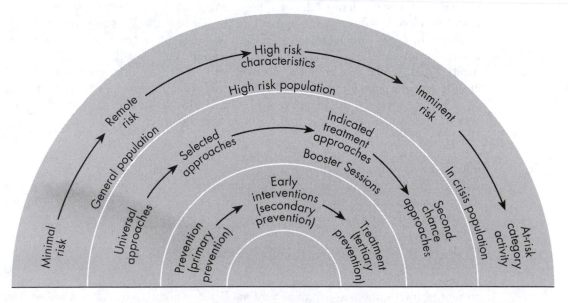

FIGURE 12.1   Risk, approaches, and prevention continuums

The Risk Continuum

The risk continuum introduced in Chapter 1 is at the top of the figure. Problems faced by young people are conceptualized as following a continuum from minimal risk to actual participation in an activity in one of the at-risk categories. Beginning at the left of Figure 12.1, a remote degree of risk is associated with certain demographic characteristics. As young people develop and mature, personal characteristics that lead to increasingly higher risk may become evident. If these personal characteristics are not modified, young people may soon be beyond remote risk and high risk and considered at imminent risk for many problems. The end of this continuum describes children or adolescents who are already engaged in one or more of the risk behavior categories discussed in earlier chapters.

The Approach Continuum

The second strand in the arch in Figure 12.1 identifies various intervention approaches to the problems that may appear at each level of risk: universal approaches, selected approaches, indicated treatment approaches, booster sessions, and second-chance approaches. Although the labels of "universal, selected, and indicated" are used in different ways in the prevention literature (for example, Mrazek and Haggerty [1994] use these terms to define levels or types of primary prevention only), we use these terms more broadly here as a way to help conceptualize the continuum of possible interventions for at-risk youth. The relative placement of each approach between the anchors of the risk continuum above reflects the relation of the approach to the level of risk. Thus a universal approach is the most appropriate type of intervention when a child exhibits minimal or remote risk. As a child moves from remote risk to high risk, a selected approach is more appropriate. As a young person moves from high risk to imminent risk and then to at-risk category activities, an indicated treatment approach and then a second-chance program are more useful. Each of the approaches in the second strand of the arch can operate in the domain of the community, family, or school, but we focus on the school setting for our examples.

Universal approaches.   Universal strategies are considered to be appropriate for all children, not just those who are presumed to be at risk. All children within a given catchment area (a community, a neighborhood, a school) may receive a common or universal intervention. All children in a low-income neighborhood, for example, are given access to a program even though some are at only minimal risk and some of their families are more affluent. All children in a classroom are engaged in interactive and cooperative learning groups rather than just those who are educationally deficient; all children are involved in a schoolwide program of positive behavioral support (Horner, Crone, & Stiller, 2001; Lewis & Sugai, 1999; see Chapter 5).

In universal school approaches, the intent is to maintain or increase the educational achievement, prosocial coping skills, and mental health of large numbers of children. Ideally, universal content is integrated throughout a comprehensive health-oriented school curriculum. Basic life-skills competencies (discussed in Chapters 13 and 14)—such as problem-solving and decision-making skills, communication and other social skills, and impulse control—help young people respond to a variety of social situations. Developmentally appropriate personal, social, and cognitive skills are important components of a universal life-skills program. These programs can be beneficial at any time in the life of a young person, but they have the greatest influence early in life. Ideally, universal programs should be an integral part of preschool, elementary, and middle school curriculums.

Selected approaches. Selected approaches are aimed at groups of young people who share some circumstance or experience that increases the probability that they will develop problems in the future. Demographic parameters, specific environmental stressors, and skill deficits indicate the need for target prevention programs. The children from low-income families who qualify for a Head Start program are perhaps the best example of a selected group defined by demographic factors. Because of their economic situation (which presumes other stressful circumstances), they are provided with an enriching pre-school experience that increases their chances for later academic success.

Specific environmental stressors also provide a useful way to target young people either when they appear to be in a vulnerable situation or during specific developmental stages. Children from families in which there has been an acrimonious divorce, mental health problems, or drug abuse or alcoholism, for example, are quite vulnerable. Individual or group counseling or school support programs are very useful interventions for these students. The transitions from elementary school to middle school and from middle school to secondary school are stressful developmental periods that are often followed by a significant increase in absenteeism, increased susceptibility to substance use and delinquency, and a sharp decline in psychological well-being (Felner et al., 1993; Lord, Eccles, & McCarthy, 1994; Reyes & Hedeker, 1993; Rudolph et al., 2001).

A third group of children appropriate for selected programs are those whose behaviors indicate deficits in skills. Sometimes these children are identified in psychological terms, such as lonely, depressed, anxious, aggressive; sometimes by educational categories, such as learning disabled or behavior disordered; and sometimes in terms of their limitations in the five Cs (critical school competencies, concept of self, connectedness, coping, and control skills, discussed in Chapter 6). Most often, these children are identified and referred because of behavior disruptions. Unfortunately, many classroom interventions designed for these children focus on reducing behaviors that disrupt the class but do not attend to behaviors such as increasing literacy skills that are also vital to the child's ability to succeed in school in the long run (O'Shaughnessy et al., 2002).

The risks, problems, and needs of the selected group must be identified before an appropriate intervention can be designed and implemented. The appropriate content for a selected approach often consists of the same social and cognitive skills that are addressed in universal approaches. Some children need increased attention, more intensive emphasis, and more applied practice to acquire these life skills. This is the case in any classroom, but school personnel need to give particular attention to students with special education classifications. Lane, Gresham, and O'Shaughnessy (2002) recommend that social skills competency interventions for children with emotional and behavioral disorders address each of the following components: skill acquisition, skill performance, removal or reduction of competing problem behaviors, and generalization and maintenance of skills. Because of their emotional, behavioral, and learning problems, children identified for special education are especially suited for selected approaches.

Booster sessions. Prevention efforts should be intensive, sequential, and comprehensive, with continued involvement over a long time period. One-shot prevention efforts are not very effective because program effects dissipate in a relatively short time (Frost & Forrest, 1995;

O'Shaughnessy et al., 2002). Recall that Kirby (2001) included "sufficient length" as 1 of 10 elements of successful pregnancy prevention programs. Short-term interventions achieve, at best, short-term results. Consequently, periodic and sequential "booster" follow-up sessions should be added to help maintain the effects of the initial intervention: Frost & Forrest, 1995). Bundy (2004) demonstrated that five-session booster lessons for the SCARE and SOAR programs (described later in the chapter) administered to randomly assigned participants nearly a year after the original programs were extremely useful in maintaining and extending the positive effects of both programs. Few programs without booster sessions have achieved positive long-term results (Durlak, 1995).

Indicated approaches.   On the right-hand side of the middle continuum in Figure 12.1 are indicated treatment approaches for individuals who are at imminent risk for problem behavior or who have actually begun to engage in the behavior. Indicated treatment approaches must be developed for young people whose underlying characteristics, problems, and behaviors are associated directly with at-risk activity. An anger reduction treatment group, for example, is an indicated treatment for hostile teens, and it is also a prevention strategy for fighting or other violence. Attitudes and skills that are particularly relevant for each at-risk category are addressed in indicated treatment approaches. Alternative behaviors and coping skills specific to the problem are also taught in indicated treatment.

Second-chance approaches.   Finally, "second-chance" interventions are needed for those children and adolescents who are already engaging in substance use, have dropped out, have become pregnant, or are engaging in violent and aggressive behaviors. Young people who have made poor choices need an opportunity to change those choices to more constructive ones; they need a second chance. The five chapters of Part 3 provide concrete examples of specific treatment interventions for specific at-risk categories.

The universal, selected, indicated, and second-chance approaches address, in sequential order, those risk factors that are the most salient contributors to young people's problems. These intervention efforts are most successful when they are comprehensive and cover a broad range of risk and protective factors. The problems of children and youth at risk have multiple antecedents, and interventions must focus on many causal factors if they are to be effective. The intent of such approaches is to set individuals on new paths as early as possible, to open opportunities, to modify life circumstances, and to aim for long-term change.

THE PREVENTION–TREATMENT CONTINUUM

Prevention, early intervention, and treatment programs also form a continuum, which is represented by the bottom strand of the arch in Figure 12.1. Conceptually, these three terms are closely aligned with the four-decade-old formulation of primary, secondary, and tertiary prevention that Caplan (1964) used to define prevention in the psychiatric field. As we mentioned earlier, Caplan used these terms to describe efforts for "reducing (1) the incidence of mental disorders of all types in a community (primary prevention), (2) the duration of a significant number of those disorders which do occur (secondary prevention), and (3) the impairment which may result from disorders (tertiary prevention)" (pp. 16–17). Caplan's terms are included on the continuum for some grounding; however, we use the prevention, early intervention, and treatment designations to more appropriately anchor our framework.

ENVIRONMENTAL SETTINGS

In the comprehensive framework we attend to the environment by including society–community, family, and school settings, and we acknowledge the relationship between these components. Intervention in each of these settings is also conceived as following a continuum from (a) early broad-based prevention to (b) early intervention efforts to coordinate support and training activities, and ultimately to (c) treatment approaches. The three rectangles in Figure 12.2 represent the three settings, and each is divided by a diagonal line to indicate that some strategies and programs are best implemented earlier in the risk continuum and some are more appropriate later. The diagonal line also suggests that some aspects of prevention need to be maintained and supported throughout the model. In some circumstances treatment begins early and may accompany prevention. Early intervention falls in the middle of Figure 12.2 and has elements of both prevention and treatment.

Society–Community

The society–community continuum interacts with both family and school continuums but encompasses the community and larger society. Prevention efforts in this setting consist of improving socioeconomic conditions; increasing the supply of low-cost housing, child care, job opportunities, and career options; providing community social support programs; and developing healthy community norms and values.

Along the early intervention portion of the continuum are community programs that involve family members and school personnel. That is, there is a need to provide social support and coordinated programs that enable community members to assist young people. There is a need to strengthen existing support for families in the schools and in community organizations. There is a need for schools to work with the community. Below the diagonal line are treatment strategies that include system-level interventions, such as empowerment and social activism. Empowering young people and helping them to develop plans for social action are a preventive approach on the individual level, but they serve as treatment on the society–community level. The target here is not individuals or even groups of individuals but rather the norms, structures, and practices of organizations, communities, society, and the nation.

Family

Prevention, early intervention, and treatment for families forms a continuum that begins with strategies designed to strengthen families—strategies that encourage interaction, consistency, communication, stability, support, and prosocial values. Prenatal and health care programs are included as well. As family problems increase, social and emotional support programs and training in parenting skills are implemented. Counseling is critical for dysfunctional families. At the extreme end of the continuum, programs designed to address child abuse and neglect, parental dysfunction, and family violence are especially important (see also Chapter 15).

School

Prevention in schools begins with adequate comprehensive preschools, compensatory programs (such as Head Start), and before- and after-school programs. All school-based efforts are enhanced and the effects prolonged if there is a strong level of collaboration

Environmental settings	Prevention	Early intervention	Treatment
Society/ community	Adequate socioeconomic conditions with housing, child care, and job opportunities and career options	Programs to increase low-risk community values and norms	Coordinated programs that link community, family, and school efforts
		Community social support programs	Community programs and strategies
Family	Programs that encourage family interaction, communication, and stability	Social and emotional support programs	
	Programs that increase supportive and pro-social values in families	Parent training	Family counseling and therapy	Specific treatment programs for child abuse and neglect, parental dysfunction, and family violence
	Prenatal and other health care provisions			
School	Preschool and compensatory educational programs (e.g., Head Start)	Universal programs that develop social and cognitive skills	Booster sessions	Second-chance programs
	Before- and after-school programs	Selected programs	Treatment for specific at-risk activities	

FIGURE 12.2   Environmental settings for a prevention, early intervention, treatment framework for at-risk children and youth

between school and home. Such collaboration is difficult to achieve due to parents' antic-ipation of being treated with cultural insensitivity, being patronized by school personnel, or being blamed for their children's difficulties. In addition, teachers may anticipate that parents will not respect their expertise, will not participate, or will blame their children's problems on the teachers (Kay, Fitzgerald, & McConaughy, 2002). Indeed, these fears are all too often realistic, and the presumed common goal of serving the child is often not enough to overcome these barriers. Rather, multicultural competence, communication skills, time, resources, empathy, and patience are also required. Kay and her colleagues (2002) describe the successful development and implementation of parent-teacher part-nerships to prevent problem development among children at risk for behavioral and emo-tional disorders. One important element of their program is the inclusion of parent liaisons, paraprofessionals from the local community who support parent-teacher interactions and facilitate and direct the meetings. In addition, a parent-teacher action research team is formed to develop plans for learning about, intervening with, and supporting the optimal development of the identified children, utilization of ground rules such as "Parents talk first, then teachers," and ongoing evaluation of all dimensions of the process.

Universal school programs for teaching social and life skills to all children begin early in this model, although the diagonal line indicates that they can be implemented at any point (see Figure 12.2). In Chapter 13 we provide detailed information about teaching these skills. The need for selected programs increases chronologically; specific early inter-vention is necessary for targeted children in specific problem situations or for those who exhibit problem behavior.

Figure 12.3 presents early intervention and treatment concepts for each of five at-risk categories (discussed in Chapters 7 through 11). The universal programs specified at the left in each box of Figure 12.3 represent the preventive efforts that are directed toward all young people. As children develop, efforts shift from universal approaches to programs aimed at selected groups or individual children experiencing the specific problem areas listed.

Selected interventions should begin by grade 3 or earlier for children who engage in risky behavior (e.g., aggressiveness, withdrawal) or who exhibit such negative emotions as depression, anxiety, or hostility. In a given third-grade classroom, quite accurate predic-tions can be made as to who will drop out of school before graduation (Slavin, 1994). Evidence also suggests that delinquency in adolescence can be predicted on the basis of early behavior patterns. Researchers have shown that a pattern of antisocial behavior estab-lished by fifth grade (Walker, Colvin, & Ramsey, 1995) or even earlier (Patterson et al., 1992) is the single best predictor of criminal behavior in adolescence. This is especially the case if the antisocial behavior occurs in a wide variety of settings and involves more than one type of act.

As young people progress through school, indicated treatment programs are required to assist those with more specific and serious concerns. Figure 12.3 also highlights second-chance programs for adolescents who have already engaged in risk category behavior.

A universal life-skills curriculum, modified and adapted for developmental skill level, cultural appropriateness, and social class variables, should be provided to all students as they move through school. Curriculum should include information on study skills and time management, how to prepare for tests, how to make friends, how to manage emer-gencies when home alone, how to avoid or report abuse, and, as the young adolescent matures, how to prepare for intimate relationships, how to prevent pregnancy and STDs, how to avoid drug use and resist peer and media pressure to engage in behavior that has

Selected programs

Demographic factors   Environmental stressors   Skill deficits

Indicated treatment programs

Underlying characteristics   At-risk behavior

Second-chance programs

At-risk activity

Dropout prevention
- Universal programs for all children
- CCBG Solution-Focused Counseling Mastery learning; cooperative learning; learning strategies
- Alternative school programs; GED/apprentice programs; Job Corps

Substance-abuse prevention
- Universal programs for all children
- Decision-making, assertiveness, and refusal skills training Motivational interviewing
- Drug rehabilitation programs

Pregnancy prevention
- Universal programs for all children
- Peer relationship and self-esteem programs
- Community- and school-based health clinics; programs for pregnant girls

Delinquency prevention
- Universal programs for all children
- Prevention programs for aggression and conduct problems; anger reduction and anti-bullying programs
- Reality therapy and restitution programs; school security and postvention

Suicide prevention
- Universal programs for all children
- Suicide-prevention programs; school crisis team
- Direct-action interventions, postvention

Grade level   Preschool   3   4   5   6   7   8   9   10   11   12

FIGURE 12.3   Early intervention and treatment for five at-risk categories negative consequences, and other life events. To be effective, these programs should be ongoing components of the curriculum rather than one-session classes. Training in problem solving, decision making, empathy, communication, assertiveness, and coping skills should also be ongoing. Teachers, with support from and in consultation with school counselors, psychologists, and social workers, should be prepared to teach cognitive and life skills, avoidance of substance use and delinquency, and sex education. Implementing such a model will have far-reaching effects for young people and for society as a whole.

PRACTICAL CONSIDERATIONS

Would such a comprehensive program be expensive? Certainly. But it is useful to consider the social costs if certain behaviors are not prevented. The costs of comprehensive prevention and intervention programs must be weighed against the costs of future residential treatment programs, medical bills, long-term incarceration, property damage, and welfare programs. When we calculate all of these costs, the expense of comprehensive prevention and early intervention becomes a bargain. To illustrate, it is estimated that in 1996 the federal government spent more than $38 billion to provide services and support to families that began with a birth to a teenager. In that same year, the federal government invested $138.1 million—less than one seventh of one billion dollars—to prevent teen pregnancy (Bess, Leos-Urbel, & Green, 2001). That is more than 275 times less than the amount the federal government spent to support families begun with a birth to a teen. Of course, the long-term costs of teen mothering calculated here did not include lost wages (and lost taxes) associated with limited education or costs associated with the increased likelihood that sons born to adolescent mothers will spend at least some time in prison. In Chapter 6 we described the parallel increases, and decreases, in funding for prisons and educational institutions, respectively. An Urban Institute study (Green, Waters Boots, & Tumlin, 1999) on the costs of protecting vulnerable and abused children found that for every $1 states spend on "other services" (including prevention, child protective services, and case management activities) more than $3 is spent to cover interventions such as out-of-home placement, adoption, and administrative costs. Several years later, a follow-up report from the Urban Institute indicated that prevention funding is still dramatically lower than intervention funding; whereas at least $1.5 billion was expended on other services, of which prevention services only constitute one part, $9.4 billion was spent on maintenance payments and services for children in out-of-home placements (Bess et al., 2001). Of course, simply withdrawing money from intervention and investing in prevention does not solve our problems. We need to continue to assist those who are already struggling while dramatically increasing our investment in prevention.

TWO UNIVERSAL PREVENTION PROGRAMS

Helpers implement universal programs to the entire population of intact groups. They are presumed to be helpful to all young people regardless of where they happen to be on the at-risk continuum, from remote risk to category behavior. That is, the populations served range from the doing well, to risky groups, to those already experiencing some level of impairment. In this section we provide examples of and discuss two broad-based programs that are helpful to all young people. The scope of both these prevention programs ranges from universal (i.e., promoting positive development for all) to targeted interventions for at-risk groups. The first is a school-based antibullying program and the second is a classroom-based psychoeducational group program. Desired outcomes include the enhancement of social competencies and the reduction of problems and risk factors. The terms "school-based" and "classroom-based" are used for convenience only. In addition to school settings, these programs can be used in preschool and after-school settings, juvenile detention facilities, and recreational and day care programs.

Antibullying Interventions

The bullying that students, parents, and educators face today differs from that of earlier years in part because of young people's access to more lethal forms of aggression. So, even when the bully is not actually accessing weapons, the perception of threat and the psychological effects are intensified.

Bullying is a specific subset of hostile aggression in which (1) there is an imbalance of power with a more powerful person or group attacking a less powerful one, (2) the behavior is intended to disturb or harm, and (3) the behavior occurs repeatedly over time. The aggressive behavior may be verbal (e.g., threats, name-calling), psychological (e.g., exclusion, rumors), or physical (e.g., hitting, kicking). Bullying can be done directly in the classroom, hallway, or playground or indirectly and anonymously through e-mail messages. The power differential may be psychological or physical. Thus bullying can take many forms but retains the same essential spirit. Bullies are characterized by the need to dominate others through hostile means, and they show little or no empathy for their victims (Ballard, Argus, & Remley, 1999). Of particular concern is frequent bullying, typically defined as bullying that occurs once a week or more. In a large World Health Organization study (Nansel et al., 2001), 30% of the sample reported frequent or moderate involvement in bullying either as a victim (over 10%), as a bully (13%), or both (over 6%). Frequency of bullying was higher in middle school grades than in secondary schools. Males were more likely than females to be both the victims and the perpetrators of bullying. However, relational aggression has emerged in the last few years as a serious problem (Crothers, Fields, & Kolbert, 2005). Simmons (2002) argues that much of girls' aggression is not captured in many studies of bullying. She notes that girls normatively use relational aggression to bully their victims, that relational aggression is characterized by high frequency and invisibility to teachers, and that girls are often reluctant to acknowledge that it occurs.

Technology has afforded young people a new, and particularly insidious, method of bullying. Referred to as electronic bullying or cyber bullying, this mode of bullying uses chat rooms, text messaging, Web pages, and e-mail to hurt others. The Internet allows users to maintain anonymity when communicating with a victim. Little research has been done on this form of bullying, but anyone familiar with e-mail can readily see the problem. A victim can receive dozens of e-mail messages, perhaps from the same bully, and assume that virtually everyone at school believes him or her to be a jerk, a loser, or anything else the bully chooses to call him or her.

Research examining personal characteristics of young people involved in bullying has consistently found that both the victims and the bullies demonstrate poorer psychological functioning than their peers. Earlier research suggested that bullies generally demonstrate greater dislike of school, higher levels of conduct problems, and have an increased risk of having a criminal record as adults (Olweus, 1993). More recent research indicates that bullies feel more comfortable in the social environment of school, are often at least moderately popular, and hold high status with their peers (Juvonen, Graham, & Shuster, 2003; Pelligrini, 2002). Ninety percent of young adolescents who were bullied, on the other hand, believed that the victimization caused them significant problems including the loss of friendships, feelings of isolation, and hopelessness (Hazler, Hoover, & Oliver, 1992). Young people who are bullied generally show higher levels of anxiety, depression, and unhappiness, and they display significant behavioral difficulties even 2 years after the bullying (Rigby, 1999; Schwartz, McFadyen-Ketchum, Dodge, Pettit, & Bates, 1998; Swearer, Song, Cary, Eagle, & Mickelson, 2001). Bully–victims, young people who are victims and then turn around and bully others, appear to suffer from more severe social and psychological problems than either bullies or victims (Haynie et al., 2001; Juvonen et al., 2003; Ma, 2001; Pelligrini, 2002; Salmivalli & Nieminen, 2002).

Fortunately, actions taken by school personnel and others can significantly reduce the occurrence of bullying (Crawford, 2002; Espelage & Swearer, 2003; Newman-Carlson & Horne, 2004; Teacher Education Institute, 2002) if they attend to the problem. Unfortunately, school personnel underestimate the prevalence of bullying, and they intervene in only one third of bullying incidents brought to their attention (Rodkin & Hodges, 2003).

Schoolwide plan.   Although individual efforts can be helpful, developing a systemwide plan is necessary to significantly reduce bullying. Begin with a clear, agreed upon definition of bullying, and make a plan for action. This plan for action should include answers to these questions:

- Does the plan develop an effective way to eliminate or reduce student-to-student put-downs?
- Are there as many opportunities for students to be recognized for prosocial, positive behaviors as opportunities to be recognized for antisocial, negative behaviors? How would the students answer this question?
- Does the plan include recognizing and promoting students' prosocial behavior and their random acts of kindness?
- Does the plan establish ways to recognize and support positive and kind acts done by staff and faculty?

Faculty and staff must be backed up in their efforts to identify and halt bullying. Inconsistent application of the plan or administrative failure to support the efforts of those implementing it will reduce student confidence and decrease effectiveness.

The purpose of the schoolwide plan is to change the context in which bullying occurs (Espelage & Swearer, 2003). Norms of looking the other way, intermittent punishment, and classroom Darwinism must be changed to norms of attending to bullying incidents, consistent application of consequences, and fostering a strong sense of community within every classroom (Newman-Carlson & Horne, 2004). In addition to responding systemwide, the plan needs to consider interventions with the specific people involved in the bullying. This includes victims, bullies, bystanders, "toadies," and parents.

The victim.   Concerned adults need to consider the bullying victim's realistic options given the particular situation and persons involved. The coping skills and support network of bullied students may need to be strengthened before the student can act more assertively on his or her own behalf. Victims of bullying often feel a great deal of shame and mistrust, which may make it harder for them to attempt to use the skills they do have. Sometimes students can be helped to identify behaviors and strategies that will reduce their risk of further bullying. The assertiveness training program described in Chapter 13 attends to one dimension that may be important for students who are bullied. Bullies can benefit from assertiveness training as well, learning appropriate ways to meet their needs for importance, validation, and esteem.

The bully.   Incidences of bullying should not be ignored, but they do vary widely in seriousness and severity. Thoughtless teasing might merit an informal discussion; group harassment with threats might need formal procedures including interviews with perpetrators and parents and possible disciplinary action. Pikas (cited in Rigby, 2000) has developed an approach known as the Method of Shared Concern, which involves a two-stage process. In the first stage, perpetrators are identified and spoken to individually. The adult shares his or her concern with the bully for the person being victimized and invites the bully to act in a constructive and responsible way to remedy the situation. No threats are used, but the adult carefully monitors subsequent behaviors. In the minority of cases where this approach is not successful and the bullying continues, the second step includes sanctions and application of consequences.

The bystander.   Observers of victimization and bullying often receive little attention. This is unfortunate because they contribute to the problem. Many want to help but are insecure and afraid that they themselves will be targeted next. Remaining silent leads to guilt and anxiety. Encouraging bystanders to discuss their feelings, along with the provision of assertiveness skills and exploration of various options for responding, can encourage them to become more active in reducing bullying. Bystanders can provide personal support to victims, show their concern, encourage the victim's efforts and accomplishments, and refuse to reinforce the bully with verbal encouragement or laughter. More direct intervention might take the form of protecting the victim and confronting the bully during the incident.

The "toadies."   There is another type of bystander who is more interested in encouraging bullying and the bully. Indeed, bullies are sometimes bolstered by the presence of "passive bullies." These participants in bullying behavior support the primary aggressor by expressing approval and encouragement. This elevates the status of the perpetrator and reinforces him or her (Ballard et al., 1999). These passive bullies should be dealt with in the same way as the overtly aggressive bully.

Parents.   Parents are essential allies in implementing a schoolwide antibullying program. Understanding the problem of bullying, the prevention program, and the definitions of bullying used by the school are all-important in parental acceptance and support of the program. In the process of learning about the program, parents may realize the importance of exploring bullying with their children in a more focused way, which may lead to surprises for the parents of both victims and bullies. Many children suffer, and dole out suffering, in silence.

The parents of bullied children need information and support to help their child. The parents of students who bully may respond in numerous ways to their child's behavior: denial, blaming the victim, the school, or society, or requesting assistance with an out-of-control child. Blaming the bully—or his or her parents—is not helpful.

A developmental and comprehensive approach to reducing bullying is important. In addition, prevention programs that are supported throughout the school building, that include consistent responses to individual behavior, and that incorporate aspects of the social context of bullying are most likely to reduce the number of young people victimized by bullying. We describe such a program next.

Group-Oriented Psychological Education Prevention

This second universal program was developed around themes and suggestions offered by Phoenix area high school students who were asked to respond to the question: "How can we decrease violence in the schools?" These students were participants in a citywide essay contest conducted by the City of Phoenix and Prudential Securities. Students from 14 high schools submitted essays with a winner selected from each school. A cash prize was given to each winner, and an overall citywide winner received an additional cash prize. In addition to providing the prize money, Prudential Securities also provided a small grant to the City of Phoenix and, subsequently, to Arizona State University to analyze the essays and to develop a violence reduction program based on the winning suggestions. Although some of the students' solutions were not applicable—psychologically, politically, or economically—the suggestions were concrete, interesting, and always thought provoking.

We (McWhirter, J. J., Herrmann, Jefferys, & Quinn, 1995) used a content analysis procedure for reviewing the winning essays, which we confirmed and validated by a similar analysis for all the submitted essays at one randomly selected school. The content analysis identified common themes regarding strategies and programs to prevent or reduce school violence. The content analysis resulted in four basic themes:

1. Increase support and encouragement through positive peer models (e.g., conflict resolution and peer mediation programs).
2. Change the structure of the school environment.
3. Increase positive adult role models, and provide better communication between school and home.
4. Develop specific classes that deal with student emotions underlying issues leading to violence (e.g., stress, turmoil, and difficulties young people face).

Students highlighted one other factor that led to developing the Group-Oriented Psychological Education Prevention (GOPEP) program. Almost all the students mentioned the need for prevention. This group of young people saw a need to begin violence reduction and other programs early and to continue them on into secondary school.

We completed an extensive review of prevention programs and discovered a host of training resources and materials on conflict resolution and peer mediation. This fact made the first suggestion superfluous. It seemed redundant to develop such a program when abundant material on this topic is already available. Suggestions two and three, which have been the focus of many prevention efforts and are important considerations, were beyond the scope of this specific project. We strongly recommended to school personnel that steps should be taken to implement them.

Because so many of the essay winners suggested the possibility of using the classroom structure to deal with underlying violence issues and because so many believed that underlying emotional issues were often the cause of violence, we decided to focus our efforts on developing programs to help young people understand and then manage their negative emotions and behavior and increase their positive ones. Thus the students' fourth suggestion led to development and validation of an anger management program.

SCARE (Student Created Aggression Replacement Education; Herrmann & McWhirter, 2001) is designed to help young adolescents manage feelings of hostility, aggression, and anger. The SCARE program teaches young people methods to control impulsive emotions, encourages them to make better decisions in responding to provocative situations, and provides them with alternatives to violent behavior. Through participation in SCARE, students first learn to recognize the problem of anger and violence in our society, then learn the necessary skills to cope with their own feelings of anger and aggression, and finally learn strategies to prevent violence and aggression from escalating in others. Because the SCARE program is the prototype for other psychoeducation programs, we will return to it for further discussion.

The other GOPEP programs include SOAR, or Students Optimistic Attitudes and Resiliency Program (Gilboy et al., 2002); ART, or Anxiety Reduction Training (Boewe & McWhirter, 2002, November); and BLOCKS, or Building Lives on Companion Knowledge Skills (Fair & McWhirter, 2002, August). These are all based on supporting evidence that various social competencies can be directly and deliberately taught to reduce negative risk factors and to increase positive protective ones, and that educating young people in psychological foundations will help to prevent negative events. The group-oriented aspect of this program is based on psychoeducational group methodology. Psychoeducational group work is a common delivery method in comprehensive prevention programs where it is intended to maximize the potential for students' healthy development and success. Thus GOPEP uses a group format to deliver the skills, although sometimes the group is a classroom-sized group.

In these GOPEP prevention programs, we have targeted children and young adolescents mostly using a cognitive-behavioral approach. As discussed earlier, research indicates that at-risk children are overly sensitive to negative interpersonal interactions. They tend to have more negative beliefs about the intentions of others and to minimize their own responsibility for problems. They also frequently misunderstand and then mislabel their own affective arousal (emotions) so that feelings such as hurt, fear, frustration, and anger become confused. Higher risk youth then subsequently respond to their own misperceived emotions, oftentimes in aggressive ways. Their solutions to perceived problems are often excessively action oriented and nonverbal, which typically worsens the problems they experience. The cognitive-behavioral training provided in GOPEP is designed to improve poor self-understanding, change frequent distortions of emotions and of perceptions around events, and enhance better problem solving.

The GOPEP programs are user-friendly prevention and intervention curriculums that provide leaders with easy-to-follow, step-by-step instructions. Currently, the four interventions focus on reducing anger, depression, and anxiety and on increasing hope and optimism, empathy, and positive relationships. Each curriculum consists of 15 group sessions with each session lasting approximately 1 hour. We designed the programs to be used by teachers, counselors, social workers, psychologists, law enforcement officers, detention center staff, scout leaders, senior citizen volunteers, and any other caring and dedicated adult who is committed to bringing about positive change in the lives of young people. The four packages deal with anger and empathy (SCARE); optimism, hope, and depression (SOAR); building and negotiating relationships (BLOCKS); and anxiety (ART).

Anger management.   Learning to deal with anger and other emotions is an important component of an antibullying program. Unfortunately, most anger reduction programs have not been empirically validated. Without validation, practitioners do not know whether their interventions are effective. More important is the possibility that the intervention is doing more harm than good. Most interventions are designed to put young people together in a group to help them reduce their anger and aggression, but this can be risky if youth are given unstructured time in which they may reinforce each others' aggression. Few anger programs have dealt with this issue, and few have been directed at the roots of aggressive and violent behavior in younger, middle-school-aged populations.

One exception is the SCARE program (Herrmann & McWhirter, 2001), which the Safe and Drug-Free Schools and Communities Agency in the U.S. Department of Education has identified as a "promising" program. The SCARE program was specifically developed to prevent violence and aggression through appropriate management of anger for early adolescents. A growing body of literature has consistently indicated that these years are critical to a young person's social development, and this time period is potentially one of the best times for prevention programs for at-risk youth. As there are a lack of aggression replacement and anger management packages available to teachers, counselors, and youth workers for this age group (McWhirter, J. J., Herrmann, Jefferys, & Quinn, 1995), curriculum was designed for broad scale implementation by such individuals.

One premise of the SCARE program is that negative actions perceived as intentional will elicit anger, and anger in turn motivates hostile behavior. Therefore, the SCARE program focuses on the reattribution of perceived offenses and the control and management of resulting anger. In recent years empirical evidence has linked high levels of anger to a number of negative social consequences, including an increased propensity to cause physical damage to oneself and others, increased psychological problems, and school-related problems (Deffenbacher, Lynch, Oetting, & Kemper, 1996). Because the literature has also indicated that anger can be effectively reduced through therapeutic intervention (Achmon, Granek, Golomb, & Hart, 1998; Deffenbacher, McNamara, Stark, & Sabadell, 1990; Moon & Eisler, 1983; Novaco, 1975), the SCARE program was constructed as a meta-theoretical treatment package focusing on anger management and coping skills for adolescents and young adults. Primary objectives embraced by the SCARE program include (a) teaching young people about emotions, including aggression and anger; (b) helping young people to recognize alternatives to violent behavior and aggressive responses; and (c) encouraging young people to make good decisions in response to provocative situations. The 15 different sessions are clustered in three distinct yet related areas: (a) recognizing anger and violence in the community, (b) managing and reducing self-expressions of anger, and (c) defusing anger and violence in others.

In recognizing anger and violence in the community, primary objectives include (a) providing a clear definition of anger and violence and (b) introducing the topic of anger and violence in a way that promotes intrigue and interest for acquiring anger management and coping skills. We know that learning is facilitated among youth who have cultivated an interest for a particular subject and who feel that the material presented to them is relevant to their lives. By combining national statistics with descriptive images obtained from popular media resources, this section aims to stimulate motivation for learning anger reduction skills and cultivates awareness that such skills are vitally important to all adolescents.

The second section, managing and reducing anger in the self, was developed to inform youth about effective prosocial strategies for managing their own aggressive impulses and feelings of anger. This section is based on Novaco's (1975, 1979) adaptation of Michenbaum's (1972) stress inoculation model, and it consists of three separate phases: (a) education and cognitive preparation, (b) skill acquisition, and (c) application training. Education and cognitive preparation provides youth with information about the cognitive, physiological, and behavioral interactions of anger arousal. They learn about internal triggers that can provoke anger and about steps they can take to effectively manage their expression of anger. Skill acquisition consists of training adolescents in cognitive-behavioral coping skills to effectively manage situations involving anger and aggression. Application training consists of practicing newly acquired skills within the context of experiential group sessions or role plays until such skills are mastered. In studies assessing the efficacy of this model, Novaco (1975, 1979) reported evidence in support of stress inoculation training for reducing anger, whereas others have reported the effectiveness of this model with adolescent populations (Hains & Ellmann, 1994; Wilcox & Dowrick, 1992).

Finally, the third section, defusing anger and violence in others, draws on an eclectic model involving skills and techniques for (a) preventing situations involving anger and violence from developing and (b) promoting peaceful resolutions to hostile situations that have developed. To promote these objectives in as many different ways as possible, this section is not grounded in any one theoretical orientation but combines techniques from different schools of thought. In a review of the treatment literature, Greenwood (1994) noted that multimodal approaches that combine several treatment modalities (e.g., cognitive skills, relaxation skills, and social skills training) are usually more efficacious than unimodal approaches. In addition, multimodal approaches are of special value when treating behaviorally disordered and "acting-out" youth. Several sessions in the defusing anger and violence in others section draw upon diverse yet complementary theoretical tenants, including sessions on verbal and paraverbal techniques, body language training (proxemics and kinesics), identifying creative alternatives to aggression, diversity appreciation training, and no-violence contracting.

Hope, optimism, depression.   SOAR (Student's Optimistic Attitudes and Resiliency Program; Gilboy et al., 2002) is a proactive program that is multitheoretical in foundation and multimodal, utilizing humanistic, cognitive, and behavioral intervention techniques. The program also addresses the diversity of learning styles and works to engage the whole child in the process of learning. The humanistic approach creates the context for SOAR. The program builds largely on the positive foundations of students, emphasizing self-development, understanding, and positive regard for each student in a supportive community. The program uses stories, metaphors, and activities to increase hope and optimism and reduce depression. The purpose of the program is to build on the strengths of every child, increasing the child's sense of control over his or her thoughts, attitudes, and attributions. It builds resiliency and promotes well-being. The SOAR program seeks to explore healthy functioning not as the absence of something wrong but as a positive and definable entity in and of itself. The cognitive-behavioral approach also plays a prominent role in SOAR as many of the sessions engage students in learning new concepts, cognitive reframing, and activities that reinforce their learning.

The program was developed to highlight principles of positive psychology, and its theoretical foundations lies in learned optimism (Seligman, 1990) and hope theory (Snyder, 1994). In the simplest sense, optimism is a process by which one looks at a glass as half full (positive) as opposed to half empty (negative). It is the meanings that we give to the events in our lives that cause us to see them as positive or negative. The theory of learned optimism posits that our attributions are a function of the permanence, pervasiveness, and personalization of our thoughts. The optimist sees failure as a unique event that does not generalize and poison other areas of personal competence. This person will see the cause in the situation (external) as opposed to being a personal deficit (internal). The pessimist's failure is viewed as a permanent flaw that generalizes to all areas of life and is the result of some internal shortcoming. A wealth of research demonstrates a predictive relationship between optimism and psychological and physical well-being in children and adults (Buchanan & Seligman, 1995). The efficacy of the learned optimism intervention has been demonstrated in research with significantly fewer depressive symptoms in the intervention group than in a comparison group. An extremely important finding from this research was that the preventive effect, in terms of decreased depression, actually grew after the program had ended (Gillham, Reivich, Jaycox, & Seligman, 1995).

The second theoretical anchor is hope theory (Snyder, 1994). Hope is generically defined as having positive expectations or the lack of negative expectations about the future (Snyder et al., 1996). More specifically, hope is operationalized by three components: (1) the process of continual internal goal setting, (2) the ability to generate multiple paths to the goals, and (3) the perseverance to reach the goals (Snyder, 1996). The hopeful individual will see the path options and have the wherewithal to pursue the paths. The theory states that hope can be instilled through an improved view of one's future and skills acquisitions (i.e., techniques of optimistic thinking).

The sequence of the programming entails three broad areas. First, it is important to place the sessions in a meaningful context that will engage the students. Second, all students are taught how to think optimistically for themselves and how to modify other thoughts and behaviors to accommodate the new skills of hope and optimism. Third, students are made aware of the relevance of their newfound optimistic strategies. The students internalize the concepts and then apply them to their interactions with others, which ultimately positively affects their identity as members of the classroom and the larger community. These three areas are integrated into the sequence with key components practiced throughout. Implementation of this program predicts a decreased incidence of depressive symptoms and, concurrently, an increase in hope.

Relationships. BLOCKS (Building Lives on Cooperation Knowledge Skills; Fair, & McWhirter, 2002) is designed to increase students' ability to negotiate successful interactions with others. Developing social skills to create successful relationships is one of the most important accomplishments of childhood (Greshman & Elliot, 1990). This is especially important with students with differences in social skill functioning. BLOCKS focuses on increasing skills such as cooperation, assertion, responsibility, empathy, and self-control. The program is multitheoretically based and utilizes multimodal interventions. BLOCKS promotes interpersonal and friendship skills, leading to better social adjustment.

The theoretical framework for this program is based on the theory of multiple intelligence (Gardner, 1983) and social learning theory (Bandura, 1993). Multiple intelligence theory, in essence, is a multiplied way of understanding intellect. According to Goleman (1995), IQ is not the only measure for success and counts for only 20% of the variance, with emotional and social "intelligence" accounting for the rest. Research demonstrates a positive relationship between social intelligences and academic performance (Elias, Gara, Schuyler, Branden-Muller, & Sayette, 1991). More important, research has shown that the acquisition of social skills can positively affect academic achievement during the time they are taught as well as in the long term.

Social learning theory (Bandura, 1973, 1993) is the second theoretical base for BLOCKS. Social learning theory explains that new behavior interacts between the environmental, behavioral, and cognitive influences in which the new skills are acquired.

Anxiety.   ART (Anxiety Reduction Training; Boewe & McWhirter, 2002) is designed to reduce fear and anxiety in participants. Anxiety and fear can either be directed toward a specific object or can be a general feeling and negative affect of worry. Anxiety inhibits cognitive abilities as well as emotional and social development. Anxiety may go undetected because it sometimes operates at a low level, yet it still influences many areas of daily functioning.

In the ART program young people reduce anxiety through a series of activities involving the creation of art. Using several different media, students create an art product and discuss their thoughts and feelings related to their productions. Each ART session activity has specific instructions that involve student reflection on specific components such as identity, feelings, environment, coping skills, and fears. The art skills involved are quite basic, and projects can be accomplished based on students' current levels of visual art skills: simple figures, simple abstract drawings, or collages of photos or magazine illustrations.

After each project, students discuss their respective pieces and what they represent. The exercises are nonthreatening while encouraging self-disclosure, connecting with group members, and cultivating feedback and support. Students recognize and confront certain fears while finding support and comfort from their peers.

CONCLUSION

The comprehensive prevention, early intervention, treatment framework presented in this chapter highlights how intervention is related to and modified by the developmental sequence through which children progress as they become increasingly at risk. Prevention efforts include universal approaches for all children as well as selected programs that attend to issues of concern that are identified early on. As children come to be increasingly at risk, they may require indicated intervention or treatments focused on specific problem areas. For youth already engaged in an at-risk category activity, treatment that includes second-chance programs may be necessary. Each of these interventions, provided for children and teenagers at a specified level of risk, can be offered in the society or community, family, and school settings. Antibullying programs and GOPEP represent two examples of effective prevention interventions.

Core Components of Programs for Prevention and Early Intervention

▲ *The Little Train*
It's three a.m. again and she wakens full of dread
Another day coming
another endurance test to mark
how many taunts, snubs, stares
a girl can bear in silence.
The clock ticks on relentlessly
then in its rhythm she begins to hear
"I think I can I think I can"
She smiles, remembering stories and laps, comfort
Smiles at herself for this lapse into silly optimism
Smiles at the thought of her teacher—
trying so hard to push this "positive thinking"
That no one will ever use . . .
Sleep finds her
Still smiling.

CHAPTER OUTLINE

▲   Specific affective, cognitive, and behavioral skills play a large part in a young person's personal and social success. Resilient youth develop social competencies that help them to negotiate life's vicissitudes and to emerge as healthy, strong, and contributing individuals. High-risk youth do not develop such competencies and frequently find themselves on a downward spiral of lowered expectations, deviant behavior, rejection by society, and a dead-end future. They have not mastered those fundamental life skills that allow them to survive and thrive in the world.

In Chapter 6 we discussed resiliency and how some young people have the ability to thrive despite exposure to severe risks. To be considered resilient, children must both experience significant negative life events that ensure their status as high risk and demonstrate successful and positive adaptations to that risk. We also highlighted five major areas—the five Cs of competency—that appear to be important in the lives of young people who are resilient. The five Cs distinguish between high-risk and low-risk young people.

In this chapter we lay out a series of prevention and early intervention strategies that are core components in improving resiliency among young people. In presenting these various programs, we use the general framework of the five Cs. This serves as a useful framework to guide our thinking. However, an intervention to improve one specific competency is likely to improve others as well.

Most of these prevention and early intervention programs are designed to be implemented with young people early in their school careers, in some instances even in preschool. The reason for this, of course, is that most problem behavior develops according to an orderly progression from less serious to more serious. Nothing precludes implementing these programs later in a young person's life if the person has not developed the competency.

Although some competency skills seem to tie in directly with specific problem behaviors presented in Chapters 7 through 11, specific problems usually do not exist in isolation from others. For example, delinquent youth are likely to have reading problems, use drugs, engage in risky sex, and join gangs (Jessor, 1993). In addition, a specific problem behavior tends to weaken protective factors such as commitment to school or attachment to parents. Improving the five Cs using some of the programs identified here will help to strengthen and increase protective factors.

CRITICAL SCHOOL COMPETENCIES

Critical school competencies consist of both basic academic skills and academic survival skills. Again, we acknowledge the very important role that good academic skills—reading, writing, arithmetic, and so forth—play in the success and happiness of citizens. Exposing young people to high-quality schools is critical for developing basic academic skills. Academic survival skills include social competency, which is critical for school survival initially and later for survival in life as the young person matures.

Social competence can be described as the ability to make use of personal resources to influence the environment and to achieve a positive outcome. Social competence is made up of a variety of skills that provide effective ways of being with others. Such skills include behaving appropriately in the classroom, the formation of relationships and friendships, nonviolent resolution of conflicts, assertiveness and resistance to peer pressure, and negotiation of relationships with adults. Without these essential skills, children and adolescents are susceptible to high-risk problem behaviors (Allsopp, Santos, & Linn, 2000; Botvin et al., 1995; Wagner, 1996). Deficits in personal, cognitive, and social skills are an underlying cause of social incompetence. So young people, especially those at risk, need specific help to acquire the social competence to cope with academic work, to make good decisions about life's options, to adopt health-promoting behaviors, to form stable human relationships, and to maintain hope about their future (see Box 13.1).

Training in Life Skills

Life-skills training programs emphasize the acquisition of generic social and cognitive skills. The theoretical foundation of these approaches consists primarily of Bandura's (1977) social learning theory and Jessor and Jessor's (1977; Jessor, 1993) problem-behavior theory. From these perspectives, deviant behaviors are seen as socially learned, functional behaviors that result from the interplay of personal and environmental factors. Skill-building training programs typically employ some combination of interpersonal communication and social skills, strategies for cognitive change, and coping mechanisms.

▲ Box 13.1

The Birthday Party

As we walked up the sidewalk to the front porch, the front door opened and Mary exclaimed, "Grama, Papa . . . Thank you for coming to my birthday party!" Said in a clear, precise, and thoroughly taught voice that only a 3-year-old can muster.

At 3 years old, Mary's social and interpersonal skills were in stark contrast to the group of inner-city children I had worked with all that afternoon. Too bad all children don't have a mother who teaches them what to say and when to say it. But if parents don't, teachers can.

The life-skills model.   With its emphasis on education and training rather than counseling and therapy, the life-skills model is ideal for use in elementary, middle, and secondary schools. Programs that include a few core elements are useful, but comprehensive programs are more effective (Dryfoos, 1994; Durlack, 1995; Lowenthal, 1996). The life-skills model can enlist the efforts of mental health counselors, psychologists, social workers, school nurses, nurse practitioners, and teachers in such varied fields as physical education, home economics, and health educators (Allsopp et al., 2000). School counselors, psychologists, and special education teachers are key participants in this plan. Life-skills modules can be incorporated into the curriculum at all developmental levels, from kindergarten through high school and in a variety of course content areas. Life-skills training can also be included in adult and continuing education programs and in parent education programs offered by the school system as well as by community colleges and community service agencies.

Training model.   Procedures for teaching life skills resemble those used in teaching any other skill. The overall task is broken down into small stages or component parts, which are taught systematically, step by step, from the simple to the more complex. Training in each session follows a five-step model: (1) instruction (teach), (2) model (show), (3) role play (practice), (4) feedback (reinforce), and (5) homework (apply). Specific tasks are presented in sequence, and frequent rewards are given for desired behavior. In this model, directed practice and an emphasis on influential models play equal parts. Although the order may vary somewhat, all five training steps are important in teaching specific skills.

1. *Teach.* Explanations and instructions are provided. A rationale for the skill is provided, and students are given oral instructions on how to perform it.
2. *Show.* The specific skill is modeled for the student. The skill can be "shown" by videotape, or the trainer or another child can demonstrate it.
3. *Practice.* The child is encouraged to imitate and use the skill by role playing in the training session. The performance is evaluated with emphasis on the correct aspects of the student's imitative behavior.
4. *Reinforce.* As the child role plays additional problem situations, feedback and encouragement are given. Further coaching is provided as needed to shape and refine the performance.

5. *Apply.* Students are requested to perform the newly acquired skill in various real-life situations. They record their experiences and report back at the next session. The characteristics of successful and unsuccessful performances are reviewed, and refinements are introduced as needed.

Components of the life-skills program can be included in regular and special education classes and in a program designed for use throughout a school or a district. To be most effective, these skills programs should start early in a child's life, such as in preschool, and continue to be reinforced throughout the young person's school career (Forness et al., 2000). Ideally, the program would be universally applied so as not to stigmatize students with limited or deficient skills. Of course, provision needs to be made to teach or reteach skills to children who miss or otherwise do not get them.

Prevention Strategy for Children: Interpersonal Cognitive Problem Solving

There are several useful models for academic survival, life, and social problem-solving skills that include "think aloud" (Camp & Bash, 1985a, 1985b, 1985c), the "skill streaming" programs (Goldstein, Sprafkin, Gershaw, & Klein, 1980; McGinnis & Goldstein, 1984, 1990), and "I can problem solve" (Shure, 1992a, 1992b, 1992c). This last program includes the interpersonal cognitive problem-solving or "I can problem solve" (ICPS) manuals for preschool, kindergarten and primary grades, and intermediate elementary grades. This cognitive problem-solving program is the result of more than 30 years of research by Spivack and Shure and their colleagues at Hahnemann University (Shure, 1999). It is designed to enhance interpersonal thinking skills that reduce or prevent high-risk behaviors. The underlying goal of the program is to help children learn *how* to think, not *what* to think.

Rebelliousness, aggressive and antisocial behavior, poor peer relationships, and poor academic achievement are important early predictors of later delinquency, alcohol and substance abuse, psychopathology, and school dropout (Shure & Spivack, 1988). Often by the third grade, schoolchildren with poor academic survival and life skills exhibit behavior that indicates a high-risk pattern for subsequent behavioral maladjustment, special school placement, academic problems, and grade retention. Considerable evidence exists to suggest that some children do not have adequate problem-solving skills. Available evidence suggests that problem solvers draw on (or are limited by) their repertoire of social behavioral and social cognitive competencies (e.g., role-taking and assertiveness skills) as well as their store of social knowledge (e.g., familiarity with social roles and conventions) in generating, evaluating, and applying potential solutions to social and interpersonal dilemmas that confront them.

Spivack and Shure (1974) investigated how these cognitive interpersonal skills might be taught and how early they could be successfully absorbed. They assumed that the earlier these skills could be learned the greater the cumulative benefit and the broader their usefulness for confronting life challenges. Focusing on African American inner-city nursery school children, these researchers found that children as young as 4 years old benefit from the program. The interpersonal cognitive problem-solving program (ICPS), later nicknamed by the children "I can problem solve," was the result.

The researchers also investigated whether the level of effective problem solving was correlated with level of intelligence, asking, in essence: Do smarter people make better problem solvers? Results suggest that general verbal skills and IQ scores are not related to effective problem solving (Spivack, Platt, & Shure, 1976). Another investigation focused on how overly impulsive (i.e., impatient and quick to act) or overly inhibited (i.e., passive and very shy) children would respond to problem-solving training. Both of these extremes are examples of children deficient in the ability to foresee the consequences of their actions and limited in solutions to interpersonal problems. Both impulsive and shy children responded well to training in interpersonal problem solving. The ICPS program has even been successfully implemented with parents being trained to work with their children on problem solving (Shure, 1996a, 1996b). The program is applicable to different age groups, social classes, and to children of diverse ethnic and racial backgrounds.

Program description.   The format of the preschool program is a script (Shure, 1992a), which is upgraded in sophistication for use in kindergarten and early elementary school (Shure, 1992b) and further upgraded for intermediate grades (Shure, 1992c). The program has a particularly strong advantage as an intervention strategy in that teachers in a typical classroom, mixing quiet and talkative youngsters in smaller groups, can easily implement it. Ideally, teachers work with small groups of 6 to 10 students for about 20 minutes per day.

As a school-based program, the ICPS intervention includes all the children in a class because even good problem solvers can get better. The classroom-based approach has several advantages: No student is left out because children initially competent in problem solving help avoid group silence; it helps those children incorrectly identified as being at low risk (the unidentified false negatives); and more youth can be reached in a shorter period of time.

It is recommended that the formal classroom curriculums be implemented on a daily basis for 4 months. However, informal use of the approach should continue throughout the time the children are in school. The ICPS manuals (Shure, 1992a, 1992b, 1992c) include formal lessons as well as specific suggestions for incorporating problem-solving approaches into ongoing classroom curriculums and interactions. Each lesson includes a stated purpose, suggested materials, and a teacher's script. The teacher's script is intended to be a flexible guideline for implementing the basic steps of the lesson. Lessons are grouped into two major categories: pre-problem-solving skills and problem-solving skills.

Pre-problem-solving skills.   Pre-problem-solving concepts set the stage for the acquisition of problem-solving skills by teaching the ICPS vocabulary, teaching cause-and-effect relationships, encouraging listening and paying-attention skills, and helping children identify feelings.

The first and second weeks of the program focus on basic word concepts that lay a foundation for problem solving. For example, the words *different* and *same* help children develop a habit of thinking about a variety of different alternatives. Kicking and hitting are the same in that they both hurt; asking is different from hurting. The words *all* and *some* help children learn to recognize that certain solutions may not be successful with all people but with some. The word *or* helps children think about more than one way to solve a problem: "I can do this" or "I can do that."

Cause-and-effect relationships are also taught. For example, "Lidia hit Denise because Denise hit Lidia first." Children learn to understand cause and effect but also to think in such a way that they will see the cause-and-effect connection between an act and its consequence. The words *because* and *why*, *might* and *maybe*, *now* and *later*, and *before* and *after* are all included and set the stage for problem-solving consequences that come later in the program.

Approximately 20 lessons are included that teach children the concept of emotions and about how people feel. Children are encouraged to identify another's feelings in a problem situation; they learn to be sensitive to feelings. Obviously, they must learn a language for emotions. They are encouraged to learn "if . . . then" logic. For example, a child learns to identify and label emotions: "If he is crying, then he is sad." Teaching feelings is important; if people's feelings are to be considered in decision making, it is necessary to identify, understand, and verbalize them.

Problem-solving skills.   Problem-solving skills are taught through lessons on alternative solutions, consequences, and solution–consequence pairs. The intermediate grade school program also includes a section on means–ends thinking, which is believed to be too advanced for younger students.

Alternative solutions lessons are designed to help children recognize problems and generate possible solutions. The goal is to stimulate children to think of as many different solutions as possible to everyday interpersonal problem situations that are presented to them. All solutions are accepted equally. Solutions are never evaluated for being "good" but are praised for being "different." Later, the children evaluate for themselves whether an idea is good or not, and why.

The objective of the consequences sessions is to help children learn to think sequentially and to engage in consequential thinking. Children are guided to think about what might happen next if a particular solution is carried out. Children are encouraged to identify consequences for their own solutions and then to decide whether the idea is good or not.

The lessons for solution–consequence pairs are designed to give children practice in linking solutions with consequences. Children are encouraged to suggest a solution to a problem and then follow it up with a consequence. They then return to the same problem for a second solution and look at the consequence of that solution, and so on. These exercises provide experience in linking a variety of pairs of solutions and consequences. For example, in trying to get a friend to leave the room, a child might say "Push him if he won't go" (solution), "but he might hit me back" (consequence), or "If I ask him" (solution), "he might go" (goal).

The curriculum for older children includes means–ends thinking. Means–ends thinking is a higher order skill that does not emerge until sometime in middle childhood. In these sessions, children are taught to elaborate or plan a series of specific actions to attain a given goal. They are encouraged to recognize and devise ways around potential obstacles. They are helped to develop a realistic time frame in constructing a means to the goal.

In addition to the formal curriculum, the teacher is encouraged to extend the approach from helping children think about hypothetical situations and their problems to helping them think about actual problems that arise during the day, including those that occur in the classroom. This informal problem-solving dialogue technique, which focuses on the real-life world of the child, contributes to another advantage of the program—generalization—that is built in as an integral part of ICPS.

In addition to the preschool and elementary school programs, ICPS curriculums have been developed for adolescents through high school and young adulthood (Spivack et al., 1976). Taken as a whole, available findings suggest that ICPS training has beneficial effects going beyond improved cognitive test performance (Shure, 1993, 1999; Shure & Spivack, 1988). Changes in social behavior have been noted, including decreases in aggressive and impulsive behavior and increases in cooperative and prosocial behavior. Behavioral gains have been achieved with numerous groups, ranging from preschoolers showing early signs of behavioral maladjustment to disturbed schoolchildren in residential treatment to juvenile delinquents (Shure, 1999). Long-term follow-up data are sparse, but initial findings suggest substantial holding power for behavioral treatment effects, at least in the early years. ICPS helps instill academic survival skills and has the potential to prevent serious behavioral problems later on.

CONCEPT OF SELF

In Chapter 6 we identified self-concept, self-esteem, and self-efficacy as the second "C" of competency. We pointed out that generally, high-risk young people tend to struggle with negative self-concepts and with low self-esteem and self-efficacy. We do know that high-risk young people have biased attributions and that these biased attributions influence their perceptions, including self-perceptions. Providing interventions to modify biased attributions is a reasonable prevention approach. One of the best early primary prevention programs was developed by Seligman and colleagues (Peterson, Maier, & Seligman, 1993; Seligman, 1990, 1993, 1994, 1995) at the University of Pennsylvania.

Training to Prevent Depression

For more than 30 years, Seligman has been a major researcher in the general area of depression, with his first contributions identifying, clarifying, and establishing the concept of learned helplessness. He also devoted major effort and energy to the opposite side of the coin, learned optimism, establishing a robust link between pessimism and eventual depression (Seligman, Schulman, DeRubeis, & Hollon, 1999). The Penn Prevention Program (PPP) sought to inoculate children against the effects of pessimism—with spectacular results. The children in the Penn Prevention Program spent a total of 24 hours learning and practicing cognitive-behavioral skills. They were also asked to practice the skills in homework assignments. Because the PPP worked so well in preventing depression when it was taught to children in schools, Seligman (1995) developed an approach to teach it to parents. This program is primarily a depression prevention program, but it helps youth improve their concept of self, which is strongly related to depression.

In this intervention, children who reported parental conflict, depressive symptoms, or both were targeted because these factors increase children's risk for future depression (Jaycox & Repetti, 1993; Nolen-Hoeksema, Girgus, & Seligman, 1992). Children who participated in the prevention program reported fewer depressive symptoms than did children in the control group immediately after the program and at a 6-month follow-up. A later study explored the program's effects after a 2-year delay (Gillham et al., 1995). The effects of the prevention program actually grew stronger after the program was over, suggesting that psychological immunization against depression can occur by teaching social and cognitive optimism skills to children.

The PPP contains two major components: a social problem-solving component and a cognitive component. The social problem-solving component focuses on interpersonal and conduct problems that are often associated with depressed children. Children are taught to think about their goals before acting. They generate lists of possible solutions for various problems and are encouraged to make decisions by weighing the pros and cons of all the options. The cognitive component is based on the theories developed by Ellis (1962, 1985, 1996),

Beck (1976), and Seligman (1990). Briefly, children are taught to identify negative beliefs and to evaluate these beliefs by examining evidence for and against them. Children are taught explanatory style and how to identify pessimistic explanations. They learn to generate alternative explanations that are more realistic and more optimistic. Finally, children are also taught behavioral techniques to enhance assertiveness, negotiation, and relaxation, as well as techniques for coping with parental conflict. The PPP also focuses on the concept of optimism, which we discussed in Chapter 12 as a component of the GOPEP program.

Optimism

Optimism is an ability to think positively about one's situation and future, even in the face of difficulty. People who are optimistic believe that they can achieve their desired goals and make the changes in their lives necessary to achieve their goals. Optimism includes positive self-talk skills, so that when one experiences a setback, he or she is able to reason through it and not catastrophize the outcome. When people do badly, they typically ask themselves, "Why?" There are three components to the answer to this question: Who is to blame? How much of life will be undermined? And, How long will it last? The first component attaches blame to the self or to the world. The second and third questions—how pervasive is the cause and how permanent is the cause—govern what people do to respond to failure. Feeling bad about oneself does not directly cause failure. However, the belief that problems undermine everything in life and that problems will last forever cause people to stop trying. Giving up leads to more failure, and more failure leads to an even more pessimistic explanatory style. Thus, in the face of a bad event, someone who is pessimistic characteristically thinks that a problem is pervasive and permanent and that he or she is personally at fault for the problem. For example, a child may attribute a poor school performance to a personal failure or inability and begin to believe that all school efforts will result in failure. This explanatory style leads to destructive actions and becomes a kind of self-fulfilling negative prophecy. Positive events are believed by pessimists to be temporary, limited, and caused by something other than their own actions.

By contrast, optimists characteristically employ an explanatory style in which they think the bad event is temporary, limited to the specific event, and with many possible causes other than themselves. This cognitive mind-set saves the person from stress and mobilizes energy toward constructive goals. When a positive event occurs, an optimist characteristically thinks that he or she had a personal hand in causing the outcome and that it is pervasive and permanent. Thus the three critical dimensions used to explain why any particular good or bad event happens are personal, permanent, and pervasive.

Internal versus external: Personal.   When events happen, children either blame themselves (internal) or blame circumstances or other people (external). Pessimistic children have a habit of blaming themselves when bad things happen and frequently explain good events by attributing them to other people or to the situation. To change the explanatory style from pessimism to optimism, and thus inoculate against future depression, children need to learn to take appropriate responsibility for events that occur in their lives but also not to blame themselves when things go wrong—because most problems are caused by a complex set of contributing factors. Some children shoulder the entire blame and think of things in black-and-white terms. This leads to overwhelming feelings of worthlessness and guilt, causing them to withdraw and further increasing their risk for depression.

Sometimes versus always: Permanent.   Pessimistic and depressed children believe the cause of bad events and the reasons for their failure are permanent. Because the cause will persist forever, bad events are always going to occur. Optimistic children believe that the causes for bad events are temporary; this serves to inoculate them against depression. For the pessimistic child, mistakes, rejections, failures, and so forth are thought of in terms of forever and always. The optimistic child explains bad events with words such as sometimes or lately or another time-limiting term.

Pessimistic and optimistic children react differently to positive events in their lives as well. Children who believe that good events have temporary causes tend to be more pessimistic than children who believe that good events have permanent causes. This is just the opposite of the explanation for bad events.

Specific versus global: Pervasive.   If the cause of the event is pervasive, its effect is distributed across many different situations in life and becomes global. Children who focus on global explanations for bad events give up on everything when they fail in one area. Pessimistic and depressed children tend to let a bad situation expand into all parts of their lives. This limits the number of positive outlets available to them and catastrophizes everything.

Children who attribute global causes to bad events need to learn to be more specific in their explanations. Instead of a test failure meaning "I am stupid," children can learn to say, "I didn't prepare very well this time." Children who think about good events as having more global causes do better in more areas of their lives. When it comes to good events, the optimist believes that the causes enhance everything they do. Pessimists believe that good events are caused by specific factors: "That just happened because she felt sorry for me." Global negative causes are pervasive and lead to despair and passivity. Seligman (1995) argues that the dimension of pervasiveness is not easily taught to children, although it is routinely taught to adults and may be used for middle and secondary school students.

Basic Skills of Optimism

The PPP has incorporated the main techniques of cognitive therapy for depression into a prevention program for people who are not depressed. The PPP helps individuals develop new skills of optimistic thinking. There are four basic skills of optimism:

Thought catching.   People must first learn to catch the negative things they say to themselves, about themselves, and about events that occur. These almost imperceptible thoughts affect behavior and mood. By learning to recognize thoughts, they can then be changed.

Evaluation.   The second skill is to evaluate the automatic and habitual thoughts or beliefs that have been identified. These can be acknowledged as being hypotheses that need to be tested rather than "Truths," and evidence can be gathered and considered to determine the accuracy of the beliefs.

Accurate explanations.   When bad events happen, more accurate explanations can be developed to challenge the automatic thoughts. By interrupting the chain of negative explanations, attitudes and mood can improve.

Decatastrophizing. Catastrophizing, or thinking about the worst possible case, is counterproductive. Most often, the worst case is very unlikely. Ruminating on potential terrible implications and the worst possible consequences creates frustration, drains energy, and interferes with correcting problems.

Identifying automatic thoughts, searching for evidence, generating alternatives, and decatastrophizing are extremely important in developing optimism and lowering pessimism and depression in children.

Application for At-Risk Problem Prevention

Early primary prevention programs can be very helpful to children. Skills for optimism can serve as a means of problem prevention. Children who drop out, and even children who attend school but have given up on themselves academically and personally, lack hope that school will benefit their future or that they can succeed in school. They may internalize their lack of success as their own fault, due to pervasive personal characteristics ("I'll never be able to read. I'm stupid."), or blame it on pervasive global factors ("Teachers don't care." "School is useless."). Teachers or school counselors could initiate classroom discussions to identify thoughts students face in response to negative school experiences (thought catching). The class can assist in evaluating sample thoughts, helping to generate accurate explanations to substitute for sample negative thoughts. Decatastrophizing can be illustrated. When working individually with students, the same series of steps can be followed, reinforcing and further personalizing optimism skills. With practice, students will begin to utilize these skills to encourage each other.

Teaching these skills to children is important, but it is equally important for the helping adults to learn and practice these skills themselves. Using these skills may improve the mental health of the helper—not an unimportant consideration given the nature of the work, the consistent drain of personal resources and energy, and the constant stress of budget cuts and limited resources. Increased optimism gives the helper more energy and greater influence as well.

Optimism can also be taught to parents. Parental (and other adult) criticism often reflects the bad habits and biases of the adult and contributes to increased pessimism in children. If parents are aware of their children's attributions, parents can provide more helpful feedback and criticism to their children. Children view ability as permanent, so blaming failure on lack of ability fosters pessimism. In contrast, blaming lack of success on conduct, effort, or attention is less malignant because these are temporary and changeable. Children can be challenged and supported in their efforts to improve conduct, increase effort, or focus attention. If they believe they lack ability, they will be at greater risk of dropout and other problems. Please see the description of the SOAR program related to enhancing optimism (Gilboy et al., 2002) described in Chapter 12.

Cognitive Restructuring

The term *cognitive restructuring*, as we use it here, simply means modifying, changing, or restructuring one's beliefs. A belief is a rule that a person applies to all situations regardless of his or her current experiences. When the belief is maladaptive, it can be unlearned to produce a new and better belief. As more adaptive beliefs replace incomplete or faulty ones, behavior changes too.

The best-known approaches to changing maladaptive beliefs or cognitive patterns are rational-emotive behavioral therapy (REBT; Ellis, 1962, 1996) and cognitive therapy (CT; Beck, 1976, 1991). Both approaches are based on the assumption that faulty cognitions cause detrimental self-evaluations and emotional distress and that these experiences lead to behavioral problems. The goal is to help people develop their cognitive ability to recognize faulty self-statements and to substitute more positive ones. There is growing evidence that children and adolescents can understand the principles of REBT (Vernon [1983] reviews the evidence) and CT (Garber, Deale, & Parke, 1986).

Rational-emotive behavior therapy (REBT).   Ellis's rational-emotive behavior therapy, the oldest and probably best known of the cognitive therapies, is based on the belief that people need to change their faulty thinking and correct irrational beliefs to lead healthier, happier lives. Ellis (1996) suggests that emotional disturbances are the result of illogical and irrational thinking in the form of internalized beliefs. Thus emotional disturbances arise from cognitive or thinking processes around an activating event. Ellis recognized, however, that emotion is complex and is tied to a variety of sensing and response processes and states.

The major assumption of REBT is that thoughts create feelings. In other words, it is not events or other people that make one feel upset or inadequate but one's belief about them. A young boy who does not succeed at football and feels depressed, for example, may assume that his poor performance has caused the depressed feeling. Ellis argues, however, that it is the assumptions about the event or the failure—the thoughts about it, not the event itself—that cause the depressed feeling.

Ellis (1985) proposes an A-B-C-D-E model as a cognitive intervention strategy. The child or adolescent learns to recognize the activating event (A), the corresponding belief (B) about the event, and the emotional and behavioral consequences (C). The counselor then helps the young person to dispute (D) the old belief system and attend to the new emotional and behavioral effects (E) of more rational thinking.

At-risk children and adolescents develop many irrational ways of thinking. These irrational thoughts lead to maladaptive behavior. Cognitive restructuring efforts are designed to help young people recognize and change these irrational beliefs into more rational ones. Attainment of this goal requires a confrontive and supportive counselor who is able to actively engage the client (Ellis, 1996).

Cognitive therapy.   Beck (1976, 1991) suggests that cognition and affect are interactive. Like Ellis, he believes that an individual's cognition about an event determines the affective response to the event. If cognitions are distorted or inaccurate, the individual's emotional response will be inappropriate.

Three elements are central to Beck's CT model: the cognitive triad, cognitive schemas, and cognitive errors. The cognitive triad is composed of thoughts that focus on three major aspects of life: view of the world, the self, and the future. When the cognitive triad is negative, the individual views the world, self, and future as negative, and depression and despair result.

A schema is like a personality trait; it is a stable cognitive pattern that an individual creates from the cognitive triad. Schemas are underlying cognitive structures that help the individual organize and evaluate information, events, and experiences. At-risk children and adolescents develop schemas that distort environmental stimuli in a negative way. Often their schemas include a derogatory self-image. Because these schemas are a person's "core beliefs," they influence both behavioral and affective responses to an event.

Dysfunctional or negative schemas are often maintained and exacerbated by faulty information processing or consistent errors in logic. These are called cognitive errors. At-risk young people make these automatic cognitive errors when they evaluate events. These errors—negativistic, categorical, absolute, judgmental—cause the person to consistently misread or misinterpret even benign experiences.

Treatment and training strategies flow directly from Beck's cognitive model. His cognitive therapy has both behavioral and cognitive components that are designed to reduce automatic negative cognitions. The client learns to challenge the assumptions that maintain the faulty cognitions. Behavioral strategies are used first in the therapeutic or training process. Positive activities are established and augmented through role playing, graduated task assignments, activity schedules, assertiveness training, and behavioral rehearsal. After these strategies are successfully used, cognitive interventions are introduced to identify, test, and modify the cognitive distortion. Clients are taught (a) to recognize the connections between cognitions, affect, and behavior; (b) to monitor negative automatic thoughts; (c) to examine evidence related to distorted automatic cognitions; (d) to substitute more realistic interpretations for distorted cognition; and (e) to learn to identify and modify dysfunctional beliefs.

Cognitive therapy is dedicated to the goal of helping clients discover maladaptive thoughts, recognize their negative impact, and replace them with more appropriate and positive thought patterns. Cognitive restructuring techniques have been successfully applied in clinical settings and are used increasingly in training modules to help at-risk young people make cognitive changes so that they can lead more productive lives.

Tyrone Baker (of Chapter 2) could benefit from cognitive change strategies. Interpersonal problem solving could help him make better decisions. Self-assessment, self-monitoring, and self-reinforcement could provide him with tools to help him delay gratification. Through cognitive restructuring, he could modify his irrational thoughts, the nature of his cognitive triad, and his negative schemas. Cognitive errors could be corrected to modify and improve his negative behavior.

CONNECTEDNESS

Connectedness with others is critical in people's lives (Hawkins et al., 1999; Smith & Sandhu, 2004) and is a major goal of more effective and comprehensive life-skills training programs. Hawkins, Catalano, and their colleagues (Catalano, Haggerty, Oesterle, Fleming, & Hawkins, 2004; Hawkins et al., 2000; Lonczak, Abbott, Hawkins, Kosterman, & Catalano, 2002) have demonstrated that environmental conditions can support the development of positive, prosocial behaviors or conversely reinforce the development of negative, antisocial behaviors. Connectedness is dependent upon an individual having the skills, opportunities, and recognition for engaging in successful behaviors. Connectedness involves both intrapersonal awareness and interpersonal skills. Both have to do with understanding self and others. The interpersonal communication skills that are core to connectedness are sometimes termed social skills, social competence, or human relations skills. Such skills in interpersonal communication are necessary for people to have effective and healthy interpersonal relationships. As we mentioned in Chapter 6, interpersonal communication skills are necessary for responsive, confident, and mutually beneficial relationships. A lack of good communication skills often leads to social isolation and rejection, which in turn results in poor psychological adjustment and a lack of connectedness. Positive adult reactions and peer acceptance are related to friendly, positive interpersonal communications, and each of these form a sense of connectedness that is critical in people's lives for sustained happiness (Lee et al., 2001; Townsend & McWhirter, 2005).

Training in Interpersonal Communication

Acquisition of basic communication skills begins in early childhood; by adolescence, teens have acquired a complex repertoire of social skills. Most programs designed to promote communication skills offer training in verbal and nonverbal communication, creation of healthy friendships, avoidance of misunderstandings, and development of long-term love relationships.

Programs to promote interpersonal communication should be developmentally appropriate. The variables that seem to play a role in the development and maintenance of interactions from age 1 to 3 years are attention to the listener, to the speaker, or to the object of interest; proximity and turn-taking with others; relevance of content; and provision of feedback from the listener. From age 3 to 5 years, behaviors that may be incorporated in training programs include the use of attention-getting cues, listener responses, reinforcement of turn-taking and mutual attention, and the use of routines to maintain attention. Mutual attention and feedback are still important skills for 6- to 8-year-olds, and appropriate role taking is developed during this age period. From ages 9 to 12, the use of positive, cooperative, and helpful communication, as opposed to negative, is important. Gazda and colleagues (1999) provide a comprehensive list of interpersonal communication and human relation skills and indicate the approximate age at which each skill is usually acquired.

Interpersonal communication skills represent the major component of many prevention programs. A particularly useful package is an integrated program of training in communication skills for adolescents (Goldstein et al., 1980) and younger children (McGinnis & Goldstein, 1984, 1990). Other useful programs have been developed for elementary school students (Cartledge & Milburn, 1986; Jackson, Jackson, & Monroe, 1983; Wiig, 1983) and for secondary school pupils (Kelly, 1982; Wilkinson & Canter, 1982). Stephens's (1992) social skills program is appropriate for both children and adolescents. Communication skills training used in prevention include the work of Cummings and Haggerty (1997), Dupaul and Eckert (1994), and Jones, Sheridan, and Binns (1993).

Jason Carter (of Chapter 4) could profit from training in communication skills. As described, he is disconnected from most other children and from most adults. His difficulty in dealing with his dysfunctional family has extended to his classroom interactions. Although parent training and family counseling approaches are probably necessary to help modify the family dysfunction, Jason's ineffective interpersonal communication is contributing to the aversive nature of his school experience. Better interpersonal communication skills would allow him to interact more positively with classmates and adults at school. This improvement could bring greater acceptance by Jason's peers and increase his self-esteem.

Assertiveness Skills

Some at-risk young people get into trouble because they are timid and withdrawn and appear to be incapable of dealing with other students, teachers, and family members in effective ways. Others express themselves in hostile, angry, aggressive ways that cause problems for people around them and ultimately for themselves. Still others find themselves going along with the crowd because they are overly susceptible to influence by their peers. They do not recognize pressure or have the skills to resist it. Many at-risk children and youth need training in general assertiveness and in specific ways to resist peer pressure.

General assertiveness training.   Assertiveness training is a psychoeducational procedure designed to reduce deficits in specific social skills and to help the individual interact more effectively with others. Assertiveness training also reduces the maladaptive anxiety that prevents young people from expressing themselves directly, honestly, and spontaneously.

Assertiveness training usually includes modules on the expression of positive feelings, the expression of negative feelings, and the ability to initiate, continue, and terminate conversations. Besides these basic interpersonal communication skills, assertiveness training focuses on limit setting and self-initiation. The person who knows how to set limits can say no to unreasonable requests. Self-initiators have the capacity to ask for what they want and to actively seek opportunities for enjoyment, advancement, and intimacy.

Nonverbal communication is also an important aspect of assertiveness training. The way a message is delivered is given as much attention as the message itself. Loudness of voice, fluency of spoken words, facial expression, body expression, interpersonal distance, and method and degree of eye contact all deliver their own messages. Students are taught to look others squarely in the eye during both positive and negative social confrontations. Looking people in the eye is a sign that one is sure of one's position, knowledge, or attractiveness in mainstream U.S. culture. Students are taught that passive behavior can be replaced by assertive techniques and that assertive responses are more adaptive than aggressive ones in handling conflict and anger. All assertiveness training programs should attend to students from cultural backgrounds in which direct eye contact is considered disrespectful or aggressive. Rather than exclude "eye contact," this component of the program as well as others should acknowledge cultural differences and provide guidance in exploring when using assertive behavior may be more or less effective.

One school-based assertiveness training program has been reported to yield extremely positive results (Smith, 1986). The children trained in assertiveness had better school attendance records than their untrained counterparts, were ill less often, scored higher in reading and math, had better self-images, and showed positive changes in those negative attitudes that predict future drug abuse. Three years after completing the program, the trained students were more resistant to peer pressure to use tobacco, alcohol, and illicit drugs. The assertiveness-trained youth also achieved higher grades than the students who were not trained in assertiveness. This social thinking and reasoning program, called STAR (Benn, 1981), provides techniques and methods to train children from grades 3 through 5 in how to respond more effectively in social conflict situations. Another program for promoting learning and understanding of self, called PLUS (Benn, 1982), is an adaptation of STAR for high school students and has demonstrated similar success.

Resistance and refusal training.   Specific resistance and refusal skills help at-risk students resist negative social influences (Herrmann & McWhirter, 1997). Resistance training focuses on helping young people (a) identify and label social influences and pressure situations and (b) develop behavioral skills to resist such influences. Skills are needed to resist various types of pressures, from those exerted by the entertainment media and advertising to those of peers. Students are taught to identify and label various forms of pressure.

Peer pressure, for instance, can take the form of teasing, friendly pressure, tricks, dares, lies, physical threats, social threats, or silence. Typical examples of each kind of pressure are demonstrated.

Students are then taught strategies for resisting pressure and for refusing to succumb to it. Particular techniques are described, demonstrated, and modeled. Students practice and observe others practicing each resistance or refusal strategy. They engage in role playing to develop competence in each technique. All of them are given opportunities to rehearse and refine their performances so that in real-life situations they can respond with confidence. Students who are trained in assertiveness develop skills to avoid use of tobacco, alcohol, and marijuana (Herrmann & McWhirter, 1997, 2000). They are less willing to use drugs after resistance training, which provides youth with the skills needed to recognize and resist the external pressures to use drugs. But developing refusal skills alone, such as the "just say 'No'" campaign, is not effective. Young people need to enhance interpersonal skills, develop better self-awareness, remain free of drug-using peers, and be assisted in developing social networks and friendships with low-risk peers for intervention to be successful in the long term.

Allie Andrews (of Chapter 1) might well profit from assertiveness and resistance training. Her interaction with her stepfather suggests that she has few ways to respond to stress, mostly acting-out and self-defeating responses. Her peer interaction hints that she may be turning to her friends for the acceptance she does not receive at home. Thus her resistance to drug use is probably quite low. Assertiveness and resistance training might help her develop the skills she needs to change her self-defeating patterns and prevent substance use.

COPING ABILITY

The fourth "C" identified in Chapter 6 is coping ability. Many at-risk young people are affected by stress and anxiety. Anxiety is associated with a number of undesirable intrapersonal and interpersonal characteristics: lack of responsiveness, inability to perform independently, overdependence on conformity, excessive concern about evaluations, and self-critical and self-defeating attitudes. Anxiety from such sources leads to chronic stress. Because many aspects of the educational process are greatly affected by anxiety and stress, providing coping methods to deal with them is particularly beneficial. Mounting evidence suggests that school-based prevention and early intervention programs have the potential of reducing future instances of serious anxiety disorders (Dadds, Spence, Holland, Barrett, & Laurens, 1997).

Relaxation and imagery are helpful tools to offset some of the negative aspects of anxiety and stress. These two techniques are combined in relaxation and imagery training (RIT), a program that promises to help at-risk children realize more of their potential (J. J. McWhirter, 1988; J. J. McWhirter & M. C. McWhirter, 1983). Similar programs improved students' test anxiety, study skills, and academic self-esteem (Wachelka & Katz, 1999).

Beneficial Relaxation

Relaxation techniques alone can reduce stress and many of its negative psychological and physical effects. Relaxation has been reported to help clients overcome fatigue, avoid negative reactions to stress, reduce anxiety, improve social skills and interpersonal relationships, and improve self-assurance (Burns, 1981). Relaxation can also help to reduce depression and improve self-esteem (Kahn, Kehle, Jenson, & Clarke, 1990). Relaxation is both effective and efficient in helping students to behave more appropriately in school, to think more positively about themselves, and to interact more positively with their peers. Relaxation also reduces anxiety—an especially important effect because anxiety is associated with dependence, hostility, low peer status, poor relationships with teachers, and aggression (McReynolds, Morris, & Kratochwill, 1989).

Relaxation techniques are useful in learning school material as well as in the social arena. A variety of studies have demonstrated the positive effects of relaxation techniques on reading, spelling, mathematics, music, and athletics (Carter & Russell, 1980; Frey, 1980; Glantz, 1983; J. J. McWhirter & M. C. McWhirter, 1983; Oldridge, 1982; Olrich, 1983; Proeger & Myrick, 1980; Zenker, 1984; Zenker & Frey, 1985). In addition to improving social and academic performance, relaxation has been used successfully as an intervention strategy for hyperactivity. Relaxation is a viable tool for increasing attention to task and decreasing impulsiveness. And relaxation training teaches young people to use the relaxation response when anxiety and fear arise.

Relaxation training promotes anxiety reduction by teaching the individual to reduce muscle tension. Essentially, relaxation training accomplishes two objectives. First, it is a means to countercondition the anxiety associated with a stressful environment. Second, it is a self-management tool. Through the self-regulation training of relaxation, children can increase their control over their lives, be responsible for their behavior, and improve their academic performance. This tool has a spin-off effect. As children gain confidence in the ability to become calm in learning and social situations, they gain approval from adults and peers, improve their attention span, are less distractible, and learn more. This procedure shows considerable promise for improving the self-management skills of children (Brennan, 1984; Rivera & Omizo, 1980).

Progressive Relaxation

Several techniques are useful in relaxation training, including biofeedback, autogenic training, meditation, the quieting reflex, and progressive relaxation. Most training in relaxation uses a procedure originally outlined by Jacobson (1938), which he referred to as progressive (deep-muscle) relaxation. Merely telling an individual to relax is not enough. Jacobson developed a more structured and concrete procedure by which the individual achieves a state of deep muscular relaxation. To achieve relaxation in a specific muscle or muscle group, the client lies down comfortably and alternately tenses and relaxes the major muscle groups. The contraction phase is then gradually decreased until it is eliminated as the individual develops awareness of and releases muscle tension.

In the relaxation technique used in RIT, the youth tenses and then relaxes various muscle groups. This procedure continues until the person is aware of the contrast between a tense and a relaxed state. Early in relaxation training it is necessary to repeat the tension and relaxation phases several times during several sessions. Eventually the need for tensing is eliminated and the individual achieves relaxation quickly. Once students develop this technique, they can relax on their own without instructions from the adult, thereby exercising a greater degree of self-control. With practice, most individuals can learn to achieve a relaxed physical and mental state within a few minutes. Lazarus (1971) and Carkhuff (1969) have published guides for conducting relaxation sessions, and elsewhere (J. J. McWhirter, 1988) we have developed relaxation strategies for younger people.

At least some of the problems faced by Paul Andrews (of Chapter 1) can be attributed to his stressful environment. The tension in his dysfunctional family and his intense dislike of school have led to angry, hostile, aggressive acting out. Adults' reactions to his behavior increase his stress. His aggressiveness and anger appear to be methods for coping with underlying anxiety. Relaxation training would enable him to cope better with his own emotional reactions to his situation. Relaxation would provide Paul with the skill needed to redirect his aggression and attend to his underlying apprehension and anxiety.

Visual Imagery

Visual imagery is an important adjunct to relaxation training. It is used to lessen tension and to enhance comfort, to engage various muscle groups, and to cue a relaxation response. The counselor or teacher might ask the child to imagine a peaceful scene, such as waves lapping on a shore at night, rocking on a porch swing, or sitting in front of a warm fireplace. Many excellent scripts and audiotapes are available to set imaginary scenes for students (Davis, Robbins-Eshelman, & McKay, 2000). Commercial tapes have music, narrative, and distinctive environmental sounds (bird songs, flowing water, rustling leaves). Of course, the subject matter of the tape or script must be appropriate to the age and environment of the targeted youth. For example, an ocean scene may be outside the experience of many students. Students must be given ample time and practice to develop skill in imagery.

Visual images in the form of guided fantasies allow the child or youth to confront areas of difficulty, to learn tasks, and to develop self-control. Through imagery, the child is guided through an event as if the activity were actually happening. The child enters a rich world of internal experiences where imagination is recruited to promote specific psychological and physiological changes to aid performance or behavior. In addition, imagery should include positive suggestions, especially when the youth is anticipating a negative outcome or condition. Positive imagery is obviously important for an at-risk child or adolescent such as Paul Andrews, who has come to expect failure and negative reactions.

Several key elements go into guided fantasy scripts for young people. The scripts should be as realistic and focused as possible and incorporate words, phrases, and situations that apply to the individual. Paul Andrews's counselor might enlist other adults as collaborators. Paul's mother could become a technical consultant and suggest words, language, and fantasies as well as key events and details that would make the fantasy a rich and realistic experience. If we were to construct a fantasy for Paul, we would follow these guidelines:

1. Help Paul use all his senses—touch and hearing as well as vision. Internal emotional and muscular cues that are experienced before and during a scene should not be neglected.
2. Set the scene as vividly as possible by describing it clearly. If specific details are available, provide them. If not, ask Paul to supply them.
3. Work from the outside environment (the classroom, the home) to the inside environment or the emotional state.
4. Guide the fantasy from Paul's viewpoint, as if he were actually in the situation. Paul is not simply observing himself as a spectator but is actually participating in the

event—feeling the emotion it arouses, thinking about it, observing others in the situation, and so forth.

5. Use positive statements and autosuggestions to help Paul develop self-reinforcing statements. Be sure to close the fantasy with a positive image.

Imagery improves learning and retention of materials in most academic subjects (J. J. McWhirter, 1988). It seems to be useful in all areas of the curriculum as it can create an appropriate readiness and mental set for learning. In the sciences and mathematics, imagery aids creative problem solving and memory. It promotes learning in the language arts by lending vitality to poetry and prose. In educational contexts imagery (a) creates a readiness to learn, (b) aids comprehension, (c) enhances memory and recall, and (d) facilitates problem solving and creative thinking.

Helping students prepare their minds, emotions, and bodies for learning may be as important as the instruction itself. Anticipation of a mental event and openness of mind create a state of readiness for whatever is to be learned. We have had success using imagery, along with other techniques, to enhance group experiences of high school students (Wenz & McWhirter, 1990).

Affirmations

In view of the generally negative cognitions of at-risk young people, use of positive affirmation to acknowledge and increase personal strengths is critical. RIT provides an opportunity for the teacher or counselor to encourage the child by making positive affirmations. These affirmations should be used consistently and frequently throughout both the relaxation and imagery segments of the program. Most children know the story *The Little Engine That Could* with its refrain of "I think I can, I think I can, I think I can." This saying can be the basis of a class discussion of other positive sayings (see Box 13.2). Children repeat these sayings to themselves to reduce stress and to build confidence. Several phrases seem particularly useful: "I can do it"; "I've studied for this test, and I'll do my best"; "I am special because . . ."; "I can relax and remember the right answer"; "I have lots of strengths." Specific phrases and sentences need to be developed from the repertoire of the at-risk children and adolescents.

Affirmations represent one technique in a wide range of useful cognitive strategies. In the following section, we attend to a number of cognitive restructuring approaches known to be helpful to children and adolescents. With the RIT program, children will begin to understand that they have the power and self-control to overcome the effects of stress and anxiety and get on with living and learning. Counselors and other adults can facilitate development of that power and that self-control.

CONTROL: STRATEGIES FOR COGNITIVE CHANGE

The final and fifth "C" denoted in Chapter 6 is control—control of decisions, control of self, and control of the future. A variety of cognitive-behavioral techniques have been devised to help children and young people develop control over their internal reactions and overt behavior. Three points in cognitive-behavioral theory are particularly important in this respect: First, cognitive events mediate behavior; therefore, a focus on cognition can be an effective approach to changing behavior. Second, young people are active participants in their own learning and can exercise control over it. And third, cognition, behavior, and the environment are related: each affects and is affected by the others. Among the cognitive-behavioral strategies with demonstrated utility in dealing with control are interventions to improve decision making.

Control of Decisions

At-risk young people are more likely to engage in rigid thinking and to perceive fewer alternatives to problems when they emerge. Thus their ability to generate and select from alternative choices of action needs to be improved. Good decision making requires that the benefits and consequences of, say, drug use or other risky behavior are clear and accurate. Unfortunately, neither all the benefits nor all the consequences of drug use (and drug abstinence) are known. Nevertheless, decision-making strategies help users to (a) define the nature of their choice, (b) enlarge the number of alternatives under consideration, (c) identify all benefits and consequences of each alternative, and (d) implement their desired alternative. Because these steps are effective with many of the root problems, they represent a valuable resource for at-risk youth as does the DECIDE model that we present next.

Early models of problem solving and decision making were based on the assumption that adequate and accurate information would lead to better choices. There was an implicit assumption that prudent choices would flow from a rational review of options. We now know that accurate information is necessary but not sufficient for effective decision making. Even for adults with substantial life experience and mature cognitive skills and abilities, the processes of problem solving and decision making are far less rational than they were once thought to be. Children and adolescents are at least as irrational as adults in their problem solving and decision making.

At the same time, young people have the potential to make competent decisions. Dodge and Price (1994) suggest that children who accurately perceive and effectively solve interpersonal problems use a five-stage sequential problem-solving, decision-making process. In stage one, they attend to relevant environmental cues. In stage two, they accurately encode and interpret these cues. In stage three, they generate many and varied solutions to the problems. In stage four, they accurately evaluate each of the solutions and determine the best possible solution. Finally, in stage five, they plan the steps necessary to carry out and actually perform the favored solution. For high-risk youth several things stand in the way of effective problem solving and decision making. These include the emotional component of most problems, the tendency to appraise situations from an egocentric perspective, the perception of limited alternatives, and failure to use systematic decision-making procedures. For example, social-cognitive deficits in aggressive children have been reported in the area of social attention and recall (stage 1), generating multiple solutions to interpersonal problems (stage 3), and performance of favored responses (stage 5). Social-cognitive distortions in antisocial children occur when errors are made in the interpretation of social stimuli (stage 2) and misjudgments are made concerning the consequences of hostile acts (stage 4; Dodge & Price, 1994).

Explicit instruction in problem-solving and decision-making processes helps to avert problems and overcome areas of limitation. The steps involved in problem solving require specific skills, which need to be learned and practiced. We have adopted a model for general problem-solving training that we call DECIDE, which is similar to that of the

DECIDES model of career counseling developed by Kinnier and Krumboltz (1984) but contains some variations for problem solving.

We developed the DECIDE model specifically for improving the skills in general problem solving for at-risk children and adolescents. DECIDE stands for the steps to be taken: (1) Define the problem, (2) Examine variables, (3) Consider alternatives, (4) Isolate a plan, (5) Do action steps, and (6) Evaluate effects. Teaching at-risk children and adolescents these six problem-solving steps will contribute to a more internal locus of control— that is, students will feel that their behavior is under their own control—and will help modify impulsive, self-defeating behavior. An internal locus of control, in turn, can improve self-esteem, increase a sense of self-efficacy, and strengthen resistance to problem behaviors. Let's look at each of these steps.

1. *Define the problem.* The problem is defined as clearly as possible and is stated as a goal to be achieved. This goal is assessed: Will it address the problem? If it is attained, does it help the individual achieve satisfaction?
2. *Examine variables.* The specifics of the total situation are examined. Background issues and environmental factors are considered, so it may be necessary to gather and appraise additional information. It is particularly important to identify the feelings and thoughts of the young person at this step. Both here and in step 1, questions and suggestions from other students in the classroom or the group are useful.
3. *Consider alternatives.* Various means of solving the problem are considered. The strengths and weaknesses of each possibility are evaluated. Again, the teacher or the counselor may call for brainstorming to generate ideas from other students about alternatives and strategies.
4. *Isolate a plan.* The alternatives are gradually narrowed down until what seems like the best response or solution remains. A plan for carrying out this alternative is prepared, and the potential consequences are considered in more detail.
5. *Do action steps.* After a plan is decided upon, action must be taken to implement it. Youngsters are systematically encouraged to follow through on the necessary steps to carry out their plan. They perform the behaviors that make up the solution plan.
6. *Evaluate effects.* Finally, children and adolescents need to evaluate the effectiveness of the solution. Teaching them to look for effects in their thoughts and feelings is important. They analyze and evaluate the outcome, review the decision, and if necessary develop another plan to achieve their goal.

Self-Management and Self-Control

Self-management and self-control are related. Self-management is the ability to maintain or alter goal-directed behavior without depending on discernable external forces. Young people with good self-management skills are able to respond to situations based on their internal standards. Self-control is an important component of self-management and refers to control over one's affective, cognitive, and behavioral reactions. It is particularly important for high-risk children and adolescents because it helps them prevent problem situations, limit negative emotional reactions, resist problematic behaviors, and delay gratification.

Training in self-management and self-control includes the following skills: (a) self-assessment (being able to compare present functioning with internal standards and evaluate significant differences between the performance and the standard), (b) self-monitoring (being attuned to and aware of one's present functioning), and (c) self-reinforcement (providing positive consequences when performance meets standards and negative consequences for failure to perform adequately).

Self-assessment.   Self-assessment is the systematic evaluation of one's own behavior to determine whether it has been adequate. Young people need to be able to evaluate and assess their behavior to improve it. Most young people evaluate themselves on the basis of standards acquired from significant others in their environment. Both parents and teachers provide young people with standards against which to evaluate their behavior in various situations. For a variety of reasons, many at-risk young people fail to acquire clear standards for self-evaluation.

Self-ratings can be used to teach youth to assess their behavior. First, the student and adult decide together which specific behavior needs to be changed. After a target behavior is identified, the next step is to devise a rating system—a scale of 0 to 10, say, or 0 to 100—by which the specific behavior can be assessed and evaluated. Paul Andrews of Chapter 1, for example, might be asked to rate his classroom outbursts by rating his underlying mood and behavior: 0 (no desire to hit or to explode) to 10 (several outbursts). Number 5 on this rating scale might be "resisted desire to hit or explode." Such a rating scale would provide Paul with a subjective measure of mood and behavior, and the self-assessment would help him to develop self-control. Although Paul has several behaviors that need to change, he needs to deal with only one behavior at a time. An attempt to change too many behaviors simultaneously would lower the probability of success and serve to confuse him. If he started out by attempting to change a single behavior, Paul's chance for success would be increased. (Workman [1982] is an excellent source of self-assessment techniques.)

Self-monitoring.   Self-monitoring is focusing attention and awareness on one's characteristics, emotions, thoughts, or behavior and is closely related to self-assessment. Self-monitoring requires students to observe their own behavior and to record it. Essentially students are taught to collect data on their own behavior. Self-monitoring helps students become more aware of their own negative and positive behaviors, putting their behavior more firmly under their own control (DiGangi, Maag, & Rutherford, 1991). Several authors (Kaplan, 1991; Shapiro & Cole, 1992; Workman, 1982) provide useful information on observation and recordkeeping forms for the self-monitoring process.

Self-reinforcement.   Self-reinforcement is the act of supplying one's own consequences for performance. Such consequences may be intangible and intrinsic (such as silent self-praise for meeting a personal goal) or tangible and external (such as buying oneself a present after meeting a personal goal). Consequences may also be negative. A negative consequence might be self-criticism or forgoing a particular pleasure.

Self-reinforcement energizes the self-management process. People anticipate and work for possible positive consequences. Self-reinforcement keeps the person on the track of establishing and pursuing goals. The effects of self-reinforcement on school performance are found to be as beneficial as those of external reinforcement (Kaplan, 1991). The self-reinforcement of behaviors conducive to learning works powerfully to improve school achievement and personal performance.

In summary, when young people are taught to assess their own behavior, to monitor their academic and personal performance, and to reinforce their improved behavior with positive consequences, their school performance is likely to improve, and their personal problems are minimized.

Control for Learning

Self-management and self-control help in the educational process too. Self-management training produces both short- and long-term gains in achievement. Students who have received this training have been found to raise their levels of academic aspirations, increase their efforts on future tasks, improve their nonacademic skills, and decrease their disruptive behaviors (Smith, Young, Nelson, & West, 1992). Self-control skills help students make adaptive attributions: Students are encouraged to take responsibility for their successes and failures by learning when failure is attributable to their own lack of effort and when success results from their own ability, efforts, and skills. These modified attributions result in enhanced efforts in similar tasks in the future.

One consistent difference between academically successful and unsuccessful students is their awareness of their own learning strategies. Many at-risk students are unaware that their learning strategies are limited or ineffective. Another way for adults to intervene in the learning process is to teach successful learning strategies to at-risk students. A learning strategy is a plan for merging cognitive skills and metacognitive ability in the process of acquiring information (Cohen & de Bettencourt, 1991; Zigmond, 1990). In this educational approach, students are taught to observe, monitor, and think about their learning strategy or plan.

Children's awareness of their cognitive strategies is correlated with enhanced performance on reading measures. That is, children who can describe the thinking processes they use as they read are able to comprehend more than students who cannot. Duffy and his colleagues recommend that teachers model their own mental processes to stimulate metacognitive skill in their students (Duffy, Roehler, & Herrmann, 1988). The purpose of instruction in metacognitive strategies is to increase students' awareness of themselves as learners, place students in control of their own learning activity, and provide them with a method to use to improve their own learning.

Reciprocal teaching is a similar learning strategy that is successful with poor learners. To implement this strategy, the teacher and a small group of students talk about the texts they read. The students take turns being "teacher" and practicing the four components of reciprocal teaching: they (a) generate questions about the content of the reading material, (b) summarize the content, (c) clarify points, and (d) predict future content on the basis of prior knowledge or clues within the text. Reciprocal teaching has improved achievement of low achievers (Lysynchuk, Pressley, & Vye, 1990; Rosenshine & Meister, 1991), providing success for students with learning problems.

CONCLUSION

Communication and life skills, cognitive change strategies, and coping techniques are critical elements in programs for prevention and early intervention. Young people who have acquired these tools have the ability to avoid problem behavior. Comprehensive training programs to teach these skills need to be instituted early and universally for all youth to prevent problems. For at-risk youth, indicated programs to teach these skills are needed as early as possible—ideally before third grade. For long-term benefits, young people need the skills reinforced over time and from a variety of people. Finally, for older children and adolescents who are at higher risk, these skills need to be included in special education classes, school counseling programs, and in community treatment programs.

School-based psychoeducational groups, peer (and cross-age) tutoring, and school mediation programs are strong environments in which to teach and reinforce these skills. By learning these skills, young people will improve their interactions with others, perform better in school, and realize their potential for a more positive future.

PEER INTERVENTIONS

▲ Dear Jenny,
I am really, really sorry that I did something to make you mad at me. If you would tell me what it is, I would change it, but you won't talk to me. Please be my friend again, I will try to be the best friend that I can be.
Kayla

▲ Dear Jenny,
It has been 2 weeks that you won't talk to me, and I still don't know what I did. Did you tell Angie and Kara something about me, because now they won't talk to me either? I can't eat or sleep, this is making me very upset. I am going to go talk to the peer helper even though we think she is weird, that's how upset I am about all of this, so you should think about what you are doing to me. Your friend (still, even though you won't talk to me).
Kayla

▲ Dear Jenny,
Jackie is actually nice, and she isn't weird at all. She asked me what a friend is, and I said that you are a friend. Hah! I would tell you more but I am going to go study with a FRIEND.
Kayla

▲ Dear Jenny,
Well, I guess this is my last note to you because after all this time of wanting to be your friend and wanting to know what I did wrong, now it doesn't matter to me anymore. I liked being your friend and you are pretty and fun, but there are girls who don't act like you and they are my friends now. If that means I'm not cool, that's OK with me. A friend is someone who talks to you and listens to you, so we aren't really friends anymore. Maybe you should talk to Jackie too and tell her how mean you are, she could probably help you be a better friend, and then you wouldn't have to hang around girls that say mean things.
Kayla
P.S. I know you are going to show this to Kara and Angie, so don't think it will shock me.

CHAPTER OUTLINE

▲   In the previous chapter, we provided a series of core interventions designed to build personal resiliency and to increase the individual competencies of young people at risk. We presented prevention strategies to be implemented in curriculum-based developmental programs in schools. In this chapter, we present major prevention strategies that utilize the power of the peer group in helping young people decrease negative and increase positive behaviors. These interventions help prevent and reduce the negative behaviors discussed earlier in this book.

IMPORTANCE OF PEERS

The history of prevention of problem behaviors included educational and "scare" approaches during the 1960s, self-esteem and ego-enhancing approaches during the 1970s, and social skills training approaches during the 1980s. Each of these approaches is necessary but not sufficient in preventing or decreasing problem behaviors. The core competency approaches described in Chapter 15, which include components of education (cognitive), self-esteem and optimism building (affective), and social skills training (behavioral), show great promise and characterize preventive interventions prevalent during the 1990s. Many of these interventions have proven efficacious in modifying the abuse of substances, in reducing teen pregnancy, and in preventing other problems. In making interventions specific, focused, and personalized, high-risk children and adolescents are aided in improving their resiliency and competency skills.

Unfortunately, for many high-risk young people, learning to be competent is not enough. For example, young people can learn resistance and refusal skills, or to "just say no." However, knowing how to say "No" is very different from actually doing so. Any discussion of prevention must include consideration of the influences of peer pressure in encouraging and maintaining problem behavior. Peer cluster theory provides one way to explain peer influence on problem behavior and models how to use peer influence to help young people overcome problems. Later in the chapter we highlight several prevention and intervention strategies designed to modify negative peer clusters or to engage youth in identifying more closely with positive peer clusters. For example, we examine cooperative learning groups with a particular emphasis on peer support networks. We also describe strategies that utilize peers to help other peers by enhancing academic and social success in school settings. We provide models for peer and cross-age tutoring, peer mediation programs, and other peer-assisted or peer-mediated interventions.

Peer Influence—For Good or Bad

As children grow older, the importance of parents decreases as a reference group and as a model for conformity (Carter & McGoldrick 2005). Interestingly, the degree of emotional closeness and values consensus between parents and youth has been directly related to problem behavior (Jessor, 1993). Although parental influence is more important for some young people than for others, peer influence becomes the dominant factor for many teenagers. Peer influence clearly can be part of the problem, but it also can be part of the solution.

Young people are very responsive to peer group comments as measures of self-worth and self-esteem. The peer group represents the transfer vehicle for transition from childhood to adulthood. It is within the peer group that the young person learns to relate to different roles and to experiment with interpersonal interaction skills that will eventually transfer to the world of adults.

The peer group exemplifies the world outside the home. Compliance, aggression, leadership, and need satisfaction are developed within peer group interaction. A teenager who is attracted to a peer group who values antisocial activity inevitably finds that resisting the encouragement of group members to engage in negative behaviors is an insurmountable task. In this situation the adolescent is faced with a decision—either abandon the relationships that provide social support or capitulate to the dictates of peer group pressure. The most consistent risk factor for urban middle school students is having friends who exhibit problem behavior (Jessor, Van Den Bos, Vanderryn, Costa, & Turbin, 1995). The most powerful protective factor is having an attitude that is intolerant of deviant behavior. Most important is the research that demonstrates that peer-mediated interventions produce positive academic outcomes for a wide range of students, including students with emotional and behavior disorders (EBD). Cross-age, same-age, and classwide peer tutoring and cooperative learning are successful peer-mediated interventions across academic subject areas and grade levels (Ryan, Reid, & Epstein, 2004).

Peer Cluster Theory

Peer cluster theory (Beauvais et al., 1996; Oetting & Beauvais, 1986) provides a way of operationalizing peer pressure, especially as it relates to problem behaviors. This theory suggests that antisocial behavior and school problems are major factors in creating deviant peer clusters. Young people who engage in troublesome behavior have a tendency to find one another. These individuals form peer cluster groups. These deviant peer cluster groups normalize, support, and encourage a wide range of deviant behaviors.

Peer cluster theory suggests that the dominant influences on an adolescent's drug use and other problem behaviors are the attitudes, beliefs, and behaviors of the young person's immediate peers (Beauvais et al., 1996; Gardner & Steinberg, 2005; Rice, Milburn, Rotheram-Borus, Mallett, & Rosenthal, 2005). According to this theory, social and environmental factors such as poverty, prejudice, family, community, and the presence of emotional stressors, as well as personality traits, values, and beliefs, provide a framework that can increase or decrease adolescents' susceptibility to problem behaviors. Against this background, the peer cluster is a dominant influence on young people's behavior. Alternative models examining the influences of peers and family patterns on adolescent delinquency and violence have suggested that the direct influence of family functioning is stronger than that suggested by peer cluster theory (Dishion, Patterson, & Griesler, 1994; Henry, Tolan, & Gorman-Smith, 2001).

A peer group can be a large or small reference group; a peer cluster is a small subset of a peer group that influences the values, attitudes, and beliefs of each member. Peers within a particular cluster are likely, in the case of a substance-using adolescent, to use the same drugs, use them for the same reasons, and use them together. These characteristics are much more specific than those implied by the term *drug lifestyle*, which can refer to heavy and occasional drug users alike. Similarly, peer clusters influence sexual behavior, delinquency, gang membership, and school dropout. Adolescents at risk of dropping out have more friends who are dropouts, more working friends, and fewer school friends than adolescents at low risk of dropping out (Ellenbogen & Chamberland, 1997). Peer pressure implies the heavy influence of a group on an individual, who usually has limited ability to resist it. Peer clusters are much more dynamic; every member of the peer cluster is an active participant in developing the norms and behaviors of the cluster. The cluster is an interactive whole. Although some members will wield more influence than others (as in any group), the group as a whole determines the behavior, attitudes, and beliefs of the entire cluster (Oetting & Beauvais, 1987).

The dynamics of peer clusters may explain why many prevention and intervention treatments fail. Most adolescents return to their original environment and former peer cluster after treatment. The norming influence of the peer cluster often can diminish or eliminate the treatment effects. Treatment strategies must consider peer clusters and provide alternatives for adolescents who may be drawn back into a peer cluster that engages in unproductive, unhealthy, or antisocial behavior. In fact, removing young people from their peer cluster alone sometimes ameliorates their problem (Oetting & Beauvais, 1987). Another alternative is providing treatment for the whole cluster, for example, in-school approaches that make use of the peer cluster. First, counselors can organize professionally led, weekly group counseling sessions for young people and their peers who use substances or show other risky behavior. Also, schools can assign young people to a form of in-school suspension that requires them to spend one or more days each week together as a group, learning why they have been having problems, learning the short- and long-term consequences, and developing the skills necessary to change. Both strategies are designed to engage the peer cluster and modify norms and attitudes that support negative behavior. But, as we have advocated for years, be cautious. The peer group may reinforce norms that adults are helpless to modify, especially if groups are provided with unstructured time. Researchers (Cho et al., 2005; Dishion, McCord, & Poulin, 1999; Gardner & Steinberg, 2005) discuss the iatrogenic effect, whereby group interventions intended to help actually cause harm because peers within groups negatively influence one another and encourage antisocial behavior. This is particularly problematic in informal and unstructured groups. To reduce the potential harmful effects of a group intervention, it is wise to keep the group structured and to include in the group some young people with prosocial attitudes or, as we discuss later, trained peer or cross-age facilitators.

Interventions that provide group treatments to high-risk, aggressive youth are particularly problematic and can inadvertently exacerbate violent tendencies. In addition, interventions that fail to incorporate caretakers and focus exclusively on children tend to be less successful. A young person who returns from treatment into the same family dynamics, as well as the same peer cluster, is unlikely to be consistently reinforced for treatment gains that were made. Adolescent violence prevention programs offering intensive counseling for high-risk children and their families are more successful in deterring juvenile crime than "scared straight" or military-like boot camps that work with the most aggressive teens. As predicted by peer cluster theory, young people with delinquent tendencies who are put together in camps or centers provide justification for criminal attitudes and values and teach one another how to commit more crimes (National Institutes of Health Consensus Development Program, 2004).

COOPERATIVE LEARNING AND PEER SUPPORT NETWORKS

Cooperative learning groups are a basic way to influence peer clusters. Any teacher can develop this approach, from the primary grades through high school and beyond. Children learn the skills of collaboration, manage conflicts and disputes, and develop a cooperative spirit with their classmates. Peer clusters lose some of their negative influence when this strategy is adopted.

The practice of grouping students by their ability to learn, as determined by some objective measure, has a negative effect on children in low-ability groups, and it tends to reinforce initial inequalities (Barr, 1992; Berliner & Biddle, 1995). Teachers treat high-ability groups differently from low-ability groups. Students with lower ability receive fewer opportunities to answer analytical questions, are given less time to respond, and receive less praise than the students in high-ability groups. These students begin to think little of their own ability. Overall, ability grouping as a practice has decidedly negative effects for children with lower ability.

Cooperative Learning

Teachers are frustrated by the wide range of skills and abilities they find in heterogeneous classrooms. Various grouping procedures (Vaughn, Hughes, Moody, & Elbaum, 2001) such as cooperative learning are one solution to this problem (Slavin et al., 1994). Cooperative learning is implemented in various ways. First, it can vary in task structure. In some programs, students work independently on a task that has been divided up. In others, students work on the task as a group. The latter format encourages peer helping and a truly cooperative learning environment. Second, cooperative learning can vary according to incentives. For example, the group's grade or reward may be the sum or average of the individual members' performances, or it may be contingent on the product that the group as a whole has created. In most cooperative learning implementations, students work in small, heterogeneous groups (usually numbering between four and six) and are rewarded according to the group's performance.

Cooperative learning groups also have the potential to provide at-risk students with a peer support group. Cooperative learning groups are a major intervention approach, and we discuss the deliberate adaptation of them to augment a peer support network. These networks are a counterpoint to negative peer clusters.

Positive Effects of Cooperative Learning Groups

Cooperative learning has several aims. First, a cooperative model is a healthy alternative to an individual competitive model. Individual competition can have devastating effects on the motivation of at-risk students. Membership in a successful group permits students to experience success with all its attendant advantages—perceptions of themselves as able to perform well, satisfaction with their performance, and the esteem of their peers—regardless of each student's personal individual performance. This experience is of particular benefit to at-risk students who have known few academic successes (see Box 14.1).

In cooperative learning groups, students are encouraged to help and support one another rather than to compete. As in most athletic activities, individual excellence is encouraged because it benefits the whole team. Both high- and low-ability children profit from the experience. The low-ability children benefit from the assistance of their peers, and high-ability children achieve a higher level of understanding after providing that assistance (Saleh, Lazonder, & De Jong, 2005). Incidentally, high-ability students in cooperative learning situations, compared to those in individualistic competitive ones, demonstrated higher achievement on factual recall and high-level reasoning measures and had higher academic self-esteem and greater cohesion (Johnson, Johnson, & Taylor, 1993).

▲ Box 14.1

Getting Smart

One teacher recently experimented with cooperative learning groups. She joined two children of middle ability with one child of high ability and one of low ability for a social studies project. They worked together cooperatively on the reading material. When they were finished with their project, she quizzed each child on the material.

The next day, when the low-ability child received his score on the test, he looked perplexed and said, "I'm not this smart." The teacher smiled and replied, "I guess you must be." She decided to continue to organize cooperative learning groups in her classroom.

Cooperative learning increases academic performance (Stevens & Slavin, 1995). Whether students are questioning factual information, discovering new concepts, or solving problems, a cooperative learning approach has been shown to develop academic skills. Students, especially those from diverse linguistic and cultural backgrounds, make significant academic gains compared to student gains in traditional settings. Classroom interaction with peers offers students many chances to use language and improve speaking skills, especially important for ESL students.

Cooperative learning encourages active learning. Extensive research and practice have indicated that students learn more when they are actively engaged in discovery and in problem solving. As students talk and reason together to solve a problem or complete a task, they become more involved in communicating and in thinking. These activities automatically engage a child in an active way that is quite different from the passive listening and learning required by most approaches (Carpenter, Bloom, & Boat, 1999).

Cooperative learning prepares students for work in today's world. Team approaches to problem solving and individual efforts to accomplish group goals and aid interpersonal harmony in the work setting are all valued skills in today's society of interdependent workplaces. Cooperative learning teaches students how to work together and builds students' social nature, social understanding, and personal efficacy.

Finally, cooperative learning groups provide an opportunity to improve race relations in the school (Davidson & Worsham, 1992). Students who work together in cooperative learning groups are more likely to value mixed racial and ethnic acquaintances and friendships and develop a respect for diversity, including greater acceptance of students with physical and learning disabilities. When students cooperate to reach a common goal, they learn to respect and appreciate each other. Ms. Bassett, Carlos Diaz's social studies teacher (see Chapter 5), is working toward this goal by placing her students in cooperative learning groups. As her students of different ethnic backgrounds work with each other, prejudice diminishes. Consequently, Carlos is now establishing friendships with other students. Dividing a class into interracial learning teams reduces prejudice by undercutting stereotypes and encouraging group members to pull together (Costa, 1991).

Cooperative learning takes numerous forms. Programs are known by names such as Learning Together, Group Investigation, Team Assisted Individualization, Student Teams-Achievement Divisions, Teams-Games-Tournaments, and Jigsaw (Slavin [1983] provides a complete review of these cooperative learning methods). These strategies are a group of instructional methods that utilize interdependence among students in the learning of content (Carpenter et al., 1999).

Cooperative learning programs have demonstrated positive affective outcomes that directly address the needs of at-risk youth: motivation, peer support, self-attributions, and self-esteem (Slavin et al., 1994; Stevens & Slavin, 1995). After 30 years of research, the evidence is impressive (Kutnick, 2005), supporting the claim that cooperative learning groups enhance academic achievement; increase positive self-esteem, internal locus of control, altruism, and perspective taking; improve intergroup relationships between students without and with disabilities, as well as the relationship between students of different cultural backgrounds; and provide positive peer support. Because they entail positive peer support, cooperative learning groups seem to be a natural way to promote feelings of connectedness among students at risk of dropping out or those who have other social and emotional problems. The potential to increase social capital and prosocial peer influence are especially important in cooperative peer learning groups.

Peer Support Networks

Grouping students together because they share a problem may increase interaction, mutual support, and camaraderie, but it can also have other unwanted effects: Positive peer models and influences on academic performance and behavior may be drastically reduced; negative peer modeling may escalate; the entire group may perform according to anti-adult and antisocial norms. Nevertheless, to be successful, classroom interactions must foster caring communities in which students feel they belong and where they believe teachers and peers support them (Carpenter et al., 1999). Support networks for psychological well-being are well documented in the literature (Peebles-Wilkins, 2003).

To increase their positive impact and to minimize their potential negative influence, we propose that cooperative learning groups be formed deliberately to increase the socioemotional supports for students (Meyer & Henry, 1993; Meyer, Williams, Harootunian, & Steinberg, 1995). We and others (Carter, Cushing, Clark, & Kennedy, 2005) have found that by purposefully and deliberately designing peer support networks, high-risk students are provided with positive peer support, which promotes their feelings of connectedness with other students and with the school. High-risk students are not identified in any formal or obvious way, but they are put in situations where they can maintain relationships with peers who provide positive models of academic performance and behavior. In this way, peer support networks are accessible to students regarded as being at risk. They also form a natural structure for psychoeducational support groups recommended by Morganett (1990, 1995) and O'Rourke and Worzbyt (1996).

In developing peer support networks, first identify students at risk. Then identify students who are more grounded, resilient, and prosocial. The five Cs of competency (see Chapter 6) can be used to help identify both groups of students.

After students have been identified, the teacher or counselor deliberately structures a cooperative learning group that also functions as a peer support network. Figure 14.1 shows a classroom grouping form that can be used to structure peer support networks. Students with the greatest support needs are targeted, and their names are put in one of the five slots in each cluster. If at all possible, only one high-risk student is included in any single group. Attempts should be made to avoid putting together individuals who form friendship bonds that are a negative influence on academic motivation, school achievement, and behavior. The other four students in each peer support network cluster should be chosen with the intent of making the group as heterogeneous as possible with regard to gender, race, ability, and achievement (for example, European American, Latino, and African American; female and male; one low, one high, and three average achievers).

For each cooperative learning peer support group, include at least one student who is generally on task in group activities and, if possible, one student who is a peacekeeper diplomat. Also, include at least one group member who might be a potential friend to the student at risk. Ideally, students in the peer support cooperative groups would be very much like the student at risk with an important exception—the potential friends are positive influences. Try to avoid individual personalities that may create negative group combinations. For example, two physically aggressive, volatile students may create a potentially explosive group; or timid or quiet students may be manipulated or intimidated by "macho" boys.

These peer support cooperative learning groups should stay together for their class cooperative learning activities for at least a 9- or 12-week grading period. Although modifications may need to be made when group combinations are not working, the intent is to put together high-risk students with less risky students to provide a peer support network.

Group 1	

Group 2	

Group 3	

Group 4	

Group 5	

Group 6	

FIGURE 14.1   Peer support network form: Classroom grouping

Elements of Cooperative Learning

After formation of the groups, it is important that the students engage in cooperative learning activities to help the interaction and mutual interdependent collaboration. In one study (Bassett, McWhirter, & Kitzmiller, 1997), we found that teachers who reported a commitment to cooperative learning groups were not really using the method. Many teachers believed that they were implementing cooperative learning when, in fact, they were missing its essence. Structured cooperative learning among students is more than just putting students into groups to learn. Students sitting together at the same table and talking with one another is not cooperative learning. Having one student do all the work on a group report while others simply put their names on it is not cooperative learning. A student who finishes a task early and helps slower students complete it is not involved in cooperative learning.

The five basic elements (Johnson, Johnson, & Holubec, 1990) essential to cooperative learning groups are positive interdependence, individual accountability, face-to-face interaction, social skills, and group process. Slavin (1991) identifies similar elements and adds a sixth: group rewards. He argues that awards accruing to the whole group are useful and powerful in building the prestige and power of the cooperative learning group.

Positive interdependence.   Students are linked with others in such a way that one cannot succeed unless the other members of the group succeed and vice versa. Goal interdependence, role interdependence, shared rewards, dependence on one another's resources, and a distributed division of labor helps ensure positive interdependence.

Individual accountability.   The performance of each individual student in the group is assessed, and the results are reported back to the student and to the group. Randomly selecting one student's work to represent the entire group or randomly asking one group member to explain a problem, solution, or concept are ways to accomplish this element. Students need to know that they can't "ride" on the backs of others.

Face-to-face interaction.   This element exists when students assist, help, support, and encourage one another's efforts to learn. Discussion of strategies and concepts, explanations of how to solve problems, teaching knowledge, and making connections between past and present information fulfill this requirement.

Social skills.   Working cooperatively requires specific social and interactional skills. Leadership, communication, trust-building, decision-making, and conflict management skills are necessary components of effective cooperative learning groups. As we have made clear elsewhere in this book, these skills have to be taught just as purposefully and precisely as academic skills. Many students have never had an opportunity to work cooperatively in a group before, and they need the social skills to do so.

Group process.   Monitoring and discussing the interactional process of the groups is necessary. Students need to become aware and be encouraged to maintain effective working relationships in their groups and to consider whether they are achieving their goals. Group maintenance, feedback about participation, and other process issues need to be developed.

To develop and increase group cohesion, productivity, and interaction, ask the cooperative learning group members to respond to these two questions after each session: What was something that each member did that helped the group today? What can each person do at the next meeting to make the group better? The 10 minutes that this processing takes provides feedback for members on their collaborative skills, allows the group to focus on group maintenance, and reminds students to use their collaborative skills consistently.

Cooperative learning groups that are deliberately structured to provide a social support network can change the way young people experience school. The social support network provides high-risk students with systematic opportunities to develop positive interaction patterns and to form friendships with peers who have been carefully selected as potential supports and friends based on personal, cultural, and social characteristics. Teaching social skills, critical thinking, and academic content is integrated in the context of group support.

PEER AND CROSS-AGE TUTORING PROGRAMS

Peer and cross-age tutors are students who teach other students in formal and informal learning situations that are delegated, planned, and directed by an educator. Peer tutoring is a one-to-one teaching process in which the tutor is of the same academic age as the partner. Cross-age tutoring involves matching an older student tutor with a younger student learner. Peer tutoring alters the environmental and social climate in a school and can enhance and increase learning. It provides a cost-effective way (Topping & Bryce, 2004) to meet the individual needs of students and to improve the performance of students who need help with their studies. Tutoring programs are designed to aid at-risk children by improving their academic performance and their emotional well-being (Arreaga-Mayer, 1998; Keller, 2002; Tansey, Santos de Barona, McWhirter, & Herrmann, 1996). Peer tutoring improves social interactions, self-concept, motivation, attitudes toward the school (Lazerson, 2005), peer status, and overall school experience (Cushing & Kennedy, 1997; Tansy et al., 1996). The concept of peer tutoring has deep roots in our educational system.

Systematic planning is a critical component of successful peer or cross-age tutoring programs. It improves thinking skills (McKinstery & Topping, 2003; Topping & Bryce, 2004), use of mathematic and scientific words and concepts (Topping, Campbell, Douglas, & Smith, 2003; Topping, Peter, Stephen, & Whale, 2004), and increases information on specialized subjects such as music, horticulture, health, safety, and social interactions (Heron, Welsch, & Goddard, 2003). Administrators, teachers, students, and families more readily accept programs that attend to readiness, preparation, selection, implementation, supervision, and evaluation components.

Well-planned programs can be integrated into schools more effectively than programs that are not well articulated from the outset (Greenwood, Carta, & Maheady, 1991). Elements essential to implementing a successful peer or cross-age tutoring program include considerations of cost, school readiness, and teacher, student, and parent preparation.

Cost-Effectiveness

Cost-effectiveness is an important consideration for administrators in the implementation of academic interventions. Levin, Glass, and Meister (1984) studied the cost-effectiveness of four educational intervention strategies designed to raise student achievement in reading and mathematics: (a) computer-aided instruction, (b) cross-age/peer tutoring, (c) reduced class size, and (d) a longer school day. When student gains and program costs were compared, peer tutoring produced math and reading gain scores more than twice those resulting from computer-aided instruction, 3 times those achieved through reducing class size from 35 to 30 students, and almost 4 times more than lengthening the school day by 1 hour. Information regarding the relative utility of peer or cross-age tutoring interventions is vital to administrators in a time of reduced resources, increased demands, and increased accountability. Young people make gains even with the brevity and low cost in time and resources (Topping & Bryce, 2004).

Readiness

Much of the success of peer tutoring depends on the readiness of the school to accept the program. Readiness is a function of both attitudinal factors and availability of resources to support the program. As administrator of the school, the principal is instrumental in allowing for program adjustments such as release time, schedule modifications, allocation of space, and active encouragement of peer tutoring. Teachers support the peer tutoring program by participating in peer selection, curriculum development, ongoing evaluation, and program development activities. Teacher readiness requires thorough training in peer tutoring methods through in-service training and ongoing consultation and supervision (Hawryluk & Smallwood, 1986). Specialized training and instruction in peer and cross-age tutoring methods for teachers are often available from school psychologists and counselors.

Counselors may encourage teachers to acquaint themselves with tutoring methods and materials through published resources, including the *Cross-Age Tutoring Handbook* (Johnson, 1977), *Tutoring for At-Risk Students* (Gaustad, 1992), *Increasing Student Productivity Through Peer Tutoring Programs* (Pierce, Stahlbrand, & Armstrong, 1984), and *Peer Tutoring: A Guide for School Psychologists* (Ehly, 1986).

Preparation

Sufficient preparation of participating individuals increases the likelihood that the peer or cross-age tutoring program will be successfully established and accepted in both the school and the community. Students may be readied for peer tutoring through written and oral information about the program. Because peer or cross-age tutoring is a nontraditional means of instruction, presenting the program and its participants in a positive light is important.

Teachers play a central role in determining the content to be taught. They also explain to tutors how to approach learning, monitor student progress, and facilitate students' interactions. To increase teachers' acceptance of and commitment to the program, training and preparation of teachers should encompass several components, including (a) understanding the purpose, advantage, and features of the peer tutoring program; (b) planning lessons and material preparation for student use; and (c) developing competence in teaching interactional and problem-solving skills to students. This training is accomplished through consultation, exposure to written material on peer tutoring, and in-service training. Teacher training includes instruction of tutoring methods, simulation exercises to familiarize teachers with student and teacher roles, modeling strategies for social and conflict resolution skills, and discussion of anticipated problems that may interfere with implementation. Our experience suggests that training programs developed for this purpose can accomplish these objectives in a minimum of three to five 40-minute training sessions if ongoing in-services, consultation, and coordination for maintenance purposes are provided.

The degree to which students are prepared to tutor is another critical element of an effective tutoring program. Children who have a fuller understanding of a task and its rationale are better prepared to perform the task themselves and better equipped to teach it to others (Barron & Foot, 1991). Students planning to tutor are better prepared when trained in various aspects of tutoring, including (a) developing and presenting instructional material, (b) recognizing and reinforcing correct learner responses appropriately, (c) providing corrective feedback effectively, (d) redirecting off-task behavior, (e) communicating with learners, and (f) working closely with teachers. Tutor preparation includes a mix of didactic instruction, practice in specific skills, and group discussion of possible problems. Tutors also benefit from ongoing training to strengthen their skills and reinforce the purpose of the program. Ongoing training can be accomplished through brief refresher training sessions offered periodically during the peer or cross-age tutoring program.

Advance preparation of parents is essential to the program's acceptance. If not properly informed, parents may perceive their child's participation in the peer or cross-age tutoring program negatively. Advance preparation of participating parents in the form of written information, group discussions, and personal contact may convert potentially doubting parents to agents of support. Because peer tutoring activities involve individual students selected from the entire class, parental consent is needed. Parents should be provided with a clear explanation of the program, reasons for their child's involvement, and safeguards against possible negative effects. Parent preparation may be accomplished through letters to parents, meetings between parents and school personnel, and presentations at meetings such as the PTA and the PTSO.

Sample Method: Pause, Prompt, and Praise

To illustrate the nature of peer tutoring, we selected one method for fuller description. The "pause, prompt, and praise" method is very helpful for tutoring oral reading. The first part of the tutoring procedure, "pause," requires the tutor to delay attention to the student's reading error for more than 5 seconds or until the end of the sentence. The second part of the procedure, "prompt," requires the tutor to supply a prompt if no self-correction occurs. The prompts are the self-correction strategies that the student learner has already learned as part of program preparation. They are often graphic or contextual clues that provide meaning. If no correct response is elicited following two prompts, the tutor supplies the correct word and moves on. The final part of the procedure, "praise," requires the tutor to verbally reinforce positive behaviors and to encourage development of independent self-correcting skills. Therefore, in addition to the general praise for behaviors such as finishing a whole page, the tutor praises self-corrections and prompts corrections made by the learner.

This method supplies the tutor with a procedure for dealing with both correct and error behavior by the reader. It encourages him or her to reinforce the desired behaviors. Perhaps more important, it allows the reader to develop independence and independent self-correction strategies. It is also a simple method for peer tutors to learn.

Program Implementations

Educational interventions such as peer or cross-age tutoring often emerge from a need to remediate students who are failing or at risk of failure. The impetus to develop new programs often reflects a sense of urgency. Initially, however, a modest peer or cross-age tutoring program is most viable. Avoid overtaxing available resources during the initial implementation stage of a program and expand later when the program is well established.

In spite of how thoroughly a program has been planned, unforeseen problems will arise. After initial startup, slight adjustments will be necessary. Administrative support is essential to the program. As well, teachers will need some release time and other forms of support to develop materials, assess and supervise program participants, and provide ongoing training (in-service and discussion groups) related to the program. Now let's take a closer look at the elements of a successful peer tutoring program.

Tutor selection.   In cross-age tutoring programs, older tutors are matched with younger partners. In peer tutoring programs, tutors and student learners (or partners) are the same age, class, or grade. When selecting tutors, consideration may be given to students with a variety of characteristics, including those who are academically accomplished and able to instruct, those who are positive role models and influential with their peers, and others who are at greater risk of school failure and may benefit academically and emotionally from their role as tutors. Each type of tutor offers a degree of assurance that the program will be accepted. The academically accomplished tutor will bring mastery of the subject matter to the tutoring session, the influential peer will popularize the program within the peer culture, and the "at-risk" tutor will provide evidence that the program is of benefit to those who tutor.

When choosing whom to include as student learners, educators might consider the degree of learning difficulties, motivation, and behavioral adjustment the learner presents. Learners with severe problems may not be good candidates for initial implementation of the program. These students may be introduced to the peer tutoring program in subsequent years, once introductory concerns are resolved and the program is established.

Once matched, it is advisable that tutor–learner interactions be observed and pairs assessed for compatibility. Supervising teachers or coordinating counselors should intervene in difficult relationships and reassign unworkable matches. This kind of support will prevent tutors and learners from feeling frustrated or discouraged with the program and will increase their enjoyment of the process.

Tutoring sessions.   The program coordinator, scheduling several 20- to 30-minute sessions each week, should develop a tutoring schedule. Tutoring schedules must be followed consistently. Failure to hold tutoring sessions at their scheduled times conveys the message that the program is unimportant relative to other activities.

Tutoring sessions typically are held in a designated area within the classroom, isolated somewhat from other student activities. This seating arrangement allows for privacy and reduces distractions but enables the teacher to directly monitor the tutoring session.

Materials.   Tutoring materials are generated by the teacher or adapted from published sources. With supervision, experienced tutors can learn to develop materials for the learner, resulting in increased understanding of the materials by the tutor and decreasing the teacher's required time commitment somewhat.

Student incentives.   Students' motivation to participate in a peer or cross-age tutoring program will not be sustained without some form of incentive. Incentives for participating in the program can be provided for both tutors and their partners on a regular basis. Although most students are motivated through immediate praise and verbal approval, school personnel can recognize student involvement by making schoolwide announcements and providing activities such as social events and learning games. Time set aside for personal reflection and discussion of students' experiences in the program is especially useful. In some schools, tutors receive elective credit for their participation in the program. Some programs recognize tutors and their partners by awarding certificates of completion and recognition. School newsletters and plaques hung in the central hallways are other ways to recognize students for their involvement. Schools can be very creative in developing incentives to enhance student involvement.

Teacher supervision.   Teachers need to meet with tutors before each session to review instructional materials. Prior to the session, the teacher ascertains that the tutor has a clear grasp of the content of the instructional material and the objectives for the learner. These meetings become shorter as the tutor demonstrates competence in the tutorial role.

Initially, after each session, the tutor meets with the teacher to discuss how the session went, the partner's progress, and any difficulties encountered. The teacher reinforces and instructs the tutor at this time. Postsession supervision is reduced as the tutor establishes competence. The motivational aspects of these meetings, however, must be kept in mind; reinforcement of tutors is an ongoing activity and is extremely important. As part of their supervisory role, teachers should directly observe the tutoring session in about one of every three or four sessions to monitor the tutoring process.

Evaluation.   Program evaluation is important to a tutor program for several reasons. Ongoing evaluation of student progress can be used to motivate both the student receiving tutoring and the tutor. Also, feedback from student performance can be used to determine aspects of the program that are effective and those that could benefit from modification. Evaluation results can be used to demonstrate the value of the program to interested parties, such as administrators faced with decisions about funding special programs or parents who express doubts about the quality of alternative educational approaches.

Evaluation activities should be linked to the goals and objectives of the program. Tutoring programs are often designed to improve the academic achievement of both the tutor and the student learner in the specific area tutored. Another common goal of tutoring programs is enhancing both students' academic self-concept. The effectiveness of a tutoring program may be gauged by whether the tutor and the learner have achieved gains in academic performance in the subject being tutored and in academic self-concept.

The use of global measures of academic achievement or self-concept for evaluating the effectiveness of the program may result in ambiguous feedback on student progress. Overall academic achievement is a composite of several academic areas (mathematics, reading, spelling, and so forth). It is unrealistic to expect change in overall academic achievement through tutoring in only one academic area. It is equally unrealistic to anticipate change in global self-concept as a result of improved performance in a specific academic area (Craven, Marsh, & Debus, 1991). Efforts to evaluate program effectiveness using global indices will underestimate the actual benefits of the program. The best way to measure the effect of the tutoring program is to evaluate academic and self-concept change specifically related to the subject tutored.

Students participating in the tutoring program should be assessed before, during, and after participating in the program. Academic achievement can be assessed through teacher-developed, curriculum-based measures that are inexpensive, directly related to the academic subject matter, and sensitive to improvement in academic performance.

Several tests designed to measure children's self-concepts have academic self-concept factors (Harter, 1985; Piers, 1984). Each of these tests mixes academic self-concept items among the other self-concept items, which does not readily allow measurement of academic self-concept alone. The Multidimensional Self-Concept Scale (MSCS) is well suited to isolating academic self-concept because its 25 academic self-concept items are not woven into the body of the instrument; rather, they are presented on a separate page and may be administered, scored, and compared to national norms without giving or scoring the entire test (Bracken, 1992). The academic scale of the MSCS, about a 5-minute test, can be used throughout the course of program participation as a measure of academic self-concept.

PEER MEDIATION PROGRAMS

Mediation is a problem-solving process that enables individuals to resolve disputes that are troublesome. In addition to being effective in some marital relationships, it is used in contract disputes (Mareschal, 2005), legal disputes (Shestowsky, 2004) and child custody disagreements (Sanchez & Kibler-Sanchez, 2004). It also has great application in school settings.

School peer mediation (Lane & McWhirter, 1992, 1996) is a mode of conflict management employed by students for the purpose of resolving conflicts. Trained peer mediators work as a team of two to facilitate problem solving between disputants. Students' involvement in the mediation process ensures practice with critical thinking, problem solving, and self-discipline. Students' participation in efforts to change their own and their peers' behavior is directly related to the developmental construct of self-regulation. Awareness of socially approved behaviors is a critical feature.

The setting for this mediation process is often the playground. Used in conjunction with traditional means of discipline, such as suspension for serious violent acts, peer mediation provides a structured forum for the resolution of in-school disputes. Student involvement in the mediation process provides practice in critical thinking, problem solving, and self-discipline. "The process of peer mediation is a self-empowering one — it enables students to make decisions about issues and conflicts that affect their own lives" (Maxwell, 1989, p. 150). This element of student participation in self and peer behavior change is directly related to the developmental construct of self-regulation. Awareness of socially approved behaviors is a critical feature of self-regulation, which involves the ability to postpone acting on a desired object or goal. Self-regulation requires being able to generate socially approved behavior in the absence of external monitors. The ability to self-regulate is a developmental skill that must be practiced regularly. School peer mediation programs provide daily opportunities for reinforcement.

Background

School peer mediation programs have sprung up across the nation in the last two decades, and many of them are based on community mediation models such as the San Francisco Community Board Program (1982). Developers of the San Francisco Community Board Program had 5 years of experience settling disputes between neighbors and businesses before introducing this school-based Conflict Manager program. In this program, students receive 16 hours of training and role-play practice. They eventually become team mediators on the playground and in the lunchroom. Similar programs now exist in almost all major cities in the United States. The assistance of a community mediation school initiative trainer, although not essential, may be valuable in training school personnel and students.

Models for both adults in the community and children in schools promote conflict mediation through the application of communication skills, listening to evoke varying perspectives, eliciting mutual contributions to the problem's eventual solution, and attending to feelings — all in an atmosphere of respect for the parties involved.

Theoretical Assumptions

Advocates of peer mediation in the schools assume that "children helping children" is a valid perspective from which to view program implementation and outcomes. A wealth of research literature supports this perspective. Peer leaders have been found to have greater credibility regarding student social interactions. They serve as potent role models and can demonstrate prosocial behaviors. Peers can create and reinforce norms supporting the notion that certain behaviors are deviant rather than acceptable, and they can promote alternatives to deviant behaviors. The student mediators who are the direct recipients of program training receive the most impact; students without direct training also benefit (Jones, 1998).

Another strength of such programs is that they emphasize student involvement and student management. Thus participants tend to feel more committed to program goals and more interested in producing change among their peers. A more specific description of benefits follows.

Benefits to Students and to the School

Both student behavior and school discipline problems improve as a result of peer mediation. McCormick (1988) reported that at-risk disputants (students who had been referred frequently for discipline problems) were observed by teachers to exhibit shifts to cooperation after experiencing peer mediation, a change supported by a 47% decrease in self-reported aggressive conflicts. Also, "at-risk students who directly participated in the program developed more 'prosocial' attitudes towards conflict, but those who had only indirect exposure to the collaborative process maintained their 'antisocial' attitudes towards conflict" (McCormick, 1988, p. 73). For example, when one at-risk student was trained as a peer mediator, his previous preference for resolving conflict in an aggressive style was replaced (over one semester as a mediator) with a reported preference for a collaborative style of dispute resolution. Such metamorphoses are also described by McCormick: "'Troublemakers' were just as enthusiastic about the problem-solving process and just as competent to guide others through it as those peer mediators who were thought to be ideal students" (p. 63).

Araki, Takeshita, and Kadomoto (1989) found that peer mediation increased empowerment and volunteerism, with both mediators and disputants developing increasing capacities for self-control. Disputants who were nonlisteners became listeners through participation in the mediation process. All students—both disputants and mediators—found a place for talking about problems, learning more about the views of others, and practicing better communication in a nonviolent, nonjudgmental atmosphere. The words of one student summarize peer mediation's impact:

> All I ever wanted to do was to fight. If someone said something to me I didn't like, I didn't think about talking, I just thought about fighting. I came into a mediation session as a disputant with four girls on the other side. I thought, "Who needs this? What am I doing here?" I just wanted to punch these girls out. I figured that the mediator would tell me what I was going to have to do. But she didn't. Instead she drew me out, listened to me. It felt so good to let it all out; then I wasn't angry anymore. I thought, "Hey, if this can work for me, I want to learn how to do it." (McCormick, 1988, p. 54)

Peer mediation also provides benefits for schools by reducing the number of discipline events. In one Hawaii school, the number of on-campus fights dropped from 83 to 19 over a 2-year period (Araki et al., 1989). At a New York school, these events declined by 50% (Koch, 1988), and an Arizona school reported a 47% decrease in the average number of aggressive incidents per month (McCormick, 1988). Finally, out of 69 mediated cases at a Milwaukee high school, 60 agreements were reached, and researchers recorded an 80% success rate for disputes mediated during the 1986–87 school year (Burrell & Vogel, 1990). As more instruments for program evaluation become available, the benefits to students and to school climate will become increasingly apparent.

Training Staff Members

The training sequence begins with presentation of the mediation program to the entire school staff. The school counselor and principal often conduct this introductory session. Given the time and resources required to implement a peer mediation program, it is very important that the initial presentation include evidence of the benefits to students and to the school. After the presentation, each staff member completes a level-of-interest questionnaire to determine his or her degree of commitment to the process. If staff support for mediation is adequate (usually 80%), training for teachers and support personnel is initiated. Elementary and middle school staff training usually requires about 8 hours. The content of this training includes communication skills that encompass active listening, reflection of feeling, message clarification, body language, giving "I" messages, brainstorming, types of questioning, and effective problem solving. The mediation sequence is identified, and adult responsibilities are delineated. Role play is used extensively with the adult staff members, as it is later with the students.

Training Student Peer Mediators

Once the adults have been trained, they plan and implement an orientation assembly to motivate students and to alert them to the qualities of a good mediator. Role plays and skits are used to outline aspects of the program and the process.

As the time for implementation nears, students who wish to become peer mediators nominate themselves or are nominated by others. Nominations may also come from counselors, teachers, and administrators. Final selection of mediators is completed by student vote. Adult staff members then train selected students, sometimes with the assistance of a community mediation training consultant. Training for elementary and middle school students consists of five half days. The adult staff members teach the communication skills that they reviewed in their own training. They guide the students through role plays not unlike those they engaged in during the adult training.

The mediation sequence is introduced and practiced until it becomes a comfortable process for the children. This sequence involves four basic stages: introduction, listening, wants, and solutions.

In the first stage of the peer mediation sequence, the student mediators introduce themselves, offer their services ("Do you need a mediator?"), and walk to a different area to cause physical and psychological separation from the initial point of conflict. When the disputants and mediators are ready, the rules are reviewed and commitment to them is elicited. An assurance of confidentiality is given to disputants by the mediators.

In stage 2 of the mediation sequence, the peer mediators listen to each disputant in turn. They reflect and restate content and feelings as they address each disputant. Because no interruptions are allowed, disputants have the opportunity to hear the others' perspectives of the conflict and their resultant feelings.

With guidance from the peer mediators, disputants express their wants in stage 3 of the sequence. As the requests are heard and restated by mediators, clarity reduces anxiety about possible hidden agendas.

In stage 4, disputants are asked what they can contribute to the resolution of the problem. The peer mediators restate and check solutions for balance. Then each disputant is asked if the proposed solution is acceptable. An important step in this phase is asking if the problem is solved. Disputants may wish to express a need to receive or to give an apology to smooth hurt feelings. The mediators then ask disputants how such a conflict could be handled differently in the future. Peer mediators close the sequence by asking former disputants to tell their friends that the conflict has been solved, thus reducing the potential for rumors. After congratulating the students on solving their problem, the peer mediators complete a mediation report form. In this last step of the sequence, the peer mediators have an opportunity to review the quality of their guidance because they do their record keeping together.

When training is complete, student mediators receive recognition and uniform T-shirts, banners, or hats at an assembly. They are then assigned to recess duty in pairs. They meet twice a week with a staff program coordinator to discuss their successes and problems, to maintain and build new skills, and to handle scheduling problems. School counselors often introduce classroom guidance curriculum activities to promote general student awareness of the peer mediators and the services they offer.

Implications

The simplicity of the peer mediation process contributes to its success. The student mediators can easily implement the steps. They also provide support for one another. In the San Francisco Community Board Program (1982) demonstration video, a young man who was formerly a "conflict maker" became a "conflict manager." Sonny had this to say about his peer mediation experience:

> I used to be a bully. I think because I wanted to get the authority—the power. Now, as a conflict manager, I get the authority and status I used to take. I've changed. Now I can feel what the kids feel, and I can help them solve their problems.

Cahoon (1988), an elementary principal, noted that her "mediators learn valuable problem-solving skills: to think logically about processing the information presented to them, to see issues impartially, and to advise without censoring. They also gain recognition for their efforts" (p. 94). Roderick (1988) emphasized a valuable aspect of school mediation programs: "Young people have many choices besides passivity or aggression for dealing with conflict . . . [through mediation] we give them the skills to make those choices real in their own lives" (p. 90).

The Ripple Effect

Program implementation results in fewer playground problems and fewer referrals to the nurse or the principal's office. Families may also experience the program's impact; parents and students in peer mediation schools report that conflict in the home is modified (Daunic, Smith, Robinson, Miller, & Landry, 2000).

Another ripple effect of peer mediation programs is a perceived improvement in school climate. For example, Jones (1998) reports that peer mediation programs had a sustained and significant impact on both staff and teacher perception of school climate at all educational levels—elementary, middle, and secondary. The program also increased students' perceptions of school as a healthy and safe environment.

Counseling Ramifications

Peer mediation helps youth develop self-regulation and other skills. When students are given an opportunity to participate in decisions relating to their own lives, more self-regulation and positive self-esteem are likely to result. School counselors can promote peer mediation programs (and are in a strong position to open up mediation training to parents as part of a school–community outreach program). Conflict resolution through peer mediation is a preventive program as well—in the form of leadership training. It is also an integral component of a school's discipline plan. Finally, it is a way to meet the communication objectives of a guidance curriculum. Regardless of its placement in the overall picture of pupil development, its importance for children and its implications for society are clear.

The conflict resolution model of peer mediation addresses the skills of listening, problem solving, oral language expression, and critical thinking. These essential skills are directly taught in the process of mediation training. They are modeled and reinforced by the peer mediators.

Carlos Diaz (of Chapter 5) would benefit in several ways from being trained as a peer mediator. The experience of being nominated by a peer, teacher, or counselor would bolster his confidence. The skills he learns as a mediator would help him to reduce the number of fights he has with peers. Providing a valuable service to his school would help him view himself as more a part of the school community. This participation might influence teacher perceptions, increasing the amount of support and positive feedback he receives from teachers. The verbal skills learned and utilized by peer mediators might enhance Carlos's language acquisition efforts. Finally, Carlos could be an effective mediator for monolingual Spanish-speaking children at the school. Given Carlos's responsibilities at home, however, staff would have to ascertain whether the time demand of the program would hinder Carlos more than the benefits would be an enhancement. Nevertheless, a young man reinforced for his contributions to the school community who is being supported in the development of useful life skills is a young man with a lowered risk of dropout.

PEER FACILITATION

Peer facilitation (sometimes referred to as peer leadership, helping, or counseling) is very helpful in increasing the impact and efficiency of professional counseling. Peer facilitation is a process in which trained and supervised students perform interpersonal helping tasks — listening, offering support, suggesting alternatives, and engaging in other verbal and nonverbal interactions — that qualify as counseling functions with similar-aged clients who either have referred themselves or have been referred by others. Like peer tutoring and peer mediation, peer facilitation appears to be a useful way to counter negative peer cluster influence (Coker & Borders, 2001). It also reinforces and supports the use of life skills.

Peer facilitation programs generally have two major components: training and service. In the training phase, adult leaders provide designated peer helpers with intensive training. In the service or implementation phase, peer leaders offer direct service to other youth.

Training Phase

The training phase usually has certain common content. Communication skills, in particular, are emphasized. Active listening, empathetic understanding, and paraphrasing are included. Equally important are the nonverbal cues that the peer helper is projecting through his or her behavior.

In addition to basic communication skills, peer leaders almost always acquire skills in problem solving and decision making. These are useful skills that they can transfer to those whom they help although peer facilitators are almost always prohibited from giving advice. Their role is to listen, to question, to reflect, and to be a friend.

The young people in training usually spend a fair amount of time learning about important community resources. For example, information on alcohol and drug use, crisis intervention programs, and treatment facilities are emphasized. Peer leaders are an important source of referrals to community agencies.

Service Phase

Peer leaders can be helpful in many areas. In addition to tutoring and mediation, discussed earlier, peer facilitators can help introduce new students to school, befriend lonely and alone children who seem to have no friends, and work with special education students. They can also provide classroom information on tobacco, alcohol, and drug abuse problems; on healthy lifestyles; and on many other topics. With training they can facilitate small discussion and support groups. Most important, they can provide supportive and caring listening to troubled youth. Peers are often the first to know when someone is considering suicide. As we discussed in Chapter 10, in every incident of school shootings, the event "leakage" was usually to another peer. Peer facilitators can make school safer by providing a link between troubled young people and caring adults.

The role of the adult supervisors is just as important in the service phase as it is in the training phase. In addition to being models of empathy, understanding, and caring, adults are necessary to coordinate and organize the program. They must be available to help the young leaders with the particularly difficult problems. Of course, problems of an extremely urgent or serious nature must be referred to responsible adults.

Successful facilitator programs attempt to involve a representative and diverse group of students as peer helpers. Using the natural helper method described earlier, students and school personnel are asked to identify those students who are perceived to be individuals other students talk to if they need help with a problem. If students perceive the peer helper group as only an elite collection of class leaders or high achievers, many of the students who are in most need of support will stay away.

Facilitation assignments can vary from helping other students with specific problems to being available to provide encouragement and support in a common office area, to assisting on a survey of student needs. Whatever the assignment, peer facilitation programs create a pool of helpers who are trained to be sensitive to student needs and concerns.

Need to Be Needed

One of the greatest human needs is to be needed. Young people can affirm their worth to themselves and to others by assuming meaningful roles. By doing too much for children, we can destroy their self-confidence and foster low self-esteem. Not infrequently, adults provide children with an environment that demands nothing of them. Then we criticize our children for not appreciating the lifestyle or the parents who provided it. In many instances, young people have been progressively denied the opportunity to be engaged in work that is important to others and therefore denied the rewards that such work produces. Children and adolescents who tutor their peers or younger children, who assist people with disabilities, who help to care for young children, who visit with the elderly, who mediate disputes, who help others to learn, and who participate in other programs to help their families, schools, and communities are filling the void that our age of technology and specialization has created in their lives. They are responding to real social needs, and they are assuming meaningful roles at the microsystemic and mesosystemic levels. In so doing, they are satisfying their own need to be needed and are more likely to see themselves as contributing members of their communities, schools, and families.

CONCLUSION

In this chapter we have described several school-based peer programs designed to directly or indirectly prevent student problems. Such programs are an effective means of reducing some of the correlates of at-risk categories: depression, interpersonal conflict, communication deficiencies, loneliness, and lack of purpose. They can be also implemented at all levels of education—elementary, middle, and secondary settings—and can be organized within a single classroom, a whole school, or an entire district. Schools can also help mobilize peer groups as a force for good. When children are encouraged to work cooperatively in small groups, they are provided with a classroom community that encourages them to discuss their work with others, accept one another's viewpoints, weigh their options, and make decisions on the basis of reasoning.

Peer tutoring, mediation, and facilitation programs provide the direct help to at-risk young people in improving academic abilities, mastering new skills, and connecting to the school environment. The peer leaders also benefit by gaining confidence and increased self-esteem. Although requiring the assistance of teachers, counselors, and administrators in a time of increasing demands and fewer resources, peer-based programs have positive effects—both current and future—that outweigh their costs.

CHAPTER 15

FAMILY INTERVENTIONS

▲ *In some families words are like
barbed wire, they cut and puncture.*

*In some families messages are like
exploding shrapnel, they rip and tear.*

*In some families secrets are like
land mines, step on one and they
erupt in explosion.*

*In some families even love and affection
are tools in the battle.*

*All war, especially the war in families, is
at once horrible and dehumanizing
and obscenely senseless.*

CHAPTER OUTLINE

▲ As discussed earlier, the nature of the family structure is shifting in response to changes in social, political, and economic conditions. More and more families are called upon to deal with the stresses of divorce, remarriage, stepchildren, and the loss of the extended family network. Even negotiating the inevitable developmental changes that are part of the family life cycle can be highly stressful and can generate family conflict. Sometimes the symptoms of family distress emerge when a reasonably healthy family goes through a difficult transition, such as the marriage of the first child. In other cases family symptomatology reflects ongoing dysfunction and emerges in response to everyday stresses.

To illustrate, a father might abuse alcohol for several weeks following a layoff, then engage in productive coping strategies, adjust to the new situation, and return to his pre-layoff, nonproblematic level of drinking alcohol. Another father may consistently go on alcoholic binges: whenever the extended family gathers, when the mother confronts him, when the children fight, or when the traffic is heavy. The patterns of behavior that the various family members use to cope with the father's drinking may in themselves represent symptoms of family dysfunction. For example, particular roles are frequently assumed by family members with an alcoholic parent (Brooks & Coll, 1994; Devine & Braithwaite, 1993). The scapegoat role is played by a child who acts out (fighting in school, setting a fire, failing a class), thus drawing attention away from the alcohol problem. The parents temporarily unite while they deal with the "problem child." Sometimes the youth whose behavior appears self-destructive and irrational is actually trying to help a family member. This also inadvertently serves to perpetuate dysfunction (see Box 15.1).

When teachers and counselors become frustrated by the destructive and aggressive behaviors of their students, it is helpful to keep in mind that these behaviors are often goal directed and represent attempts to meet needs (see our discussion of goals of misbehavior in Chapter 9). Much behavior originates in response to the family dynamics to which the students return every night.

▲ Box 15.1

The School Slut

He was always angry with her. Every aggressive retort, every call from the school, every violation of curfew drew his rage like flies to butter. But the failing grades, her reputation as the
"school slut," and the constant battles were all worth it. Because as long as his attention was
focused on his anger with her, it would not be directed at her sister, the "good" daughter. And
he wouldn't come into her sister's bedroom. Her sister wouldn't be forced to endure those long
nights, the hideous emptiness, the vomiting afterward. At least, this much she could control.

And that's one reason the rage overwhelmed and consumed her 10 years later; that's
one reason the tears in my office were so torrential that her whole body convulsed with agony.
Because 10 years later, her sister said, "It was happening to me too."

It is a mistake, however, to attribute all student problems to some growing malevo-
lence in the American family. As we have indicated, the family is changing in response to
societal trends over which the individual family has little control. Society too often appears
eager to blame families for individual problems, as evidenced by attempts to solve those
problems by "fixing" families. Blaming families diverts attention from the fact that our
society lacks a coherent national family policy and that the structural supports required for
family life are grossly inadequate (Kagan & Weissbourd, 1994; Lott, 2002). In this chapter
we describe interventions for individual families as one point of entry for addressing the
problems of youth at risk. These interventions are family counseling, parent support
groups, parent education, and parent training.

FAMILY COUNSELING

Working with the entire family is often the optimal approach for dealing with young people
at risk for dropout, substance use, pregnancy, delinquency, suicide, or other problems.
When a child or adolescent is contemplating or engaged in life-threatening behavior, it is
of utmost importance that the family be involved in efforts to avert the problem. In general,
family counseling is appropriate (a) when the presenting problems are affected by and affect
the family system, (b) when the child or adolescent is living in the family or is working
through unfinished business with the family and is in contact with them even though not
living at home, and (c) when both the counselor and the client agree that family counseling
is an appropriate intervention.

Family counseling is not always a viable option. The following questions are often
considered in exploring the option of family counseling: Does the family have resources
such as transportation? Are there any language or cultural factors that might prohibit or discourage the family members from availing themselves of counseling services? Is the family
willing and able to commit to attending counseling sessions? Is there a family member who
has access to counseling services through an employee assistance program or some other

work benefit? Discussion of these questions and familiarity with community resources will set the stage for appropriate referrals.

Referring the Family for Counseling

For many family members, attending a counseling session is tantamount to acknowledging severe mental illness within the family. When a teacher or counselor believes that a particular family might benefit from family counseling, several steps can be taken to lay a foundation for success. First, the family needs to know why. On what basis has the referring professional made this decision? The identified problem—that is, the behavior of the child that attracted attention—should be explained in specific and concrete terms. For example, Lidia Diaz's teacher (Chapter 5) might say: "For three weeks now, Lidia has been withdrawn and quiet. She seems to be avoiding her school friends, she's refusing to participate in class, and she has cried at school three or four times this week. When I asked her how things were going at home, she simply stared at the floor and said, 'It's probably my fault anyway.' This is so different from Lidia's usual behavior that I thought it was important to contact you to talk about some possible ways to help her." Notice that Lidia's teacher does not assign blame or sound judgmental; nor does she draw conclusions from her observations.

A second step in family referral is to help the family understand that family counseling may help in the achievement of mutual goals. Counseling provides an opportunity for the family to work as a cohesive unit; the needs of all family members are considered in developing solutions to problems. Potential benefits include more appropriate behavior by the "problem child," increased responsibility among family members for voicing their opinions and feelings, better grades for the children, and more support and less stress for all family members. The teacher or counselor who knows the general nature of the problem can identify the benefits appropriate to the specific situation.

Family members are often more accepting of recommendations for counseling if they have a sense of what to expect. When Jason Carter (of Chapter 4) was first seen as a client, he asked the family counselor, "Where's your black couch? Aren't you going to write down everything I say?" Adults, too, may have misconceptions. The teacher or counselor can dispel some of the mystique surrounding counseling by discussing some of the common reasons families go to a counselor and what the process might be like. Common reasons include problems with discipline and communication, lack of trust among family members, school problems, and tension related to divorce, dating, or remarriage of a parent. There are many approaches to family counseling, and individual therapists vary in style even if they ascribe to the same approach.

Families should be encouraged to ask potential counselors, "What do you expect of your clients?" "How long have you been practicing, and what are your credentials?" "What can we expect of you?" "How do you structure your counseling sessions?" "How can we make best use of our time and money here?" "Do you have experience working with families like ours?" A family that has a sense of its own role in the therapeutic process may be more willing to consider the option of counseling.

Some families resist counseling because they are unsure how to begin the process. Let them know that once they call for an appointment, it may be anywhere from a day to a month or more before they have their first session. This first session may be an intake session during which a counselor gathers information about the family's background and history. The family may work with the intake counselor and in later sessions may be

▲ Box 15.2

In the Waiting Room

A tragedy occurred a few years ago in one of Kansas City's local hospitals. A woman of Hmong descent was standing in the waiting room of the hospital with her seriously ill infant. As she stood reticent in a corner waiting to be helped, the baby died in her arms. When the staff behind the reception desk realized what had just happened, they were aghast. They wondered why she had not approached them to ask for assistance.

The simple truth was this: Hmong people do not approach a majority group without first being summoned (Maltbia, 1991).

assigned to a different counselor. If families are unprepared for this sometimes drawn-out process, they may become frustrated and discontinue prematurely.

Some parents may want to meet with the counselor first without their children. Some counselors may request such an arrangement; others may refuse it. This decision depends on the theoretical orientation and judgment of the counselor. Encourage parents to let the counselor know their preference.

Teachers and counselors are more likely to be successful in referring families for counseling if they are knowledgeable about a variety of local counseling agencies and practitioners. It is especially important to make referrals that are consistent with the family's cultural and language needs. The importance of multicultural competence is increasingly reflected in professional ethics codes and accreditation standards, but all counselors do not have multicultural training. And certainly many agencies do not have counselors fluent in languages other than English. When a counselor or teacher approaches an ethnic minority family, it is important to consider that counseling as we know it has historically been a Western, White, middle- and upper-class phenomenon. Recent immigrants, in particular, will need a thorough explanation of the nature of counseling and may need time to consider whether it is consistent with their cultural values and practices (see Box 15.2).

When referrals are made for family counseling, the family should be provided with accurate information about agencies and practitioners, including addresses, phone numbers, specializations, and whether the agency adjusts fees to the client's ability to pay. Follow up with the family and find out what might help them to take action if they haven't followed through with the referral. For those who follow through, ask for feedback regarding the counseling facility for the benefit of future families.

The Nature of Family Counseling

In family counseling, problems are examined within the context of the family interactions, or system. Problems are viewed not as the result of individual issues but as the consequence of the complex dynamics that characterize every family system. Often, the family comes to a counselor expecting that the "problem child" will be fixed. The family counselor's first task is to assist family members to recognize that a family system is composed of a number of both positive and negative interlocking relationships. Family members must be helped to understand their contribution to the maintenance of the identified client's symptoms. Finally, the family must agree to work together to change their situation.

Working with the entire family is advantageous in many ways. It enables the counselor to establish a more accurate perspective on the problem. The counselor may discover, for example, that what has been described by a 15-year-old son as cruel authoritarianism is a belated attempt by his parents to impose control over curfew limits and homework completion. A mother who describes herself as loving and affectionate may truly believe she is so—in comparison with her own unavailable and hostile mother. But the objections and disagreements of her family can be a way to clarify the words *loving* and *affectionate* and the expectations that surround them. Watching arguments in progress provides the counselor with a picture of the family's interaction that no series of descriptions could convey. In addition to enhancing problem identification, working with the whole family makes problem solving more cohesive, efficient, and timely. The outcome of family counseling depends on many variables, including the therapist's skill, the willingness of family members to exert effort and take risks, their willingness and ability to take responsibility for their behavior, and the range of coping skills they possess.

Strategies in Family Counseling

In the 1950s Gregory Bateson and others at the Mental Research Institute (MRI) developed a communication framework for working with families. Focusing on the family as a system (see Chapter 4), family counseling attends to the interactional styles of family members. Notable members of this group include Paul Watzlawick, John Weakland, and Don Jackson, as well as Virginia Satir and Jay Haley. Jackson, Satir, and Haley, and to some extent Murray Bowen and Salvador Minuchin and most other system family theorists, share four core concepts: (1) two major tasks are involved in the process of forming and maintaining a relationship, deciding what the rules of the relationship are and negotiating who actually makes the decisions regarding the rules; (2) the exchange of messages is accomplished through the task of setting rules and negotiating who has control over the rules; (3) the basic elements of the interactional process are the messages that form the substance of communications between people in the relationship; and, finally, (4) messages have two major aspects, the communication (the content of the message) and the metacommunication (the message about the message).

Thus family counselors attempt to understand the family by analyzing the communication and metacommunication aspects of the interactions. They identify problems through observation of the family's interactions, including such behaviors as seating arrangement, control of the children, who speaks most and least frequently, and so forth. They also sometimes employ techniques that include "paradoxical messages" and "prescribing the symptom." Paradoxical messages direct the family to do something that seems opposite to the stated goal; they are particularly useful with resistant families. For example, a family might be directed to refuse to cooperate during a session. The family has the choice of either cooperating (to maintain control vis-à-vis the counselor) or continuing their lack of cooperation and thereby give the counselor therapeutic leverage because they are following a directive.

The counselor who prescribes the symptom asks the family to continue their problem behavior, perhaps because "I don't yet understand it well enough." This technique is also beneficial with resistant families because in order to resist they must change their problem behavior. Relabeling or reforming consists of describing the problem behavior in such a way that makes it sound positive. A therapist might relabel an adolescent's use of foul language, for example, as a creative way of directing her parents' attention away from her school performance. After establishing that this teen is creative and purposeful, the therapist can draw upon her creativity to devise more effective means of getting what she wants.

Other family counselors focus on the structural context of the family interaction. They examine the organizational dynamics and boundaries both within the family system and between the family and the environment. Boundaries can be seen as a manifestation of the rules and regulations governing the system and separating the system from its environment. How the family regulates and modifies these boundaries is of interest to the family counselor. Two fundamental concepts are "differentiation of self" and "triangulation." A chronic high level of anxiety within a family causes tension to escalate. If unchecked, this tension eventually exceeds the capacity of the family's normal coping mechanisms, and a variety of family symptoms result. Differentiation of self is the individual's ability to discriminate between emotional and cognitive processes and to achieve independence from the emotional climate of the family. Highly differentiated family members can respond to conflict on a cognitive level on the basis of conscious beliefs and values, whereas the undifferentiated individual responds in an emotional and unstable manner. The greater the differentiation of self, the more effectively the family member can cope with anxiety. The failure of family members to differentiate is termed "fusion." Fusion, that is, a low level of differentiation, is characterized by inability to separate emotional from intellectual interaction.

Poorly differentiated family members are more likely to be part of a family triangle. Triangulation occurs when the anxiety in a two-person system is more than the system can handle and a third person is engaged in the system to diffuse the tension. Triangulation is a specific type of enmeshment (see Chapter 4). For example, to diffuse marital tension, the mother establishes a close "friendship" with her daughter and together they exclude the father. Triangulation generally increases problematic communication within a family.

As a family moves through the stages of the family life cycle (see Chapter 4), it changes structurally to accommodate changing roles and tasks. Such adaptation occurs through the renegotiation and modification of boundaries. Clear boundaries fall between enmeshed and disengaged boundaries and allow for optimal functioning. Family subsystem boundaries that are pervasively enmeshed or consistently rigid, especially those between the parent and child subsystems, are the primary basis for dysfunction.

By identifying the boundaries and transactional patterns within the family system and subsystems, the family counselor affects the goal of therapy, which is to change the structure of the family so that it is more consistent with the developmental needs of its members. One technique to do this is to present the family with a scenario and assign roles to the individual members. The roles require them to act out new patterns of behavior. This changes the behavior patterns that support the symptom and alters the sequences between family members, thereby restructuring the family system.

There are several ways in which a family counselor might work with the Carter family of Chapter 4. For example, the counselor might help the Carter family identify the sequence of acts in which the family's problems are embedded. The counselor would note the relationships among Lois's constant negative affect, lack of eye contact with her husband, fatigue, and refusal to ask for what she wants and needs; Doug's telling Jason, "If you . . . , I'll. . . ." without ever following through, his black-and-white views of Jason, the "bad one," and Christie, the "good one," and his sarcastic tone when he talks to his wife; Jason's feeble attempts to cheer up his mother, his belligerence toward his father, and his rapt attention whenever his parents interact; Christie's subtle teasing of Jason, her aloof primness when asked a question, and her fingernail biting. The counselor might attempt to understand how these behaviors maintain or threaten the power balance in the family and might view each symptom as a tactic employed by one person to deal with the others. He or she would see Jason's acting out as his way of defining his relationship with his parents: Jason sets the pace and they respond. The counselor might direct Jason to continue to misbehave at school and at home (assuming his misbehaviors are not dangerous or harmful) and ask him to keep a log of each misbehavior, noting why he chose each behavior when he did. This use of symptom prescription gives Jason the choice of cooperating with the others, setting the stage for change, or resisting the therapist by reducing his symptoms.

In another approach the counselor would focus on helping each of the Carters to separate emotionality from objective thinking. He or she would begin by looking for clear and well-defined boundaries between family members. The counselor might view Doug's anger at his wife and his feelings of inadequacy as overriding his cognitive knowledge of the importance of consistency and consequences in discipline. He or she might view Lois's guilty feelings as an indication of her inability to separate her own feelings and behavior from those of her son. The unexpressed anger between Lois and Doug is diffused and focused on Jason, with the result that Doug feels excluded by both his wife and his son. The counselor might help the couple to express and explain their feelings to each other objectively. As the process of triangulation diminished, the members of the family would achieve a greater degree of differentiation.

Another approach would acknowledge the sociocultural context in which the Carter family operates. The counselor might conceptualize the problem in terms of two stressors: a developmental transition (Jason is entering adolescence) and an idiosyncratic problem (Lois is chronically depressed). The family's dysfunction is a result of their failure to renegotiate boundaries in response to these stressors. In light of the enmeshed boundaries between Jason and his mother and the lack of a defined parental subset, the counselor might work to increase the strength of the parental subset by engaging Doug and Lois in tasks together. He or she might ask Jason and Christie to reverse roles as a means of unbalancing the homeostasis and creating an opportunity for change.

Each of these strategies or techniques shares an emphasis on the family as a system. A systems framework is often a major foundation for family counseling. But in what other ways might we be helpful to families with youth at risk? We now consider alternatives to family counseling.

ALTERNATIVES AND ADJUNCTS TO FAMILY COUNSELING

For a number of reasons, family counseling is not always the best way to pursue change. Families can gain the support, knowledge, and skills they need to address their problems through a number of other channels. As mentioned earlier (see Chapter 12), practitioners are more likely to be helpful when they implement interventions that have been empirically supported. Unfortunately, even fewer family-based approaches have been submitted to an expert panel scientific review than individual or school-based interventions. Kumpfer and Adler (2003), in an extensive review of reviews, identified a number of principles of effective family-focused programs to help practitioners judge whether a program is worth selecting. Counselors can then adapt programs that best match their clients age, gender, developmental level, or culture (see Box 15.3). In this section we describe several alternatives to family counseling.

▲ Box 15.3

Principles of Effective Family-Focused Interventions

1. *Recruitment and Retention.* Family recruitment and retention (in the range of 80 to 85%) is possible with the use of incentives—food, child care, transportation—plus rewards for homework completion, attendance, and graduation.

2. *Scope and Content.* Comprehensive, multicomponent interventions that address family relations, communication, and parental monitoring are more effective in modifying risk or protective factors than are single-component programs.

3. *Target.* Family-focused programs that emphasize family strengths, resilience, and protective factors are more effective for improving family relationships than child-focused or parent-focused programs.

4. *Focus.* Family programs tailored to the cultural traditions of the family are most effective when they produce cognitive, affective, and behavioral changes in family dynamics or the environment.

5. *Training Methods.* Skills training methods that use interactive techniques—role play, active modeling, family and skill practice sessions—along with homework activities and videos or CDs of effective and ineffective parenting skills increase client satisfaction and program effectiveness compared to didactic lecturing and simple discussion.

6. *Trainer or Leader.* The effectiveness of the program is highly tied to the trainer's personal efficacy and confidence, affective characteristics of genuineness, warmth, humor, and empathy, and ability to structure sessions and be directive.

7. *Parent/Family Dysfunction.* When parents are very dysfunctional, interventions beginning early in the life cycle are more effective. In addition, increased dosage or intensity (25 to 50 hours of intervention) is necessary with higher-risk families than with low-risk families (5 to 24 hours).

8. *Timing and Development.* Family programs should be age and developmentally appropriate with new versions available as children mature; they need to address appropriate risk and protective factors when the family is receptive to change.

9. *Empowerment.* Developing a collaborative process where family members are encouraged to find their own solutions is effective and also builds a supportive relationship and reduces parent resistance and dropout.

Source: Adapted from Kumpfer and Adler, 2003.

Multisystemic Therapy

Multisystemic therapy (MST) has emerged as a leading intervention for adolescent delinquent behavior (Henggeler, 1999). Working from a socioecological model of human development, MST counselors focus on providing parents with skills to effectively monitor and discipline their children and on increasing family cohesion. MST discourages continued contact with peers who provide reinforcement for delinquent behavior; it promotes contact with prosocial peers (Henggeler, 1999; Huey, Henggeler, Brondino, & Pickrel, 2000). When treating conduct problems in young people, helpers must involve multiple systems in treatment and should attend to negative or positive roles that peers play in undermining or facilitating intervention.

The Family Checkup

The Family Checkup (FCU) is a brief family intervention developed by our friends and colleagues Tom Dishion and Elizabeth Stormshak at the University of Oregon (Dishion et al., 2002; Stormshak & Dishion, 2002). The FCU is based on principles of motivational interviewing (Miller & Rollnick, 2002; see also Chapter 8) and is designed for families experiencing mild to severe problems.

The FCU consists of three sessions conducted with the parent(s) or caregiver(s) and the child or children. The first session is an interview that takes place in the home when possible so that the family is observed in their usual and familiar setting. The second session consists of an assessment of multiple dimensions of the family, including communication, discipline and other aspects of parenting, characteristics of each family member, functioning in home and school settings, and peer relationships. In the third session, the family is presented with feedback that is designed to facilitate several goals: supporting and enhancing positive parenting by identifying strengths and weaknesses; reducing harm by identification of impending, serious events, such as a suicide attempt or school expulsion, and preventing such problems through provision of concrete recommendations; tailoring feedback to maximize motivation for change; and supporting motivation for change through identification of family strengths and resources. During the feedback session, parents provide a self-assessment of their family, and the clinician clarifies and contributes to this assessment using the information gained through the prior assessment stage. This session culminates in the collaborative development of a menu of options that emerge logically from the assessment and feedback. The menu of options targets changes that the family perceives as important and includes specific behaviors that the parents want to engage in on their own (e.g., meeting the parents of the children's friends, initiating Family Game Night once a week). The menu may also include parent education, parent training, support groups, or individual, couples, or family therapy.

Because this three-step model places a strong emphasis on forming a trusting relationship with the family and collaborative identification of concerns, families who may have initially resisted a recommendation for family therapy are often willing to pursue this option after a Family Checkup. There are multiple positive outcomes associated with the Family Checkup, including reductions in family conflict, increased parental monitoring, and reduced substance use and problem behavior over time (Dishion, Nelson, & Kavanagh, 2003; Dishion et al., 2002; Stormshak & Dishion, 2002).

Multidimensional Treatment Foster Care

Current research supports multiple interventions aimed first at the family but also toward other parts of the environment. Behavior modification procedures used in halfway houses, for instance, have had immediate results but produce few long-lasting changes after teenagers return to their natural environments. Association with prosocial peers and inclusion in a functional, well-adjusted family are both key factors in socializing youth. Close interaction with deviant peers, even while in a treatment program, often increases problematic behavior (Dishion, McCord, & Poulin, 1999). Youth outside of a functional family system are also less likely to thrive.

The Multidimensional Treatment Foster Care (MTFC) program combats these two risk factors by recruiting community foster families to be members of a treatment team that monitors daily family and child activities, monitors peer associations, and tracks school behavior of the high-risk, delinquent youth in the program (Chamberlin, Fisher, & Moore, 2002). These high-risk young people might otherwise be placed in institutional settings with little intervention or monitoring. The program illustrates how multidimensional and ecologically oriented interventions can be very effective for some of our most at-risk adolescents.

The program responds to the whole ecology of children's lives. The foster parents receive increased financial compensation in comparison to general foster parents, are considered to be primary members of the treatment team, receive more than 20 hours of pre-service training, attend weekly training and technical assistance meetings, and have 24-hour, 7-days-a-week on-call access to psychological support staff. The children in the program, who would otherwise be placed in an institutional setting, receive services within a structured, supportive, teaching-oriented family environment; are closely supervised with regard to their whereabouts, activities, and peer associations; receive daily monitoring of their participation and progress in school; receive social skills building from a skills trainer; and receive individual therapy. The young person's family of origin receives intensive training and support, has 24-hour, 7-days-a-week access to program staff, receives family therapy, and is provided with aftercare services (e.g., ongoing support and consultation). The young person's school is involved in a collaborative support meeting to set up a system before the youth is enrolled and receives support monitoring the child or young adolescent's behavior at school through use of a school "card" on which attitude, homework completion, and attendance are all evaluated. The performance ratings on the school card are checked nightly by MTFC foster parents and are linked with a three-level point system to reinforce positive behavior and decrease problematic behavior.

In follow-up studies MTFC youth spent 60% fewer days incarcerated than control participants, had 50% fewer subsequent arrests, ran away from the program 3 times less often, returned to live with parents or relatives more often, and had significantly less hard drug use (Chamberlin et al., 2002). The program cost (nearly $130 per day) is substantially less than standard youth detention (Chamberlin et al., 2002).

Parent Education and Training

Parent training in child management is a promising family intervention strategy (Kosterman et al., 2000; Kumpfer & Tait, 2000). It is most effective, however, if parents learn to recognize and deal with the signs of risk before their child reaches adolescence. Training in behavior modification, in management of rewards and consequences, and in communication skills is most effective with younger children whose behavioral problems have not yet developed into serious misbehavior. If children are already extremely negative, parent training is relatively less effective in reducing the children's offenses, perhaps because the behaviors have already become part of the young persons' repertoire because they have already identified with deviant peers or because they have achieved a high level of autonomy (Dishion, Capaldi, & Yoerger, 1999).

Parent education and training refers to programs, support services, and resources offered to parents and caregivers that are designed to provide support and increase skills and efficacy for raising a family in a healthy and constructive manner. Teachers, counselors, and other human service professionals can often provide effective prevention and intervention in the form of parent education and training. The parents of a student who is acting out sexually may shy away from discussing sex, birth control, and sexually transmitted diseases. The parents of a student who doesn't turn in homework may lack a consistent system for monitoring school progress. The parents of a student who is belligerent and aggressive may have lost control of their child. These issues and others may be effectively addressed by educating parents on dealing with specific aspects of their children's behavior. Family-oriented programs designed to prevent chemical dependency and to strengthen families by teaching parents behavioral management, effective discipline, sex education, nutrition, and family budgeting can be very effective (Ashery, Robertson, & Kumpfer, 1998; Kumpfer, 1998; Kumpfer & Alvarado, 1995). Cultural appropriateness is critical to the success of parent training programs (Kumpfer & Alvarado, 1995; Norwood, Atkinson, Tellez, & Saldana, 1997). Three useful programs are the Effective Black Parenting Program, Los Niños Bien Educados (http://www.ciccparenting.org), and Positive Indian Parenting (http://www.hcc.ohio-state.edu/famlife/nnfr/ctf/curricul/97.html). A fourth well-researched program, Family Effectiveness Training, including bicultural effectiveness training (BET; Szapocznik, Santisteban, Kurtines, Perez-Vidal, & Hervis, 1984; Szapocznik, Santisteban, Rio, Perez-Vidal, & Kurtines, 1986b), is discussed later. In addition, an important focus for the teacher, counselor, or parent-trainer in getting acquainted with the family is to understand the family culture, values, identity, and practices. Expectations regarding child behavior and accepted modes of child discipline are often associated with culture although level of acculturation influences traditional values and practices (Crunkilton, Paz, & Boyle, 2005; Harvey & Hill, 2004).

Before we describe specific parent education and training programs, a few basic principles of parenting can go a long way to help parents be more effective. Two of our "favorite" parenting principles are: the Premack principle and logical consequences.

The Premack principle.   The Premack principle, or Grandma's Rule, is a relatively simple and highly effective guide that parents can quickly put to good use (J. J. McWhirter, 1988). The Premack principle tells us that "for any pair of responses, the more probable one will reinforce the less probable one" (Premack, 1965, p. 132). In other words, behaviors that youngsters are quite likely to perform (playing videogames, riding a bike, watching television, talking on the telephone) can serve as reinforcements for those behaviors that they are less likely to perform (completing homework, drying dishes, caring for younger siblings, cleaning their rooms). As Grandma might put it: First you work, then you play. The parents' task is to identify what their child wants to do and then require that a less-favored activity occur first: "Clean your desk and then we can play a game." "Pick up the room before you go out to play." or "Do the dishes before you watch television."

Application of the Premack principle is most effective when parents break down tasks into subtasks (e.g., clean desk; put away all loose books and papers; put away all crayons, pens, and pencils; dust desktop; water plant on desk), and sometimes it is also helpful to reward the performance of each subtask. Frequent small rewards provide more effective reinforcement than infrequent, large rewards. Parents should provide rewards immediately after the behavior is accomplished, reward the behavior only after it occurs, and the reward should always be accompanied with verbal praise. Parents will hear rationalizations ("But my show will be over by the time I finish the dishes!"), and they are guaranteed to hear many more if they give in to them.

Logical consequences.   Carrying out a system of logical consequences not only encourages children to take responsibility for their behavior but can greatly reduce the amount of arguing (see Box 15.4). Consider the Carter family of Chapter 4. Doug Carter is unhappy with the fact that Jason stays up very late on weekends watching television. Because he stays up so late, Jason sleeps late the following morning, leaving his chores undone until the afternoon or forgetting them altogether. Jason's behavior is only one of the problems here; the other problem is that his behavior has no logical consequences. A logical consequence of staying up very late is to be quite tired when one is roused from sleep to do one's chores. By allowing Jason to sleep late, his parents condone his late-night TV habits. By requiring Jason to get up and do his chores no matter what time he goes to bed, his parents would give Jason responsibility for deciding how late to stay up (reducing the likelihood of a "But I'm 13 years old!" argument) and still have the satisfaction of knowing his work is done (reducing the likelihood of a "You live in this house too" argument).

If logical consequences are to work, parents must be prepared to apply them without fail. Table 15.1 provides some sample behaviors and their logical consequences. Each consequence is modified according to the severity of the misbehavior and the number of times the behavior recurs after consequences have been applied. If a child continues to leave toys about the house, for example, the parents may remove the toys for 2 or more days at a time. Children should always know the logical consequences of their misbehaviors and be informed when the consequences are changing. With older children, parents may draw up a contract that specifies, for example, rules for using the family car and consequences of failure to follow those rules. By signing the contract, families formalize the agreement and establish a clear standard of conduct.

Family Effectiveness Training

José Szapocznik and his associates (1986a, 1989, 2000) present a prevention model for Hispanic families of preadolescents who are at risk for drug abuse. This program is based on the premise that intergenerational family conflict related to the acculturation process may exacerbate existing maladaptive patterns of interaction in families and contribute to drug use. It is one of only a few empirically tested programs that directly address cultural differences. The three components of family effectiveness training (FET) are designed to change maladaptive interactional patterns and to enhance the family's ability to resolve intergenerational and intercultural conflict.

The first component, family development, helps the family to negotiate their children's transition to adolescence. Family members learn constructive communication skills and take increased responsibility for their own behaviors. Parents develop the skills to direct their

▲ Box 15.4

Eat Your Dinner!

Parents once brought a 4-year-old to us who stubbornly clenched her teeth and refused to eat when she didn't like the dinner she was served. She often threw her food on the floor. Her parents responded in a number of ways—arguing with the little girl, arguing with each other, threatening the girl, or rewarding each bite—and typically concluded by cleaning up the mess and providing an alternative meal. Mealtime had become "a living hell."

At first the parents were horrified when we informed them that the logical consequence of such behavior was to let her go without eating until the next meal was served. But finally they conceded that she really would not be harmed by her hunger pains and agreed to try this approach. Upon their daughter's next refusal to eat, they explained to her that if she threw her dinner on the floor, she would get nothing to eat until breakfast. When she promptly and predictably flipped her dinner to the floor, her parents were prepared. They didn't yell or argue or rush to clean it up. Instead, they calmly reminded her that it would be a long time until breakfast and finished their own dinner before attending to the mess she had made. She kept them awake most of the night with her tearful cries, but they didn't back down.

The next day she ate breakfast and lunch without incident (lunch, eaten at day care, had never been a problem), and dinner the next evening was relatively peaceful. She complained about the food, but she ate most of it. The next evening she once again overturned her plate and endured the same logical consequence. She cried for only 2 hours that night. Two months later her parents reported that she had never again overturned her plate and was eating at least a small portion of everything they served her.

TABLE 15.1   **Sample Logical Consequences**

Action	Consequence
Leaving toys out	The toys are taken away for one day; only one toy allowed out at a time
Talking on the phone too long	All calls are limited to 3 minutes for 2 days
Fighting over a bike	The bike is taken away for a day and the children must play peacefully together for 30 minutes
Violating family curfew	Staying home the next evening or weekend
Stealing from a store	Apologizing to the store manager; returning the item; working to earn the cost of the item and giving the money to the store, a church, or a charity organization

children in a democratic rather than an authoritarian style. This component also includes drug education for the parents so that they can effectively teach their children about drugs.

The second component, bicultural effectiveness training (BET; Szapocznik et al., 1984, 1986b), is designed to bring about family change by temporarily placing the blame for the family's problems on the cultural conflict within the family. Alliances are established between family members through the development of bicultural skills and mutual appreciation of the values of their two cultures. BET helps the family handle cultural conflicts more effectively and reduces the likelihood that conflicts will occur. BET is itself an excellent parent training program of obvious value to families of nonmajority cultures.

The third component of FET is brief strategic family counseling (Szapocznik & Williams, 2000), the most experiential aspect of this model. The FET counselor meets with the family for 13 two-hour sessions and assists the family in addressing conflicts and improving relationships. The FET model may be modified to deal with issues other than drug use. One final parent education and training program is now described. This one is based on European American norms, but it has potential benefits for other cultural groups as well.

Parent Effectiveness Training

Parent effectiveness training (PET; Gordon, 1970, 1977) is a method of parent training based on two principles stressed by the psychologist Carl Rogers: unconditional positive regard and empathy. A fundamental premise of the method is that everyone in the family can "win," with power negotiated and shared by parents and children. Although the program was originally designed for parents of problem children, its contents are also valuable for parents of well-functioning children. The PET program teaches parents skills in confrontation, conflict resolution, active listening, and giving I-messages. Training provides parents with an opportunity to practice and refine those skills throughout the sessions. These skills enable parents to communicate more effectively with their children and to resolve problems constructively (J. J. McWhirter & Kahn, 1974; Wood & Davidson, 1993).

A PET training course is typically 24 hours in duration, ordinarily presented in eight weekly 3-hour sessions. Brief presentations, group discussions, audiotapes, dyads for skill practice, role playing, workbook assignments, and textbook reading are among the training methods used. Gordon continues to develop new applications for his ideas (1989), and in 1997 he published a home study version of his program (see Gordon, 2000). Core components of the program include problem ownership, active listening, I-messages, and mutual problem solving.

Problem ownership. In accord with the PET model, parents are trained to identify whether the parent, the child, or the relationship (both parent and child) have ownership of the problem. Determining who owns the problem sets the stage for problem resolution. The child owns the problem when he or she is blocked in satisfying a need but his or her behavior does not interfere with the satisfaction of the parent's needs. A parent owns the problem when the child's attempts to satisfy a need interfere with the parent's needs. The relationship owns the problem when neither the child nor the parent is able to satisfy his or her needs. Problem solving is achieved via three different pathways; the choice of pathway depends on problem ownership. Active listening is used when the child owns the problem, sending I-messages is used when the parent owns the problem, and mutual problem solving is used when both own the problem.

Active listening. The purpose of active listening is to communicate a deep sense of acceptance and understanding to the child. The parent tries to understand what the child is feeling and to communicate empathy to the child. The affective and emotional dimensions of the communication process are reflected in eye contact, tone of voice, and body movement. If parents reflect their children's feelings accurately, the children will feel understood, freed from the emotion of the problem, and better able to deal with the problem. When children amplify and fully express their thoughts and feelings at the heart of the problem, they are moving toward the desired goal and often are able to suggest their own solutions. Sometimes active listening helps children accept an unchangeable situation (e.g., the family must move to a new apartment) and gives them a chance to get their feelings out and experience genuine acceptance.

Active listening requires getting inside the child, viewing the world through his or her eyes, and communicating that understanding. Essentially, then, the parent must respond to both the words that the child uses and the feelings that lie behind the words. The following examples demonstrate the skill.

Child 1 (crying): Tommy took my truck away from me.

Parent 1: You sure feel bad about that. You don't like it when he does that.

Child 1: Yeah, it makes me mad.

Child 2: Boy, do I have a lousy teacher this year. I don't like her. She's an old grouch.

Parent 2: Sounds like you are really disappointed with your teacher.

Child 2: I sure am; I miss being in Mrs. Chang's class. She liked me.

In each illustration, the parent has accurately understood the child, and the child has responded by verifying the parent's accuracy and elaborating on the feeling. Each interchange sets the stage for a continued and meaningful conversation.

Parents should never use active listening to draw out and then put down the child ("Oh, so you want to flunk and go back with Mrs. Chang, do you?"). Parents sometimes begin active listening but subsequently slam the door shut because their own attitudes get in the way or because of lack of time. At other times, parents simply echo a message to the child without empathy. Over time, this will result in demoralization and mistrust.

Sending I-messages. When the parent determines that he or she owns the problem—that is, his or her needs are directly and tangibly affected—there are several possible responses. For example, the parent can modify the environment, him- or herself, or the child directly. With younger children, changing the environment often promotes a change in the child's behavior and solves the parent's problem. Such changes may include enriching the environment (bringing out crayons and paper or scheduling times for friends to come over and play), simplifying the environment (turning down or turning off the television or requiring that one activity be cleaned up before another is initiated), or substituting one activity for another (tag on the front lawn instead of wrestling in the living room).

Parents who own the problem may also decide to change themselves. For example, a father might decide that he will work on becoming more tolerant of noise in the house and will follow through and supervise his children more after asking them to do a task; a mother might reduce the amount of pressure she puts on her children to behave in a particular manner.

Finally, the parent can seek to modify the child directly. Sometimes parents use spanking or some other form of punishment, which may produce short-term compliance but is detrimental in the long term (Gershoff, 2002). Verbal punishment is also ineffective; it typically consists of derogatory labeling or put-down statements: "You are so lazy." "You are a real pest." "You are no good; you just want to be a mean person don't you!" This kind of communication is called "You-messages."

Rather than punishment or ineffective you-messages, a simple I-message is a powerful tool in modifying a child's behavior. In an I-message the adult clearly expresses to the child the problem and the feelings about the problem while letting the child know that the adult owns the problem. Often the child is willing to modify behavior based on the adult's feelings. An I-message is less apt to provoke rebellion and resistance, and it places the responsibility on the child for changing behavior. The following examples demonstrate the contrast between you-messages and I-messages.

You-message: You didn't do your chores this morning. You are so lazy and irresponsible!
I-message: I'm angry because you didn't do your chores.
Comment: The focus is on the problem of the chores and not on the character or personality of the child. The parent's feelings of annoyance and anger are not directly expressed in the you-message; the anger is clear and direct in the I-message.
You-message: Stop being such a pest. You're always interrupting your mother and me when we are talking.
I-message: I am frustrated with you because I want to finish my conversation with your mother and you keep interrupting us; this has been happening a lot lately.
Comment: The I-message communicates the parent's feelings, puts responsibility on the child for the behavior, and does not lower the child's self-esteem.

By sending an I-message, the adult anticipates that the child will understand the adult's problem, respect the adult's needs, and therefore discontinue acting in a negative way. Frequently an I-message is adequate for modifying the child's behavior. Occasionally it is necessary to follow the I-message with a change in the environment. For example, after communicating frustration at being interrupted, the father could require the child to go play in another room until he has finished the conversation with the child's mother.

Mutual problem solving.   Mutual problem solving is the PET strategy used when the problem is owned by both child and parent; that is, when the needs of both the child and the adult are being blocked by a problem. Too often solutions to problems and conflicts result in a win–lose situation. The loser (adult or child) feels defeated, and regardless of who loses the child is denied opportunities to develop behavior that is self-disciplined, sensitive to others, and inner directed.

Gordon (1970) recommends following a six step, no-lose method whenever an adult and a child encounter a conflict-of-needs situation. In this way the parent and the child can construct a solution that is acceptable to both of them. These steps are common to many problem-solving models.

1. *Identify and define the conflict.* It is important to determine whether the disagreement is actually over the issue at hand. Sometimes the conflict is really over a different matter and the current problem reflects another concern. Both parent and child need to be clear on the nature of the conflict.

2. *Generate possible solutions.* Both parent and child need to indicate as many alternative solutions as possible. The child should be encouraged and praised for identifying solutions even when they don't seem feasible.
3. *Evaluate the alternative solutions.* The feasibility and potential effectiveness of each solution is critically evaluated. Both the adult and the child should consider the consequences of the various solutions and decide which solutions they can live with. The parent does not stop being the parent at this step. For example, the parent should not enter into false "equal" arrangements in which the child also picks out the mother's clothes or the child gets to use profanity every time the parent does.
4. *Decide on and get commitments for the most acceptable solution.* Both must agree to commit themselves to the solution, including modifying their own behavior as needed.
5. *Work out ways of implementing the solution.* The adult and the child must agree upon who is going to do what and when it is to be done.
6. *Follow up and evaluate how the solution worked.* After an agreed-upon time limit, parent and child review the solution to determine satisfaction with it. If the parent is consistent about following up when the problem and the solution are "easy," the child will be more trusting and willing to try out solutions that demand more risk or effort on the child's part.

By engaging the child in the process of mutually solving the problem, over time, both parent and child will be more satisfied, and the child will learn to anticipate problems and generate solutions independently. Thus conflicts can be resolved in a healthy manner that builds a relationship that is mutually satisfying, constructive, and loving.

Effective parenting derives from a philosophy in which respect for the child is uppermost. This means respecting individuality, uniqueness, complexity, idiosyncratic potential, and capacity for making choices. This philosophy is expressed in effective communication. Of course, these skills are just as important to the effective teacher or counselor as they are to parents (Gordon, 1989). The PET program, like all parent training programs, reflects a particular set of values and assumptions. Exploration of parent values is an important prerequisite to carrying out any parent training program.

In addition to the multiple parent education and training programs just reviewed, it is important to consider programs specifically for other caretakers—such as guardians and foster parents—who are often underrepresented in the family intervention treatment literature. Foster parents and foster families play key roles in many young people's lives and may play a critical role in the lives of high-risk youth.

Parent Support Groups

The final alternative or adjunct to family counseling is participation in a parent support group. These groups are also very useful to foster parents and others serving in primary caretaking roles. Many parents would benefit from experiencing a sense of accompaniment with other parents who have "been there" or are currently "in the same boat." Each new generation of parents deals with issues that their own parents never imagined. Your grandparents, for example, are unlikely to have had a son (i.e., your father) who came home with a pierced nipple. Many of the underlying issues are the same, however, and are related to the movement through the family life cycle: dealing with stress, change, loss, and anger; problems of communication, discipline, and authority; and passing down values and traditions. Especially in light of the decline of the extended family network, a parent support group is an ideal way for parents to express their concerns and learn what other parents have experienced and attempted. It also allows parents to share the pain and frustration as well as the joys and successes of raising children. Parent support groups are available through local churches, YMCAs, schools, counseling agencies, day-care centers, and workplaces. Many areas of the country also have local parent crisis lines or Parents Anonymous groups, which can provide information about parent support groups.

One parent support group that is active throughout the United States is ToughLove. ToughLove is a self-help group for parents and guardians of teenagers who are uncontrollable, addicted, abusive, or otherwise in trouble with the school or the law. With more than 1,500 groups, this organization provides ongoing support, assistance in crises, and referrals to professionals, as well as many practical ideas for helping teenagers stop their self-destructive behavior. Parents are encouraged to make their own plans for addressing their teenager's behavior. The group functions as a sounding board, a source of suggestions, and a backup support team. One ToughLove mother we know enlisted the help of other ToughLove parents in planning a constructive confrontation with her drug-abusing daughter. One of the other couples provided an alternate place for the daughter to stay for a week in case she decided she could not stay with her mother after the confrontation. The same mother had just posted fliers for a ToughLove parent in another part of the country whose runaway son had been seen locally.

Alateen and Al-Anon family groups are broad-based teen and family support groups that operate throughout the country. Teens or families of alcoholics meet together much like the members of Alcoholics Anonymous. Participating teens and families learn about alcoholism and are helped to achieve a loving detachment from the alcoholic, to increase their self-esteem and independence, and to rely on the group for encouragement and support. Through sharing their common problems, members of alcoholics' families discover that they are not alone and that they have the ability to cope with their situation.

Parent support groups can provide invaluable information and support for parents and guardians who feel hopeless, angry, and alone in dealing with the problems of their troubled children. ToughLove, Alateen, and Al-Anon provide support for family members who may feel trapped in an impossible situation. These are only three such groups; there are literally thousands of others. There are support groups for parents of children with problems ranging from spina bifida and cerebral palsy to bipolar disorder and schizophrenia. Teachers and counselors can assist families by keeping informed about these resources and by encouraging families to contact local chapters of these support groups. Refer to our website for more information, e-mail, and web addresses for many of the organizations mentioned.

CONCLUSION

A family systems framework is a realistic and viable way to view the problems of troubled children and adolescents. Too often work with an individual provides only partial solutions. All young people live in a montage of overlapping systems: families, schools, neighborhoods, larger communities, the nation. Family counselors address the family as a system in order to change dysfunctional patterns of behavior and communication. Parent training and parent support groups provide alternatives and adjuncts to family counseling. Counselors, teachers, and other helping professionals can be of invaluable assistance by providing these services or by helping families gain access to such programs.

REFERENCES

Aber, J. L., Jones, S. M., Brown, J. L., Chandry, N., & Samples, F. (1998). Resolving conflict creatively: Evaluating the developmental effects of a school-based violence prevention program in neighborhood and classroom context. *Development and Psychopathology, 10,* 187–213.

Achmon, J., Granek, M., Golomb, M., & Hart, J. (1998). Behavioral treatment of essential hypertension: A comparison between cognitive therapy and biofeedback of heart rate. *Psychosomatic Medicine, 51,* 152–164.

Adams, D., & Hamm, M. (1994). New designs for teaching and learning: *Promoting active learning in tomorrow's schools.* San Francisco: Jossey-Bass.

Adler, A. (1930). *The education of children.* South Bend, IN: Gateway.

Adler, A. (1964). *Social interest: A challenge to mankind.* New York: Capricorn.

Advocates for Youth. (1994). *Adolescent sexual behavior, pregnancy, and parenthood.* Washington, DC: Author. Retrieved July 8, 2002, from http://www.health.state.ok.us/program/ahd/FP2002.pdf.

Advocates for Youth and Sexuality Information & Education Council of the United States. (1999). *Poll on America's attitudes toward sexuality education.* Washington, DC: Hickman-Brown.

Aksamit, D. (1990). Mildly handicapped and at-risk students: The graying of the line. *Academic Therapy, 25,* 277–289.

Alan Guttmacher Institute. (1994). *Sex and America's teenagers.* New York: Author.

Alan Guttmacher Institute. (1999). *Teenage pregnancy: Overall trends and state-by-state information.* New York: Author.

Alan Guttmacher Institute. (2004). *Parents' beliefs about condoms and oral contraceptives.* Retrieved September 28, 2005, from www.agi-usa.org/pubs/journals/3605004.pdf.

Albee, G. W. (1995, February). The answer is prevention. *Psychology Today,* 60–64.

Alessi, N. E., McManus, M., Brickman, A., & Grapentine, L. (1984). Suicidal behavior among serious juvenile offenders. *American Journal of Psychiatry, 141,* 286–287.

Algozzine, B., & Kaye, P. (Eds.). (2002). *Preventing problem behaviors: A handbook of successful prevention strategies.* Thousand Oaks, CA: Corwin Press.

Allen, M., & Ashbaker, Betty, Y. (2004). Strengthening schools: Involving paraprofessionals in crisis prevention and intervention. *Intervention in School and Clinic, 39*(3), 139–146.

Allen, M., Burt, K., Bryan, E., Carter, D., Orsi, R., & Durkan, L. (2002). School counselors' preparation for and participation in crisis intervention. *Professional School Counseling 6*(2), 96–102.

Allen, M., Jerome, A., White, A., Marston, S., Lamb, S., Pope, D., & Rawlins, C. (2002). The preparation of school psychologists for crisis intervention. *Psychology in the Schools, 39,* 427–439.

Allsopp, D. H., Santos, K. E., & Linn, R. (2000). Collaborating to teach prosocial skills. *Intervention in School and Clinic, 35*(3), 141–146.

Ambrosio, T., & Schiraldi, V. (1997). *From classrooms to cellblocks: A national perspective.* Washington, DC: The Justice Policy Institute.

Ameri, A. (1999). A decade and a half later, still a crude drug with underappreciated toxicity, *Pediatrics, 109,* 284–290.

American College of Obstetricians and Gynecologists. (1993). Special needs of pregnant teens. *ACOG patient education pamphlet no. AP103.* Washington, DC: Author.

American Psychiatric Association. (2000). *Diagnostic and statistical manual of mental disorders* (4th ed., text rev.). Washington, DC: Author.

American Psychological Association Presidential Task Force on Violence and the Family. (1996). *Violence and the family.* Washington, DC: Author.

American Psychological Association Task Force on Psychological Intervention Guidelines. (1995). *Template for developing guidelines: Interventions for mental disorders and psychological aspects of physical disorders.* Washington. DC: Author.

American Social Health Association. (1995). *Gallup study: Teenagers know more than adults about STDs, but STD knowledge among both groups is low.* Research Triangle Park, NC: The Association.

Amrein, A. L., & Berliner, D. C. (2002, March 28). High-stakes testing, uncertainty, and student learning. *Education Policy Analysis Archives*, 10(18). Retrieved July 1, 2002, from http://epaa.asu.edu/epaa/v10n18/.

Anderegg, M. L., & Vergason, G. A. (1992). Preparing teachers for their legal responsibilities in facing school-age suicide. *Teacher Education and Special Education*, 15, 295–299.

Anderson, C. A., & Dill, K. E. (2000). Violent video games can increase aggression. *Journal of Personality and Social Psychology*, 78(4), 772–790.

Anderson, J. D. (1994, March–April). Breaking the silence: Creating safe schools for gay youth. *Student Assistance Journal*, 21–23.

Anderson, S., Cavanagh, J., Hartman, C., & Leonard-Wright, B. (2001). *Executive excess 2001: Layoffs, tax rebates, the gender gap*. Boston, MA: Institute for Policy Studies and United for a Fair Economy.

Annie E. Casey Foundation. (2005). *KIDS COUNT databook*. Retrieved November 8, 2005, from www.aecf.org/kidscount/sld/databook/jsp.

Annis, H. M., Schober, R., & Kelly, E. (1996). Matching addiction outpatient counseling to client readiness for change: The role of structured relapse prevention counseling. *Experimental and Clinical Psychopharmacology*, 4(1), 37–45.

Anooshian, L .J. (2005). Violence and aggression in the lives of homeless children: A review. *Aggression and Violent Behavior*, 10, 129–152.

Ansley, L. (1997, August 13–14). Just keeps getting worse. *USA Weekend*, p. 5.

Apter, T. (1990). *Altered loves: Mothers and daughters during adolescence*. New York: St. Martin's Press.

Araki, C. T., Takeshita, C., & Kadomoto, L. (1989). *Research results and final report for the dispute management in the school project*. Honolulu, HI: University of Hawaii at Manoa, Program on Conflict Resolution. (ERIC Document No. ED312750)

Arbona, C. (2000). The development of academic achievement in school aged children: Precursors to career development. In R. Lent & S. Brown (Eds.), *Handbook of counseling psychology* (3rd ed., pp. 270–309). New York: Wiley.

Arendell, T. (1995). *Fathers and divorce*. Thousand Oaks, CA: Sage.

Arnold, D. S., O'Leary, S. G., Wolff, L. S., & Acker, M. M. (1993). The parenting scale: A measure of dysfunctional parenting in discipline situations. *Psychological Assessment*, 5(2), 137–144.

Arnold, M. S. (1995). Exploding the myths: African-American families at promise. In B. B. Swadener & S. Lubeck (Eds.), *Children and families "at promise"* (pp. 143–162). Albany, NY: State University of New York Press.

Arreaga-Mayer, C. (1998). Increasing active student responding and improving academic performance through classwide peer tutoring. *Intervention in School and Clinic*, 34(2), 89–94, 117.

Ashery, R., Robertson, E., & Kumpfer, K. (Eds.). (1998). *Drug abuse prevention through family interventions*. Rockville, MD: National Institutes of Health.

Astone, N., & McLanahan, S. (1991). Family structure, parental practices, and high school completion. *American Sociological Review*, 56, 309–320.

August, G. J., Realmuto, G. M., Winters, K. C., & Hektner, J. M. (2001). Prevention of adolescent drug abuse: Targeting high-risk children with a multifaceted intervention model—The early risers "skills for success" program. *Applied and Preventive Psychology*, 10, 135–154.

Ballard, M., Argus, T., & Remley, T. P. (1999). Bullying and school violence: A proposed prevention program. *NASSP Bulletin*, 83, 38–46.

Band, S. R., & Harpold, J. A. (1999, September). School violence: Lessons learned. *FBI: Law Enforcement Bulletin*, 68, 9–16.

Bandura, A. (1973). *Aggression: A social learning analysis*. Englewood Cliffs, NJ: Prentice-Hall.

Bandura, A. (1977). *Social learning theory*. Englewood Cliffs, NJ: Prentice-Hall.

Bandura, A. (1986). *Social foundations of thought and action*. Englewood Cliffs, NJ: Prentice-Hall.

Bandura, A. (1993). Perceived self-efficacy in cognitive development and functioning. *Educational Psychologist*, 28(2),117–148.

Bandura, A., Pastorelli, C., Barbaranelli, C., & Caprara, G. V. (1999). Self efficacy pathways to childhood depression. *Journal of Personality and Social Psychology*, 76, 258–269.

Barber v. State, 592 So.2d 330 (Fla. App. 2nd Dist. 1992).

Barlow, D. H., Allen, L. B., & Choate, M. L. (2004). Toward a unified treatment for emotional disorders. *Behavior Therapy*, 35, 205–230.

Barr, R. (1992). Teachers, materials, and group composition in literacy instruction. In M. J. Dreher & W. H. Slater (Eds.), *Elementary school literacy: Critical issues*. Norwood, MA: Christopher-Gordon.

Barron, A. M., & Foot, H. (1991). Peer tutoring and tutor training. *Educational Research*, 33, 174–185.

Bassett, C., McWhirter, J. J., & Kitzmiller, K. (1997). *Teacher implementation of cooperative learning groups*. Unpublished manuscript, Arizona State University, Tempe.

Battin-Pearson, S., Newcomb, M. D., Abbott, R. D., Hill, K. G., Catalano, R. F., & Hawkins, J. D. (2000). Predictors of early high school dropout: A test of five theories. *Journal of Educational Psychology, (92)*3, 568–582.

Bauer, A. M. (2001). "Tell them we're girls": The invisibility of girls with disabilities. In P. O'Reilly, E. M. Penn, & K. deMarrais (Eds.), *Educating young adolescent girls* (pp. 29–45). Mahwah, NJ: Erlbaum.

Baumeister, R. F., Bushman, B. J., & Campbell, W. K. (2000). Self-esteem, narcissism, and aggression: Does violence result from low self-esteem or from threatened egotism? *Current Directions in Psychological Science, 9*(1), 26–29.

Baumrind, D. (1993). The average expectable environment is not good enough: A response to Scarr. *Child Development, 64*, 1299–1317.

Baumrind, D. (1995). *Child maltreatment and optimal caregiving in social contexts.* New York: Garland.

Bearman, P., & Moody, J. (2004). Suicide and friendships among American adolescents. *American Journal of Public Health, 94*, 89–95.

Beauvais, F., Chavez, E. L., Oetting, E. R., Deffenbacher, J. L., & Cornell, G. R. (1996). Drug use, violence, and victimization among White American, Mexican American, and American Indian dropouts, students with academic problems, and students in good academic standing. *Journal of Counseling Psychology, 43*(3) 292–299.

Beck, A. T. (1976). *Cognitive therapy and emotional disorders.* New York: International Universities Press.

Beck, A. T. (1991). Cognitive therapy: A 30 year retrospective. *American Psychologist, 46*(4), 368–375.

Beck, A. T., Kovacs, M., & Weissman, A. (1979). Assessment of suicidal intention: The scale for suicidal ideation. *Journal of Clinical and Consulting Psychology, 47*, 343–352.

Beck, A. T., Ward, S. H., Mendelson, M., Mock, J., & Erbaugh, J. (1961). An inventory for measuring depression. *Archives of General Psychiatry, 4*, 561–571.

Beck, A. T., Weissman, A., Lester, D., & Trexler, L. (1974). The measurement of pessimism: The hopelessness scale. *Journal of Consulting and Clinical Psychology, 42*, 861–865.

Becker, E. (1981). *The denial of death.* New York: Free Press.

Becker-Lansen, E., & Rickel, A. U. (1995). Integration of teen pregnancy and child abuse research: Identifying mediator variables for pregnancy outcome. *Journal of Primary Prevention, 16*(8), 39–53.

Bell, N. J., & Bell, R. W. (Eds.). (1993). *Adolescent risk taking.* Newbury Park, CA: Sage.

Bellanti, C. J., & Bierman, K. L. (2000). Disentangling the impact of low cognitive ability and inattention on social behavior and peer relationships. *Journal of Clinical Child Psychology, 29*(1), 66–75.

Bellotti v. Baird, 428 U.S. 132 (1979).

Belsie, L. (2001). USA: America by the numbers: Surprise: More nuclear families. *The Christian Science Monitor, 93*(97), 1, 5.

Bender, W. N., Shubert, T. H., & McLaughlin, P. J. (2001). Invisible kids: Preventing school violence by identifying kids in trouble. *Intervention in School and Clinic, 37*(2), 105–111.

Benn, W. (Ed.). (1981). *STAR: Social thinking and reasoning.* Irvine, CA: Irvine Unified School District.

Benn, W. (Ed.). (1982). *PLUS: Promoting learning and understanding of self.* Irvine, CA: Irvine Unified School District.

Bennett, B. E., Bryant, B. K., VandenBos, G. R., & Greenwood, A. (1990). *Professional liability and risk management.* Washington, DC: American Psychological Association.

Berliner, D. (2001, January 28). *Our schools vs. theirs: Averages that hide the true extremes.* Education Policy Project CERAI-01-02, Center for Education Research, Analysis, and Innovation. Milwaukee: University of Wisconsin–Milwaukee.

Berliner, D. C., & Biddle, B. J. (1995). *The manufactured crisis: Myths, fraud, and the attack on America's public schools.* Reading, MA: Addison-Wesley.

Berman, A. L., & Cohen-Sandler, R. (1983). Suicide and malpractice: Expert testimony and the standard of care. *Professional Psychology: Research and Practice, 14*, 6–19.

Bernstein, J., & Mishel, L. (1994). Trends in the Low-Wage Labor Market and Welfare Reform: The Constraints on Making Work Pay. Washington, DC: Economic Policy Institute.

Bernstein, N. (1996). *Treating the unmanageable adolescent: A guide to oppositional defiant and conduct disorders.* Northvale, NJ: Jason Aronson.

Berry, E. H., Shillington, A. M., Peak, T., & Hohman, M. M. (2000). Multi-ethnic comparison of risk and protective factors for adolescent pregnancy. *Child and Adolescent Social Work, 17*, 79–96.

Besner, H. F., & Spungin, C. I. (1995). *Gay and lesbian students: Understanding their needs.* Washington, DC: Taylor & Francis.

Bess, R., Leos-Urbel, J., & Green, R. (2001). *The cost of protecting vulnerable children II: What has changed since 1996?* The Urban Institute. Retrieved July 10, 2002, from www.urban.org.

Beyth-Marom, R., Fischhoff, B., Jacobs, M., & Furby, L. (1989). *Teaching decision making to adolescents:*

A *critical review*. Washington, DC: Carnegie Council on Adolescent Development.

Bickel, R., Howley, C., Williams, T., & Glascock, C. (2001). High school size, achievement equity, and cost: Robust interaction effects and tentative results. *Education Policy Analysis Archives, 9*(40). Retrieved October 8, 2001, from http://epaa.asu.edu/epaa/v9n40.html.

Bilchik, S. (1999, August). *OJJDP research: Making a difference for juveniles*. Washington, DC: Office of Juvenile Justice and Delinquency Prevention, 1–22.

Birch, S., & Ladd, G. W. (1997). The teacher–child relationship and children's early school adjustment. *Journal of School Psychology, 35*, 61–79.

Blake, C., Wang, W., Cartledge, G., & Gardner, R. (2000). Middle school students with serious emotional disturbances serve as social skills trainers and reinforcers for peers with SED. *Behavioral Disorders, 25*, 280–298.

Blue Shield of Virginia v. McCready, 457 U.S. 465 (1982).

Blumenthal, S. J. (1990). Youth suicide: Risk factors, assessment, and treatment of adolescent and young adult suicidal patients. *Psychiatric Clinics of North America, 13*(3), 511–556.

Blumstein, A., Cohen, J., & Farrington, D. P. (1988). Criminal career research: Its value for criminology. *Criminology, 26*, 1–35.

Blustein, D. L., Juntunen, C. L., & Worthington, R. L. (2000). The school-to-work transition: Adjustment challenges for the forgotten half. In S. Brown & R. W. Lent (Eds.), *Handbook of counseling psychology* (3rd ed., pp. 435–470). New York: Wiley.

Blustein, J., Levine, C., & Dubler, N. N. (Eds.). (1999). *The adolescent alone: Decision making in health care in the United States*. New York: Cambridge University Press.

Boewe, M. I., & McWhirter, J. J. (2002, November). *ART: Anxiety reduction training.* Trainer's manual and student workbook. (Treatment Manual) Tempe, AZ: Arizona State University.

Bogust v. Iverson, 10 Wis. 2d 129, 102 N.W. 2d 228 (1960).

Bongar, B. (1992). Effective risk management and the suicidal patient. *Register Report, 18*(6), 22–27.

Bor, W., & Sanders, M. R. (2004). Correlates of self-reported coercive parenting of preschool-aged children at high risk for the development of conduct problems. *Australian and New Zealand Journal of Psychiatry, 38*, 738–745.

Borum, R. (1996). Improving the clinical practice of violence risk assessment: Technology, guidelines, and training. *American Psychologist, 51*, 945–956.

Borum, R. (2000). Assessing violence risk among youth. *Journal of Clinical Psychology, 56*, 1263–1288.

Botvin, G. J., Schinke, S., & Orlandi, M. S. (Eds.). (1995). *Drug abuse prevention with multiethnic youth*. Thousand Oaks, CA: Sage.

Boyer, D., & Fine, D. (1992). Sexual abuse as a factor in adolescent pregnancy and child maltreatment. *Family Planning Perspectives, 24*(1), 4–11.

Bracken, B. A. (1992). *Multidimensional self-concept scale*. Austin, TX: Pro-Ed.

Bray, J. H. (1999a). From marriage to remarriage and beyond: Findings from the Developmental Issues in StepFamilies Research Project. In E. M. Hetherington (Ed.), *Coping with divorce, single-parenting and remarriage: A risk and resiliency perspective* (pp. 253–271). Hillsdale, NJ: Lawrence Erlbaum Associates Publishers.

Bray, J. H. (1999b). Stepfamilies: The intersection of culture, context, and biology. Monographs of the Society for Research in Child Development, 64, No. 259, 210–218.

Bray, J. H. (2001). Therapy with stepfamilies: A developmental systems approach. In D. D. Lusterman, S. H. McDaniel, C. Philpot (Eds.), *Integrating family therapy: A casebook* (pp. 127–140). Washington, DC: American Psychological Association.

Brennan, T. R. (1984). The reduction of disruptive classroom behavior of emotionally disturbed adolescents through the use of a relaxation procedure. (Doctoral dissertation, Columbia University Teachers College, 1983). *Dissertation Abstracts International, 44*, 3347A.

Brewster, K. L., Cooksey, E. C., Guilkey, D. K., & Rindfuss, R. R. (1998). The changing impact of religion on the sexual and contraceptive behavior of adolescent women in the United States. *Journal of Marriage and the Family, 60*(2), 493–504.

Bridge, J. A., Goldstein, T. R., & Bren, D. A. (2006). Adolescent suicide and suicidal behavior. *Journal of Child Psychology and Psychiatry, 47*, 372.

Brock, S. E., Sandoval, J., & Lewis, S. (2001). *Preparing for crises in the schools: A manual for building school crisis response teams* (2nd ed.). New York: Wiley.

Brody, J. L., & Waldron, H. B. (2000). Ethical issues in research on the treatment of adolescent substance abuse disorders. *Addictive Behaviors, 25*, 217–228.

Bronfenbrenner, U. (1979). *The ecology of human development: Experiments by nature and design*. Cambridge, MA: Harvard University Press.

Bronfenbrenner, U. (1989). Ecological systems theory. *Annals of Child Development, 6*, 187–249.

Brooks, V., & Coll, K. (1994, April 12–16). *Troubled youth: Identification and intervention strategies.* Paper presented at the national convention of the American Alliance for Health, Physical Education, Recreation, and Dance, Denver, CO.

Brown, J. D., Halpern, C. T., & L'Engle, K. L. (2005). Mass media as a sexual super peer for early maturing girls. *Journal of Adolescent Health, 36,* 420–427.

Brown, L. M., & Gilligan, C. (1992). *Meeting at the crossroads: Women—psychology and girls' development.* Cambridge, MA: Harvard University Press.

Brown, S. S., & Eisenberg, L. (Eds.). (1995). *The best intentions: Unintended pregnancy and the well-being of children and families.* Washington, DC: National Academy Press.

Brown, T., & Swenson, S. (2005). Identifying basic needs: The Contexual Needs Assessment. *International Journal of Reality Therapy, 24,* 7–10.

Bruce, M. (1995). Brief counseling: An effective model for change. *The School Counselor, 42*(5), 353–364.

Buchanan, G. M., & Seligman, M. E. P. (Eds.). (1995). *Explanatory style.* Hillsdale, NJ: Erlbaum.

Buchman, D. D., & Funk, J. B. (1996). Video and computer games in the '90s: Children's time commitment and game preference. *Children Today, 24,* 12–16.

Bundy, A. (2004). Efficacy of booster session maintenance in an anger prevention program and an optimistic resiliency program. Doctoral Dissertation, Arizona State University.

Burman, L. E., Rohaly, J., & Maag, E. (2002). EGTRRA: Which provisions spell the most relief? Urban Institute. Retrieved [9-18-05] from http://www.urban.org/url.cfm?ID=310510.

Burns, L. E. (1981). Relaxation in the management of stress. In J. Marshall & C. L. Cooper (Eds.), *Coping with stress.* London: Gower.

Burrell, N., & Vogel, S. (1990). Turfside conflict mediation. *Mediation Quarterly, 7*(3), 237–251.

Bushman, B. J., & Anderson, C. A. (2001). Media violence and the American public: Scientific facts versus media misinformation. *American Psychologist, 56*(6/7), 477–489.

Bushweller, K. (1995, May). The resilient child. *The American School Board Journal,* 18–23.

Butts, J. (2002). *The rise and fall of the American youth violence: 1980–2000.* Washington, DC: Urban Institute.

Cahoon, P. (1988). Mediator magic. *Education Leadership, 45*(4), 92–95.

Cambone, J., Weiss, C. H., & Wyeth, A. (1992). *We're not programmed for this: An exploration of the variance between the ways teachers think and the concept of shared decision making in high schools.* Cambridge, MA: Harvard University, National Center for Educational Leadership.

Camp, B. W., & Bash, M. S. (1985a). *Think aloud: Increasing social and cognitive skills—A problem-solving program for children, classroom program grades 1–2.* Champaign, IL: Research Press.

Camp, B. W., & Bash, M. S. (1985b). *Think aloud: Increasing social and cognitive skills—A problem-solving program for children, classroom program grades 3–4.* Champaign, IL: Research Press.

Camp, B. W., & Bash, M. S. (1985c). *Think aloud: Increasing social and cognitive skills—A problem-solving program for children, classroom program grades 5–6.* Champaign, IL: Research Press.

Camp, C. G., & Camp, G. M. (1999). *The corrections yearbook, 1998.* Middletown, CT: Criminal Justice Institute.

Campbell, C. A., & Dahir, C. A. (1997). *National standards for school counseling programs.* Alexandria, VA: American School Counselors Association.

Campfield, K. M., & Hills, A. M. (2001). Effects of timing of critical incident stress debriefing (CISD) on posttraumatic symptoms. *Journal of Traumatic Stress, 14,* 327–340.

Canada, G. (1995). *Fist stick knife gun: A personal history of violence in America.* Boston: Beacon Hill.

Canetto, S. S., & Lester, D. (1995). Gender and the primary prevention of suicide mortality. *Suicide and Life-Threatening Behavior, 25*(1), 58–69.

Capaldi, D. M., & Patterson, G. R. (1991). Relation of parental transition to boys' adjustment problems: Mothers at risk for transitions and unskilled parenting. *Developmental Psychology, 27,* 489–504.

Caplan, G. (1964). *Principles of preventive psychiatry.* New York: Basic Books.

Capuzzi, D. (1994). *Suicide prevention in the schools: Guidelines for middle and high school settings.* Alexandria, VA: American Counseling Association.

Capuzzi, D., & Golden, L. (1988). *Preventing adolescent suicide.* Muncie, IN: Accelerated Development.

Capuzzi, D., & Gross, D. R. (1996). "I don't want to live": The adolescent at risk for suicidal behavior. In D. Capuzzi & D. R. Gross (Eds.), *Youth at risk: A prevention resource for counselors, teachers, and parents* (2nd ed., pp. 253–282). Alexandria, VA: American Counseling Association.

Carey v. Population Services International, 431 U.S. 678 (1977).

Carkhuff, R. R. (1969). *Helping and human relations, Vol. 1.* New York: Holt, Rinehart & Winston.

Carlson, L., Grossbart, S., & Stuenkel, J. K. (1992). The role of parental socialization types on differential family communication patterns regarding consumption. *Journal of Consumer Psychology, 1*(1), 31–52.

Carpenter, C. D., Bloom, L. A., & Boat, M. B. (1999). Guidelines for special educators: Achieving socially valid outcomes. *Intervention in School and Clinic, 34*(3), 143–149.

Carter, B., & McGoldrick, M. (2005). *The expanded family life cycle: Individual, family, and social perspectives (3rd. Ed.).* Boston: Allyn & Bacon.

Carter, E., & McGoldrick, M. (Eds.). (2004). *The expanded family life cycle: Individual, family, and social perspectives* (3rd ed.). Needham Heights, MA: Allyn & Bacon.

Carter, E. W., Cushing, L. S., Clark, N. M., & Kennedy, C. H. (2005). Effects of peer support interventions on students' access to the general curriculum and social interactions. *Research and Practice for Persons with Severe Disabilities, 30,* 15–25.

Carter, J. L., & Russell, H. (1980). Biofeedback and academic attainment of LD children. *Academic Therapy, 15,* 483–486.

Cartledge, G., & Milburn, J. F. (Eds.). (1986). *Teaching social skills to children: Innovative approaches* (2nd ed.). New York: Pergamon Press.

Carville, J. (1996). *We're right, they're wrong: A handbook for spirited progressives.* New York: Random House.

Caspar, L., & Bianchi, S. (2002). Single-mother families. In Continuity and change in the American family (pp. 95–121). Thousand Oaks: Sage.

Catalano, R. F., Haggerty, K. P., Oesterle, S., Fleming, C. B., & Hawkins, J. D. (2004). The importance of bonding to school for healthy development: Findings from the Social Development Research Group. *Journal of School Health, 74*(7), 252–261.

Catalano, R. F., & Hawkins, J. D. (1996). The social development model: A theory of antisocial behavior. In J. D. Hawkins (Ed.), *Delinquency and crime: Current theories* (pp. 149–197). New York: Cambridge University Press.

Center, Y., Wheldall, K., Freeman, L., Outhred, L., & McNaught, M. (1995). An experimental evaluation of Reading Recovery. *Reading Research Quarterly, 30,* 240–263.

Center for Disease Control. (2002). *Teen birth rates decline in all states during the 1990's.* Retrieved August 7, 2002, from http://www.cdc.gov/nchs/releases/02facts/teenbirths.htm.

Centers for Disease Control and Prevention. (1997). HIV/AIDS Surveillance Report 1997. *MMWR Weekly, 46*(1), 1–39.

Centers for Disease Control and Prevention. (1998a, March 20). Suicide among Black youths—United States, 1980–1995. *MMWR Weekly, 47*(10), 193–106.

Centers for Disease Control and Prevention. (1998b). Trends in sexual risk behaviors among high school students: United States, 1991–1997. *MMWR Weekly, 47,* 749–752.

Centers for Disease Control and Prevention. (2000, June 9). Youth risk behavior surveillance—United States, 1999. *MMWR Weekly, 49*(SS05), 1–96.

Centers for Disease Control and Prevention. (2001, November 2). Youth tobacco surveillance—United States, 2000. *MMWR Weekly, 50*(SS04).

Centers for Disease Control & Prevention. (2002). Trends in sexual risk behaviors high school students—United States, 1991–2001. (MMWR); September 26, 2002; 51(38); 856–859.

Centers for Disease Control and Prevention. (2002, September 26). Trends in sexual risk behaviors high school students—United States, 1991–2001. *MMWR Weekly, 51*(38), 856–859.

Centers for Disease Control and Prevention. (2005). *Associations of body mass index and perceived weight with suicide ideation and suicide attempts among U.S. high school students.* Retrieved September 14, 2005, from http://archpedi.amaassn.org/cgi/content/short/159/6/513.

Centers for Disease Control and Prevention, National Center for Health Statistics. (2003). *Health, United States, 2003 trend tables.* Retrieved February 29, 2005, from http://www.cdc.gov/nchs/products/pubs/pubd/hus/listables.pdf.

Cerel, J., Roberts, T. A., & Nilsen, W. J. (2005). Peer suicidal behavior and adolescent risk behavior. *Journal of Nervous and Mental Disease, 193*(4), 237–243.

Chamberlain, P., Fisher, P. A., & Moore, K. J. (2002). Multidimensional treatment foster care: Applications of the OSLC intervention model to high-risk youth and their families. In J. B. Reid, G. R. Patterson, & J. Snyder (Eds.), *Antisocial behavior in children and adolescents: A developmental analysis and model for intervention* (pp. 203–218). Washington, DC: American Psychological Association.

Chambless, D. L., & Hollon, S. D. (1998). Defining empirically supported therapies. *Journal of Consulting and Clinical Psychology, 66,* 7–18.

Cheng, W. D. (1996). Pacific perspective. *Together, 24*(3).

Chenneville, T. (2000). HIV, confidentiality, and duty to protect: A decision-making model. *Professional Psychology: Research and Practice, 31*, 661–670.

Child Trends, Inc. (1996). *Facts at a glance.* Washington, DC: Author.

Children's Defense Fund. (1995). *The state of America's children yearbook.* Washington, DC: Author.

Children's Defense Fund. (2000). *The state of America's children yearbook 2000.* Washington, DC: Author.

Children's Defense Fund. (2001a). *Weakening economy and vanishing safety net also clouds news of last year's decline in child poverty.* Retrieved April 17, 2002, from http://www.childrensdefense.org/release010925.htm.

Children's Defense Fund. (2001b). *Fair Start-FAQs.* Retrieved April 7, 2002, from http://www.childrens-defense.org/fairstart-faqs.htm.

Children's Defense Fund. (2001c). *Facts on youth, violence and crime.* Retrieved from http://www.childrensdefensc.org/ss_ydfs_viocrime.php on May 10, 2002.

Children's Defense Fund. (2001d). *The state of America's children yearbook.* Retrieved from http://www.childrensdefense.org/keyfacts.htm on July 29, 2002.

Children's Defense Fund. (2002, June). *Suicide among children.* Report presented at the annual conference of the National Education Association, New York.

Chizmar v. Mackie, 896 P.2d 196 (Alaska, 1995).

Cho, H., Hallfors, D. D., & Sanchez, V. (2005). Evaluation of a high school peer group intervention for at-risk youth. *Journal of Abnormal Child Psychology, 33,* 363–374.

Christenson, S. L., & Thurlow, M. L. (2004). School dropouts: Prevention considerations, interventions, and challenges. *Current Directions in Psychological Science 13*(1), 36–39.

Chronister, K. M., McWhirter, B. T., & Kerewsky, S. D. (2004). *Prevention from an ecological framework.* In R. K. Conyne & E. P. Cook (Eds.), *Ecological counseling: An innovative approach to conceptualizing person–environment interaction* (pp. 315–338). Alexandria, VA: ACA Press.

Cicchetti, D., Rogosch, F. A., Lynch, M., & Holt, K. D. (1993). Resilience in maltreated children: Processes leading to adaptive outcome. *Development and Psychopathology, 5,* 629–647.

Clark, A. J. (1994). Conflict resolution and individual psychology in the schools. *Individual Psychology: Journal of Adlerian Theory, Research, and Practice, 50*(3), 329–340.

Clark, D. B., & Sayette, M. A. (1993). Anxiety and the development of alcoholism. *The American Journal on Addictions, 2*(1), 59–76.

Clarke-Stewart, K. A., Gruber, C. P., & Fitzgerald, L. M. (1994). *Children at home and in day care.* Hillsdale, NJ: Erlbaum.

Clausen, J. A. (1993). *American lives: Looking back at the children of the great depression.* New York: Free Press.

Clay, M. M. (1985). *The early detection of reading difficulties.* Exeter, NH: Heinemann.

Cohen, D. K., McLaughlin, M., & Talbert, J. E. (1993). *Teaching for understanding: Challenges for policy and practice.* Hoboken, NJ: Jossey Bass.

Cohen, M. (1998). The monetary value of saving a high risk youth. *Journal of Quantitative Criminology, 14*(1), 5–33.

Cohen, S. B., & de Bettencourt, L. V. (1991). Dropout: Intervening with the reluctant learner. *Intervention in School and Clinic, 26,* 263–271.

Coie, J. D., Watt, N. F., West, S. G., Hawkins, J. D., Asarnow, J. R., Markman, H. J., Ramey, S. L., Shure, M. B., & Long, B. (1993). The science of prevention: A conceptual framework and some directions for a national research program. *American Psychologist, 48*(10), 1013–1022.

Coker, J. K., & Borders, L. D. (2001). An analysis of environmental and social factors affecting adolescent problem drinking. *Journal of Counseling & Development, 79,* 200–208.

Colangelo, N., & Assouline, S. G. (1995). Self-concept of gifted students: Patterns by self-concept, domain grade level, and gender. In F. J. Mönks (Ed.), *Proceedings from the 1994 European council on high ability conference* (pp. 66–74). New York: Wiley.

Coleman, J. (1991). *Parental involvement in education.* Policy Perspectives, U.S. Department of Education.

Coleman, J. S., & Hoffer, T. (1987). *Public and private high schools: The impact of communities.* New York: Basic Books.

Coley, R. J. (1995). *Dreams deferred: High school dropouts in the United States.* Princeton, NJ: Educational Testing Service.

Comeau, N., Stewart, S. H., & Loba, P. (2001). The relations of trait anxiety, anxiety sensitivity and sensation seeking to adolescents' motivations for alcohol, cigarette, and marijuana use. *Addictive Behaviors, 26,* 803–825.

Comer, J. P. (Ed.). (1996). *Rallying the whole village: The Comer Process for reforming education.* New York: Teachers College Press.

Conchas, G. Q. (2001). Structuring failure and success: Understanding the variability in Latino school engagement. *Harvard Educational Review, 71*(3), 579–589.

Contreras, J., & Kerns, K. A. (2000). Emotion regulation processes: Explaining links between parent–child attachment and peer relationships. In K. A. Kerns, J. M. Contreras, & A. M. Neal-Barnett (Eds.), *Family and peers: Linking two social worlds* (pp. 1–25). Westport, CT: Praeger.

Conyne, R. K. (2004). Prevention groups. In J. L. DeLucia-Waack, D. A. Gerrity, C. R. Kalodner, & M. T. Riva (Eds.), *Handbook of group counseling and psychotherapy* (pp. 621–629). Thousand Oaks, CA: Sage.

Conyne, R. K., & Cook, E. P. (2004). *Ecological counseling: An innovative approach to conceptualizing person–environment interaction.* Alexandria, VA: American Counseling Association.

Cope-Farrar, K. M., & Kunkel, D. (2002). Sexual messages in teens' favorite prime-time TV programs. In J. D. Brown, J. R. Steele, & K. Walsh-Steele (Eds.), *Sexual teens, sexual media* (pp. 59–78). Mahwah, NJ: Erlbaum. Costa, A. L. (Ed.). (1991). *Developing minds: A resource book for teaching thinking.* Alexandria, VA: Association of Supervision and Curriculum Development.

Costa, F. M., Jessor, R., Fortenberry, J. D., & Donovan, J. E. (1996). Psychosocial conventionality, health orientation, and contraceptive use in adolescence. *Journal of Adolescent Health, 18,* 404–416.

Costa, L., & Altekruse, M. (1994). Duty-to-warn guidelines for mental health counselors. *Journal of Counseling & Development, 72*(4), 346–350.

Cowley, C., & Tillman, F. (2001). Adolescent girls' attitudes toward pregnancy: The importance of asking what the boyfriend wants. *Journal of Family Practice, 50*(7), 603–607.

Cranston, K. (1991). HIV education for gay, lesbian, and bisexual youth: Personal risk, personal power, and the community of conscience. *Journal of Homosexuality, 22*(3/4), 247–259.

Craven, R. G., Marsh, H. W., & Debus, R. L. (1991). Effects of internally focused feedback and attributional feedback on enhancement of academic self-concept. *Journal of Educational Psychology, 83,* 17–27.

Crawford, J. (2002). *Obituary: The Bilingual Education Act, 1968–2002.* Education Policy Studies Laboratory. Retrieved October 20, 2002, from http://www.asu.edu/educ/epsl/~LPRU/features/article2.htm

Crawford, N. (2002, October). New ways to stop bullying. *APA Monitor, 33*(9), 64.

Crothers, L. M., Field, J. E., & Kolbert, J. B. (2005). Navigating power, control, and being nice: Aggression in adolescent girls' friendships. *Journal of Counseling & Development 83*(3), 349–354.

Crunkilton, D., Paz, J., & Boyle, D. P. (2005). Culturally competent intervention with families of Latino youth at risk for drug abuse. *Journal of Social Work Practice in the Addictions, 5*(1/2), 113–131.

Cuban, L. (1989). At-risk students: What teachers and principals can do. *Educational Leadership, 45*(5), 29–33.

Cummings, C., & Haggerty, K. P. (1997). Raising healthy children. *Educational Leadership, 54*(8), 28–30.

Cunningham, C. E., Bremner, R., & Boyle, M. (1995). Large group community-based parenting programs for families of preschoolers at risk for disruptive behaviour disorders: Utilization, cost effectiveness, and outcome. *Journal of Child Psychology and Psychiatry, 36*(7), 1141–1159.

Cushing, L. S., & Kennedy, C. H. (1997). Academic effects of providing peer support in general education classrooms on students without disabilities. *Journal of Applied Behavior Analysis, 30,* 139–151.

Dadds, M. R., Spence, S. H., Holland, D. E., Barrett, P. M., & Laurens, K. R. (1997). Prevention and early intervention for anxiety disorders: A controlled trial. *Journal of Consulting and Clinical Psychology, 65,* 627–635.

Daly, E. J., III, Duhon, G. J., & Witt, J. C. (2002). Proactive approaches for identifying and treating children at risk for academic failure. In K. L. Lane, F. M. Gresham, & T. E. O'Shaughnessy (Eds.), *Interventions for children with or at risk for emotional and behavioral disorders* (pp. 18–32). Boston: Allyn & Bacon.

Darroch, J. E., Landry, D. J., & Oslak, S. (1999). Age differences between sexual partners in the United States. *Family Planning Perspectives, 31*(4), 160–167.

Daunic, A. P., Smith, S. W., Robinson, T. R., Miller, M. D., & Landry, K. L. (2000). School-wide conflict resolution and peer mediation programs: Experiences in three middle schools. *Intervention in School and Clinic, 36*(2), 94–100.

Davalos, D. B., Chavez, E. L., & Guardiola, R. J. (1999). The effects of extracurricular activity, ethnic identification, and perception of school on student dropout rates. *Hispanic Journal of Behavioral Sciences, 21*(1), 61–77.

Davidson, N., & Worsham, P. (Eds.). (1992). *Enhancing thinking through cooperative learning.* New York: Teachers College Press.

Davis, L., Johnson, S., Miller-Cribbs, J., & Saunders, J. (2002). A brief report: Factors influencing African-American youth decisions to stay in school. *Journal of Adolescent Research, 17,* 3.

Davis, M., Robbins-Eshelman, E., & McKay, M. (2000). *The relaxation and stress reduction workbook* (3rd ed.). Oakland, CA: New Harbinger.

Davis, T. E., & Osborn, C. J. (2000). *The solution-focused school counselor: Shaping professional practice.* Ann Arbor, MI: Edwards Brothers.

de Shazer, S. (1990). What is it about brief therapy that works? In J. K. Zeig & S. G. Gilligan (Eds.), *Brief therapy: Myths, methods, and metaphors* (pp. 90–99). New York: Brunner/Mazel.

Deater-Deckard, K., Dodge, K. A., Bates, J. E., & Pettit, G. S. (1998). Multiple risk factors in the development of externalizing behavior problems. *Development & Psychopathology, 10,* 469–493.

DeBaryshe, B. D., Patterson, G. R., & Capaldi, D. M. (1993). A performance model for academic achievement in early adolescent boys. *Developmental Psychology, 29,* 295–804.

Deffenbacher, J. L., Lynch, R. S., Oetting, E. R., & Kemper, C. C. (1996). Anger reduction in early adolescents. *Journal of Counseling Psychology, 43*(2), 149–157.

Deffenbacher, J. L., McNamara, K., Stark, R. S., & Sabadell, P. M. (1990). A comparison of cognitive-behavioral and process-oriented group counseling for general anger reduction. *Journal of Counseling Development, 69,* 167–172.

Delligatti, N., Akin-Little, A., & Little, S. G. (2003). Conduct disorder in girls: Diagnostic and intervention issues. *Psychology in the Schools, 40,* 183–192.

Department of Justice. (2005). Retrieved September 6, 2005, from http://ojjdpncjrs.org.

Devieux, J. G., Malow, R. M., Ergon-Perez, E., Samuels, D., Rojas, P., Khushal, S. R., & Jean-Gilles, M. (2005). A comparison of African American and Cuban American adolescent juvenile offenders: Risky sexual and drug use behaviors. *Journal of Social Work Practice in the Addictions, 5,* 69–83.

Devine, C., & Braithwaite, V. (1993). The survival role of children of alcoholics: Their measurement and validity. *Addiction, 88,* 69–78.

Diaz Reyes v. United States, 770 F. Supp. 58 (D.P.R. 1991), aff'd without op., 971 F.2d 744 (1st Cir.), cert. denied, 504 U.S. 957 (1992).

Dickerson, B. J. (1995). *African American single mothers: Understanding their lives and families.* Thousand Oaks, CA: Sage.

DiClemente, R., Wingood, G. M., Crosby, R., Sionean, C., Cobb, B. K., Harrington, K., Davies, S., Hook, E., III, & Kim, M. (2001). Parental monitoring: Association with adolescents' risk behaviors. *Pediatrics, 107,* 1363–1369.

Dielman, M. B., & Franklin, C. (1998). Brief solution-focused therapy with parents and adolescents with ADHD. *Social Work in Education, 20,* 261–268.

Dielman, T. E. (1994). School-based research on the prevention of adolescent alcohol use and misuse: Methodological issues and advances. *Journal of Research on Adolescence, 4,* 271–293.

Diemer, M. A., & Blustein, D. L. (in press). Critical consciousness and career development among urban youth. *Journal of Vocational Behavior.*

Diener, E., & Diener, C. (1996). Most people are happy. *Psychological Science, 7*(3), 181–189.

DiGangi, S. A., Maag, J. W., & Rutherford, R. B., Jr. (1991). Self-graphing of on-task behavior: Enhancing the reactive effects of self-monitoring on on-task behavior and academic performance. *Learning Disabilities Quarterly, 14,* 221–230.

Dishion, T. J., Andrews, D. W., & Crosby, L. (1995). Antisocial boys and their friends in early adolescence: Relationship characteristics, quality, and interactional process. *Child Development, 66,* 139–151.

Dino, G., Kamal, K., Horn, K., Kalsekar, I., & Fernandes, A. (2004). Stage of change and smoking cessation outcomes among adolescents. *Addictive Behaviors. 29*(5), 935–940.

Dishion, T., Capaldi, D., & Yoerger, K. (1999). Middle childhood antecedents to progression in male adolescent substance use: An ecological analysis of risk and protection. *Journal of Adolescent Research, 14,* 175–206.

Dishion, T. J., & Bullock, B. M. (2001). Parenting and adolescent problem behavior: An ecological analysis of the nurturance hypothesis. In J. G. Borkowski, S. L. Ramey, & M. Bristol-Power (Eds.), *Parenting and the child's world: Influences on academic, intellectual, and social–emotional development* (pp. 231–249). Hillsdale, NJ: Erlbaum.

Dishion, T. J., & Kavanagh, K. (2002). The Adolescent Transitions Program: A family-centered approach. In J. B. Reid, J. J. Snyder, & G. R. Patterson (Eds.), *Antisocial behavior in children and adolescents: A developmental analysis and the Oregon Model for*

Intervention (pp. 257–272). Washington, DC: American Psychological Association.

Dishion, T. J., Kavanagh, K., Schneiger, A., Nelson, S., & Kaufman, N. (2002). Preventing early adolescent substance use: A family-centered strategy for public middle school. In R. L. Spoth, K. Kavanagh, & T. J. Dishion (Eds.), Universal family-centered prevention strategies: Current findings and critical issues for public health impact [Special Issue]. *Prevention Science, 3,* 191–201.

Dishion, T. J., McCord, J., & Poulin, F. (1999). When interventions harm: Peer groups and problem behavior. *American Psychologist, 54,* 755–764.

Dishion, T. J., & McMahon, R. J. (1998). Parental monitoring and the prevention of child and adolescent problem behavior: A conceptual and empirical formulation. *Clinical Child and Family Psychology Review, 1,* 61–75.

Dishion, T. J., Nelson, S. E., & Kavanagh, K. (2003). The family check-up with high risk young adolescents: Preventing early-onset substance use by parent monitoring. *Behavior Therapy, 34*(4), 553–571.

Dishion, T. J., Nelson, S. E., & Yasui, M. (2005). Predicting early adolescent gang involvement from middle school adaptation. *Journal of Clinical Child and Adolescent Psychology, 34,* 62–74.

Dishion, T. J., Patterson, G. R., & Griesler, P. C. (1994). Peer adaptation in the development of antisocial behavior: A confluence model. In L. R. Huesmann (Ed.), *Aggressive behavior: Current perspectives* (pp. 61–95). New York: Plenum.

Dishion, T. J., & Stormshak, E. (2002). *An ecological approach to child clinical and counseling psychology.* Washington DC: American Psychological Association.

Dittus, P. J., & Jaccard, J. (2000). Adolescents' perceptions of maternal disapproval of sex: Relationship to sexual outcomes. *Journal of Adolescent Health, 26*(4), 268–278.

Dixon, A. C., Schoonmaker, C. T., & Philliber, W. W. (2000). A journey toward womanhood: Effects of an afrocentric approach to pregnancy prevention among African-American adolescent females. *Adolescence, 35,* 425–429.

Dodge, K. A., & Price, J. M. (1994). On the relation between social information processing and socially competent behavior in early school-aged children. *Child Development, 65,* 1385–1397.

Drazen, S. M. (1994, August). *Factors influencing student achievement from early to mid-adolescence.* Paper presented at the meeting of the American Psychological Association, Los Angeles.

Dreikurs, R. (1964). *Children: The challenge.* New York: Hawthorne.

Dreikurs, R. (1967). *Psychology in the classroom.* New York: Harper & Row.

Dryfoos, J. G. (1990). *Adolescents at risk: Prevalence and prevention.* New York: Oxford University Press.

Dryfoos, J. G. (1994). *Full-service schools: A revolution in health and social services for children, youth, and families.* San Francisco: Jossey-Bass.

Dubow, E., Edwards, S., & Ippolito, M. (1997). Life stressors, neighborhood disadvantage, and resources: A focus on inner-city children's adjustment. *Journal of Clinical Child Psychology, 26,* 130–144.

Duffy, G., Roehler, L., & Herrmann, B. A. (1988). Modeling mental processes helps poor readers become strategic readers. *Reading Teacher, 41,* 762–767.

DuPaul, G. J., & Eckert, T. L. (1994). The effects of social skills curricula: Now you see them, now you don't. *School Psychology Quarterly, 9*(2), 113–132.

DuRant, R. H., Rome, E. S., Rich, M., Allred, E., Emans, S. J., & Woods, E. R. (1997). Tobacco and alcohol use behaviors portrayed in music videos: A content analysis. *American Journal of Public Health, 87*(7), 1131–1135.

Durlak, J. A. (1995). *School-based prevention programs for children and adolescents.* Thousand Oaks, CA: Sage.

Durrant, M. (1995). *Creative strategies for school problems: Solutions for psychologists and teachers.* New York: Norton.

Duvall, E. M., & Miller, B. C. (1985). *Marriage and family development* (6th ed.). New York: Harper & Row.

Dynarski, M., & Gleason, P. (2002). How can we help? What we have learned from recent federal dropout prevention evaluations. *Journal of Education for Students Placed at Risk, 7*(1), 43–69.

Eccles, J. S., & Midgley, C. (1989). Stage/environment fit: Developmentally appropriate classrooms for early adolescents. In R. E. Ames & C. Ames (Eds.), *Research on motivation in education* (Vol. 3, pp. 139–186). San Diego, CA: Academic Press.

Eccles, J. S., Midgley, C., & Adler, T. (1984). Grade-related changes in the school environment: Effects on achievement motivation. In I. G. Nicholls (Ed.), *The development of achievement motivation* (pp. 283–331). Greenwich, CT: JAI Press.

Eccles, J. S., Midgley, C., Wigfield, A., Buchanan, C. M., Reuman, D., Flanagan, C., & MacIver, D. (1993). Development during adolescence: The impact of stage environment fit on young adolescents' experiences in schools and in families. *American Psychologist 48*(2), 90–101.

Edelman, M. W. (1987). *Families in peril: An agenda for social change.* Cambridge, MA: Harvard University Press.

Educational Testing Service. (2005). *One-third of a nation: Rising dropout rates and declining opportunities.* Retrieved September 28, 2005, from www.ets.org/research/pic/onethird.pdf.

Ehly, S. (1986). *Peer tutoring: A guide for school psychologists.* Washington, DC: National Association of School Psychologists.

Eisenberg, N., Fabes, R. A., Nyman, M., Bernzweig, J., & Piñuelas, A. (1994). The relations of emotionality and regulation to children's anger-related reactions. *Child Development, 65,* 109–128.

Ekstrom, R. B., Goertz, M. E., Pollack, J. M., & Rock, D. A. (1986). Who drops out of high school and why? Findings from a national study. *Teacher's College Record, 87,* 356–373.

Elias, M. J., Gara, M. A., Schuyler, T. F., Branden-Muller, L. R., & Sayette, M. A. (1991). The promotion of social competence: Longitudinal study of a preventative school-based program. *American Journal of Orthopsychiatry, 61,* 409–417.

Ellenbogen, S., & Chamberland, C. (1997). The peer relations of dropouts: A comparative study of at-risk and not at-risk youths. *Journal of Adolescence, 20,* 355–367.

Ellis, A. (1962). *Reason and emotion in psychotherapy.* New York: Stuart.

Ellis, A. (1985). *Overcoming resistance: Rational-emotive therapy with difficult clients.* New York: Springer.

Ellis, A. (1996). *Better, deeper, and more enduring brief therapy: The rational emotive behavior therapy approach.* New York: Brunner/Mazel.

Elmore, R., Peterson, P. L., & McCarthy, S. J. (1996). *Restructuring in the classroom: Teaching, learning, and school organization.* San Francisco: Jossey-Bass.

Entwisle, D., & Alexander, K. (1992). Summer setback: Race, poverty, school composition, and mathematics achievement in the first two years of school. *American Sociological Review, 57,* 72–84.

Epkins, C. C. (2000). Cognitive specificity in internalizing and externalizing problems in community and clinic-referred children. *Journal of Clinical Child Psychology, 29,* 199–208.

Esbensen, F. (2000). Preventing adolescent gang involvement [Youth Gang Series Bulletin], *Bulletin of the Office of Justice Programs.* Washington DC: U.S. Department of Justice, Office of Juvenile Justice and Delinquency Prevention.

Espelage, D. L., & Swearer, S. M. (2003). Research on school bullying and victimization: What have we learned and where do we go from here? *School Psychology Review, 32,* 365–383.

Evans, W. P., Marte, R., Betts, S., & Silliman, B. (2001). Adolescent suicide risk and peer related violent behaviors and victimization. *Journal of Interpersonal Violence, 16*(12), 1330–1348.

Ewing v. Goldstein, 15 Cal. Rptr. 3d 864 (Cal. Ct. App. 2004), review denied (Nov. 10, 2004).

Fad, K. S. (1990). The fast track to success: Social-behavioral skills. *Intervention in School and Clinic, 26*(1), 39–43.

Fair, C. A., & McWhirter, J. J. (2002, August). *BLOCKS: Building lives on cooperative knowledge skills.* Trainer's manual and student workbook. (Treatment Manual) Tempe, AZ: Arizona State University.

Fashola, O. S., & Slavin, R. E. (1998). Effective dropout prevention and college attendance programs for students placed at risk. *Journal of Education for Students Placed at Risk, 3*(2), 159–183.

Fassinger, R. E. (2000). Gender and sexuality in human development: Implications for prevention and advocacy in counseling psychology. In S. D. Brown & R. W. Lent (Eds.), *Handbook of counseling psychology* (3rd ed., pp. 346–378). New York: Wiley.

Federal Bureau of Investigation. (2000). *Hate crime statistics.* Retrieved September 13, 2002, from http://www.fbi.gov/ucr/ucr.htm.

Federal Interagency Forum on Child and Family Statistics. (2005). *America's children: Key national indicators of well-being 2005.* Retrieved November 8, 2005, from http://childstats.gov/americaschildren/index/asp.

Fehon, D. C., Grilo, C. M., & Lipschitz, D. S. (2005). A comparison of adolescent inpatients with and without a history of violence perpetration: Impulsivity, PTSD, and violence risk. *Journal of Nervous and Mental Disease, 193,* 405–411.

Feijoo, A. N. (1999). *Teenage pregnancy, the case for prevention: An updated analysis of recent trends & federal expenditures associated with teenage pregnancy.* Washington, DC: Advocates for Youth.

Felner, R. D., Brand, S., Adan, A. M., Mullhall, P. F., Flowers, N., Sartain, B., & DuBois, D. L. (1993). Restructuring the ecology of the school as an approach to prevention during school transitions:

Longitudinal follow-ups and extensions of the School Transitional Environment Project (STEP). *Prevention and Human Services, 10*, 103–136.

Ferguson, E. D. (2001). Adler and Dreikurs: Cognitive-social dynamic innovators. *Journal of Individual Psychology, 57*(4), 324–341.

Fergusson, D. M., & Lynskey, M. T. (1995). Childhood circumstances, adolescent adjustment, and suicide attempts in a New Zealand birth cohort. *Journal of American Child and Adolescent Psychiatry, 34*(5), 612–621.

Fergusson, D. M., & Woodward, L. J. (2002). Mental health, educational, and social role outcomes of adolescents with depression. *Archives of General Psychiatry, 59*(3), 225–231.

Fernandez v. Baruch, 52 N.J. 127, 244 A2d 109 (1968).

Fincham, F. D. (1994). Understanding the association between marital conflict and child adjustment: Overview. *Journal of Family Psychology, 8*(2), 123–127.

Fincham, F. D., Grych, J. H., & Osborn, L. N. (1994). Does marital conflict cause child maladjustment? Directions and challenges for longitudinal research. *Journal of Family Psychology, 8*, 128–140.

Finkelhor, D., Mitchell, K. J., & Wolak, J. (2000). *Online victimization: A report on the nation's youth.* Washington, DC: National Center for Missing and Exploited Children.

Finn, J. D., Gerber, S. B., & Boyd-Zaharias, J. (2005). Small classes in the early grades, academic achievement, and graduating from high school. *Journal of Educational Psychology, 97*(2), 214–223.

Flannery, D. J., Williams, L. L., & Vazsonyi, A. T. (1999). Who are they with and what are they doing? Delinquent behavior, substance use, and early adolescents' after school time. *American Journal of Orthopsychiatry, 69*, 247–253.

Flores, E., Cicchetti, D., & Rogosch, F. A. (2005). Predictors of resilience in maltreated and nonmaltreated Latino children. *Developmental Psychology, 41*, 338–351.

Foley-Nicpon, M., & Kerr, B. (2005). Preserving the promise: A typical day at TARGETS. In B. Kerr & S. R. Kurpius (Eds). *Handbook for Counseling Girls and Women, Volume II.* (pp. 12–24.) Mesa, AZ: Nueva Science Press

Ford, C. A., Thomsen, S. L., & Compton, B. (2001). Adolescents' interpretations of conditional confidentiality assurances. *Journal of Adolescent Health, 29*, 156–159.

Foreman, T., & Bernet, W. (2000). A misunderstanding regarding the duty to report suspected abuse. Child

Maltreatment. *Journal of the American Professional Society on the Abuse of Children, 5*, 190–196.

Forness, S. R., Serna, L. A., Neilsen, E., Lambros, K., Hale, M. J., & Kavale, K. A. (2000). A model for early detection and primary prevention of emotional or behavioral disorders. *Education and Treatment of Children, 23*(3), 325–345.

Forrest, J. D., & Samara, R. (1996). Impact of publicly funded contraceptive services on unintended pregnancies and implications for Medicaid expenditures. *Family Planning Perspectives, 28*, 188–195.

Fraser, M. W. (1996). Aggressive behavior in childhood and early adolescence: An ecological-developmental perspective on youth violence. *Social Work, 41*(4), 347–356.

Freeman, A., & Dolan, M. (2001). Revisiting Prochaska and DiClemente's stages of change theory: An expansion and specification to aid in treatment planning and outcome evaluation. *Cognitive and Behavioral Practice, 8*, 224–234.

Freeman, B. (1995). Power motivation and youth: An analysis of troubled students and student leaders. *Journal of Counseling and Development, 73*, 661–671.

Freire, P. (1998). *Pedagogy of the oppressed* (M. B. Ramos, Trans.). New York: Continuum. (Original work published 1970)

French, S. A., Story, M., Remafedi, G., Resnick, M. D., & Blum, R. W. (1996). Sexual orientation and prevalence of body dissatisfaction and eating disordered behaviors: A population-based study of adolescents. *International Journal of Eating Disorders, 19*(2), 19–26.

Frey, H. (1980). Improving the performance of poor readers through autogenic relaxation training. *Reading Teacher, 33*, 928–932.

Frost, J. J., & Forrest, J. D. (1995). Understanding the impact of effective teenage pregnancy prevention programs. *Planning Perspectives, 27*, 188–195.

Fry, D. P. (1993). The intergenerational transmission of disciplinary practices and approaches to conflict. *Human Organization, 52*, 176–185.

Fuligni, A. J., & Hardway, C. (2004). Preparing diverse adolescents for the transition to adulthood. *The Future of Children, 14*. Retrieved November 17, 2005, from www.futureofchildren.

Fuller, B., Kagan, S. L., Loeb, S., Carroll, J., McCarthy, J., Kreicher, G., Carrol, B., Cook, G., Chang, Y., & Sprachman, S. (2002). *New lives for poor families? Mothers and young children move through welfare reform.* Retrieved [4-18-05] from http://pace.berkeley.edu/gup_ex_sum.pdf.

Funk, J. B., Baldacci, H. B., Pasold, T., & Baumgardner, J. (2004). Violence exposure in real-life, video games, television, movies, and the Internet: Is there desensitization? *Journal of Adolescence, 27,* 23–39.

Gangi, R., Schiraldi, V., & Ziedenberg, J. (1998). *New York state of mind: Higher education vs. prison funding in the Empire State, 1988–1998.* Washington, DC: The Justice Policy Institute.

Garbarino, J. (1994). *Raising children in a socially toxic environment.* San Francisco, CA: Jossey-Bass.

Garbarino, J. (1998). The stress of being a poor child in America. *Child and Adolescent Psychiatric Clinics of North America, 7*(1), 105–119.

Garber, J., Deale, S., & Parke, C. (1986, November). *The coping with depression pamphlet revised for adolescents: Comprehensibility and acceptability.* Paper presented at the annual meeting of the Association for the Advancement of Behavior Therapy, Chicago.

Gardner, H. (1983). *Frames of mind: The theory of multiple intelligences.* New York: Basic Books.

Gardner, M., & Steinberg, L. (2005). Peer influence on risk taking, risk preference, and risky decision making in adolescence and adulthood: An experimental study. *Developmental Psychology, 41,* 625–635.

Garfield, S. L. (1994). Research on client variables in psychotherapy. In A. E. Bergin & S. L. Garfield (Eds.), *Handbook of psychotherapy and behavior change* (4th ed., pp. 190–228). New York: Wiley.

Garrison, C., Addy, C., & Jackson, K., et al. (1992). Major depressive disorder and dysthymia in young adolescents. *American Journal of Epidemiology, 135,* 792–802.

Gaustad, J. (1992). Tutoring for at-risk students. *Oregon School Study Council Bulletin, 36*(3), 1–74. (ERIC Document Reproduction Service No. ED353642)

Gazda, G. M., Asbury, F. R., Balzer, F. J., Childers, W. C., Phelps, R. E., & Walters, R. P. (1999). *Human relations development: A manual for educators* (6th ed.). Boston: Allyn & Bacon.

Gelles, R.J. (1997). *Intimate violence in families.* Thousand Oaks, CA: Sage.

Gentile, D. A., Lynch, P. J., Linder, J. R., & Walsh, D. A. (2004). The effects of violent video game habits on adolescent hostility, aggressive behaviors, and school performance. *Journal of Adolescence, 27,* 5–22.

Gershoff, E. T. (2002). Corporal punishment by parents and associated child behaviors and experiences: A meta-analytic and theoretical review. *Psychological Bulletin, 128,* 539–579.

Gilboy, S. F., McWhirter, J. J., & Wallace, R. (2002). *SOAR: Students' optimistic attribution and resiliency program: A depression prevention and amelioration program.* Unpublished manuscript, Arizona State University.

Gillham, J. E., Reivich, K. J., Jaycox, L. H., & Seligman, M. E. P. (1995). Prevention of depressive symptoms in schoolchildren: Two-year follow-up. *Psychological Science, 6,* 343–351.

Gingerich, W. J., & Wabeke, T. (2001). A solution-focused approach to mental health intervention in school settings. *Children and Schools, 23,* 33–47.

Glantz, K. (1983). The use of relaxation exercises in the treatment of reading disability. *Journal of Nervous and Mental Disease, 171*(12), 749–752.

Glasser, W. (1965). *Reality therapy: A new approach to psychiatry.* New York: Harper & Row.

Glasser, W. (1972). *The identity society.* New York: Harper & Row.

Glasser, W. (1976). *Positive addiction.* New York: Harper & Row.

Glasser, W. (1984). Reality therapy. In R. J. Corsini (Ed.), *Current psychotherapies* (3rd ed., pp. 320–353). Itasca, IL: Peacock.

Glasser, W. (1990). The quality school. *Phi Delta Kappan, 72,* 425–435.

Glasser, W. (1998). *Choice theory: A new psychology of personal freedom.* New York: HarperCollins.

Glasser, W. (2001). *Counseling with choice theory: The new reality therapy.* New York: HarperCollins.

Glasser, W. (2002). *Unhappy teenagers: A way for parents and teachers to reach them.* New York: HarperCollins.

Glimps, B. J. (2005). Students who are gay, lesbian, bisexual, or transgender. *Current Issues in Education* [Online] 8(16). Retrieved November 2, 2005, from http://cie.ed.asu.edu/volume8/number16/.

Glosoff, H. L., Herlihy, B., & Spence, E. B. (2000). Privileged communication in the counselor–client relationship. *Journal of Counseling & Development, 78,* 454–462.

Glynn, T., Crooks, T., Bethune, N., Ballard, K., & Smith, J. (1992). Reading Recovery in context: Implementation and outcome. *Educational Psychology, 12*(3/4), 249–261.

Goldfield, M. (1997). Race and labor organization in the United States. *Monthly Review, 49*(3), 80–97.

Goldhaber, D. (2002). *What might go wrong with the accountability measures of the "No Child Left Behind Act"?* The Urban Institute. Retrieved May 29, 2002, from http://www.edexcellence.net/NCLB conference/.

Goldstein, A., Sprafkin, R., Gershaw, N. J., & Klein, P. (1980). *Skill streaming the adolescent: A structured learning approach to teaching prosocial behavior.* Champaign, IL: Research Press.

Goldstein, A. P. (1996). *The psychology of vandalism.* New York: Plenum Press.

Goldstein, A. P., Harootunian, B., & Conoley, J. C. (1994). *Student aggression: Prevention, management, and replacement training.* New York: Guilford Press.

Goleman, D. P. (1995). *Emotional intelligence: Why it can matter more than IQ for character, health and lifelong achievement.* New York: Bantam Books.

Golub, A., & Johnson, B. D. (2001). *The rise of marijuana as the drug of choice among youthful adult arrestees.* Washington, DC: U.S.. Department of Justice, National Institute of Justice, Research in Brief.

Good, T. L., & Brophy, J. E. (1994). *Looking into classrooms* (6th ed.). New York: HarperCollins.

Gordon, R. (1987). An operational classification of disease prevention. In J. A. Steinberg & M. M. Silverman (Eds.), *Preventing Mental Disorders.* Rockville, MD: U.S. Department of Health and Human Services.

Gordon, T. (1970). *Parent effectiveness training.* New York: Wyden.

Gordon, T. (1977). *Leader effectiveness training.* New York: Putnam.

Gordon, T. (1989). *Teaching children self-discipline . . . at home and at school: New ways for parents and teachers to build self-control, self-esteem, and self-reliance.* New York: Random House.

Gordon, T. (2000). *Parent Effectiveness Training: The Proven Program for Raising Responsible Children.* Three Rivers Press, New York, New York.

Gormley, W. T. (1995). *Everybody's children: Child care as a public problem.* Washington, DC: Brookings Institution.

Gould, M. S., Greenberg, T., Velting, D. M., & Shaffer, D. (2003). Youth suicide risk and preventive interventions: A review of the past 10 years. *Journal of American Academy of Child and Adolescent Psychiatry, 42*(4), 386–405.

Gould, M. S., & Kramer, R. A. (2001). Youth suicide prevention. *Suicide and Life Threatening Behavior, 31* (Suppl.), 6–31.

Gould, M. S., & Shaffer, D. (1986). The impact of suicide in television movies: Evidence of imitation. *New England Journal of Medicine, 315,* 690–694.

Goyette-Ewing, M. (2000). Children's after school arrangements: A study of self-care and developmental outcomes. *Journal of Prevention & Intervention in the Community, 20,* 55–67.

Gragg, K. M., & McWhirter, E. H. (2003). Women, domestic violence, and career counseling: An application of social cognitive career theory. *Journal of Counseling & Development 81*(4), 418–424.

Green, R., Waters Boots, K., & Tumlin, C. (1999). *The cost of protecting vulnerable children.* The Urban Institute. Retrieved June 8, 2002, from www.urban.org.

Greenwood, C. R. (1999). Costs and benefits of early childhood intervention. *Office of Juvenile Justice and Delinquency Prevention, No. 94.* Washington, DC: U.S. Department of Justice.

Greenwood, C. R., Carta, J. J., & Maheady, L. (1991). Peer tutoring programs in the regular classroom. In G. Stoner, M. R. Shinn, & H. M. Walker (Eds.), *Interventions for achievement and behavior problems* (pp. 179–200). Washington, DC: National Association of School Psychologists.

Greenwood, P. W. (1994). What works with juvenile offenders: A synthesis of the literature and experience. *Federal Probation, 58*(4), 63–67.

Gresham, F. M., & Elliott, S. N. (1990). *Social skills rating system manual.* Circle Pines, MN: American Guidance Service.

Grossman, D. C., Mueller, B. A., Riedy, C., Dowd, M. D., Villaj-Prodzinski, J., Nakagawara, J., Howard, J., Thiersch, N., & Harruff, R. (2005). Gun storage practices and risk of youth suicide and unintentional firearm injury. *JAMA: Journal of the American Medical Association, 293*(6), 707–714.

Grossman, J. A., & Kruesi, M. (2000). Innovative approaches to youth suicide prevention: An update of issues and research findings. In R. Marris, S. Canetto, J. McIntosh, & M. Silverman (Eds.), *Review of suicidology, 2000* (pp. 170–201). New York: Guilford Press.

Grossman, J., Hirsch, J., Goldenberg, D., & Libby, S. (1995). Strategies for school-based response to loss: Proactive training and postvention consultation. *Crisis, 16*(1), 18–26.

Grubb, W. N. (1999). *Learning and earning in the middle: The economic benefits of sub-baccalaureate education.* New York: Community College Research Center, Columbia University. Retrieved April 28, 2002, from http://www.tc.columbia.edu/,iee/ccrc/papers/grubb1.pdf.

Grunbaum, J. A., Kann, L., Kinchen, S., Ross, J., Hawkins, J., Lowry, R., Harris, W. A., McManus, T., Chyen, D., & Collins, J. (2004, May 21). Youth risk behavior surveillance—United States, 2003. *MMWR, 53*(SS-2). Retrieved January 12, 2006, from www.cdc.gov/mmwr/pdf/ss/ss5302.pdf.

Gunasekera, H., Chapman, S., & Campbell, S. (2005, October 10.). Sex and drugs in popular movies: An analysis of the top 200 films. *Journal of the Royal Society of Medicine, 10,* 464–470.

Gysbers, N. C., & Henderson, P. (2006). *Developing and managing your school guidance and counseling program* (4th ed.). Alexandria, VA: American Counseling Association.

Hack, M., Youngstrom, E., & Cartar, L., et al. (2004, October). Behavioral outcomes and evidence of psychopathology among very low birth weight infants at age 20 years. *Pediatrics, 114*(4), 932–940.

Haffner, D. (1994). *Sexuality education and contraceptive instruction in U.S. schools.* Paper prepared for the Committee on Unintended Pregnancy. Washington, DC: Institute of Medicine.

Haggerty, R. J., Sherrod, L. R., Garmezy, N., & Rutter, M. (Eds.). (1994). *Stress, risk, resilience in children and adolescents: Processes, mechanisms, and interventions.* New York: Cambridge University Press.

Hains, A. A., & Ellmann, S. W. (1994). Stress inoculation training as a preventative intervention for high school youths. *Journal of Cognitive Psychotherapy, 8*(3), 219–232.

Halpern, D. F. (2005, July–August). Psychology at the intersection of work and family: Recommendations for employers, working families, and policymakers. *American Psychologist, 60*(5), 397–409.

Hanna, F. J., Hanna, C. A., & Keys, S. G. (1999). Fifty strategies for counseling defiant aggressive adolescents: Reaching, accepting, and relating. *Journal of Counseling & Development, 77,* 395–404.

Hanson, M., & Peterson, D. S. (1993). *How to conduct a school recovery support group.* Portland, ME: J. Weston Walch.

Harding, A. K., Gray, L. A., & Neal, M. (1993). Confidentiality limits with clients who have HIV: A review of ethical and legal guidelines and professional policies. *Journal of Counseling and Development, 71,* 297–305.

Harlow, L. L., Newcomb, M. D., & Bentler, P. M. (1986). Depression, self-derogation, substance use, and suicide ideation: Lack of purpose in life as a mediational factor. *Journal of Clinical Psychology, 42*(1), 5–21.

Harris, S. M. (1995). Psychosocial development and black male masculinity: Implications for counseling economically disadvantaged African American male adolescents. *Journal of Counseling and Development, 73,* 279–287.

Harter, S. (1985). *Manual for the Self-Perception Profile for Children (revision of the Perceived Competence Scale for Children).* Denver, CO: University of Denver.

Harter, S. (1990). Causes, correlates and the functional role of global self-worth: A life-span perspective. In R. Sternberg & J. Kolligian (Eds.), *Competence considered* (pp. 67–97). New Haven, CT: Yale University Press.

Harvey, A. R., & Hill, R. B. (2004). Africentric youth and family rites of passage program: Promoting resilience among at-risk African American youths. *Social Work, 49,* 65–74.

Haveman, R., & Wolfe, B. (1994). *Succeeding generations.* New York: Russell Sage Foundation.

Hawkins, J. D., Catalano, R. F., Kosterman, R., Abbott, R., & Hill, R. (1999). Preventing adolescent health-risk behaviors by strengthening protection during childhood. *Archives of Pediatric Adolescent Medicine, 153,* 226–234.

Hawkins, J. D., Herrenkohl, T. I., Farrington, D. P., Brewer, D., Catalano, R. F., Harachi, T. W., & Cothern, L. (2000). *Predicators of youth violence.* Washington, DC: U.S. Department of Justice, Office of Juvenile Justice and Delinquency, Juvenile Justice Bulletin.

Hawryluk, M. K., & Smallwood, D. L. (1986). Assessing and addressing consultee variables in school-based behavioral consultation. *School Psychology Review, 15,* 519–528.

Haynie, D. L., Nansel, T., Eitel, P., Crump, A. D., Saylor, K., Yu, K., & Simons-Morton, B. (2001). Bullies, victims, and bully victims: Distinct groups at-risk. *Journal of Early Adolescence, 21*(1), 29–50.

Hazler, R., Hoover, J., & Oliver, R. (1992). What kids say about bullying. *The Executive Educator, 14,* 20–22.

Henggeler, S. W. (1999). Multisystemic treatment of serious clinical problems in children and adolescents. *Clinician's Research Digest, 21,* 1–2.

Henry, D. B., Tolan, P. H., & Gorman-Smith, D. (2001). Longitudinal family and peer group effects on violent and non-violent delinquency. *Journal of Child Clinical Psychology, 16,* 203–220.

Henshaw, S. K. (1998). Abortion incidence in the United States, 1995–1996. *Family Planning Perspectives, 30,* 263–270.

Herek, G. M., Gillis, J. R., Cogan, J. C., & Glunt, E. K. (1997). Hate crime victimization among lesbian, gay, and bisexual adults. *Journal of Interpersonal Violence, 12,* 195–215.

Heron, T. E., Welsch, R. G., & Goddard, Y. L. (2003). Applications of tutoring systems in specialized subject areas: An analysis of skills, methodologies, and results. *Remedial and Special Education, 24,* 288–300.

Herrmann, D. S., & McWhirter, J. J. (1997). Refusal and resistance skills for children and adolescents: A selected review. *Journal of Counseling and Development, 75,* 177–187.

Herrmann, D. S., & McWhirter, J. J. (2000). *SCARE: Student created aggression replacement education* (2nd ed.). Trainer's manual and student workbook. Dubuque, IA: Kendall/Hunt.

Herrmann, D. S., McWhirter, J. J., & Sipsas-Herrmann, A. (1997). *The relationship between dimensional self-concept and juvenile gang involvement: A focused examination.* Unpublished manuscript, Arizona State University.

Hess, R. S. (2000). Dropping out among Mexican-American youth: Reviewing the literature through an ecological perspective. *Journal of Education for Students Placed at Risk, 5*(3), 267–289.

Hilton, J., Desrochers, S., & Devall, E. L. (2001). Comparison of role demands, relationships, and child functioning in single-mother, single father, and intact families. *Journal of Divorce & Remarriage, 35*(1/2), 29–56.

HIV Epidemiology Program. (1996, February). *Young men's survey: Los Angeles, August 1994–January 1996.* Paper presented to Los Angeles County Adolescent HIV Consortium, Los Angeles, CA.

H. L. v. Matheson, 450 U.S. 398 (1981).

Hockaday, C., Crase, S. J., Shelley, M. C., & Stockdale, D. F. (2000). A prospective study of adolescent pregnancy. *Journal of Adolescence, 23,* 423–438.

Hoffman, E. (1994). *The drive for self: Alfred Adler and the founding of individual psychology.* Reading, MA: Addison-Wesley.

Holinger, P. C., Offer, D., Barter, J. T., & Bell, C. C. (1994). *Suicide and homicide among adolescents.* New York: Guilford Press.

Holleran, L. K., & Jung, S. (2005). Acculturative Stress, Violence, and Resilience in the lives of Mexican-American Youth. *Stress, Trauma, and Crisis: An International Journal, 8*(2–3), 107–130.

Holloman, F. W. (1993). Estimates of the population of the United States by age, sex, and race. U.S. Bureau of the Census, *Current population reports, Series P-25,* No. 1095.

Hopkins, B. R. (1989, February). Counselors and the law. *Guidepost,* p. 13.

Hopkins, B. R., & Anderson, B. S. (1985). *The counselor and the law* (2nd ed.). Alexandria, VA: American Association for Counseling and Development.

Hora, P. F., Schma, W. G., & Rosenfeld, J. T. A. (1999). Therapeutic jurisprudence and the drug treatment court movement: Revolutionizing the criminal justice system's response to drug abuse and crime in America. *Notre Dame Law Review, 74*(2), 439–538.

Horner, R. H., Crone, D. A., & Stiller, B. (2001). *The role of school psychologists in establishing positive behavior support: Collaborating in systems change at the school-wide level.* National Association of School Psychologists. Retrieved July 10, 2002, from http://www.naspcenter.org/teachers/IDEA_pbs.html.

Horner, R. H., & Sugai, G. (2000). School-wide behavior support: An emerging initiative [Special issue]. *Journal of Positive Behavioral Interventions, 2,* 231–233.

Howell, J. C. (1998). *Youth gangs: An overview.* Washington, DC: U.S. Department of Justice, Office of Justice Programs, Bulletin of the Office of Juvenile Justice and Delinquency Prevention.

Hser, Y., Grella, C. E., Hubbard, R. L., Hsieh, S., Fletcher, B. W., Brown, B. S., & Anglin, D. (2001). An evaluation of drug treatments for adolescents in 4 US cities. *Archives of General Psychiatry,* 689–695.

Huesmann, L. R., Moise-Titus, J., Podolski, C., & Eron, L. D. (2001). *Longitudinal relations between children's exposure to television violence and their aggressive and violent behavior in young adulthood: 1977–1992.* Washington DC: American Psychological Association. Retrieved December 15, 2002, from http://www.lionlamb.org/research_articles/ctvout.2001.~ver12_pdf.pdf.

Huey, S. J., Jr., Henggeler, S. W., Brondino, M. J., & Pickrel, S. G. (2000). Mechanisms of change in multisystemic therapy: Reducing delinquent behavior through therapist adherence and improved family and peer functioning. *Journal of Consulting and Clinical Psychology, 68,* 451–467.

Hughes, J. N., & Hasbrouck, J. E. (1996). Television violence: Implications for violence prevention. *School Psychology Review, 25,* 134–151.

Hull-Blanks, E. E., Kerr, B. A., & Kurpius, S. E. (2004) Risk factors of suicide ideation attempts in talented, at-risk girls. *Suicide & Life Threatening Behavior, 34*(3), 267–276.

Human Rights Campaign Foundation. (2004). *Gay teens and school.* Retrieved November 2, 2005, from www.hrc.org.

Hunt-Morse, M. C. (2002). *Adolescent mothers' psychosocial development: Implications for parenting.* Unpublished doctoral dissertation, University of Oregon.

Hyman, I. A., & Perone, D. C. (1998). The other side of school violence: Educator policies and practices that may contribute to student misbehavior. *Journal of School Psychology, 36*(1), 7–27.

Jackson, M. S., Bass, L., & Sharpe, E. G. (2005). Working with youth street gangs and their families: Utilizing a nurturing model for social work practice. *Journal of Gang Research, 12,* 1–18.

Jackson, N., Jackson, D., & Monroe, C. (1983). *Getting along with others: Teaching social effectiveness to children.* Champaign, IL: Research Press.

Jacobson, E. (1938). *Progressive relaxation* (2nd ed.). Chicago: University of Chicago Press.

Jaffe v. Redmond, 116 S.Ct. 1923 (1996).

Jaffee, S. R. (2002). Pathways to adversity in young adulthood among early childbearers. *Journal of Family Psychology, 16,* 38–49.

James-Burdumy, S., Dynarski, M., Moore, M., Deke, J., Mansfield, W., & Pistorino, C. (2005). *When schools stay open late: The national evaluation of the 21st Century Community Learning Centers Program.* Final Report. Document No. PR05-12. Princeton, NJ: Mathematica Policy Research, Inc.

Janosz, M., LeBlanc, M., Boulerice, B., & Tremblay, R. E. (2000). Predicting different types of school dropouts: A typological approach with two longitudinal samples. *Journal of Educational Psychology, 92*(1), 171–190.

Jarjoura, R. G., Triplett, G. P., & Brinker, G. P. (2002). Growing up poor: Examining the link between persistent childhood poverty and delinquency. *Journal of Quantitative Criminology, 18*(2), 159–187.

Jaycox, L. H., & Repetti, R. L. (1993). Conflict in families and the psychological adjustment of preadolescent children. *Journal of Family Psychology, 7,* 344–355.

Jessor, L. D., & Jessor, S. L. (1977). *Problem behavior and psychosocial development: A longitudinal study of youth.* New York: Academic Press.

Jessor, R. (1991). Risk behavior in adolescence: A psychosocial framework for understanding and action. *Journal of Adolescent Health, 12,* 597–605.

Jessor, R. (1993). Successful adolescent development among youth in high-risk settings. *American Psychologist, 48,* 117–126.

Jessor, R., Van Den Bos, J., Vanderryn, J., Costa, R. M., & Turbin, M. S. (1995). Protective factors in adolescent problem behavior: Moderator effects and developmental change. *Developmental Psychology, 31,* 923–933.

Jeynes, W. (2002). The relationship between the consumption of various drugs by adolescents and their academic achievement. *American Journal of Drug Alcohol Abuse, 28,* 15–35.

Jimerson, S., Egeland, B., Sroufe, L. A., & Carlson B. (2000). A prospective longitudinal study of high school dropouts: Examining multiple predictors across development. *Journal of School Psychology, 38*(6), 525–549.

Jobes, D. A., & Berman, A. L. (1993). Suicide and malpractice liability. Assessing and revising policies, procedures and practice in outpatient settings. *Professional Psychology: Research and Practice, 24,* 91–99.

Johnson, D. W., & Johnson, R. T. (1988). Critical thinking through structured controversy. *Educational Leadership, 45,* 58–64.

Johnson, D. W., & Johnson, R. T. (1989). *Cooperation and competition: Theory and research.* Edina, MN: Interaction.

Johnson, D. W., Johnson, R., & Holubec, E. (1990). *Circles of learning: Cooperation in the classroom.* Edina, MN: Interaction.

Johnson, D. W., Johnson, R. T., & Taylor, B. (1993). Impact of cooperative and individualistic learning on high-ability students' achievement, self-esteem, and social acceptance. *Journal of Social Psychology, 133*(6), 839–844.

Johnson, K. (2000). *School crisis management: A hands-on guide to training crisis response teams* (2nd ed.). Alameda, CA: Hunter House.

Johnson, S. (1977). *Cross-age tutoring handbook. Corcoran Unified School District, AC.* (ERIC Document Reproduction Service No. ED238826)

Johnson, S. M., & Boles, K. C. (1994). The role of teachers in school reform. In S. A. Mohrman & P. Wohlstetter (Eds.), *School-based management: Organizing for high performance* (pp. 109–137). San Francisco: Jossey-Bass.

Johnston, L. D., O'Malley, P. M., & Bachman, J. G. (2000). *National survey results on drug use from the Monitoring the Future study, 1975–1999. Volume I: Secondary school students.* Ann Arbor, MI: University of Michigan.

Johnston, L. D., O'Malley, P. M., & Bachman, J. G. (2003). *The Monitoring the Future national survey results on adolescent drug use: Overview of key findings, 2002* (NIH Publication No. 03-5374). Bethesda, MD: National Institute on Drug Abuse.

Jones, C. A. (1998, November). *Preventing school violence: A review of the literature.* Paper presented at the annual meeting of the Mid-South Educational Research Association, New Orleans, LA.

Jones, R. N., Sheridan, S. M., & Binns, N. R. (1993). Schoolwide social skills training: Providing preventive services to students at-risk. *School Psychology Quarterly, 8*(1), 57–80.

Jones, T. S. (1998). Research supports effectiveness of peer mediation. *The Fourth R, 82*, 1–25.

Jordan, K. M. (2000). Substance abuse among gay, lesbian, bisexual, transgender, and questioning adolescents. *School Psychology, 29*, 201–206.

Juhnke, G. (1997). After school violence: An adapted critical incident stress debriefing model for student survivors and their parents. *Elementary School Guidance & Counseling, 31*(3), 163–170.

Juvonen, J., Graham, S., & Shuster, M. A. (2003). Bullying among young adolescents: The strong, the weak, and the troubled. *Pediatrics, 112*(6), 1231–1237.

Kagan, S. L., & Weissbourd, B. (Eds.). (1994). *Putting families first: America's family support movement and the challenge of change.* San Francisco: Jossey-Bass.

Kahn, D. J., Kazimi, M. M., & Mulvihill, M. N. (2001). Attitudes of New York City high school students regarding firearm violence. *Pediatrics, 107*(5), 1125–1132.

Kahn, J. S., Kehle, T. J., Jenson, W. R., & Clarke, E. (1990). Comparison of cognitive-behavioral, relaxation, and self-modeling intervention for depression among middle-school students. *School Psychology Review, 19*, 195–210.

Kaiser Family Foundation. (2005). *Sex on T.V. 4.* Retrieved December 1, 2005, from http://www.Kaisernetwork.org/.

Kalichman, S. C. (1999). *Mandated reporting of suspect child abuse: Ethics, law, and policy* (2nd ed). Washington, DC: American Psychological Association.

Kalichman, S. C., & Brosig, C. L. (1993). Practicing psychologists' interpretations of compliance with child abuse reporting law. *Law and Human Behavior, 17*, 83–93.

Kaminer, Y. (2005). Cognitive group therapy for aggressive boys. *Journal of the American Academy of Child & Adolescent Psychiatry, 44*, 843.

Kamps, D., & Kay, P. (2001). Preventing problems through social skills instruction. In R. Algozzine & P. Kay (Eds.), *What works: How schools can prevent behavior problems.* Thousand Oaks, CA: Corwin Press.

Kann, L., Kinchen, S. A., Williams, B. I., Ross, J. G., Lowry, R., Hill, C. V., Grunbaum, J., Blumson, P. S., Collins, J. L., & Kolbe, L. J. (1998, August). *Youth risk behavior surveillance—United States, 1997* (Report No. SS-3). Washington, DC: U.S. Government Printing Office.

Kaplan, J. S. (1991). *Beyond behavior modification: A cognitive-behavioral approach to behavior management in the school.* Austin, TX: Pro-Ed.

Karcher, M. J. (2004). Connectedness and school violence: A framework for developmental interventions. In E. Gerler (Ed.), *Handbook of school violence* (pp. 7–42). Binghamton, NY: Haworth Press.

Karoly, L. A., Kilburn, M. R., & Cannon, J. S. (2005). *Early Childhood Interventions: Proven Results, Future Promise* . RAND Labor and Population Research Brief (MG-341-PNC, 2005). Retrieved [5-25-06] from http://www.rand.org/pubs/research_briefs/2005/RAND_RB9145.pdf.

Kaufman, P. Alt, M. N., & Chapman, C. (2001). *Dropout rates in the United States: 2000.* National Center for Education Statistics. Retrieved July 17, 2005, from http://nces.ed.gov/pubsearch/pubsinfo.asp?pubid52002114.

Kay, P., Fitzgerald, M., & McConaughy, S. H. (2002). Building effective parent–teacher partnerships. In B. Algozzine & P. Kay (Eds.), *Preventing problem behaviors: A handbook of successful prevention strategies* (pp. 104–125). Thousand Oaks, CA: Corwin Press and Council for Exceptional Children.

Kazdin, A. E. (1994). Interventions for aggressive and antisocial children. In L. D. Eron, J. H. Gentry, & P. Schlegel (Eds.), *Reason to hope: A psychosocial perspective on violence and youth* (pp. 341–382). Washington, DC: American Psychological Association.

Kellam, S. G., Ling, X., Merisca, R., Brown, C. H., & Ialongo, J. (1998). The effect of the level of aggression in the first grade classroom on the course and malleability of aggressive behavior into middle school. *Development and Psychopathology, 10*, 165–185.

Keller, C. L. (2002). A new twist on spelling instruction for elementary school teachers. *Intervention in School and Clinic, 38*(1), 3–7.

Kellogg, N. D., Hoffman, T. J., & Taylor, E. R. (1999). Early sexual experiences among pregnant and parenting adolescents. *Adolescence, 34*(134), 293–303.

Kelly, J. (1982). *Social skill training.* New York: Springer.

Kelly, J. (2005, June). Washington's mixed gang signals. *Youth Today*, p. 6.

Kessler, R. C., Wang, P., & Zaslavsky, A. M. (2005). Prevalence and treatment of mental disorders: Reply. *New England Journal of Medicine, 353*(11), 1184.

Key, J. D., Barbosa, G. A., & Owens, V. J. (2001). The second chance club: Repeat adolescent pregnancy prevention with a school-based intervention. *Journal of Adolescent Health, 28*, 167–169.

Kim, M., Ohls, J., & Cohen, R. (2001). *Hunger in America 2001: Local report prepared for Food for Survival, Inc.* (3503). Princeton, NJ: Mathematica Policy Research, Inc.

King, K. A., Price, J. H., Telljohann, S. K., & Wahl, J. (2000). Preventing adolescent suicide: Do high school counselors know the risk factors? *Professional School Counseling, 3,* 255–262.

Kinnier, R. T., & Krumboltz, J. D. (1984). Procedures for successful career counseling. In N. Gysbers (Ed.), *Designing careers: Counseling to enhance education, work and leisure.* San Francisco: Jossey-Bass.

Kirisci, L., Vanyukov, M., & Tarter, R. (2005). Detection of youth at high risk for substance use disorders: A longitudinal study. *Psychology of Addictive Behaviors, 19,* 243–252.

Kirby, D. (2000). School-based interventions to prevent unprotected sex and HIV among adolescents. In J. L. Peterson & R. J. DiClemente (Eds.), *Handbook of HIV prevention* (pp. 83–101). New York: Kluwer Academic Press.

Kirby, D. (2001). *Emerging answers: Research findings on programs to reduce teen pregnancy.* Washington, DC: National Campaign to Prevent Teen Pregnancy.

Kirby, D., Short, L., Collins, J., Rugg, D., Kolbe, L., Howard, M., Miller, B., Sonenstein, F., & Zabin, L. S. (1994). School-based programs to reduce sexual risk behaviors: A review of effectiveness. *Public Health Reports, 103*(3), 339–360.

Kiselica, M. S. (1995). *Multicultural counseling with teenage fathers.* Thousand Oaks, CA: Sage.

Klein, D., Lewinsohn, P. M., Rohde, P., Seeley, J. R., & Shankman, S. A. (2003). Family study of co-morbidity between major depressive disorder and anxiety disorders. *Psychological Medicine, 33*(4), 703–714.

Klein, D. N., Lewinsohn, P. M., Rohde, P., Seeley, J. R., & Olino, T. M. (2005). Psychopathology in the adolescent and young adult offspring of a community sample of mothers and fathers with major depression. *Psychological Medicine, 35*(3), 353–365.

Klein, K., Forehand, R., & the Family Health Project Research Group. (2000). Family processes as resources for African American children exposed to a constellation of sociodemographic risk factors. *Journal of Clinical Child Psychology, 29*(1), 53–65.

Kliewer, W., & Sandler, I. N. (1992). Locus of control and self-esteem as moderators of stress-symptom relations in children and adolescents. *Journal of Abnormal Child Psychology, 20,* 393–413.

Kling, K. C., Hyde, J. S., Showers, C., & Buswell, R. (1999). Gender differences in self-esteem: A meta-analysis. *Psychological Bulletin, 125,* 470–500.

Knitzer, J., Steinberg, Z., & Fleisch, B. (1990). *At the schoolhouse door: An examination of programs and policies for children with behavioral and emotional problems.* New York: Bank Street College of Education.

Knoester, C., & Haynie, D. L. (2005). Community context, social integration into family, and youth violence. *Journal of Marriage and Family, 67,* 767–780.

Koch, M. (1988). Resolving disputes: Students can do it better. *NASSP Bulletin, 72*(504), 16–18.

Korinek, L., Walther-Thomas, C., McLaughlin, V. L., & Williams, B. T. (1999). Creating classroom communities and networks for student support. *Intervention in School and Clinic, 35,* 3–8.

Kortering, L. J., & Braziel, P. M. (1999). School dropout from the perspective of former students. *Remedial and Special Education, 20*(2), 78–83.

Kosterman, R., Hawkins, J. D., Guo, J., Catalano, R. F., Abbott, R. D., Russell, S., & Joyner, K. (2000). Adolescent sexual orientation and suicide risk: Evidence from a natural study. *American Journal of Public Health, 91,* 1276–1282.

Kovacs, M. (1981). Rating scales to assess depression in school-aged children. *Acta Paedopsychiatrica, 46,* 305–315.

Kovacs, M., & Beck, A. T. (1977). An empirical-clinical approach toward a definition of childhood depression. In J. G. Schulterbrandt & A. Raskin (Eds.), *Depression in childhood: Diagnosis, treatment, and conceptual models* (pp. 1–25). New York: Raven.

Kovacs, M., & Devlin, B. (1998). Internalizing disorders in childhood. *Journal of Child Psychology and Psychiatry, 39,* 47–63.

Kozol, J. (1991) *Savage inequalities: Children in America's schools.* New York: Crown.

Kozol, J. (1992). *Savage inequalities: Children in America's schools.* New York: Harper Perennial.

Kozol, J. (2005). *The shame of the nation.* New York: Crown.

Krajewski, S. S., Rybarik, M. F., Dosch, M. F., & Gilmore, G. D. (1996). Results of a curriculum intervention with seventh graders regarding violence in relationships. *Journal of Family Violence, 11,* 93–112.

Kraut, R. Lundmark, V., Patterson, M., Kiesler, S., Mukopadhyay, T., & Scherlis, W. (1998). Internet paradox: A social technology that reduces social involvement and psychological well-being? *American Psychologist, 53,* 1017–1031.

Kumpfer, K. (1998). Selective prevention interventions: The strengthening families program. In R. Ashery, E. Robertson, & K. Kumpfer (Eds.), *Drug abuse prevention through family interventions* (pp. 160–207). Rockville, MD: National Institutes of Health.

Kumpfer, K. L., & Alder, S. (2003). Dissemination of research-based family interventions for the prevention of substance abuse. In Z. Sloboda & W. J. Bukoski (Eds.), *Handbook of drug abuse prevention* (pp. 75–119). New York: Kluwer Academic/Plenum.

Kumpfer, K. L., & Alvarado, R. (1995). Strengthening families to prevent drug use in multiethnic youth. In G. J. Botvin, S. Schinke, & M. A. Orlandi (Eds.), *Drug abuse prevention with multiethnic youth* (pp. 255–294). Thousand Oaks, CA: Sage.

Kumpfer, K. L., Molgaard, V., & Spoth, R. L. (1996). The strengthening families program for the prevention of delinquency and drug abuse. In R. D. Peters & R. J. McMahon (Eds.), *Preventing childhood disorders, substance abuse, and delinquency* (pp. 241–267). Newbury, CA: Sage.

Kumpfer, K. L., & Tait, C. M. (2000). Family skills training for parents and children, *Bulletin of the Office of Justice Programs*, pp. 1–11. Washington, DC: U.S. Department of Justice, Office of Juvenile Justice and Delinquency Prevention.

Kupersmidt, J. B., Burchinaal, M., & Patterson, C. J. (1995). Developmental patterns of childhood peer relations as predictors of externalizing behavior problems. *Development & Psychopathology, 7*, 825–843.

Kupersmidt, J. B., Coie, J. D., & Dodge, K. A. (1990). *The role of poor peer relationships in the development of disorder*. In S. R. Asher & J. D. Coie (Eds.), *Peer rejection in childhood*. New York: Cambridge University Press.

Kurpius, S. E., Kerr, B., & Harkins, A. (Eds.). (2005). *Handbook for counseling girls and women, Volume l. Talent, Risk, and Resiliency*. Mesa, AZ: Nueva Science Press.

Kutnick, P. (2005). Co-operative learning: The social and intellectual outcomes of learning in groups. *European Journal of Special Needs Education, 20*, 117–121.

Ladd, G. W., & Burgess, K. B. (2001). Do relational risks and protective factors moderate the linkages between childhood aggression and early psychological and school adjustment? *Child Development, 72*(5), 1579–1601.

Ladd, G. W., Kochenderfer, B. J., & Coleman, C. C. (1996). Friendship quality as a predictor of young children's early school adjustment. *Child Development, 67*, 1103–1118.

LaFave, W. R., & Scott, A. W. (2002). *Substantive criminal law*. St. Paul, MN: West.

Lambda Legal (2005). Making schools safe for gay, lesbian, bisexual and transgendered youth: A resource guide. Retrieved [11-15-06] from http://www.lambdalegal.org/cgi-bin/iowa/news/online.html?record=1123.

Lanctot, N., & Smith, C. A. (2001). Sexual activity, pregnancy, and deviance in a representative urban sample of African-American girls. *Journal of Youth and Adolescence, 30*, 349–372.

Lane, K. L., Gresham, F. M., & O'Shaughnessy, T. E. (Eds.). (2002). *Interventions for children with or at risk for emotional and behavioral disorders*. Boston: Allyn & Bacon.

Lane, P. S., & McWhirter, J. J. (1992). A peer mediation model: Conflict resolution for elementary and middle school children. *Elementary School Guidance and Counseling, 27*(1), 15–24.

Lane, P. S., & McWhirter, J. J. (1996). Creating a peaceful school community: Reconciliation operationalized. *Catholic School Studies, 69*(2), 31–34.

Lapan, R. T., Gysbers, N. C., & Petroski, G. F. (2001). Helping seventh graders be safe and successful: A statewide study of the impact of comprehensive guidance and counseling programs. *Journal of Counseling & Development, 79*, 320–330.

Laursen, E. K., & Birmingham, S. M. (2003). Caring relationships as a protective factor for at-risk youth: An ethnographic study. *Families in Society 84*(2), 240–246.

Lazarus, A. A. (1971). *Behavior therapy and beyond*. New York: McGraw-Hill.

Lazerson, D. B. (2005). Detention home teens as tutors: A cooperative cross-age tutoring pilot project. *Emotional & Behavioural Difficulties, 10*, 7–15.

Lee, R. M., Draper, M., & Lee, S. (2001). Social connectedness, dysfunctional interpersonal behaviors, and psychological distress: Testing a mediator model. *Journal of Counseling Psychology, 48*, 310–318.

Lee, R. M., & Robbins, S. B. (1995). Measuring belongingness: The Social Connectedness and Social Assurance Scales. *Journal of Counseling Psychology, 42*, 232–241.

Lee, R. M., & Robbins, S. B. (1998). The relationship between social connectedness and anxiety, self-esteem, and social identity. *Journal of Counseling Psychology, 45*, 338–345.

Lee, R. M., & Robbins, S. B. (2000). Understanding social connectedness in college women and men. *Journal of Counseling and Development, 78*, 484–491.

Levin, H., Glass, G., & Meister, G. (1984). *Cost effectiveness of four educational interventions, Project Report No. 84-A11*. Stanford, CA: Institute for Research on Educational Finance and Governance.

Levin, M. L., Whitaker, D. J., Miller, K. S., & May, D. C. (1999). Teenage partners' communication about sexual risk and condom use: The importance of the parent–teenager discussions. *Family Planning Perspectives, 31,* 117–121.

Levy, S. R., Jurkovic, G. L., & Spirito, A. (1995). A multi-systems analysis of adolescent suicide attempters. *Journal of Abnormal Child Psychology, 23,* 221–234.

Lewinsohn, P., Rohde, P., & Seeley, J. K. (1993). Psychosocial characteristics of adolescents with a history of suicide attempts. *Journal of American Society of Child Adolescent Health Care, 4,* 106–108.

Lewinsohn, P., Rohde, P., Seeley, J., & Fischer, S. (1993). Age-cohort changes in the lifetime occurrence of depression and other mental disorders. *Journal of Abnormal Psychology, 102,* 110–120.

Lewis, T. J., & Sugai, G. (1999). Effective behavior support: A systems approach to proactive schoolwide management. *Focus on Exceptional Children, 31*(6), 1–24.

Lind, M. (2001). Thinking aloud: The case for a living wage. *New Leader, 84*(5), 12–14.

Lipschitz, A. (1995). Suicide prevention in young adults. *Suicide and Life-Threatening Behavior, 25*(1), 155–169.

Lipsey, M. W., Wilson, D. B., & Cothern, L. (2000, December). *Effective intervention for serious juvenile offenders.* Washington, DC: U.S. Department of Justice, Office of Justice Programs, Bulletin of the Office of Juvenile Justice and Delinquency Prevention.

Lockwood, L. (2000). Where are the parents? Parents' criminal responsibility for the acts of children. *Golden Gate University Law Review, 30,* 497–498.

Lodge, J., Harte, D. K., & Tripp, G. (1998). Children's self-talk under conditions of mild anxiety. *Journal of Anxiety Disorders, 12,* 153–176.

Loeber, R., Burke, J., Mutchka, J., & Lahey, B. (2004). Gun carrying and conduct disorder: A highly combustible combination? *Archives of Pediatric and Adolescent Medicine,158,* 138–145.

Loeber, R., & Farrington, D. P. (1998). *Serious and violent juvenile offenders: Risk factors and successful interventions.* Thousand Oaks, CA: Sage.

Lonczak, H. S., Abbott, R. D., Hawkins, J. D., Kosterman, R., & Catalano, R. F. (2002). Effects of the Seattle Social Development Project on sexual behavior, pregnancy, birth, and sexually transmitted disease outcomes. *Archives of Pediatrics and Adolescent Medicine, 156*(5), 438–447.

Lord, M. (1999, October). The violent-kid profile. *U.S. News* [Online]. Retrieved August 2001 from www.usnews.com

Lord, S. E., Eccles, J. S., & McCarthy, K. A. (1994). Surviving the junior high school transition: Family processes and self-perceptions as protective and risk factors. *Journal of Early Adolescence, 14*(2), 162–199.

Lorion, R., Price, R., & Eaton M. (1989). The prevention of child and adolescent disorders: From theory to research. In D. Shaffer, I. Philips, & N. B. Enzer (Eds.), *Prevention of mental disorders, alcohol and other drug use in children and adolescents* (pp. 55–95). Office of Substance Abuse Prevention and American Academy of Child and Adolescent Psychiatry, Prevention Monograph No. 2 (DHHS Publication No. ADM 89-1646). Rockville, MD: Office of Substance Abuse Prevention.

Lott, B. (2002). Cognitive and behavioral distancing from the poor. *American Psychologist, 57,* 100–110.

Lowenthal, B. (1996). Integrated school services for children at risk: Rationale, models, barriers, and recommendations for implementation. *Intervention in School and Clinic, 31*(3), 154–157.

Lunenburg, F.C. (2000). America's hope: Making schools work for all children. *Journal of Instructional Psychology, 37*(1), 39–47.

Luthar, S. S. (1999). *Poverty and children's adjustment* (Vol. 41, Developmental Clinical Psychology and Psychiatry). Thousand Oaks, CA: Sage.

Luther, S. S., & Latendresse, S. J. (2005). Children of the affluent: Challenges to well-being. *Current Directions in Psychological Science, 14,* 49–53.

Lykken, D. T. (2001). Parental licensure. *American Psychologist, 56,* 885–894.

Lynskey, M., & Hall, W. (2000). The effects of adolescent cannabis use on educational attainment: A review. *Addiction, 95,* 1621–1630.

Lysynchuk, L. M., Pressley, M., & Vye, N. J. (1990). Reciprocal teaching improves standardized reading-comprehension performance in poor comprehenders. *Elementary School Journal, 90,* 469–484.

Ma, X. (2001). Bullying and being bullied: To what extent are bullies also victims? *American Educational Research Journal, 38*(2), 351–370.

MacSwan, J., & Pray, L. (2005). Learning English bilingually: Age of onset of exposure and rate of acquisition of English among children in a bilingual education program [Online]. *Bilingual Research Journal, 29*(3). Retrieved November 1, 2005, from http://brj.asu.edu/.

Maeroff, G. I. (1998). Altered destinies: Making life better for school children in need. *Phi Delta Kappan, 79*(6), 425–432.

Mahoney, J. L. (1998). The prediction and prevention of crime: Developmental antecedents and turning points. *Dissertation Abstracts International: Section B: The Sciences & Engineering. 58*(8-B), 4492.

Maine, S., Shute, R., & Martin, G. (2001). Educating parents about youth suicide: Responses to suicidal statements, attitudes, and intention to help. *Journal of Suicide and Life Threatening Behavior, 31*, 320–332.

Mallon, G. P. (1998). *We don't exactly get the welcome wagon: The experiences of gay and lesbian adolescents in child welfare systems.* New York: Columbia University Press.

Maltbia, G. (1991). Cultural diversity as a labor management issue. *Employee Assistance Program Exchange, 21*(5), 26.

Manlove, J. (1998). The influence of high school dropout and school disengagement on the risk of school-age pregnancy. *Journal of Research on Adolescence, 8*, 187–220.

Mannheim, C. I., Sancilio, M., Phipps-Yonas, S., Brunnquell, D., Somers, P., Farseth, G., & Ninonuevo, F. (2002). Ethical ambiguities in the practice of child clinical psychology. *Professional Psychology: Research and Practice, 33*, 24–29.

Maples, M. F., Packman, J., Abney, P., Daugherty, R. F., Casey, J. A., & Pirtle, L. (2005, Fall). Suicide by teenagers in middle school: A postvention team approach. *Journal of Counseling & Development, 83*(4), 397–405.

Mareschal, P. M. (2005). What makes mediation work: Mediators' perspectives on resolving disputes. *Industrial Relations: A Journal of Economy & Society, 44*, 509–517.

Martin-Baró, I. (1994). *Writings for a liberation psychology.* Cambridge, MA: Harvard University Press.

Marttunen, M. J., Aro, H. M., & Lonnquist, J. K. (1993). Precipitant stressors in adolescent suicide. *Journal of the American Academy of Child and Adolescent Psychiatry, 32*(6), 1178–1183.

Marzen, T. J., O'Dowd, M. K., Crone, D., & Balch, T. J. (1985). Suicide: A constitutional right? *Duquesne Law Review 1*, 56–100.

Massey, O. T., Armstrong, K., Boroughs, M., Henson, K., & McCash, L. (2005). Mental health services in schools: A qualitative analysis of challenges to implementation, operation, and sustainability. *Psychology in the Schools, 42*, 361–372.

Mattison, R. E. (2000). School consultation: A review of research on issues unique to the school environment. *Journal of American Academy of Child and Adolescent Psychiatry, 39*(4), 402–413.

Maxwell, J. (1989). Mediation in the schools. *Mediation Quarterly, 7*, 149–154.

Mayou, R. A., Ehlers, A., & Hobbs, M. (2000). Psychological debriefing for road traffic accident victims: Three year follow-up of a randomized controlled trial. *British Journal of Psychiatry, 176*, 589–593.

Mazza, J. J., & Eggert, L. L (2001). Activity involvement among suicidal and non-suicidal high-risk and typical adolescents. *Suicide and Life-Threatening Behavior, 31*(3), 265–281.

McCambridge, J., & Strang, J. (2004). The efficacy of single-session motivational interviewing in reducing drug consumption and perceptions of drug-related risk and harm among young people: Results from a multi-site cluster randomized trial. *Addiction, 99*, 39–52.

McCormick, M. (1988). *Mediation in the schools: An evaluation of the Wakefield Pilot Peer Mediation Program in Tucson, Arizona.* Washington, DC: American Bar Association.

McCreanor, T., & Watson, P. (2004). Resiliency, connectivity and environments: Their roles in theorising approaches to promoting the well-being of young people. *International Journal of Mental Health Promotion 6*(1), 39–42.

McCubbin, H. I., & McCubbin, M. A. (1988). Typologies of resilient families: Emerging roles of social class and ethnicity. *Family Relations, 37*, 247–254.

McDevitt, T. M. (1996). *Trends in adolescent fertility and contraceptive use in the developing world.* [IPC/95-1]. Washington, DC: U.S. Bureau of the Census.

McGee, J., & DeBernardo, C. R. (1999, May/June). The classroom avenger: A behavioral profile of school-based shootings. *The Forensic Examiner,* 16–18.

McGinnis, E., & Goldstein, A. P. (1984). *Skillstreaming the elementary school child: A guide for teaching prosocial skills.* Champaign, IL: Research Press.

McGinnis, E., & Goldstein, A. P. (1990). *Skillstreaming in early childhood: Teaching prosocial skills to the preschool and kindergarten child.* Champaign, IL: Research Press.

McGloin, J. M., & Widom, C. S. (2001). Resilience among abused and neglected children grown up. *Development and Psychopathology, 13*, 1021–1038.

McGowan, S. (1991, October). Confidentiality: Breaking a sacred trust. *Guidepost,* pp. 14–15.

McGuire, J. M., Parnell, T. F., Blau, B. I., & Abbott, D. W. (1994). Demands for privacy among adolescents in multimodal alcohol and other drug abuse treatment. *Journal of Counseling & Development, 73*(1), 74–78.

McIntosh, J. L. (2000). Epidemiology of adolescent suicide in the United States. In R. W. Maris, S. S. Canetto, J. L. McIntosh, & M. M. Silverman (Eds.), *Review of Suicidology, 2000* (pp. 3–33). New York: Guilford Press.

McKinstery, J., & Topping, K. J. (2003). Cross-age peer tutoring of thinking skills in the high school. *Educational Psychology in Practice, 19*, 199–217.

McLean, P., & Taylor, S. (1994). Family therapy for suicidal people. *Death Studies, 18*(4), 409–426.

McLloyd, V. C. (1989). Socialization and development in a changing economy: The effects of paternal job and income loss on children. *American Psychologist, 44*(2), 293–302.

McMillen, M. M., Kaufman, P., & Whitener, S. D. (1995). *Dropout rates in the United States: 1995*. Washington, DC: National Center for Education Statistics.

McNeely, C., Nonnemaker, J., & Blum, R. (2002). Improving the odds: The untapped power of schools to improve the health of teens. *Journal of School Health, 72*(4). Available at www.allaboutkids.umn.edu.

McReynolds, R. A., Morris, R. J., & Kratochwill, T. R. (1989). Cognitive-behavioral treatment of school-related fears and anxieties. In J. N. Hughes & Robert J. Hall (Eds.), *Cognitive-behavioral psychology in the schools* (pp. 434–465). New York: Guilford Press.

McWhirter, B. T. (1990). Loneliness: A review of current literature, with implications for counseling and research. *Journal of Counseling and Development, 68*(4), 417–422.

McWhirter, B. T., & Burrow-Sanchez, J. J. (2004). Preventing and treating affective disorders in children and adolescents. In D. Capuzzi & D. Gross (Eds.), *Youth at risk: A prevention resource for counselors, teachers, & parents* (4th ed., pp. 147–179). Alexandria, VA: American Counseling Association.

McWhirter, B. T., McWhirter, J. J., Hart, R., & Gat, I. (2000). Preventing and treating depression in children and adolescents. In D. Capuzzi & D. Gross (Eds.), *Youth at risk: A prevention resource for counselors, teachers, & parents* (3rd ed., pp. 141–169). Alexandria, VA: American Counseling Association.

McWhirter, E. H. (1994). *Counseling for empowerment*. Alexandria, VA: American Counseling Association.

McWhirter, E. H. (1997, April). Empowerment, social activism, and counseling. *Counseling & Human Development, 29*(8), 1–11.

McWhirter, E. H. (2001, March). Social action at the individual level: In pursuit of critical consciousness. Invited keynote address, 5th Biennial conference of the Society for Vocational Psychology, Houston, TX.

McWhirter, J. J. (1988). *The learning disabled child: A school and family concern* (2nd ed.). Lanham, MD: University Press of America.

McWhirter, J. J. (2002). Will he choose life? In L. B. Golden (Ed.), *Case studies in child and adolescent counseling* (3rd ed., pp. 81–89). New York: Merrill/Prentice-Hall.

McWhirter, J. J., & Kahn, S. E. (1974). A parent communication group. *Elementary School Guidance and Counseling, 9*(2).

McWhirter, J. J., Herrmann, D. S., Jefferys, K., & Quinn, M. M. (1995). *Violence prevention programs*. Phoenix: Prudential Securities/City of Phoenix.

McWhirter, J. J., McWhirter, B. T., McWhirter, A. M., & McWhirter, E. H. (1994). High- and low-risk characteristics of youth: The five Cs of competency. *Elementary School Guidance & Counseling, 28*(3), 188–196.

McWhirter, J. J., McWhirter, B. T., McWhirter, A. M., & McWhirter, E. H. (1995). Youth at-risk: Another point of view. *Journal of Counseling and Development, 73*(5), 567–569.

McWhirter, J. J., & McWhirter, E. H. (1989). Poor soil yields damaged fruit: Environmental influences. In D. Capuzzi & D. Gross (Eds.), *Youth At Risk: A Resource for Counselors, Teachers and Parents* (pp. 19–40). Alexandria, VA: AACD Press.

McWhirter, J. J., & McWhirter, M. C. (1983). Increasing human potential: Relaxation and imagery training (RIT) with athletic and performing art teams. *Personnel and Guidance Journal, 62*(3), 135–138.

McWhirter, P. T. (1998). Risk factors associated with adolescent alcohol, tobacco, marijuana, solvent inhalant, and cocaine use. *National Institute on Drug Abuse Research Monograph, 179*, 202.

McWhirter, J. J., & McWhirter, R. J. (1988). Legal considerations for the practitioner. In D. Capuzzi & L. B. Golden (Eds.), *Preventing adolescent suicide*. (pp. 436–464). Muncie, IN: Accelerated Development.

McWhirter, R. J. (2006). The criminal lawyer's guide to immigration law : Questions and answers (2nd ed.). Chicago, IL: Criminal Justice Section, American Bar Association.

Meggert, S. S. (2000). Who cares what I think: Problems of low self-esteem. In D. Capuzzi & D. R. Gross (Eds.), *Youth risk: A prevention resource for counselors, teachers, and parents* (3rd ed., pp. 109–136). Alexandria, VA: American Counseling Association.

Meier, D., & Wood, G., et al. (2004). *Many children left behind: How the No Child Left Behind Act is damaging our children and our schools*. New York: Beacon Press.

Melchert, T., & Burnett, K. F. (1990). Attitudes, knowledge, and sexual behavior of high-risk adolescents: Implications for counseling and sexuality education.

Journal of Counseling and Development, 68(3), 293–298.

Metalsky, G. I., & Joiner, T. E. (1992). Vulnerability to depressive symptomatology: A prospective test of the diathesis-stress and causal mediation components of the hopelessness theory of depression. *Journal of Personality and Social Psychology*, 63(4), 667–675.

Metalsky, G. I., Joiner, T. E., Hardin, T. S., & Abramson, L. Y. (1993). Depressive reactions to failure in a naturalistic setting: A test of the hopelessness and self-esteem theories of depression. *Journal of Abnormal Psychology*, 102(1), 101–109.

Metcalf, L. (1995). *Counseling towards solutions: A practical solution-focused program for working with students, teachers, and parents.* New York: Center for Applied Research in Education.

Meyer, L. H., & Henry, L. A. (1993). Cooperative classroom management: Student needs and fairness in the regular classroom. In J. W. Putnam (Ed.), *Cooperative learning and strategies for inclusion: Celebrating diversity in the classroom* (p. 116). Baltimore: Paul H. Brookes.

Meyer, L. H., Williams, D. R., Harootunian, B., & Steinberg, A. (1995). An inclusion model to reduce at-risk status among middle school students: The Syracuse experience. In I. M. Evans, T. Cicchelli, M. Cohen, & N. P. Shapiro (Eds.), *Staying in school: Partnerships for educational change* (pp. 83–110). Baltimore: Paul H. Brookes.

Michenbaum, D. (1972). Clinical implications of modifying what clients say to themselves. *Research Reports in Psychology*, 42. Waterloo, Ontario, Canada: University of Waterloo.

Middlebrook, D. L., LeMaster, P. L., Beals, J., Novins, D. K., & Manson, S. M. (2001). Suicide prevention in American Indian and Alaska Native communities: A critical review of programs. *Suicide and Life Threatening Behavior*, 31, 32–49.

Miller, D. B., & MacIntosh, R. (1999). Promoting resilience in urban African American adolescents: Racial socialization and identity as protective factors. *Social Work Research*, 23, 159–169.

Miller, M., Azrael, D., & Hemenway, D. (2002). Firearm availability and unintentional firearm deaths, suicide, and homicide among 5–14 year olds. *Journal of Trauma*, 52(2), 267–275.

Miller, T. R., & Blincoe, L. J. (1994). Incidence and cost of alcohol-involved crashes in the United States. *Accident Analysis and Prevention*, 26(5), 583–591.

Miller, W. R., & Rollnick, S. (2002). *Motivational interviewing: Preparing people for change* (2nd ed.). New York: Guilford Press.

Miller-Kahn, L., & Smith, M. L. (2001, November 30). School choice policies in the political spectacle. *Education Policy Analysis Archives*, 9(50). Retrieved July 4, 2002, from http://epaa.asu.edu/epaa/v9n50.html.

Mitchell, J. J. (1996). *Adolescent vulnerability: A sympathetic look at the frailties and limitations of youth.* Calgary, Alberta, Canada: Detselig Enterprises Ltd.

Mize, J., & Pettit, G. S. (1997). Mothers' social coaching, mother–child relationship style, and children's peer competence: Is the medium the message? *Child Development*, 68, 291–311.

Moffitt, T. E., Caspi, A., Dickson, N., Silva, P., & Stanton, W. (1996). Childhood-onset versus adolescent-onset antisocial conduct problems in males: Natural history from ages 3 to 18 years. *Development and Psychopathology*, 8, 399–424.

Montagne, M., & Scott, D. M. (1993). Prevention of substance use problems: Models, factors, and processes. *International Journal of the Addictions*, 28, 1177–1208.

Moon, J. R., & Eisler, R. M. (1983). Anger control: An experimental comparison of three behavioral treatments. *Behavior Therapy*, 14, 493–505.

Moon, M., McFarland, M. W., Kellogg, T., Baxter, M., Katz, M., MacKellar, D., & Valleroy, L. (2000). HIV risk behavior of runaway youth in San Francisco: age of onset and relation to sexual orientation. *Youth and Society*, 32(2), 184–201.

Moore, D. D., & Forster, J. R. (1993). Student assistance programs: New approaches for reducing adolescent substance abuse. *Journal of Counseling and Development*, 71, 326–329.

Moore, J. (2005, July). Quality in after-school programs: After-school project of the Robert Wood Johnson Foundation. *Youth Today.* (For a free 79-page copy contact JoAnne Vellardita at vellardita@theafterschoolproject. org)

Moore, J., & Hagedorn, J. (2001). *Female gangs: A focus on research.* Youth Gang Series Bulletin. Washington, DC: U.S. Department of Justice, Office of Justice Programs, Office of Juvenile Justice and Delinquency Prevention.

Moore, K. A., Morrison, D. R., & Greene, A. D. (1997). Effects on the children born to adolescent mothers. In R. A. Maynard (Ed.), *Kids having kids: Economic costs and social consequences of teen pregnancy* (pp. 145–180). Washington, DC: Urban Institute Press.

Morganett, (Smead) R. S. (1990). *Skills for living: Group counseling activities for elementary students.* Champaign, IL: Research Press.

Morganett, (Smead) R. S. (1995). *Skills for living: Group counseling activities for elementary students* (2nd ed.). Champaign, IL: Research Press.

Moskos, M. A., Achilles, J., & Gray, D. (2004). Adolescent suicide myths in the United States. *Crisis: The Journal of Crisis Intervention and Suicide Prevention,* 25(4), 176–182.

Mossman, D. (1994). Assessing predictions of violence: Being accurate about accuracy. *Journal of Consulting and Clinical Psychology, 62,* 783–792.

Mrazek, P. J., & Hagerty, R. J. (Eds.). (1994). Reducing risks for mental disorders: *Frontiers for preventive intervention research.* Washington, D.C.: National Academy Press.

Mulhall, P. F., Stone, D., & Stone, B. (1996). Home alone: Is it a risk factor for middle school youth and drug use? *Journal of Drug Education, 26,* 39–48.

Mulroy, E. A. (1995). *The new uprooted: Single mothers in urban life.* Westport, CT: Auburn House/Greenwood.

Mulvey, E. P., & Cauffman, E. (2001). The inherent limits of predicting school violence. *American Psychologist, 56*(10), 797–802.

Murphy, J., & Duncan, B. (1997). *Brief interventions for school problems: Collaborating for practical solutions.* New York: Guilford Press.

Murphy, J. J. (1997). *Solution-focused counseling in middle and high schools.* Alexandria, VA: American Counseling Association.

Musick, J. S. (1993). *Young, poor, and pregnant.* New Haven, CT: Yale University Press.

Nansel, T. R., Overpeck, M., Pilla, R. S., Ruan, W. J., Simons-Morton, B., & Scheidt, P. (2001). Bullying behaviors among U.S. youth: Prevalence and association with psychosocial adjustment. *Journal of American Medical Association, 285*(16), 2094–2100.

National Campaign to Prevent Teen Pregnancy. (2001, May). *Emerging answers: Research findings on programs to reduce teen pregnancy.* Washington, DC: Author.

National Campaign to Prevent Teen Pregnancy. (2005). *The What if? project: What if teen birth rates in each state had not declined between 1991 and 2002?* Retrieved September 28, 2005, from www.teenpregnancy.org/whycare/whatif.asp.

National Campaign to Prevent Teen Pregnancy/Child Trends. (2005). *Not yet: Programs to delay first sex among teens.* Retrieved September 28, 2005, from www.teenpregnancy.org/works/pdf/NotYet.pdf.

National Center on Addiction and Substance Abuse. (2005). *Criminal neglect: Substance abuse, juvenile justice and the children left behind.* Retrieved September 14, 2005, from www.casacolumbia.org/pdshopprov/files/JJreport.pdf.

National Center for Children in Poverty. (2002). *Low-income children in the United States: A brief demographic profile.* Retrieved May 9, 2002, from http://cpmcnet.columbia.edu/dept/nccp/ycpf.html.

National Center for Chronic Disease Prevention and Health Promotion. (2000). *Adolescent and school health: Prevent alcohol and drug use.* Retrieved October 5, 2005, from http://www.cdc.gov/nccdphp/dash/alcoholdrug.htm.

National Center for Education Statistics. (2001). *The condition of education 2001.* U.S. Department of Education (NCES 2001-072). Washington, DC: Government Printing Office.

National Center for Health Statistics. (2000). *Deaths: Final data for 1998.* Washington, DC: U.S. Department of Health and Human Services.

National Commission on Excellence in Education. (1983). *A nation at risk: The imperative for educational reform.* Washington, DC: U.S. Government Printing Office.

National Data Evaluation Center (2005). *Reading Recovery and Descubriendo la Lectura National Statistical Abstract 204-2005* (NDEC Rep. No. 2005-14). Columbus: The Ohio State University.

National Institutes of Health Consenses Development Program. (2004). *Preventing violence and related health-risking social behaviors in adolescents* (Draft Statement). Retrieved September 28, 2005, from http://consenses.nih.gov/ta/023/youthviolenceDRAFTstatement101504.pdf.

National Organization on Adolescent Pregnancy, Parenting, and Prevention. (1995). *Pregnancy, poverty, school, and employment.* Bethesda, MD: Author.

Neihart, M., Reis, S. M., Robinson, N. M., & Moon, S. M. (2002). *The Social and Emotional Development of Gifted Children: What Do We Know?* Washington, DC: National Association for Gifted Children.

Newcomb, M. D., & Bentler, P. M. (1989). Substance use and abuse among children and teenagers. *American Psychologist, 44*(2), 242–248.

Newman-Carlson, D., & Horne, A. M. (2004). Bullybusters: A psychoeducational intervention for reducing bullying behavior in middle school students. *Journal of Counseling & Development, 82*(3), 259–267.

Nie, N. H., & Erbring, L. (2000). *Internet and society.* Stanford Institute for the Quantitative Study of Society. Retrieved July 26, 2002, from http://www.stanford.edu/group/siqss/Press_Release/Preliminary_Report.pdf.

N. O. L. v. District of Columbia, 674 A.2d 498 (Dist. of Columbia, 1996).

Noell, J. W., & Ochs, L. M. (2001). Relationship of sexual orientation to substance use, suicidal ideation, suicide attempts, and other factors in a population of homeless adolescents. *Journal of Adolescent Health, 29*(1), 31–36.

Nolen-Hoeksema, S., Girgus, J. S., & Seligman, M. E. P. (1992). Predictors and consequences of childhood depressive symptoms: A 5-year longitudinal study. *Journal of Abnormal Psychology, 101,* 405–422.

Norton, D. G. (1994). Education for professionals in family support. In S. L. K. Kagan & B. Weissbourd (Eds.), *Putting families first: America's family support movement and the challenge of change* (pp. 401–440). San Francisco: Jossey-Bass.

Norwood, P. M., Atkinson, S. E., Tellez, K., & Saldana, D. C. (1997). Contextualizing parent education programs in urban schools: The impact on minority parents and students. *Urban Education, 32*(3), 411–432.

Novoco, R. W. (1975). *Anger control: The development and evaluation of an experimental treatment.* Lexington, MA: Heath.

Novaco, R. W. (1979). Anger and coping with stress. In J. Foreyt and D. Rathjen (Eds.), *Cognitive behavior therapy: therapy, research and practice.* New York: Plenum Press.

Obiakor, F. E. (2001). *It even happens in "good" schools: Responding to cultural diversity in today's classrooms.* Thousand Oaks, CA: Sage.

O'Connor, M. F. (1992). Psychotherapy with gay and lesbian adolescents. In S. H. Dworkin & F. J. Gutierrez (Eds.), *Counseling gay men and lesbians: Journey to the end of the rainbow* (pp. 3–22). Alexandria, VA: American Association of Counseling and Development.

Oden, S., Schweinhart, L., & Weikart, D. P. (2000). *Into adulthood: A study of the effects of Head Start.* Ypsilanti, MI: High/Scope Educational Research Foundation.

Oetting, E. R., & Beauvais, F. (1986). Peer cluster theory: Drugs and the adolescent. *Journal of Counseling and Development, 65,* 17–22.

Oetting, E. R., & Beauvais, F. (1987). Peer cluster theory, socialization characteristics, and adolescent drug use: A path analysis. *Journal of Counseling Psychology, 34*(2), 205–213.

Office of Community Oriented Policing Services, U.S. Department of Justice. (2005). *School vandalism and break-ins: Problem-oriented guides for police.* Retrieved September 17, 2005, from www.cops.usdoj.gov/mime/open.pdf?Item=1560.

Office of Elementary and Secondary Education. (2000). *Education for homeless children and youth program: Title VII, subtitle B of the McKinney-Vento homeless assistance act. Report to Congress, Fiscal Year 2000* (EDD00014). Washington, DC: U.S. Government Printing Office.

Office of Juvenile Justice and Delinquency Prevention. (2005). *Juvenile arrests 2002.* Retrieved September 14, 2005, from www.ncjrs.org/pdffiles1/ojjdp/204608.pdf.

Office of the Surgeon General. (2001). *Youth violence: A report of the Surgeon General.* Retrieved May 10, 2002, from http://www.surgeongeneral.gov/library/youthviolence/youvioreport.htm.

Oldridge, O. A. (1982). Positive suggestion: It helps LD students learn. *Academic Therapy, 17,* 279–287.

Olfson, M., Shaffer, D., Marcus, S. C., & Greenberg, T. (2003). Relationship between antidepressant medication treatment and suicide in adolescents. *Archives of General Psychiatry, 60,* 978–982.

Olrich, F. (1983). A whole person spelling class. *Academic Therapy, 19,* 73–78.

Olweus, D. (1993). Bully/victim problems among schoolchildren: Long term consequences and an effective intervention program. In S. Hodgins (Ed.), *Mental disorder and crime* (pp. 317–349). Thousand Oaks, CA: Sage.

Orlinsky, D. E., Grawe, K., & Parks, B. K. (1994). Process and outcome in psychotherapy: Noch einmal. In A. E. Bergin & S. L. Garfield (Eds.), *Handbook of psychotherapy and behavior change* (4th ed., pp. 270–376). New York: Wiley.

O'Rourke, K., & Worzbyt, J. C. (1996). *Support groups for children.* Bristol, PA: Accelerated Development.

Orthner, D. K., & Randolph, K. A. (1999). Welfare reform and high school dropout patterns for children. *Children and Youth Services Review, 21*(9/10), 881–900.

O'Shaughnessy, T. E., Lane, K. L., Gresham, F. M., & Beebe-Frankenberger, M. E. (2002). Students with or at risk for emotional and behavioral difficulties: An integrated system of prevention and intervention. In K. L. Lane, F. M. Gresham, & T. E. O'Shaughnessy (Eds.), *Interventions for children with or at risk for emotional and behavioral disorders* (pp. 3–17). Boston: Allyn & Bacon.

Osofsky, J. D. (1997). *Children in a violent society.* New York: Guilford Press.

Otto, R. (1992). The prediction of dangerous behavior: A review and analysis of "second generation" research. *Forensic Reports, 5,* 103–133.

Overby, K. J., & Kegeles, S. M. (1994). The impact of AIDS on an urban population of high-risk female minority adolescents: Implications for intervention. *Journal of Adolescent Health, 15,* 216–227.

Papolos, D., & Papolos, J. (1999). *The bipolar child*. New York: Broadway Books.

Patterson, G. R. (1993). Orderly change in a stable world: The antisocial trait as a chimera. *Journal of Consulting and Clinical Psychology, 61*, 911–919.

Patterson, G. R., Crosby, L., & Vuchinich, S. (1992). Predicting risk for early police arrest. *Journal of Quantitative Criminology, 8*(4), 335–355.

Patterson, G. R., De Baryshe, B. D., & Ramsey, E. (1989). A developmental perspective on antisocial behavior. *American Psychologist, 44*(2), 329–335.

Patterson, G. R., Reid, J. B., & Dishion, T. J. (1992). *Antisocial boys*. Eugene, OR: Castalia.

Patterson, G. R., Reid, J. B., & Dishion, T. J. (1998). Antisocial boys. In J. M. Jenkins & K. Oatley (Eds.), *Human emotions: A reader* (pp. 330–336). Malden, MA: Blackwell.

Pedlow, C. T., & Carey, M. P. (2004). Developmentally appropriate sexual risk reduction interventions for adolescents: Rationale, review of interventions, and recommendations for research and practice. *Annals of Behavioral Medicine, 27*, 172–184.

Peebles-Wilkins, W. (2003). Support networks and well-being. *Children & Schools, 25*, 67–68.

Pelligrini, A.D. (2002). Bullying, victimization, and sexual harassment during the transition to middle school. *Educational Psychologist, 37*(3), 151–163.

People v. Brac, 167 P.2d 535 (1946).

Peterson, C., Maier, S., & Seligman, M. (1993). *Learned helplessness*. New York: Oxford.

Pettit, G. S. (2004). Violent children in developmental perspective: Risk and protective factors and the mechanisms through which they (may) operate. *Current Directions in Psychological Science, 13*, 194–197.

Pettit, G. S., Bates, J. E., & Dodge, K. A. (1997). Supportive parenting, ecological context, and children's adjustment: A seven-year longitudinal study. *Child Development, 68*, 908–923.

Pfeffer, C. R., Hurt, S. W., Kakuma, T., Peskin, J. R., Siefker, C. A., & Nagabhairava, S. (1994). Suicidal children grow up: Suicidal episodes and effects of treatment during follow-up. *Journal of the American Academy of Child and Adolescent Psychiatry, 33*, 225–230.

Pfeffer, C. R., Normandin, L., & Kakuma, T. (1994). Suicidal children grow up: Suicidal behavior and psychiatric disorders among relatives. *Journal of the American Academy of Child and Adolescent Psychiatry, 33*, 1087–1097.

Phillips, V., McCullough, L., Nelson, C. M., & Walker, H. M. (1992). Teamwork among teachers: Promoting a statewide agenda for students at risk for school failure. *Special Services in the Schools, 6*(3/4), 27–49.

Pierce, M. (2002). No child left behind? A faculty response to President Bush's education bill. *Harvard Graduate School of Education News*. Retrieved May 29, 2002, from http://www.gse.harvard.edu/news/features/pierce07012002.html.

Pierce, M. N., Stahlbrand, K., & Armstrong, S. B. (1984). *Increasing student productivity through peer tutoring programs*. Austin, TX: Pro-Ed.

Piers, E. V. (1984). *Piers-Harris children's self-concept scale—Revised edition*. Nashville, TN: Counselor Recordings and Tests.

Pinnell, G. S., Lyons, C. A., DeFord, D. E., Bryk, A. S., & Seltzer, M. (1994). Comparing instructional models for the literacy education of high-risk first graders. *Reading Research Quarterly, 29*, 8–39.

Plunkett, M., & Mitchell, C. M. (2000). Substance use rates among American Indian adolescents: Regional comparisons with Monitoring the Future high school seniors. *Journal of Drug Issues, 30*, 575–592.

Pong, S., & Ju, D. (2000). The effects of change in family structure and income on dropping out of middle and high school. *Journal of Family Issues, 21*(2), 147–169.

Population Reference Bureau. (2004.) *Child poverty in rural America*. Retrieved September 28, 2005, from www.prb.org/pdf04/ChildPovertyRuralAmerica.pdf.

Premack, D. (1965). Reinforcement theory. In D. Levin (Ed.), *Nebraska Symposium on Motivation: 1965*. Lincoln: University of Nebraska Press.

Prilleltensky, I. (1997). Values, assumptions and practices: Assessing the moral implications of psychological discourse and action. *American Psychologist, 52*(5), 517–535.

Princeton Survey Research Associates. (1997, March). *National omnibus survey questions about teen pregnancy*. Association of Reproductive Health Professionals and the National Campaign to Prevent Teen Pregnancy. Washington, DC: Author.

Princeton Survey Research Associates. (2001). *Condom advertising on television*. Menlo Park, CA: Henry J. Kaiser Family Foundation. Retrieved March 25, 2003, from http://www.kff.org/content/2001/3135/SurveySnapshot.pdf.

Prochaska, J., Velicer, W., DiClemente, C., & Fava, J. (1988). Measuring processes of change: Application to the cessation of smoking. *Journal of Consulting and Clinical Psychology, 56*, 520–528.

Prochaska, J. O., & DiClemente, C. C. (1983). Stages and processes of self-change of smoking: Toward an integrative model of change. *Journal of Consulting and Clinical Psychology, 51*, 390–395.

Prochaska, J. O., & DiClemente, C. C. (1986). Toward a comprehensive model for change. In W. R. Miller & N. Heather (Eds.), *Treating addictive behaviors.* New York: Plenum Press.

Prochaska, J. O., & DiClemente, C. C. (1992). Stages of change in the modification of problem behaviors. In J. O. Prochaska (Ed.), *Progress in behavior modification* (pp. 184–218). New York: Academic Press.

Proeger, C., & Myrick, R. (1980). Teaching children to relax. *Florida Educational Research and Development Council Research Bulletin, 14*, 51.

Prothrow-Stith, D. (2001). Youth, risk, and resilience: Community approaches to violence prevention. In J. M. Richmond & M. W. Fraser (Eds.), *The context of youth violence: Resilience, risk, and protection* (pp. 97–114). Westport, CT: Praeger.

Pryor, D. B., & Tollerud, T. R. (1999). Applications of Adlerian principles in school settings. *Professional School Counseling, 2*(4), 299–304.

Public Agenda. (2005). *All work and no play? Listening to what kids and parents really want from out-of-school time.* Retrieved September 28, 2005, from http://www.publicagenda.org/research/pdfs/all_work_no_play.pdf.

Queralt, M. (1993). Risk factors associated with completed suicide in Latino adolescents. *Adolescence, 28*(112), 831–850.

Radkowsky, M., & Siegel, L. J. (1997). The gay adolescent: Stressors, adaptations, and psychosocial interventions. *Journal of Clinical Psychology, 17*, 191–216.

Rak, C. F., & Patterson, L. E. (1996). Promoting resilience in at-risk children. *Journal of Counseling and Development, 74*, 368–373.

RAND Corporation. (2004). *Watching sex on television predicts adolescent initiation of sexual behavior.* Retrieved September 28, 2005, from www.rand.org.

Randell, B., Eggert, L. L., & Pike, K. (2001). Immediate post intervention effects of two brief youth suicide prevention interventions. *Suicide and Life-Threatening Behavior, 31*(1), 41–61.

Range, L. M., Leach, M. M., McIntyre, D., Posey-Deters, P. B., Marion, M. S., & Kovac, S. H., et al. (1999). Multicultural perspectives on suicide. *Aggression and Violent Behavior, 4*(4), 413–430.

Reddy, M., Borum, R., Berglund, J., Vossekuil, B., Fein, R., & Modzeleski, W. (2001). Evaluating risk for targeted violence in schools: Comparing risk assessment, threat assessment, and other approaches. *Psychology in the Schools, 38*(2), 157–172.

Remafedi, G., French, S., Story, M., Resnick, M., & Blum, R. (1998). The relationship between suicide risk and sexual orientation: Results of a population-based study. *American Journal of Public Health, 88*(1), 57–60.

Reminger, K., Hidi, S., & Krapp, A. (Eds.). (1992). *The role of interest in learning and development.* Hillsdale, NJ: Erlbaum.

Renninger, S. M., Veach, P. M., & Bagdade, P. (2002). Psychologists' knowledge, opinions, and decision-making processes regarding child abuse and neglect reporting laws. *Professional Psychology: Research and Practice, 33*, 19–23.

Resnick, M. D., Bearman, P. S., Blum, R. W., Bauman, K. E., Harris, K. M., Jones, J., Tabor, J., Behring, T., Sieving, R. E., Shew, M., Ireland, M., Bearinger, L. H., & Uldry, J. R. (1998). Protecting adolescents from harm: Findings from the National Longitudinal Study on Adolescent Health. *Journal of the American Medical Association, 278*(10), 823–832.

Reville, P. (2002). No child left behind? A faculty response to President Bush's education bill. *Harvard Graduate School of Education News.* Retrieved May 29, 2002, from http://www.gse.harvard.edu/news/features/reville07012002.html.

Reyes, O., & Hedeker, D. (1993). Identifying high-risk students during school transition. *Prevention in Human Services, 10*(2), 137–150.

Rice, E., Milburn, N.G., Rotheram-Borus, M.J., Mallett, S., & Rosenthal, D. (2005). The effects of peer group network properties on drug use among homeless youth. *American Behavioral Scientist, 48*, 1102–1123.

Richardson, D., Hammock, G., Smith, S., Gardner, W., & Signo, M. (1994). Empathy as a cognitive inhibitor of interpersonal aggression. *Aggressive Behavior, 20*, 275–289.

Riche, M. F. (2000). America's diversity and growth: Signposts for the 21st century: Family life. *Population Bulletin, 55*(2), 26–28.

Rigby, K. (1999). Peer victimization at school and the health of secondary school students. *British Educational Psychology, 68*, 95–104.

Rigby, K. (2000). Effects of peer victimisation in schools and perceived social support on adolescent well-being. *Journal of Adolescence, 23*, 57–68.

Rivera, E., & Omizo, M. M. (1980). The effects of relaxation and biofeedback on attention to task and impulsivity among male hyperactive children. *Exceptional Child, 27*(1), 41–51.

Rivers, I., & D'Augelli, A. R. (2001). The victimization of lesbian, gay, and bisexual youths. In A. R. D'Augelli & C. J. Patterson (Eds.), *Lesbian, gay, bisexual identities and youth: Psychological perspectives* (pp. 199–223). New York: Oxford University Press.

Roberts, S. (1994, December 24). Gap between rich and poor widens in New York. (p.3). *New York Times.*

Robertson, D., & Mathews, B. (1989). Preventing adolescent suicide with group counseling. *Journal for Specialists in Group Work, 14*(1), 34–39.

Robin Hood Foundation. (1996). *Kids having kids.* Washington, DC: Author.

Robinson Kurpius, S. E., Kerr, B., & Harkins, A. (Eds). (2004). *Handbook for counseling girls and women: Talent, risk, and resiliency.* Mesa, AZ: MTR Nueva Science.

Robinson Kurpius, S. E., Kerr, B., & Harkins, A. (Eds). (2005). *Handbook for counseling girls and women: Ten years of gender equity research at Arizona State University. Vol. 1: Talent, risk and resiliency. Vol. 2: Talent development.* Mesa, AZ: MTR Nueva Science.

Robinson, W. L., Watkins-Ferrell, P., Davis-Scott, P., & Ruch-Ross, H. S. (1993). Preventing teenage pregnancy. In D. S. Glenwick, & L. A. Jason (Eds.), *Promoting health and mental health in children, youth, and families* (pp. 99–124). New York: Springer Publishing Co.

Roderick, T. (1988). Johnny can learn to negotiate. *Educational Leadership, 45*(4), 86–90.

Rodkin, P. C., & Hodges, E. V. E. (2003). Bullies and victims in the peer ecology: Four questions for psychologists and school professionals. *School Psychology Review, 32,* 384–400.

Roe v. Wade, 410 U.S. 113 (1973).

Rohde, P., Lewinsohn, P.M., Klein, D.N., & Seeley, J.R. (2005). Association of parental depression with psychiatric course from adolescence to young adulthood among formerly depressed individuals. *Journal of Abnormal Psychology, 114,* 409–420.

Romano, J. L., & Hage, S. M. (2000). Prevention and counseling psychology: Revitalizing commitments for the 21st century. *The Counseling Psychologist, 28,* 733–763.

Rose, S., Bisson, J., & Wessely, S. (2001). Psychological debriefing for preventing post traumatic stress disorder (PTSD) (Cochrane Review) [Abstract]. *Cochrane Library, 4.*

Rosenshine, B., & Meister, C. (1991, April). *Reciprocal teaching: A review of nineteen experimental studies.* Paper presented at the annual meeting of the American Educational Research Association, Chicago.

Ross, J. G., Saavedra, P. J., Shur, G. H., Winters, F., & Felner, R. D. (1992). The effectiveness of an after-school program for primary grade latchkey students on precursors of substance abuse. *Journal of Community Psychology, OSAP Special Issue,* 22–38.

Rosser, R., Stevens, S., & Ruiz, B. (2005). Cognitive markers of adolescent risk taking: A correlate of drug abuse in at-risk individuals. *Prison Journal, 85,* 83–86.

Rotheram-Borus, M. J., & Langabeer, K. A. (2001). Developmental trajectories of gay, lesbian, and bisexual youths. In A. R. D'Augelli & C. J. Patterson (Eds.), *Lesbian, gay, and bisexual identities and youth* (pp. 97–128). New York: Oxford University Press.

Rothstein, R. (2004). *Class and schools: Using social, economic and educational reform to close the Black-White achievement gap.* Washington DC: Economic Policy Institute.

Rowley, W. J., & MacDonald, D. (2001). Counseling and the law: A cross-cultural perspective. *Journal of Counseling & Development, 79,* 422–429.

Roy, A. (1983). Family history of suicide. *Archives of General Psychiatry, 40,* 971–974.

Roy, A. (2001). Consumers of mental health services. *Suicide and Life-Threatening Behavior, 31*(1, Supplement), 60–83.

Rudolph, K. D., Lambert, S. F., Clark, A. G., & Kurlakowsky, K. D. (2001). Negotiating the transition to middle school: The role of self-regulatory processes. *Child Development, 72*(3), 929–946.

Russell, S. T., & Joyner, K. (2001). Adolescent sexual orientation and suicide risk: Evidence from a natural study. *American Journal of Public Health, 91,* 1276–1282.

Ryan, C. (2001). Counseling lesbian, gay, and bisexual youths. In A. R. D'Augelli & C. J. Patterson (Eds.), *Lesbian, gay, bisexual identities and youth: Psychological perspectives* (pp. 223–250). New York: Oxford University Press.

Ryan, C., & Futterman, D. (1998). *Lesbian & gay youth: Care & counseling.* New York: Columbia University Press.

Ryan, J. B., Reid, R., & Epstein, M. H. (2004). Peer-mediated intervention studies on academic achievement for students with EBD: A review. *Remedial & Special Education, 25*(6), 330–341.

Sadker, M. P., & Sadker, D. M. (1987). *Teachers, schools, and society.* New York: Random House.

Saleh, M., Lazonder, A. W., & De Jong, T. (2005). Effects of within-class ability grouping on social interaction, achievement, and motivation. *Instructional Science, 33,* 105–119.

Salmivalli, C., & Nieminen, E. (2002). Proactive and reactive aggression among school bullies, victims, and bully-victims. *Aggressive Behavior, 28*(1), 30–44.

San Francisco Community Board Program, Inc. (1982). *School initiatives* [video]. San Francisco: Author.

Sanchez, E.A., & Kibler-Sanchez, S. (2004). Empowering children in mediation: An intervention model. *Family Court Review, 42*, 554–575.

Sander, J. B., & McCarty, C. A. (2005). Youth depression in the family context: Familial risk factors and models of treatment. *Clinical Child and Family Psychology Review, 8*(3), 203–219.

Santa Rosa Health Care Corp. v. Garcia, 964 S.W.2d 940 (Tex. 1998).

Savin-Williams, R. C. (1994). Verbal and physical abuse as stressors in the lives of lesbian, gay male, and bisexual youths: Associations with school problems, running away, substance abuse, prostitution, and suicide. *Journal of Consulting and Clinical Psychology, 62*(2), 261–269.

Savin-Williams, R. C. (1995). Lesbian, gay male, and bisexual adolescents. In A. R. D'Augelli & C. J. Patterson (Eds.), *Lesbian, gay, and bisexual identities over the lifespan* (pp. 165–189). New York: Oxford University Press.

Savin-Williams, R. C., & Rodriguez, R. G. (1993). A developmental, clinical perspective on lesbian, gay male, and bisexual youths. In T. P. Gullotta, G. R. Adams, & R. Montemayor (Eds.), *Adolescent sexuality: Advances in adolescent development* (pp. 77–101). Newbury Park, CA: Sage.

Scarr, S., Phillips, D., & McCartney, K. (1990). Facts, fantasies, and the future of child care in the United States. *Psychological Science, 1*(1), 26–35.

Scheier, L. (2001). Etiologic studies of adolescent drug use: A compendium of data resources and their implications for prevention. *Journal of Primary Prevention, 22*, 125–168.

Schliebner, C. T., & Peregoy, J. J. (1994). Unemployment effects on the family and the child: Interventions for counselors. *Journal of Counseling & Development, 72*(4), 368–372.

Schorr, L. B. (1997). *Common purpose: Strengthening families and neighborhoods to rebuild America.* New York: Doubleday.

Schultz, D., Izard, C. E., Ackerman, B. P., & Youngstrom, E. A. (2001). Emotion knowledge in economically disadvantaged children: Self-regulatory antecedents and relations to social difficulties and withdrawal. *Development and Psychopathology, 13*, 53–67.

Schwartz, D., McFadyen-Ketchum, S. A., Dodge, K. A., Pettit, G. S., & Bates, J. E. (1998). Peer group victimization as a predictor of children's behavior problems at home and in school. *Development and Psychopathology, 10*, 87–99.

Seastrom, M. M., Gruber, K. J., Henke, R., McGrath, D. J., & Cohen, B. A. (2002). *Qualifications of the public school teacher workforce: Prevalence of out-of-field teaching, 1987–88 to 1999–2000* (NCES Publication No. 2002-603). Washington, DC: U.S. Department of Education, National Center for Education Statistics.

Seidman, E., & French, S. E. (1997). Normative school transitions among urban adolescents: When, where, and how to intervene. In H. J. Walberg & O. Reyes, et al. (Eds.), *Children and youth: Interdisciplinary perspectives. Issues in Children's and Families Lives, Vol. 7* (pp. 166–189). Thousand Oaks, CA: Sage.

Seligman, M. (1990). *Learned optimism.* New York: Knopf.

Seligman, M. (1993). *Helplessness: On depression, development, and death.* San Francisco: Freeman.

Seligman, M. (1994). *What you can change and what you can't.* New York: Knopf.

Seligman, M. E. P. (1995). *The optimistic child: A revolutionary program that safeguards children against depression and builds lifelong resilience.* New York: Houghton Mifflin.

Seligman, M. E. P., Schulman, B. S., DeRubeis, R. J., & Hollon, S. D. (1999). The prevention of depression and anxiety. *Prevention & Treatment, 2*, article 8. Retrieved June 15, 2002, from http://journals.apa.org/prevention/volume2/pre0020008a.html.

Sergiovanni, T. J. (1994). *Building community in schools.* San Francisco: Jossey-Bass.

Sergiovanni, T. J. (2001). *The principalship.* Needham Heights, MA: Allyn & Bacon.

Sewell, K. W., & Mendelsohn, M. (2000). Profiling potentially violent youth: Statistical and conceptual problems. *Children's Services: Social Policy, Research, and Practice, 3*, 147–169.

Sexton, T. L., & Whiston, S. C. (1994). The status of the counseling relationship: An empirical review, theoretical implications, and research directions. *The Counseling Psychologist, 22*, 6–78.

Shannon, P. (1989). The struggle for control of literacy lessons. *Language Arts, 66*, 625–633.

Shapiro, E. S., & Cole, C. L. (1992). Self-monitoring. In T. H. Ollendick & M. Hersen (Eds.), *Handbook of child and adolescent assessment* (pp. 124–139). New York: Pergamon Press.

Shapiro, E. S., & Cole, C. L. (1994). *Behavior change in the classroom: Self-management interventions.* New York: Guilford Press.

Sharan, S. (Ed.). (1994). *Handbook of cooperative learning methods.* Westport, CT: Greenwood.

Shearer, C. (1990, January 17). Bankrupt: Education reforms costly. *State Press* (Tempe, AZ), p. 3.

Shedler, J., & Block, J. (1990). Adolescent drug use and psychological health: A longitudinal inquiry. *American Psychologist, 45,* 612–630.

Sheley, J., McGee, A., & Wright, J. (1992). Gun-related violence in and around inner-city schools. *American Journal of Diseases of Children, 146,* 677–682.

Shestowsky, D. (2004). Procedural preferences in alternative dispute resolution: A closer, modern look at an old idea. *Psychology, Public Policy, and Law, 10,* 211–249.

Shortt, A. L., Barrett, P. M., & Fox, T. L. (2001). Evaluating the FRIENDS program: A cognitive-behavioral group treatment for anxious children and their parents. *Journal of Clinical Child Psychology, 30*(4), 525–535.

Shubert, T. H., Bressette, S., Deeken, J., & Bender, W. N. (1999). Analysis of random school shootings. In W. N. Bender, G. Clinton, & R. L. Bender (Eds.), *Violence prevention and reduction in schools* (pp. 97–101). Austin, TX: Pro-Ed.

Shure, M. B. (1992a). *I Can Problem Solve (ICPS): An interpersonal cognitive problem solving program (preschool).* Champaign, IL: Research Press.

Shure, M. B. (1992b). *I Can Problem Solve (ICPS): An interpersonal cognitive problem solving program (kindergarten/primary grades).* Champaign, IL: Research Press.

Shure, M. B. (1992c). *I Can Problem Solve (ICPS): An interpersonal cognitive problem solving program (intermediate elementary grades).* Champaign, IL: Research Press.

Shure, M. B. (1993). I Can Problem Solve (ICPS): Interpersonal cognitive problem solving for younger children. *Early Child Development and Care, 96,* 49–64.

Shure, M. B. (1996a). *Raising a thinking child: Help your young child to resolve everyday conflicts and get along with others.* New York: Pocket Books.

Shure, M. B. (1996b). *Raising a thinking child workbook.* New York: Pocket Books.

Shure, M. B. (1999, April). Preventing violence: The problem solving way. *Juvenile Justice Bulletin,* 1–11.

Shure, M. B., & Spivack, G. (1988). Interpersonal cognitive problem solving. In R. H. Price, E. L. Cowen, R. P. Lorion, & J. Ramos-McKay (Eds.), *14 ounces of prevention: A casebook for practitioners* (pp. 69–82). Washington, DC: American Psychological Association.

Simmons, R. (2002). *Odd girl out: The hidden culture of aggression in girls.* New York: Harcourt Books.

Simons, R. L., Whitbeck, L. B., Conger, R. D., & Melby, J. N. (1991). The effect of social skills, values, peers, and depression on adolescent substance use. *Journal of Early Adolescence, 11*(4), 466–481.

Sinclair, M. F., Hurley, C. M., Evelo, D. L., Christenson, S. L., & Thurlow, M. L. (2002). Making connections that keep students coming to school. In B. Algozzine & P. Kay (Eds.), *Preventing problem behaviors: A handbook of successful prevention strategies* (pp. 162–182). Thousand Oaks, CA: Sage.

Sitlington, P. L., & Frank, A. R. (1993). Dropouts with learning disabilities: What happens to them as young adults? *Learning Disabilities Research and Practice, 8*(4), 244–252.

Sklar, H. (1995). *Chaos or community? Seeking solutions, not scapegoats for bad economics.* Boston: South End Press.

Sklare, G. (1997). *Brief counseling works: A solution focused approach for school counselors.* Thousand Oaks, CA: Corwin Press.

Slavin, R. (1983). *Cooperative learning.* New York: Longman.

Slavin, R., & Madden, N. (1989). What works for students at risk: A research synthesis. *Educational Leadership, 46*(5), 4–13.

Slavin, R. E. (1991). Cooperative learning and group contingencies. *Journal of Behavioral Education, 1*(1), 105–115.

Slavin, R. E. (1993). Ability grouping in the middle grades: Achievement effects and alternatives. *The Elementary School Journal, 93*(5), 535–552.

Slavin, R. E. (1994). Preventing early school failure: The challenge and the opportunity. In R. E. Slavin, N. L. Karweit, & B. A. Wasik (Eds.), *Preventing early school failure: Research, policy and practice* (pp. 1–12). Boston: Allyn & Bacon.

Slavin, R. E., Karweit, N. L., & Wasik, B. A. (Eds.). (1994). *Preventing early school failure: Research, policy, and practice.* Boston: Allyn & Bacon.

Small, M. A., Lyons, P. M., & Guy, L. S. (2002). Liability issues in child abuse and neglect reporting statutes. *Professional Psychology: Research and Practice, 33,* 13–18.

Smith, C. (1996). The link between childhood maltreatment and teenage pregnancy. *Social Work Research, 20*(3), 131–141.

Smith, D. C., & Sandhu, D. S. (2004). Toward a positive perspective on violence prevention in schools: Building connections. *Journal of Counseling & Development, 82*(3), 287–293.

Smith, D. J., Young, K. R., Nelson, J. R., & West, R. P. (1992). The effect of a self-management procedure on the classroom academic behavior of students with mild handicaps. *School Psychology Review, 21,* 59–72.

Smith, J. C., Mercer, J. A., & Rosenberg, M. L. (1989). Hispanic students in the Southwest, 1980–82. In *Alcohol, drug abuse, and mental health administration, Report of the Secretary's Task Force on Youth Suicide, Volume 3: Prevention and interventions in youth suicide* (pp. 196–205). DHHS Pub. No. (ADM) 89-1623. Washington, DC: U.S. Government Printing Office.

Smith, K. (2002). *Who's minding the kids? Child care arrangements: Spring 1997.* Current Population Reports. Washington, DC: U.S. Census Bureau.

Smith, M. J. (1986). *Yes, I can say no.* New York: Arbor House.

Smith, S. W., & Daunic, A. P. (2002). Using conflict resolution and peer mediation to support positive behavior. In B. Algozzine & P. Kay (Eds.), *Preventing problem behaviors: A handbook of successful prevention strategies* (pp. 162–182). Thousand Oaks, CA: Sage.

Smith, T. (2000). *Data from the general social survey.* Chicago, IL: University of Chicago National Opinion Research Center.

Smylie, M. A., & Tuermer, U. (1992). *Hammond, Indiana: The politics of involvement v. the politics of confrontation.* Claremont, CA: Claremont Graduate School, Claremont Project VISION.

Snyder, C. R. (1994). *The psychology of hope: You can get there from here.* New York: Free Press.

Snyder, C. R., Sympson, S. C., Ybasco, F. C., Borders, T. F., Babyak, M. A., & Higgins, R. L. (1996). Development and validation of the State Hope Scale. *Journal of Personality and Social Psychology, 2,* 321–335.

Snyder, H. N. (2000, December). Juvenile arrests 1999. *Bulletin of the Office of Justice Programs,* pp. 1–11. Washington, DC: U.S. Department of Justice, Office of Juvenile Justice and Delinquency Prevention.

Solantaus, T., Leinonen, J., & Puramaki, R. L. (2004). Children's mental health in times of economic recession: Replication and extension of the family economic stress model in Finland. *Developmental Psychology, 40*(3), 412–427.

Sommers-Flanagan, J., & Sommers-Flanagan, R. (1998). Assessment and diagnosis of conduct disorder. *Journal of Counseling & Development, 76,* 189–197.

Spergel, I., Curry, D., Chance, R., Kane, C., Ross, R., Alexander, A., Simmons, E., & Oh, S. (1996). *Gang suppression and intervention: Problem and response.* Research Summary, Office of Justice Programs, Office of Juvenile Justice and Delinquency Prevention. Washington, DC: U.S. Department of Justice.

Spivack, G., Platt, J. J., & Shure, M. B. (1976). *The problem solving approach to adjustment.* San Francisco: Jossey-Bass.

Spivack, G., & Shure, M. B. (1974). *Social adjustment of young children.* San Francisco: Jossey-Bass.

SRI International. (1997, December 11) *Charter School Effectiveness. Legislative Analyst's Office: Perspectives and issues 1996–97.* Menlo Park, CA: Author.

Starbuck, D., Howell, J. C., & Lindquist, D. (2001, December). Hybrid and other modern gangs. *Bulletin of the Office of Juvenile Justice and Delinquency Prevention.* Washington, DC: U.S. Department of Justice, Office of Justice Programs.

State v. Tritt, 23 Utah 365, 463 P.2d 806 (1970).

Stephens, S. (2001). The effectiveness of Motivational Enhancement Therapy in adolescent smoking cessation. *Dissertation Abstracts International, 62* (2-B).

Stephens, T. M. (1992). *Social skills in the classroom* (2nd ed.). Odessa, FL: Psychological Assessment Resources.

Stern, S. R. (2005) Messages from teens on the big screen: Smoking, drinking, and drug use in teen-centered films. *Journal of Health Communication, 10*(4), 331–346.

Stevens, R. J., & Slavin, R. E. (1995). The cooperative elementary school: Effects on students' achievement, attitudes, and social relations. *American Educational Research Journal, 32*(2), 321–351.

Stivers, C. (1990). Promotion of self-esteem in the prevention of suicide. *Death Studies, 14,* 303–327.

Stormshak, E. A., Bierman, K. L., & The Conduct Problems Prevention Research Group. (1998). The implications of different developmental patterns of disruptive behavior problems for school adjustment. *Development and Psychopathology, 10,* 451–468.

Stormshak, E. A., & Dishion, T. J. (2002). An ecological approach to clinical and counseling psychology. *Clinical Child and Family Psychology Review, 5,* 197–215.

Straus, M. B. (1994). *Violence in the lives of adolescents.* New York: Norton.

Styron, T., Hanoff-Bulman, R., & Davidson, L. (2000). "Please ask me how I am": Experiences of family homelessness in the context of single mothers' lives. *Journal of Social Distress & the Homeless, 9*(2), 143–165.

Sue, D. W., & Sue, D. (2003). *Counseling the culturally diverse: Theory and practice* (4th ed.). New York: Wiley.

Sugai, G., & Horner, R. H. (1999). Discipline and behavioral support: Preferred processes and practices. *Effective School Practices, 17*(4), 10–22.

Sugai, G., & Horner, R. H. (2001). Features of an effective behavior support at the school district level. *Beyond Behavior, 11*(1), 6–19.

Sullivan, M., & Wodarski, J. S. (2002). Social alienation in gay youth. *Journal of Human Behavior in the Social Environment, 5*(1), 1–17.

Sutton, M. J., Brown, J. D., Wilson, K. M., & Klein, J. D. (2002). Shaking the tree of knowledge for forbidden fruit: Where adolescents learn about sexuality and contraception. In J. D. Brown, J. R. Steele, & K. Walsh-Childers (Eds.). *Sexual teens, sexual media* (pp. 25–55). Hillsdale: NJ: Erlbaum.

Swadener, B. B., & Lubeck, S. (Eds.). (1995). *Children and families at promise: Deconstructing the discourse of risk.* Albany: State University of New York Press.

Swaim, R. C., Oetting, E. R., Edwards, R. W., & Beauvais, F. (1989). Links from emotional distress to adolescent drug use: A path model. *Journal of Consulting and Clinical Psychology, 57,* 227–231.

Swearer, S., Song, S. Y., Cary, P. T., Eagle, J. W., & Mickelson, W. T. (2001). Psychosocial correlates in bullying and victimization: The relationship between depression, anxiety and bully/victim status. *Journal of Emotional Abuse, 2* (2/3), 95–122.

Sweeney, T. J. (1998). *Adlerian counseling: A practitioner's approach* (4th ed.). Philadelphia: Taylor & Francis.

Szapocznik, J., & Williams, R. A. (2000). Brief strategic family therapy: Twenty-five years of interplay among theory, research and practice in adolescent behavior problems and drug abuse. *Clinical Child and Family Psychology Review, 3*(2), 117–135.

Szapocznik, J., Santisteban, D., Kurtines, W. M., Perez-Vidal, A., & Hervis, O. (1984). Bicultural effectiveness training: A treatment intervention for enhancing intercultural adjustment in Cuban-American families. *Hispanic Journal of Behavioral Sciences, 6,* 317–344.

Szapocznik, J., Santisteban, D., Rio, A., Perez-Vidal, A., & Kurtines, W. M. (1986a). Family effectiveness training (FET) for Hispanic families. In H. P. Lefley & P. B. Pedersen (Eds.), *Cross-cultural training for mental health professionals.* Springfield, IL: Charles C Thomas.

Szapocznik, J., Santisteban, D., Rio, A., Perez-Vidal, A., & Kurtines, W. M. (1986b). Bicultural effectiveness training (BET): An experimental test of an intervention modality for families experiencing intergenerational/intercultural conflict. *Hispanic Journal of Behavioral Sciences, 8*(4), 303–330.

Szapocznik, J., Santisteban, D., Rio, A., Perez-Vidal, A., & Kurtines, W. M. (1989). Family effectiveness training: An intervention to prevent drug abuse and problem behaviors in Hispanic adolescents. *Hispanic Journal of Behavioral Sciences, 11*(1), 4–27.

Tang, M., & Cook, E. P. (2001). Understanding relationship and career concerns of middle school girls. In P. O'Reilly, E. M. Penn, & K. deMarrais (Eds.), *Educating young adolescent girls* (pp. 213–229). Mahwah, NJ: Erlbaum.

Tansy, M., Santos de Barona, M., McWhirter, J. J., & Herrmann, D. S. (1996). Peer and cross-age tutoring programs: Counsellor contribution to student achievement. *Guidance and Counselling, 12*(1), 21–24.

Taqi-Eddin, K., Macallair, D., & Schiraldi, V. (1998). *Class dismissed: Higher education vs. corrections during the Wilson years.* San Francisco, CA: Justice Policy Institute.

Tarasoff v. Regents of the University of California, et al., 17 Cal. 3d 425, 551 P2d 334 (1976).

Taylor, B., Pressley, M., & Pearson, D. (2000). *Research-supported characteristics of teachers and schools that promote reading achievement.* Ann Arbor, MI: Center for the Improvement of Early Reading Achievement.

Teacher Education Institute. (2002). *Bully prevention in schools: On-line course for teachers.* Retrieved December 15, 2002, from http://www.teachereducation.com/course_outlines/graduate_online/bully_gradon_outline.htm.

Thomas, S. P., & Smith, H. (2004). School connectedness, anger behaviors, and relationships of violent and nonviolent American youth. *Perspectives in Psychiatric Care, 40*(4), 135–148.

Thompson, E. A., & Eggert, L. L. (1999). Using the suicide risk screen to identify suicidal adolescents among potential high school dropouts. *Journal of the American Academy of Child and Adolescent Psychiatry, 38*(12), 1506–1514.

Thomson, E., Hanson, T., & McLanahan, S. (1994). Family structure and child well-being: Economic resources vs. parental behaviors. *Sociological Forces, 73,* 221–242.

Tidwell, R., & Corona Garrett, S. (1994). Youth at risk: In search of a definition. *Journal of Counseling and Development, 72,* 444–446.

Tolan P. H., & Gorman-Smith, D. (1997). Families and the development of urban children. In H. J. Walberg & O. Reyes (Eds.), *Children and youth: Interdisciplinary perspectives. Issues in children's and families' lives* (Vol. 7, pp. 67–91). Thousand Oaks, CA: Sage.

Tolan, P. H., & Guerra, N. G. (1994). Prevention of delinquency: Current status and issues. *Applied & Preventive Psychology, 3,* 251–273.

Tomlinson-Keasey, C., & Keasey, C. B. (1988). "Signatures" of suicide. In D. Capuzzi & L. Golden (Eds.), *Preventing adolescent suicide* (pp. 213–245). Muncie, IN: Accelerated Development.

Topping, K. J., & Bryce, A. (2004). Cross-age peer tutoring of reading and thinking: Influence on thinking skills. *Educational Psychology, 24,* 595–621.

Topping, K. J., Campbell, J., Douglas, W., & Smith, A. (2003). Cross-age peer tutoring in mathematics with seven- and 11-year olds: Influence on mathematical vocabulary, strategic dialogue and self-concept. *Educational Research, 45,* 287–308.

Topping, K. J., Peter, C., Stephen, P., & Whale, M. (2004). Cross-age peer tutoring of science in the primary school: Influence on scientific language and thinking. *Educational Psychology, 24,* 57–75.

Townsend, K. C., & McWhirter, B. T. (2005). Connectedness: A review of current literature, with implications for counseling, assessment, and research. *Journal of Counseling & Development, 83*(2), 191–201.

Trei, L. (2002, April 10). Child care left out of feminist revolution, Strober says. *Stanford Report.* Retrieved April 4, 2005, from http://ed.stanford.edu/suse/news-bureau/displayRecord.php?tablename=notify1&id=10.

Triantafillou, N. (1997). A solution-focused approach to mental health supervision. *Journal of Systemic Therapies, 16,* 305–328.

Uhlmann, E., & Swanson, J. (2004). Exposure to violent video games increases automatic aggressiveness. *Journal of Adolescence, 27,* 41–52.

United States v. Chase, 301 F.3d 1019 (9th Cir. 2002).

United States v. Glass, 133 F.3d 1356 (10th Cir. 1998).

United States v. Hayes, 227 F.3d 578 (6th Cir. 2000).

United States v. Juvenile, 347 F.3rd 778, 787 (9th Cir. 2003).

U.S. Census Bureau. (2001). *Census 2000 Supplementary Survey.* Washington, DC: Demographic Surveys Division.

U. S. Census Bureau (2002). Who's minding the kids? Child Care Arrangements: Winter 2002. Retrieved March 12, 2005, from http://www.census.gov/population/www/socdemo/childcare.html.

U.S. Conference of Mayors. (2001). *A status report on hunger and homelessness in America's cities: 2001.* Washington, DC: National League of Cities.

U.S. Department of Agriculture, Economic Research Service. (2005). *Rural children at a glance.* Retrieved September 28, 2005, from www.ers.usda.gov/publications/EIB1.pdf.

U.S. Department of Commerce. (1997). *March 1997 population survey.* U.S. Department of Commerce News (CB99-115). Washington, DC: Author.

U.S. Department of Education. (1998). *National educational goals panel report.* Washington, DC: Author.

U.S. Department of Education. (2000). *Safeguarding our children: An action guide.* Washington, DC: U.S. Government Printing Office.

U.S. Department of Health and Human Services. (1998). *New tools for HIV care: STD treatment.* Rockville, MD: Health Resources & Services Administration.

U.S. Department of Health and Human Services. (2002). *Substance abuse—A national challenge: Prevention, treatment and research at HHS* [Fact sheet]. Retrieved October 8, 2005, from http://www.cdc.gov/nccdphp/dash/alcoholdrug.htm.

U .S. Office of Juvenile Justice and Delinquency Prevention. (2005). *Overcoming barriers to school reentry.* Retrieved September 28, 2005, from www.ncjrs.org/pdffiles1/ojjdp/fs200403.pdf.

Valleroy, L. A., MacKellar, D., & Jacobs, T. (1996). *HIV and risk behavior prevalence among young men who have sex with men sampled in six urban counties in the USA.* Presented to the 11th International Conference on AIDS, Vancouver, BC.

van Dalen, A., & Glasserman, M. (1997). My father, Frankenstein: A child's view of battering parents. *Journal of American Child and Adolescent Psychiatry, 36,* 1005–1007.

Vaughn, S., Hughes, M. T., Moody, S. W., & Elbaum, B. (2001). Instructional grouping for reading for students with LD: Implications for practice. *Intervention in School and Clinic, 36*(3), 131–137.

Velez, W., & Saenz, R. (2001). Toward a comprehensive model of the school leaving process among Latinos. *School Psychology Quarterly, 16*(4), 445–467.

Ventura, S., & Curtin, S. C. (1999). Recent trends in teen births in the United States. *Statistical Bulletin, 80*(1), 2–12.

Ventura, S. J., Martin, J. A., Curtin, S. C., Mathews, T. J., & Park, M. M. (2000). Births: Final data for 1998. *National Vital Statistics Reports, 48*(3). Hyattsville, MD: National Center for Health Statistics.

Ventura, S. J., Matthews T. J., & Hamilton, B. E. (2002). Teenage births in the United States: state trends, 1991–2000, an update. *National Vital Statistics Reports, 50.* Atlanta, GA: Centers for Disease Control.

Vernon, A. (1983). Rational-emotive education. In A. Ellis & M. Bernards (Eds.), *Rational-emotive approaches to the problems of childhood.* New York: Plenum Press.

Vickers, H. S. (1994). Young children at risk: Differences in family functioning. *Journal of Educational Research, 87*(5), 262–270.

Wachelka, D., & Katz, R. C. (1999). Reducing test anxiety and improving academic self-esteem in high school and college students with learning disabilities. *Journal of Behavior Therapy and Experimental Psychiatry, 30,* 191–198.

Wagner, W. G. (1996). Optimal development in adolescence: What is it and how can it be encouraged? *The Counseling Psychologist, 24*(3), 360–399.

Walker, H. M., Colvin, G., & Ramsey, E. (1995). *Antisocial behavior in school: Strategies and best practices.* Pacific Grove, CA: Brooks/Cole.

Walker, L. E. A. (1990). Psychological assessment of sexually abused children for legal evaluation and expert witness testimony. *Professional Psychology: Research and Practice, 21,* 344–353.

Walker, L. E. A. (1996). *Abused women and survivor therapy: A practical guide for the psychotherapist.* Washington, DC: American Psychological Association.

Watkins, K. P., & Durant, L. (1996). *Working with children and families affected by substance abuse: A guide for early childhood education and human service staff.* West Nyack, NY: Center for Applied Research Education.

Watt, D., & Roessingh, H. (1994). ESL dropout: The myth of educational equity. *Alberta Journal of Educational Research, 40*(3), 283–296.

Way, N., & Leadbeater, B. (1999). Pathways toward educational achievement among African American and Puerto Rican adolescent mothers: Reexamining the role of social support from families. *Development and Psychopathology, 11,* 349–361.

Wayne, A. (2002, June 13). Teacher inequality: New evidence on disparities in teachers' academic skills. *Education Policy Analysis Archives, 10*(30). Retrieved July 4, 2002, from http://epaa.asu.edu/epaa/v10n30/.

Webster-Stratton, C. (1997). From parent training to community building. *Families in Society: The Journal of Contemporary Human Services, 78,* 156–171.

Webster-Stratton, C., Reid, M. J., & Hammond, M. (2001). Preventing conduct problems, promoting social competence: A parent and teacher training partnership in Head Start. *Journal of Clinical Child Psychology, 30*(3), 283–302.

Weinstein, B., Levine, M., Kogan, N., Harkavy-Friedman, J., & Miller, J. M. (2000). Mental health professionals' experiences reporting suspected child abuse and maltreatment. *Child Abuse & Neglect, 24,* 1317–1328.

Weisz, J. R., Sweeney, L., Proffitt, V., & Carr, T. (1993). Control-related beliefs and self-reported depressive symptoms in late childhood. *Journal of Abnormal Psychology, 102,* 411–418.

Wenz, K., & McWhirter, J. J. (1990). Enhancing the group experience: Creative writing exercise. *Journal for Specialists in Group Work, 15*(1), 37–42.

Werch, C. E., & DiClemente, C. C. (1994). A multicomponent stage model for matching drug prevention strategies and messages to youth stage of use. *Health Education Research: Theory & Practice, 9,* 37–46.

Werner, E. E. (1995). Resilience in development. *Current Directions in Psychological Science, 4*(3), 81–82.

Werner, E. E., & Smith, R. S. (1992). *Overcoming the odds: High risk children from birth to adulthood.* Ithaca, NY: Cornell University Press.

Whisman, M. A., & Kwon, P. (1993). Life stress and dysphoria: The role of self-esteem and hopelessness. *Journal of Personality and Social Psychology, 65*(5), 1054–1060.

White, R., Algozzine, B., Autette, B., Marr, M. B., & Ellis, E. (2001). Unified discipline: A school-wide approach for managing problem behavior. *Intervention in School and Clinic, 37,* 3–8.

Whiteman, T. L., Borkowski, J., Keogh, D., & Weed, K. (2001). *Interwoven lives: Adolescent mothers and their children.* Mahwah, NJ: Erlbaum.

Wiehe, S. E., Garrison, M. M., Christakis, D. A., Ebel, B. E., & Rivara, F. P. (2005). A systematic review of school-based smoking prevention trials with long-term follow up. *Journal of Adolescent Health, 36*(3), 162–169.

Wiig, E. H. (1983). *Let's talk: Developing prosocial communication skills.* Columbus, OH: Merrill.

Wilcox, D., & Dowrick, P. W. (1992). Anger management with adolescents. *Residential Treatment for Children and Youth, 9*(3), 29–39.

Wilens, T. E., Biederman, J., Bredin, E., Hahesy, A. L., Abrantes, A., Neft, D., Millstein, R., & Spencer, T. J. (2002). A family study of high-risk children of opiod- and alcohol-dependent parents. *American Journal on Addictions, 11*(1), 41–51.

Wilke, M. (2001). *Changing standards: Condom advertising on American television a special report of the Kaiser Daily Reproductive Health Report* (Publication Number 3139). Menlo Park, CA: Henry J. Kaiser Family Foundation.

Wilkinson, J., & Canter, S. (1982). *Social skills training manual: Assessment, program design, and management of training.* New York: Wiley.

Wilson, J. Q. (1993). *The moral sense.* New York: Macmillan.

Winicki, J. (2004). Children in homes below poverty: Changes in program participation since welfare reform. *Children and Youth Services Review, 25*(8), 651–668.

Winiki, J. (2003). Children in homes below poverty: Changes in program participation since welfare reform. *Children and Youth Services Review, 25,* 651–668.

Wohlstetter, P., & Smyer, R. (1994). Models of high-performance schools. In S. A. Mohrman & P. Wohlstetter (Eds.), *School-based management: Organizing for high performance* (pp. 81–107). San Francisco: Jossey-Bass.

Wolin, S., & Wolin, S. (1993). *The resilient self: How survivors of troubled families rise above adversity*. New York: Random House.

Wood, C., & Davidson, J. (1993). Conflict resolution in the family: A P.E.T. evaluation study. *Australian Psychologist, 28*(2), 100–104.

Woolfenden, S. R., Williams, K., & Peat, J. K. (2002). Family and parenting interventions for conduct disorder and delinquency: A meta-analysis of randomized controlled trials. *Archives of Disease in Childhood, 86*(4), 251–256.

Workman, E. (1982). *Teaching behavioral self-control to students*. Austin, TX: Pro-Ed.

World Health Organization. (1999). *Partners in life skills education: Conclusions from a United Nations Inter-Agency meeting*. Geneva: Author.

Wright, D. M. (1975). Criminal aspects of suicide in the United States. *North Carolina Central Law Journal, 7*, 156–163.

Wubbolding, R. E. (2000). *Reality therapy for the 21st century*. Philadelphia: Brunner-Routledge.

Wycoff, S., Bacod-Gebhardt, M., Cameron, S., Brandt, M., & Armes, B. (2002). Have families fared well from welfare reform? Educating clinicians about policy, paradox, and change. *Family Journal: Counseling & Therapy for Couples & Families, 10*(3), 269–280.

Yokota, F., & Thompson, K. M. (2000, May 24–31). Violence in G-rated animated films. *Journal of the American Medical Association, 283*, 2716–2720.

Younge, S. L., Oetting E. R., & Deffenbacher J. L. (1996). Correlations among maternal rejection, dropping out of school, and drug use in adolescence. *Journal of Clinical Psychology, 52*, 96–102.

Youngstrom, E., Wolpaw, J. M., Kogos, J. L., Schoff, K., Ackerman, B., & Izard, C. (2000). Interpersonal problem solving in preschool and first grade: Developmental change and ecological validity. *Journal of Clinical Child Psychology, 29*(4) 589–602.

Zenker, E. (1984). In the dark about teaching spelling? Just relax! *Academic Therapy, 20*(2), 231–234.

Zenker, E., & Frey, D. (1985). Relaxation helps less capable students. *Journal of Reading, 28*(4), 242–244.

Ziedenberg, J., & Schiraldi, V. (1999). *The punishing decade: Prison and jail estimates at the millennium*. Center on Juvenile and Criminal Justice. Retrieved June 18, 2002, from http://www.cjcj.org/pubs/punishing/punishing.html.

Zigmond, N. (1990). Rethinking secondary school programs for students with learning disabilities. *Focus on Exceptional Children, 23*(1), 1–22.

Zill, N., Morrison, D., & Coiro, M. J. (1993). Long-term effects of parental divorce on parent–child relationships, adjustment, and achievement in young adulthood. *Journal of Family Psychology, 7*, 91–103.

Zorn, T. (2001). Millennium dreams: 21st century EEO practices for federal employees. *Public Manager, 30*(2), 20–24.

NAME INDEX

SUBJECT INDEX

21st Century Community Learning Centers, 36

A

Abortion, 55
Abstinence, 169
Academic achievement, 93
 suicide and, 213
Academic skills
 basic/survival, 113
 control for learning and, 278
 critical competencies and, 258–263
 tutoring programs and, 289–294
Accidents, latchkey children and, 76
Acid rock music, 187
Action, "Stages of Change" metatheory and, 155
Active listening, parent effectiveness training and, 317
ADA (Americans With Disabilities Act), 129
Addiction. See Substance use
Adjudicated youth, school participation and, 130
Adlerian model, 170–178
Adolescent development, 161
Adolescents of color. See Children/adolescents of color
Adult caring relationships, 122
AFDC (Aid to Families with Dependent Children), 28
Affirmations, 274
Affluence, ennui and, 32
After-school programs, 102
 latchkey children and, 77
Aggression in families, 182
Aging (life cycle), 70
AGMs (attention-getting mechanisms), 171, 175
AIDS, 56, 159
 statistics and, 167
Aid to Families with Dependent Children (AFDC), 28
Al-Anon, 320
Alateen, 320
Alcohol use, 6, 145
 families and, 77, 78
 suicide and, 212
Alternative education programs, 137
Americans With Disabilities Act (ADA), 129
Andrews family, 10–12, 45, 55
 coping and, 118
 parenting styles and, 84–86
 relaxation training and, 273
 self-assessments and, 277
 self-esteem/self-efficacy and, 115
 substance use and, 147, 148

 suicide and, 220
 working poor and, 25
Anger, suicide and, 215
Anger management, 252
Antisocial behavior, 179–207
 origins of, 185–193
 society and, 185
Anxiety, combatting, 255
Approach continuum, 239–241
ART program, 251, 255
Assertiveness skills, 269–271
Assumed inadequacy, 173, 176
At risk, 235
 defined, 6–9, 88
 ecological model, 17–20
 overview, 1–21
 problems/issues, 13
 tree metaphor, 14–17
At-risk categories
 socioeconomic status and, 31
 tree metaphor and, 16
At-risk category activity, 7, 9
At-risk children/youths
 individual characteristics of, 107–122
 statistics and, 5
At-risk continuum, 7
At-risk society, 5
Attention, misbehavior and, 171, 175
Attention-getting mechanisms (AGMs), 171, 175
Attitudes, 16

B

Baker family, 28–30, 31
 cognitive change strategies and, 268
 curricula and, 136
 delaying gratification and, 119
 reality therapy and, 202
 resiliency and, 112
 substance use and, 147, 148
 treatment programs and, 234
Barbiturates, 146
Beck Hopelessness Scale (BHS), 224
Before-school programs, 102
Behavior, 16
 changes in, suicide warning signs and, 220
 purposiveness of, 170
BET (bicultural effectiveness training), 313, 316
BHS (Beck Hopelessness Scale), 224